An overview of the Buddhist teaching.

Mahāyāna Myths and Stories

THE COMPLETE WORKS OF SANGHARAKSHITA include all his previously published work, as well as talks, seminars, and writings published here for the first time. The collection represents the definitive edition of his life's work as Buddhist writer and teacher. For further details, including the contents of each volume, please turn to the 'Guide' on pp.665–9.

COMPLETE WORKS 16 **COMMENTARY**

Sangharakshita

Mahāyāna Myths and Stories

EDITED BY VIDYADEVI

Windhorse Publications
169 Mill Road
Cambridge
CB1 3AN
UK

info@windhorsepublications.com
www.windhorsepublications.com

Cover design by Dhammarati
Cover images: Back flap: © Clear Vision Trust Picture Archive; front: *Universal Gateway*, Chapter 25 of the *Lotus Sutra*, text inscribed by Sugawara Mitsushige, Kamakura period, 1257. Metropolitan Museum of Art
Frontispiece image of Nagini courtesy of Varaprabha
Typesetting and layout by Ruth Rudd
Printed by Bell & Bain Ltd, Glasgow

British Library Cataloguing in Publication Data:
A catalogue record for this book is available from the British Library.

ISBN 978-1-909314-88-7 (paperback)
ISBN 978-1-909314-89-4 (hardback)

CONTENTS

FOREWORD

Urgyen Sangharakshita introduced me to the strange and wonderful world of Mahāyāna *sūtras* with his three lecture series on the *White Lotus Sūtra*, the *Sūtra of Golden Light,* and the *Vimalakīrti-nirdeśa*. These were later transformed into books, and now you have all three in your hand. In them, Sangharakshita taught me how to read Mahāyāna *sūtras*, how to love them, and even, to a certain extent, how to live them, and for that I'll always be grateful.

Perhaps what I learned from them more than anything else was that there is more to the Dharma life than grasping certain ideas and practising certain techniques. It's also a matter of engaging the imagination. Of *seeing* imaginatively. Of *understanding the world* through the imagination. The three *sūtras* are highly imaginative. They don't explain the practicalities of the spiritual life – mindfulness, the five precepts, how to meditate. Instead, they invite us to re-imagine our lives, and they do this with the aid of stories, descriptions of fantastic, Utopian worlds, gorgeous imagery, and magic. This may seem a long way from the classic Buddhist aim of 'seeing things as they really are', the quest to find the truth. But what *is* the truth, and where do we find it?

> Things need not have happened to be true. Tales and adventures are the shadow truths that will endure when mere facts are dust and ashes and forgotten.

This, from the fantasy writer Neil Gaiman, could just as well be said of Mahāyāna *sūtras* as of fantasy novels. Sangharakshita is interested in the 'shadow truths' that the *sūtras* express, and in helping us to see how they play out in our own lives. He could have simply asked us to read the *sūtras*, of course, but most of us probably wouldn't have done that, and if we had tried we would almost certainly have found them incomprehensible. The shadow truths in Mahāyāna *sūtras* are hidden in the darkness of an alien culture and literary style, and we need someone who can throw light on them for us.

A young man runs away from home, for reasons we're not told, and goes to live in foreign lands. He doesn't do well. For ten, twenty, fifty years, he roams aimlessly around, working just to feed and clothe himself, getting more destitute the older he gets. Meanwhile, his father becomes rich. But not happy. All the time he is thinking of his lost son, secretly holding the pain of his loss in his heart. One day the son wanders back – unawares – to his native land, right back, in fact, to where his father now lives. This is the first half of one of the parables from the *White Lotus Sūtra*, and Sangharakshita devotes a whole lecture to it ('The Myth of the Return Journey'). In the *sūtra* the parable is introduced to depict 'Hīnayāna' Buddhists, who are like the son – they don't realize that all the wealth of the Mahāyāna is theirs. This is an ancient argument that, although of historical interest, doesn't really concern us spiritually. But stories cannot be contained by one meaning, and Sangharakshita takes the parable out of its historical context and illuminates its shadow truth for us. I was in my early twenties when I first heard this lecture, and I strongly identified with the son: his poverty, his aimlessness, his emptiness, his loneliness; all were mine. But what Sangharakshita showed me was that I was the father too. Yes, I was poor, but I was also rich.

In his lecture 'History versus Myth in Man's Quest for Meaning', Sangharakshita offers a way for us to understand the meaning of Mahāyāna *sūtras*:

> Reading the Mahāyāna scriptures, we are emancipated from the contingent and the determinate, from time, space, and causality, from historical reality. We experience archetypal reality, myth, the realm of undefined meanings.

[handwritten marginal notes:] is it because the chars lack personality + pers' drives? interesting but, how?

An undefined meaning is a truth that can't be expressed in conceptual terms. It's rather like Gaiman's 'shadow truth': its meaning can't be seen in the clear light of reason and logic, but is glimpsed in the mists and shadows of images, stories, poems, songs and magical events.

A bodhisattva named Ruciraketu is grappling with a problem. As he's thinking about it, his house enlarges to become a palace made of jewels, filled with exquisite perfumes. In each of the four directions appears a great throne, and on each throne sits a Buddha. The whole universe is flooded with light, divine flowers rain down, beautiful music resounds, and all beings throughout the whole universe are filled with happiness. The four Buddhas give Ruciraketu the solution to his problem. This episode, from the *Sūtra of Golden Light*, is the kind of passage that I might read and move on from: Ruciraketu had a question, which the four Buddhas answered. Simple. But in his lecture 'The Bodhisattva's Dream', Sangharakshita showed me that the magical episode preceding the resolution to his problem isn't merely a piece of superfluous baroque ornamentation, but is essential to what follows. Ruciraketu's problem couldn't be resolved on its own level. That's the nature of problems (as opposed to difficulties, which *can* be resolved by means of effort and intelligence). His house expanding to become a palace and all that follows describes the ascent of his consciousness into the archetypal realm, from where his problem is no longer a problem for him. (The four Buddhas' 'solution' to his problem is the problem viewed from the archetypal realm.) The reason I'm telling you all this now, when you could just as well read Sangharakshita's brilliant exposition, is because of its effect on me. Up until then I'd viewed my spiritual problems as negative. They were holding me up, blocking my progress on the path to Buddhahood, and I wished that I didn't have them. On hearing Sangharakshita's lecture I realized that they weren't *blocking* the path, they *were* the path. They weren't *in* the way, they *were* the way. Rather than needing to rid myself of them, I needed to cherish them, painful as they might be.

In the quotation above, Sangharakshita says that, in reading Mahāyāna *sūtras*, we experience archetypal reality. He went on to say that

> we can experience the archetypal realm only because we ourselves are, on another level, archetypal beings. If we really allow ourselves to become absorbed in a Mahāyāna *sūtra*, we become part of it.

We exist, then, on different levels. We're the poor son and we're the rich father. We're sitting at home trying to solve a thorny problem and we're also in a jewel palace listening to divine music. We tend to identify more with what we might call the sense-based level of our being, as if that were the 'real' world, but the archetypal realm is every bit as real. Perhaps more real. I'm reminded of some lines from one of the Estonian poet Jaan Kaplinski's poems:

> I could have said: I stepped from the bus.
> I stood on the dusty roadside where
> a young maple and dog-roses grew.
> But really, I leaped into the silence,
> and there was no land, no surface to step on.[1]

Although both descriptions are true, Kaplinski states that one is truer than the other: 'I *could* have said ... but *really* ...'. Similarly, I think what Sangharakshita expresses in these lectures is that the world of the Mahāyāna *sūtras* – the Profound Buddha Region, as the *Sūtra of Golden Light* puts it – is closer to reality than is our sense-based level of consciousness.

Five hundred youths visit the Buddha. They each bring a parasol, which they offer to him. The Buddha magically transforms the parasols into one great canopy, which covers the whole universe. Everything in the universe can clearly be seen reflected in the interior of the canopy, and the voices of all the Buddhas are heard reverberating in the space beneath it. Thus begins the *Vimalakīrti-nirdeśa*, and thus begins Sangharakshita's wonderful exploration of it. I was fortunate to be present when he gave these lectures, and I seemed to have the experience of living in both realms simultaneously as I sat there in the East-West Centre in London in 1979. I *could* have said that I was sitting in a lecture hall with about a hundred others, listening to Sangharakshita speak, but *really* I was in Vimalakīrti's house, with Mañjuśrī, Śāriputra, and the thousands of other beings – human and divine. Both were true, but one was truer than the other.

Dharmachari Ratnaguna
Manchester
September 2016

The Drama of Cosmic Enlightenment

PARABLES, MYTHS, AND SYMBOLS
OF THE WHITE LOTUS SŪTRA

I

THE UNIVERSAL PERSPECTIVE OF MAHĀYĀNA BUDDHISM

The myths which Buddhism has inherited from the ancient Hindu tradition tell many stories of Indra, the king of the gods, who lives in a magnificent palace in the 'Heaven of the Thirty-Three'. In his palace Indra has many treasures, and among those treasures, the legends say, is a net. Now this net is no ordinary net. For one thing, it is made entirely of jewels. What is more, this net of jewels has a number of wonderful and extraordinary characteristics. And one of these characteristics is that when you look into the facets of any one jewel, you can see all the other jewels reflected in it. Each and every jewel in the net reflects all the others, so that 'all the jewels shine in each, and each shines in all'.

In the *Avataṃsaka Sūtra*, the Buddha likens the whole universe to Indra's net of jewels.[2] So what is the basis for this comparison? At the simplest level we could say that just as Indra's net consists of innumerable jewels of all shapes, sizes, and degrees of brilliance, so the universe consists of innumerable phenomena of various kinds. But the Buddha takes the analogy further, and in doing so challenges the very way we see things. We usually experience the things that make up the universe as being completely separate and distinct from one another, and we can hardly imagine seeing things in any other way. A mountain, a bicycle, an ant, a block of flats, a policeman – just a mass of separate objects – this is how we see the world. But in reality, so the Buddha says, it is not like that at all. From his point of view – that is, from the point of view of the highest spiritual experience – everything

The nagas symb the subconscious.

in the universe, great and small, near and far, reflects everything else. All things reflect one another, mirror one another – in a sense they even contain one another. This truth applies not only throughout space but also throughout time, so that everything that happens anywhere is happening here, and everything that happens at any time is happening now. Time and space are transcended, all the categories of logic and reason are superseded, and the world we 'know' is turned upside down.

Indra's net is not the only traditional illustration of this law of mutual reflection. In the Mahāyāna Buddhist countries of the Far East, a particular teaching from the scriptures has been quoted so often that it has entered deeply and intimately into the literature of these countries, and even into their everyday lives. The saying goes: 'Each and every single grain of dust in the universe contains all the Buddha worlds of the ten directions of space and the three periods of time' (the three periods of time being past, present, and future).[3] This might at first sight seem to be rather a strange and exotic insight, but we do have something like it nearer home, in the poetry of William Blake:

> To see a World in a Grain of Sand,
> And a Heaven in a Wild Flower,
> Hold Infinity in the palm of your hand,
> And Eternity in an hour.[4]

We are all too likely not to take this familiar verse seriously. If we think about it at all, we probably think, 'Oh well, it's not that Blake actually saw the world in a grain of sand. It's just a figure of speech, a flight of poetic fancy.' But Blake was not just a poet; he was also a visionary, a mystic. These lines suggest that he really did see, or at least glimpse, the world as it really is, the world as the Buddha describes it through the simile of Indra's net of jewels.

As the Buddha taught that everything is interconnected in this way, it is perhaps not surprising to discover that his own teaching, the Dharma, is itself like Indra's net. The teachings of Buddhism, like everything else, form a network of connections, a net of jewels, and each facet throws light on all the others. This means – to look at it the other way round – that we can't *fully* understand any one aspect of the Dharma unless we understand the whole of it. When we reach some understanding of a doctrine that is new to us, we may think that we can just add it to

Buddha protected by nagas (snakes)
p protecting the wisdom of subcons

our stock of knowledge like adding a pebble to a heap of pebbles, but in fact this is impossible. Whenever we encounter a new teaching, we have to go back and look again at everything we already 'know' in the light of our new understanding. Every single insight into the truth that we have modifies, at least subtly, all our previous insights.

So each time we discover a new way of exploring the Buddhist path, our understanding is completely transformed. And the avenues of exploration open to us are numerous. For example, we can see spiritual development in terms of evolution, using anthropology, biology, and history to trace the progress of what I have termed the 'higher evolution of man'.[5] We can bring a Western psychological approach to bear on the practical problems that we encounter in the course of our spiritual development. Western philosophy and the arts also give us rich sources of inspiration; and meanwhile the traditional formulations of Indian Buddhism remain open to us as well. Each exploration of human growth and development sheds light on the whole process.

The *White Lotus Sūtra*, which is a product of the Mahāyāna, the second great phase of Indian Buddhism, explores the Dharma through parables, myths, and symbols – in other words, through archetypes, through what Jung calls the collective unconscious. But why does the *White Lotus Sūtra* take this particular mode of expression? To understand this, we need to take a look at the history of Buddhism and see how the Mahāyāna developed its universal perspective.

Buddhism began in India some 2,500 years ago. The Buddha, Śākyamuni, was born and brought up as Siddhartha, prince of the Śākyan clan, in what is now southern Nepal. In the years following his Enlightenment, he travelled and taught throughout what was known in those days as the Middle Region, which corresponds to the present day Indian states of Bihar and Uttar Pradesh, an area about the size of England and Wales. And after his death, during the 1,500 years his teaching lasted in India, it spread throughout the whole vast subcontinent and beyond, crossing deserts and seas to penetrate practically the whole of Asia. It even reached westwards as far as Antioch and Alexandria, and this without the benefit of modern transport and communication systems.

As well as travelling so far afield, Buddhism changed greatly during the period of its development in India. The fundamental things, the essential Dharma, remained the same, but the way the teachings were presented and interpreted changed over the years. There were three great phases of development, each lasting roughly five hundred years: the Hīnayāna, the Mahāyāna, and the Vajrayāna. Mahāyāna is a Sanskrit word meaning great way, or great vehicle (from *mahā*, 'great', and *yāna*, 'way' or 'vehicle') – the great way or vehicle to Enlightenment. The Mahāyāna was not a particular school or sect of Buddhism, as some writers make out, but a phase of development which came to represent a certain approach to Buddhism. The term Mahāyāna is often contrasted with that given to the first phase of Buddhism, Hīnayāna, which means little way – and this gives us a clue to the approach that Mahāyāna Buddhism took. Whoever coined the terms 'little way' and 'great way' was obviously making a contrast. But what is being contrasted? What difference is being pointed out?

According to popular belief, the difference between the Hīnayāna and the Mahāyāna is simple. The Hīnayāna, people say, teaches that you should devote yourself simply to the attainment of your own Enlightenment, completely ignoring the needs of others. The Mahāyāna, again according to popular opinion, teaches the opposite – that you should forget all about yourself, devoting your energies solely to helping other beings to tread the path to Enlightenment. This assessment of the contrast is both crude and misleading. It manages to give the impression that the Mahāyānist is a model of transcendental politeness, forever holding the door of Enlightenment open for other people to pass through – a gross distortion of the truth of the Mahāyāna's position. For the Mahāyāna simply – but profoundly – realizes that concern for the welfare and the spiritual development of other people is an integral part of one's own spiritual development. Indeed, to be concerned with one's own development but completely uninterested in that of other people is self-defeating in the long run.

The Mahāyāna vision sees that all forms of life in the universe on all levels, and perhaps especially on the human level, are, like Indra's net, interrelated and interactive. Indeed, the Mahāyāna takes the image a step further. The net is not static, for the individual jewels that make it up are in motion, and the whole net, each and every jewel, is heading in one direction. Admittedly, some jewels are a little further ahead, and some are lagging behind, for the net is after all very large. Some jewels are big and bright, while others are smaller and less lustrous, and some, unfortunately, are even dragging in the mud, so that they seem to have lost their beauty and look more like ordinary pebbles than jewels. But

The Buddha has come when the Dharma dies out.

they are all moving towards the same goal, and they are all, directly or indirectly, in contact with one another.

The urge to Enlightenment, the urge to something above and beyond the world, is innate in all life, but it is a blind urge, like that of a plant groping for the light. The Mahāyāna's greatest spiritual hero, the bodhisattva – a being (*sattva*) dedicated to the attainment of Enlightenment or awakening (*bodhi*) – is one in whom the urge to grow which is present in every living being has become self-conscious. The bodhisattva is thus the embodiment of the Higher Evolution. Realizing that the urge to develop spiritually is potential in all living beings, a bodhisattva feels a sense of solidarity with other beings, and could not possibly ignore them and think only in terms of his or her own salvation. Bodhisattvas therefore dedicate themselves to Enlightenment not just for their own sake but for the sake of all living beings whatsoever. For the Hīnayāna, by contrast, the ideal Buddhist is the *arhant*, the sage or saint who has destroyed all passions and reached Nirvāṇa, but whose spiritual career is at no stage concerned with other beings. Like bodhisattvas, *arhants* have become conscious of the urge to spiritual growth, but their progress is limited because they are unaware that all living beings share the potential for Enlightenment.

Evidence of the contrast between the bodhisattva and the *arhant* is plentiful in the Mahāyāna scriptures, but for a really vivid impression you have only to look at the Buddhist paintings and sculptures produced in India and China, and now preserved in temples and museums throughout the world. The bodhisattva is usually depicted as a beautiful young man (or woman) sitting on a delicate lotus flower. He has a graceful figure, long flowing locks, and many fine ornaments. The *arhant*, on the other hand, is usually an old man with a bald head and bushy eyebrows. Clad in a shabby monastic robe, he leans wearily on a knotted staff. No lotus seat for him – he is usually standing on solid rock, or sometimes, for a change, floating on the ocean. The bodhisattva represents the ideal in all its perfection and purity, the abstract ideal not stained or touched by anything of the world, but lifted above it. The *arhant*, by contrast, represents the realization of the ideal under the conditions and limitations of space and time, the stress of history. No wonder the *arhant* has a weather-beaten, worn look.

We can find an interesting parallel to this in the way Christian art depicts the angels and the saints. The angels are usually represented as sleek, graceful, well-groomed young men with long curly hair and wings. They are often playing on musical instruments, and they have sweet, innocent expressions which make it clear that they have never sinned. They don't even know what sin is – they're as innocent as that. The saints, on the other hand, are usually old and worn and rather ugly. They certainly do know what sin is, even if they have succeeded after many struggles in overcoming it or at least in holding it down. And unlike the angels, they suffer; they're usually shown being crucified upside-down, or beheaded, or shot full of arrows, or roasted on a gridiron. Again, on the one hand you have the archetypal, the ideal, and on the other, the realization of the ideal in the concrete conditions of human historical existence.

But contrary to appearances (as depicted in art) bodhisattvas don't have an easy time of it. They are committed to cultivating spiritual qualities through all sorts of practices, and in particular through the practice of the six *pāramitās*. *Pāramitā* usually gets translated as 'perfection' or 'virtue', but 'discipline for the attainment of Enlightenment' gives a better idea of what the term means.

The first of these disciplines for the attainment of Enlightenment is *dāna* – giving or generosity. According to Mahāyāna tradition you can give in many ways, ranging from the comparatively gross to the comparatively refined and subtle.[6] First, and most obviously, you can give material things – food, clothing, shelter, and so on. Secondly, there's the giving of education and culture. The third kind of giving is psychological – the giving of fearlessness. So many people suffer from profound feelings of insecurity, and the bodhisattva should resolve those feelings – it's as though the bodhisattva has to be a sort of psychotherapist on the transcendental plane. Fourthly, the bodhisattva also gives the gift of the Dharma, the Truth. And this isn't just a matter of handing people a little tract and saying, 'Go away and read this.' Giving the Dharma means sharing your own understanding of the truth of things as far as it goes, and pointing, perhaps, to the greater understanding of others with more experience. The final gift – which is also, we may say, the all-inclusive gift – is the giving of yourself in your relationships with other people. You

a part of yourself and hold the rest back. The bodhisattva

tman's words, 'When I give I give myself.'[7]

eaching of the Buddha that his followers in the

heart, it is this one – they have learned not just to

be generous, but even to be overwhelmingly generous. They usually practise some form of generosity every day. I lived for many years among Buddhists in the East, and I can testify that generosity is one of the most attractive features of life there. When I was first settling in Kalimpong, I stayed with a Burmese Buddhist and his wife, and I soon discovered that I had to be careful what I said, because if I admired anything it was at once given to me – my attempts to refuse were to no avail. This was simply the Burmese Buddhist way of treating a guest. Later on, when I had my own hermitage in Kalimpong, I used to go down to Calcutta and meet up with my old Buddhist friends, especially Buddhist monks from Sri Lanka, Thailand, Vietnam, and Japan. As soon as I came through the door, two or three monks would already be asking, 'What do you need?' 'Are you short of anything? – A typewriter, paper, money?' 'Do you need a fountain pen? – Have this one!'

It will perhaps take some time for Western Buddhists to imbibe this spirit of generosity; but generosity is certainly a quality which any practising Buddhist, any would-be bodhisattva, needs to cultivate. As they sometimes say in the Mahāyāna countries, never mind if you can't meditate, never mind if you can't read or understand the scriptures. You can at least give. If you can't do that, you're not on the path to Enlightenment in any sense.

The second discipline, *śīla*, is often translated – not very fortunately – as 'morality', but the literal translation is 'uprightness'. The aspects of the bodhisattva's conduct which this discipline deals with are expressed in the form of precepts, or guidelines, which can be applied to every action of body, speech, and mind. There are many sets of ethical precepts, the most widely known of which is a set of five precepts that are practised throughout the Buddhist world. The first of these five precepts is an undertaking to refrain from taking life. The bodhisattva is careful not to injure even the humblest of other living beings, or, to put it more positively, he or she cultivates what Albert Schweitzer calls 'reverence for life' – reverence for the uniqueness of everything that lives.[8] The bodhisattva reflects, 'I have not called life into being, nor can I replace it when it is destroyed, so I have no right to take it, or to harm it in any way.' With this in mind, the bodhisattva tries as far as possible to be vegetarian. The second precept that the bodhisattva observes is traditionally phrased 'undertaking to refrain from taking what is not given' – in other words, one abstains from any

Diff bet unconscious + subconscious
in buddhism

kind of theft or fraud. In following the third precept, one undertakes to abstain from sexual misconduct. These three are the precepts which concern the ethics of bodily action.

The fourth precept gives guidance on the ethics of speech. The bodhisattva undertakes not only to be truthful, but to tell the truth with great love and affection, taking into account the feelings and needs of the listener. Also, whether speaking to one person or to many people, the bodhisattva speaks in a way that promotes harmony, concord, and unity. In short, the bodhisattva practises real communication.

Now Buddhist ethics are concerned not just with the actions of body and speech, but also with the actions of the mind. The fifth precept is therefore devoted to the preservation of 'mindfulness' with all that that implies – awareness, vitality, mental alertness, presence of mind, and so on. Practising this precept means avoiding anything which might diminish your awareness. This traditionally refers to over-indulgence in alcohol and drugs, but anything that may be used as a drug can be added to the list.[9]

The third practice of the bodhisattva is *kṣānti.* It is difficult to translate *kṣānti* by any one English word because it means a number of things. It means patience: patience with people, patience when things don't go your way. It means tolerance: allowing other people to have their own thoughts, their own ideas, their own beliefs, even their own prejudices. It means love and kindliness. And it also means openness, willingness to take things in, and, especially, receptivity to higher spiritual truths. It's very difficult to be truly receptive. Even when we hear something crucial from the spiritual point of view, it's quite likely that we won't really take it in. We may receive it on an intellectual level, but just play around with the idea, not letting it sink into the depths of our being. Prejudices or negative emotions may stop the truth halfway. There are so many barriers, so many obstacles, which *kṣānti* needs to overcome.

The fourth *pāramitā* is *vīrya* – energy or vigour, 'energy in pursuit of the good'.[10] *Vīrya* consists primarily in the effort to get rid of negative emotions like anger, jealousy, and greed, and to foster positive emotions like love, compassion, joy, and peace. This means practising the 'four exertions': preventing the arising of unarisen unskilful mental states; eradicating arisen unskilful mental states; developing unarisen skilful mental states; and maintaining arisen skilful mental states.[11] *Vīrya* is needed not just for this kind of 'exertion', however, but for the practice of all the disciplines leading to the attainment of Enlightenment, even the practice of *kṣānti*; in fact, without energy we can do nothing.

The fifth *pāramitā*, *samādhi*, presents us with another untranslatable term. It has three distinct levels of meaning. On one level it means concentration in the sense of the unification of all your psychic energies, the bridging of all the schisms in your being. Then there's *samādhi* in the sense of the personal experience of ever higher levels of consciousness, the kind of experience you may have when you meditate. This level of *samādhi* includes the development of what the Buddhist tradition calls 'supernormal powers' – telepathy, clairaudience, clairvoyance, and so on. In the third and highest sense, *samādhi* is the experience of Reality itself, or at least receptivity to the direct influence of Reality. This experience may begin in the form of flashes of insight – perhaps of the kind William Blake had when he 'saw the world in a grain of sand'.

The sixth discipline is *prajñā* – wisdom. Buddhist tradition speaks of three kinds of wisdom. The first kind is traditionally called 'wisdom from hearing'. This is the wisdom we gain by listening to teachers of the Dharma and reading scriptures – wisdom gained at second-hand, as it were. The next kind of wisdom is that which we gain when we reflect on what we have heard and apply our own original thought to it. The third kind of wisdom arises when we meditate on our reflections, and incidentally it coincides with the highest level of *samādhi*.[12] Wisdom in this sense has four levels. The truths it reveals are profound and subtle, and here I will mention them only briefly. Firstly, we develop the wisdom which sees that conditioned existence, the mundane world, is essentially painful and unsatisfactory (*duḥkha*), impermanent (*anitya*), and insubstantial or devoid of selfhood (*anātman*).[13] Secondly, we see that Nirvāṇa, the Unconditioned, is devoid of suffering, impermanence, and insubstantiality, and possesses the opposite characteristics: bliss and happiness, permanence (eternity, if you like), and true being, true selfhood. With the arising of the third kind of wisdom, we see that the very distinction between the conditioned and the Unconditioned is only provisional – being part of the structure of thought, it is not ultimately valid. With this kind of wisdom we see the emptiness of the distinction between the conditioned and the Unconditioned. With the fourth kind of wisdom – which has been developed particularly by the Zen tradition – we go even further. We see the emptiness of the very concept of emptiness itself: the emptiness, the relativity, of all concepts, including those of Buddhism.[14]

So these are the disciplines which the bodhisattva has to practise.[15] Together they make up what is perhaps the noblest way of life ever proposed to humanity, a perfectly balanced and comprehensive scheme of spiritual development. Giving and uprightness provide for the other-regarding and the self-regarding aspects of the spiritual life, for altruism and individualism. Patience and vigour provide for the cultivation of the 'feminine' and 'masculine' virtues. And meditation and wisdom provide for the internal and the external dimensions, the subjective and objective aspects, of the Enlightenment experience.

Despite the guidance which the Mahāyāna gives the spiritual aspirant through the teaching of the six *pāramitās*, you will sometimes hear it said that it is the Hīnayāna which is meant for people who are prepared to make an effort to help themselves, whereas the Mahāyāna is for people who want everything to be done for them by the bodhisattvas. According to this way of thinking, the Hīnayāna, the 'little way', is so called because it is addressed to an élite group, whereas the Mahāyāna, the 'great way', is addressed to the masses. Again, this distinction is both crude and misleading. As a universal religion, Buddhism addresses itself not to any particular group or community, but potentially to each and every human being. As the Hīnayāna and the Mahāyāna are both stages in the development of Buddhism, both are addressed to all individuals, so we can't distinguish between them in this respect. At the same time, there is a difference, which will perhaps become clear with the help of a parable.

Let's suppose that there is a famine somewhere, a terrible famine of the kind that still happens in Africa. People are gaunt and emaciated, and there is terrible suffering. In a certain town in the country which has been struck by this famine there live two men, one old, one young, who each have an enormous quantity of grain, easily enough to feed all the people. The old man puts outside his front door a notice which reads: 'Whoever comes will be given food.' But after that statement there follows a long list of conditions and rules. If people want food they must come at a certain time, on the very minute. They must bring with them receptacles of a certain shape and size. And holding these receptacles in a certain way, they must ask the old man for food in certain set phrases which are to be spoken in an archaic language. Not many people see the notice, for the old man lives in an out-of-the-way street; and of those who do see it, a few come for food and receive it, but others are put off by the long list of rules. If food is only available on those terms it seems less troublesome to starve. When the old man is asked why he imposes so many rules, he says, 'That's how it was in my grandfather's time whenever there was a famine. What was good enough for him is certainly good enough for me. Who am I to change things?' He adds that if people really want food they will observe any number of rules to get it. If they won't observe the rules they can't really be hungry.

Meanwhile the young man takes a great sack of grain on his back and goes from door to door giving it out. As soon as one sack is empty, he rushes home for another one. In this way he gives out a great deal of grain all over the town. He gives it to anyone who asks. He's so keen to feed the people that he doesn't mind going into the poorest, darkest, and dirtiest of hovels. He doesn't mind going to places where respectable people don't usually venture. The only thought in his head is that nobody should be allowed to starve. Some people say that he's a busybody, others that he takes too much on himself. Some people go so far as to say that he's interfering with the law of karma. Others complain that a lot of grain is being wasted, because people take more than they really need. The young man doesn't care about any of this. He says it's better that some grain is wasted than that anyone should starve to death.

One day the young man happens to pass by the old man's house. The old man is sitting outside peacefully smoking his pipe, because it isn't yet time to hand out grain. He says to the young man as he hurries past, 'You look tired. Why don't you take it easy?' The young man replies, rather breathlessly, 'I can't. There are still lots of people who haven't been fed.' The old man shakes his head wonderingly. 'Let them come to you! Why should you go dashing off to them?' But the young man, impatient to be on his way, says, 'They're too weak to come to me. They can't even walk. If I don't go to them they'll die.' 'That's too bad,' says the old man. 'They should have come earlier, when they were stronger. If they didn't think ahead that's their fault. Why should you worry if they die?' But by this time the young man is out of earshot, already on his way home for another sack. The old man rises and pins another notice beside the first one. The notice reads: 'Rules for reading the rules'.

No doubt you've already guessed the meaning of the parable. The old man is the *arhant*, representing the Hīnayāna, and the young man is the bodhisattva, representing the Mahāyāna. The famine is the human predicament, the people of the town are all living beings, and the grain is the Dharma, the teaching. Just as in principle both the old man and the young man are willing to give out grain to everybody, so in principle both the Hīnayāna and the Mahāyāna are universal, meant for all. But in practice we find that the Hīnayāna imposes certain conditions. To practise Buddhism within the Hīnayāna tradition, even today, if you're taking it at all seriously, you must leave home and become a monk or nun. You must live exactly as the monks and nuns lived in India in the Buddha's time. And you mustn't change anything. The Mahāyāna doesn't impose any such conditions. It makes the Dharma available to people as they are and where they are, because it is concerned solely with essentials. It's concerned with getting the grain to the people, not with any particular manner in which this is to be done. The Hīnayāna expects people to come to it, so to speak, but the Mahāyāna goes out to them.

This difference between the Hīnayāna and the Mahāyāna goes back to the early days of Buddhist history. About a hundred years after the Buddha's death, his disciples disagreed about certain issues so strongly that the spiritual community was split in two. Indeed, they disagreed about the very nature of Buddhism itself. One group of disciples held that Buddhism was simply what the Buddha had said. The four noble truths, the Noble Eightfold Path, the twelve links or chain of conditioned co-production, the four foundations of mindfulness; this was Buddhism. But the other group argued that this was not enough. Yes, all these teachings did form part of Buddhism, but the example of the Buddha's life could not be ignored. The Buddha's teaching revealed his wisdom, but his life revealed his compassion, and both together made up Buddhism.

The Hīnayāna is descended from the first group of disciples, the Mahāyāna from the second. The Mahāyāna derives its inspiration not only from the Buddha's teaching but also from the way he lived his life. This is why the Mahāyāna stresses both wisdom and compassion, saying that compassion inevitably arises from true wisdom. It would be going too far to say that the Hīnayāna is completely without compassion, but the Hīnayāna scriptures rarely mention it, and certainly do not give it equal place with wisdom. But the Mahāyāna scriptures say, 'Wisdom and Compassion are the two wings of the bird of Enlightenment, and with one wing only it cannot fly.'

The life story of the Buddha shows that he didn't wait for people to come to him. He didn't just sit under the bodhi tree and wait for disciples. During the forty-five years following his Enlightenment he travelled far and wide to seek people out and teach them. And if someone came to see him, the Buddha would take the initiative in the conversation. He would greet the newcomer and put them at their ease, so that they felt welcome. This was the living example of the Buddha.

In the same spirit the Mahāyāna goes out to meet people. For example, in all the Mahāyāna Buddhist countries – China, Japan, Tibet, Mongolia – the scriptures were translated from the Indian languages into the local language from the very first. Tibet didn't even have a written alphabet when Buddhism first arrived there. The first Tibetan Buddhists created a literary language so that they could translate the texts and the Tibetan people could read them for themselves. But in the Theravāda countries of South-East Asia (Theravāda being one school of the Hīnayāna tradition), the scriptures all remained in Pāli, the original ancient Indian dialect, which is a dead language, as Latin is. If you wanted to study them you had to become a monk, go and live in a monastery, and learn Pāli, before you could read so much as a sentence of the Buddha's teaching for yourself. It's only very recently, under Western influence, that the Pāli Buddhist scriptures have begun to be translated into the languages of Sri Lanka, Burma, and Thailand. A Sinhalese monk once told me that he thought English Buddhists were very lucky. 'You have translations of nearly all the Pāli texts,' he explained, 'but we've only just started translating them into Sinhalese' – which does seem quite astonishing.

So the Mahāyāna literally speaks the language of the people it is addressing – Tibetan, Chinese, English, or whatever is appropriate. But more than this, it also tries to speak the appropriate language in a metaphorical sense. Metaphorically speaking, whether we speak English, Hindi, Greek, or whatever, we express ourselves in two main languages: the language of concepts and the language of images. The language of concepts is the language of intellect and rational thought, the language of science and philosophy. But the language of images is the language of the imagination, the language of the emotions. It's the language of poetry, the language of myth and symbol, simile and metaphor. Concepts address the conscious mind, but images appeal to the unconscious depths that – as modern psychology has made us aware – are within us all.

The Buddha himself spoke both the language of concepts and the language of images. Sometimes he expounded his teaching in a highly abstract, intellectual fashion, and sometimes he spoke in beautiful metaphors and parables – the parable of the raft, the parable of the blind men and the elephant, the parable of the ever-smouldering anthill, and a hundred others.[16] But as it developed, the Hīnayāna forgot the language of images, and spoke more and more exclusively in the language of concepts, until poetry and metaphor were completely banished. Take, for example, the Abhidharma literature of the Theravādins, which consists of seven massive works, some of them in many volumes.[17] They contain psychological analysis, classification of mental states, descriptions of mental functions, and so on – all in severely conceptual style. It is the proud boast of the Abhidharma that in all those thousands of pages there is not a single figure of speech.[18]

The Mahāyāna, on the other hand, continued to speak both the language of concepts and the language of images, and it spoke them both ever more eloquently, as the hundreds of Mahāyāna scriptures show. Amongst the conceptual works are the Perfection of Wisdom *sūtras*, which number more than thirty, some many hundreds of pages long and others comparatively short. The oldest and most important is probably the *Aṣṭasāhasrikā*, the *Perfection of Wisdom in Eight Thousand Lines*. The *Hṛdaya*, the *Heart Sūtra* ('heart' in the sense of 'essence' – the essence of the Perfection of Wisdom) is well known, and so is the *Vajracchedikā*, the 'Diamond Cutter', and both are much recited in the Mahāyāna monasteries of the Far East. All these scriptures are concerned with one topic – *śūnyatā*, Voidness, Reality – the highest level of Wisdom, the perfection of the sixth discipline of the bodhisattva. However, *śūnyatā* is presented in these conceptual works not as a concept but as the *absence* of all concepts. In fact, this literature speaks the language of concepts in such a way as to transcend all concepts whatsoever.

There's a mysterious legend attached to the origin of the Perfection of Wisdom *sūtras*. It is said that the great Mahāyāna teacher and sage Nāgārjuna retrieved them from the depths of the ocean, where they had been kept in secret by the *nāga* kings since the days of the Buddha. This story, which obviously has a symbolic significance, is often depicted in Buddhist art. We see Nāgārjuna floating on a little raft in the middle of the ocean, and a mermaid-like creature with long flowing green hair emerging from the sea with a heavy book in her hands. This is the beautiful daughter of the *nāga* king who lives in the depths of the sea. She hands over the long-treasured text to the great teacher, and he triumphantly bears it back to dry land, writes commentaries on it, and makes it more and more widely known. This is the legend. We don't know exactly when Nāgārjuna lived – probably in the first century of the Christian era – but it is certain that his teaching of the Perfection of Wisdom was a factor in the rise of the Mahāyāna.

The *Laṅkāvatāra Sūtra*, the 'Holy Entry of the Good Teaching into Lanka', which is set on the island of Lanka, where the Buddha goes to preach to the king of the *rākṣasas*, is also written almost exclusively in conceptual language. This text, popular in medieval times with Chinese Buddhist intellectuals, is one of the most difficult of all the *sūtras*, containing highly abstruse psychological and metaphysical teachings.[19]

Then there's the *Gaṇḍavyūha Sūtra*, the 'Scripture of the Cosmic Array', which is part of a larger work called the *Avataṃsaka Sūtra*, the 'Flower Ornament Scripture', traditionally known as the king of the *sūtras*. The *Gaṇḍavyūha Sūtra* describes the pilgrimage of a young man called Sudhana who visits more than fifty people – men, women, old, young, holy, not so holy – in the course of his search for wisdom and Enlightenment. Sudhana learns something from everyone he meets, until eventually he finds the bodhisattva Maitreya, who is living in the Vairocana tower in southern India. It is here that Sudhana receives his final instruction, his final initiation. He is admitted to the tower by Maitreya, and inside the tower he has a wonderful vision. He sees that all the phenomena in the universe are contained in the tower, and the tower is contained, or reflected, in every single thing in the universe. Once again, it's Indra's net of jewels. The form of the *sūtra* is all about images – it's a sort of Buddhist *Pilgrim's Progress* – but its content is mainly conceptual.[20]

The *Vimalakīrti-nirdeśa*, the 'Exposition of Vimalakīrti', speaks the language of both concepts and images, maintaining a beautiful balance and blending of the two. It tells the dramatic story of the meeting between Mañjuśrī, the Bodhisattva of Wisdom, and Vimalakīrti, a wise old householder of Vaiśālī, a town of north-eastern India. In a scene which is often depicted in Chinese Buddhist art, the two come together and have a terrific debate, the sound of which echoes down through Buddhist history.[21]

Some Mahāyāna scriptures speak the language of images almost entirely. There's the *Lalitavistara*, for example – the 'Extended Account of the Sports or Games'. Now we may be forgiven for wondering what kind of spiritual text this might be. And it may come as a surprise to learn that the sports or games are those of the Buddha, that we have here a *sūtra* which offers us what we may say is the Buddha's playful nature. The *Lalitavistara* recounts various incidents of the Buddha's career which were to him 'child's play', incidents in which he acted freely, easily, naturally, spontaneously – in other words, in a truly spiritual manner. So this *sūtra* is a kind of biography of the Buddha, but it is not biography as we usually understand the term, because it contains a great deal of what scholars like to call 'legendary material'. But this is not just 'false history': the *Lalitavistara* speaks the language of images, and the events it describes must be taken on a symbolic level.[22]

There are also the three Pure Land *sūtras*, which consist entirely of strings of images, with hardly any conceptual material at all. They describe the Happy Land of Amitābha, the Buddha of Infinite Light, with its deep blue ground and its criss-crossing golden cords, and its wonderful jewel trees, which the *sūtras* lovingly describe, branch by branch, flower by flower, and even petal by petal. One of these *sūtras* is used to aid visualization of the Pure Land in the context of meditation, and all three are the basis of the Pure Land school of Buddhism, which is traditional in China and Japan; followers of this school all aspire to rebirth in this archetypal Happy Land.[23]

So to the *Saddharma Puṇḍarīka*, the *Sūtra of the White Lotus of the Good Dharma*. This also speaks almost exclusively in the language of images. Although the *sūtra* is very long, its conceptual content is absolutely minimal. The *White Lotus Sūtra*, therefore, appeals not to the head but to the heart, not to the intellect but to the imagination. Its parables, perhaps the most significant in the entire range of Buddhist canonical literature, are famous throughout the Buddhist East, and it is also replete with myths and symbols. In form it's a sort of drama, even a sort of mystery play. It has for its stage the entire cosmos, and the action lasts for millions of ages. The *dramatis personae* consist of the Buddhas and bodhisattvas, *arhants*, gods, demons, and men – in fact, all sentient beings whatsoever. And the atmosphere of the *sūtra* is very strange, an atmosphere of miracle and marvel. In fact, as the *sūtra* unfolds, what we see is a sort of transcendental sound and light show – there seems no other way to describe it. As for the theme of the drama, it is a very great one indeed. It is Enlightenment – not just the Buddha's Enlightenment, or the disciples' Enlightenment, but the Enlightenment of all sentient beings whatsoever. Hence our title: *The Drama of Cosmic Enlightenment.*

1

QUESTIONS AND ANSWERS

THE DOCTRINE OF MUTUAL INTERPENETRATION

Is the doctrine of the mutual interpenetration of all phenomena a logical development of the doctrine of conditionality, or does it represent an entirely new vision of existence?

It does not represent an entirely new vision so much as a new expression of the Buddhist vision. The doctrine of interpenetration is concerned with the nature of ultimate reality, which can be approached in various ways. The *pratītya-samutpāda* (conditioned co-production) doctrine takes a phenomenological approach ('this being, that becomes' and so on).[24] That phenomenology has certain metaphysical implications which are not brought out in the Theravāda but emerge in the Mahāyāna, especially in the Madhyamaka's interpretations of the *śūnyatā* teaching. The fact that all phenomena, all *dharmas*, are reducible to *śūnyatā* was already there in the *pratītya-samutpāda* teaching; the Madhyamaka simply drew attention to it. Multiplicity was thus reduced to unity, for *dharmas* are many and *ś... ıtā* – at least for the purposes of discourse – is one. Subse... ioners of the Yogācāra school came to see Reality not in ... but in terms of the One Mind.[25] In reducing the multi- ... enomena to absolute mind, however, they too thought ... n of multiplicity to oneness, diversity to unity.
... *Avataṃsaka Sūtra* (which, like all Mahāyāna ... ascribed to the Buddha) was satisfied neither

with the original Hīnayāna position nor with the subsequent standpoint of the Yogācāra. To use Western terminology, he saw that both unity and multiplicity are just concepts. Given that the nature of reality is ultimately inexpressible through concepts, the question is how to use those concepts at least to hint at its nature. In the *Avataṃsaka Sūtra*, therefore, the concepts of unity and diversity are combined to give at least a more adequate expression of the nature of reality. All things are not seen in the one, nor is the one seen in all things, but rather each individual thing is seen in every other individual thing.

So could the contemplation of the doctrine of mutual interpenetration be more useful to Dharma practice than the doctrine of śūnyatā*?*
Until you have reached a relatively refined level of spiritual practice, there is little point in exploring metaphysical subtleties. While you are still finding it difficult to concentrate the mind, or practise mindfulness in the affairs of everyday life, it is more important to focus on basic principles. If anything, I would concentrate on impermanence, which does ultimately imply *śūnyatā*, and also has a direct connection with *pratītya-samutpāda*, and therefore with the possibility of spiritual progress. Close study of the *pratītya-samutpāda* doctrine inevitably involves arriving at some understanding of *śūnyatā*, because *śūnyatā* is a metaphysical statement of the implications of conditioned co-production.

ched

Does that mean that it is never appropriate to reflect on śūnyatā*? Perhaps the doctrine was only useful as a way of dealing with the highly conceptual state of medieval Buddhism? But if it is redundant, why continue to chant the* Heart Sūtra*?*
If you *do* want to reflect on *śūnyatā*, one way of looking at it is to bear in mind that the word, which literally means emptiness, really means 'empty of all concepts'. It is a reminder to us that ultimate reality is empty of concepts, in that all our conceptual constructions are inadequate to express it. In that sense, the doctrine of *śūnyatā* is never inappropriate, never out of date. That is not to say, however, that you need to be acquainted with all the highly technical, purely metaphysical expositions of the teaching of *śūnyatā*. You have to bear in mind what the point of it really is from a practical point of view.

Are there any Buddhist practices designed to cultivate the type of vision that Indra's net expresses?
In his book *The Essence of Buddhism*, Suzuki describes a demonstration given by a great Chinese master to explain the doctrine of mutual interpenetration. The master arranged mirrors and candles all round the room in such a way that every mirror reflected all the candles, and also all the other mirrors.[26] The model is inadequate, because it is static, but you could try to imagine all the mirrors and candles in motion – that would give some idea of what mutual interpenetration is like.

Probably the best way of developing insight into reality through this particular way of looking at it would be to read a text rather than reflecting on the philosophical doctrine. While in a relatively concentrated state of mind, you could read to yourself a chapter of the *Avataṃsaka Sūtra*.[27] The original *sūtras* give a much better feeling for the nature of that particular outlook than any of the more doctrinal expositions.

Apart from the Avataṃsaka Sūtra *and your example from William Blake, are there any significant descriptions of the mutual interpenetration of all phenomena in other cultures and religions?*
The question hinges on what you mean by phenomena. There are certain phenomena within the range of Buddhist experience which do not seem to occur within the range, for example, of orthodox Christian thought or experience, so that the statement that all things are mutually interreflecting would have a more restricted meaning within a Christian context than within a Buddhist one. Sometimes Christians speak in terms of Christ bearing all the sins of the world, as though all the sins are reflected in him, but not very much is said about Christ being reflected in every human being, or in material things. It's true that in a verse from a Gnostic gospel, Jesus is represented as saying, 'Split the wood and there am I; lift the stone and there am I', but that text is not included in the Authorized Bible.[28]

So this does seem to be a distinctively Buddhist way of expressing a certain insight, and one which took time to develop. The *Avataṃsaka* teaching of interpenetration comes as the culmination of some centuries of the development of Buddhist thought. There are perhaps analogies in the various mystical traditions. Some of the more poetic Sufi mystics, who think of ultimate Reality in terms of the 'Beloved', speak of seeing the face of the Beloved reflected in all phenomena, which perhaps comes some way towards the Buddhist conception.[29] Plato also gave some thought to the question of unity and multiplicity, and seemed in the *Parmenides* to opt for unity as real and diversity as unreal.[30]

Is there some suggestion of the doctrine of mutual interpenetration in the Hermetic idea 'as above, so below'?[31]

I suppose there is a similarity in a general way, but the Hermetic idea is about correspondence, not mutual reflection. It is perhaps misleading even to say that mutual interpenetration is reflection; it is more that each and every thing is actually present in each and every other thing. Mutual interpenetration breaks down the whole idea of separate 'thingness', just as the *śūnyatā* concept of Insight does.[32]

Returning to Blake, you have mentioned that his poem in the Auguries of Innocence *is comparable in principle to the theme of the* Gaṇḍavyūha Sūtra. *How closely did his vision approach that of the* Gaṇḍavyūha, *and what particular circumstances or abilities led him to develop such a vision? Did he have access to any concentration or meditation practices, or did he develop any such methods himself?*

As far as I know, Blake never engaged in anything comparable to meditation practice, but we must not forget that he was an artist, and an artist does concentrate very intensely. He also had a natural visionary faculty, and a very positive attitude towards life in a highly elevated sense. How he got the idea of the world in a grain of sand it is impossible to say. Perhaps he just saw things like that, just as he saw the angel in the tree. Perhaps the things he wrote about came directly from his personal experience, even though he was well versed in the alternative traditions of his day. He seems to have been an unusually gifted person almost from birth.

Much as I admire Blake, however, it seems to me that his vision does not really go very far towards that of the *Avataṃsaka Sūtra*. But you might find the *Avataṃsaka Sūtra* quite overwhelming and baffling; Blake, being more accessible, might be more useful to you. The only way to find out would be to steep yourself in Blake's writings for a while, then do the same with the *Avataṃsaka Sūtra*, and see how you felt. Perhaps you would have a sense of a deeper understanding of things through reading the *Avataṃsaka Sūtra*, or on the other hand you might feel out of your depth, and get more from reading Blake. Perhaps we do need such bridges and links from our own tradition to prepare us spiritually and even intellectually for the Buddhist texts. Without this preparation the deeper insights of Buddhism may remain for us just matters of philosophy in the narrow intellectual sense, with no real bearing on our own lives.

HOW DO WE ENCOURAGE THE URGE TO ENLIGHTENMENT?

You say that there is an urge to Enlightenment which is immanent in all life, and which becomes self-conscious in the bodhisattva. Is there some conflict between that urge to Enlightenment and the ego's habitual resistance to new experience? You mention this in The Religion of Art.[33] *It seems to me that much of my behaviour, and that of those with whom I study the Dharma, is motivated more by the ego's resistance than by the urge to Enlightenment. How do we encourage the urge to Enlightenment to become our dominant motivation?*

We know that life on this planet has evolved from lower to higher levels, so we are probably justified in speaking of an urge to progress in this way. A being may not necessarily want to evolve, but it may be virtually forced to in order to survive. This applies to species in the collective sense, and it is similar on the human level. We have an urge to reach higher levels, perhaps produced through the force of circumstances, but at the same time the whole of our past and present experience is holding us back. In the case of the ordinary, worldly person, the urge to progress to a higher level has not become conscious in the individual sense; he or she just goes along with the general tide of humanity. In some people, however, there develops a partly conscious urge to go beyond, to achieve something better. This urge is usually vague and unsure to start with, but the more it develops, the more conflict there is between that immanent urge to grow and the resistance that your being as it already is puts up to further development.

We could perhaps divide people into three categories. There are the Stream Entrants[34] for whom there is no real conflict. Yes, they may have problems to resolve, but they cannot slip back. At the other end of the scale there are people who are not yet individuals, but just group members who will grow if the group grows but not otherwise. In between are those who have developed some glimmering of individuality, and therewith some individual aspiration to reach a higher level of development. They can be pulled forward by that ideal, but also pulled back by the group working through their own group nature, or their 'ego', as you term it.

The function of the teacher, or spiritual friend, is to encourage individuality and responsibility, to try to detach the nascent individual from the overwhelming influence of the group, and encourage everything in him or her that leads away from the group. That may mean encouraging them to meditate, to develop positive emotions, to free themselves from neurotic and dependent relationships, to go on retreats, to live in a single-sex community, to be open with other people, or many other things, depending on the person and the circumstances. You need to be careful not to develop a formula and apply it to everybody; you should try to respond to the person's actual needs, and help them along the path they have already started to follow, if that is a path leading to growth and development. It feels good to get people going along exactly your own path, but perhaps they need to do things differently. You need to get to know someone quite well to know what their needs are and see clearly what step they need to take next. If you do not think in terms of leading or guiding the other person, but just in terms of being a good friend to them, everything else will grow out of that.

IS IT POSSIBLE TO EMBODY THE BODHISATTVA IDEAL?

You contrast the image of the sixteen-year-old youth, the bodhisattva, with the battered old monk who is the arhant, *suggesting that the youth symbolizes the ideal in the abstract, whereas the old man symbolizes the ideal in terms of historical limitations. Does that mean it is impossible to have the fully mature altruism of the bodhisattva ideal in concrete historical circumstances?*

The bodhisattva is not young as distinct from being old, but eternally young, which means that the youthfulness of the bodhisattva represents something outside time and space. In the case of the *arhant*, it is scarcely possible to speak of someone as eternally old (unless you think of God the Father, the Ancient of Days), so the *arhant* is not just somebody who is old, but somebody who has become old – at least, this is my way of interpreting it. I regard the beautiful, youthful figure of the bodhisattva as representing the transcendental spiritual ideal as it exists outside space and time, and the *arhant* as that same ideal incorporated within the historical process, manifesting under the conditions of space and time.

The very fact of those conditions means that the ideal cannot manifest fully. Even if you have realized that the eternally youthful bodhisattva represents you as a human being, can you manifest that spiritual ideal fully in your life? Your life has only a certain length, and you have only two arms, two legs, and one pair of hands. There is so much to do, and so much that you cannot do. So within the historical process the ideal cannot actually be manifested fully by any individual, not even by the Buddha. The historical Buddha died. To manifest the ideal fully he would have had to go on living for ever and ever, and living everywhere. A limitation is automatically imposed if you are existing under the conditions of space and time, as an ordinary human being. This is what the *arhant* represents, and this is why I speak of him as being a bit battered and bowed. The ideal is there but – from the particular point of view I adopt here – it is there as manifested under the conditions of space and time.

The Mahāyāna usually paints a picture of the arhant *as the spiritual individualist. Is that what you are saying?*
No, I am adopting a different point of view, leaving aside the traditional Mahāyāna way of looking at the *arhant*, except in terms of iconography. I am looking at the iconography afresh, and asking myself what it is saying. What does it mean to juxtapose the figures of the bodhisattvas and the *arhants*? In the Christian context, what does it mean to juxtapose these beautiful, youthful angels and these old, emaciated saints? To me, the one is the ideal existing outside time towards which one is striving all the time, and the other is the same ideal as limited by space and time, struggling to express itself despite these limitations. You can see it shining through. Sometimes, although the poor old *arhant* or saint is so worn down, old and wrinkled, at the same time there is something of the youthful expression of the bodhisattva there. This is not of course the way the *arhant* is viewed within the Mahāyāna tradition, but my own particular interpretation.

The contrast reminds me of the distinction between the different kāyas of a Buddha.[35]
Yes. The *sambhogakāya* represents the ideal of Buddhahood as existing without any limitations. The *dharmakāya* takes that process a step further; the limitations disappear to such an extent that the Buddha himself disappears, because even the notion 'Buddha' is a limitation in respect of the ultimate spiritual ideal.

THE GIFT OF FEARLESSNESS

I am aware of how much fear affects my behaviour and inhibits me from making contact with other people. Fear seems to affect other people in this way too. Does this explain the emphasis on fearlessness in the list of the things that the bodhisattva gives?
The bodhisattva's giving of fearlessness seems to suggest that people are badly in need of it. Fear is produced by a sense of separateness, or ego, for want of a better term. You should not be surprised to experience fear in all sorts of situations. It is just an indication of the fact that you experience yourself as a self, as an ego; whenever you experience yourself in that way there is the possibility of fear. Until you have transcended the sense of separateness there will be fear, because you are bound to be afraid of whatever threatens you. The gift of fearlessness is therefore ultimately the gift of Insight into egolessness, and this is why it is so important. It could even be called an aspect of the gift of the Dharma, in the sense of some actual experience of Insight, not just the words of the Dharma.

Fearlessness is placed between culture and the Dharma in the list of the bodhisattva's gifts. Is that significant?
Well, fearlessness comes after the gift of culture because it is beyond culture. But if 'the gift of the Dharma' means the Dharma in its fullest sense, I would say that the gift of fearlessness is included in that. Perhaps the two gifts can be distinguished, because whereas the gift of the Dharma is verbal, fearlessness is communicated directly in terms of personality: you give fearlessness to others by being fearless yourself.

Does that mean being egoless yourself?
Yes, exactly. Being brave is something different. Bravery is acting as though you are not afraid even though you are, something we often

have to do if we can't manage anything better. It is to some extent a spiritual quality to be able to act as though you are not afraid when you are, because it means that to some extent you have transcended the ego feeling. You are not allowing the fear – the ego sense – to dominate you completely. You may not be able to stop it affecting your emotional experience, but at least you are not letting it affect your behaviour too much.

There are specific practices which address craving and hatred. Would it be useful to address fear in the same sort of way?
Fear would seem not to be a primary emotion in the way that greed and hatred are. In a way, fear is included in them. But there are some specific practices for eliminating fear, like the Vajrayāna practices which involve going to meditate in the cremation ground at night.[36] People sometimes keep skulls and bones around them as a reminder, although you can become hardened to their presence, if you are not careful, so that they become mere objects which do not produce any effect.

Perhaps from time to time you should expose yourself to situations of which you are rather afraid. Take the example of giving a talk for the first time. You feel reluctant and nervous. You are afraid of failing, afraid of what other people will say, afraid of making a fool of yourself. But you get over that first experience, and the time comes when you can deliver a talk without any experience of fear at all. That indicates that the ego has been overcome, at least to some extent.

A QUESTION OF ATTITUDE

What is the source of the story about the famine, the old man, and the young man?
I think I may have adapted it from a story told to me by a *bhikkhu* friend in India, so it is semi-traditional.

It is fifteen years since you gave this talk, and during that time the Theravāda has been taught more widely in the West. Would you modify the parable in any way if you were to tell it now? Is there more proselytizing on the part of the Hīnayāna these days?
Things *have* changed over the last few years, partly because Buddhists from different schools have had more contact with each other, at least

in the West, and partly because of certain political and cultural events, like the fact that so many Tibetan Buddhists have left Tibet.

But proselytization is not necessarily indicative of a bodhisattva attitude; indeed, the word itself is slightly pejorative in the same kind of way as 'Hīnayāna'. Very often Buddhist monks and teachers from all Buddhist countries tend to spread just their own culture. Their motives are religio-nationalistic rather than purely spiritual, so their proselytizing cannot really be classified as an expression of bodhisattva-like outward-goingness.

In fact, in terms of attitudes towards the propagation of Buddhism in the modern world, there is not really much difference between any of the schools, regardless of what they call themselves. They have all got some representatives, whether monastic or lay, who have a genuine feeling for other people and wish to share the Dharma with them, whether they are teaching it in Theravāda, Tibetan, or Zen terms. And I am quite sure that in all the major schools and traditions there are at least a few people who have some spiritual experience, some inner strength, and who go out to others with the Dharma on that basis, just as there are also those who are anxious to gather disciples, or spread their own national Buddhist culture, or even just rake in the money. The important thing to realize is that you can only really go out to others spiritually when you have something to give. It is unwise for any Buddhist to go out to teach others just because he or she feels like it. Your outward-goingness must be a natural expression of your spiritual experience and spiritual strength.

So do you think this difference between a Hīnayāna attitude and a Mahāyāna attitude is mainly a question of spiritual maturity? Is it the case that, whichever school you follow, you will reach a point of spiritual maturity on the basis of which you will want to go out to people?
I think that is true, but there is far greater traditional support for one in that position within the Mahāyāna, in the historical sense, than within the Hīnayāna. In the oldest Pāli texts, which speak of the Buddha's own example, there is the same outward-going basis, at least in principle, that is found in the Mahāyāna. Many Buddhist schools in Theravāda countries, however, do not go back that far, so their followers do not get the support for going out to others that a Mahāyānist in a similar position would have. The bodhisattva ideal is certainly known in

Theravāda countries, but it is an exception to the rule, whereas in Mahāyāna countries it is the rule for spiritual life.

But we must not allow ourselves to be misled by labels. Someone may be teaching the Dharma on the basis of the Pāli scriptures, but their teaching may not necessarily be a narrowly Hīnayānistic form of Buddhism. In the same way, a lama may be teaching in terms of the Mahāyāna or the Vajrayāna, but he is not necessarily communicating a Mahāyānistic or Vajrayānistic attitude. Often there is a correspondence, but equally often there is not. We must be able to read the real message that is being conveyed, regardless of the particular language. You may meet a Theravāda *bhikkhu* who assures you that you should devote yourself entirely to your own salvation and Enlightenment, and not bother about other people, but he may be most kind and considerate towards you. On the other hand, you may meet a lama who recommends that you should devote yourself, as a bodhisattva, to saving millions of human beings, but who is very selfish and self-centred in his own behaviour. One must not be misled by words or professions.

Obviously 'Hīnayāna' is a pejorative term. What did the Hīnayāna schools call themselves?
Oddly enough, they seem not to have used a collective term to describe themselves. Each Hīnayāna school – the Theravāda, the Sarvāstivāda, the Mūlasarvāstivāda, the Mahāsāṃghikas, and the Bahuśrutīyas – seems to have thought of itself just as that school, so that they had no collective designation to distinguish themselves from the Mahāyāna. Perhaps they just thought of themselves as 'the Buddhist schools'.

Do you think they identified themselves with each other as having certain factors in common at the time, or has that become clear in retrospect?
There must have been some sense of solidarity. They do seem to have been aware that they differed from the Mahāyāna, and from the evidence we have it would seem that they quite consciously refused to accept the Mahāyāna *sūtras* as the word of the Buddha. As they did not use any collective term, and as we cannot use 'Theravāda' in all circumstances – because the doctrines of the various schools differed – we must make do with the rather uncomfortable word Hīnayāna, even though we are well aware of its limitations and slightly pejorative character.

the mud, the flowers bloom out of the water, so that their petals are pure and unstained. Because of this, the lotus has become a symbol of purity – purity in the midst of impurity. It has come to symbolize the presence of the Unconditioned in the midst of the conditioned – if you like, the presence of the spiritual in the midst of the worldly – unstained by the conditions in which it appears. So the title of the *sūtra* is suggesting that although the real truth appears in the midst of the world, it is not tainted by any worldly considerations.

The word *sūtra* (Pāli *sutta*) is the most common term for a Buddhist scripture, so that Buddhists refer to the *sūtras* just as Christians might speak of the Bible. But although it tends to be used so generally, *sūtra* has a specific meaning. It comes from a word meaning 'thread', so it suggests a number of topics strung together on a common thread of discourse. The form of a *sūtra* is almost always the same. First you get a description of where the discourse was given, what was going on, and who was present. That is followed by the main body of the text, which usually consists of a teaching of the Dharma, the real truth, by the Buddha himself. The *sūtra* then ends with an account of the effect of the Buddha's teaching on the people listening.

In some of the Pāli *suttas*, although the Buddha is present, he stays in the background and one of his disciples speaks, in which case the text ends with the Buddha giving his approval to what the disciple has said, thus making the discourse his own, as it were.[37] Sometimes, especially in Mahāyāna *sūtras*, it is not even a question of the Buddha giving his approval. A disciple may be doing the actual speaking, but he speaks under the direct inspiration of the Buddha, so that in truth the Buddha is speaking through him. But however it is spoken, it is important to understand that whatever is said in the body of a *sūtra* is not just issuing from the ordinary level of consciousness. It isn't something that has been worked out intellectually. It isn't a proof or an explanation of something in the mundane sense. It is a truth, a message, even a revelation, issuing from the depths of the Enlightened consciousness, the depths of the Buddha nature. This is the essential content of any Buddhist scripture, and this is its purpose: to communicate the nature of Enlightenment and show the way leading to its realization.

So we can translate the complete title of this particular communication of the Enlightened mind as 'the Scripture of the White Lotus (or if you like the Transcendental Lotus) of the Real Truth'. We could scarcely hope to convey in English all the associations of the Sanskrit words, so the translation is only approximate, but it will do.

As a literary document, the *White Lotus Sūtra* – to revert to the short version of the title – belongs to the first century of the Christian era, that is, five hundred years after the death of the Buddha. But although we know when the *sūtra* was first written down, this, of course, does not give us any clue as to when it was first composed. It is hard for us to imagine, but for practically the whole of that first five-hundred-year period the Buddha's teaching was passed on by word of mouth. Not a word of it was written down. Indeed, there is no evidence that the Buddha himself *could* read and write. In those days writing was not a very respectable accomplishment. Corrupt businessmen who wanted to keep a record of their international transactions might write things down, but it was not a proper occupation for religious people. So the Buddha just used to teach in the form of discourses, and people would listen to what he had to say, commit it to memory, and then repeat it to their own disciples. In this way the teachings of Buddhism – and of Hinduism too – were passed on from generation to generation, like the lighted torch passed from one runner to another before the start of the Olympic Games.

But eventually Indian Buddhists did start to write down the Buddha's teachings. We don't really know why. Perhaps memories had grown weaker since the Buddha's day. Perhaps people didn't feel so confident, and felt there was a danger that the teachings would be lost if they were not written down. Or perhaps reading and writing had become more respectable, so that it was natural to make the teachings available in written form. But whatever the reason, in the first century CE there was a general writing down of the teachings, and the *White Lotus Sūtra* was among the teachings that became scriptures – 'scripture' literally meaning a written document – at that time.

The teachings of Buddhism were written down in various languages – Sanskrit, Pāli, Prakrit, Apabhraṃśa, Paiśāci, and so on[38] – and the *White Lotus Sūtra* was one of the first to be written down in Sanskrit. But although Sanskrit is the language of ancient India, it doesn't necessarily follow that India was where the text was first written down. By this time Buddhism, especially Mahāyāna Buddhism, had spread into central Asia, and it may have been there that the *White Lotus Sūtra* was first recorded. After all, we know that the Pāli scriptures originated from Sri Lanka, not India, at around the same time. But wherever the *White Lotus Sūtra* was written down, it was written in a mixture of two kinds of Sanskrit: 'Pure' Sanskrit and 'Buddhist Hybrid' Sanskrit. Pure Sanskrit follows the rules laid down by the grammarian Pāṇini, so it is sometimes called Pāṇinian Sanskrit. Buddhist Hybrid Sanskrit (sometimes simply called Mixed Sanskrit) is Sanskrit mixed with Prakritisms to produce a less 'correct', more colloquial language.

So the *sūtra* is written in a combination of these two kinds of Sanskrit. It also combines prose and verse, the prose being in Pure, Pāṇinian, Sanskrit and the poetry in Hybrid Sanskrit. This already makes the text quite distinctive. What makes it curious, not to say odd, from a literary point of view, is its structure. The prose and verse come alternately – first you get a prose passage of a few pages, and then comes a passage in verse. The curious thing is that the verse passage repeats almost exactly what has just been said in prose (with a few contractions and expansions). Some scholars would have it that the verse sections are older than the prose, but there's no real proof of that. The whole work, both prose and verse, is divided into twenty-seven chapters, or twenty-eight in some versions, and makes quite a substantial volume.

The original texts of many Buddhist scriptures have been lost, but in the case of the *White Lotus Sūtra* we are fortunate. Copies were discovered in the nineteenth century, and there have been more recent discoveries too – in Nepal, where several copies were unearthed, in the sands of the desert of central Asia, and in Kashmir, where copies were found only a few decades ago. There are also ancient translations of the work into Chinese, Tibetan, and other languages. The standard Chinese translation is the work of Kumārajīva, one of the greatest of all Buddhist translators and scholars, who lived in the fourth and fifth centuries CE, during the Tang dynasty, a time when Buddhism was thriving in China. For hundreds of years Kumārajīva's translation exerted an influence on Chinese culture comparable to that of the Authorized Bible on English culture, and it is still considered by the Chinese to be a masterpiece of their classical literature. And as well as making such an impact on the literary world, Kumārajīva's great achievement also inspired many Chinese artists, resulting in the development of a whole tradition of illustrating well-known scenes from the *sūtra*.

Until fairly recently, only one complete translation of the *sūtra* had been published in English. This was the work of the Dutch scholar

Hendrik Kern, published in the Sacred Books of the East series in 1884, and still in print. As this was the first translation, and as in those days people didn't know the real meaning of a number of important Buddhist technical terms, it isn't surprising that Kern's version is less than perfect, although it is very good for its time. It's rather unimaginative, and it contains some extremely odd footnotes. For one thing, the translator seems to be obsessed by the idea that the whole of Buddhism can be explained in terms of astronomy. He also tries to make out that Nirvāṇa is quite literally equivalent to the state of physical extinction: Enlightenment equals death, in other words. Very odd. A much more readable, although incomplete, version of the *sūtra* became available in 1930 in the form of a translation of Kumārajīva's Chinese text made by Bunnō Katō and revised by Professor William Soothill, an English missionary who lived for a time in China. Although Soothill was a Christian, he does succeed in conveying the devotional fervour and the spiritual mood of the original text.[39]

The first sentence of the text is translated in the same way in whatever version you read. Indeed, the opening words are the hallmark of any Buddhist *sūtra*, and the English translation, with its distinctive, slightly antiquated form, has a sort of magic about it, like 'Once upon a time'. When we hear or read the words 'Thus have I heard' (*evaṃ mayā śrutaṃ* in Sanskrit), we know at once that a teaching of the Buddha is to follow. But who has 'heard'? Who is the speaker? According to tradition it is Ānanda. Ānanda was the Buddha's cousin, his disciple, and for twenty years his constant attendant and travelling companion. And Ānanda is said to be the principal source of the oral tradition. We are told that his memory was so good that he was able to remember almost word for word whatever the Buddha said, and pass it on to the other disciples. If he happened to be out on an errand when the Buddha gave a teaching, he would get the Buddha to repeat it to him so that he had stored away in his memory a collection of everything that the Buddha had ever said.

I must confess that when I first came into contact with Buddhism, I did tend to wonder whether such a thing was possible. But during my twenty years in India, I certainly did meet both Indians and Tibetans who could reel off hundreds and hundreds of pages of scriptures by heart. And later, when I came back to England, I got to know somebody with a memory almost like a tape recorder. He would say, 'On the eighth of July three years ago, you said...' and would proceed to reel off, word for word, exactly what I had said – the order in which I had touched on certain topics, the logical stages of the argument, all the illustrations I had used, everything – together with the time of day and the circumstances. So I thought to myself, 'If it is possible for someone in London in the twentieth century to have such a phenomenal memory, no doubt it was possible in ancient India too,' and I became convinced that the Buddha did have in Ānanda someone with this extraordinary capacity to remember discourses and conversations.

But although these words, 'Thus have I heard', have a literal, historical significance, they also suggest something more esoteric. In reality, the Buddha is not outside us. The Buddha nature is not outside us, but within us – 'This very body the Buddha', as the Zen tradition has it.[40] And we could say that there's not just an Ānanda outside, in the realm of history; there's also an Ānanda inside us. And just as the historical Ānanda listened to the Buddha, so the Ānanda inside us hears the voice of truth within. Ānanda, we could say, is our own ordinary mind listening to the utterance of our own Enlightened consciousness. It's as though within us we have two consciousnesses, a lower one and a higher one. The lower consciousness usually ignores the higher one and goes its own way, or maybe doesn't even know that the higher one exists. But if that lower consciousness just stops and listens for a while, if it is receptive, it becomes aware of the voice of the higher consciousness. Like Ānanda listening to the voice of the Buddha, our ordinary mind can be receptive to the higher mind, the Enlightened mind, within us. Taking this line of thought a bit further, we can say that the whole drama of cosmic Enlightenment takes place not only without, on the stage of the cosmos, but also within, in the recesses of our own heart.

Although the opening words of the *sūtra* may be very familiar, once we are past them we find ourselves in a very unfamiliar world indeed. The world of the Mahāyāna *sūtra* is almost the kind of thing you find in science fiction, on a more spiritual, transcendental level. So before we delve into the parables, myths, and symbols of the *sūtra*, we need an introduction to this strange world. You probably won't make much sense of it, and I'm afraid I'm not going to offer much help. I'm just going to relate some of the events described in the *sūtra* and leave them to make their own effect, however strange, however bizarre, however unintelligible. For your part, just read it like a story. And whatever you do, don't think. Don't try to work it all out. Don't ask yourself what it all means. Just let your mind stop ticking and take it all in. If you want to set your intellect to work on it, you can do that later on. For the moment, just absorb the content of the *sūtra* as though you were watching a film in the darkness. This is something transcendentally surrealistic, and you really haven't a hope of working it all out, so just let your rational mind go to sleep for a while and allow the pictures to have their effect. And don't be afraid of allowing yourself to feel.

The *sūtra* opens on the Vulture's Peak. In geographical terms, the Vulture's Peak is an enormous rocky crag where the Buddha used to stay when he wanted to get away from it all. From there he could see for many miles around. In those days he would have been able to see, far in the distance, the tens of thousands of roofs of Rājagṛha, the capital city of Magadha, which was one of the great kingdoms of northern India at that time. But there are no roofs there now. You can still visit the Vulture's Peak, and it still commands a magnificent view, but there is no city any more. All you can see is dense leopard-inhabited jungle, and here and there a few ancient Buddhist, Jain, and even prehistoric Cyclopean ruins.[41]

Symbolically speaking, the Vulture's Peak represents the summit of earthly existence. Go beyond it, and you're in the world of the transcendental, the world of the purely spiritual. So when the *sūtra* describes the Buddha as seated on the Vulture's Peak, it is placing him halfway between heaven and earth. And he is surrounded there by tens of thousands of disciples of various kinds. We are told that there are twelve thousand *arhants*, those who have reached Nirvāṇa in the Hīnayāna sense of the destruction of passions, without positive knowledge and illumination. Then there are eighty thousand bodhisattvas, and also tens of thousands of gods and other non-human beings with their retinues.

And we are told that the Buddha delivers to this huge assembly a great discourse on infinity, a very popular Buddhist topic. He speaks eloquently for a long time, and everybody is deeply moved. Indeed, the effect of the Buddha's teaching is such that beautiful flowers of many colours start raining down from the heavens, and the whole universe shakes and trembles in six different ways. Then, having finished his discourse, the Buddha enters into deep meditation; and while he is meditating, there comes forth from a spot between his eyebrows a brilliant ray of pure white light. It's like a great searchlight sweeping all around the universe so that it is possible to see hundreds of millions of miles into the depths of space. In that intense light innumerable world systems are discovered in all the directions of space. And in every world system can be seen much the same thing as is going on in this one: a Buddha preaching, surrounded by disciples, and bodhisattvas practising the six great disciplines.

So this is the spectacle revealed by the ray of light which issues from the Buddha as he sits there meditating. Naturally the great assembly is astonished, and everybody wonders what it means, and what is going to happen. The bodhisattva Maitreya, the future Buddha, as he is sometimes called, enquires of Mañjuśrī, who is the wisest of the bodhisattvas, traditionally regarded as the incarnation of Wisdom, 'What is going on? What does this great occurrence signify?' And Mañjuśrī says, 'I believe – in fact I'm sure – it means that the Buddha is about to proclaim the *White Lotus Sūtra*.'

And as Mañjuśrī says this, the Buddha slowly emerges from his meditation. He opens his eyes and says, as though speaking to himself, 'The Truth in its fullness is very difficult to understand.' So difficult is it, he says, that only the Buddhas, only the fully Enlightened ones, are able to understand it. Only they, *and no one else*, can understand the Truth in its fullness (which may be a salutary reflection for us). Everybody else, the Buddha tells the assembly, has to approach the truth gradually, step by step; and the Buddha takes this into account in his teaching. He takes people by the hand and leads them one step at a time. First he teaches the *arhant* ideal of gaining Nirvāṇa in the sense of the extinction of passions, and only then, when that has been achieved and understood, does he expound the higher, more Mahāyānistic ideal of the realization of perfect Buddhahood through following the career of the bodhisattva.

If he revealed the highest truth all at once, the Buddha goes on to explain, people would be so terrified that they would be unable to receive and assimilate it. Incidentally, this is rather like what happens at the point of death, according to the *Tibetan Book of the Dead*. In that instant, Reality in its fullness dawns on the mind in one blinding flash.[42] If the mind could bear it, that moment could be the dawning of Enlightenment itself, but it is too much for the mind to bear, and it just shrinks back, terrified, and falls to ever lower levels of reality until it finds a level where it feels at home. Because people are afraid of Reality in this way, although the Buddha knows the full Truth, he can't take the risk of revealing it to his disciples all at once. He has to take them so far and then show them the next stage, until eventually they reach the ultimate goal. On this occasion, he looks round the assembly and says that he's not sure whether even now everybody present is ready to hear what he has to say. For there is, he now reveals, something more for them to learn. Even the *arhants* among them do not yet know the highest Truth.

This revelation provokes a dramatic incident. Five thousand of the disciples present simply get up and walk out. They murmur among themselves, 'Something more to learn? That's impossible. We're Enlightened, we've got Nirvāṇa. What more could there possibly be to learn? What is the Buddha talking about? Maybe he's getting a bit senile. Something more to learn? – not for us!' And with that they give the Buddha a perfunctory bow, just for old times' sake, and out they all go, shaking the dust of the assembly from their sandals.

This is a trap into which we can fall only too easily. Mistaking intellectual understanding for true knowledge, we can fool ourselves into thinking that there's no further to go, nothing more to learn. And of course as soon as we start thinking like that, we can't possibly learn any more. This is the biggest danger of all, and many people, like the five thousand disciples, succumb to it. I'm reminded of an episode in English religious history when Oliver Cromwell had dealings with a number of religious sectaries who got into a terrific argument over some knotty points of scripture. They were so obstinate, so immovable, that in the end Cromwell wrote to them, in desperation, 'Reverend Sirs, I beseech you, in the bowels of Christ, think it possible you may be mistaken.'[43]

In the *sūtra*, however, the Buddha doesn't say anything; he just lets the disciples leave. And when they have gone, he simply says, 'Now the assembly is quite pure.' In other words, now everyone present is receptive, prepared to consider that there may be something more for them to learn. So the Buddha goes on to reveal the highest Truth to this pure assembly. He tells them that his previous teaching of the three *yānas* is only provisional, an expedient made necessary by the diversity of temperaments among his disciples. Now these three *yānas* are not the Hīnayāna, the Mahāyāna, and the Vajrayāna. I'm afraid that in Buddhism we get lots of terms with double meanings. The *yānas* the Buddha is talking about here are a different set – consisting of the *śrāvakayāna* (the way of the disciple), the *pratyekabuddhayāna* (the way of the 'privately Enlightened' one), and the *bodhisattvayāna* (th way of the bodhisattva).

I don't want to go into technicalities here[44] – it's more important to grasp the general principle that between them these three *yānas* symbolize different possible approaches to Enlightenment. The first two are different forms of spiritual individualism – the first perhaps being a bit more negative than the second – and the third is of course the bodhisattva ideal. When the Buddha says that his teaching of these three *yānas* was only provisional, he means – as he goes on to explain – that in reality there is only one way, *ekayāna*. This is the Great Way, the Mahāyāna, the way leading to perfect Buddhahood. All roads lead to Rome; all the *yānas*, all the different ways – individualistic and altruistic – are useful up to a point, but ultimately they all converge into *the* Way. In other words, there is only one process of Higher Evolution, and all participate in it to the extent that they make an effort to develop. The Buddha tells the assembly that if anyone offers even a flower with faith and devotion, they are already – in principle – on the path to Buddhahood. One thing leads to another. A small act of faith leads to a bigger act of faith, a small practice of the Way leads to a bigger practice, and in this manner, step by step, you gradually begin to tread the Great Way, the one way leading to perfect Enlightenment. There is no good deed, no humanitarian act, that falls outside the scope of the Way.

On hearing this teaching Śāriputra, the oldest and wisest of the Buddha's disciples, is filled with joy. Although he is old, he is prepared to learn. His only regret, he says, is that he has spent so long at a lower level of understanding. But the Buddha encourages him, and tells him that at a time in the distant future he too will realize supreme Enlightenment as a perfect Buddha. He even tells him what his name will be. But not all the disciples are like Śāriputra. Some of them are rather disturbed and perplexed by the new teaching. Have they been wasting their time? Was the old practice completely useless? What should they do next?

To reassure them, the Buddha tells the first of the great parables of the *sūtra*, the parable of the burning house. And we see here for the first time the effect of symbolism. Four leading elders who were still in doubt after hearing the Buddha's abstract statement of the higher teaching are now convinced. They now realize that they can go beyond the stage of eradication of negative emotions, and proceed to positive illumination, supreme Knowledge, Wisdom, Enlightenment ... and they

d. One of them, Mahākāśyapa, gives expression to their parable on their behalf, the parable – or myth – of the

parable has been told, the Buddha praises the four elders, oceeds to shed more light on the way he leads sentient beings to Enlightenment. We already know that he teaches step by step, holding back the highest truth until his disciples are ready to hear it. Now we learn that he also adapts his teaching to suit the varying capacities of different people. To illustrate this, he tells two more parables: the parable of the rain-cloud and the parable of the sun. He follows the parables by predicting that Mahākāśyapa and the other elders will also become perfect Buddhas, even announcing what their names will be.

Then, turning from the future to the past, and once more addressing the whole assembly, the Buddha tells them about another Buddha, a Buddha who lived millions and millions of years before his own time. The Buddha tells the story because the career of this Buddha in some respects paralleled his own. The majority of the followers of this Buddha, too, had followed the Hīnayāna path of the *arhant*. Only sixteen of them – they were his own sons from the period before he became a monk – had aspired to perfect Buddhahood as bodhisattvas. But sooner or later, the Buddha says, all the followers of this Buddha would enter the Great Way, the Mahāyāna. To illustrate this, the Buddha tells the parable of the magic city – and as we will not be looking at this parable in depth, I will recount it briefly here.

A party of travellers is bound for a place called Ratnadvīpa ('Place of Jewels'), and has employed a guide to show them the way through the dense forest. It is a very difficult, dangerous road, and long before they have reached their destination the travellers become exhausted, and say to their guide, 'We can't go another step. Let's all go back.' But the guide thinks, 'That would be a pity. They've come so far already. What can I do to persuade them to keep going?' Well, apparently the guide has some sort of magic power, because what he does is conjure up a magic city. He says to the travellers, 'Look! There's a city right here in front of us. Let's rest there and have something to eat, and then we'll decide what to do next.' The travellers, of course, are only too pleased to stop and have a rest. They have a meal and spend the night in the magic city, and in the morning they feel much better, and decide that they will carry on with their journey after all. So the guide makes the magic city disappear and leads the travellers on to their destination, the Place of Jewels.[45]

The meaning of the parable is not hard to fathom in the context of the *sūtra*. The guide is of course the Buddha, and the travellers are his disciples. The Place of Jewels is supreme Enlightenment, and the magic city is the Hīnayāna Nirvāṇa – Nirvāṇa as the comparatively negative state of freedom from passions, without positive spiritual illumination. And, as the parable suggests, the Buddha first of all speaks in terms of Nirvāṇa in the ordinary psychological sense. Only when this teaching has been assimilated – only when the disciples have rested in the magic city – does he lead them on to the higher spiritual goal of perfect Buddhahood, the Place of Jewels.

We could use the same parable to describe the process of teaching meditation. When people first come along to learn to meditate, they quite often ask, 'What is the goal of meditation?' You wouldn't usually reply, straight off, 'Well, the goal of meditation is to become like a Buddha,' because that's the last thing most people want to be. They're not interested in anything religious or spiritual; they just want peace of mind in the midst of their everyday life and work. And it's perfectly true to say that meditation gives you peace of mind. But when they've been meditating for some time, and they start to experience peace of mind through meditation, then they might ask, 'Well, is this all, or is there something more to meditation?' That would be the right time to say, 'Yes, there is something more. Peace of mind in the ordinary psychological sense is not the final goal of meditation, but only an intermediate stage. Beyond it there's a spiritual goal – Enlightenment, knowledge of the Truth, knowledge of Reality – which in Buddhist terms is called perfect Buddhahood.' Here 'peace of mind' is the magic city in which the traveller is nourished and rested for the long journey to Enlightenment.

When the Buddha has told the parable of the magic city, we begin to see the effect of all these parables on the audience. More and more disciples come forward to confess their previously limited understanding and announce their acceptance of the new teaching. The Buddha predicts that the monk Pūrṇa, together with five hundred other distinguished *arhants*, will gain supreme Enlightenment, and in their joy these *arhants* also tell a parable, the parable of the drunkard and the jewel. More and more disciples are then predicted to perfect Buddhahood, and eventually all the Hīnayāna disciples are converted, and decide to aspire to supreme Enlightenment as bodhisattvas.

There are, of course, thousands of bodhisattvas already present, bodhisattvas who have followed the Great Way from the beginning. The Buddha now turns to them, and impresses upon them that the *White Lotus Sūtra* is tremendously important and must be preserved at all costs. The text should be read, recited, copied, expounded, and even ceremonially worshipped, the Buddha says. And all the bodhisattvas promise to protect the *sūtra*.

Then, suddenly, something extraordinary happens – extraordinary even by the standards of this extraordinary *sūtra*. In the midst of the assembly, from the depths of the earth, there springs up a stupa, a colossal, unbelievably magnificent stupa which towers into the sky. A stupa is a monument which is made to contain the relics – fragments of bone and so on – of the Buddha or one of his disciples. Following a pre-Buddhistic practice, the first stupas were very simple – just a mound of earth, a sort of tumulus. But the stupa which appears out of the earth in the *White Lotus Sūtra* is made not of brick, not of stone, not even of marble, but of the seven precious things – gold, silver, lapis lazuli, moonstone, agate, pearl, and carnelian. What is more, it is beautifully decorated with flags and flowers, and it is emitting light, fragrance, and music in all directions.

One can just imagine the scene. There are all these astonished disciples – only the Buddha isn't astonished – and this enormous stupa towering into the sky. And as they all gaze up at the stupa in amazement, from the midst of it there comes forth a thunderous voice which cries, 'Excellent, excellent, Śākyamuni! You are well able to preach the *White Lotus Sūtra*. All that you say is true.' (Śākyamuni of course is the Buddha, whom we can call 'our' Buddha because he appeared in our world.) At this the disciples are absolutely agog. What does it all mean? Whose is the voice? Whose is the stupa? So the Buddha explains that the stupa contains the preserved body of a very ancient Buddha called Abundant Treasures (Prabhūtaratna in Sanskrit), who lived millions upon millions of years ago. During his lifetime Abundant Treasures had made a vow that after his death, the stupa in which his remains were enshrined would spring forth wherever the *White Lotus Sūtra* was being expounded. What is more, he had vowed that he himself would bear testimony to the truth of the teaching.

The whole assembly is very impressed by this explanation, and they ask if it isn't possible for the stupa to be opened so that they can see the body of this ancient Buddha, still miraculously preserved after millions of years. But Śākyamuni tells them that it's not as easy as all that. According to another vow that Abundant Treasures made, Śākyamuni has to fulfil a certain condition before the preserved body of the ancient Buddha can be seen. The condition is that Śākyamuni must summon into his presence all the Buddhas who have ever emanated from him, and who are now teaching the Doctrine throughout the universe. And at once Śākyamuni proceeds to fulfil the condition, so that the assembly's wish can be granted. Once more he sends out a great ray of light which reveals the Buddhas in all the universes in the ten directions of space. And at once those Buddhas understand that this is a signal, and tell their own bodhisattvas, 'Now I've got to go on a journey to the Sahā-world, millions of miles across the universe, because Buddha Śākyamuni has sent for me.'

In Buddhism, each Buddha-world, each universe, has got a name. Ours is called the Sahā-world, 'the world of endurance', because here there's a lot to be endured. According to the Buddhist scriptures, our world is not a particularly good one; there are lots of other worlds with Buddhas and bodhisattvas where conditions are much better. So Śākyamuni doesn't want these incoming Buddhas to see the imperfection of his own little universe, and sets about preparing it for their arrival. He transforms the whole earth into brilliant blue light, like lapis lazuli, with golden cords stretching across it to mark off the blue ground into squares. Inside these squares, we're told, there spring up beautiful trees made entirely of jewels – trunk, branches, leaves, flowers, fruit – and thousands of feet tall. The earth, which is strewn with all sorts of heavenly flowers, smokes with sweet-smelling incense. And to complete the purification process, all the gods and men who are not part of the assembly are transferred somewhere – we're not told precisely where, but they're sort of bundled out of the way – and all the villages, towns and cities, mountains, rivers, and forests, disappear.

Hardly is this transformation completed when five hundred Buddhas arrive from the different directions of space, each accompanied by a great bodhisattva, and take their seats on five hundred magnificent lion thrones under five hundred jewel trees. Such is the scale of things that they completely take up all the available space, and the Buddhas have barely begun to arrive. So Śākyamuni hastily purifies untold millions of worlds in all the directions of space, and they are all instantly occupied by streams of incoming Buddhas, who take their seats beneath jewel trees and pay their respects to the Buddha Śākyamuni by offering a double handful of jewel flowers.

Now that all these millions of Buddhas, with their attendant bodhisattvas, are gathered together in one place, the condition laid down by Abundant Treasures has been fulfilled. So Śākyamuni floats up into the sky until he is level with the great door of the stupa, draws back the bolt, and flings open the door with a sound like thunder to reveal the body of Abundant Treasures within. And even though the body of the ancient Buddha is millions upon millions of years old, it is perfectly preserved, seated cross-legged within the stupa. Awe-struck at the sight, the assembly take up handfuls of jewel flowers and scatter them so that they rain down over the two Buddhas.

And it turns out that it is not just that Abundant Treasures' body has been perfectly preserved. The ancient Buddha is actually still alive after all these years, and he asks Śākyamuni to come and share his throne. So Śākyamuni goes to sit next to Abundant Treasures in the stupa – this deeply symbolic and significant scene became a favourite one with Chinese Buddhist artists. The whole assembly, looking up into the sky at the two Buddhas, desires to be raised up to the same level, so Śākyamuni exerts his supernormal powers and lifts all the assembly, all the millions of Buddhas and bodhisattvas, up into the air until they are level with himself and Abundant Treasures.

At this point, Śākyamuni cries out in a loud voice, 'Who among you is able to preach the *White Lotus Sūtra* in the Sahā-world? The time of my death is at hand. To whom can I entrust the Lotus of the True Law?' There then follows a whole series of episodes – possibly added to the *sūtra* after the main body of it was completed – which I am going to omit, partly for the sake of brevity, and partly because they rather break up the continuity of the action. After these diversions, two bodhisattvas come forward in response to the Buddha's demand, and promise that they will preserve and spread the *White Lotus Sūtra* after the Buddha's death. And all the *arhants* who have been predicted to perfect Buddhahood give a similar pledge.

Attention now turns to two nuns who are present, standing a little to one side. These are Mahāprajāpatī, the Buddha's aunt and foster-mother, and Yaśodharā, his wife in the days before he left home, both of whom became nuns after the Buddha's Enlightenment, under his guidance. They are feeling rather sorrowful because nothing has so far been said about Enlightenment for them, but the Buddha assures them that they are sure of becoming perfectly Enlightened one day. In response, they too pledge to protect the *White Lotus Sūtra*.

There are many irreversible bodhisattvas in the assembly – 'irreversible' in that they have gone so far on the path that they cannot fall back into lower states, and are irrevocably bound for perfect Buddhahood. They now announce that they are determined to make the *White Lotus Sūtra* known throughout the whole universe, and they join the rest of the assembly in begging the Buddha to have no anxiety about the *sūtra's* future, even in the dreadful days which lie ahead. A dark age is approaching, they say, a time of war and confusion, bloodshed and evil, but they tell the Buddha, 'Do not worry. Even in the terrible age that is coming, we shall remember the teaching. We shall preserve it, we shall protect it, and we shall propagate it.'

We are swiftly made aware that the preservation of the *sūtra* will be no easy task. The bodhisattva Mañjuśrī comments that it is a tremendous responsibility, and the Buddha agrees, and goes on to list four qualities which the bodhisattvas who want to fulfil this mission must have. First, they must be perfect in conduct. Second, they must confine themselves to 'proper spheres of activity' – which means that they must avoid unsuitable company and dwell inwardly in the true nature of reality. Third, they must maintain happy, peaceful states of mind, unaffected by zeal or envy. And fourth, they must cultivate feelings of love towards all living beings. The Buddha explains these four qualities in some detail, and then tells another parable, the parable of the wheel-rolling king, or universal monarch. (A 'wheel-rolling' king is one who sets turning the wheel of the Dharma, that is, one who rules according to the Buddha's teaching.)

The story goes like this. There was once a king who went to war because he wished to extend his domain. His soldiers fought so heroically that the king was very pleased with them, and gave them all the rewards they deserved. He gave them houses, land, clothes, slaves, chariots, gold, silver, gems – in fact, everything he had in his palace. The only thing he didn't give away was the magnificent crest jewel that he wore in his own turban. Eventually, however, he was so pleased with the soldiers' bravery that he took the crest jewel itself and handed it over to them. So, as the Buddha goes on to explain, he himself is like the wheel-rolling king. Seeing the efforts that his disciples have made to practise his teachings, seeing how bravely they have fought against Māra, he rewards them with more and more teachings and blessings. In the end, keeping nothing back, he gives them the supreme teaching, the *White Lotus Sūtra*.[46]

Having heard this parable, the great bodhisattvas who have come from other world systems with their own Buddhas offer their services too. But Śākyamuni says, 'No, your services are not necessary. I have innumerable bodhisattvas here in my own Sahā-world, and they will protect the *White Lotus Sūtra* after my death.' As he says this, the universe shakes and trembles, and from the space underneath the earth there issues an incalculable host of irreversible bodhisattvas. One by one they salute in turn all the Buddhas present, and sing their praises. Although this takes an extraordinary length of time – fifty minor aeons, during which the whole assembly stays completely silent – it actually seems, through the power of the Buddha, as though only a single afternoon has passed.

When all the salutations and songs are over, the Buddha Śākyamuni and the four leaders of the great host of irreversible bodhisattvas exchange greetings. The implication seems to be that Śākyamuni is claiming all these newly appeared bodhisattvas as his own disciples. The assembly can scarcely believe it. The Buddha assures them, 'Yes, these are indeed my own disciples, and they have been following the Great Way for a very long time. You haven't seen them before because they live under the earth.' But this isn't good enough for the perplexed disciples. They say, 'Look here. You gained Enlightenment under the bodhi tree at Bodh Gaya only forty years ago. How can you possibly have trained such a fantastic number of bodhisattvas in that time? A few hundred, a few thousand even, we could believe – but this many? And they seem to belong to past ages and to other world systems too. How can you possibly claim them all as your disciples? It's as ridiculous as a young man of twenty-five pointing to a crowd of wizened centenarians and saying that they are all his sons.'

The Buddha, of course, has a reply to all this scepticism. And this reply is a central revelation, as the Mahāyāna sees it, making this scene the climax of the whole drama of cosmic Enlightenment. The Buddha says that he did not really gain Enlightenment only forty years ago. In fact, he says, he gained Enlightenment an uncountable, incalculable number of millions of ages ago. In other words, he makes the rather staggering claim that he is eternally Enlightened. By now it is obvious that this is no longer the historical Śākyamuni speaking, but the universal, cosmic principle of Enlightenment itself. All these millions of ages, he says, he has been teaching and preaching in many different forms, and in many different worlds. He has appeared as Dīpaṅkara Buddha, Śākyamuni Buddha, and so on. He is not really born, does not really attain Enlightenment, does not really die, but only appears to do so, just to encourage people. If he stayed with them all the time, he says, people would not appreciate him or follow his teaching. And to illustrate this, he tells the parable of the good physician.

This great declaration that the Buddha is eternally Enlightened produces a tremendous effect on the assembly. Hosts of disciples attain various spiritual insights, powers, understandings, and blessings, while flowers, incense, and jewels rain down from the sky, celestial canopies are raised on high, and countless bodhisattvas sing the praises of all the Buddhas – a display which provides an apt setting for the Buddha's next teaching. For he now explains that the development of faith in his eternal life, faith in the sense of an emotional response, is equivalent to the development of wisdom. Such faith, we may say, is wisdom expressed in emotional terms. If you have this sort of faith, you will see and hear the universal Buddha on the spiritual Vulture's Peak eternally preaching the *White Lotus Sūtra*. What is more, the Buddha says, the merits of listening to the *White Lotus Sūtra* are very great, and the merits of preaching it even greater – and of course it's very demeritorious to disparage the *sūtra* in any way.

This warning introduces the episode of the bodhisattva Never Direct. Never Direct, the Buddha says, was a bodhisattva who lived millions of years ago. He used to go around saying to people, 'It is not for me to direct you. You are free to do anything you like. But I would advise you to take up the bodhisattva career so that ultimately you may become perfect Buddhas.' Now some of the people on the receiving end of this got very fed up with Never Direct. Why on earth should they want to become Buddhas? Many of them became so angry that they abused the bodhisattva, hit him with sticks, pelted him with stones, and generally gave him a very rough time indeed. Nothing daunted him, however, and not bearing his abusers any ill will, Never Direct would just retreat to a safe distance and continue to cry out, 'It is not for me to give you any direction. You will all become Buddhas.' This is how he got his nickname, Never Direct. Śākyamuni ends the story by saying that he himself was Never Direct in a previous life, and some of those who were his persecutors in those days are now his disciples.

At this point it's the turn of the irreversible bodhisattvas from under the earth to speak. They also promise to protect the *White Lotus Sūtra*, and say that they will preach it throughout the whole universe. Their promise sparks off all manner of marvels and wonders. The Buddha-fields in all the directions of space begin to shake and tremble, and all the inhabitants of those distant worlds look down into the Sahā-world and see it revealed, like looking down through the depths of the water and seeing something at the bottom. They see the Buddhas Śākyamuni and Abundant Treasures seated on their joint lotus throne in the middle of the stupa, and they see the countless millions of great bodhisattvas.

Śākyamuni is joyfully hailed by all the gods, who shower down flowers, incense, and jewels which merge in a huge mass, like clouds massing together, and form a jewelled canopy which covers the whole sky. Marvel upon marvel takes place, until all the worlds in the universe are seen to reflect one another like millions of mutually reflecting mirrors, and interpenetrate one another like innumerable beams of intersecting coloured light. Eventually all these universes, with all their beings, all their Buddhas and bodhisattvas, are fused into one harmonious Buddha-field, one cosmos wherein the principle of Enlightenment reigns supreme.

For one last time the Buddha extols the merits of the *sūtra*, and reminds the assembly of the importance of preserving it and propagating it. Then he rises from his lion throne in the midst of the sky and places his right hand in blessing on the heads of the countless irreversible bodhisattvas. At last, requesting the Buddhas present to return to their own domains, he says, 'Buddhas, peace be upon you. Let the stupa of the Buddha Abundant Treasures be restored as before.' Everybody rejoices – and thus the great drama concludes.

2

QUESTIONS AND ANSWERS

THE SYMBOLISM OF THE WHITE LOTUS

What is the symbolical significance of the name White Lotus Sūtra*? Does the title relate to the content of the sūtra? Most translators call it simply the* Lotus Sūtra – *is this inexactitude?*

When you take the full title, *Saddharma Puṇḍarīka Sūtra*, the emphasis needs to be on *Saddharma*. It is not just the Dharma, but the real Dharma, the true Dharma, because it contains a higher revelation in respect of the unity of the three *yānas*, and in respect of the eternity of the Buddha. I wouldn't like to say that calling it the *White* Lotus of the true Dharma was *just* a flowery addition, but Indian Buddhists were very fond of that kind of style – there is also the *Karuṇā Puṇḍarīka Sūtra*, the *White Lotus of Compassion Sūtra*.[47]

You can look at the symbolism of the lotus – that it blooms, that it grows out of the mud, and so on – but that can really be applied to any *sūtra*, because any *sūtra* represents the transcendental truth in that kind of way. So although no doubt you *could* give an exegesis of the title in such a way as to demonstrate the whole teaching of the *sūtra*, in my view that would not originally have been intended to be the case. As I say, the emphasis should really be on the fact that the *sūtra* embodies the *saddharma*, the real teaching of the Buddha; the 'White Lotus' just makes the title more pleasing and evocative.

Strictly speaking *puṇḍarīka* is 'white lotus', just as *utpala* is 'blue lotus', but sometimes *puṇḍarīka* is used simply to mean lotus. I have seen these lotuses growing in India. They are white tinged with pink, bigger than a water-lily, and their petals are large and slightly blowsy, not spiky like the petals of water-lilies.

The sūtra is often called the Threefold Lotus Sūtra. *What relationship do the preceding and succeeding* sūtras *bear to the* White Lotus Sūtra?
They are apparently apocryphal works of Chinese composition. They have their own value – some of the imagery in the introductory *sūtra* is quite extraordinary – but in a way they are superfluous, because the *White Lotus Sūtra* stands complete in itself and needs no introduction or conclusion. I have not worked out any doctrinal connection, but no doubt that could be done, or has been done.

You call these two sūtras apocryphal. But isn't any Mahāyāna text claiming its descent from the Buddha through some revelation 'apocryphal'?
Chinese works such as these are apocryphal in that they purport to be translated from Sanskrit, and have an array of names of translators, dates, and places of translation, but these details amount to deception, for the works are not in fact translations at all. This distinguishes them from Mahāyāna *sūtras* which are apocryphal in the Indian sense. Unlike the Indians, the Chinese had a highly developed critical sense which they applied to their own literature and to Buddhist works, so they would have been aware of stylistic differences, and that certain words came into use at a certain time. They had a sophisticated ability to discriminate in this way which did not become common in Europe until after the Renaissance.

WHERE DID THE MAHĀYĀNA *SŪTRAS* COME FROM?

In The Eternal Legacy, *you say that the Mahāyāna* sūtras *are revealed, directly or indirectly, by the Buddha's* sambhogakāya *('body of glory'), and you also say that we are not to think of the* sūtras *as necessarily being delivered at one particular time and place.*[48] *Were the* sūtras *composed by Enlightened disciples, or do we have to believe that a germ of them at least was uttered by the historical Buddha?*
Well, we cannot regard the Mahāyāna *sūtras* in their present form as having been delivered by the historical Buddha Śākyamuni. It may well

be, however, that some of the teachings contained in the *sūtras* do go back to Śākyamuni, and perhaps even some of his actual words are embedded in them. This is noticeable in, for example, the *Lalitavistara*,[49] in which quite extensive passages of what would seem to be the teaching of the historical Buddha are embedded in this very colourful Mahāyāna *sūtra*. The difference in style and approach can be seen very easily, because the quotations are in rather sober vein whereas the rest of the text is highly mythic and poetic. Although there are examples like this, however, as a whole the *sūtras* cannot possibly be regarded as representing the actual discourses of the historical Buddha. So what was the genesis of the Mahāyāna *sūtras*? If they were not the utterance of the historical Buddha, whose utterance were they? Certainly they purport to be the utterance of the historical Buddha, though saying that raises all sorts of questions, because the ancient Buddhists did not distinguish the historical from the non-historical, so they would not have been able to think of a *sūtra* as having been given by a non-historical as distinct from a historical Buddha. They did not use those categories. But from our point of view, where did those *sūtras* originate?

If the *sūtras* are a communication from the Enlightened mind, as they appear to be no less than the Pāli scriptures, we can only assume that certain gifted disciples had experiences of communication from the Buddha in the sense of the trans-historical essence of Buddhahood. They would then have written down this communication as best they understood it in the form of the Mahāyāna *sūtras*, attributing those *sūtras* in all sincerity to the Buddha himself. It is not that they were deliberately composing something of their own which they proceeded to put into the mouth of the Buddha. That would have been entirely foreign to their way of thinking. Perhaps there were different levels of inspiration, so that sometimes what purported to be the utterance of the *sambhogakāya* actually sprang from a rather lower level of inspiration, but in the case of some Mahāyāna *sūtras* we cannot resist the impression that, as far as we are able to judge, they sprang from as high a level of inspiration as we encounter in the Pāli canon with respect to utterances which seem to be those of the historical Buddha. So it would seem that the Mahāyāna *sūtras*, broadly speaking, originated in the spiritual experience of spiritually gifted disciples who were able to reach a level corresponding to that of the Buddha's own spiritual attainment, and receive there, so to speak, a communication from the Buddha which they thereafter embodied, perhaps sometimes in their own language, in what we know as the Mahāyāna *sūtras*.

So the sūtras *were esoteric, 'non-public', writings composed by Enlightened disciples?*
The impression I have is not that they were withheld from ordinary people or other members of the spiritual community any more than the Hīnayāna *suttas* were. You must remember that many of the Mahāyāna *sūtras* were produced at a period when writing had become much more common than it was in the Buddha's day. The *sūtras* were committed to writing, or even perhaps originally composed in written form – they do not bear the hallmarks of oral traditions as the Pāli *suttas* do. This means that they would automatically have had a wider circulation than was possible for a teaching that was transmitted orally and had to be learned from the lips of a teacher with whom you were in personal contact.

Many Mahāyāna *sūtras* have colophons extolling the virtues of copying and distributing the *sūtra*, which would suggest that Mahāyāna *sūtras* were definitely not thought of as esoteric documents in the way that the Vinaya was. According to the Vinaya, it is an offence to teach the Dharma to one who is not a *bhikkhu*,[50] but the Mahāyāna *sūtras* issue no such prohibition; in fact, you are encouraged to transmit the *sūtra* to as many sentient beings as possible, an attitude which is of course in accordance with the bodhisattva ideal.

But the White Lotus Sūtra *does emphasize the dire consequences of disparaging the* sūtra. *The Buddha goes so far as to say:*

> *'Those who slander this* sūtra
> *If I told the tale of their evils*
> *I could not exhaust them in a whole kalpa.*
> *For this cause and reason*
> *I especially say to you*
> *Amongst undiscerning people*
> *Do not preach this* sūtra.'[51]

Presumably not preaching the sūtra *to the undiscerning would save them from the consequences of hearing it yet being unreceptive to it, or even disparaging it. The implication is that it is better not to hear the Dharma at all than to hear it and react against it. Is this so? If it is, should all forms of transmission of the Dharma be given only to those likely to be receptive rather than being given indiscriminately in the form of books, public talks, and so on?*

We can't take such an extreme warning at face value. This kind of statement appears in Mahāyāna *sūtras* for a mixture of reasons. Mahāyāna *sūtras* were not accepted by Hīnayānists – to use that term – as genuine *Buddhavacana*,[52] and sometimes the Hīnayānists seem to have criticized the *sūtras*, or even slandered them, as the Mahāyānists would see it. The warnings of this kind which the Mahāyāna *sūtras* contain are therefore partly polemical in intent. At the same time, they are partly the expression of a genuine concern for people's spiritual well-being, a concern that people should not be put in a position of rejecting something which it can only do them harm to reject.

You have to be very careful about this. It is not as though there is some avenging deity waiting to punish you. If you are not receptive to the truth, however, or if you get into the habit of closing your mind to something that you cannot immediately accept and understand, you do come to be in a parlous condition, spiritually speaking. The Mahāyāna *sūtras* are really saying that it is not skilful to present a pupil with teachings which, given their general attitude and mental make-up, they cannot but reject. If those teachings bear the label 'Buddhism', they can only come to the conclusion that Buddhism is not for them. People should not be fed teachings in such quantities that they are quite unable to digest them and are bound to vomit them up.

On the other hand, you also need to be careful in another way. In the twentieth century there was a great controversy in the Church between the Anglicans and the Roman Catholics. A Catholic priest produced a pamphlet called *Reserve in Communicating Religious Knowledge*,[53] which suggested that if, for instance, someone who was interested in Catholicism came round to see a priest, the priest should not talk about Catholic dogmas like the infallibility of the pope all at once, because that would be bound to put the visitor off. The advice was that the priest should say first the kind of thing that the visitor would be able to accept more readily, such as that the Catholic Church teaches that we should love our enemies. The other doctrines or dogmas should be kept in reserve, in recognition of the fact that they were not very acceptable to someone who was just beginning to be interested in the Catholic Church. When the Anglicans got hold of this pamphlet, of course they at once accused the Catholic Church of hypocrisy, of not being open with people about its true beliefs.

In a way, though, the Catholic priest had a point. If you try to explain certain things to people before they are prepared, you may simply scare them away. The fact is that people progress very slowly on the spiritual path, and at the beginning they are just not prepared for the teachings pertaining to the later stages of the path. On the other hand, there is also something in the accusation of hypocrisy. You could use this 'reserve in communicating religious knowledge' in a way that was not quite honest and straightforward. So this is a matter of some tact and delicacy.

For instance, suppose someone at a meditation class asked you 'Do Buddhists not believe in God?' If you replied, 'Oh no, lots of Buddhists believe in God,' that would not be straightforward and honest. But suppose you knew that if you were to say that Buddhists do not believe in God – full stop – then that person would never come to the class again, how should you reply? It is a difficult question. I suggest that you should temporize, using that word positively. You could say, for example, 'The word "God" can be understood in a number of different ways. Nowadays there is a lot of discussion even among Christians as to what God really means, even as to whether there *is* a God. In Buddhism we do not pronounce very readily about matters concerning ultimate Reality, and from the Christian point of view God is a statement of ultimate Reality. We prefer to concentrate on the actual practice of ethics and meditation, with a view eventually to having a deeper understanding of these things for ourselves, out of our personal experience.' If you were to answer in this way, you would be neither hypocritical nor untrue to the Buddhist tradition.

Sometimes people want to corner you and force you to make a statement one way or the other, but you should not allow this to happen. Sometimes you have to say, 'Buddhism is a vast subject. It is not easy even for those who have been practising it for some time to understand it. Just take it bit by bit. Concentrate on observing the precepts, practising meditation, and reflecting on whatever teachings appeal to you most. Leave the others aside if you find them too difficult or unacceptable. We would not insist that you sign the thirty-nine articles of Buddhism on the spot, even if we had them!'

You said that the White Lotus Sūtra *may have been written down in central Asia. How much central Asian influence is evident in the* sūtra, *in terms of its cosmology or even its spiritual content?*
The question is perhaps better applied to Mahāyāna *sūtras* in general than specifically to the *White Lotus Sūtra*. It has been suggested that Mahāyāna imagery, particularly the concept of Amitābha and the Pure Land of the *Sukhāvatī-Vyūha Sūtras*, does owe something to Iranian influences.[54] There are anticipations of the jewel trees of the Pure Land in the *Dīgha Nikāya* of the Pāli canon, for example,[55] and it would seem likely that this idea of jewel trees in magnificent gardens is of Babylonian origin. We know that Aśoka was in contact with the Persian empire, and Persian artisans apparently came to India to build his palace – which seems to have been modelled on that of Persepolis – for those highly polished columns can only have been produced by Persian craftsmen. So it seems quite possible that some of the later, more legendary *suttas* in the *Dīgha Nikāya* belonging to that period (one hundred years after the Buddha) do reflect the Persian influence in their imagery.

DON'T TAKE IT TOO SERIOUSLY

You have referred to the Mahāyāna sūtras *as works of symbolic religious art, and recommended that we should see them as giving us a glimpse into an archetypal world rather than providing an actual pattern of Buddhist living. So what is the best approach to studying this non-conceptual material?*
It is very difficult to say. The main thing is to avoid literalism. You should familiarize yourself with the letter of the text, but not take it too literally. Many people approach almost any Buddhist material in a very literalistic way, grasping the letter tightly and often missing the spirit completely.

I am afraid I will be misunderstood, but I would almost advise that you should not take it too seriously. Read it in the way that you would read good poetry, or a good novel. Enjoy it; immerse yourself in it. You can get down to a study of what the details mean, and what the deeper significance of the *sūtra* might be, later on. To begin with, it is very important to allow the work as a whole to have some impact on you, to try to experience it as a whole rather than getting lost in the details. It is also important to read the *sūtra* itself, and use a commentary to throw light on it, rather than the other way round.

A TWOFOLD MESSAGE

The White Lotus Sūtra *seems to consist of two main revelations: that there is in truth only one spiritual path, and that what we perceive as the historical Buddha is really an expression of eternal Enlightenment. Chapters 1 to 10 seem to be an independent drama providing a setting for and an amplification of the first revelation; chapters 11, 15, and 16 then provide a setting for the second revelation. Do you think there might originally have been two independent teachings which were brought together to form the twin nuclei of the* White Lotus Sūtra*?*

Leaving aside the miscellaneous cluster of chapters at the end, the *sūtra* does naturally fall into these two parts, but that is no reason to regard them as having been originally independent works. Although they have their distinctive themes, the two sections do seem to hang together. One corresponds to the relative *bodhicitta* and the other to the absolute *bodhicitta*. One is concerned with the spiritual path which exists in time and is followed in time, and the other pertains to ultimate reality, as embodied in the Buddha, which exists outside space and time. I do not have an impression of discontinuity or of two independent *sūtras* having been soldered together to make a single work, and as far as I know this has not been suggested by any scholar who has made a study of the work. I think that you are correct in detecting the difference of theme between the two sections, but that distinction represents the basic structure of the *sūtra*, and conveys its twofold message.

CAN WORSHIP OF THE *SŪTRA* LEAD TO ENLIGHTENMENT?

The sūtra *talks of faith as the emotional equivalent of wisdom, and recommends worship of the* sūtra *as a practice. Some Buddhists seem to see homage to the* White Lotus Sūtra *as their only practice. Could this ever be a full path to Enlightenment?*

I suppose it depends what you mean by worship of the *White Lotus Sūtra*. I think that true worship of the *sūtra* could be at least an *approach* to the path to Enlightenment, but I am not sure how easily worship of a text would come to people in the West. It is not impossible, but it is a little foreign to our tradition. Text worship does feature prominently in some religions, particularly in Sikhism. Sikhism has no images, but has as the object of worship the *Adi Granth* (which they call the

Guru Granth Sahib), the volume of the Sikh scriptures. Sikhs place a beautifully printed volume of this text on a silken cushion, or on a canopied throne, and they make offerings to it, just as described in the Mahāyāna *sūtras*, where the practice probably originated.

You could adopt the practice of keeping a scripture open on the shrine, with a little glass case to protect it from incense smoke. It would be suitable for Dharma Day in particular, but it would be appropriate at all times if you wanted to represent all of the Three Jewels in the shrine-room. The symbol of the Buddha jewel is the image, and the symbol of the Sangha jewel is the presence of the spiritual community, but to symbolize the Dharma jewel, a book is needed.

Nichiren,[56] *of course, teaches the practice of reverence for the* sūtra. *It seems almost like a form of Pure Land Buddhism, with devotion offered to the* White Lotus Sūtra *rather than to Amitābha. Could this practice actually lead the practitioner to an insight into the* sūtra?

The standard Buddhist teaching is that the five spiritual faculties, which include faith, must be balanced. For a time one particular faculty may predominate, but in the end they need to be in equilibrium. As I see it, there is no question of alternative paths, as is sometimes suggested in Hinduism. If you start off travelling the path of devotion, sooner or later you have to bring in the path of wisdom; the one reinforces the other.

WHO IS TO JUDGE WHAT IS PROFOUND?

In the sūtra *the Buddha explains to the assembly that the truth is very difficult to understand, and has to be approached gradually. Do you accept the Mahāyāna's suggestion that its teachings are more profound than those that historically precede it? Are the* Heart Sūtra *and the* White Lotus Sūtra *more profound than the teachings of the Pāli canon?*

That is a very difficult question. Who is to judge what is profound? Someone studying a verse of the *Dhammapada*, for example, might see the whole Truth in that, even though others could not. Sometimes the implications of an apparently simple saying are absolutely vast.

Perhaps you might say that some texts or sayings are obviously more profound than others, but it is very difficult to make a blanket statement. Certainly some Mahāyāna teachings are more *elaborate* than others. For instance, the Mahāyāna *sūtras* have gone into the *śūnyatā* teaching in a much more thoroughgoing fashion than any Pāli text. Perhaps you need some acquaintance with the Mahāyāna to be able to appreciate the depths of some of the Buddha's teaching in the Pāli scriptures. The depth may be there, but for various reasons it is not so well articulated.

The linguistic resources of the Mahāyāna were far greater, because a Buddhist vocabulary had been developed and refined by that time, and confusions had been resolved. The Buddha had to make do with the language used by the people around him who did not have his Enlightenment experience. He had to use the same language, but try to use it in his own way. When the Mahāyāna *sūtras* were composed hundreds of years later, Buddhists had developed a language of their own which was more adequate to express their insights and intuitions.

So you would not accept the sūtra's *suggestion that it is explicating a fuller teaching?*
It is fuller in relation to the classical Hīnayāna, but the classical Hīnayāna does not necessarily coincide with certain teachings of the historical Buddha as recorded in the existing Pāli canon. Assuming that the teachings of the Pāli canon are properly understood, it could not be said that the Mahāyāna goes beyond them.

THE *TRIKĀYA* DOCTRINE AND THE *WHITE LOTUS SŪTRA*

How radical would the idea of an eternal Buddha have been when it emerged? What stage of development would the trikāya *doctrine*[57] *have reached at the time of the* White Lotus Sūtra?
The distinction between the *rūpakāya* of the Buddha and the *dharmakāya* occurs even in the Pāli canon, although the Theravāda uses the term *dharmakāya* rather literalistically: in their view, the Buddha is the *dharmakāya* simply because he is the embodiment of all the teachings contained in the Tripiṭaka. So the concept of the *dharmakāya* as distinct from the *rūpakāya* was part of general Buddhist teaching before the *White Lotus Sūtra*, but it was the *White Lotus Sūtra* which brought it into prominence and placed it at the centre of the teaching, showing how important it was to see that the Buddha was the *dharmakāya* in the fullest sense, not just the *rūpakāya*.

The development of the *trikāya* doctrine seems to have emerged in later Mahāyāna *sūtras*. The earlier ones distinguish between the *rūpakāya* and the *dharmakāya*, but make no mention of a *sambhogakāya*. Sometimes what came to be called the *sambhogakāya* shades into the *dharmakāya*, but there is no sharp differentiation between them as there came to be later in the *trikāya* doctrine, which is associated with the Yogācāra.

In the White Lotus Sūtra *it is almost as if the eternal Buddha is both* sambhogakāya *and* dharmakāya.
Yes. If the Buddha is to be an actor in a drama of cosmic Enlightenment, he has to have a form; he can hardly appear as a featureless *dharmakāya*. In that way the Buddha has a *sambhogakāya*-type presentation, although in fact he is the *dharmakāya*. Perhaps it is not advisable to distinguish too sharply between the three *kāyas*.

THE ĀNANDA WITHIN

You suggest that the speaker of the sūtra *could be said to be the Ānanda within. Could this mean that in a sense we have heard the* White Lotus Sūtra *before because it is an innate memory?*
You could perhaps consider it in terms of the Platonic doctrine of reminiscence, or the doctrine of mutual interpenetration. It is perhaps not too far-fetched to say that there is within you a level of receptivity on which you are listening to the Truth represented by the *sūtra*.

The corollary is that the Buddha is teaching within one's own mind. Given your reservations about any suggestion that one is already a Buddha, is this a useful image?
I think it can be if you bear in mind the limitations of that static way of looking at things. I think such phrases as 'the Enlightened mind within' are to be avoided because they are misleading if they are taken literally. A human being is a potential Buddha in the sense that if he or she makes a sufficient effort, he or she can attain Enlightenment. But it is not as if there is just a thin layer separating you from Buddhahood, so that you have just got to get through that layer and hey presto! there you are, Enlightened. It is a big mistake to think of immanent Buddhahood as any kind of possession.

As far as we know, the Buddha himself did not use the language of potentiality or immanence, and I am very doubtful as to whether it is a skilful language for us to use. No doubt it does express an actual spiritual experience at a certain level, but anyone who is not very spiritually advanced is likely to misunderstand, and would be better off hearing that, by making sufficient effort, they can eventually attain a state called Enlightenment. We are all 'potentially Enlightened', but that is not to say that we are literally Enlightened at this moment in any sense that is comprehensible to us.

The idea of the Ānanda within struck a chord with me. I wonder if identifying with Ānanda rather than with the Buddha gets the benefits of the language of potentiality without some of the risks?
Ānanda is a much more modest figure, because at the time of his association with the Buddha he was only a Stream Entrant, not yet fully Enlightened; so yes, perhaps you can much more safely identify with Ānanda.

Where did the language of potentiality come from?
It is used in India outside Buddhism – in a way it is the language of the Upaniṣads. One Upaniṣad says, 'I am Brahman, I am the Absolute'[58] – there is that direct identification. But whether the Upaniṣads had a historical influence on the Mahāyāna it is difficult to say. It could be that the language of Buddhism was influenced by the thought of the Upaniṣads, or it could be that there was a parallel development.

ALL ONE PATH

The sūtra *speaks of three vehicles culminating in one Buddha vehicle. Is this principle of progressive levels unique to this* sūtra, *or is it found in earlier teachings?*
It is not really so much a question of levels as of *yānas*. What are thought of as different ways with different goals all merge into one way. They can perhaps be regarded as successive stages of one path, but the point is that it is one path – all these apparently different paths are reduced to one path. This is one of the two distinctive teachings of the *White Lotus Sūtra* which afterwards became the heritage of the whole of the Mahāyāna.

At the time of the Buddha there was only one path, but in the period before the rise of the *White Lotus Sūtra*, the distinction between the *arhant* and the Buddha had hardened into separate paths. The *White Lotus Sūtra* was an expression of a reaction against this separation, and effectively brought the paths back together again.

In our own day we are doing something similar, on a certain level, in the way in which we bring together the lay and the monastic, which had become so widely separated, into one Going for Refuge.[59]

THE POSITIVE AND NEGATIVE ASPECTS OF THE PATH TO NIRVĀṆA

You mention that the Hīnayāna Nirvāṇa is simply the eradication of the passions. Would it really be possible to eradicate all passions without developing Insight?

No, I don't think so. Even if you were to think just in terms of eradicating the passions, and had no thought of gaining *bodhi*, the attainment of *bodhi* would still be part of the process of eradicating the passions, although your mode of expressing that experience would be limited. There is no doubt, however, that when in the Pāli canon Sāriputta is asked to say what *nibbāna* is, he gives a purely negative definition, saying simply that it is the cessation of *lobha, dosa*, and *moha*.[60] But there are other passages in the Pāli canon which tell a different story.

In fact, the path to Nirvāṇa, in whatever formulation, always has both a positive aspect and a negative aspect. In the intermediate stages there is a cessation of something unskilful and also a coming into existence and increase of something skilful. As you progress up the spiral path the positive and the skilful gradually increase as they counterbalance the negative and unskilful. By extension from that, Nirvāṇa is certainly the cessation of everything unskilful, but it is also the plenitude of everything skilful. The Hīnayāna often left out the second part of the statement.

Why should they have done that if they had genuine spiritual attainments? Would it have been some sort of skilful means?

That's a circular argument, because you are assuming that they had some genuine spiritual attainment when perhaps they did not. Perhaps there had been a deterioration and on that account they thought just in negative terms. We know so little about the general historical situation, the social and cultural conditions, that it is very difficult to speculate. The fact is that the Theravādins presented the Dharma in increasingly negative terms to the neglect, right down to the present day, of much more positive formulations which are to be found in the Pāli canon itself. A classic example is that of the twelve positive *nidānas*, which were completely ignored in expositions of the Dharma until the time of Mrs Rhys Davids.[61] Another case is that of the *Itivuttaka*,[62] which tails off at the end into an increasingly negative presentation of the spiritual life, the latter sections being apparently later productions. It is obvious that this tendency to negativity happened, but we are completely in the dark about the psychological, spiritual, and cultural reasons as to why it happened.

WHY WALK OUT?

At the beginning of the sūtra *five thousand disciples walk out, and the assembly is thus purified. Why didn't the Buddha just preach to the whole assembly, contacting those who were receptive and not contacting those who were not?*

You have to consider what the *sūtra* is trying to do. It is a drama, and in a drama there has to be action. I think the author of the *sūtra* wanted to dramatize the disciples' rejection of the truth offered to them to emphasize that this is what can happen. You can be so full of your own imagined spiritual attainments that you even close your ears to what the Buddha has to say and walk out. As a human being you have that freedom, and some people unfortunately exercise it. This is the point that is being emphasized.

Might the incident also indicate an awareness on the part of the Buddha that it is harder to teach an audience that includes people who are not receptive?

Yes, the fact that there are certain people present who are resistant does affect the atmosphere of a whole group. If you are speaking to a group, it is impossible to ignore a section of it which is in disagreement with the rest of the group. If most of an audience is very attentive and one section is restless, that interferes with the total empathy between speaker and audience.

ARE LAY PEOPLE EXCLUDED?

The Buddha predicts to Enlightenment arhants *such as Śāriputra, numerous* bhikṣus, bhikṣuṇīs *like Mahāprajāpatī and Yaśodharā, evil-doers such as Devadatta, and non-human beings such as a* nāga *princess, but no lay people. Why is this, and could it be the reason for the emphasis on lay people in the* Vimalakīrti-nirdeśa*?*

You would have thought in view of the universalism of the Mahāyāna that laymen and laywomen would also be predicted to Enlightenment, so it is rather an odd omission. Perhaps, as you say, the *Vimalakīrti-nirdeśa* makes up for that, although it would not have done so in a conscious way. Perhaps particular Mahāyāna *sūtras* do have responsibility for particular approaches or emphases.

I am sure that the *sūtra* does not intend deliberately to exclude lay people. It is one of the earlier Mahāyāna *sūtras*, so perhaps there is still an over-emphasis on monasticism carried over from the Hīnayāna which has not been fully permeated by the Mahāyāna spirit, as though the author has not completely transcended his Hīnayāna background. It is not so easy to bring everything that you have inherited from the past into line with your real position.

TRANSCENDING TIME

The body of the Buddha Abundant Treasures can only be revealed when all the Buddhas who have emanated from Śākyamuni are present. What is the meaning of this episode? And are the emanations people who have become Buddhas as disciples of Śākyamuni, or are they magical emanations?

This coming together of the ancient Buddha and the present Buddha represents Enlightenment's transcendence of time. The coming together of Buddhas (which are magical emanations, to answer your question) is the corresponding transcendence of space. The significance of the episode is that time and space are beginning to be transcended.

When Śākyamuni purifies the whole world and it turns into lapis lazuli ground with golden cords, have we gone up to an even higher level, to enter a sort of Sukhāvatī?

It is more a question of feeling than doctrine. As you read the *sūtra*, what do you feel? Do you feel as though you are rising to a higher level? Later on there is that episode where the Buddha literally raises the whole assembly to a higher level, and the symbolism is obvious, but as you go through the *sūtra*, you must be mindful and examine your own responses. Do you feel uplifted by a certain passage? Does it seem to raise you to a higher level of experience? You must consult your own experience.

3
TRANSCENDING THE HUMAN PREDICAMENT

As human beings, we live in two quite different worlds. Some of the time we live in the world of rational thought, the world of science, philosophy, concepts, and systematic generalizations from experience. But some of the time we live in a very different world indeed: the world of the unconscious, the world of poetry, myths, and symbols. It is the need for both these aspects of human nature to be involved in the spiritual life which leads to the narrating of the first parable of the *White Lotus Sūtra*.

At first, as we have seen, the Buddha is reluctant to speak at all, because the truth of things is so difficult to understand, but at length he is persuaded to attempt an explanation. In clear conceptual terms he tells the disciples that his teaching of the eradication of negative emotions – which they, *arhants* that they are, thought was the be-all and end-all of spiritual achievement – is just the start. It's just a way of getting people going on the spiritual path. There is, the Buddha now reveals, a higher spiritual goal which consists not just in the eradication of the negative emotions, necessary as that may be, but in the attainment of positive spiritual knowledge and Enlightenment: Perfect Buddhahood. And the way to attain this higher goal is to practise the bodhisattva ideal, working towards Enlightenment not just for the sake of individual emancipation, but so as to contribute to the cosmic process of Enlightenment, the Enlightenment of all sentient beings.

On hearing this, of course, a number of the disciples present simply cannot entertain the idea and leave forthwith – and many of those who stay are thrown into confusion. Will they have to abandon everything they have been taught so far? Have they been wasting their time? They may understand the new teaching in a rational, intellectual way, but their hearts are not convinced. Although he himself wholeheartedly accepts the new teaching, Śāriputra, the greatest and wisest of the disciples, is aware that many of the others are still perplexed, and he speaks on their behalf. Can the Buddha explain things to them in another way? In response to this appeal, the Buddha says that he will tell a story, remarking that 'intelligent people through a parable reach understanding'. Sometimes it is not easy to understand things when they are put in a dry, abstract, conceptual manner, but with the help of a story much becomes clear. And the story the Buddha tells is the parable of the burning house:

Once upon a time there was a great elder, a very rich old man who lived in a huge mansion with his hundreds of servants and his many children. The story does not speak of wives or mothers, but we know that the elder had as many as thirty children, and they were all quite young. The house in which they lived had once been magnificent, but now it was old and tumbledown. The pillars were decaying, the windows were broken, the floorboards were rotting, and the walls were crumbling. And in the nooks and crannies of this tumbledown house there lurked all sorts of ghosts and evil spirits.

One day the house suddenly caught fire. Because it was so old and the timbers were so dry, the whole building was burning merrily in no time. As it happened, the elder was safe outside the house when the fire started, but his children were playing inside. Too young to realize that they were in danger of being burned to death, they just carried on playing and made no effort to escape.

The elder was very afraid for his children, of course, and wondered how on earth to save them. At first he thought of carrying them out of the house one by one, for he was strong and able, but he soon realized that it would be impossible to get them all out in time. Instead, he decided to try calling out to the children. He shouted, 'The house is on fire! You're in terrible danger! Come out quickly!' But the children had no idea what their father could mean by danger. They just carried on playing their games, glancing at the elder occasionally as they ran to and fro, but taking no serious notice of him at all.

The elder saw that there was no time to lose, for the house would crash to the ground at any minute. In desperation he hit upon another plan. He would try to trick the children into coming out of the house. Knowing the different nature of each child, he knew that they liked different kinds of toys, some liking one kind and some preferring another. So he called out to them, 'Come and look at the toys I have brought for you! There are all kinds of carts, some drawn by deer, some drawn by goats, and some drawn by bullocks, and they are all standing just outside the gate. Come quickly and look!' And although the children had been deaf to all his warnings, this time they heard him. They all came rushing and tumbling helter-skelter out of the burning house, pushing and shoving each other in their eagerness to get the new toys.

When the elder was sure that all the children were safely out of the house, he sat down with a great sigh of relief; and at once, of course, the children came clamouring round him demanding the toys he had promised them. The elder was extremely fond of his children, and wanted to give them whatever their hearts desired. And, fortunately, he was extremely wealthy – in fact his wealth was infinite – so he could afford to give them the best of everything. Instead of the carts of different kinds which he had promised them, therefore, he gave to each of them a magnificent bullock-drawn cart, bigger and better than they could have imagined in their wildest dreams. Although he had promised them one thing and gave them something else, this was not deceitfulness on his part, because it was motivated by his desire for the welfare and the safety of his children.

So this is the parable of the burning house.[63] In a way there is no need to say any more, because a parable speaks directly in its own symbolic language. It means just what it says it means, and we simply have to let it all sink in. It can be useful, however, to dwell on the events of the story and see what significance they have for us.

The elder, of course, is the Buddha, the Enlightened One, and the mansion in which he lives is the world – not just this earth, but the whole universe, the whole of conditioned existence, all worlds. The mansion – the universe – is inhabited by many beings – not just human beings, according to Buddhism, but beings of all kinds, some less developed than mankind and some even more developed. And just as the mansion is old and decayed, this universe is subject to all kinds of imperfections. For a start, it is impermanent, changing all the time. We cannot stay in it for long; it is more like a hotel than a home. The mansion has ghosts in the corners too, which suggests that this world of ours is haunted. Haunted by what? By the past. We like to think that we live in the present, but more often than not the ghosts of the past are all around us. We may think that we are experiencing objectively existing beings and situations, but often they are really the projections of our unconscious minds, the ghosts of the past that we carry along with us all the time.

In the parable the mansion catches fire at a certain time, but in reality the mansion of the world is constantly blazing and burning. The use of fire as a symbol is very common in Buddhism, and in Indian religion generally. The Buddha used it in a teaching known as the Fire Sermon which he gave not long after his Enlightenment, on an occasion when he was speaking to a company of his disciples who had previously been 'matted-hair' ascetics and whose main religious practice had been fire-worship. No doubt the Buddha was alluding to their previous practice when he led a thousand of them to the top of a hill and said to them, 'The whole world is ablaze. The whole world is burning. Burning with what? It is burning with the fire of craving and neurotic desire. It is burning with the fire of anger, hatred, and aggression. It is burning with the fire of ignorance, delusion, bewilderment, and lack of awareness.'[64] This was surely not just an *idea* of the Buddha's, not just a concept he happened to think up. He surely saw the world, as though in a vision, just like this. Perhaps before he spoke he had been looking down from the hilltop into the jungles below, and had seen a forest fire burning in the distance. Then he may have seen, in his spiritual vision, that not only was the forest burning, but the houses were burning, people were burning, the mountains were burning, the earth was burning, the sun, moon, and stars were burning – everything conditioned was burning with the threefold fires of craving, hatred, and delusion.

Fire, incidentally, far from being just a negative symbol in Buddhism, has many positive associations. It is associated with change – in fact fire, the process of combustion, *is* change, and not just change but transformation. In Indian spiritual life fire is therefore a symbol not just of destruction but also of renewal and spiritual rebirth. In Vedic times, long before the Buddha, people placed offerings on a fire altar to ascend in the subtle form of smoke to the realms of the gods. The rite of cremation involves a similar transformation, reducing the physical body to ashes but – or so the ancient Indians believed – sending the subtle aspect of being, the 'soul', to the moon or to the sun, to the world of the fathers or to the world of the gods. In Hinduism the cremation ground is the domain of Śiva the Destroyer, who is the god not only of destruction but also of spiritual rebirth, because before you can build up you must break down. And the flames which surround the wrathful deities of Tibetan Buddhism also symbolize a transformation by fire – the fiery breaking through of the spirit of Enlightenment into the darkness and ignorance of the world.

But fire is a threat to the children in the mansion; in fact they are in danger of burning to death. Who do the children represent? Obviously they represent living beings, especially human beings – that is to say, especially ourselves. In the context of the *sūtra* they represent the Hīnayāna disciples, those who are following lower spiritual ideals. More generally speaking, we can say that they represent all those who have evolved only up to a certain point and have some distance – maybe a great distance – still to go.

The children in the parable are in danger of being burned to death. The implication is that human beings are in danger – *we* are in danger. What does this mean? It could mean that we are in danger of remaining within the world, within the process of conditioned existence, the cycle of birth, death, and rebirth as illustrated by the Tibetan wheel of life.[65] The danger is that if we carry on turning round and round within the wheel we must inevitably suffer, at least sometimes. But the symbolism could also mean that we are in danger of getting stuck at a lower level of development. Unfortunately this happens to very many people, and it isn't always entirely their own fault. The human organism, biologically, psychologically, and even spiritually speaking, has a natural tendency to grow. In fact, to grow is the nature of life itself. Life in all its forms wants to unfold its inner potentialities, and if any living thing cannot do this it feels miserable, or at least uneasy and dissatisfied. People are often so restricted by their circumstances that they simply cannot grow – indeed, they sometimes feel that they cannot even breathe. All sorts of unpleasant and uncontrollable factors press in on them from all sides. They strangle them, stifle them, and make them feel that they are not developing as they should and could, so that they feel not only frustrated and restricted, but miserable, resentful, and unhappy in every way.

In the parable, of course, the person trying to rescue the children from danger is their father. If the 'father' here meant the begetter of the children, this might seem to imply that the Buddha is a kind of creator god, the creator of the world, of men and women, and all living beings. But this 'father' simply stands for someone older, more experienced, and more highly evolved. He is like the 'cultural father' of some so-called primitive cultures where you have both a biological father, who begot you, and a cultural father – usually your mother's brother – who is responsible for educating you and bringing you up. (In modern societies the biological father fulfils both roles, but this is not an invariable rule.) So there is no implication of theism here.

The elder's first impulse when the fire starts is to rush into the house and carry the children out – he would be strong enough to do that – but on reflection he dismisses the idea. This goes to show that however willing and able you may be, you just cannot save people, spiritually speaking, by force. You could conceivably drag someone out of a burning building against their will, but it is impossible to make anybody evolve against their will. Yes, you can drag them to meditation classes, you can drag them into church. You can force them to recite the Creed and read the Bible. You can intimidate them into not doing this or not doing that. But you cannot make them evolve against their will. By its very nature the Higher Evolution is a voluntary process, something *you* do because *you* want to do it.

Unfortunately, this is sometimes forgotten. Some religious teachers hold the view that what people really need to make them grow spiritually is discipline – and these teachers are only too willing to dish it out, and give their disciples a very tough time indeed. Of course, there is no shortage of people who are ready to accept this sort of discipline. It is not difficult to find ways of conditioning people along certain lines. This kind of conditioning, however, is a very different thing from real spiritual development. So Buddhism does not force, it does not compel, it does not intimidate, and it doesn't have recourse to discipline in this almost military sense of the term, because trying to force people to develop is self-defeating. Throughout the history of Buddhism, therefore, Buddhist teachers have been very tolerant. Buddhism has never tried to force anybody to do anything.

So in the end the elder gives up the idea of rescuing the children and instead tries calling out to them. Now this call is full of meaning. It represents the call of Truth, the call, if you like, of the divine. Turning to the Hindu tradition again, we find the symbolism of the call beautifully expressed in the medieval Hindu story of Krishna (Kṛṣṇa) and his flute. Krishna is one of the great spiritual figures of Hinduism, a demigod said to be an incarnation of Vishnu (Viṣṇu) the Preserver, and he is surrounded by all sorts of myths and legends. The story of Krishna's flute is set in an Indian village called Vrindavana where the people live by herding cows. Just imagine the scene. It is a dark night with no moon and the whole village is sound asleep. The cows are all shut in their stalls for the night, and everywhere – the little thatched mud-walled huts, the fields and the forest – is absolutely still. Then, suddenly, in the midst of the darkness, in the midst of the silence, from the depths of the forest there comes a sound, faint but sweet and shrill, a sound that seems to come from an infinitely remote distance – the sound of a flute. Even now in India you can sometimes have this experience. You can be all by yourself in the midst of the countryside, with no one for miles around, and all of a sudden, out of the dark and the silence, there comes the sound of a flute.

Now although the sound of the flute is very faint and distant, it does not go unheard in the village of Vrindavana. Almost as though they have been expecting to hear it, the wives of the cowherds – the *gopīs* – wake up, and know at once that Krishna is calling them. Without making a sound, without telling anybody, they get up and steal out of their houses, along the streets of the village, and into the forest. Leaving their husbands and their children, their pots and their pans, their cows and their goats, they all go stealing away, rushing away as soon as they are at a safe distance, to dance with Krishna in the heart of the forest.[66]

In this story Krishna is a symbol of the divine, and the *gopīs* represent the human heart, or the human soul if you like; and the sound of Krishna's flute is the call of the divine, sounding from the very depths of existence. In fact, most of us hear such a call at some time in our lives. It may come in a moment of quietness when we are out in the country, or through an experience of great art, literature, or music. Perhaps we may hear it after some tragic event, or perhaps when we are just rather weary of life. At such a time we may hear the call, the call which is sometimes termed the voice of the silence,[67] the voice of something beyond. But even if we have heard this call very clearly, what usually happens is that we ignore it. Indeed, the very idea that there might have been a voice vaguely worries us. We don't know where it came from, or what mysterious region it might be calling us to. And if we follow it into unknown territory, we are afraid that we will have to give up all sorts of things that we are attached to. So we tell ourselves that we were imagining things, or that it was just a dream, and go on living and working and enjoying ourselves as though we had never heard anything at all.

Quite often, of course, we are much too busy enjoying ourselves even to hear the call, like the children in the parable. They almost completely ignore their father's calls because, the Buddha says – and we can imagine him saying this with a smile – they are absorbed in their games. We are absorbed in our games – the psychological games, spiritual games, and cultural games that we play almost all the time. We are so fascinated by our little games of success, prestige, popularity, ego-tripping dressed up as self-fulfilment, and so on, that even though we hear the call of the divine, the voice of the Buddha, we just go on playing.

And like the children in the burning house, we are not only playing our games, but running to and fro from one game to another. We are restless, anxious, incapable of staying anywhere for long. We constantly want to change the game we are playing or to change our partner – in more ways than one – so we end up running backwards and forwards in desperation. Just one thing occasionally stops us in our tracks. In the story, you may remember, the children just occasionally glance at their father as they run past. Similarly, as we run to and fro playing our little games, we do give the odd glance in the direction of religion.

So what is the elder to do? Force is out of the question and the children will not respond to a direct appeal. In the end his only alternative is to have recourse to a stratagem – in plain words, to play a trick. This kind of 'trick', which benefits the person on which it is played, is known in Buddhism as *upāya-kauśalya* – 'skilful means'.[68] The elder knows that the children are very fond of toys, so he decides to persuade them to come out of the burning house by promising them carts of different kinds to play with: deer carts, goat carts, and bullock carts. These three different kinds of cart represent, technically speaking, the three 'vehicles', the three *yānas* – the *śrāvakayāna*, the *pratyekabuddhayāna*, and the *bodhisattvayāna* – that is, the *arhant* ideal, the ideal of private Enlightenment, and the bodhisattva ideal.[69] Less technically, the carts stand for different formulations of the Buddha's teaching, or even different sectarian forms of Buddhism adapted to the needs of different temperaments.

Be good to have clarity on meanings.

Although the children take no notice of their father's warnings of danger, as soon as he promises them all these marvellous toys, out they come rushing. Their eager response to being promised their favourite kind of toy says something very perceptive about how religions appeal to people. It seems to suggest – bearing in mind what the toys represent – that a subjective and sectarian approach to the truth is much more attractive for many people than a more objective, universal approach. And this does seem to be the case in practice. It is certainly the more exclusive forms of religion that exert the most powerful emotional appeal. If your opening gambit is, 'Well, look, this is how I see it. Other people see things differently, but we're maybe all right from our own point of view. Let's go forward together,' that is no way to convince the average person. The way to get a following is to put it about that yours is the only true religion and all the others are just plain wrong. This explains why it is that the forms of Buddhism which in the course of history have become the most exclusive – that is, exclusive by Buddhist standards – have become the most popular in the West.

A sectarian approach may be more popular, but does this mean that it is necessary? Do we have to follow a particular path believing it to be the only true way, and only later on in our spiritual experience come to a broader outlook, like the *arhants* in the *sūtra*? If we look at our situation it is really questionable whether this is actually possible for us. In the Buddha's day no doubt it *was* possible. His disciples would have been able to learn and practise one teaching at a time. There was no writing in those days, at least not for religious purposes, so the Buddha did all his teaching orally. The disciples couldn't just pick up books about religion, and they certainly didn't go to other teachers, so they knew only what the Buddha taught them.

Even in more recent times, different forms of religion existed independently in different parts of the world – even in different parts of the same country – so it was perfectly possible to stick to one teaching or sect and ignore all the others completely. Until comparatively recently you could be a Christian in the West and never have heard of Buddhism or Hinduism, and you could be a Buddhist in the East and never hear the name of Christianity from one year to the next.

The world is now a very different place. Nowadays, everybody can study everything. All the spiritual teachings are available in written form – 'Who runs, may read,' as John Keble said[70] – so it is no longer possible to keep people away from a teaching for which they are not ready. This means that people get hold of all sorts of teachings which, because they are not spiritually developed enough, they can only misunderstand and misinterpret. This just can't be helped. With improved communication and transport, the world is becoming a smaller place all the time. All religions, even all sects, are increasingly to be found everywhere, so it's no longer possible to follow any one and ignore all the others – at the very least we'll know about them from books or hearsay.

In this situation, the only thing to be done is for religions to try to see the parable of the burning house in its universal perspective. We all need to try to recognize that all the ways are different aspects of one and the same path, the path to perfect Buddhahood, the path to Enlightenment. Of course differences of temperament still exist, but sectarianism is no longer needed to cater for them. It is quite enough to choose a method of spiritual practice appropriate to our needs – for example, an appropriate method of meditation. We don't need to belong to a sectarian organization that excludes all the others. We don't need to be 'Theravādin' or 'Zen' or 'Mahāyānist' – why not just be Buddhist? And Buddhism itself can be interpreted very broadly. According to the Buddha's own criterion, Buddhism is whatever conduces to the Enlightenment of the individual. The Buddha alone among religious teachers seems to have understood that religion is really the process of the evolution and development of the individual. Sectarian organizations tend to lose sight of this, and in fact many of them express for the most part merely negative emotions, and we would be better off without their exclusivity and intolerance.

You notice that, in their eagerness to get their own particular carts, the children come out of the house pushing and shoving one another. In the same way, in our rush to get out of the house and grab the toy we want, instead of going out side by side or hand in hand, we jostle and shove all the others who are doing the same thing. We may not actually persecute anybody – at least not if we are Buddhists – but at the same time we may not exactly radiate positive feelings towards other people following other paths. This, as we have seen, needs to change, and in fact the parable goes on to show that as you progress on your chosen path it does change. Once the children are all outside, the elder gives each of them the very best kind of cart – or even one and the same cart – bigger and better than anything they could ever have imagined.

Here is the indication that the closer people come to the goal, the more their paths converge.

People get into the spiritual life in different ways – some through music, art, or poetry, some through social service, some through meditation, some through the desire to resolve pressing psychological problems. Some people are attracted to Zen, others to the Theravāda. We all have our own personal idiosyncracies, so we are naturally attracted by different things in the beginning. But as we get more and more deeply into our chosen approach, we realize that it is changing us. We begin to notice that our idiosyncracies of temperament – even those which led us to this particular approach – are being resolved. In the end we come to realize through our own experience that all forms of art, all forms of religion, are means for the higher evolution of humanity. By participating in any of them we ourselves are evolving, and other people are also evolving, even though their interests and preoccupations are different from our own. We are all evolving together, all participating in the same process of the Higher Evolution, the process – in Buddhist terms – of cosmic Enlightenment; this is really the message of the parable of the burning house.

So does this mean that the parable is teaching universalism? It is, after all, saying that the distinction between the different *yānas* is illusory, that in reality there is only one *yāna*. But is this universalism? Well, I understand universalism as saying that all religions teach the same thing and that there is therefore no difference between them.[71] The doctrines may appear to differ, but universalists would say that this is only a matter of words – the substance is the same – and they would back this up by trying to equate doctrines from different religions. For example, they would say that the Christian Trinity – Father, Son, and Holy Ghost – corresponds to the Buddhist *trikāya* (*dharmakāya, sambhogakāya, nirmāṇakāya*) and the Hindu *trimūrti* (Brahmā, Viṣṇu, Maheśvara). This kind of wholesale system of equations – the very substance of universalism – often leads to very forced interpretations.

It is clear enough that the parable of the burning house does not teach universalism in this sense. It doesn't say that all religions teach the same thing; they obviously teach different things. Moreover, some religions are more advanced than others – universal religions, for example, being more advanced than ethnic religions. And whereas the universalist would claim that all religions are totally true in all respects, the Buddhist would say that there are some teachings which pass currency as religious but – because they are not true – are not really religious at all. The orthodox Christian doctrine of eternal punishment is an example of such a teaching.

The parable is not even saying that all the *yānas* of Buddhism teach the same thing. What it does maintain very definitely is that all the different ways are part of the same 'stream of tendency', to use an expression of Matthew Arnold's.[72] Everyone is trying to get out of the same burning house. Indeed the parable emphasizes movement, escape; it is dynamic, unlike the static teaching of universalism. The universalist fixes systems of belief into patterns which have to rely heavily on intellectual resemblances, whereas the parable of the burning house can rely on the unity of the evolutionary process.

Another general consideration arising out of this parable, and one which must be addressed as it constitutes the main theme, is the idea of escape as a model for the spiritual life. The elder's sole concern is that the children should escape from the burning house. Does this mean that the parable is teaching escapism? Well, obviously enough, it is – in a sense. A lot of people would say that this is typical of the way religions encourage us to run away from the problems of the world, and even from our own problems. And, they would say, this is particularly true of Buddhism. After all, look at the Buddha – leaving his wife and child like that, ducking out of his responsibilities and obligations! Some would say that Christians stay in the world and try to make it into a better place, try to help the sick and care for the needy, whereas Buddhists just sit around meditating, ignoring the sins and sufferings all around them. Pure escapism!

But is escape morally wrong? Suppose you were literally trapped in a burning house. There you would be, standing at the upstairs window, surrounded by smoke and flames. Along would come the fire brigade, and you would escape, either by jumping into a net or by being carried down a ladder. Would your friends say afterwards, 'You shouldn't have done that. That was sheer escapism'? Buddhism simply sees that our situation is one of pain and suffering – or at least limitation, imperfection, frustration – and says, 'Get out of it.' This is just acting realistically, like escaping from that burning house.

Perhaps the word 'escape' is the wrong one. The word traditionally means 'to gain one's liberty by flight', 'to get safely out of', and so on, but in the nineteenth century it gained a new usage – 'mental or emotional distraction from the realities of life' – and it is this which has given birth to the notion of escap*ism*: 'the tendency to seek or practice of seeking such distraction'. The burning house in the parable represents the predicament in which we find ourselves as human beings. Given the connotations of the language of escape, it would perhaps be better to speak of *transcending* this human predicament rather than escaping from it. The parable is showing us how we can transcend our present state, how we can grow from a lower, less satisfactory state of existence to a higher, more satisfactory state.

This is not to say, of course, that there is no such thing as escapism, but we need to understand what escapism really is. Not everybody is prepared to make the kind of effort that the process of growth and development requires – *that* is what we try to escape from. When we try to avoid situations which demand that we go beyond ourselves, when we try to forget our human predicament, when we try to secure an easy life – these are the times when we are really being 'escapist'. Escapism is stagnation, even regression. Sometimes, it is true, religious activity – of the kind which involves lip service but no effort towards personal change – is escapism, though there is less of this these days simply because fewer people are involved in religion of any kind. Nowadays it is more usually non-religious activities that provide outlets for escapism. For many people work is escapism, politics are escapism, even the arts are escapism. Reading is escapism. Watching television is escapism. Sex is escapism. In short, any kind of life that involves no positive, deliberate effort to evolve is escapism – which means, if you think about it, that escapism is the rule rather than the exception. And of course, escapism of this kind is the last thing that the parable of the burning house teaches. It is concerned above all with growth, development, evolution.

Today the burning house is burning more merrily than ever; we only have to open our newspapers or turn on the radio any day of the week to know that. So the whole question of escape – or rather the whole question of transcendence, growth and development into a higher state – becomes more urgent than ever, both for the individual alone and for the individual as part of a spiritual community. Conventional religion as it has come down to us is no longer very useful to us. Even traditional Eastern Buddhism is no longer very useful, either to us in the West or even to people in the East.

Still, there is no need to despair. It is always darkest before the dawn, as the old saying goes. Potentially at least we are on the threshold of an age when the world will be one world, a time when there will be a single world community, a single human culture to which all existing cultures will contribute their best. Enlightenment will be the one universally recognized goal for every human individual, and the way of the Higher Evolution will be the one universally recognized way to reach it. But this will not happen automatically. It will happen only to the extent that the individual human being tries to grow – and we can start to make that effort right now. If we take heed of the message of the parable of the burning house, even here, even now, we can transcend the human predicament.

3
QUESTIONS AND ANSWERS

'JUST TELL ME WHAT TO BELIEVE.'

Before hearing the parable of the burning house, Śāriputra says to the Buddha:

> *On first hearing the Buddha's preaching,*
> *In my mind there was fear and doubt*
> *Lest it might be Māra acting as Buddha,*
> *Distressing and confusing my mind.*

Then later he says:

> *It is the World-honored One who preaches the true Way;*
> *The Evil One has no [such] truths [as] these.*
> *Hence I know for certain that*
> *This is not Māra acting as Buddha,*
> *But because I had fallen into nets of doubts,*
> *I conceived it as the doing of Māra.*[73]

I wonder if some Hīnayānists did think that the Mahāyāna was the work of Māra? Śāriputra represents the Hīnayāna, doesn't he?
Yes. It is quite possible that some followers of the Hīnayāna schools did not merely say that the Mahāyāna *sūtras* were not *Buddhavacana*, but

went so far as to say that they were the work of Māra. There is no direct evidence, but this could be indirect evidence.

But what sort of person thinks in this way, considering the matter more broadly? After all, you are quite right to be on your guard against misrepresentations of the Buddha's teaching; there is nothing wrong with that. But the type of Hīnayānist represented by Śāriputra here would seem to be the sort of person who is so desperately afraid of not getting it right that he clings fast to his own particular orthodoxy and is closed to any other way of looking at things, even within his own spiritual tradition, and very quick to suspect that some other way of looking at his own tradition is the work of the devil. This suggests great insecurity.

Many people in the Western world during the Middle Ages and even during the Reformation had this sort of attitude. They were so afraid of falling into heresy, so concerned to be completely orthodox Catholics, that they would sometimes say to the Church, 'Just tell me what to believe.' Sometimes dogmatic Communists behave in this way too. They are so anxious to follow the exact party line that they are even prepared to change, believing one thing one day and another thing the next as the party line changes. This does suggest great personal insecurity, and a lack of faith in one's own powers of judgement.

THE COUNTERFEIT DHARMA

When Śāriputra receives his prediction to Enlightenment, and in the later predictions, the Buddha foretells the duration of what is called the 'counterfeit Dharma',[74] what does this mean? Does it correspond to anything in the history of Buddhism, or point to any real future danger?
To the best of my knowledge the counterfeit Dharma is that form of Buddhism in which the outward appearances are kept up but the inner spirit is lost. It is tempting to identify that with the Hīnayāna, and perhaps the Hīnayāna did exemplify it in some respects, but in some cases you find Mahāyāna practitioners also just keeping up appearances and losing the spirit. It happens in Zen; it can happen in any form of Buddhism. It is not possible to point to any particular period, although perhaps it has happened in some periods more than others.

We may find personally that there may be times when what we are practising is a counterfeit Dharma; we are going through the motions but the spirit is lacking. At other times our heart may really be in it, and then it is the real Dharma. It is not a fixed thing. It is akin to the third fetter, reliance on rules and rituals as ends in themselves.[75] So you can't say that any one particular form of Buddhism represents a counterfeit Dharma. Any individual Buddhist can practise his form of Buddhism in such a way that, so far as his life is concerned, it is a counterfeit Dharma.

GIVING MORE THAN YOU PROMISED

The Buddha asks Śāriputra if the elder has been guilty of a falsehood in giving the great carts of the precious substances to his children equally. Śāriputra replies:

> *Even if that elder did not give them one of the smallest carts, still he is not false. Wherefore? [Because] that elder from the first formed this intention: 'I will by tactful means cause my children to escape.' For this reason he is not false.*[76]

Is this more or less saying that the end justifies the means?
No, I don't think it means that at all. Suppose someone comes along to a Buddhist centre to learn meditation. If they ask whether meditation will give them happiness, you are likely to say that it will. The centre does not exist for the sake of making people happy in the limited sense that the person had in mind when they asked the question, but it is not untrue to say that if you practise Buddhism it will make you happy, even in the sense that that person understands that particular term.

It is that sort of point which is being illustrated here. If you give someone more than you had promised them, you are not failing to keep your promise. If you told someone that if they came outside you would give them a bag of sweets, and you actually gave them two bags of sweets, would you have told a lie? Technically you would have, perhaps, but not ethically. You have given more than you promised; you have more than kept your word. Certainly this passage is not to be understood as condoning lies, even in a good cause.

Śāriputra does say that even if the elder had not given the children any carts at all, he would still not have been lying, because his intention was to help the children to escape.

Yes, because the escape was what he really gave them – a greater gift than any cart.

THE COSMIC LAW

The previous chapter of the sūtra *says, 'All things abide in their fixed order, hence the world abides forever.'*[77] *What does this mean?*

The Sanskrit here is *dharma-sthitiṃ*, *dharma* in this context meaning 'cosmic law'. The cosmic law is established according to a certain order; it is not random or fortuitous, but proceeds in certain ways. So this phrase does not mean that the Dharma is fixed in the sense of eternalism, but that its proceeding in a certain way is fixed. The speaker is seeing existence in terms of a certain undeviating order, seeing it especially, perhaps, in terms of the cyclical order and the spiral order. These are fixed in the sense that if you develop a mental state which pertains to the round you will not experience the fruits of the spiral, and vice versa. You can rely on that just as you can rely on the law of gravity. If you jump into the air, you will come down. The law of gravity will not suddenly be suspended so that you go floating up into the air – it is a fixed law, a determinate law, a law that endures. So this is an affirmation of Buddhism's faith in the Dharma, or cosmic law, for want of a better term. You can think of it in terms of the five *niyamas*;[78] they too can be depended upon not to change.

In a footnote to the text, the Chinese master Zhiyi is quoted as saying '*Dharma-niyāmatā*, law-order or fixed position, indicates suchness. Because of standing on reality, all laws (or beings) abide forever, and therefore every phenomenon also has an unshakeable and everlasting existence.'[79] Of course you must not think of the thing as separate from the reality or suchness in which it is said to abide – that would be to abstract and reify the concept of suchness. And the phenomena are not unchanging – that is the area of possible confusion – but fixed only in that the process which they represent can be relied upon to go on in that particular way.

4
THE MYTH OF THE RETURN JOURNEY

The parable of the burning house gives us the metaphor of life as predicament, or even as trap, but this is of course only one way of looking at it. Human existence is multi-faceted, deep and mysterious, difficult to understand. 'Wonders are many, and none is more wonderful than man' chants the chorus of Sophocles' play *Antigone*.[80] Throughout history, facets of the nature and purpose of human life have been reflected by symbols and similes from which have arisen myths, legends, and stories – and these in turn have crystallized into epic poems, novels, dramas, and parables. The mystery of human life always having been the compelling preoccupation of humanity, the great works of ancient and modern literature which concern some aspect of human existence are read and reread, even after hundreds and thousands of years.

Some of these great works see human life in terms of conflict, or even warfare. Homer's *Iliad*, for example, tells the story of the battle between the Greeks and the Trojans over Helen of Troy, a battle involving not just men and women but even gods and goddesses. Two or three hundred years after the *Iliad* another epic was written, perhaps not so eminent from a literary point of view, but very, very much longer: the *Mahābhārata*. This was composed by the Indian poet and sage Vyāsa, and gives an account of the battle between the Kauravas and their cousins the Pandavas for possession of their ancestral kingdom. Northern Europe produced the anonymous eighth century Anglo-Saxon epic *Beowulf*, which recounts the battles of the hero Beowulf against three terrible adversaries: the fiendish monster Grendel, Grendel's still more fiendish mother, and the dragon. Even from comparatively modern times we have one of the very greatest of all epic poems, Milton's *Paradise Lost*, whose main theme is the War in Heaven, the battle between Satan and the Messiah. In all these works life is seen in terms of conflict. Life is a battle – between right and wrong, between light and darkness, between heaven and hell, between conscious and unconscious – and the battleground is the human heart.

But human existence can also be seen as a riddle, a mystery, or even a problem, and this is how the book of Job in the Bible sees it. Job has been brought up to believe that God rewards the good for their virtue – and punishes the wicked – here in this very life. But although Job is conscious of no evil in himself, he suffers, and it seems that his suffering is the punishment of God. Why should the just man be ground into dust while the unjust man 'flourishes like the green bay tree'? To make sense of life Job needs to know the answer. The same kind of question plagues Shakespeare's Hamlet, confronted with the murder of his innocent father by his villainous uncle. When Hamlet asks his famous question, 'To be or not to be?', life itself has become a problem.

There are many other ways of viewing human existence. However, of all the symbols and similes for life, perhaps the most popular and significant is that of the journey or pilgrimage. Life is not only a battle, not only a problem. It is a journey: a journey from the cradle to the grave, from innocence to experience, from the depths of existence to the heights, from darkness to light, from death to immortality. We find life seen as a journey in a great number of works: the *Odyssey*, the *Divine Comedy, Monkey, Pilgrim's Progress, Wilhelm Meister, Peer Gynt*, and countless others.

The *White Lotus Sūtra* gives its own account of human life as a journey. The parable of the return journey, which occurs in chapter 4, is related not by the Buddha but by four great elders. They have heard the Buddha tell the assembly that Śāriputra is now so far advanced on the path that he is sure to reach the highest goal of all – not just emancipation from his own individual sin and suffering but Buddhahood itself. Amazed and delighted to learn that the spiritual life has a higher aim, the existence of which they had not hitherto suspected, the four great elders say they feel as though they have quite unexpectedly acquired a priceless jewel, and in chorus they give expression to their feelings in a parable.[81]

They say that once upon a time there was a man who left his father and went away into a distant country. He lived there for a long time – perhaps as long as fifty years – and during all that time he was miserably poor. Roaming around, doing a job here and a job there, he lived from hand to mouth, and all he ever possessed were the clothes he stood up in.

Meanwhile, his father was leading a very different kind of life. He was a businessman, and he met with such success in his various trading ventures that he became extremely rich. His trade took him from place to place until he finally settled in another country, where he continued to heap up riches – gold, silver, jewels, and grain. He had slaves and workmen and journeymen, horses and carriages, cows and sheep. He even had elephants – and in the East if you possess elephants you really are rich. He also, inevitably, had dozens of dependants and followers clustering around him in the hope of some reward. His influence in business – money-lending, agriculture, commerce – spread far and wide, and he lived the life of a merchant prince.

But despite his growing wealth and all his business activities, the rich man never stopped missing his son. How was the boy? Would they ever meet again? Sorrowful at their long separation, his one hope was that one day his son would come home to inherit the wealth due to him. 'After all,' the rich man thought, 'I am getting old, and one day I must surely die.'

All this time the son continued to roam from one town to the next, from one kingdom to the next, until one day, quite by chance, he came to the place where his father was living – although of course he had no idea that he was anywhere near his father. As he was passing, or rather skulking, through the streets keeping a lookout for odd jobs which would earn him a few coppers for food, he saw an enormous house, and sitting in the doorway he saw what seemed to be a very rich man. He was surrounded by an enormous company of people, all waiting on him, or waiting for him. Some had bills in their hands and others had great bundles of money that they wanted to give him. Others had presents, and maybe some had bribes.

The rich man was sitting in the gateway on a magnificent throne – even his footstool was ornamented with gold and silver. He was handling millions of gold pieces, just running his fingers through them, and someone was standing behind him fanning him with a yak's tail. In India a yak's tail is one of the symbols of royalty and divinity, so you would only be fanned with one if you were very, very rich indeed, and had been exalted almost to the plane of divinity. Not only that, he was sitting under a magnificent silk canopy which was inlaid with pearls and flowers, and hung all round with garlands of jewels. He really was a magnificent sight.

When the poor man saw this rich man seated there on his throne, in all this state, he was absolutely terrified. He thought he must have come upon the king, or at the very least some great nobleman. 'I'd better be off,' he said to himself. 'I'm much more likely to get work in the streets of the poor. If I stay here they might make me into a slave.' And he hurried away, without the faintest idea that the rich man was his own father.

But the rich merchant no sooner saw that wretchedly poor man at the edge of the crowd of followers than he knew that this was his son, come back after all these years. What a relief! Now he would be able to hand over his wealth to its rightful inheritor and die happy. Joyfully he called a couple of servants and told them to run after the poor man and bring him back. But when they caught up with the poor fellow he was more terrified than ever. 'They've been sent to arrest me. I'm probably going to have my head cut off!' he thought – and he was so afraid that he fell to the earth in a dead faint.

His father was rather surprised at this, but he began to see that all those years he had been living in riches, his son had been living in poverty, and this had created a great psychological difference between them. The boy was obviously not used to being in contact with the rich and powerful. But the faithful father thought, 'Never mind. However low he may have sunk, he is still my son,' – and he resolved to find a way of restoring their relationship. In the meantime, things being as they were, he decided that it would be better to keep his son's identity secret. He therefore called another servant and instructed him to tell the poor man that he was free to go. Hardly believing his luck, the poor man went off with all speed to seek work in the poorest quarter of the town.

But he was followed by two of his father's men, chosen for their humble appearance. When they caught up with him, the men offered him work, as the rich man had instructed them to do. The job would be to clear away a huge heap of dirt that had accumulated at the back of the mansion, and the wages would be double the normal rate. The poor man accepted this proposal at once, and went off to work with

— Yical integration —

the two men. Day after day he shovelled the heap of dirt and removed it in baskets to a distant place. He found lodging in a straw hovel right next to the mansion, so close that the rich man could see it from his window. The rich man would often look out and think how strange it was that he should be living in a beautiful mansion while his son lived in squalor so near by.

One day, when the poor man had been working at the mansion for quite some time, the rich man put on dirty old clothes and, taking a basket in his hands, managed to have a talk with his son. 'Don't think of working anywhere else', he said, 'I'll make sure you've got plenty of money. If there's anything you need – a pot, a jug, some extra grain, anything like that – just ask me. I've got an old cloak in the cupboard; you can have that if you like. Just don't worry about a thing. You've been working well and I'm pleased with you. You seem honest and sincere, not like some of the rogues I've got working for me. In fact – well, I'm an old man – you look to me as your own father, and I'll treat you just like my own son.'

So for a number of years the poor man carried on clearing away the heap of dirt, and he got into the habit of going in and out of the mansion without thinking twice, although he continued to live in his old straw hovel. Then it happened that the old man became ill, and knew that he was soon going to die. He called the poor man and said, 'I feel that I can trust you completely now, just as I would my own son, so I'm going to hand over to you the management of all my affairs. You'll do everything on my behalf.' And from that day onward the poor man was the rich man's steward, and looked after all his investments and transactions. As before, he went freely in and out of the mansion but continued to live in his old hovel. Even though he was handling all this wealth, he continued to think that he was poor, for as far as he knew the money was not his, but his master's.

But as time went on, the poor man changed. His father, who watched him constantly, saw that he was gradually becoming accustomed to handling riches, and feeling ashamed that in the past he had lived so miserably. It became obvious that the poor man had begun to want to be rich himself. By this time the rich man was very old and weak indeed, and he knew that his death was near. So he sent for all the people in the city – the king's representative, the merchants, his friends, his distant relations, ordinary citizens, and country folk from round about – and when they were all gathered, he presented his son to them and told them the whole story. When he had finished, he handed over all his wealth to his son, who, of course, could hardly believe his good fortune.

In the context of the *White Lotus Sūtra*, this parable has a specific meaning which the four elders explain as soon as they have finished telling the story. Until now, they confess, they have been contented with an inferior spiritual ideal. Now, in his kindness and generosity, the Buddha has revealed to them the ideal of attaining supreme Enlightenment not for themselves alone but for the benefit of all sentient beings, and in this way has made them heirs to all his spiritual treasures. Like the son in the parable, the four elders feel overjoyed at the wealth which they have so unexpectedly gained.

The four elders' explanation takes us quite a long way, but with a little imagination we can go much further, even much deeper. We can start by reflecting on the strangely familiar ring of this story. You may well be thinking, 'I'm sure I've heard that story somewhere before.' Thinking back, you may be pretty sure that you haven't read the *White Lotus Sūtra* – it isn't the sort of thing you can read one weekend and then forget about – so why does the parable of the return journey seem so familiar? The reason, as you may have realized, is that it resembles a much more widely known parable: Jesus' parable of the prodigal son.[82] This parable is told by Jesus of Nazareth to elucidate a different point, and it has a different ending, but in general outline the two stories are the same. In both parables there is an affectionate father and a son who runs away; in both parables the runaway son lives miserably for a while before returning to the bosom of his father; and in both parables the position of servant is contrasted with the position of son.

These are the similarities between the parables; there are also significant differences between them. Perhaps the most important of these differences is that in the gospel parable the prodigal son appears to be guilty of wilful disobedience, whereas in the *White Lotus Sūtra* the son seems to go astray just through carelessness and forgetfulness. This illustrates a crucial difference between Christianity and Buddhism, Christianity seeing the human condition in terms of sin, disobedience, and guilt while Buddhism sees it more in terms of forgetfulness, unmindfulness, and ignorance.

Another parable about a father and a son, belonging to roughly the same period as the parable of the return journey, constitutes an even

significant

It actually feels like this is a good point to stop!

more interesting parallel. It occurs in the apocryphal Acts of the Apostle Thomas, an essentially Gnostic work extant in Greek translation as well as in the original Syriac. Modern translators call the story the 'Hymn of the Pearl', but the text gives it the title 'Song of the Apostle Judas Thomas in the Land of the Indians'.[83] Saint Thomas, one of the twelve Apostles, is traditionally known as the Apostle to India because he is supposed to have visited India soon after the death of Jesus, and this parable is said to have been composed while he was imprisoned there. Whether he had much contact with Buddhism, and whether the 'Hymn of the Pearl' owes anything to the parable of the return journey, we can only speculate.

The parable says that in the East there live a father and his son. The son is quite happy living in the wealth and splendour of 'the kingdom of his father's house', but one day his father sends him on a mission to the land of Egypt, to bring back the one pearl which lies, encircled by a great dragon, in the midst of the sea. When he reaches Egypt, the son finds the dragon and waits for him to go to sleep so that he can take the pearl. But the Egyptians become suspicious of this stranger, even though he is disguised in Egyptian garments, and they give him a drugged drink which causes him to lose his memory. Forgetting that he is the son of a king, forgetting all about the pearl, he enters the service of the king of Egypt. And eventually, living with the Egyptians, eating their food and drinking their drink, he becomes more and more like them. In the end, we are told, he falls into a deep sleep. His father in the East, who knows what is happening, becomes anxious, and sends his son a letter – in the form of a bird – reminding him of his mission. And as soon as he receives the letter, the son comes to his senses, enchants the dragon, and seizes the pearl. He returns home in triumph, and his father receives him with great joy.

Each of these parables, the return journey, the prodigal son, and the 'Hymn of the Pearl', has its own wealth of symbolism, but they all share the same central symbol. They all begin with a separation between a father and a son; this is the event from which everything else follows. So what is meant by this separation of father and son? Who or what are the father and the son?

Well, we could say that the father represents what may be called the higher self (although we need to be careful not to take the expression too literally), and the son is the lower self. And just as the son is separated from his father, the lower self is separated – or, in more contemporary language, *alienated* – from the higher self. Here, by the way, is another metaphor for the human condition: alienation. We are alienated from our own higher selves, our own better natures, our own highest potentialities. We are alienated from Truth, from Reality. And just as the son went not just a short distance away from his father, but to an altogether different part of the world, so the alienation between the higher self and the lower self is severe. Indeed, the schism between the two is complete; there is no contact of any kind between them.

We may say that the condition of the human race is one of alienation from Truth, but when did this condition begin? The son lives in a distant country for many years, which suggests that the alienation is of long standing. But if we take the parable literally, the implication is that although it may have happened a long time ago, it did happen at a certain point in time. This is the view of orthodox Christianity, which teaches that Adam and Eve lived happily in the garden of Eden, in harmony with God and in obedience to his commands, until Adam took a bite of the apple, at which point mankind fell from grace and became alienated from God.

Buddhism holds a different view. According to the Buddha you can go back and back in time for millions of years, millions of ages, but you will never come to an absolute first beginning of things. However far back you go, you can still go further. You will never get back to a point before the point at which time begins. So the beginning of the parable is not in time at all, but completely outside time. This means that the 'return journey' is not a journey back into the past, but a journey out of time altogether, a journey which transcends time. It is very important to understand this.

In the books about Zen which people are so fond of reading, there are all kinds of strange and wonderful – and apparently meaningful – expressions, all kinds of appealingly snappy little mondos and koans. One of these Zen sayings – which is of course absolutely true – speaks of 'your original face before you were born'. The Zen masters are apparently rather fond of asking their disciples, at a moment's notice, to show them their original face before they were born. 'Come on!' they demand, 'Show it to me. I want to see it.' Of course the hapless disciple usually fails miserably, as hapless disciples tend to in these stories, written as they apparently are by the masters. The disciple tends to tackle the problem by sitting down and thinking about yesterday, the day before, the week before, a month ago, two months ago, a year ago, two years ago, twenty years ago, thirty years ago – until they get back to the day they were born. If they can get back past *that*, they think, they will encounter their original face.

This is all wrong. To think that before a certain point in time there was the original face and after that there was no original face is a complete misunderstanding. The expression may seem to mean this, but if we go trying to track down the original face in the past, if we take this expression 'original' or the word 'before' literally, we are not really practising Zen, but just regressing in the psychoanalytical sense. The past is no nearer to Enlightenment than the present or the future, because time has nothing to do with Enlightenment. We are 'born', in the Zen sense, out of time, and our original face also exists out of time, so the Zen expression 'seeing your original face' has nothing to do with going back in time, or with going forward in time, or with standing still at the present moment of time. When Zen speaks of seeing your original face before you were born, it means going outside time altogether, rocketing through time and coming up on the other side in a dimension where there is no time at all, no past, present, or future. That is where the original face is to be seen, and nowhere else. That's where it 'is' all the time.

So there is no question of going back in time to enquire into the beginning of our state of alienation. We are alienated from reality here and now, and all we have to do is overcome this alienation from reality. And we can't do that just by going back and back into the past because we are still running on the rails of the alienation itself. We have to take a leap, a crosswise leap – a jump from the top of the pole, to use another Zen expression – to land, if we're lucky, in the absolute.

This is the point of the Buddha's famous parable of the poisoned arrow – another parable connected with war – which is told in the Pāli canon.[84] The Buddha says that a soldier was wounded in battle by a poisoned arrow. Fortunately there is a surgeon on hand, but when he tries to take the arrow out, the wounded man says, 'Just a minute! Before I let you take out that arrow I want to ask a few questions. Who shot this arrow? Was he a Brahmin, a Kṣatriya, or a Vaiśya? Was he dark or fair? Was he young or old? What sort of bow was he using? And what sort of arrow is it? – A wooden one? An iron one? If it's wood, what

Perhaps similar to not fixating on fault in a conflict. But instead on how you yourself react.

sort of wood is it made from? – Oak? Cedar? Where does the feather come from? Is it a goose feather or a peacock feather? Answer all these questions, and then you can take out the arrow.'

Long before his questions were answered, of course, the soldier would be dead from the poison in the arrow. The important thing is to get rid of the arrow, not to enquire where it came from. In the same way, if we try to go back and back all the time – 'How did the world begin? How did we get into such a mess? What was I in my last birth? What are the roots of my neurosis?' – there is no end to it. We could go step by step back into the past and still be walking in millions of years. What we need to do is just see our present alienated, neurotic, conditioned, negative state, and rise above it, go soaring up into eternity, into a spiritual dimension. This is the message of the poisoned arrow. Likewise, the 'return journey' of the son is not about going back in time, but about going beyond time.

The son, who represents the lower self, wanders from place to place looking for work, for the simple reason that he needs food and clothing. He has no higher ideals. He has none of his father's ambitions of succeeding in trade and commerce. Translating this into modern terms (borrowed from Abraham Maslow's book *Towards a Psychology of Being*),[85] the lower self is 'need-motivated'. Everything the son does is out of his subjective need, out of his craving. By contrast, the father – the higher self – is 'growth-motivated'. The parable expresses this in terms of his accumulation of riches, but this is in no way to imply that it is glorifying capitalism or anything like that; as a parable, its meaning is symbolic. The father, the higher self, accumulates wealth until he possesses all conceivable spiritual riches and qualities.

Although he is so rich, the father is not happy because he is thinking of his son *all the time*. What can we infer from this? It tells us that the higher self never loses its awareness. It's conscious all the time. Although we may completely forget the higher self, the higher self never forgets us. But at the same time – this is the mystery – we are it. An image may help to make this clear. Imagine an enormous subterranean chamber all lit up from within. We are living in a tiny chamber next to – indeed part of – the big one. A pane of glass which is transparent only from one side separates the two chambers, so that although someone in the large illuminated chamber could see everything going on in the little chamber, from the little chamber we can see nothing at all of what is going on in the large chamber. In fact, we have no idea that there is a large chamber. But although cramped in our little chamber we may forget, even be oblivious to, the existence of the large chamber, the large chamber always has a window onto the little chamber. Even though the lower self forgets the higher self, the higher self is the higher self *of* the lower self.

The parable says that the poor man roams from one town to another and one country to another until he eventually reaches the place where his father is living. So he is already on his way back to his father, although he does not know it. It is his need for food and clothing, his craving, which drives him from place to place and brings him almost to his father's door. What are we to make of this?

Let's look at an example. A man has a certain psychological problem. He's so worried about it that he just can't sleep, and sleeping tablets don't help. He is really getting desperate for some peace of mind. One day he meets a friend who says, 'I know what will help you. You need to meditate.' By this stage the man is ready to try anything, so he asks where he can learn to meditate and goes along to a class. His only concern is to get rid of the problem and get some sleep. But at the meditation classes he starts to hear about something new: Buddhism. At first he is not particularly interested, but after a few months – rather to his surprise – he finds himself not just trying to get peace of mind but trying to follow the spiritual path. After a while he even starts thinking in terms of Enlightenment. So when did he take the first step in that direction? It was when, driven by his need for peace of mind, he joined the meditation class. In the same way the poor man, driven by his basic needs, made his way to his father's door without knowing it. This is the first stage of the return journey.

When the poor man eventually arrives at his father's door, his father is sitting outside surrounded by gold, jewels, and flowers. The poetic description of the rich man – who represents the higher self – is highly significant. He is a glorious archetypal figure, a god, even a Buddha, so he is described with light and colour, jewels and brilliance. But how does the poor man react? He is so terrified at the sight that he wants to run away. He thinks that he has come upon a king or nobleman, not recognizing in this glorious figure his own father. This goes to show that the alienation between the lower self and the higher self is quite severe. Even when the two confront each other, the lower self does not

This reminds me of my fear of GFR.

recognize the higher self as its own higher self, but thinks it is something strange and foreign. Such a confrontation occurs when we come face to face with an embodiment of the spiritual ideal. Whenever we read a description or see an image of the Buddha – or some god or saint – we think, or our lower self thinks, 'This has nothing to do with me. I'm down here, poor and humble. I'm not like that. I don't have those qualities.' The theistic systems which believe in a personal creator god, and indeed all dualistic systems, encourage this attitude.

We could call this the stage of religious projection. We project outwards all the qualities which are buried deep down in the depths of our own nature, not realizing that they are our own. As we see it, these glorious external figures are endowed with all the qualities which we lack. We are poor and they are rich. This religious projection is a step in the right direction; indeed, it is the next stage of the journey. It is a positive thing because it enables us to see spiritual qualities in a concrete way. But the projection must be resolved. These qualities belong to us – not to our ego, but to the deepest and truest depths of our being – and we must claim them as our own.

As yet, however, the son does not recognize his father, although his father immediately recognizes him and sends messengers to bring him back. But the poor man is terrified, thinks he is going to be arrested, and faints away. This reminds me of the account of the death experience given in the *Tibetan Book of the Dead*. At the time of death, so the text says, the Clear Light, a white light of absolutely unbearable brilliance, like a million suns, suddenly bursts on the vision of the dying person.[86] This light is the light of Reality, the light of Truth, the light of the Void. If we recognize that this is no light bursting upon us from without, but the light of our own intrinsic mind, our own true self, unfolding from deep within, if we can realize our oneness with that light, then we gain Enlightenment on the spot. But what happens? The light comes – blinding, terrible, overpowering – and most dying people shrink back in fear. 'Human kind cannot bear very much reality.'[87] This is true not only at the moment of death, but at all those moments when we encounter a truth that seems more than we can possibly bear.

The poor man, you notice, is not just terrified. His imagination is working overtime. He thinks that he is being arrested: already in his mind's eye he can see the block and the executioner's axe. His first thoughts are of imprisonment, slavery, violent death. Only too often

Definitely reminds
me of my fears re
GFR

Be
good
to think
what
those
fears
are

when we come in contact with the Truth, it seems not liberating but
an imprisonment, a limitation, or at least a nuisance. We do not want
to change our ideas, or to change ourselves, and in that diseased state
the liberating truth seems to us confining and narrow. Not only that,
like the poor man in the parable we are afraid of dying. When the
lower self – the I, the ego – comes in contact with Reality, it thinks,
as it were, 'I'm for the chop. I'm finished; this is the end of me,' and
so it shrinks back.

So the rich man lets his son slope off, but of course he has not given
up hope, and by some clever planning he manages to get his son clearing
away the heap of dirt at the back of his mansion. Now according to the
interpretation of the parable which the four elders give, the son's clearing
away dirt represents the narrow, selfish type of religious life which is
aimed at individual development to the exclusion of any concern for
others. The four elders identify this sort of approach with the Hīnayāna,
the lesser teaching which they have so recently renounced, but this is
perhaps a little extreme. A better – or at least more contemporary –
interpretation would suggest that the clearing away of the dirt represents
the process of psychoanalysis, the heap of dirt representing all the
repressions which the alienated person uncovers during analysis. The
sūtra mentions that it takes twenty years to clear away the dirt, which
seems rather a long time, but resolving repressions, negative emotions,
complexes, and all the rest of it is rather time-consuming, so analysis
does sometimes take as long as that.

And eventually, while the process of removing the dirt continues, the
father manages to speak to his son, and confidence springs up between
them. As this trust develops, the poor man begins to enter the rich
man's mansion without hesitation, but he continues to live in his own
hovel. So what does this mean? On one level it refers to the scholar,
the academic specialist in comparative religion. He knows the texts,
sometimes in the original languages, and he knows the teachings, even
the higher teachings. Sometimes he even claims to know the esoteric
teachings. In other words, he goes in and out of the mansion without
hesitation, knowing exactly what is there – but he does not live there
himself. He still lives in the straw hovel which represents all the things he
is really interested in as an academic: promotion within his department;
his annual increment; prestige within his profession; controversy and
brisk exchange of articles and opinions with other scholars.

On a higher level, the poor man's going in and out of the mansion without hesitation refers to the average follower of religion. Such people are undoubtedly sincere and have perhaps had genuine religious experience – they go in and out of the mansion, as it were – but their home is elsewhere. Even though they have some spiritual experience, maybe during the weekly meditation class, they are preoccupied most of the time with mundane things. In one of his books William James, the great psychologist and author of *The Varieties of Religious Experience*, discusses the question, 'What is a religious person?' He says that a religious person is not one who has religious experiences – anybody can have those – but one who makes religious experiences the centre of their existence. It is not important where we visit; what is important is where we permanently live, or at least where we live most of the time – in other words, where our real centre of interest lies. As the Gospel says, 'Where your treasure is, there will your heart be also.'[88]

When the rich man falls sick, he hands the management of his affairs over to the poor man, who thus becomes familiar with riches but still continues to live in the hovel. This element of the parable represents the theist, or the theistically inclined mystic, and the dualistic approach in general. Such a person may have great, overwhelming, uplifting spiritual experiences, but they all seem to come from outside, not from within. The mystic says, 'These experiences are not mine; they are the gifts of God.'

Once you reach this stage of the journey, only time is required. The rich man sees that his son is becoming used to riches and ashamed of his poverty, that he aspires to be rich himself. In other words, the alienation of lower self from higher self is becoming less and less. When the rich man is at the point of death, the alienation is practically over, with just a thin thread remaining; the lower self and the higher self are almost one. And when at last the rich man acknowledges the poor man as his son, he dies, and there are no longer two – father and son, rich man and poor man – but only one, a rich man who was once a poor man. In other words, unity between the lower self and the higher self has been completely restored. The return journey has been accomplished.

Our journey also is nearly accomplished. The four elders who have told the parable compare themselves to the son – and the Buddha, of course, is the father. Formerly, they say, they had not dared to think in terms of becoming like the Buddha, thinking only of following his verbal teaching, which had seemed to indicate a lesser goal, the goal of individual emancipation, the goal of the destruction of negative emotions. But they now realize, they say, that that is not enough, for there are all sorts of positive qualities to be developed. It is not enough to have Wisdom; you need Compassion too. It is not enough to be an *arhant*; you can become like the Buddha himself. You can follow the bodhisattva path; you can aspire to supreme Enlightenment.

In other words, the four elders wake up to the truth of the Higher Evolution of man. They realize that the Buddha is not something unique and unrepeatable, but a forerunner, an example of what others too can become if only they make the effort. They realize that the religious life is not just a personal affair in a negative limited sense, but part of a cosmic adventure – and this is what we too have to try to realize. Religion, when properly understood, is not something remote from life, not just a dull, churchy little backwater, but life become conscious of its own upward tendency, its own tendency to grow and develop. And whether we know it or not, we are all involved, directly or indirectly, in this upward tendency of life. Each one of us is the poor man in the parable, the son who has run away; but each one of us also, if we only knew it, is the rich man, the father. And each one of us is making, even at this very moment, the return journey.

4
QUESTIONS AND ANSWERS

THE MYTH OF THE FALL

It seems to me that there are two complementary models which describe the predicament of man: the conceptual, linear model of the Higher Evolution, and the cyclical myth of the Fall, of descent and return, the latter developed, for example, by Blake in the Four Zoas. *To what extent is the myth of the Fall in accord with the Dharma?*

It is not in accord with the Dharma. There is a myth of a fall in Buddhist literature, in the *Aggañña Suttanta* of the *Dīgha Nikāya* in the Pāli canon,[89] but that is not a fall from the absolute, so to speak, but from a higher to a lower plane of being within the mundane sphere. The *sutta* describes how at the beginning of the world period beings remaining from a previous cycle of evolution and involution, attracted by the evolving material universe, descend and become merged with it. So far the picture is identical with that of other traditions. The difference is that Buddhism does not regard this fall as a fall from a state of perfection. Indeed, in Buddhism there can be no question of such a fall. By definition a Buddha *cannot* fall; there is no fall from the state of Enlightenment. There can only be a fall from relatively higher to relatively lower states within *saṃsāra*.

Buddhism does not recognize an ultimate first beginning, so there can be no question of everything starting with an original fall of man. There is also no question of a return journey in the sense of going back into the past. It is going 'back' to something which is outside time. You can think of the absolute as being above you, or as being deep within you, or even as something which you have left behind, but you cannot help putting it in some relation to space and time. Within the Buddhist context, therefore, the return journey is not literally a journey to something which was there in the beginning. You return to it not by travelling backwards in time but by going out of time altogether. We can think of the absolute as being 'above' the temporal process, which is spatial terminology, or we can think of it as being 'before' the temporal process, which is temporal terminology. If one of these ways of thinking has more emotional resonance for you than the other, make use of whichever is appropriate – but be careful how you interpret it in conceptual terms.

But if you take the myth of the fall not literally or as doctrine but symbolically, is there anything wrong with that approach?
Well, you can think of the fall as occurring outside time. Really the fall occurs at every instant. There is a fall every time craving arises in dependence on feeling, instead of faith.[90]

Why does the idea of a return journey have such a strong emotional appeal?
One reason might be that it suggests the real possibility of contact between yourself and what you are seeking, or even that you are in contact with the ideal already in a vestigial way. Perhaps also it has something to do with the experience of very early childhood. Maybe you unconsciously hearken back to those very early days of 'oceanic oneness'.

But surely it is not just a matter of 'going back to the womb'? Isn't it more that you make use of that impulse but turn it around and allow it to move you in the direction you really need to take?
When you get in touch with the emotions bound up with that very early state, that must be a positive thing, because you can then link something very deep and basic in yourself with your spiritual quest, your spiritual aspirations.

Perhaps from time to time it would be a good thing to try to get back in contact with those early childhood feelings. I think in almost all cases they must have been intensely pleasurable, though perhaps they were all too quickly overlaid with much less pleasurable experiences. A baby gets immense emotional satisfaction from the experience of relative oneness with its mother; in fact, our relationship with our mother is probably the most important emotional experience in our life, leaving aside spiritual developments. This is perhaps not a very popular point of view, but I think that in the course of our adult relationships we are often only trying to recapture that early pleasurable experience, which in almost all cases was so intensely blissful, so secure, so satisfying, so uncomplicated. We could probably not have survived very long without it.

How might one get back in touch with those early feelings?
You can just try to remember them. It is not really a question of remembering specific experiences; that is perhaps not possible unless something traumatic happened to you. It is more like recollecting the feeling of the state before anything traumatic happened. There is a theory that your first really traumatic experience occurs when you are weaned, and this is not surprising. Watch a mother and you will see that she is totally absorbed in her baby; it is almost a lover-like relationship. On the receiving end of that, the baby probably feels great, and really enjoys the experience. Everybody has gone through that at some stage, and it must have left a trace in the psyche which perhaps still persists. It is good to get in touch with that.

So the return journey myth could be a synthesis of those early feelings and the feeling of wanting to be an individual, wanting to develop spiritually?
Yes. It is important to carry your emotions, especially your more basic and primitive emotions, along with you.

LOOKING FOR A DEEPER MEANING

The Christian religious tradition gained inspiration from earlier literature by interpreting the myths and parables of that literature allegorically. I have in mind the Christian interpretations of the Greek myths as they came down to them particularly through the Metamorphoses *of Ovid.*
Well, I think that usually Christian thinkers were more concerned with giving allegorical interpretations of Old Testament myths and legends.

Some took the view that the gods and goddesses of Greek and Roman mythology were simply demons. It was the Greeks themselves, the Neoplatonists, who started the allegorization of their own myths.

What is the function of allegory?

Strictly speaking, allegory means the personification of certain abstract qualities which are then made to behave in a way that illustrates the relationships between those qualities. Suppose, for example, that you want to describe some sort of moral conflict. Perhaps you call your hero Everyman. Someone called Temptation comes along and tries to persuade him to do something, but then another character called Good Counsel advises him not to do it. Conscience might intervene and reinforce what Good Counsel says, but then Pleasure comes along and Everyman is swayed in the other direction. That is the distinct literary form called allegory. One of the best-known allegories in English is the *Pilgrim's Progress*.

When we speak of the allegorization of myths and legends, though, we are not really thinking of that specific form; we are using the term in a very loose, perhaps even incorrect, way. The basic purpose of the so-called allegorization of myths, legends, and symbols is to try to evoke from them a meaning which is deeper and more acceptable than the surface meaning. This kind of allegorization is extremely important as a means of preserving continuity of tradition and reflecting the developing spiritual consciousness of the individual or group. Suppose, say, as an ancient Greek you know various stories about the gods and goddesses, but some of the actions of the gods and goddesses are in conflict with your own moral sense. What are you to do? At first sight it seems that the options are either to stifle your moral sense and continue to take those stories literally, or to heed the dictates of your moral sense to such an extent that you reject the myths and legends on moral grounds. But there is a third option, a middle way. You can interpret the myths and legends in such a way that your moral sense, your developing spiritual sense, is no longer offended. That is really what this type of 'allegorization' is all about. It enables you to stay in touch with your own tradition and faithful to it while not having to accept it in a literal sense which is offensive to you. You are able to grow and at the same time you stay in contact with your tradition. This is an almost universal process, because as people develop, the old myths in their literal forms become unacceptable.

For instance, at one point in the *White Lotus Sūtra* we find the Buddha putting out his tongue and encircling the universe with it.[91] This is really quite grotesque, and offends our aesthetic sense, but can we take it literally? We could say that the *sūtra* is illustrating the power and importance of speech in a way that the ancient Indian mentality evidently found acceptable, but that we cannot accept. We are not happy with the imagery, and certainly cannot take it literally, so we have to do the best we can with it by allegorizing it.

To what extent are the parables found in the White Lotus Sūtra *intended by their author to be interpreted allegorically?*
It is very doubtful whether the authors of parables consciously distinguish their many different levels of meaning. To take another example, commentators on Shakespeare's plays have read all sorts of profound meanings into them, interpreting their imagery and the significance of the various characters, but it is very doubtful whether those meanings were consciously present to Shakespeare's mind when he composed the plays. That is not to say that those meanings cannot validly be found there; it is almost as though Shakespeare had a higher perception which included those meanings in a non-conceptual way.

It is much the same with the author of the parables, myths, and symbols of the *White Lotus Sūtra*. You *can* construct a myth or legend, but that is an artificial procedure which probably will not have the same kind of impact. Some poets have tried to create myths of their own, but they are usually not very successful. Most poets wisely prefer to give some shape to traditional material.

So to what extent can the sūtra *be interpreted allegorically after perhaps first absorbing it on a more imaginative, non-rational level?*
You will start interpreting it, allegorizing it, when you feel a need to do so. If you don't feel a need to do so, don't bother. I think a lot of people reading the parables, myths, and symbols of the *White Lotus Sūtra* will quite spontaneously start trying to interpret them as a means of engaging with the material at a deeper level. And if you do this you do reach a deeper and fuller experience of those parables, myths, and symbols. It is not that you cease to experience them as parables, myths, and symbols – indeed, after allegorizing them you should experience them more profoundly and more strongly.

Has Buddhist tradition had recourse to allegory in any particular texts?
I don't think that Buddhist myths and symbols have been studied in this way in the East, as far as I can recollect. More often than not they were just taken literally. Eastern people did not feel any incongruity; they could perhaps take quite literally the statement that the Buddha protruded his tongue and it encircled the universe. Not having that sort of faith, we are obliged to allegorize so that we don't feel alienated from the *sūtras*. Allegorization usually comes with a certain amount of intellectual sophistication.

Is there a risk of losing something of the complexity and ambiguity of an image by going for one-to-one correspondences?
It is not such a simple matter as a one-to-one correspondence. The more deeply you go into a myth or symbol the more you realize how multi-faceted and multi-layered it is. It is not a question of saying it means this, so you can forget about the myth itself because now you have grasped in conceptual terms what it was trying in its inadequate way to say. That is much more like allegorization in the strict sense: a woman *en déshabillé* represents Temptation with a capital T, full stop. In the case of real myths and parables it is not as simple as that.

THE SYMBOLISM OF SERVANTS AND SONS

This parable introduces the symbolism of the servant and the son. In the West being a servant has become quite discredited, and the relationship between son and father is not flourishing either. What do servants and sons symbolize in a spiritual context?
A servant is one who serves. Why should you serve, from a spiritual point of view? What does service mean? Service means that you do something for somebody else, more often than not something which he could just as well do for himself. In the old days a servant polished his master's shoes. The master was presumably capable of polishing his own shoes, but the servant did it. So why is one the servant and the other the master? You could say that it is because one has more money than the other, but I would say that that is not a real servant and master relationship. Such a relationship really implies that the master is superior and perhaps the servant even gains by serving him. The servant cannot do what the master is able to do, so he does for him things which he could perhaps

do for himself but which he should not be allowed to do because he has more important duties to perform. Understanding this, the servant gladly serves him so that he can devote himself to something which the servant is incapable of doing. If servant and master share the same ideals, service to the master is the servant's way of serving those ideals. Without the servant, the master could not devote himself to the ideals so fully. This is the *natural* servant-master relationship. If it is based merely on economic considerations, it can obviously be exploitative.

In the old days the bond between master and servant was bound up with feudal loyalty, and that had many positive elements. As the servant you did not have the resources and strength to protect yourself, but you placed yourself under the protection of your feudal superior and he guarded your life, perhaps with his own life sometimes. In return for that, you placed yourself at his disposal in certain other respects. It was a natural relationship in which you recognized his superiority in a certain sense.

In India, even in pre-Buddhistic times, the disciple served his teacher, living with him – in his house if he was a householder and in the monastery if he was a monk – and serving him. The Tibetan language has a word which means both 'disciple' and 'servant'. That was also the custom in some of the Western monastic orders, and the system survived in some of the English universities of medieval foundation; there were 'sizars' who served in the college in return for free board, lodging, and tuition. Going back to India, under the Vedic tradition, if you wanted to be accepted by someone as a disciple you went to his house, gathering some sticks on the way which you offered to him on your arrival. This expressed your readiness to serve the teacher, because you would expect to serve him if he taught you. You would go and fetch water, gather sticks, perhaps take the cattle out to graze. Only when you had done all that would you sit down at the teacher's feet and listen to him expounding the Vedas.

Clearly we are out of touch with that tradition. These days, influenced by the predominance of egalitarian ideas, people don't like to think that anybody is superior to them in any essential way, and therefore they don't like to serve in this basic, genuine sense. This kind of service was the rationale behind the relationship between the *upāsaka* and the *bhikṣu*, but unfortunately in recent times this has developed into a situation where the *bhikṣu* lives the Buddhist life vicariously on the layman's behalf, and the layman just makes merit by serving the *bhikṣu* instead of trying to follow the spiritual path himself.

As far as the relationship between father and son goes, I think that in modern times very few people know what it means to be a son. In ancient times the man regarded his son as himself reborn, as his heir, even as the one whose services after his death were going to ensure that he went to heaven. People did not understand the nature of conception; it was thought that the impregnation of the female was like planting seed in a field. Not being regarded as a joint product of both parents, the child, especially the son, had a very close relationship with the father. This emerges in ancient literature, and sometimes even in more recent writing. In some Victorian novels the deep attachment of the father to the son, sometimes in an unhealthy way, is very evident.[92]

It is the instinct of the father to have a son like himself, in whom he can see a continuation of himself. Sometimes, therefore, fathers are very attached to their sons – often without the son's realizing it – trying to live their lives and fulfil their ambitions through them. These days fathers are often denied that sort of satisfaction. Sometimes their sons even take a delight in doing the very things their father does not want them to do, and of course this results in a loss of contact between father and son.

The man – or woman – who wants to be an individual has to make a break, in a sense, with both father and mother. At the same time, he or she needs to try to maintain some kind of positive connection without forfeiting his or her individuality, and that is not easy. There is sometimes a struggle between parents and children – the children wanting to be individuals, and the parents wanting to dominate the children and live their lives through them. We are in a difficult position these days. Perhaps in the old days, when it was inevitable that the son would follow in the father's footsteps, things were more straightforward.

SYMBOLISM AND LITERALISM

Is the teaching of the Tibetan Book of the Dead *to be taken literally, or as a symbolic account of the psyche shrinking from reality, regardless of the after-death state?*

I think it can be taken in both ways. Govinda makes the point that the so-called *Book of the Dead* is also a book of the living, something that in principle can be practised in the present life.[93] With regard to the after-death experiences I think there are certain details which need not be taken literally; for instance, the 'seven times seven days' is clearly symbolical. But from the accounts in various traditions, and even the modern secular accounts of people coming back from death-like experiences, it seems that something like the brief contact with Reality described in the *Tibetan Book of the Dead* does take place. There are even descriptions of contact with what seem to be angels, spiritual guides, Buddhas, and so on. We can thus take the content of the after-death experience as described in the *Tibetan Book of the Dead* as broadly corresponding to the facts, though we do not necessarily have to accept all the details, some of which may be symbolical or pertaining more to Tibetan culture than to the actual spiritual experience.

You mentioned in passing the Clear Light of the Tibetan Book of the Dead. *In some texts the Clear Light is taken to be synonymous with* śūnyatā. *What is the correspondence?*
The expression *śūnyatā* is not to be taken literally. The Unconditioned is empty with regard to the conditioned, but it is not literally void, literally empty. One of the ways of expressing that is by thinking in terms of light, thinking of the Void as a luminous void – though of course that sort of thinking also has its limitations, because it encourages us to think of Reality as being something like the sun, to put it crudely. The sun is a very good symbol – our experience of the sun is a very positive thing – but as a symbol it has its limitations. The light of the sun shines from a definite limited area, but when we speak of the Clear Light of the Void, do we really mean that Reality is circumscribed in space and rays are coming out of it? It is just not possible to take the image literally without limiting the Reality itself. It has therefore sometimes been described in terms of pure light without any actual source, light of the highest possible intensity distributed equally everywhere. The light of the sun diminishes the further away it is from its source, and presumably we cannot think of the light of *śūnyatā* in that way.

Are there sources within other religious traditions which speak of Reality in terms of light?
In Sufism Reality is often spoken of in terms of light, and the approaches to it in terms of stages of increasing brilliance. There are also some verses in the Koran which speak of light upon light, and in one of Saint

Paul's epistles he speaks of going from glory to glory. In the Pāli canon too there is the idea of the higher heavenly realms as being realms of increasing brilliance, with presumably the top, the transcendental, having the greatest brilliance of all.[94]

So would Reality still have that expansiveness, like the sun's radiance which expands outwards?
Yes, but into what would Reality expand?

The image of an evenness of light seems a bit flat – it has no dynamic quality.
I suppose it does seem flat – but why do we need to feel that dynamic quality? Perhaps we need both evenness and expansiveness. One is Reality in terms of space; the other is Reality in terms of time. Perhaps we need the idea of light without any boundary, with a high degree of brilliance evenly distributed, but we also need within that the light which is increasing in brilliance all the time. That does sound logically contradictory, but perhaps that cannot be helped. It's a bit like the difference between the relative and the absolute *bodhicitta*.

HOW DO WE OVERCOME THE FEAR OF CHANGE?

In the parable the son is afraid when he first encounters his father with all his wealth. In connection with this, you say that that which is liberating seems to us confining. How can we overcome the fear of change?
You need the help and encouragement of your spiritual friends. When I was staying in Wales, I was watching the baby lapwings learning to fly. The babies were scared of flying, but in the end they would flap their miserable wings and get airborne, and then there would be a terrific flurry of wings as they were caught up in an air current and swept away. All the time the parents would be hovering nearby uttering cries of encouragement until the baby got the hang of it and began to enjoy soaring around. The parents sometimes needed to give vigorous encouragement for quite a long time before the baby took to the air.

Your spiritual friends need to function in the same sort of way. They need to say, 'Come on, you can do it! You're not going to kill yourself! Give up that habit. Move out of that situation. It's OK, you'll survive.'

This is where spiritual friends can be really helpful, especially spiritual friends who have already gone through the same kind of experience and know what it's like.

Do you think that one of the functions of puja is to help to overcome this kind of fear?
It's one of the functions of all spiritual practices. The difference is that it is possible to resist a spiritual practice and not let it take its effect, whereas a spiritual friend will not necessarily tolerate that kind of resistance.

GUARDIAN ANGELS

In the lecture you speak of a higher self and a lower self, and say that the lower self can forget the higher self but the higher self will not forget the lower self. In what sense will the higher self not forget the lower self?
Although I have used those expressions, you mustn't think of the higher self as being really separate; this kind of language is not very Buddhistic, although I think I am justified in using it. The higher self is aware of the lower self in the sense that you are aware of yourself at a deeper level, a level at which an experience of something like Reality, or at least a higher level of consciousness, still persists. Since it is higher, it can, so to speak, look down on the lower. It's rather like a one-way mirror; you can look through and see another person, but they can't see you.

Does that higher self have a guiding function in your life even though you are not aware of it? I have heard of people having experiences in which they felt they had met spiritual guides which they took to be an aspect of themselves which was guiding them.
Yes, you can think in those terms. There is the guardian angel, the genius (in the Roman sense), the patron saint – these are all ways of looking at that particular experience. The important thing to realize is that the 'guardian angel' is really you – and that is extremely difficult to realize, because the mere fact that you think of it as something objective means that you don't experience it as you. You can *think* that it is you, but that is a completely different thing. The minute that you start to really *feel* that it is you, very strange things start happening within you. The 'he' or the 'it' becomes 'I', which means that it is transformed at least to some extent.

If the higher self has, as it were, paternal feelings towards the lower self and therefore appears in the form of a guide, why does it only appear occasionally in a definite form? Why do we not hear that voice more often?
Because the lower self is the lower self – and some selves are lower than others. In some people the lower self is further removed from the higher self, and hears its voice less clearly or frequently. This is really just a question of spiritual status. Why are you not Enlightened? Why do you not normally dwell in the third *dhyāna*? There are ten thousand reasons. Why are you what you are?

Bearing in mind the dangers of using the language of potentiality and immanence, in what respect can the higher self be said to be there if you are not actually experiencing it?
The language which speaks of thinking that you are already a Buddha is dangerous and to be avoided, but it is quite positive to think in terms of a guardian angel (rather than a Buddha or even a bodhisattva) which is invisible but hovering near. There is a very real possibility of contact with that. The possibility of contact with the Buddha, on the other hand, is rather remote for the time being; thinking of yourself as being a Buddha can only be purely abstract and theoretical. Thinking that you have an angel which is your slightly higher self is much more real and accessible, something you can really have some feeling for.

Is it good actually to invoke your guardian angel?
It could be. You will just have to try it and see whether it works for you. Some people might feel a bit foolish invoking their guardian angel, or, to use a Buddhist term, their *puṇya devatā*. But a Sinhalese Buddhist friend of mine often used to say, when things were going well, 'Ah, that must be my *puṇya devatā*,' – this being a personification of one's own previous good karma helping one out in the present. He seemed to think of it very much as a sort of guardian angel.

How does this idea fit in with the practice of visualizing a Buddha or bodhisattva? When you visualize your yidam, *are you really coming into contact with an inferior emanation of the Buddha or bodhisattva?*
Yes, you could look at it like that.

When you are visualizing, is it appropriate, then, to feel that this is your guardian angel?
If you visualize successfully, it is formally (in both senses of the term) a Buddha or bodhisattva, but your actual experience is much more akin to an experience of your guardian angel. It is sometimes said that Buddhas and bodhisattvas have three forms – a *devatā* form, a bodhisattva form, and a Buddha form – so perhaps you could think of the *devatā* form as corresponding to the guardian angel.

Fear of meeting Reality directly could perhaps inhibit the visualization of the form as Buddha or bodhisattva. But I would rather like to meet a guardian angel…
Yes. For many people the danger is not shrinking from ultimate reality but continuing to think of it in purely conceptual terms to such an extent that they are cut off from any slightly higher experience at all. It is much better actually to experience your guardian angel on a comparatively low level than just to have highly abstract thoughts about Buddhahood and ultimate reality. An ounce of practice and experience is worth a ton of theory and conceptualization.

Do you have any suggestions about how to contact a guardian angel?
You have to find a point of contact. Look in literature and art, and see whether there is any figure of that kind that attracts you. It might be a figure from Egyptian mythology, or even from a novel or a painting. Take that as your starting point. If it attracts you, you must have some affinity for it; it must mean something to you.

A MATTER OF TIME?

You said of the stage of the parable at which the son is becoming familiar with the riches of his father that this was the stage of religious dualism, and that from now on the final stages of the son's journey were 'just a matter of time'. How can the transition from dualism to Insight be said to be just a matter of time?
I didn't mean that it is an automatic process. It is just a matter of time assuming that you are keeping up your spiritual practice, at least from a Buddhist point of view. If your spiritual practice is Christian, you may just remain stuck in that duality and think that the riches that you

are observing don't belong to you but to somebody else. Within the Buddhist context, however, if you keep up your practice, it will gather momentum and you will find yourself moving from the stage of dualism to the stage of oneness, so to speak.

PSYCHOLOGY AND THE SPIRITUAL LIFE

Using the Buddha's story of the man struck by a poisoned arrow, you say that there is no point in trying to go back to the roots of our neuroses; the important thing is to transcend them here and now. Later, commenting on the son shifting the pile of dirt, you suggest that this could refer to the psychoanalytical process. This shifting of the dirt does seem to be a useful preparatory stage in breaking down the son's alienation from the father. How useful are psychological techniques in the context of spiritual practice, and what are their limits and risks?

I think such techniques may be useful within the context of spiritual life. Outside that context, however, they don't seem to do much good, perhaps because they have become ends in themselves. If human beings are basically spiritual, no method or technique that doesn't recognize that is going to help very much. Some useful preparatory work may be done, but even that will be vitiated by the fact that there is no recognition that we are basically spiritual beings.

You can't say, 'Let's deal with these mundane problems and leave aside any sort of spiritual consideration.' Indeed, you can't ignore the basically spiritual nature of human beings when dealing with them in any way, perhaps not even the physical. Can you really help people even to a limited extent by treating them as machines?

The great risk is simply that of losing sight of the ultimate spiritual objective. If a psychoanalyst is trying to help someone to be happy, but thinks of happiness in purely mundane terms, perhaps they can't really do all that much for the person. A lot of people seem to have an analyst not as someone who is helping them to get over their problems so that they will be in a better state of mind, but as an ongoing institution, like having a doctor or a lawyer. To think that you will always need your analyst isn't very encouraging from the Buddhist point of view. Perhaps in that case you might suspect that the analyst also needs you.

So if you don't have an intuition of a higher spiritual reality towards which to grow, you can't really successfully engage in psychological techniques?

Well, sometimes so-called psychological problems are spiritual problems. Someone may go to the doctor apparently with some sort of illness, but perhaps what they are really suffering from is malnutrition. In the same way someone may come along with what seem to be psychological problems, but what they are actually suffering from is spiritual starvation. In that case there is not much point in trying to tackle the psychological problems in terms of psychoanalysis without spiritual nourishment. It is spiritual nourishment and friendship that they really need; then at least some of the problems may go away.

When I hear about counselling and other techniques, I notice in myself both a definite interest in them and a feeling that what is really lacking is a more wholehearted use of the more obviously spiritual practices that we already have: puja, confession, recitation of sūtras, *spiritual friendship. I do feel attracted to these psychological techniques, but I suspect that it is not an entirely healthy attraction.*

That suspicion is probably justified; it's all too easy to wander off along bypaths. If there is some method or technique we know that we can bring in, well and good, but we should not start to have wholesale recourse to these things, giving meditation and puja a minor place. The danger is that we may start relying more on these techniques than on the Dharma and traditional Buddhist practices.

But even when people have built up authentic meditation experience through years of practice, they often seem still to have deeply rooted reactive patterns of behaviour which are at odds with their meditation experience. Year after year these patterns seem to go untouched and unchanged. Are there areas, in our communication with other people for instance, that meditation doesn't affect?

I think meditation does resolve such areas if you can get into it deeply enough and for long enough, but this is often not possible. If your circumstances are not conducive to intensive meditation, you may need to tackle your problems on their own level. Your spiritual friends may be the best people to help you do that, pointing out things that you can't see yourself. Perhaps in extreme cases professional help may be needed, but as far as possible you should look to your friends. Of course, for a friend to be able to point out basic patterns in this way they need to know you very well, and have a strong positive feeling for you; and you need to be able to trust them too. This implies a considerable degree of friendship. If you don't normally function in this way as a friend, it is perhaps because you are not yet sufficiently a friend. We could do a lot more for one another in this way.

5
SYMBOLS OF LIFE AND GROWTH

In England we have four distinct seasons – spring, summer, autumn, and winter – but this particular pattern is not universal. In northern India, which provides the backdrop for the *White Lotus Sūtra*, there are three seasons in the year, of about four months each. There's the cold season, when by Indian standards it's cold all the time, a bit like an English summer without the rain. Then there's the hot season, which is very hot indeed. There's no rain at all, not even a drop, and it seems to get hotter and hotter and hotter. The leaves drop off the trees, and all the vegetation turns brown and dry; the earth is baked brick-hard; and towards the end of the hot season great fissures appear in the ground, some of them so wide and deep that you have to be careful as you walk along not to fall into them. Cows wandering in search of food kick up a thick dust which turns the whole atmosphere a dull yellow.

Then, come July, before your very eyes the rainy season begins. One minute the weather is hot and bright, the next, with miraculous speed, a huge dark cloud appears, blotting out the sun, and within a few minutes the whole sky is overcast, deep greyish-blue turning almost black. On every side lightning flickers and flashes, and terrible crashes of thunder roll from one end of the sky to the other. Then you hear a great sound, like the rushing of a tremendous wind, and down comes the rain. It comes down in great bucketfuls for days and days and days. Water swirls underfoot all the time, and the ground is a great sea of mud. The rivers turn yellow and overflow their banks. Here and there in the villages the mud walls of the huts collapse, and sometimes whole villages are swept away.

But then, just a few days after the rainy season has begun, a wonderful thing happens. Just like magic, the yellow, parched land suddenly becomes entirely green, and vegetation of every kind springs up. The rice fields are filled with emerald shoots, and even the most stunted bushes and shrubs burst into leaf. The bamboo and the plantain shoot up inches in a single night. Every shrub, every tree, every bush, every plant, starts to grow.

After so many months of intense heat and dryness, the start of the rainy season in India is greeted with a joy which it is hard to imagine English people feeling for April showers. The Indian monsoon comes as a tremendous relief, the worker of a magical transformation. The scene is often represented in art, especially in the Moghul miniature paintings, and described in Pāli and Sanskrit literature. It is also depicted in the parable called the rain-cloud, also known as the parable of the plants, which occurs in the fifth chapter of the *White Lotus Sūtra*. In Soothill's translation from Kumārajīva's Chinese version, this is what the Buddha says:

> It is like unto a great cloud
> Rising above the world,
> Covering all things everywhere,
> A gracious cloud full of moisture;
> Lightning-flames flash and dazzle,
> Voice of thunder vibrates afar,
> Bringing joy and ease to all.
> The sun's rays are veiled,
> And the earth is cooled;
> The cloud lowers and spreads
> As if it might be caught and gathered;
> Its rain everywhere equally
> Descends on all sides,
> Streaming and pouring unstinted,
> Permeating the land.
> On mountains, by rivers, in valleys,
> In hidden recesses, there grow
> The plants, trees, and herbs;

Trees, both great and small.
The shoots of the ripening grain,
Grape vine and sugar-cane.
Fertilized are these by the rain
And abundantly enriched;
The dry ground is soaked,
Herbs and trees flourish together
From the one water which
Issued from that cloud,
Plants, trees, thickets, forests,
According to need receive moisture.
All the various trees,
Lofty, medium, low,
Each according to its size,
Grows and develops
Roots, stalks, branches, leaves,
Blossoms and fruits in their brilliant colours;
Wherever the one rain reaches,
All become fresh and glossy.
According as their bodies, forms
And natures are great or small,
So the enriching (rain),
Though it is one and the same,
Makes each of them flourish.
In like manner also the Buddha
Appears here in the World,
Like unto a great cloud
Universally covering all things;
And having appeared in the world,
He, for the sake of the living,
Discriminates and proclaims
The truth in regard to all laws.
The Great Holy World-honoured One,
Among the gods and men
And among the other beings,
Proclaims abroad this word:
'I am the Tathāgata,
The Most Honoured among men;

I appear in the world
Like unto this great cloud,
To pour enrichment on all
Parched living beings,
To free them from their misery
To attain the joy of peace,
Joy of the present world,
And joy of Nirvāṇa.
Gods, men, and every one!
Hearken well with your mind,
Come you here to me,
Behold the Peerless Honoured One!
I am the World-honoured,
Who cannot be equalled.
To give rest to every creature,
I appear in the world,
And, to the hosts of the living,
Preach the pure Law, sweet as dew;
The one and only Law
Of deliverance and Nirvāṇa.
With one transcendent voice
I proclaim this truth,
Ever taking the Great-Vehicle
As my subject.
Upon all I ever look
Everywhere impartially,
Without distinction of persons,
Or mind of love or hate.
I have no predilections
Nor any limitations;
Ever to all beings
I preach the Law equally;
As I preach to one person,
So I preach to all.
Ever I proclaim the Law,
Engaged in naught else;
Going, coming, sitting, standing,
Never am I weary of

Pouring it copious on the world,
Like the all-enriching rain.
On honoured and humble, high and low,
Law-keepers, and law-breakers,
Those of perfect character,
And those of imperfect,
Orthodox and heterodox,
Quick witted and dull witted,
Equally I rain the Law-rain
Unwearyingly.'[95]

There is no need to comment on the specific details of this parable; the general meaning is obvious enough. But before moving on to consider the parable's implications, I want to comment on the kind of symbolism it introduces, the symbolism of life and growth. Now clearly the parables that we have met so far are also symbols of life and growth. In the parable of the burning house, the children – that is to say sentient beings – are depicted as moving from a state of potential suffering to a state of everlasting bliss, peace, and happiness. In the parable of the return journey the poor man comes closer and closer to the rich man, becomes more and more like him, and is in the end acknowledged as his son and heir. So in both these parables there is growth, onward and upward movement. In fact, we could say that the whole *White Lotus Sūtra* is a symbol of life and growth, for it depicts a universe in which every living thing is moving upwards. *Arhants* are becoming bodhisattvas, bodhisattvas are becoming Buddhas – all individual beings whatsoever are moving in the direction of Enlightenment. However, the parable of the rain-cloud can be singled out specifically as a symbol of life and growth for an obvious reason – because it compares the whole process of spiritual development to the unfolding of a plant.

Plant symbolism is much more common in Buddhism than is generally supposed. In fact, the first symbol for humanity to emerge from the Enlightened consciousness of the Buddha was a symbol of this kind. If we go back to the time just after the Buddha's Enlightenment, we find that he was at first hesitant about going out to teach the truth he had discovered. It was so difficult and subtle – would anyone else ever be able to understand it? The scriptural records tell us that at that point the Buddha looked out over the world and saw a vision of the whole mass of humanity just like a great bed of lotuses.[96] Many of the lotus plants were not just deep down in the water, but right deep down in the mud, so submerged that you could hardly see their buds. But others, the Buddha saw, had begun to grow, so that at least the tips of their buds had emerged above the surface of the water. Other buds stood free of the water and were starting to unfurl their petals. And a very few were on the point of bursting into bloom. Through this beautiful vision of the different stages of development, the Buddha realized that there were at least some individuals who could flower in the sunlight of his teaching, and set out to share his vision of reality.

If we turn to a period much later in the Buddhist tradition, we find in Tibetan Buddhism a similar sort of symbolism. According to Tibetan tradition there are a number of psychic centres (which the Tibetans call 'wheels') – four, five, or sometimes seven – situated at different points along the spinal column within the human body: one at the stomach, one at the solar plexus, one at the heart, one at the throat, one at the head, and so on. These psychic centres are symbolized by lotuses of different sizes and colours, and with different numbers of petals. Practitioners who use this symbolism say that in meditation – especially in certain esoteric meditation practices – a powerful current of upward-moving energy is generated within the body. This current is called in Buddhist Sanskrit *chandali* – 'the fiery one'. It corresponds to the Tibetan *tummo*, usually translated as 'psychic heat', and the Hindu *kuṇḍalinī*, 'the coiled-up one' (an evocative term for 'coiled-up' potential energy). In all these traditions this potential energy is often represented as a serpent. As the energy passes up the spinal column, it activates the different centres, and the lotus flowers open – the higher up the centre, the bigger and more beautiful the lotus. Leaving aside the question of whether we can take the symbolism of the psychic centres and the current of energy literally or whether it is metaphorical, the lotus here clearly symbolizes the whole process of spiritual development.

White Tāra is one of the most popular of the archetypal bodhisattvas of Buddhist tradition. As her name suggests, she is completely white in colour – a beautiful, graceful, smiling figure, usually seated in *siddhāsana* and clad in the silks and jewels of a bodhisattva. In her left hand she holds a whole spray of lotuses. And here there is a very interesting point to notice. The spray of lotuses consists of a closed lotus bud, a half-open bud, and a fully open flower. Now these lotuses could represent, for example, the Buddhas of the three times – the past, the present, and the future. No doubt the symbolism is rich and capable of many interpretations. But the simplest and most obvious meaning is that White Tārā's three lotuses represent the process of growth and unfoldment which is the spiritual life.

This kind of symbolism, then, is frequently found in the Buddhist tradition. But why – in chapter 5 – does the *White Lotus Sūtra* suddenly start talking in terms of plants and their growth? Well, you could say that it just happened like that – it was an accident – but I don't personally believe that. I believe that this kind of symbolism is introduced at this point in the *sūtra* for a very definite purpose. It is there to correct a mistake which it is only too easy to make if we take certain details of the previous parables – the burning house and the return journey – too literally, a mistake which may lead us to misinterpret the whole process of the spiritual life.

In the parable of the burning house the children are persuaded to come from the inside of the building to the outside. In the myth of the return journey the poor man comes from a distant country to his father's city, and then to his father's mansion. In both parables, then, there is a change of place, a journey, a movement in space. Now the characteristic feature of movement in space is that the moving object changes its position but does not itself change. In other words, the change that takes place is external, not internal. So if we take the parables literally, the danger is that we will understand the process of spiritual development not in terms of internal change, but in terms of external change. This means that – consciously or semi-consciously – we will think of the self as having experiences, traversing changes, but itself remaining unchanged.

This misunderstanding does represent a very real danger, and one that we are all likely to encounter or even succumb to. It is easy enough to study the history of Buddhism. It is easy enough to become acquainted with all the doctrines and study the different stages of the path. The danger is that we may start to mistake our intellectual journey through those stages for real experience. We may be aware that our understanding of Nirvāṇa itself is only theoretical, but it may not be so obvious that our knowledge and understanding of the earlier stages is also quite theoretical. If we are not careful we will not be aware that we are not passing through them in actual experience, but only mentally, that is, externally. There's no internal change taking place at all.

For example, many books on Buddhism refer to the Buddha's Noble Eightfold Path – there's no getting away from it, and quite rightly so – but it is very often misrepresented. We are given a picture of a path divided into eight stages, and encouraged to think of ourselves traversing it stage by stage. But it isn't like that at all. Following the Noble Eightfold Path is in practice much more like putting forth, one after another, eight successive shoots or branches. This is reflected in the term for the Eightfold Path in Pāli (*aṭṭhāṅgikamagga*) and Sanskrit (*aṣṭāṅgikamārga*). *Aṅga* does not mean a step or stage, but a limb, shoot, or branch, so following the Eightfold Path is not at all like climbing a ladder rung by rung, but more like rising up as the sap rises up through a tree when the rain falls.[97]

Taking the analogy further, we could say that the first of these shoots, Perfect Vision, or transcendental consciousness, is like the rain. When you get your first glimpse of transcendental consciousness, your first experience above and beyond the limitations of your ordinary self, like rain spreading through the soil it gradually permeates and influences all other aspects of your being. It spreads to your emotional life, your speech, your activities, your way of earning a living, your mental state – your whole way of life.

So practising the Noble Eightfold Path is not a matter of following a path step by step, but of imbibing a certain inspiration, having a certain experience, and then allowing that to permeate all aspects of your being until you are permanently saturated in that experience at all levels. At that point of perfect and complete transformation, you reach the eighth step of the transcendental Eightfold Path, perfect *samādhi*, and you attain the Enlightenment of a Buddha.

It is to stop us from mistaking external change for internal change, from mistaking intellectual understanding for personal experience, that the *White Lotus Sūtra* adds to the symbol of the journey the symbol of the plant. The symbol of the journey apparently has two factors: the path itself and the person treading the path. In the symbolism of the plant, however, these two factors come together to produce a single factor. The plant itself is the process of development, so there is no possibility of any misunderstanding. Instead of thinking of ourselves as traversing the path, we now think of ourselves as plants, as living, growing things. The only question that arises is that of what stage we have reached. Are we still buds, submerged in the water or the mud, are we half-open flowers, or are we even in full bloom?

Whatever stage a plant has reached, it needs both rain and sun to help it to grow. It is appropriate, then, that sun imagery is also introduced in the *White Lotus Sūtra*, in a parable which follows directly after the parable of the rain-cloud: the parable of the sun and moon. The Buddha does not elaborate upon this parable, and it is so short that it is in fact more like a simile than a parable. This is Kern's translation from the Sanskrit:

> And further, Kāśyapa, the Tathāgata, in his educating creatures, is equal and not unequal. As the light of the sun and moon, Kāśyapa, shines upon all the world, upon the virtuous and the wicked, upon high and low, upon the fragrant and the ill-smelling; as their beams are sent down upon everything equally, without inequality; so, too, Kāśyapa, the intellectual light of the knowledge of the omniscient, the Tathāgatas, the Arhats, &c., the preaching of the true law proceeds equally in respect to all beings in the five states of existence, to all who according to their particular disposition are devoted to the great vehicle, or to the vehicle of the Pratyekabuddhas, or to the vehicle of the disciples. Nor is there any deficiency or excess in the brightness of the Tathāgata-knowledge up to one's becoming fully acquainted with the law.[98]

The sun and moon are of course universal symbols, and like plant and flower symbolism they feature frequently in Buddhist tradition. In Tantric Buddhism, the sun is embodied especially in the figure of Vairocana, who occupies the centre of the mandala of the Five Buddhas.[99] His name means simply 'illuminator'. In the Vedas, the pre-Buddhist scriptures, Vairocana is one of the names of the sun, and in Japanese Buddhism he is known as Dainichi, 'the great sun Buddha'. Iconographically he is represented as being brilliant white in colour, like the sun at its midday brightest, and he is shown holding his emblem, the eight-spoked golden wheel of the Dharma. His fingers make the 'wheel-turning gesture', the *dharmacakra-pravartana*, which is associated with the Buddha's first teaching at Sarnath, and represents the dissemination of the truth in all possible directions, just like the beams of the sun shining in all directions of space. The lotus throne on which Vairocana is sitting is supported by lions, the lion itself being a solar symbol. Furthermore, according to Indian mythology, when the lion roars in the jungle at night, all the other beasts fall silent. The Buddha, we are told in the scriptures, preaches his Dharma with a lion-like roar, *siṅgha-nāda*; when Truth is given utterance by the Buddha, all partial truths or untruths fall silent.[100]

In the *White Lotus Sūtra* too, the sun is a symbol for the Buddha's teaching. In some respects the meaning of its symbolism in the *sūtra* is identical to that of the rain-cloud. Both are indispensable to the life and growth of the plant. And both are absolutely impartial; this is stressed in both parables. The rain-cloud gives the same moisture, and the sun gives the same light and heat, to each and every plant on the Earth. The cloud doesn't give some plants a heavier shower of rain than others. The sun doesn't treat some plants to a purer or a brighter light. In the same way, in principle the Buddha gives the same teaching, communicates the same reality, the same higher state of consciousness, to all living beings. The teaching has different forms, just as the rain consists of individual drops and the sunshine of individual rays, but all the forms have one and the same meaning, just as each raindrop is made of water and each sunbeam is made of light.

The quality of impartiality is particularly drawn out in the parable of the rain-cloud. The word the Buddha uses to describe the rain is *ekarasa* (*eka* meaning 'one', and *rasa* meaning 'taste', 'juice', or 'essence'). This same word is used in a similar connection in another parable, one which occurs in the Pāli scriptures: the parable of the great ocean.[101] The Buddha says that wherever you go in the great ocean, you can scoop a handful of water and it will have the same taste: the taste of salt. Likewise, whatsoever part of his teaching you take up, it will have one taste: the taste of freedom. In other words, whatever aspect of the Buddha's teaching you practise, it has one essence, one purpose, one effect – to help you to get free from your conditioning. There are many different presentations of the Buddha's teaching. There are the lists: the Eightfold Path, the five spiritual faculties, the three Refuges. There are the teachings about suffering, impermanence, and no-self. And there are all sorts of methods of practice: the mindfulness of breathing, the *mettā bhāvanā*, the contemplation of the impurities, the *brahma vihāras*. But all these many teachings, traditions, and practices have just one aim: to help individual human beings to become free from their conditioning.

From this the important corollary follows that the Buddha's teaching is not to be identified with any one formulation. It is not possible to say that the Buddha's teaching is the Noble Eightfold Path and just that, or the contents of the Pāli canon and just that. The Buddha's teaching is not just Zen, or just Theravāda, or just what Professor so-and-so says it is. Buddhism cannot be identified with any one individual formulation, much less with any one individual school or sect. The Buddha's teaching or message can only be identified with that spirit of liberation, of freedom from conditionedness, that pervades all these formulations, just as the taste of salt pervades all the waters of the ocean. Whether it is the teaching of the Eightfold Path or the teaching of the bodhisattva ideal, whether it is this meditation practice or that, if it helps us to become free from our conditioning, it is part and parcel of the Buddha's teaching.

When we read about Buddhism, it is very important not only to remember this but to try really to feel it; otherwise all our studies and knowledge will be in vain. When we read the scriptures or hear about the Buddha's teaching, it is not enough just to pay attention to the words, the ideas and concepts. What really matters is to feel, through the concepts, through the images and symbolism, that which informs and gives life to them all – the experience of emancipation from all conditions whatsoever. In other words, we are trying to feel at least to some degree the absolute consciousness of the Buddha, the Enlightened consciousness from which all the teachings originally came.

Now, although the rain falls on all alike, and the sun shines on all alike, the plants themselves are all different and they grow in different ways. A nut grows into a tree, and a seed into a flower; a rose bush produces big red blossoms whereas a crocus bulb produces small yellow ones. Some plants shoot up in the air, others creep along the ground, and others clasp bigger and stronger plants. They all grow according to their own nature. And it is just the same, the parable suggests, with human beings. They all receive the same truth, they all hear what is in principle the same spiritual teaching, and they all grow. But the strange, astonishing, and wonderful thing is that they all grow in different ways. They all grow according to their own nature. People may all hear the same teaching, believe in the same teaching, and follow the same path, but they do what seem to be completely different things. Some become more and more deeply involved in meditation, so that in the end they are spending most of their time meditating and have hardly any contact with other people. Others take up social work. Others burst into song, write poetry, or paint pictures. And others, perhaps the majority, simply go on being themselves. They do not display any specific talent, but just become more and more individual. The paradox is that although we each become more and more different from one another as we grow and develop, at the same time we also become more and more like one another: more aware, more sensitive, more compassionate; in a word, more alive.

This means that in the spiritual life there can be no question of regimentation. It is reasonable to expect that, with a little endeavour, all human beings will grow, but it is unreasonable to expect all human beings to grow in the same way. This, unfortunately, is often forgotten. When we discover something that we ourselves find very helpful to our own development, we tend to think that everybody else should also find it helpful. Indeed, if we are not careful, we even start insisting that they must find it helpful. Or, conversely, we discover that something is not helpful to us, at least at present, and therefore refuse to recognize that it is helpful to other people.

It is this kind of fixed attitude which leads to sectarianism in Buddhism. When people hit upon a helpful approach to their spiritual development, rather than just making use of it, they are quick to declare that the school or method they have discovered *is* Buddhism. If you don't follow this school, they say, you can't really be a Buddhist. This is just as bad as orthodox Christianity, and indeed represents a carrying over of Christian attitudes into Buddhist life.

I must confess that I found a lot of this sort of thing in the English Buddhist movement when I came back in 1964 after spending twenty years in the East. For instance, there were some people who – quite rightly – found meditation very helpful indeed, and devoted a number of hours every day to practising it. And because they found meditation so helpful, they used to declare that the practice of studying the scriptures – or reading about Buddhism at all – was completely useless. In their opinion, nobody who called themselves a Buddhist should be expected, or even allowed, to do anything other than meditate.

But there were other people, I found, who preferred to study. And these people, who tended to be rather bookish, would say that people in the West, being tense and full of problems, and rather difficult in all sorts of ways, were simply not ready for so sublime a spiritual practice as meditation, and ought to stick to reading books. Some people went so far as to say that meditation was dangerous, and that if you insisted on doing it at all, five minutes at a time was quite enough. Other people again were against anything ceremonial or colourful. They did not find ritual helpful themselves, for one reason or another, so they tended to say that it was bad for everybody.

We need to be careful not to get stuck in fixed ideas about which particular Buddhist school is best, or which kind of Buddhist practice is best. Furthermore, we need to examine our fixed ideas about what 'Buddhism' is, and even what 'religion' is. Again we can take as our reference point the parables of the *White Lotus Sūtra*, which say that the rain falls and the sun shines on the good and the bad alike. But in applying this to our own situation, I want to put it rather differently: the rain falls and the sun shines on the *religious* and the *secular* alike.

For a couple of thousand years in the West, all cultures and communities were 'officially' religious. This meant that you could only develop higher states of consciousness through traditional religious means: prayer, meditation, the sacraments, and so on. If you wanted to evolve, you had to be a religious person and do it in the religious way. You had to be a pious church-goer, or a religious scholar, or a mystic.

But a great change has taken place. It began at the time of the Renaissance, when thinkers, philosophers, and artists started separating – some would say emancipating – themselves from the tutelage of religion. Then, after the Industrial Revolution, the whole process speeded up, and today in most Western countries – and the change is spreading to the East as well – communities and cultures are secular rather than religious. Art is secular art; it has no direct connection with conventional or traditional religion. And literature is very definitely secular literature.

But despite this split between the religious and the secular, the Higher Evolution is still possible. In the modern world, especially in the West, it can take place not only in religious but also in secular terms. Indeed, in the West today spiritual progress is more likely to take place within a secular context than within a conventional religious one. All that is traditionally or conventionally associated with the word 'religion' has little appeal now for the vast majority of thinking people. One can even go so far as to say, to put it bluntly, that those who go to church are probably not very interested in religion, and those who are very interested in religion are unlikely to go to church.

It might be better, therefore, to present the Higher Evolution of man not in conventional religious terms at all, but in secular terms. Perhaps more people would then be attracted to the teachings and benefit from them. It may be that one day we shall have to conclude that in sticking to traditional religious forms, including Eastern religious forms, we are being unimaginative and unrealistic, and perhaps even excluding – or at least not encouraging – some people who could benefit from the teachings of the Higher Evolution.

The rain falls and the sun shines on the religious and the secular alike. Both rain and sunshine help all plants to grow in their own way. In everything that we have seen so far, the two parables are similar. But there is a distinction between them, although this distinction does not exactly amount to a difference. The symbolism of the rain-cloud and the symbolism of the sun are complementary. The rain-cloud gives moisture, whereas the sun gives light and heat. To borrow terms from the Chinese tradition, the rain-cloud is *yin*, associated with the depths, with the earth, and the sun is *yang*, associated with the heights, with the sky. And in terms of human development, the individual is quite literally like the plant. Just as the plant taps its moisture up from the earth, and gets its heat and light from the sky, so the developing human being must be nourished from below, from the unconscious depths, and also from above, from the supra-conscious heights.

To translate this into more simple terms, we must be nourished through both emotion and reason. Usually presentations of Buddhism in the West emphasize the rational aspect, or even give the impression that Buddhism is exclusively rational. We are told about Buddhist thought and philosophy, Buddhist metaphysics, psychology, and logic; and sometimes it all seems very dry and academic. The other side, however, the side represented by myth, symbol, and the imagination, the emotions and vision, is no less important, and for many people perhaps even more important. This is why we need to absorb texts which appeal to our emotions, like the parables, myths, and symbols of the Mahāyāna in the *White Lotus Sūtra*.

It is not enough to understand the Buddha's teaching intellectually. Anybody who has the ability to read – and a moderate intelligence – can do that. We have to ask ourselves again and again not just 'Do I know?

Do I understand?' but 'Do I feel? Do I vibrate with this?' We might even ask ourselves 'Do I really feel like a plant at the end of the hot season? Is this how I feel after a day's work or after I've been immersed in the ordinary daily round? Do I feel all dry and withered? Do I feel in need of nourishment? Do I really feel ready to take something in?' When you come in contact with the truth, with the Buddha's teaching, do you actually feel as though you are being refreshed by a great shower of rain? Do you really feel that you are going to drink something in after having been dry and thirsty for a long time?

Again, when you come in contact with the Dharma, do you really feel that the sun has come out? During the months of winter it is not unusual to feel dull and tired, and even miserable, because the sky is grey with fog and mist, and you are cold. You look forward to the spring sunshine, to your summer holiday, to the first beautiful, warm, bright weekend when you feel that spring is really on the way. When you see the buds begin to open and the flowers blooming in the parks and gardens, you can hardly help but feel a lifting of the heart. You feel as though a new spirit were rising within you.

But do you feel like this when you come into contact with the Buddha's teaching? Do you feel as though you are drinking in spiritual sunshine? If you do not respond in this way, your approach is still just intellectual. It is important that we should actually feel ourselves living, feel ourselves growing just like the plant when the rain falls and the sun shines, feel ourselves expanding. If we feel like this, our birth as human beings is not in vain, for we will ourselves be symbols, living symbols, of life and growth.

5
QUESTIONS AND ANSWERS

A STRANGE FUSION OF INDIVIDUALITY AND UNIVERSALITY

You say that as people grow they get more and more different from each other, but paradoxically they also get more and more like each other. I can understand how if you are moving towards deep spiritual experience the element of similarity comes in. It is not so obvious, though, why people get more and more different from each other. I can see from people around me that they do, but how and why?

Suppose you have a number of lamps made of some semi-translucent material with patterns and designs on it. Inside each lamp there is a light, and as you turn up the light and it gets brighter, not only does the lamp give off more light, but the pattern in the lamp becomes clearer and clearer. In the same way, when the light of Enlightenment shines through you, it lights up your features, your distinctive individuality, all the more clearly. That's the only way I can explain it.

Don't you notice this with people? Maybe they haven't gained Enlightenment, but they have progressed over the years, and you do see something shining from them or through them more brightly than before. Don't they seem, in that paradoxical way, much more themselves? It is not as though their individuality has merged into something non-individual, or even supra-individual, so that they become featureless. On the contrary, they seem much more themselves than ever before; there is a strange fusion of individuality and universality. You could even say that people who are less developed are more like each other on the level of form, so to speak, than those who are more developed.

As I see it, we are differentiated by our conditioning, by all the things that limit us and make us distinct. Isn't there a contradiction between the universal experience coming through and the biases in the individual that limit its expression?

But, paradoxically again, it is the individual that expresses the universal. If there wasn't that limited form, what medium could there be for the expression of universal experience?

Isn't personality made up of merit, your positive actions in the past, even in past lives, as well as conditioning?

Yes, there is not simply your mundane, conditioned personality, but also that more skilful 'merit-produced' personality which provides a vehicle – admittedly inadequate – for the expression of whatever higher consciousness, or even Enlightenment experience, you have attained. Without that, the higher experience could not express itself at all on the mundane plane.

I'm not sure that this 'paradox' between the unique individual and the unique universal really *is* a paradox. A paradox has been defined as 'truth standing on its head to attract attention', something which is logically self-contradictory. The idea of the coalescence of the individual and the universal is not a paradox in that way.

Perhaps the term universal itself can be misleading – we tend to think of something abstract and common, which is not the best way to think of it. When the individual attains the universal, it is not as though the individual is merged into something which is non-individual. From a spiritual point of view, universality is the way in which the individual behaves. For instance, when the individual is developing *mettā* towards all living beings, he or she is adopting a universal attitude – the individual *is* universal *mettā*,[102] you might say – but it is an *individual* being universal. Perhaps only an individual can be universal. A tree can't be universal, a stone can't be universal, not even a monkey or a mackerel can be universal, but a human being can be universal, because a human being is – or potentially can be – an individual, and universality is an attitude that pertains essentially and distinctively to the individual.

[margin note: sounds a bit like juxtaposing some thing with something so diff to shine light on its truth + uniqueness]

We tend to think of the universal as being like a great hole in the ground into which the individual falls, or a great ocean in which the individual loses himself, but that is taking what is essentially a metaphorical expression literally. We think of the universal as somehow extended in space, but actually universality is a quality of the functioning of the individual – or perhaps even that is too static. You could say that universality is one of the ways in which an individual functions, not a thing into which the individual disappears. Any apparent contradiction between the notion of the individual and the notion of the universal arises when we make the universal something abstract and then reify it. There is no such *thing* as the universal, you might say, from a spiritual point of view.

Isn't it the case that in the logical sense universals are just useful abstractions?
Yes, that's true. There is a great debate in philosophy from the time of Plato onwards as to whether the existence of universals is real or notional.

What you are calling the universal attitude is quite different from that, isn't it? You seem to be describing an attitude which applies in practice to an indefinite range of particulars. Wouldn't all universals work in that way? For example, we all experience the colour red in different ways, but we describe that experience in universal terms.
Yes, there is the quality of redness, but actually we never encounter redness, only red objects.

In the same way, are we talking about a similar kind of universal which can't exist apart from individuals manifesting it?
No, it's not quite like that, although it's similar. Universality – a universal attitude – in the context of the spiritual life is essentially an activity, whereas a concept like redness is not an activity but a 'thing', in the sense of a mental object. What I am really saying is that we need to get away from the idea or associations of 'thingness' when we speak of the individual and the universal in the context of spiritual life. It is not that the individual considered as an entity merges in another greater entity. It is more that that individual starts functioning in a particular way.

So, taking the example of mettā, *if you feel* mettā *in practice you feel it towards the people you meet, although in principle you are open to anybody.*
Yes. You are not experiencing an abstract, universal, cold *mettā*. You are behaving in a certain way towards people that you meet, or whom you imagine. You don't merge in with a concept called universality; you just behave in the same spirit of *mettā* with everybody you meet. This is a more practical, more down to earth way of seeing it, a less abstract mode of expression.

EXPERIENCING THE CHAKRAS

In the course of one's spiritual development, could one expect to have eventually a physical or psychical experience of release of energy at those places in the body corresponding to the traditional locations of the psychic centres?
You could expect that, very broadly speaking. For instance, if you do suddenly feel emotionally unblocked, and feel very positive, powerful feelings expanding, you might well have a sensation of release at the heart centre. Some people might even have a visual experience of a lotus bursting open, or a ball of light expanding. There can be many variations according to temperament on the same basic spiritual or physico-psycho-spiritual experience.

There are a number of traditional ways of describing the chakras. Govinda outlines several of the Buddhist ones in *Foundations of Tibetan Mysticism.*[103] Of course, there are discrepancies between the different systems, and still more differences between the various Hindu versions. Some accounts are so literalistic that they seem to suggest that you have to go through a graded course, and see your chakras, with exactly the right number of petals, quite literally opening. That sort of imagery, however, only suggests a certain type of experience which can take other forms. The essential feature of the experience is a release of energy on a higher level, a bursting open, a flowering. There is a flowering of your being, of your energies, at successively higher levels, and you can experience this in different ways. This much is obvious in that Buddhists, Hindus, and Jains all have the same sort of symbolism. The symbolism varies, however, and each text is remarkably specific. They can't all be right if you are going to take them on a literalistic level.

Are there different traditions as to the positions of the chakras, or is it possible to locate them?
It seems to be reasonably constant that very low, gross emotions are felt round about the navel, more subtle emotions are experienced at the heart centre, and energies connected with speech and communication are experienced at the throat. Still more subtle energies are experienced at the forehead, and the most subtle of all at the crown of the head. That is very much how it feels, isn't it? If you get really angry, you feel it low down in your body. If you feel strong devotional feelings, it is as though your heart expands; sometimes you can feel an actual sensation at that spot.

To develop the emotions as one does in the mettā bhāvanā *practice, should one concentrate on the heart chakra at the centre of the body, or on the organic heart, which is a little off centre?*
Buddhist texts are careful to distinguish between the organic heart and the heart chakra, and it is the chakra which should be the focus of meditation practice. The Tibetan tradition teaches that the chakras should be visualized on the surface of the body, so that, for example, the syllables *oṃ āḥ hūṃ* are visualized at the forehead, throat, and heart on the surface of the body. When a mantra is visualized at the heart centre, it is visualized on the surface, but when in addition to that you also visualize the mantra of, say, Mañjughoṣa, that is visualized as inside the body on the same level as the surface mantra. So in a sense there are two heart centres: a surface one and a deeper one.

Some teachers say that you should not think too much in terms of the human body, maintaining that the chakra system gives a model of development which is framed after the physical body but is not to be identified with it. Other teachers, especially perhaps the Hindus, seem to take it quite literally.

Which way would you advise us to take it?
I would suggest taking it as a model but not overlooking the possibility that the model correlates in certain ways with the physical body and its energies. Mr Chen, one of my teachers in Kalimpong, used to say that the 'wheels', as he called them, had nothing to do with the physical, gross body, but were present only in the subtle body. In a way there are three bodies, if you include the further development which the Vajrayāna calls

the wisdom body. According to Mr Chen the yogic practices concerned with the chakras and the subtle nerves are a means of activating and building up the subtle body, just as certain other practices bring to life the wisdom body.

But the gross body does have its systems, and perhaps these correspond to some extent with the features of the subtle body. Even if you think of the different chakras and nerves as being located in the physical body, however, they are not to be identified with physical organs or physical energies. Thinking in that way is simply a means of concentration.

Where would the astral body come into that?
What is usually called the astral body would seem to be a subtle material counterpart of the physical body, intermediate between the physical body and the subtle body I have just described. From what I gather, it would seem that you are born with an astral body, whereas the subtle body is more something which is built up as a result of spiritual effort.

So someone in a higher state of consciousness would not perceive your subtle body unless it had been consciously developed?
They might see that you had the potential to develop it, but they would not see you as actually possessing it in that moment of time, just as they might see that you were Enlightened in the depths of your being, but would also see that you had not actually realized that in the present.

Where does the aura come in?
There is an aura of every level of your being. Your physical body is surrounded by a cloud of fine dust – minute particles of skin and so on – all the time; and it also gives off various electrical currents. That is the aura of the physical body. Then there is the aura in a higher sense, the corresponding influence of those higher, more subtle bodies which under certain conditions may actually become visible in radiant form.

The main point is that you should not think of a body of any level as something absolutely discrete, as though there is an edge to your physical body beyond which there is 'non-body'. If you could see yourself through a sufficiently powerful microscope, you wouldn't be able to see where your body ended; it would just fade into a cloud of minute particles. The sharp edge you see with the naked eye simply isn't there – there is just a finer and finer aura extending out into space – and the situation is similar on other levels.

'SECULAR SPIRITUALITY'

You suggest that it might be best to present the Higher Evolution in secular rather than religious terms. What could this mean in practice, assuming that it would not just be presenting the Buddhist vision in language that avoids the use of the word Buddhism and traditional Buddhist concepts. What, for example, would be the place of devotional practices in such an approach? Would you still speak in terms of the 'secular'?

I don't actually like the word 'secular' – it's almost as bad as 'religious'. It has an air of the disgruntled, the offensively rationalistic. In making this suggestion I was thinking about the present state of affairs in the West. The decline of Christianity in the West has meant that the creative energies of a lot of people have passed outside the sphere of traditional religion to find independent expression in the field of the arts. This has produced a 'secular spirituality' which is secular only in the sense that it is not traditionally religious and does not have the support of an existing tradition. The result has been that much of the really vital spiritual life of the last two hundred years has expressed itself in artistic and not necessarily religious terms.

I certainly didn't mean that we should switch to a hard, dry, semi-scientific language, eschewing everything which is emotional, imaginative, or inspirational. I was thinking not so much in terms of scientific secular thought, but more in terms of trying to establish some connection with expressions which are basically spiritual but which are not part of the traditional Christian religion. We need not jettison traditional Buddhist language altogether, but perhaps we should have one or two alternative languages at our disposal. We don't always realize the extent to which newcomers to Buddhism are put off, or at least puzzled, by lectures peppered with Pāli and Sanskrit terms. Perhaps we should be trying to develop, with the help of some of the great Western thinkers and writers of the past, an indigenous language which will enable us to express our essentially Buddhist vision in a more imaginative and effective way.

I understand what you're saying, but I can't help thinking that a really thorough appreciation of Kant or Schopenhauer, Keats or Shelley, is almost as rare an interest in this country as Buddhism. I can't see how adopting the language of a very small, high-culture élite would reach a wider audience.

Well, Buddhism would at least reach an audience, however small, that is not being reached at present, but yes, I agree. However, I don't think that 'traditional Buddhist language' can just be imported. In the long term we need to develop a completely indigenous, yet faithfully Buddhist language, as the Chinese, the Tibetans, and the Japanese have done. Meanwhile we have to use our peculiar mixture of jargons – bits of Pāli, Sanskrit, Tibetan, and adaptations from the 'alternative' culture.

It is perhaps wrong to contrast 'religious' and 'secular'. Although Keats can be described as a secular poet, he sometimes expresses the spirit of religion. The secular has nothing to do with the form of conventional religion, but its spirit may be deeply religious in a non-traditional way. The secular language I have in mind is the language of the poet and the artist refined still further for the purposes of Buddhism, as an alternative to traditional Buddhist language translated into English. I don't mean just quoting poets, but taking their expressions and using them to express Buddhist ideas and Buddhist truths. Obviously the language would be subtly altered in the process, and that alteration would be a refinement inasmuch as Buddhism expresses a vision which goes beyond that particular poet. Poets themselves use the words of ordinary language, but they refine them to express their particular vision. They use ordinary words but combine them in a fresh and original way, to communicate something new, something individual. Buddhists could take the process a stage further. Of course, to do this you would need a highly developed sense of the English language as used by its greatest practitioners, and at the same time some depth of spiritual experience.

6

FIVE ELEMENT SYMBOLISM AND THE STUPA

In every part of the world the landscape has its own distinctive appearance, shaped by the forces of nature and the design of mankind. To the natural scene – mountains, hills or plains, barren desert or lush forest – human beings contribute architectural features of many kinds: mud huts or thatched cottages, magnificent pyramids, soaring church spires or clusters of skyscrapers, even enormous slag-heaps and smoking factory chimneys.

Since its beginnings in India, Buddhism has spread over an area extending from the deserts of central Asia in the west as far as the islands of Japan in the east, from the icy, windswept tablelands of Tibet in the north right down to the sun-drenched tropical island of Sri Lanka in the south. The natural features of all these areas are very different, and so are their architectural features, but wherever you travel throughout this vast area there is one type of architectural monument which is found everywhere: on bleak mountain tops, in pleasant wooded valleys, in the midst of vast plains and by the seashore. This ubiquitous Buddhist monument is the stupa.

Over the years the stupa has assumed a number of different forms, sometimes so different that it is almost impossible to tell that they spring from the same origins. There are stupas made of brick and stupas made of stone. Some are even made of precious metals – gold and silver – and studded with precious gems. Some stupas are so large that it would take you ten minutes to walk all the way round them, while others are so small that you can hold them in the palm of your hand.

Interesting as the history of the stupa is, however, it is not its place in the history of Buddhist art that concerns us here, but its profound symbolic significance. The stupa is one of the richest and most complex symbols in the whole field of Buddhism, especially of Mahāyāna Buddhism, and it also happens to be a symbol which occurs – very dramatically – in the *White Lotus Sūtra*.

The stupa makes its appearance in the eleventh chapter of the *sūtra*, roughly halfway through – not reckoning the chapters that seem to be later additions – so that it divides the whole *sūtra* into two great halves. The first half is dominated by the parables – the burning house, the return journey, the rain-cloud. But although the second half, including the appearance of the stupa, does include the occasional parable, it is almost completely taken over by myth and symbol, and by what we might call cosmic phantasmagoria. To generalize further, the first half is concerned with the way to Enlightenment, especially the Mahāyāna, the great way, and with the progress of the bodhisattva along that way. The second half, by contrast, is concerned with Enlightenment, the goal. It is dedicated to the Buddha, and the concept of the Buddha-field, the spiritual world in which the Buddha 'reigns'.

Becoming more abstract still, we can say that in the first half of the *sūtra* we see the whole of existence *sub specie temporis*, under the form of time, whereas in the second half we see existence *sub specie æternitatis*, as it always was, is, and will be above and beyond time, in the dimension of eternity. The first half of the *sūtra* therefore depicts spiritual perfection everlastingly in the process of attainment, whereas the second half depicts perfection eternally attained. And the stupa stands in between the two, not to separate them but to unite them, for the symbol of the stupa contains both time and eternity. But before we can go any further, we need to ask a basic question. What *is* a stupa?

The word *stūpa* is Sanskrit, and literally means 'the top'; thus it comes to refer both to the crown of the head and to the gable – the top – of a house. Oddly enough, although the Indian word is rich in symbolic associations, it is etymologically connected with our much more ordinary English word 'stump'. But the etymological definition barely gives us a clue as to what the Buddhist symbol of the stupa might represent. A more useful starting point is the stupa's historical development.

If we probe right back to the origins of the stupa, we find that it is as old as Buddhism itself, indeed far older. Its origins go directly back to the ancient Indian burial mound, to the pre-Buddhistic practice of heaping earth over the ashes of the heroic dead. The *Mahāparinibbāna Sutta* tells us that in accordance with this ancient practice, the Buddha himself directed shortly before his death that a stupa should be erected over his remains.[104] The *sutta*, the discourse from the Pāli canon which describes the Buddha's last days and death, goes on to give an account of how the Buddha's instructions were carried out. His body was placed on hundreds of logs which had been drenched in oil and ghee, and the pyre was set ablaze. It burned for a very long time, but when at last the flames had died down the Buddha's lay disciples made a reverent search through the cooling ashes to find any small fragments of bone still remaining. The monks may have had sufficient equanimity to do without a physical memento of their great teacher, but the lay disciples had the very human desire – if it is a failing, it is a forgivable one – to preserve whatever relics they could.

Unfortunately, no sooner had the relics been gathered together in a stone jar than a great quarrel arose among the disciples. If we take the representations of the scene in early Buddhist art literally, it would seem that the Buddha's ashes were barely cold when the different parties to the dispute were almost ready to go to war with one another to decide who would take possession of them.[105] Surprising as such a reaction to the death of a great teacher may seem, there is clearly something highly symbolic about it, for this is not the only incident of this kind in Buddhist tradition. After the death of the great yogi Milarepa, after his withdrawal from the mundane plane, his disciples were apparently just as greedy for relics as the Buddha's were. With characteristically apocalyptic and magnificent symbolism, the Tibetan legend[106] describes how Milarepa's relics condensed into a brilliant globe of light which hovered above the heads of the disciples. When they tried to catch hold of it, it rose up into the air out of their reach; as soon as they lowered their grasping hands, it came a fraction lower – tantalisingly close but always evading their grasp. Whether or not this literally happened, the symbolism is obviously of great significance.

In the Buddha's case, many tribes and cities, and even kings and chiefs, laid claim to his relics. For instance, the Śākyas, the Buddha's own tribe, said, 'The Buddha was born amongst us. If anyone has a right to the relics, surely we have.' But the Mallas said, 'He may have been born in Śākya territory, but it was our people he lived among and taught for so long. We certainly have a right to the relics.' And so it went on, tribe after tribe putting forward their respective claims. It took the intervention of a learned Brahmin to remind the disciples that it was unseemly, to say the least, for them to quarrel over the Buddha's relics as soon as he was dead. Brought to their senses in this way, the disciples at last settled the quarrel by dividing the relics into eight equal portions, one for each tribe that had put in a claim. Each of these communities built a stupa over their share of the relics. A stupa was also built over the jar in which the relics had been contained, and a tenth stupa was built for the embers.

The fact that this quarrel took place among the lay followers of the Buddha – the monks apparently having nothing to do with it – suggests that the practice of the worship of the relics of great men was not so much a part of the Buddha's own teaching as an ethnic practice which was still popular among his lay followers. Be that as it may, it is certainly the case that after the death of the Buddha the veneration and decoration of stupas rapidly became – and remained – a highly popular religious practice, to the extent that for hundreds of years after the Buddha's death the building, worship, and decoration of stupas was the principal religious practice of the laity. There were no temples in those days, and no images. The laity did not meditate or go to live in the jungle like the monks. So what religious practice could they do? They could make offerings to the stupas, and venerate the relics therein, and in this way keep alive the memory of the Buddha and the great example he had shown.

Although the *Mahāparinibbāna Sutta* tells us that the Buddha directed his followers to build a stupa for his relics, it says nothing about how the Buddha wanted this to be done. It is a tradition coming down from Tibetan sources which gives us a few details. The story goes that when the Buddha told them to build a stupa, the disciples naturally asked in what form it should be made. In reply the Buddha did not say anything, but gave a practical demonstration. He took his outer yellow robe and folded it in two and two again until the cloth formed a rough cube. Then he took his begging-bowl, which of course was round, turned it upside-down, and put it on top of the robes. 'Make my stupa like this,' he said.[107] And the evidence of the archaeological remains of Buddhist sites in India suggests that this shape – a square base topped by a hemisphere – was indeed the oldest form of the stupa.

At first the monks, the full-time followers of the Buddha, were not too happy about relic and stupa worship, but it became so widespread and popular among the laity that eventually they had to accept the practice as orthodox. Indeed, according to records like the *Kathā-vatthu*, some of the monks explicitly ascribed great devotional and spiritual value to the practice of worshipping relics and stupas.[108] By the time of the great king Aśoka, the third century BCE ruler of the Magadha kingdom who spread his rule all over India and founded the Maurya empire, the practice was very firmly established. Aśoka himself, according to all the accounts we have of him, was a great builder of stupas. The legends say that he built eighty-four thousand stupas in a single day – rather a tough job even for Aśoka. We are told that to make this possible, Aśoka's spiritual preceptor stretched out his hand into the sky and held back the sun until the great work was finished – a variant of the Old Testament Joshua legend.[109]

From the time of Aśoka, stupas became ever larger and more elaborate, and they were the objects of more and more fervent devotion. Archaeologists have discovered stupas which at first were comparatively small, maybe only fifteen or twenty feet across, then enlarged again and again by the simple expedient of putting another layer onto the basic structure of the cube and hemisphere. Not only did the stupas become bigger; some of them 'migrated' overseas. Buddhists in Sri Lanka, in Burma, and in central Asia, started building their own stupas, some of them bigger and better even than the Indian ones. Only the great stupa at Borabadur is bigger than those built in Sri Lanka during the first century of the Christian era, the period when the *White Lotus Sūtra* was written down.

Here is Kern's version – not perhaps as poetic as could be wished – of the passage which describes the sudden appearance of the stupa in the middle of the *sūtra*:

> Then there arose a Stūpa, consisting of seven precious substances, from the place of the earth opposite the Lord, the assembly being in the middle, a Stūpa five hundred yoganas in height and proportionate in circumference. After its rising, the Stūpa, a meteoric phenomenon, stood in the sky sparkling, beautiful, nicely decorated with five thousand successive terraces of flowers, adorned with many thousands of arches, embellished by thousands

of banners and triumphal streamers, hung with thousands of jewel-garlands and with hour-plates and bells, and emitting the scent of Xanthochymus and sandal, which scent filled this whole world. Its rows of umbrellas rose so far on high as to touch the abodes of the four guardians of the horizon and the gods. It consisted of seven precious substances, viz. gold, silver, lapis lazuli, Musāragalva, emerald, red coral, and Karketana-stone. This Stūpa of precious substances once formed, the gods of paradise strewed and covered it with Mandārava and great Mandāra flowers. And from that Stūpa of precious substances there issued this voice: Excellent, excellent, Lord Śākyamuni! thou hast well expounded this Dharmaparyāya of the Lotus of the True Law. So it is, Lord; so it is, Sugata.[110]

So this is the stupa which appears in the *sūtra* – no doubt an idealized version of the sort of monument which could be seen all over India at the time the *sūtra* was written down. But although we have placed the stupa in its historical context, this does not completely answer the question of what a stupa is. We still need to ask ourselves what it *represents*, what it symbolizes. And the answer to this question is bound up with the symbolism of the five elements.

The five elements are the traditional ones – earth, water, fire, air, and ether or space. However, we must take these terms not literally but symbolically. When we take the five elements symbolically, what do we have in mind? What did the builders of the stupas have in mind? The answer, in a word, is energy.

Earth in this sense is not the dark, moist substance you scoop up from the ground. As a symbol, earth represents energy in a state of contraction and cohesion. The earth element is the principle of solidity, that which makes everything stick together, a bit like the law of gravity. So earth represents energy locked up, blocked, even frozen, petrified, crystallized. In the same way, water as a symbolic element is not the stuff you drink. It is energy in a state of oscillation or undulation – not completely blocked, but at the same time not truly free. It just goes backwards and forwards, backwards and forwards, between two points. This is the energy represented by the element water. Then, what does fire represent? Fire, of course, always rises upwards. When you kindle a fire, it never burns downwards – at least not of its own accord – but always goes straight up. So fire symbolizes energy moving upwards, ascending, sublimating if you like. Fourthly, air symbolizes energy which is not just expanding and ascending, but also descending and spreading out on both sides. In other words, air is energy in a state of expansion, diffusing itself in all directions of space from one central point.

The symbolism of the element which for lack of an apt English word we have to translate as 'ether' or 'space' is much more difficult to explain. In the Sanskrit it is *ākāśa*, a word which is derived from a root meaning 'to shine' and which is sometimes applied to the sky. But in its real meaning *ākāśa* represents the primordial energy of which the other four – earth, water, fire, air – are grosser manifestations. They are like waves of different shapes, forms, and configurations, while the ether – the space, the *ākāśa*, the brightness, the shining – is like the sea itself. In some contexts – just to hint at the true nature of *ākāśa* – it stands halfway between what we call matter and what we call spirit or consciousness.[111]

So the five elements symbolize different states of physical energy. We can see and experience them in the external world; everything is composed of these qualities of solidity, fluidity, temperature, air, and space. And we experience them in ourselves, in the human body. Earth, we could say, is the quality of solidity and resistance of bone and muscle. Water is the fluid quality of blood and lymph. Fire is the heat, the temperature of the body. Air is the intake of oxygen and the exhalation of carbon dioxide. And all of these are contained in the space which the body occupies.

Of course we have mental, psychical energies as well as physical energies, and these mental energies are also represented by the five elements. Looked at in terms of psychical energy, earth represents a state of psychological energy blockage, emotional blockage. When you are emotionally blocked, how do you feel? You feel contracted and constricted, shut up in yourself, all stiff and rigid and lifeless, like a mental corpse. This is the earth state. It is like that of a man so tightly bound that he is unable to stir hand or foot. He may just about be able to wiggle his little toe or blink his eyes, but that's all.

Water represents a state of extremely limited mobility, like that of ice which has just started to thaw. In this state your energy feels just slightly free; blockages have been removed at least to the extent that you can move a little from side to side. This state is like that of someone whose

Are we kept 'trapped' by the confines of our ego, needs, perceptions?

limbs are free, but who is imprisoned in a tiny cell only big enough for them to be able to pace backwards and forwards. Your energy is only partially liberated, so that you can just go backwards and forwards, or round and round in a narrow closed circle. This is the state in which most people live.

Fire represents a state of liberation of energy in an upward direction. Here energy is being sublimated, and in this state you feel inspired, as though you are being lifted up, or exalted, as though you are walking on air. The 'fire state' is like that of someone whose cell encloses them on all sides but has no roof. It is open to the sky, open to the stars, and the captive is perfectly free to move in that direction; all they have to do is rise up into the air.

And air is energy in the process of becoming completely liberated. All hindrances and psychological blockages are removed. You feel that you are expanding in all directions, transcending your narrow limited individuality or selfhood. This state is like that of someone whose prison walls have suddenly fallen down so that they are absolutely free to go in any direction they like. In fact the metaphor begins to break down here, because as an individual the ex-prisoner can only go in one direction at a time, but in the state symbolized by the element air you can expand yourself simultaneously to all the quarters of space, which means transcending your own individuality.

And how does *ākāśa* – ether or space – fit into the picture? What can it possibly represent? To put it in a very general way, we can say that *ākāśa* is the higher dimension within which all these movements take place. The non-movement of earth, the undulating, oscillatory movement of water, the ascending movement of fire, the expanding movement of air – all these take place within *ākāśa*, a dimension which is higher still, and which contains and includes them all.

Taking this symbolism still further, we can say that the five elements also symbolize five different kinds of people. Earth symbolizes the psychologically and emotionally damaged person. Water symbolizes the so-called normal person: a person who has a certain amount of free energy but functions within narrow limits, in a repetitive, reactive manner. Fire symbolizes the artist, the poet, the musician, the free thinker, and the meditator, because they are rising up, sublimating, ascending. Air symbolizes the mystic, who is engaged all the time essentially in transcending the self. And space symbolizes the fully illumined sage who has accomplished that process of self-transcending – in other words, the Buddha.

According to tradition each of the five elements is associated with a colour. Earth is associated with yellow, water with white, fire with bright flaming red, air with a beautiful pale green, and space with blue, or sometimes a golden-flame colour. And the elements are also associated with certain geometrical forms: earth with the cube, water with the sphere, fire with the cone or pyramid, air with a bowl-shape or saucer-shape, like the dome of the sky turned upside down, and space with a flaming jewel-like shape.[112]

There are many other sets of correlations. For instance, according to some systems of yoga the five elements are correlated with the five psychic centres within the human body. Earth is correlated with the lowest psychic centre, the one between the anus and the genitals, water with the centre at the solar plexus, fire with the heart centre, air with the throat centre, and space with the centre at the top of the head. There is also a correlation of the five elements with the five Buddhas. But although the symbolism of the elements is such a fascinating subject in itself, it is time we applied it to our original question: what is a stupa?

The five elements as represented by different geometrical forms and by different colours can be combined to give earth, a yellow cube; water, a white sphere; fire, a red cone or pyramid; air, a green bowl or saucer; and space, a flame-coloured jewel-like shape – some translators call it an acuminated sphere but it actually looks more like a jewel. These coloured forms, arranged one on top of another in an order of increasing subtlety and release of energy, give the basic structure of the stupa. The stupa symbolizes, therefore, the progressive liberation of energy, the process of growth and development, the Higher Evolution. It thus embodies in architectural terms the entire meaning of Buddhism in general and the *White Lotus Sūtra* in particular. Small wonder that the stupa is so widespread, and so much an object of fervent devotion.

In the course of centuries the basic structure of the stupa has undergone many adaptations, some with a definite spiritual basis, others merely architectural or cultural. One of these changes in particular relates to a specific aspect of the symbolism of the elements: their correlation with the psychic centres of the human body.

Imagine in front of you a human being seated cross-legged as though in meditation, and a stupa which is the same height as the seated person.

If you identify the positions of the psychic centres up the person's spinal column, and look across to the stupa, you will find that the centres correspond with the successive geometrical forms. Now imagine that another cube, smaller than the cube at the base of the stupa, is placed between the sphere and the cone. If the whole six-shape structure thus created is hollow, so that the cross-legged human being can sit inside it, his or her eyes will be on a level with that second smaller cube, so that if the cube happens to be transparent, the eyes will be visible through it.

Now this may remind you of something. If you have ever been to Nepal, or if you have seen photographs of the stupas there, you will surely be reminded of the typical Nepalese stupa. On these stupas, on each side of the *harmikā*, as the second, higher cube is called, a pair of eyes is painted. When you see these stupas rising above the landscape in the distance, with these eyes on the sides, they produce a very strange effect indeed, especially because the stupas are so enormous that they completely dominate the landscape. The eyes look down at you with a slightly disapproving frown which seems not to be imaginary.

The presence of these pairs of eyes serves to remind us that the stupa is correlated with the human body itself, that the elements of the stupa correspond to the psychic centres, and that both represent an upward, progressive movement, a movement of spiritual evolution. But why should that second cube have been put there at all? Indeed, why should the cone, the saucer, and the jewel have been added to the two original simple elements, the cube and the sphere? And why is the conical part of the Nepalese stupa divided into sections which make it look as if it consists of a number of rings of gradually diminishing diameter?

We can answer all these questions in terms of yin-yang symbolism. The terms yin and yang are not Indian but Chinese, and they represent a polarity of universal validity and importance; they also happen to be quite well known in the West, and I am making use of them for this reason. In considering the parables of the rain-cloud and the sun, we saw that the yin principle is associated with the earth, with water, with the depths, whereas the yang principle is associated with the sky, with fire, with the heights. Yin is the negative, passive principle – the 'feminine' principle, to use that term in a very specific way. Yang is the active, masculine principle, the positive principle. Yin is symbolized by the moon; yang is symbolized by the sun. Yin is emotion, the unconscious; yang is reason, the conscious mind. Yin is life; yang is light. Yin, if you like, is the lower evolution; yang is the Higher Evolution. In the course of the evolution of the individual, yin and yang must be harmonized, synthesized. The plant, as we have seen, is the joint product of soil and rain on the one hand, and of space and sunlight on the other. In much the same way, the growing individual is nourished by both yin and yang forces.

Now how does this tie up with the stupa? The pre-Buddhistic burial mound consisted simply of a great heap of earth, a tumulus, a barrow, a place where the remains of heroes, kings, and sages were enshrined, and which was the focus for the rites of the cult of the dead. This heap of earth came naturally to be associated with the earth, and therefore with the womb of Mother Nature, and the maternal in general. In its original form, then, the stupa was a symbol of the yin principle. The earliest Buddhist stupas, made up of the cube and the sphere or hemisphere, still had this association with yin, for both the cube and the sphere are yin symbols, or lunar symbols.

So where did the smaller cube come from? And what is the origin of the triple umbrella by which in many stupas the cube is surmounted? These two symbols come from an ancient Indian, pre-Buddhistic cult parallel to the cult of the dead: the cult of the sun. Of the many solar symbols of ancient India, two were of particular importance: the sacred fire and the sacred tree. The sacred fire burned on the hearth of every orthodox follower of the Vedas, and it also burned in the middle of the village, on a cubiform brick altar in a small shrine, an idealized hut. This hut often stood at the foot of the sacred tree of the village, a peepul or a banyan tree, for the tree was also a solar symbol. So the *harmikā*, the second cube of the stupa, symbolizes the original fire altar, and the umbrella by which it is surmounted is a stylized version of the sacred tree.

So we can see how the stupa gradually developed, two solar symbols, the fire altar, and the umbrella or tree, being superimposed upon two lunar symbols, the cube and the sphere or hemisphere. Subsequently, the saucer and the cone came to be placed on top of the cube and the sphere. So the stupa is not just an arrangement of the symbols of the five elements in ascending order. It is also a synthesis of Indian solar and lunar symbolism, and a synthesis of the principles of yin and yang. It represents, we may say, a synthesis of the different aspects, the opposite poles, of our own being, of our own unruly nature.

A standard stupa consists of seven essential parts. At the bottom is the square base, the *medhī*, which – whether it is a simple cube or a number of steps or terraces (usually four) – represents the earth element, the yin principle.

Next comes the hemispherical portion, which is known in Sanskrit as the *aṇḍa*, literally 'egg', or the *garbha*, the receptacle, the treasury, the womb – names alive with symbolism. In the case of the Sinhalese stupa (known as the *dagoba*, a corruption of the Sanskrit *dhātu garbha*, or 'repository of relics'), this 'hemispherical' portion is actually bell-shaped, a feature which gives the Sinhalese stupas their distinctive beauty. In the Tibetan stupa, the *chorten*, the same bell-shape is found – but turned upside-down. It assumes a chalice-like shape which is exactly the same as that of the vase of immortality, the *amṛta kalaśa* (Sanskrit) or *bumpa* (Tibetan) which is held by Amitāyus, the Buddha of Eternal Life. This association with the vase of immortality represents the receptivity of the lunar principle to the solar principle, of yin to yang – or even the lunar principle as transformed by the solar principle. Remember too that this portion of the stupa symbolizes the water element, and therefore once again symbolizes the yin principle.

The third part of the standard stupa is the cube which originated from the Vedic fire altar. It is in this section, known as the *harmikā*, that relics would be enshrined. The Buddha's physical body was consumed by fire, just as his selfhood, we may say, was consumed in the fire of his spiritual practice and realization. So this portion of the stupa symbolizes the fire element, and therefore the yang principle.

The fourth portion, the spire, *kunta* – both umbrella and tree – developed over a long period of time until it finally consisted of thirteen rings of diminishing diameter placed one on top of another to represent the thirteen *bhumis* – stages of spiritual progress – traversed by the bodhisattva on the way to Enlightenment. In China, this one portion of the stupa, the original fire portion, was separated from the rest to become what we know in the West as the pagoda, a very characteristic feature of the Chinese landscape. It would appear that if the original stupa, the cube and the sphere, symbolized only the yin principle, the pagoda went to the opposite extreme and became a symbol of just the yang principle. We could say, however, that as the pagoda does stand on the earth, which is yin, a balance is still maintained. With the earth itself as its base, the pagoda doesn't need a separate architectural base. Although, geometrically considered, this portion of the stupa represents the fire element, in the seven-section stupa fire is already represented by the *harmikā*, so the spire comes to stand for the air element. In either case, whether symbolizing fire or air, it represents the yang principle.

The fifth section is the saucer or bowl. This originally represented space or ether, which is a synthesis of yin and yang, but here it becomes a pure white moon crescent, and symbolizes the yin principle in a highly purified and sublimated form. Sixthly comes a red solar disc, which represents the yang principle, also in highly purified and sublimated form.

Last of all, a flame-coloured or rainbow-coloured jewel grows out of the red solar disc. This symbol is found not only on the top of stupas but also surmounting the heads of Buddha-images of all countries and all periods, recalling the original meaning of the word *stupa*, the crown of the head. The *uṣṇīṣa* – which Western translators rather inelegantly call the 'bodhic protuberance' – sometimes looks like a flame springing up from the Buddha's head, and sometimes like a lotus bud growing there. The significance of the *uṣṇīṣa* is the same as the flame-coloured jewel at the top of the stupa: complete, total synthesis of yin and yang. And what is a synthesis at the highest possible level of the principles of yin and yang? Enlightenment itself: this is the true meaning of the flame-coloured jewel.

It is not surprising, in view of all these considerations, that the stupa is sometimes considered to be the most important of all Buddhist symbols, even more important, both historically and doctrinally, than that other well-known symbol, the Buddha-image. It is not surprising that the stupa makes this sudden dramatic appearance right in the middle of the *White Lotus Sūtra*. You may remember that when the stupa appears, the Buddha's disciples entreat him to open it, so Śākyamuni rises up into the air and draws the bolt of the door halfway up the stupa. The bolt draws back, the gates open with a sound like thunder, and inside the stupa is revealed the body of the ancient Buddha Abundant Treasures, still intact after countless years. Abundant Treasures then invites Śākyamuni to share his seat, so the two Buddhas sit side by side within the stupa. What does this mean? It must mean something. Every single image in the *sūtra* has a meaning. We could say that, as Abundant Treasures is the Buddha of the remote past, and Śākyamuni is the Buddha of the present, this incident represents the coming together of the past and the present. Past and present have become one.

But the episode has an even more profound significance. We are told that Abundant Treasures is the Buddha of the past; but what past? Not a thousand years ago, not a million years ago, but, we are told, uncounted, uncountable, unfathomable, incalculable myriads of myriads of years ago. Now when you pile it on like that, what you are really getting at is that this Buddha is beyond time altogether. He is not just the Buddha from the remote past, but the *primordial* Buddha, the Buddha from the metaphysical beginning of things – which means no beginning at all. In other words, Abundant Treasures is the eternal Buddha, above the past, above the present, above the future, out of time altogether. This means that when Śākyamuni, the Buddha of the present, takes his seat within the stupa by the side of the eternal Buddha, Abundant Treasures, the dimension of time and the dimension of eternity coalesce. In containing both Abundant Treasures and Śākyamuni, the stupa contains both time and eternity. So the stupa as it occurs in the *White Lotus Sūtra* at this point does not represent just a general synthesis of the yin and yang principles, on howsoever high a level. It represents the highest and most total synthesis of all: the synthesis of time and eternity.

6

QUESTIONS AND ANSWERS

HOW THE STUPA BEGAN

Why didn't one of the arhants *intervene to stop the quarrel between the disciples? What is the significance of the Brahmin?*
The incident does seem to suggest that at that stage the Brahmins had closer connections with the laity than the *bhikkhus* did; that seems a little strange, but it may have been the case. Another possibility that occurs to me is that at that time people may still have been using the terms Brahmin and *bhikkhu* interchangeably; there may not have been the hard-and-fast distinction between the *bhikkhu* and the non-*bhikkhu* that arose later. The *Dhammapada* points to this, describing the Brahmin and the *bhikkhu* in almost identical terms.[113] So Doṇa, the man who intervened, could have been a Brahmin in the spiritual sense, not the caste sense. Clearly he had respect for the Buddha and his teaching. He could have been a *paribbājaka* (Pāli) who hadn't joined the sangha in the formal sense, if in fact there was a formally constituted sangha of the coenobitical type at that time. Of course, this is just a hypothesis.

You mention that eight stupas were built over the Buddha's remains. Is that a historical piece of information, or is it mythical?
Well, it isn't obviously mythical in that it doesn't involve anything that might not have happened. If we were being told that ten million stupas

were built, that would certainly sound legendary or mythical, but eight stupas is a rather modest number. And the account does come in the Pāli canon itself.[114] I think we can take it that those stupas were actually erected. We know for certain that by the time of Aśoka the stupa had become quite elaborate, which presupposes a considerable period of development – and Aśoka was separated from the Buddha by only one hundred and fifty years.

You suggest that stupa worship was entirely a lay practice in the early centuries, only adopted by monks later. I find it hard to believe that the bhikkhus *wouldn't have felt naturally drawn to express their devotion to their teacher by leaving flowers at the stupa containing his remains.*
Perhaps – before we go any further – we shouldn't speak so much of stupa worship as of *relic* worship. In the early days the point of stupas was simply that they enshrined relics. Later on, stupas were built which didn't enshrine relics but just commemorated the Buddha, or a certain event in his life which had occurred on the spot where the stupa was built. They might contain some article associated with the Buddha, but not an actual relic. And eventually stupas became objects of worship in their own right, especially when they started incorporating images of the Buddhas and the bodhisattvas.

In the *Mahāparinibbāna Sutta* the Buddha is represented as telling Ānanda not to bother with the disposal of the remains of the Tathāgata, because there were devout lay people who would look after that.[115] This suggests that the Buddha thought that the *bhikkhus* should be getting on with their meditation and not concerning themselves with the cult of relics. It does seem, however, that *bhikkhus* became involved in this cult quite early on. Some schools, like the Chaityavādins, especially concerned themselves with the cult of the stupa and emphasized its importance. So even if the worship of the stupas containing relics was more or less the prerogative of the lay people to begin with, it very quickly spread to the *bhikkhus* and *bhikkhunīs*.

Are any of the teachings of the Chaityavādins still available?
There are some works which contain references to their beliefs. For instance, there is the commentary on the *Kathā-vatthu* of the Abhidharma Piṭaka. The *Kathā-vatthu* itself refutes the doctrines of certain schools but without naming the schools concerned, but the commentary

identifies the Chaityavādins as one of those schools. So from that source, assuming it to be reliable, we do have some idea about the teachings of the Chaityavādins. And we do know that they attached special importance to the worship of stupas.

There are also references to the worship of stupas throughout the *Mahāvastu*, which is the work of the Lokottaravādins.[116] There are some very striking carvings representing the worship of the stupa by the lay people of Amaravati in south India. By the time of Aśoka, stupas had become much more elaborate than they were in earlier days. People didn't just worship the stupas – they decorated them, festooning them with garlands of flowers, scarves, flags, streamers, and little bells, just as described in the *White Lotus Sūtra*.

An example of an Aśokan period stupa is still preserved intact – the great stupa of Sanchi, in the former state of Bhopal, halfway between Bombay and Delhi. The stupa is hemispherical in shape, built of brick and stone, and surrounded by a massive stone railing (built as a copy of an original wooden railing) pierced by four magnificent decorated gates which face the four cardinal points. These gates symbolize the universality of Buddhism which is proclaimed in all directions to all beings whatsoever in all the quarters of space. They are elaborately carved with scenes from the life of the Buddha, his previous lives (the *Jātakas*),[117] and so on. The Buddha himself does not appear in these bas-reliefs because he was simply never represented at this stage of Buddhist art. There are trees, flowers, buildings, other people, disciples, animals, a rich and lavish profusion; but the Buddha himself, even in those scenes which depict his own life, his Enlightenment, his birth and so on, is not depicted.

Why is that?

It was thought in the early days of Oriental studies that the Buddha was not depicted because artists did not feel confident enough to represent him properly, but it has since been pointed out that they represented everything else beautifully, so why not the Buddha? We now know that artists did not represent the Buddha on principle. In those days the Lokottaravādin school of Buddhism was very strong, and they held that the Buddha was not an ordinary human being, but a transcendental principle – ineffable, indescribable, unrepresentable. For these strictly metaphysical or spiritual reasons, the artists did not represent the

Buddha, and in the place where the Buddha would have been they put a symbol. If the scene was of the Buddha being born, he was represented by a pair of footprints, the *śrīpāda*. The Buddha preaching his first sermon was illustrated by a Wheel of the Law, a *dharmacakra*, perhaps on a throne supported by lions. His Enlightenment was represented by a bodhi tree. If the scene represented the Buddha moving about, a parasol or umbrella might be shown, and if the scene was the death of the Buddha – the *parinirvāṇa* – this was marked by the presence of a stupa.

Incidentally, although the great stupa is the best preserved of the many stupas originally built at Sanchi, it was in another of the stupas there that relics were found enshrined – not relics of the Buddha, but relics of his two chief disciples Śāriputra and Maudgalyāyana. By one of those rather strange historical accidents, these relics, in their original little steatite boxes, with the names of the two disciples engraved on them, spent some ninety years in the Victoria and Albert Museum, having been removed by a British archaeologist before the people of India started caring very much about Buddhism. They were returned to India, to the Maha Bodhi Society, after Indian independence, and re-enshrined at Sanchi in the course of a ceremony presided over by the Prime Minister of India, Pandit Nehru.

BUILDING STUPAS IN THE WEST

How appropriate is it to build stupas in the West?
I think stupas would look better than skyscrapers and blocks of flats. They could be a pleasing feature of the landscape, not necessarily in a completely traditional form, but having some link with tradition, based on the traditional five element structure.

Could a building be made in the form of a stupa?
In some parts of the Buddhist world, in China and in Tibet, temples, sometimes even monasteries, have been built in the form of stupas. Pagodas, which are also essentially stupas, do have chambers containing images on every storey; in this way the pagoda is not just a reliquary but also a temple. Sometimes they have even been used as libraries for sacred books. But personally I like the idea of a stupa being solid, a monument having no use. Not being able to use it – even as a temple – you can only worship it.

I've felt for some time an urge to build a stupa. I feel that a coloured element stupa would have an immediate impact, but a seven element yin-yang stupa might lend itself to more aesthetic architecture. Have you any thoughts about the most appropriate form for the West?
I am quite happy for us to have stupas of many types and varieties; I see no reason for sticking to just one. I would prefer them to approximate to the original solid architectural model rather than the temple or palace-like forms found in China and Japan; and we should perhaps start with simple forms rather than elaborate ones. I like the Sinhalese bell-shaped ones and the Tibetan chorten types. I think the elongated Thai stupas look very graceful. I also like the simple, solid ones, just a square base with a hemisphere on top. We could build all sorts of stupas, but whatever we build should be aesthetically pleasing; the proportions should be harmonious. I think multicoloured stupas might look too gaudy. In Sri Lanka stupas are usually whitewashed, and that looks very beautiful against the brilliant green background of the landscape. Tibetan stupas are whitewashed too, and Burmese ones are often gilded, which is also beautiful.

As for the Nepalese-style stupas with eyes, they are very distinctive, and they look magnificent, but they are absolutely enormous. They are all right in the landscape of Nepal, but I have a feeling that in this country, at least until the symbolism of the stupa is established, they would look rather bizarre.

I feel that stupas have quite an immediate impact. In building them, would we be trying to appeal just to Buddhists, or making something attractive and meaningful even to people who know nothing at all about its significance?
Well, you can't ignore the feelings and responses of non-Buddhists, and I can't help feeling that they might consider a four-coloured stupa a bit gaudy and tasteless. Personally I like the white stupa. I would also like to see really big stupas being built, the bigger the better. The setting is quite important too – the stupa needs to blend with the surrounding environment. In Nepal they have small stupas in the courtyards of temples and monasteries; we could do that in the West too, and circumambulate them on festival days.

You say that reliquary keeping is a human failing, but a forgivable one. Surely, if relics can help you connect with the Buddha and his teaching, keeping them has its positive aspect?

In a broader sense, the keeping of mementoes and souvenirs can be something of a weakness – because you are attached to them when perhaps you ought just to throw them away and think of the future rather than the past. This is the kind of thing I was referring to. The temptation is to treat relics as fetishes, to keep them not out of strong feelings of devotion, but as talismans, sources of magical protection. Buddhists in the past have done this, and present-day Buddhists continue to do it. And, of course, the same thing has happened in the West. Cathedral museums in Italy are full of hundreds of relics which don't seem to mean anything to anyone any more, but which meant a lot to people in the Middle Ages, when princes and churches used to have vast collections of them. Apparently various ecclesiastical commissions have sorted out these relics and declared at least ninety-five per cent of them to be fakes; there are still an embarrassing number of heads of John the Baptist and drops of milk of the Virgin Mary. That is how things can degenerate. What is a relic, after all? Do all these arms and legs and skulls really help you to connect?

If you go to the Dominican Priory in Siena you can see the head of Saint Catherine, a shrivelled little head in a little glass case. It is interesting, in a way, to think that this is the head of Catherine, that formidable lady of the fourteenth century who bossed the popes of the day and dragged them down from Avignon to Rome to do their duty, but I don't know whether it helps you to feel more closely in contact with Saint Catherine from a spiritual point of view. I would much rather read Father Raymond's biography of her, written from the perspective of someone who knew her intimately for many years of her life. That brings you far closer to the woman than just seeing what is left of her head.

There is not so much of this arm and leg business in Buddhism – Buddhist relics are usually less gruesome. They often take the form of tiny bits of bone, or even pearl-like objects called *śarīras*, which are believed to be secreted in the bones of Enlightened people. A *bhikkhu* from Singapore once told me some extraordinary stories from his personal experience about these relics. Apparently they can multiply and transfer themselves from one place to another – he would put these little pearl-like objects in a drawer, and five minutes later there would be ten times as many. He told me the story very solemnly, and I didn't feel inclined to disbelieve him.

If one came into possession of one of these śarīras, *should one make it a centrepiece for a shrine, say?*

Normally relics of that sort are enclosed in stupas. If the stupa was small enough it could be kept on the shrine – though the bigger the stupa the better. Usually it would be kept quite separately from the shrine, because if the *śarīra* does represent the Buddha, it would be like having two Buddhas on the same shrine. But if you couldn't build a large stupa, then you could certainly make a miniature one and have it on the shrine.

Śarīras are obviously a particularly subtle form of relic, but in general Buddhist relics, although they come from the physical body of the original person, are not usually the crude bits and pieces of it to be found in the reliquaries of the West. One exception to this might be the Tibetan and Chinese practice of mummifying the bodies of spiritual teachers. This seems almost the wrong sort of emphasis – was he his body? Perhaps some people do feel inspired to see the gilded mummy of Huineng, for instance; perhaps they feel spiritually more in touch. Maybe one shouldn't lay down rules for other people in this respect. But personally I am not very much stirred by relics, though I am quite happy about stupas.

The image of Abundant Treasures preserved intact in his stupa reminds me of the Egyptian pharaohs mummified in their pyramids. Could these be two cultural variations of the human desire to preserve the leader?

Perhaps there *is* something in human beings that makes them want to preserve the physical presence of their leaders. In some primitive communities they bury you under the floor of the hut, don't they? And Lenin was preserved in the way they used to preserve saints, so that people could go along to pay their respects and look at his embalmed body through a little window. It seems rather strange. Perhaps it comes from a deep-seated belief that the *mana* – the primitive power and energy attached to that person – somehow lingers on in the physical body and can be preserved by the tribe or the group.

I think in the case of the Egyptian pyramids the idea was rather different. The ancient Egyptians thought that your physical body had to be preserved intact to ensure the continuation of your subtle body in the other world. The building of the pyramid and the preservation of the body was for the sake of the person being entombed, the Pharaoh or whoever it was who could afford such a tomb, not for the sake of the group he left behind.

THE INNER EXPERIENCE OF INFINITE SPACE

You say that ākāśa *– space – comes halfway between matter and consciousness. What do you mean by that?*
To begin with, 'space' is really quite a misleading translation – perhaps 'firmament' would be nearer. One could say perhaps that if earth, water, fire, and air represent the gross material, *ākāśa* represents the subtle material, so in that sense it is midway between the material and the conscious, between matter and consciousness. It is even, in a way, a bit like the collective unconscious – though don't take that too literally.

Break down barriers?

Can you say why?
Well, it isn't really an objective, external dimension. Some ancient Hindu texts speak of the '*ākāśa* of the heart', the space you experience when you enter into your own heart, which makes it an inner dimension, not an external one. But if it is in between matter and consciousness, in a sense it is neither subjective nor objective, but a higher dimension of being accessible from within rather than from without. For instance, in the series of the four *arūpa dhyānas* there is the sphere of infinite space, but this is something that you experience in the *dhyāna* state, something you close your eyes and experience rather than open your eyes and see. At the same time, it is still mundane; it isn't the transcendental dimension.

But you seem to equate ākāśa *with some sort of transcendental experience – or am I taking it too literally?*
In the context of five element symbolism, *ākāśa* does represent the transcendental. But when you have a stupa with five, six, or more elements, *ākāśa* on its own does not have to represent the transcendental.

Is the distinction between the arūpa dhyāna *of 'infinite space' and the* arūpa dhyāna *of 'infinite consciousness'*[118] *that the one is objective and the other subjective?*
Yes. The way it happens is that first you become aware of infinite space. This is not the literal, external space of the universe, which even Western scientists cannot be sure is either finite or infinite, but the inner *experience* of infinite space. The experience you have at this stage is of complete freedom from obstruction, the feeling that you can move unimpeded in any direction. But at the same time that you experience this, you are *conscious* that you are experiencing it, so that you are experiencing space and also consciousness of space. Having achieved that, you proceed to separate, so to speak, the consciousness of space from space itself, so that you are left just with consciousness. You reflect that just as space is without limit, so your consciousness is likewise free from obstruction, or, in a sense, infinite. In that way you make the transition from the first to the second *arūpa dhyāna.*

But how do you reflect in the arūpa dhyānas*?*
Well, you can't take literally this notion that in the *dhyānas* beyond the first one there is absolutely no mental activity. It is often said that you develop the higher *dhyānas* and then come back to the first *dhyāna* in order to allow the re-arising of *vitarka* and *vicāra*,[119] so that you can develop Insight. This is not untrue, but it is grossly literalistic. What really happens is that, remaining poised in the higher *dhyānas*, you allow a very subtle type of *vitarka/vicāra* to arise; and it arises without any real detriment to your experience of that higher state of consciousness. It is with the help of that very subtle mental activity – so subtle that it may not even feel like mental activity, but more like just seeing – that you develop transcendental insight. And in much the same way you experience the difference between the so-called sphere of infinite space and the so-called sphere of infinite consciousness.

When you correlate the five elements of the stupa with the five psychic centres, you say that the addition of the harmikā *is at the level of the eyes. But on the basis of the correlation it would actually seem to come between the navel and the solar plexus. Could you explain this?*
In *Foundations of Tibetan Mysticism* Lama Govinda goes into the correlation between the elements of the stupa and the chakras in some

detail, if you're interested to find out more.[120] But you're right – the different correspondences don't always fit together. Interpolating the Vedic altar (which becomes the *harmikā*), for example, dislocates the system. Perhaps you could say that when the eyes are painted on the side of the *harmikā*, pictorial considerations have taken over, and you have to ignore the rest of the symbolism, or at least not insist on too close a correspondence.

There just are inconsistencies in symbolism sometimes. When different ideas are incorporated into the symbol, it has to lose some of its original significance to incorporate the new element. For example, in the case of the pagoda, just one element of the original stupa, the fire element, is subdivided into a number of different storeys to become a complete stupa in itself; in a way, that is a complete distortion of the original.

You say that the Vedic hearth and the parasol were incorporated into the stupa after the initial architectural form had been determined. When I was in India I noticed that nearly every Buddhist monument had some Hindu object of worship nearby. Is it possible that the hearth which forms part of the stupa represents not the universal integrating the ethnic, but the ethnic overcoming the universal? Could the Brahmins have included the Vedic hearth to make the stupa into a place of Hindu worship?

To the best of my knowledge, which derives mainly from Govinda, those elements were incorporated by the Buddhists themselves. When it comes to art and architecture even a universal religion has to make use of ethnic elements, at least initially, just as in terms of language you have to make use of whatever words are available and gradually give them your own meaning. That is rather different from the deliberate building of Hindu shrines next to Buddhist monuments which you do see in modern times.

The umbrella, for instance, is a pre-Buddhistic Hindu symbol, though it continues to be an emblem of sovereignty even today; the president of India has a white umbrella held over him on ceremonial occasions, just as in ancient times. When Buddhism adopted the symbolism of the umbrella, the sovereignty it symbolized became spiritual sovereignty over the three worlds.

The path of the Higher Evolution can be seen as five progressive stages of consciousness. Can these be correlated with the five element symbolism of the stupa?

I think probably they can, though you might have to do some violence to one or the other in order to correlate them effectively. Broadly speaking, the stupa does represent both the higher and the lower evolution, fire and air superimposed on earth and water, the solar superimposed on the lunar.

This superimposition of the solar on the lunar seems to me to say something about the nature of Buddhism. I have come to think that religions can be regarded either as solar or as lunar. I think of Christianity, for instance, more as a lunar religion, because it is based on the conception of birth and death and resurrection. Christ is the risen God, originating from the pagan god of harvest, god of spring, and so on. There are associations with the cycle of the year, and all sorts of agricultural and vegetative connections; this is all lunar symbolism.

Buddhism, by contrast, seems to be entirely a solar religion. You don't get any of this birth, death, and rebirth imagery at all – in fact, the cycle of birth and death is something that one seeks to be emancipated from. Buddhist symbolism is associated with the hero who fights with the forces representing the material world – the womb, the mother, the earth – to win his way to the higher path.

But how would your emphasis on spiritual androgyny, on the integration of 'male' and 'female', fit in with that idea?

I don't see the feminine principle and the masculine principle in this context – yin and yang – as equal. I see the integration as consisting not in the balance of the one against the other, but in the absorption of yin within yang, much as in Tantric Buddhist art you see the tiny figure of the *ḍākinī* clinging onto the much larger figure of the Buddha. If you have the yin and the yang as equal and opposite, you need a third element to synthesize them. As it is, there is no third element, so the two can only be synthesized by the stronger, or the higher, incorporating the other. You don't have the lower evolution and the Higher Evolution side by side, balancing each other; the lower evolution is incorporated into

makes me think of the child within us.

the Higher Evolution. This is the great distinction, as far as I can see, between Buddhism and Taoism.

Does that have implications for practice in terms of the masculine qualities in relation to the feminine qualities?

In some ways it does. Supposing you decide you are lacking in the feminine qualities and want to develop them, well, development is an active process, so you are going to have to take some initiative to develop those feminine qualities. According to the Mahāyāna, *vīrya* is necessary with regard to all the *pāramitās*.[121] Yes, it is a separate *pāramitā* in its own right, but it also exists on the level of all the other *pāramitās* – you need *vīrya* even to develop *kṣānti*. To be very paradoxical, you need to be a man in order to be a woman: to be at her best, a woman needs some masculine qualities. How is she to bring her natural womanly yin qualities to perfection without some element of yang?

7
THE JEWEL IN THE LOTUS

Stupas are to be found all over the Buddhist world, but we are now going to turn to something which is found mainly in one Buddhist country, albeit a very well-known and important one: Tibet. You only have to look at the map to see that Tibet is a truly enormous country, easily bigger than France and Spain put together. But although Tibet is so large, it is very thinly populated. Until recently we were rather in the dark as to the exact number of Tibetans, but it would now seem that there are between two and three million people scattered throughout that vast area. There are hardly any cities, and not even many villages, because many of the people, especially in the east and north, lead a nomadic existence, roaming from place to place with their horses and their felt tents, their flocks and their herds. And I'm sorry to say that quite a lot of these nomads, even though they are Buddhists, live by robbery.

This makes journeying in Tibet a hazardous undertaking. When you have been travelling for hundreds of miles through wild country dotted with enormous rocks behind any of which someone might be hiding with a gun, it's a relief to realize that you are approaching civilization again, or at least some tiny hill village. And you're likely to see signs that you are near to human habitation long before you see a house or a person. You may well see a chorten, a Tibetan stupa, roughly built of stones and whitewashed – but these are common even out in the wilds of Tibet. What will tell you for sure that you are near a village is much more likely to be a long, low dry-stone wall which appears on your right-hand side as you go along the track. On the wall there will be painted, in yellow, red, blue, and green, a series of characters – as tall as you are if the wall is high enough. And if you can make out the Tibetan script, you will see that the syllables spell out a Sanskrit phrase, always the same one: *oṃ maṇi padme hūṃ*. Wherever you go throughout Tibet, wherever there are people living, you will be almost sure to find a '*maṇi* wall' – or at least that was how it was in the old days, before the Chinese invasion.

In the days before anyone in Tibet had even heard of Chairman Mao, not only did they paint and engrave and carve *oṃ maṇi padme hūṃ* on these long stone walls, but they also used wooden blocks to print *oṃ maṇi padme hūṃ* on long strips of paper which they wound round and round and put into cylinders inside the ritual objects which we in the West call prayer wheels, but which the Tibetans have always called *maṇi* wheels. This same phrase was also printed onto innumerable prayer flags which fluttered from long bamboo poles outside not only every monastery but every single habitation, so that the phrase *oṃ maṇi padme hūṃ* was wafted by the breeze across all Tibet. You could probably even hear the phrase in the air, for it was recited every day by hundreds and thousands of people. If you went out for an evening stroll in a Tibetan village you would be sure to meet people walking along the road, their rosary in one hand, their prayer wheel in the other, murmuring as they went along: *oṃ maṇi padme hūṃ, oṃ maṇi padme hūṃ*.

So this phrase *oṃ maṇi padme hūṃ* obviously has some great significance. What it means, and how it connects with the *White Lotus Sūtra*, is the main theme of this chapter. But the first thing to say about the phrase is that it is a *mantra*. Mantra is a familiar enough word, but one that is often misunderstood – and the popular translation 'mystic phrase' is not really much help. If we look at the traditional derivation of the word – what Guenther calls the symbolic etymology, as opposed to the scientific etymology – we find that it is formed from two parts: *man*, which means mind, and *tra*, a verb meaning 'to protect'. So a mantra is 'that which protects the mind', because it protects – and also develops and matures – the mind of the person reciting it and meditating upon its meaning.

In strict philological terms, however, mantra comes from a word meaning 'to call' – even 'to call out' or 'to call down' – in other words, to invoke. Mantras are phrases used to invoke the dormant spiritual forces within our own minds; indeed, in a sense, they are the names of these spiritual forces. For in Buddhist tradition such forces spontaneously assume archetypal forms – forms of Buddhas and bodhisattvas, forms of guardian deities, forms of *ḍākas* and *ḍākinīs* – and every single one of these forms has his or her own mantra. When you recite a mantra, you set up vibrations to which Reality starts responding, and the appropriate Buddha or bodhisattva form appears. The form, the shape, of the Buddha or bodhisattva represents the 'shape symbol' of the spiritual energy concerned, and the mantra represents its corresponding sound symbol – we could put it like that. (In fact, since each of the archetypal figures has a particular colour – some being bright red, others deep blue, other pure white, others a beautiful green – and colour is a form of light, we could call the shape symbol also a light symbol.)

To avoid any confusion, I should point out that there are two kinds of bodhisattva, broadly speaking. One kind is the individual historical human being who has vowed to work towards supreme Enlightenment for the sake of all beings, and is at one of the ten stages of the bodhisattva career.[122] The second kind is the archetypal bodhisattva, a 'personification' or 'embodiment' of a particular aspect of Enlightenment. You can think of Enlightenment in the abstract, in general, but you can also think of it concretely, in terms of particular aspects: a wisdom aspect, a compassion aspect, a power aspect, and so on. All these are ways in which you can look at and experience Enlightenment. Different bodhisattvas embody, or 'personify', though not in any artificial sense, one or another of these aspects of Enlightenment or Buddhahood: Mañjuśrī represents wisdom, Vajrapāṇi represents power, Vajrasattva represents beginningless purity, and so on. Bodhisattvas of this sort, which are not historical human beings, though they may appear or be represented in human form, are called bodhisattvas of the *dharmakāya*, the *dharmakāya* being one particular term for ultimate reality.

The aspect of reality invoked by *oṃ maṇi padme hūṃ*, the mantra which resounds throughout Tibet, is compassion, and it is embodied, even crystallized, in the form of Avalokiteśvara. He is perhaps the most famous of all the great bodhisattvas, worshipped, meditated upon, and invoked not only in Tibet but throughout the Mahāyāna Buddhist world, and even here and there in Theravādin Sri Lanka. The *White Lotus Sūtra* devotes a whole chapter to him, so we may say that Avalokiteśvara himself is one of the symbols of the Mahāyāna in this *sūtra*. And the *maṇi padme* of his mantra translates as 'the jewel (in the) lotus'.[123]

The meaning of the mantra coincides with the meaning of one of the parables of the *White Lotus Sūtra* which also happens to be concerned with a jewel. This parable – which we will call the parable of the drunkard and the jewel – occurs in the eighth chapter of the *sūtra*, and like the myth of the return journey, it is told by some of the assembly in response to something they have heard.

At the beginning of this chapter the Buddha predicts his disciple Pūrṇa to supreme Enlightenment, declaring that in the distant future Pūrṇa will become a Buddha called Radiance of the Truth – appropriately enough for a disciple who stands out among all the others as the greatest preacher, famed far and wide for his eloquence. In previous chapters of the *sūtra* other disciples have been predicted to supreme Enlightenment, and different worlds have been 'assigned' to them, some of them unthinkably remote from our own. The difference in the case of Pūrṇa's prediction is that apparently he is to become a Buddha in this very world itself, in millions and millions of years time. But it seems from what the Buddha goes on to say that in those days the world will be a very different place from what it is now. Indeed, it will have changed so much that it will be a 'pure world', to use the technical term – a world free from certain imperfections, an ideal world.

The Indian Buddhist tradition has its own ideas as to what constitutes perfection so far as a world is concerned. For a start, according to the *sūtra*, the whole world will be perfectly flat. For some reason, the Indians seem to have objected to any irregularity in the earth's surface – all those untidy mountains and hills all over the place breaking up the beautiful, smooth contours of the horizon – so flatness is a desirable quality of a perfect world. And not only will the world be flat; it will be so transformed as to be hardly recognizable. It isn't going to be made up of the earth and stone we're used to; instead, it will be composed entirely of the seven precious things – gold, silver, and so on.

The *sūtra* goes on to say – and some people find this a very interesting feature indeed – that in those days divine vehicles will be stationed in the sky. Does this have a familiar ring? Not only that, but the division between the world of men and the world of the gods will be completely broken down, so that there is no barrier between the ordinary human world and the world of the gods, which we might call the archetypal realm. Human beings on the earth will be able to look up and see the gods, and the gods will be able to look down on them. There will be regular contact between them. And there will be no places of suffering in the world of those days, nor even the sound of any torment and distress.

The *sūtra* also says that at that time in the world there will be no women – a provocative-sounding statement, to say the least. But of course it doesn't mean that the world will contain men but not women; what it means is that there will be no distinction of sex among the beings of the earth – neither men nor women, but just human beings. And those human beings will be born (or rather reborn) not by the present rather crude arrangements but by what is called apparitional birth. People will just spring into existence, blossom naturally out of thin air. Having been born in that way, it is not surprising to find that they will live – according to the *sūtra* – a purely spiritual life. They will have no gross physical bodies but what are called mental bodies, spiritual bodies, and they will be self-luminous, brilliant, and able to fly through the air at will. With no gross physical bodies, they will have no need for gross physical food, but will feed on just two things: delight in the Buddha's teaching and delight in meditation. Of course – and this is hardly surprising in the circumstances – there will be a great many bodhisattvas. And, the *sūtra* adds as a crowning touch, there will also be many stupas, all made of the seven precious things.

Having given this glowing account of the world as it will be when Pūrṇa becomes a Buddha, the Buddha Śākyamuni proceeds to predict to Perfect Buddhahood five hundred other disciples. Delighted, naturally enough, by the prediction, these five hundred disciples say that they feel as though they have suddenly gained possession of something wonderful, and they tell a story – the parable of the drunkard and the jewel:

> World-honored One! It is as if some man goes to an intimate friend's house, gets drunk, and falls asleep. Meanwhile his friend, having to go forth on official duty, ties a priceless jewel within his garment as a present, and departs. The man, being drunk and asleep, knows nothing of it. On arising he travels onward till he reaches some other country, where for food and clothing he expends much labor and effort, and undergoes exceedingly great hardship, and is content even if he can obtain but little. Later, his friend

> happens to meet him and speaks thus: 'Tut! Sir, how is it you have come to this for the sake of food and clothing? Wishing you to be in comfort and able to satisfy all your five senses, I formerly in such a year and month and on such a day tied a priceless jewel within your garment. Now as of old it is present there and you in ignorance are slaving and worrying to keep yourself alive. How very stupid! Go you now and exchange that jewel for what you need and do whatever you will, free from all poverty and shortage.'[124]

So this is the parable – no doubt the meaning is clear enough – and this is our introduction to the symbol of the priceless jewel, which will lead us, by way of a general look at jewel symbolism in the Mahāyāna, to the jewel in the lotus. But first, there is another aspect of the parable which is worth noting. We have in this story, which begins with a man getting drunk and falling asleep, an example of a kind of symbolism which is used not only in Buddhist literature but in spiritual traditions throughout the world. We have encountered it already in the Gnostic 'Hymn of the Pearl', in which the king's son goes down into Egypt in quest of the pearl, but, drugged by the Egyptians, forgets who he is and what he is doing, and eventually sinks into a profound slumber.

In the Gnostic tradition, as in all the others, both drunkenness and sleep are symbols for lack of awareness, lack of any true human self-consciousness. This, we may say, is the state that most people are in most of the time. If humanness is characterized by awareness and self-consciousness, most people do not really live in a human state, but in a state of torpor, darkness, and ignorance more like that of an animal. To become a true human being, to achieve a state of awareness and self-consciousness, is in fact very difficult, and we usually need at least some outside help. It's just like when we are sound asleep, and go on sleeping and sleeping, as some people do, until late in the morning or even early in the afternoon. The alarm clock may ring, but we don't hear it. What we need is someone to come along and shout 'Wake up!' But if we're really fast asleep and dreaming, even a shout, however loud, may not be any use. We may need someone to come along, take us by the shoulder, and give us a really good shake. And this is all that religion really is, all that it really has to do. Religion is just that shout, just that shake, to wake us up out of our sleep, even out of our drunken stupor, of ignorance and unawareness.

In our sleepy, drunken state we don't really know who we are, or what we are; we don't know our own true nature. We think – we dream – that we are poor, limited, contingent, conditioned, and consequently we suffer. But in truth, like the man in the parable, we have the priceless jewel in our possession all the time; all we need to do is wake up to that fact.

Although in the parable the jewel is tied in the sleeping man's garment by his friend before he sets off to work, this detail is not to be taken too literally. The beginning of the parable, like the beginning of the myth of the return journey, and that of all parables and fairy stories, takes place outside time. So the jewel doesn't literally come into our possession at a certain point in time. It's there all the time – that is to say, outside time altogether. It's only our realization that we have the jewel that occurs in time.

Its origin outside time is, of course, not the only similarity between this parable and the myth of the return journey. In both parables the hero – if we can call him that – goes away to a distant country, where he suffers hardship on account of poverty; and in both parables the hero ends up possessed of riches, riches that have really been his all the time. At the same time, however, there are also significant differences between the two parables. For one thing, the father and son relationship of the return journey suggests a more extreme degree of alienation than the relationship between the two friends – two equals – in the parable of the jewel and the drunkard. An even more important difference is in the manner in which the two poor men become rich. In the myth of the return journey the poor man is gradually introduced to riches, and gets used to going in and out of the mansion without fear, until at last he learns that the riches of which he is steward are really his own inheritance. But in the parable of the drunkard and the jewel the transition is much more abrupt. One minute the man is destitute and suffering, and the next minute – because his benefactor doesn't beat about the bush – he is rich.

This profound difference between the two parables corresponds to two different methods that may be used by the guru or teacher to guide the disciple in the spiritual life: the gradual method and the sudden method. In the gradual method, the teacher says, to begin with, 'Don't strain yourself too much. You don't need to bother about Nirvāṇa or Enlightenment. Just steady your mind, be peaceful, enjoy life more.' So the disciple is led step by step, and only after many years have gone by does the teacher start talking about Enlightenment. But in the sudden method the teacher confronts the disciple with the truth immediately. There is no chance to prepare, no preamble – just 'This is it; it's right here; it's this.' Which method the teacher uses depends entirely on the temperament of the pupil. If he or she is easygoing and immersed in the things of the world, then obviously the gradual method is going to be the one to use. But if the disciple is a more heroic type and can stand the shock, then the guru doesn't hesitate to use the sudden method.

This difference between the gradual and the sudden also applies to the two aspects of the Buddha's Noble Eightfold Path, the Path of Vision and the Path of Transformation. The Path of Vision is the initial spiritual experience; you see, even if only for an instant, that you have the jewel, that you are the jewel. The Path of Transformation is the application of that experience to every aspect of your life, the gradual adjustment to the fact that you are in possession of that jewel.

It's rather like what happens when you suddenly inherit a large sum of money or win the football pools – and if this hasn't happened to you yet, no doubt you can imagine it. You hear the news – maybe you get a telegram or a solicitor's letter – that you've got half a million pounds. What a shock! What a surprise! All of a sudden you're rich, incredibly rich. For a while you may be so stunned that, although you've got all that money in the bank, you don't know what to do with it. Then comes the adjustment. Slowly you reorganize your life to suit your new status. Maybe you move into a bigger house, maybe you buy a better car; everything starts changing because you are rich. In the same way, you may be so overwhelmed at first by the vision, by the spiritual experience, that you don't know what to do with it. It could well be that you will be your usual crude self for quite a while until, little by little, you start to be transformed in the light of that great experience. It takes a long time to work it out in detail, to reorientate your life around that supreme fact, that supreme experience.

So what is this jewel which we discover that we have, or that we are? Well, the symbol of the jewel, like all symbols, does not have a meaning, not in a cut-and-dried sense. You can't take symbols and say, 'Here's a jewel, it means this. Here's a lotus, it means that.' Symbols are always suggestive, evocative, not to be reduced to any one cut-and-dried meaning. With this proviso in mind, let's try to feel – not understand but feel, or even experience – what the jewel signifies.

To put it briefly and broadly, the jewel signifies our own true nature, what we really are. To be a little rash, we could even say that it symbolizes the true self – if we use the word in the Jungian rather than the Vedantic sense.[125] This jewel, this true self, this true nature of ours, is hidden, concealed. In the parable it is concealed in the man's clothing, but in the case of most of us it would probably be more accurate to say that it's covered in mud. But whether the layers are of clothing or of mud, this kind of symbolism suggests that we don't exist just on one level, but on a number of levels, some superficial, others deeper. And the jewel represents the deepest level of all, the bedrock of our being. Or, to reverse the terminology, it represents a level above individuality in the ordinary sense of the term, a level which is even outside time altogether.

Finding the jewel means coming into contact with the deepest level of our own being, and this suggests that most of the time, in fact all the time, we are *not* in contact with that deepest level of ourselves. Not only are we out of contact with it; we don't even know that it exists. We live merely from the surface of our being, not from the depths. But when we find the jewel we come into contact with that deepest layer of ourselves, that level which exists outside time. And this doesn't mean just touching that layer and then breaking off again, but establishing permanent contact with it and living out of the depths of that experience.

The parable describes the jewel as priceless, and this is exactly what it is. The word has to be taken quite literally, with the full force of its meaning behind it. This means that contact with the true self, contact with the bedrock of one's own being, is absolutely the most important thing in one's life. Money isn't the most important. Success isn't the most important. Popularity isn't the most important. Knowledge isn't the most important. Culture isn't the most important. Religion isn't the most important. Meditation isn't the most important. 'What is a man profited if he shall gain the whole world, and lose his own soul?' The most important thing in life, the most precious thing in the whole world, is contact with one's own true self, between the surface of one's being and its depths. This is more precious than the whole world – and by world is meant here not other people, but one's own material and intellectual possessions. This is the priceless jewel, not to be sacrificed for anything whatsoever, otherwise one will have had the worst of the bargain.

But why is it the jewel that symbolizes the true self? The most obvious reason is that the jewel is the most precious of all material things, so that it is a worthy symbol of the true self, which is infinitely precious. Then, the jewel is bright, shining, brilliant; and the true self is like this too, although its brilliance is of a completely different kind, for it comes from within rather than being reflected from without. The true self, one's own true being, is self-luminous, conscious, aware. In fact, even to say that it is conscious is not correct, because it does not possess consciousness as a quality, something which is as it were stuck on from outside and able to be removed. In its very nature our own true being is pure transparent consciousness, with no distinction between subject and object.

Another quality which makes the jewel a fitting symbol for the true self is that it cannot be made dirty. It may lie hidden in dust and dirt for ages upon ages, but when the dirt is removed the jewel shines and sparkles as clean and bright as ever. In the same way, our own true nature is essentially pure. It may be hidden for the greater part of our lives by passions of various kinds – ignorance, anger, bigotry, and so on – but once those defilements are removed, it shines forth in all its original splendour. In truth it has not been defiled at all.

The symbol of the jewel has many different facets and many different forms. One of the best known is the *cintāmaṇi*, usually translated as the 'wish-fulfilling' jewel. This particular symbolism comes from Indian mythology, but all the mythologies, the folklore, and the fairy stories of the world have such objects – things that grant every wish of your heart, every desire. Just like Aladdin's lamp, you hold it in your hand and say, 'I wish…', and your wish comes true. When you've recovered from your surprise, you hold it again and wish again – and again your wish comes true. It is a universal dream of humanity to have some jewel, or some magic pot or magic lamp, or magic *anything*, that will give you whatever you want. Indian mythology tells of a wish-granting tree, a wish-fulfilling cow, and a wish-fulfilling pot – it is all much the same sort of symbolism – and also of the *cintāmaṇi*, the wish-fulfilling gem.

In the Buddhist tradition the wish-fulfilling gem has come to symbolize the *bodhicitta*, the bodhisattva's aspiration to gain Enlightenment for the benefit of all beings; and this tells us something about the nature of Enlightenment. Once you have Enlightenment, you have everything. All your wishes, all your desires, all your aspirations, are fully satisfied. Enlightenment, even in the primitive, rudimentary form of the *bodhicitta*, is the true *cintāmaṇi*, the true wish-fulfilling gem. The *cintāmaṇi* is often represented in Buddhist art as a brilliant, shining jewel with flames bursting out of it, because the *bodhicitta*, the bodhisattva's will to Enlightenment, is on fire with activity and burns up all adventitious defilements of the mind.[126]

But the *cintāmaṇi* is not the only example of jewel symbolism in Buddhism; the jewel is very protean. Splitting into three, it produces the Three Jewels – the Buddha jewel, the Dharma jewel, and the Sangha jewel – which are the three highest values of Buddhism, or one great value looked at from three different points of view. It also symbolizes the transcendental as the *vajra* or *dorje*, which is both diamond and thunderbolt, both indestructible and capable of destroying absolutely anything.

The jewel is also a solar symbol, an embodiment of the yang principle, and where there is yang, there is always yin. And the lotus, being associated with water, is a yin symbol. If anything, the lotus is an even more popular symbol in Buddhist tradition than the jewel, and its symbolism is too vast for us even to touch on all its aspects. But broadly speaking, we can say that the lotus has both a macrocosmic significance and a microcosmic significance; that is to say, it represents the universe as a whole and also the individual being. And just as the lotus consists of many layers of petals, some without, some within, so both the universe and the individual consist of many different layers, many different levels, some lower and others higher. So in this way the lotus comes to represent the whole process of development, of unfoldment stage by stage, level by level, degree by degree, from the bottom to the top – development both cosmic and human. Sometimes the lotus represents the lower evolution, sometimes, in a more rarified form, it represents the Higher Evolution, and sometimes it represents both the lower evolution and the Higher Evolution taken together.

Having said all this, we must be careful not just to settle down into thinking, 'So, the lotus represents the process of evolution.' Symbols such as this do not have any one unchanging meaning; it is not so much a question of understanding a symbol as of allowing yourself to be influenced by it. So what kind of influence does a lotus have? It must represent something rich and colourful, something growing, complex, beautiful, harmonious, delicate, pure; in other words, something ideal.

If these are the associations that the jewel and the lotus bring with them individually, what does the combination of the two – the jewel *in* the lotus – represent? Macrocosmically speaking, the jewel in the lotus means that the Unconditioned exists in the midst of the conditioned. The Real exists in the midst of the unreal. Light exists in the midst of darkness, even though we may not be able to see that light because we are blind or because our eyes are closed. So in its depth the universe is based on a principle that is ultimately spiritual, and this principle is working itself out in the universe in the course of the whole process of life.

From a microcosmic perspective, the jewel in the lotus means that Enlightenment, Buddhahood, spiritual perfection, is immanent in the depths of our own hearts. If we take our courage into both hands, if we plunge right down into the depths of our own being, underneath our thoughts about this and that, underneath our emotions, underneath our conditioned reflexes, underneath our reactions, if we go even deeper than the personal subconscious, even deeper than the collective unconscious, we shall encounter the Buddha nature itself. This is the microcosmic meaning of the jewel in the lotus.

In the mantra of Avalokiteśvara, the jewel in the lotus is enclosed by those mysterious syllables *oṃ* and *hūṃ*. Very briefly, in this context *oṃ* is the absolute, the Unconditioned, the transcendental as it is in itself, entirely unconnected with the world; and *hūṃ* is the same absolute as manifested in the world, descending into it, permeating it, moving it from within. *Oṃ* and *hūṃ* are the alpha and omega, the beginning and end, but a beginning that is before time and an end that is after time. So *oṃ* is what we might call the 'abstract universal', *hūṃ* is the 'concrete universal', and the words *maṇi padme*, the jewel in the lotus, indicate how the abstract becomes concrete.

Of course, *oṃ maṇi padme hūṃ* is not just a symbolic phrase; it is a mantra, and when it is recited, a bodhisattva appears: Avalokiteśvara, the Bodhisattva of Compassion. He also appears in the *White Lotus Sūtra*, making his appearance in chapter 24 of the Sanskrit text (chapter 25 in the Chinese version). This is one of those chapters of the *sūtra* which is not an integral part of the drama of cosmic Enlightenment. In the history of Buddhist canonical literature, different traditions have circulated various texts which have gradually been collected together, so that texts and traditions which were originally independent have come to be anthologized and written down in one overall 'portmanteau' text. It would seem that the Avalokiteśvara chapter was originally an independent *sūtra* in its own right, and was drawn into the orbit of the *White Lotus Sūtra*, along with a great deal of other miscellaneous material included in the last four or five chapters, because of the *sūtra*'s great popularity and prestige.

Avalokiteśvara has a number of different forms, one of the most famous of which is perhaps rather bizarre from the Western point of view, because it has eleven heads and a thousand arms. There are eleven heads because there are eleven directions of space – the centre, north, south, east, and west, and the four intermediate points, plus the zenith and the nadir – and Compassion is omnipresent, and looks in all directions. There are a thousand arms because there is so much to be done to relieve suffering that a thousand arms at the very least are necessary. Really an infinite number is required.

How did such a strange figure originate? According to one version of the legend, once upon a time Avalokiteśvara was sitting on Mount Potalaka, where the myths say he usually lives in southern India, and looking out over the world. And everywhere he looked, he saw terrible suffering. He saw people being oppressed by unjust kings, led off to execution, tortured, beheaded. He saw people being burned, people being devoured by wild beasts, people being bitten by serpents and dying painful deaths, people drowning at sea, and many, many people suffering from disease, sickness, old age, bereavement, and separation. Seeing how much humanity suffered, he felt this suffering so deeply, so bitterly, so intensely, that he experienced a terrible tension, and under the strain his head suddenly split into eleven fragments, each of which became a head. The heads came together, and a thousand arms appeared to relieve and succour all the people suffering throughout the world. We can see the meaning of this symbolism very clearly, because this is how you can actually feel when you see so much suffering around you; you feel as though your head could split into eleven pieces and your arms could multiply a thousandfold and stretch out in all directions to render aid. This is the sort of compassion that Avalokiteśvara represents.

In another legend associated with Avalokiteśvara's compassion, we are told that on one occasion, seeing all the suffering in the world, Avalokiteśvara could not restrain himself from weeping bitterly. He wept so profusely that a great pool of tears formed, which spread and spread until it was a huge, shining lake of pure crystal-clear water. And from that lake there sprang up a pure white lotus; the petals slowly opened, and inside was a beautiful white goddess with a white lotus in her hand. This was the 'goddess' Tāra, the female bodhisattva Tāra, who is sometimes described as being born out of the tears of Avalokiteśvara, and is thus known as his spiritual daughter. An even more delicate, tender figure than Avalokiteśvara himself, she represents the quintessence of compassion.[127]

The form of Avalokiteśvara you are most likely to see represented iconographically is perhaps the four-armed form, the *Ṣaḍakṣarī* Avalokiteśvara. *Ṣaḍakṣarī* means 'possessing six syllables', and these six syllables are those of the mantra: *oṃ ma ṇi pa dme hūṃ*. In Tantric Buddhism, Avalokiteśvara assumes a wrathful form known as Mahākāla, 'Great Time' – the destroyer of ignorance, anger, hatred, and everything conditioned. But in China, where Avalokiteśvara was introduced through the *White Lotus Sūtra*, something very different happened to him. Once he – or rather she – was established there the originally masculine bodhisattva became a feminine form called Guanyin, the most popular of all the Chinese bodhisattvas.[128]

Why is Avalokiteśvara so called? This question, asked by the bodhisattva Akṣayamati, opens the Avalokiteśvara chapter of the *White Lotus Sūtra*. In fact the name's etymology tells us that Avalokiteśvara can be interpreted in two quite different ways: as 'the one who looks down on the world', looks down, that is to say, in compassion, and as 'the one who listens', the one who hearkens to cries of distress. In response to Akṣayamati's question, however, the Buddha does not delve into etymology, but simply says that Avalokiteśvara is so called because out of compassion he responds to all those who invoke his name, and delivers them from difficulties and dangers both physical and spiritual. The long account which follows of all the various plights from which Avalokiteśvara can save human beings clearly presents him as a popular saviour figure. The Buddha goes on to say that Avalokiteśvara assumes different forms in which to preach the Dharma according to the temperaments and requirements of different beings, sometimes taking the form of a Buddha, sometimes the form of a bodhisattva, and sometimes even the form of one or another of the Hindu gods. Having had his question answered at considerable length, Akṣayamati presents Avalokiteśvara – who we now learn is actually present – with a magnificent golden necklace, and then sings a hymn of praise, one of the most beautiful in the whole range of Mahāyāna Buddhist literature.[129]

Now the form of Avalokiteśvara, whether it has a thousand arms or four arms, is a shape symbol, space symbol, *light* symbol, and his mantra is a sound symbol, but although they converge on it from different directions, they are both symbols of the compassion aspect of Enlightenment. So how do you bring the two together? How do you meditate on them?

The meditation practice is quite complex. First of all you go for Refuge – to the guru (this comes first in Tibetan Buddhism), then to the Buddha, the Dharma, and the Sangha. But you do not go for Refuge on your own. You go taking with you, as it were, all living beings. You imagine them also as Going for Refuge, because all life is ultimately heading in the direction of Enlightenment. Then you invoke blessings onto yourself, aspiring or praying that your body, speech, and mind may be transformed, and that you may make spiritual progress. After that you take the bodhisattva vow, vowing that you will gain Enlightenment not just for your own sake but for the sake of Enlightening, benefiting, helping, all other living beings, and that you will practise the six perfections as a means of achieving that end.

Then follows a stage of reflection. First you reflect, using a Sanskrit formula, that all things whatsoever in the universe are by nature pure. You see no impurity anywhere; the whole world is pure, and everything in it is pure. Then, having reflected in this way, you reflect, 'I too am pure, a pure being in a pure world. In my essential nature I am pure.'

Next, out of the depths of space, out of the depths of Reality, you conjure up the figure of Avalokiteśvara. First of all you see a lotus throne, and on that a moon disc, or moon mat as it is sometimes called. And then on the moon mat you see – visualize, feel, experience – yourself as Avalokiteśvara. In some forms of visualization practice you visualize the Buddha or bodhisattva in front of you, different from you, but in this practice you visualize yourself as the bodhisattva. You imagine yourself as Avalokiteśvara, your body the colour of a conch shell or crystal, your face smiling.

The figure – your figure – has four arms, and the lower two have their hands joined at the heart. So here is some more symbolism. These hands symbolize the jewel in the lotus: the fingers symbolize the lotus, and the two thumbs together are the jewel. This incidentally is why, according to Buddhist tradition, the salutation is made not with fingers pressed together (which is the brahminical form of salutation) but with the fingers separated and the thumbs together to make a jewel in a lotus. Whenever you greet someone in that way, you remind yourself that there is a jewel – Enlightenment potentiality – in him or her as well as in yourself.

Of the upper pair of hands, one hand holds a crystal rosary, to tell the beads as you recite the mantra, and the other holds a lotus, which is a symbol here of spiritual rebirth. The two feet are in *vajrāsana*, one on top of the other. And the body of Avalokiteśvara – your own body – is decked with silks and jewels. You have long blue-black hair, with a top-knot on which is sitting a little figure of Amitābha, the Buddha of Infinite Light, because he is the 'spiritual father' of Avalokiteśvara, the head of the Lotus family. (All Buddhas and bodhisattvas belong to one of five 'Buddha families', and this is the basis of a lot of Buddhist symbolism.)[130] Having visualized yourself as Avalokiteśvara in this way, you invoke upon yourself, as Avalokiteśvara, the blessings of Amitābha, regarding him as the guru, and you pray that you will quickly gain Buddhahood for the sake of all.

Having done that – and it is quite an involved exercise, which takes quite a long time – you just let go. Dropping everything, you stay in a state free from thought for as long as is necessary, and then, when you are ready, you return to visualization. Inside your heart you visualize a horizontal moon lotus, and on top of that a red *hrīḥ*, the seed mantra of Amitābha, and encircling this the six syllables of the mantra, *oṃ ma ṇi pa dme hūṃ*, in the appropriate colours. From the syllables there issue rays of light, which call down the compassion and blessing of the Buddhas.

Next, in this version of the full practice, you start reciting *oṃ maṇi padme hūṃ*. Even the simple recitation has its own value, but if you want to do the practice thoroughly, you do the whole visualization first, and only then begin to recite *oṃ maṇi padme hūṃ*. In the context of this particular practice it is recited at least five hundred times, but you can keep going for an hour or two, or even the whole day. Then, having come to the end of your recitation, you dissolve into light the throne on which you are sitting, the lotus, and the moon disc, and this light merges into you. The practice is then brought to an end with a dedication of merit. You say, 'May whatever merits, whatever benefits, I have gained from this practice be shared by everyone.'

Having come to the end of the practice, you thereafter think of the place you live in, your surroundings, as being the Pure Land itself, the Paradise of Avalokiteśvara. You are living in a transfigured world because you are a transfigured being. And having become transmuted into Avalokiteśvara, all the time, whatever you do, you recollect the Buddha of Infinite Light. You think constantly about the guru who is, as it were, on your head. Whatever you do, wherever you go in the world, whoever you speak to, all the time, day and night, after doing this exercise, you undertake to act with compassion for all living beings. If you can practise this visualization and mantra recitation in this way, you gradually become completely transformed. You become radiant, a jewel, even the jewel, and the world in which you have your being, your environment, becomes your lotus. Practising, experiencing, realizing, in this way, you yourself become – you yourself *are* – the jewel in the lotus.

7
QUESTIONS AND ANSWERS

MANTRAS AND MAGIC

Have Buddhist mantras incorporated sound symbols from other traditions?

It seems that in medieval times in India – let's say from the third to the eleventh century of the Common Era – there was a sort of twilight zone which was not exactly Hindu and not exactly Buddhist. In that zone there were a lot of mantras around, mantras that were used in connection with the worship of ethnic divinities and the performance of magic rites – in other words mantras used for more or less mundane purposes. Some of these mantras were definitely taken over by Buddhists and 'spiritualized'; you find a lot of them, with their associated visualizations, in the Buddhist Tantras, especially in Tibet. So no doubt Buddhism did take over a lot of material, not exactly from Hinduism, which hardly existed in the modern sense in those days, but from the Indian ethnic religion and folklore.

It's rather as if Christianity, on coming to the West from Palestine, had incorporated the Greek and Roman gods and goddesses, the village sprites and so on. In a sense, of course, it sometimes did: mythological figures do appear, heavily disguised, as Christian saints – or sometimes not so heavily disguised. Some saints just had the names of pagan gods with 'Saint' put before them – Saint Dionysus, for instance.

So is it possible to trace a historical development of Buddhist mantras?
I doubt it very much, for the simple reason that we do not have the information to do it. Don't forget that Indian history, including religious history, is very poorly documented indeed.

How is it that mantras can spark off a particular quality? Do they just gather around them a number of associations, or is there something in the mantra itself – or is it impossible to say?
It is probably impossible to say what exactly happens, but there is no doubt that each mantra has a very special, almost indefinable quality which is quite distinctive and recognizable. You could try to see what happens when you recite a mantra, especially one you have not recited before.

THE SUDDEN METHOD

In contrasting the myth of the return journey and the parable of the jewel in the lotus, you talk about how the guru chooses either the sudden or the gradual approach depending on the temperament of the pupil. Is it useful for us to think in these terms?
No. I think that such terms can be misleading, and I no longer use them. To paraphrase Huineng's words in the *Platform Sūtra*,[131] there is no such thing as the quick path and the slow path. It is simply that some attain Enlightenment more quickly than others. Some practise more intensively than others, and therefore cover the same psychological and spiritual ground more quickly.

Sometimes people understand the short path to mean a path that somehow cuts out all the long and difficult preliminary stages, but that is wishful thinking. All the stages must be traversed, because they are determined by the very conditions under which development of any kind takes place. You can't make a growing plant jump certain stages of development, but by giving it extra nourishment you may cause it to grow more quickly.

Have any of your teachers used the 'sudden method' with you, confronting you with ultimate Reality?
I don't think that any of my teachers ever deliberately and consciously confronted me with an ultimate truth – perhaps their methods were

more subtle than that. Indeed, the matter is more subtle than it perhaps appears to be. Ultimate truth, after all, can be presented in any terms. You are presented with it every moment of your life. When you change the flowers in your room because you see that they are faded, you are confronted with the ultimate truth of impermanence. Sometimes, of course, life presents us with situations in which we are more likely than usual to confront ultimate truth. It confronts us when we are bereaved or suffer some other dreadful loss, when our health is seriously affected, when we suddenly realize something unpleasant about ourselves for the first time, or see that we have been tormenting ourselves about something unnecessarily.

And have you ever used the 'sudden method' yourself?
Well, I have sometimes put a certain point to somebody, or brought them up against a certain fact about themselves, a little more sharply than usual. You do have to be quite careful, because some people take things very seriously, and a few words spoken quite lightly and casually can have a devastating effect. If you do feel that you have said something quite clearly, but quite gently, to someone a number of times, and they don't seem to have grasped the point, you may need to put it a little more strongly or directly. It depends on how well you know them, and what degree of confidence they have in you.

ARCHETYPAL IMAGERY

I am struck by the contrast between the highly idealized visionary landscapes of the White Lotus Sūtra*'s Pure Land, with the flat land, the jewel trees, the golden cords, and so on, and the concrete nature of the imagery of much Chinese and Japanese art and literature, where mountains, lakes, and natural incidents like frogs jumping into ponds become central subjects. Do these differences spring from different levels of cultural experience, from different temperaments, or from cultural differences?*
You are speaking of one particular type of Chinese and Japanese art. There is another kind which endeavours to illustrate the Pure Land quite literally, with all the jewel trees and so on. I think the kind of art you are thinking of is distinctively a product of the Zen tradition. It's just a different way of looking at things, not necessarily more or

less profound, but perhaps appealing to some temperaments more than others. Personally I prefer the more literal representations of the Pure Land, with all the jewel trees and singing birds and gold and silver ornaments, which seem to have a more 'archetypal' (for want of a better term) quality.

Colours, especially jewel-like colours, do have a certain psychological and spiritual significance of their own; they do seem to give you some intimation of the higher, more archetypal levels of existence, something that the more naturalistic type of Japanese and Chinese art is rarely able to do. You could say that this naturalistic type of art tries to penetrate beyond the archetypal into the sphere of reality itself; and it can sometimes do that, but only in the hands of a very great artist who is also a Zen master. Otherwise it all falls rather flat: you have just got a picture of a nice little tree by a nice little stream, with a nice little monk sitting underneath it on a nice little rock. That kind of art is rather hit or miss; instead of going beyond the archetypal plane into the transcendental, it sometimes falls short even of the archetypal.

THE NEED FOR ELOQUENCE

Is it significant that it is Pūrṇa, who is renowned for his eloquence, who will be the Buddha of this world once it is purified? Could the sūtra *be saying that what this world needs more than anything is people who are eloquent in the teaching of the Dharma?*

This reminds me of something written by Dr Ambedkar, the leader of the ex-Untouchables in India who led their conversion to Buddhism. Writing about the decline of religion he said, in effect, that a religion will decline if it doesn't have universally valid principles, or if it doesn't have simple principles that can be easily explained to a lot of people. Then, he went on to say, a religion will decline if it doesn't have eloquent and capable preachers.[132] Your principles may be as universally valid as you like, they may be as simple as you like, but you will still need human beings to put them across. No doubt the word 'eloquent' is not to be taken too literally; the point is to be able to communicate effectively, whether the language you use is flowery or simple. Unless you have preachers, living human beings, who can communicate in this way – whether personally or through the books they write – your principles, however universal and simple they are, are just not going to get across, and the religion will decline, or perhaps not even get started at all.

So eloquence is needed in any world – certainly in any world in any way resembling our own – in which the Dharma is being propagated. Of course, there are other worlds where the Dharma is communicated by other means – through beautiful odours, for example.[133]

HOW THE ABSTRACT BECOMES CONCRETE

You say that oṃ *is the abstract universal,* hūṃ *is the concrete universal, and the jewel in the lotus shows how the abstract becomes concrete. Can you say a bit more about this?*

Well, an abstract universal is a universal which is a concept without any definite content, whereas a concrete universal is a universal which is not separable from its various particular instances, and which expresses itself through them. These are terms of Hegelian philosophy[134] which have passed into general currency to some extent.

But perhaps we can approach it from a slightly different angle. For instance, take the concept of impermanence. When we first come across it, this is likely to be just an abstract universal as far as we are concerned. We accept it in theory, but we haven't yet embodied it in our lives. The more we actually embody it in all the different activities of our lives, the more concrete that particular universal becomes. Our realization of the concept of impermanence is transformed from a purely intellectual understanding into something which we understand through our actual experience. Of course, don't take this too literally – it is not that *oṃ* only represents an intellectual understanding. But at one level the mantra does represent that type of transition. To use Buddhist terms, it is really a transformation of *vijñāna* into *jñāna* or *prajñā*.[135]

As for the jewel and the lotus, these two between them fully represent the path, which is a process of the unfolding of potentiality through which abstract understanding is transformed into concrete realization.

Could the symbol also relate to the three levels of wisdom: hearing, reflecting, and meditating?[136]

Yes indeed, because what you merely hear, what you know in the ordinary abstract way, is quite different from *prajñā*, which is a matter of actual insight and realization. The intermediate stage is the stage of reflection, the stage of turning the knowledge over in your mind, incorporating it, making it your own.

QUESTIONS OF VISUALIZATION

You describe, at least in outline, the Avalokiteśvara visualization practice. I thought that such practices were generally not to be discussed with anyone who does not actually do the practice?
Well, the description of the image is just like looking at a picture. It is not intended as an initiation or anything like that; it is just a conjuring up of an inspiring image, and should be taken in that spirit. Any little details of the practice added just fill out the picture.

The particular practice you described involves visualizing yourself as Avalokiteśvara, but in some other practices one visualizes the bodhisattva in front of one. Is there any principle behind this distinction?
The broad principle to bear in mind is that inasmuch as your experience is bifurcated into a subject and an object, any spiritual practice that you do is conditioned by those limits. If you visualize, say, Avalokiteśvara, as being outside yourself, that is only half the truth, or not even half the truth. You also have to visualize him within you. You have to visualize Avalokiteśvara as the subject as well as the object, and eventually you need to be able to bring the two together. Whether you start with the subjective pole or the objective pole is perhaps a matter of temperament, but there is both a subject and an object in your experience, and both have to be transformed. When you are visualizing Avalokiteśvara out there, you must remember that he is also in here; and when you are visualizing him in here, you must remember that he is also out there. This is the basic principle you need to bear in mind.

Is it really a good idea to continue visualizing yourself as the bodhisattva when you have finished doing the meditation practice? Might it not be a bit fanciful?
Well, if you haven't transformed yourself into the bodhisattva in the course of the practice, it is bound to be fanciful. But there is nothing wrong with thinking of yourself as the bodhisattva and trying to behave accordingly even if you have not realized yourself as the bodhisattva in the meditation. Whether it is advisable or not depends on the

circumstances you are in. I think that it is only advisable to try to sustain the feeling that you are the bodhisattva if your circumstances are very propitious. If you were to try it in your everyday life, it would probably set up too great a tension between what you were trying to do and the circumstances in which you were trying to do it.

8
THE ARCHETYPE OF THE DIVINE HEALER

In this study of the parables, myths, and symbols of the *White Lotus Sūtra*, I have nowhere defined the terms parable, myth, and symbol; this has been quite deliberate. It suits the nature of parables, myths, and symbols to allow their nature to emerge not from any formal definition but rather from concrete examples. We have not been trying to understand the parables, myths, and symbols intellectually, with our conscious minds; we have rather sought to experience them and allow them to speak to our hidden, even secret, depths.

Now we come to something similar, but not quite the same: an archetype, the archetype of the Divine Healer. And again I will not try to define the term 'archetype'. It has been popularized in recent decades through the work of Jung and his followers, but it is noticeable that in his writings about archetypes, Jung himself is chary of giving a formal clear-cut definition of what the archetype is. Sometimes he seems to say one thing, and sometimes another. So, following in his footsteps, I am not going to define either archetypes in general or the archetype with which we are particularly concerned, the archetype of the Divine Healer. Instead, through different examples, we will attempt to conjure up, to call forth, different manifestations of this archetype, and even try to see them before our inner eyes.

First of all we are going to conjure up an archetype from ancient Egypt. Thoth is a very complex figure, like all the major Egyptian deities. He is a lunar divinity, associated with the moon rather than with the sun, and he is represented with a human body and a bird head, the head of the sacred Egyptian bird, the ibis, with a long curved bill. Thoth's ibis head is sometimes surmounted by a lunar crescent, and sometimes by a crescent with a lunar disc superimposed upon it – the full moon and the crescent moon together. In a sense Thoth is the wisest and the most intelligent of all the gods, and in a sense he is the best. He is the inventor of all arts and sciences, and indeed the originator of culture and civilization. He is especially the inventor of writing, in this case of hieroglyphic writing, and he is also the inventor of medicine. He is the Divine Healer of the Egyptian pantheon.

In Egyptian mythology and legend, Thoth is especially associated with the goddess Isis and the gods Osiris and Horus, who constitute a well-known trinity. In some legends Thoth appears as Osiris' vizier and scribe. Even after Osiris' tragic death at the hands of the forces of darkness, Thoth remained faithful to his memory, helping Isis to purify Osiris' dismembered body. When Horus, the infant son of Isis and Osiris, was stung by a great black scorpion, it was Thoth, the Divine Healer, who drove out the poison from the bite. Later on Thoth is said to have cured Horus of a tumour and healed a wound inflicted on the god Set.

The ancient Greeks considered Hermes, the messenger of the gods, to be the counterpart of Thoth in their own mythology, but Thoth is much more like the Greek divinity Apollo. Admittedly Thoth is a lunar divinity whereas Apollo is a solar divinity, but Apollo, like Thoth, is the patron of the arts and the sciences, and of music and poetry in all their forms, and Apollo too is associated with the divine art of healing. In the case of Apollo this is apparently one of the consequences of his being a solar divinity, because sunlight is necessary to health and healing.

Although Apollo has these healing attributes, however, the real Greek god of healing is Asklepios, who, significantly, is the son of Apollo by a mortal maiden, and therefore a demigod. Asklepios is sometimes represented in the form of a serpent, but he is more usually depicted as a tall, well-built, middle-aged man with a noble, dignified appearance, and an extremely wise and compassionate expression. Some of the images of Asklepios are among the most impressive, from a spiritual point of view, that have come down to us from classical antiquity. We know that the Gandhāran image of the Buddha was modelled on the Graeco-Roman Apollo, who was usually represented in the form of a beautiful young man in the prime of life, but perhaps the Gandhāran artists might have achieved even more impressive results if they had used the figure of Asklepios as a model.[137]

In Greek legend there are many stories of the miraculous cures wrought by Asklepios. It is even reported that his divine gift of healing was so great that he could not only restore the sick to health, but even bring the dead back to life. Not unnaturally, the King of the Dead became angry, because fewer and fewer people were arriving in his realm, and even those who arrived there were being rudely plucked back by Asklepios. So the King of the Dead went to Zeus, the King of the Gods, and complained bitterly that he was being deprived of his dues; and Zeus, who apparently had just one way of settling things, hurled a thunderbolt – and that was the end of Asklepios. Apollo, Asklepios' father, was furious, and slew the Cyclops who had forged the thunderbolt with which Zeus had destroyed Asklepios. Zeus then punished Apollo, of course, and so it went on, just as it does on Earth among human beings.

Asklepios was worshipped a good deal in ancient Greece; the important and powerful cult of this Divine Healer resulted in the many statues of him which have survived down to the present time. What is particularly interesting about the cult of Asklepios is that it was both a religion and also a system of therapeutics. The doctors in ancient Greece were priests of Asklepios, and served at a number of celebrated sanctuaries which were both centres of religious worship and centres of healing. These great sanctuaries were built outside towns, on sites which were especially healthy, and there people used to go for treatment and worship, because the two were the same.

Upon your arrival at a sanctuary as a patient you would be ceremonially purified, so as to be free from sin, and then given a series of baths. You would be required to abstain completely from food, and you would offer up sacrifice to Asklepios. Then, on a night appointed by the priest-physicians, you would sleep in the temple, perhaps with your head near the feet of the image of Asklepios. After all this preparation, and no doubt with great faith and expectation in your heart, and great hopes of a cure from disease, in the midst of your sleep you would have a dream in which Asklepios himself would appear and give you some advice, either about your complaint or general advice. In the morning you would tell the dream to the attendant priests, and they would give treatment according to their interpretation of it.

A few years ago I had the opportunity of visiting the most famous of all these old sanctuaries, the sanctuary at Epidaurus. As I walked around the archaeological site, which was strewn with votive tablets offered by people who had been cured of their diseases all those thousands of years ago, I found, very much to my surprise, that the atmosphere of the place was truly remarkable. There was something calm, peaceful, positive, and wholesome in the air; one could well imagine that a great sanctuary of healing had been established on that spot.

The archetype of the Divine Healer also, of course, appears in Buddhism. In the Buddhist scriptures, both Pāli and Sanskrit, the Buddha has a number of titles. In English we almost invariably call him the Buddha, but in the original sources there are many other ways in which the Buddha is addressed or referred to – the Tathāgata, the Jina, Bhagavan, Lokajyeṣṭha, and so on. Among these titles is *Mahābhaiajya*. *Mahā* means 'great', and *bhaiajya* is 'physician', so *Mahābhaiajya* is the Great Physician. This is very significant, and suggests something that we ought never to forget: that human beings are most of the time, if not all the time, psychologically and spiritually sick, and in need of healing. The Buddha is the healer of the disease of humanity, and his teaching, the Dharma, is the medicine that he gives humanity to swallow. That medicine sometimes tastes bitter, but it is certainly efficacious.

A formula found in ancient Indian medical works analyses sickness and health in fourfold terms: disease, the cause of the disease, the state of being healthy, and the regimen leading to the state of good health. Now the four noble truths, those central teachings of Buddhism, are said by some scholars to be derived from this formula. The truth of suffering corresponds to the state of disease; the truth of the origin of suffering corresponds to the aetiology of the disease; the truth of the cessation of suffering, Nirvāṇa, corresponds to the state of being cured, of being made whole; and the truth of the way leading to the cessation of suffering corresponds to the regimen leading to a cure.

The Buddha's role as spiritual healer is stressed in a number of his teachings and parables. There is the parable of the man wounded by the poisoned arrow, in which the Buddha appears as the physician wishing to pluck the arrow of suffering from the poisoned wound of humanity.[138] The commentator Buddhaghosa went even further, saying quite tersely, even bluntly, 'The worldling is like a madman.' (The word used is *puthujjana*, which is usually translated 'worldling', and refers to ordinary people – that is to say, those who have not yet become Stream Entrants). We could guess that this simile was meant to suggest that everybody who is not at least a Stream Entrant is plain mad – not even just neurotic, or a little bit touched, but stark staring mad.[139] This implies that the Buddha is not just a doctor, but the world's best mental doctor; and his teaching could perhaps be described as transcendental psychotherapy.

As we have seen in considering Avalokiteśvara, the state of Enlightenment has a number of different aspects – a wisdom aspect, a compassion aspect, a power aspect, a purity aspect, and so on. In the same way Enlightenment has its healing aspect; it is just like a great balm dropping down upon the wounds of humanity. This healing aspect is personified in the figure of Bhaiṣajyarāja or Bhaiṣajyaguru, the King of Healing or Teacher of Healing, who appears sometimes as a bodhisattva, and sometimes as a Buddha. As a Buddha he is known as Vaiḍūryaprabha, which means 'azure radiance', or, translating very literally, the 'radiance of the semi-precious stone lapis lazuli'. In Tibetan Buddhist art this Buddha of Healing is depicted more or less in the same way as Śākyamuni Buddha, but with a deep brilliant blue complexion rather than a golden one. He wears the monastic robe like Śākyamuni, and in his hand he bears as his distinctive emblem an *amlaki* fruit. Translators of Sanskrit and Tibetan texts call this fruit an emblematic myrobalan – that's apparently its botanical name. I must confess that I have never come across a myrobalan, whether emblematic or otherwise, or, come to that, an *amlaki* fruit, but this particular fruit is renowned in Indian legend for its medicinal properties, so it is appropriate that it is the distinctive badge of this Buddha or bodhisattva.

In Tibetan Buddhism Bhaiṣajyarāja has eight forms, known as the eight Medicine Buddhas, a very popular set sometimes to be seen in Tibetan painted scrolls, with a main central figure and around him the seven subsidiary forms. As in ancient Greece, there is in Tibet, or at least there was until very recently, a connection between religion and medicine, and many lamas were physicians. Near Lhasa there were special medical monasteries where medical lamas received their training. Tibetan medicine is in a sense a continuation of the Indian system of medicine which is called *āyurveda*. *Āyur* is 'life', and *veda* means 'science', so in India medicine is traditionally called 'the science of life' – not just the science of curing disease, but the science of how to live healthily, how to live physically in the best possible way. It calls to mind the system of treatment in the ancient days in China, when you paid your doctor when you were well, and stopped paying him when you fell sick.

Tibetan Buddhist medicine includes Chinese elements such as acupuncture. It also makes extensive use of consecrated pills of various kinds, and of mantras. Not only in Tibet but in many parts of the Buddhist world the monks traditionally dabble – in many cases that is the only word – in medicine, sometimes successfully, sometimes, unfortunately, not so successfully. Usually, whether in Tibet or Sri Lanka, China or Burma, the treatment is a combination of herbal remedies, often very efficacious, and faith healing or what we might call spiritual healing. In this respect traditional Buddhist medicine in the East, especially in Tibet, is not unlike that of the priests of Asklepios in the ancient Western world.

Bhaiṣajyarāja or Bhaiṣajyaguru, the King or Guru of Healing, appears as a Buddha, that is to say in Buddha form, in a canonical text that bears his name.[140] In this *sūtra* the Buddha relates to Ānanda how ages and ages ago Bhaiṣajyarāja made twelve great vows, as a result of which he established in the East what is traditionally known as a Pure Land, where all beings who came to be born there would live free from disease. Bhaiṣajyarāja appears in bodhisattva form in the *White Lotus Sūtra*, in chapters 10, 12, and 22 (or 23 in the Chinese version). In chapter 10 he takes no active part, but is simply the bodhisattva through whom the Buddha Śākyamuni addresses the eighty thousand great leaders of the assembly on the importance of preserving the *White Lotus Sūtra*. In chapter 12 Bhaiṣajyarāja is one of the two bodhisattvas who assure the Buddha that after his *parinirvāṇa* they will propagate the *White Lotus Sūtra* amongst all sentient beings in all directions of space.

Having played a very minor role in these two chapters, in chapter 22 Bhaiṣajyarāja moves to the centre of the stage. This chapter is not, strictly speaking, a part of the drama of cosmic Enlightenment; like the Avalokiteśvara chapter, it probably represents an incorporation into the *sūtra* of independent, possibly later, material. Traditionally, however, this chapter does form part of the *sūtra*, and it is of interest for a number of reasons. In it a certain bodhisattva asks the Buddha about Bhaiṣajyarāja, the King of Healing, and the Buddha tells his story. He tells it at some length, so we will content ourselves with just a few details.[141]

In the remote past, ages and ages ago, Bhaiṣajyarāja was the disciple of a Buddha called Radiance of the Sun and the Moon. This ancient Buddha preached the *White Lotus Sūtra*, and Bhaiṣajyarāja was greatly delighted by it. Overwhelmed with joy, he wanted to express his gratitude to Radiance of the Sun and the Moon in an extraordinary and unprecedented manner. He thought, 'Everybody offers flowers, incense, flags, decorations, and money. What can I offer that is most precious, that is most dear, to which I am most attached?' And at that moment, in a flash of inspiration, he decided to sacrifice his own body.

He did not act impulsively, but prepared himself by drinking gallons of scented oil until his whole body exuded fragrance. Soaking his robes in oil as well, he then set fire to himself by spontaneous combustion, and burned like a lamp for twelve thousand years in honour of the Buddha, until he eventually died. When he was reborn and grew up, the Buddha Radiance of the Sun and the Moon, in whose honour he had burned himself, was still alive and still preaching. Bhaiṣajyarāja became his chief disciple, and after the *parinirvāṇa* of that Buddha he superintended his cremation, attended to all the ceremonies, and erected for his relics eighty-four thousand stupas. Having erected eighty-four thousand stupas, most people would think that that was quite enough even for a Buddha, but this particular bodhisattva still wanted to do something more. This time he set fire to his two arms, which burned for seventy-two thousand years. This was the bodhisattva who is now Bhaiṣajyarāja.

According to this chapter, which is not universally accepted as canonical, the Buddha says that if you worship a stupa by burning a hand, a finger, or even a toe, that is more meritorious than offering all your possessions. This may seem a shocking note to strike, and may even sound rather un-Buddhistic. After all, the Buddha is supposed to have said in his very first discourse, 'Avoid extremes. Don't inflict suffering on yourself. Don't practise either self-mortification or self-indulgence. Follow a middle path.' If we take it at face value, it seems that in this chapter the Buddha himself has strayed away, at least in precept, from the middle way.

At the same time the idea of offering oneself up as a sacrifice in this way may have a familiar ring. It is reminiscent of the cases of those Vietnamese monks who some years ago burned themselves in Vietnam. I was in India at the time, and I remember seeing pictures of these monks burning themselves. One particularly impressive colour picture depicted an old monk sitting cross-legged in the open street. His whole body was blazing – apparently he had soaked himself in petrol – but he was just sitting there perfectly upright, with calm features, as though he was meditating. The old man left a letter behind saying why he was doing this, and apparently carried it out completely self-possessed, calm, and mindful.[142]

If you heard about this incident or others – there were seven altogether, six monks and one nun – you may have wondered why they set themselves on fire in this way. The reason was simple. They did it because they wanted to draw attention to the fact that in Vietnam there was no religious freedom for Buddhists. In those days there was a Roman Catholic regime in Vietnam, and Buddhism, though it was the religion of the majority of the people, was practically prohibited. I came to know quite a lot about the situation because at the time I had staying with me in Kalimpong a number of Vietnamese monks. I had in fact become aware of the situation in Vietnam some time earlier when one of the monks translated into Vietnamese one of my books, a short biography of Anagarika Dharmapala, the founder of the Maha Bodhi Society and the reviver of Buddhism in modern India.[143] The Vietnamese monk told me that when he went back to Vietnam in a few months time he would get it printed and published. When I saw him again about six months later I naturally enquired about his translation of my book, and he said, 'I'm sorry to tell you it could not be published. I'm afraid the local Catholic bishop has prohibited it. We're not free in our own country. Buddhism is the traditional religion, but we're not free.'

Some time later, the Buddhists in Saigon wanted to celebrate the Buddha's birthday, but they were refused permission by the Catholic authorities. They were not even given permission to fly the Buddhist flag, and that upset them because only a few weeks earlier the Cardinal Archbishop's birthday had been celebrated and the Vatican flag was flying everywhere. All the major educational institutions were Catholic, and admission required conversion to Catholicism. These monks felt that the only way they could protest against the systematic discouragement, or even persecution, of Buddhism by the regime was to take the dramatic action of sacrificing themselves. In this way they would draw the attention of the whole world to the fact that Buddhism was suppressed and persecuted in Vietnam by the dominant Catholic minority.

The ideological background, even the spiritual background, of their action was provided by this chapter of the *White Lotus Sūtra*. Vietnamese Buddhism, though we don't hear much about it, is a singular and distinctive form of Buddhism. It combines two major Chinese forms of Buddhism: Chan (which we know better as Zen) and Pure Land Buddhism, which we know by the Japanese term Shin. And not only is the *White Lotus Sūtra* highly honoured in Buddhist China and its cultural dependencies – including Korea, Japan, and Vietnam – but in China and Vietnam monks even go so far as to emulate, symbolically, the self-immolation of Bhaiṣajyarāja. On the crowns of the shaven heads of Chinese and Vietnamese monks can be seen a number of scars which show where, at the time of their Bodhisattva ordination, pellets of perfumed wax were placed on their heads and lit. During this procedure, mantras and prayers are chanted loudly, and the monks kneel with their crowns as it were on fire while five or seven pellets of wax burn down into the scalp. Some say that it is very painful, but they bear the pain, clenching their fists and trying to concentrate on the mantras. Some say they do not feel anything at all. This ritual, from which every Vietnamese or Chinese monk and nun bears the scars, derives from this particular chapter of the *White Lotus Sūtra*.

When I was in India I knew a Chinese monk who used to burn himself all the time. He lived at Kuśinagara, the place of the Buddha's death. He spent all his time up a tree – he lived on a little platform, and people brought him food. Every few days he would put a candle on his arm or on some other part of his body, light it, and let it burn down into the flesh. He was absolutely covered with burns. I'm not saying that this was very Buddhistic; in fact, the local Buddhists weren't really happy about what he was doing – they thought he was going to extremes. But he was very highly venerated by all the Hindus in the surrounding villages. They thought he was a really holy man, and they weren't so impressed by the other Buddhist monks, who didn't burn themselves in this way.

Un-Buddhistic as it may appear to be, the form that the protest of those Vietnamese monks took was not arbitrary, but can be understood against a background of the Chinese Buddhist tradition, which includes the *White Lotus Sūtra*. And we can learn something from their action.

It is a reminder to us that we should be prepared even to sacrifice our lives for the Dharma if necessary. It is very easy for us to forget this because, frankly, we have it so easy. In some countries today it is very difficult to follow a religion (using the term 'religion' just for the sake of convenience). People are driven underground and live in fear of a knock on the door. Here, however, we can follow anything we like – this religion, that religion, no religion, do as we please – and we do not always appreciate our good fortune. Not appreciating the rights that we enjoy, we become lazy, even indifferent. We are not always aware that under certain circumstances we could be placed in a situation where we would have to choose between our religion and death. Perhaps this is the real meaning of this Bhaiṣajyarāja chapter of the *White Lotus Sūtra*, whether or not it is a later incorporation. It really asks whether we are prepared, if circumstances require it, even to give our lives for the sake of the spiritual principles that we believe in. It is not a question of throwing away our life, of making some grand, spectacular, theatrical gesture, but rather of being prepared to stick to our principles even at the cost of life itself.

To move from general considerations of the symbolism of healing to the parable of the good physician itself, this occurs in chapter 15 of the *sūtra* (chapter 16 of the Chinese version), the chapter which constitutes the climax of the whole drama of cosmic Enlightenment. To set the scene, what has just happened (in the previous chapter) is the appearance from the space below the earth – accompanied by a great trembling and quaking throughout the universe – of a great host of irreversible bodhisattvas. They greet the Buddha Śākyamuni as their teacher, and he greets them as his sons, his disciples. The whole assembly is amazed, and they murmur among themselves, 'The Buddha gained Enlightenment only forty years ago. How could he possibly have trained such an incalculable host of universal bodhisattvas in such a short space of time? Not only that, but some of them belong to past ages and other world systems.' They just cannot understand how all these irreversible bodhisattvas who have suddenly appeared can be the Buddha Śākyamuni's disciples.

In reply to these doubts the Buddha says that in fact he did not gain Enlightenment just forty years ago, but an incalculable number of millions of ages ago. This is his great revelation to his disciples, to the assembly, to humanity, of his eternal life, of the fact that in truth he transcends time; and with this revelation the *sūtra* is lifted from the plane of time up into the plane of eternity. It is not now Śākyamuni, the historical Buddha, speaking, but the *Buddha principle*. He says that he is eternally Enlightened, and is teaching all the time, in many different forms, in many different world systems, appearing now as Dīpaṅkara, now as Śākyamuni, and so on. He is not really born, and does not really attain Enlightenment – because Enlightenment is not limited to the plane of time.

He also says that he does not really die, but only appears to do so. It is just a physical body that disappears. The Buddha principle, the Buddha nature, does not disappear, but is eternally present even though invisible. The physical body disappears after a certain length of time not just because the Buddha has grown old, but for a definite reason: to encourage people. If he remained physically present all the time, the Buddha explains, people would not appreciate him and therefore would not follow his teaching. It is to illustrate this point that he tells the parable of the good physician:[144]

Once upon a time there was a good physician who was highly skilled in the art of healing and able to cure all sorts of diseases. He had many sons – ten, or twenty, or even a hundred. One day the good physician went away to a distant country, and while he was away his sons got into his dispensary and drank some of the medicines there, probably thinking that they would do them good. Those medicines happened to be poisonous, however, and having drunk them the sons became delirious and fell to the ground. As they rolled on the ground in their delirium, their father returned.

Not all the sons had been equally affected by the poison. Some had lost their senses completely, but others were still able to recognize their father and explain to him what had happened. The physician at once went out among the fields and hills, and gathered all sorts of herbs. These he pounded and mixed to prepare a medicine which he gave to his sons to bring them out of their delirium. The sons who were still sensible to some extent took the antidote and gradually recovered; but those who had lost their senses refused to take it. The poison had entered so deeply into their systems that they were almost incoherent, but the physician managed to gather from their ravings that they were very glad to see him and wanted to be cured, but that they utterly refused to take any more medicine.

Seeing that the situation was desperate, the physician decided that he had better play a trick. He said, 'Look here, my boys. I'm very old, and the time of my death is at hand. I'm going to go away to a distant place, but I'll leave my medicine with you. If you take it, you'll surely get better, but that's up to you.' And off he went, leaving the sons in their delirium. Some time later, a messenger came to the boys with the news that their father was dead. Believing this false message (which had of course been sent by the physician, who was alive and well), the sons were greatly distressed. 'Now our father is dead there is no hope of a cure,' they lamented. Their grief was such that at last they came to their senses. Realizing that the medicine that their father had left for them was good, they drank it and were cured. When he heard of their recovery, their father at once came back to show them that he was alive and well after all.

This is the parable of the good physician. The physician, of course, is the Buddha himself, and his ten, or twenty, or a hundred sons are sentient beings in general, and his disciples in particular. The good physician goes to a distant country, so that he is separated from his sons. This separation, like that of the son who goes away from his father in the myth of the return journey, and that of the drunken man who is separated from his friend in the parable of the drunkard and the jewel, represents the state of alienation from one's true nature.

The delirium into which the sons are thrown in their father's absence represents the negative emotions and distorted views of Reality by which we are overpowered. The fact that the sons become delirious through drinking their father's poisonous medicines suggests that, just as medicines do good if they are taken properly, so in the same way there is nothing wrong with the emotions, nothing wrong with thought, nothing wrong with the physical body; it is the way they are misused that causes the trouble. It is even the same with the Dharma. The Buddha leaves the Dharma with us, as it were, having preached it, and the Dharma is meant to help us, but if we misuse it, it can do us harm.

I remember meeting once on a retreat I was leading a woman who was delighted with one particular Buddhist teaching, the *anātman* doctrine. That was what had converted her to Buddhism. 'There's no self, there's no soul. There's no I, no me. I am not...' – she went on and on in this way. But after being on retreat for a few days, she came to me rather thoughtfully and said, 'I've just discovered something in my meditation. Now I know why I like the no-self doctrine. It's because I hate myself. I like to feel I'm not there. I like to cancel myself out. It's just an expression of my self-hatred.' As she discovered, she had been making the wrong use of that particular teaching.

Sometimes we ought perhaps to ask ourselves what it is in Buddhism that especially appeals to us. Is it all that glamorous ritual? All those lovely flowers on the shrine, those beautiful images, brightly polished and shining with Brasso? Is it all that meditation, where we can sit in a lovely, peaceful atmosphere and glide away into some nice, comfortable, dreamy, womb-like state? Or is it all those books we can read, and all those interesting intellectual things we can find out about the five *skandhas* and the eighty-four different types of consciousness – is that the sort of thing that we like? Is that what Buddhism means to us? Or is it all that beautiful Buddhist art, all those lovely thangkas which those poor dear lamas are still painting in India all along the Himalayas? We have to ask ourselves what it is that we like – and examine our motives.

The herbal medicine which the physician makes for his sons when he discovers their condition is, of course, the Dharma. The parable says that those of the sons who are not completely delirious are persuaded to take the medicine. Those who have lost their senses, however, although they say that they want to be cured, adamantly refuse to take the medicine. This is a very common situation. When I was in India, I used to meet lots of Hindus, and when a Hindu came to see me, far from making polite conversation about the weather, he would more often than not say, as though his whole heart was in it, 'Swamiji, please tell me how I can become Enlightened in this very life, right now if possible.' Such a request is of course highly unlikely to be serious; it is simply good religious form to ask this sort of question. The petitioner would be horrified if you really gave him an answer and expected him to follow your advice. People ask for a teaching, or a cure, but it is often the last thing they want.

This reminds me of a story from Japan about a devout old woman who was a follower of the Pure Land school. When she died, she did not want to be born again in this dirty, wicked old world. She wanted to be reborn in a beautiful purple and gold lotus flower in the Pure Land of the Buddha of Infinite Light, and just sit there for ages upon ages listening to the Buddha preaching. She wanted to die quickly and be reborn in this paradise, so her prayers and meditations had a certain urgency. Every morning she used to go to the temple and prostrate herself in front of a great image of the Buddha of Infinite Light, saying, 'Oh Lord Buddha, please take me quickly! Please take me away from this wicked world. I'm so fed up with it. I just want to die and be reborn in your Pure Land.'

There was a certain monk in that temple who noticed her behaviour – you could hardly help noticing it because she used to pray very loudly – and he decided to test out her fervent devotion. One day he stationed himself behind the image and waited for the old woman to come. Sure enough, she came in, bowed down and prostrated herself, and cried, 'Oh Buddha of Infinite Light, please take me. Please take me to your Pure Land.' And then a voice came booming out from behind the image, 'I shall take you now!' When she heard the Buddha's voice, as she thought it to be, the lady let out a shriek and fled, wailing, 'Won't the Buddha let me have my little joke?'

So, like the sons in the parable, people may say they want a cure, but they are not always ready to accept the remedy that is offered. Just as it was their grief at their father's supposed death that brought the sons to their senses, it often takes a painful experience to jolt us into awareness. The suggestion is that it is impossible for us to evolve through continual joy and happiness. There need not be pain and stress all the time, but there can be no serious development, no Higher Evolution, for the vast majority of people without some suffering to spur them on. This is not to say, unfortunately, that there is no suffering without development.

The main point of the parable of the good physician is quite simple. It says that we are most likely to develop when we realize that we are on our own. There is no God to save us, nor even any Buddha to help us. We are just potential individuals, and as such we can evolve only by our own efforts. By its very nature the Higher Evolution is an individual affair, involving an individual effort. It is not that we should have no contact with others who are similarly striving – such contact is rewarding, stimulating, and inspiring – but it is no substitute for our own effort.

The biggest compliment that a father can pay his children – a compliment which some fathers unfortunately are not willing to pay – is to leave them alone to make their own mistakes and garner their own experience. In the same way, the biggest compliment that the Buddha pays humanity is to disappear. If we want to find him, we will have to rise to a higher level, to the level of Eternity, on which he is always preaching this same *White Lotus Sūtra*. And how do we rise up to that higher level? If we truly open ourselves to the influence of the parables, myths, and symbols of the *White Lotus Sūtra*, and even allow ourselves to be carried away by them, we are sure to find ourselves in a different world – a world of timeless truth, a world of Buddhas and bodhisattvas. We will witness a great drama, the drama of cosmic Enlightenment – the drama which is going on all the time. Not only that: we ourselves are part of the drama. All living beings, in fact, are part of the drama. One day, remote as it may seem at present, we too shall be predicted by some divine voice to supreme Enlightenment.

We usually think that it is time to listen when somebody speaks, but the real time to listen is when somebody stops speaking. The real time to listen is when there is absolute silence. For if we listen to the silence long enough it will not be an ordinary sound that we shall hear. We shall hear the voice of the Buddha, the voice of the eternal Buddha, and then we shall experience for ourselves the parables, myths, and symbols of the *White Lotus Sūtra*.

8
QUESTIONS AND ANSWERS

THE INTERPRETATION OF DREAMS

The priests at Epidaurus diagnosed illness by means of the interpretation of dreams. Is this something we could make use of?
I am sure that dreams tell you about your mental state, and this must have some bearing on your physical state; but whether you can literally draw diagnoses and methods of cure from your dreams as the Greeks seem to have done I'm not so sure. Perhaps the key to it is interpretation. It is not enough just to have a dream; you need a priest or an interpreter to tell you what it means. I don't imagine that the Greeks used to wake up in the morning and say to the priest, 'Asklepios came to me and said I should take such-and-such medicine'; I don't think it was as straightforward as that. Whatever your dream was, the priest would not necessarily take it literally. Even if you dreamed of a small bottle, it wouldn't necessarily be a bottle of medicine – it could be a bottle of spring water, and the priest might prescribe that you should drink water or go and bathe in a spring. There would be an interaction between the surface meaning of the symbol and the priest's own knowledge of medicine.

Interpretation was similarly needed in the case of the Greek oracles, because the message as delivered by the priestess in trance was usually very obscure. There was a particular class of priest whose responsibility it was to interpret the oracle and write it down in Greek hexameters;

it was their interpretation that was really the oracle as far as you were concerned.

Of course, your dreams do put you in touch with a deeper level of your being. Sometimes you do know deep down what you ought to do to get better. For instance, although your rational mind is telling you that you are much too busy for a holiday, you may know that what you really need is a rest, sunshine, and fresh air.

WHAT DO YOU MEAN BY SACRIFICE?

The Buddha tells the story of how Bhaiṣajyarāja, in a previous life, burnt himself as an offering to the Buddha Radiance of the Sun and Moon. The Buddha goes on to say that if anyone burns even a finger or a toe in homage to a Buddha's stupa, that is more efficacious than giving whole cities, or one's own children, as offerings.[145] *Notwithstanding your interpretation of this episode, it still seems rather un-Buddhistic. Might this not be a case of an ethnic practice or attitude finding its way into Buddhism?*
If you take the practice literally, it certainly doesn't seem to be in accordance with the spirit of the Buddha's teaching, but I would prefer to take it more metaphorically. The context is highly legendary and mythical after all. I would rather take it as meaning that not only should you dedicate your whole life to the Dharma, but also you should be prepared to sacrifice your life for the sake of the Dharma, if necessary.

So there is no need for people to burn themselves?
According to one explanation, the practice of burning oneself at the time of ordination originated when Buddhism was at the height of its popularity in China. At that time so many people wanted to become monks and nuns because it was an easy living that some sort of trial became necessary.

That suggests a failure on the part of those already ordained. Why couldn't they just refuse to ordain people on spiritual grounds? I don't see how such sacrifice of human values to something abstract is defensible as a Buddhist practice.
Well, what do you mean by sacrifice? Is that rather barbaric practice

actually sacrifice in the Buddhist sense of the term? Indeed, is sacrifice part of Buddhist terminology at all? Surely Buddhism speaks in terms of growth and development, not of sacrifice. Sacrifice has connotations which are really rather un-Buddhistic.

Might the burning practice be intended as a reminder of the sufferings of all sentient beings?
I think that if your realization of the suffering of sentient beings is so limited that you need to be reminded of it in that way, you are probably not ready for spiritual or monastic life as yet.

Well, it could be symbolic of your realization of suffering.
Hardly symbolic – you do actually burn the cones of wax and it does actually hurt.

Isn't it a common part of the initiation rites of primitive societies that pain is inflicted on the people being initiated?
Yes, that's true. The explanation – which Gurdjieff, interestingly enough, spoke about at length – is that pain helps you to remember.[146] It creates such a strong impression on you that if you experience it at a certain important juncture in your life – a time when you are given certain important instructions, for example – you are much more likely to remember everything that is said.

Also, of course, in certain primitive communities the pain that is inflicted is a trial of strength or endurance. Among the Native Americans rites of this kind were very common. Such trials might be all right on the ethnic level, but are they really appropriate within the spiritual community? Surely you should be sensitive enough to suffering and mindful enough not to need to have whatever lessons you learn stamped on your memory with the help of an associated painful experience.

I certainly don't think any such practice should be taken up in the West. On the other hand, I don't want to encourage people to be too soft, too little able to bear hardship and suffering. All too often people tend to shrink even from inconvenience and discomfort, not to speak of pain and suffering. There is no point in inflicting pain and suffering on ourselves just to prove that we can bear it, but we should be able to bear hardship and even suffering for the sake of our own spiritual development, or for the sake of spreading the Dharma.

Are there any practices which we could *usefully take up to help us develop an ability to endure hardship?*
There are two kinds of activity which may help: activities which are both stamina-building and spiritually significant, and activities which develop powers of endurance but have no spiritual significance. For instance, you could decide to do a thousand prostrations every day during a solitary retreat, and that would both test your endurance and strengthen your feeling for Going for Refuge; but if you were just to go outside your retreat hut every day and spend an hour lifting up a big heavy stone and putting it down again, that would test your endurance but would have no particular spiritual significance.

Perhaps our daily routine should be such that we are strengthened rather than weakened. Not too many mornings lying in bed; not taking things too easily; not too many holidays; not too many visits to the cinema. Quite apart from the question of distraction, all this can be very weakening. Under modern conditions we can end up rather weak creatures if we're not careful. We very rarely have to work hard day after day, week after week, month after month, as many people in the world still have to do just to survive. We very rarely work for the Dharma with that sort of vigour and indifference to hardship and discomfort.

So should we be careful that our living situations do not become too comfortable?
It depends what you mean by comfort. The princess in the fairy tale was uncomfortable even though she had dozens and dozens of mattresses because there was one pea right at the bottom. Yes, our surroundings should be clean and tidy, aesthetically pleasing and convenient, but not so comfortable as to be luxurious. Simplicity is the key word: we need to avoid extravagance in all its forms. Spending a lot of money on food or clothes – or even haircuts – is just not necessary.

BALANCING ARCHETYPAL AND HISTORICAL

Did the emphasis of the Mahāyāna on the Buddha as representing the cosmic principle lead to a devaluation of the human state?
I am not sure about that, but the historical Buddha did rather get overshadowed by the archetypal Buddha in the Mahāyāna. I think it is very important to keep a balance – to be aware of both the historical

and the archetypal Buddha. After all, we do live mainly on the historical plane. If all our attention is concentrated on the archetypal Buddha but we are not actually living on the archetypal plane, we have an almost purely conceptual understanding of the archetypal, while being alienated to some extent from the historical, alienated from our actual position rooted in space and time, in history. If we are not really rooted in history, or don't appreciate the fact that we are rooted there, we are less likely to grow as human beings.

Buddhists in the West need to attempt the feat of being aware of the Buddha as a historical personality and at the same time having a glimpse of the archetypal Buddha which is above and beyond the historical. Mahāyāna Buddhists do tend to lose the historical in the archetypal – you meet Tibetan Buddhists who have never heard of Śākyamuni. On the other hand the Hīnayānists tend to lose the archetypal in the historical, not that they have a particularly vivid apprehension even of the historical Buddha.

Can we study the archetypal through the historical?
Yes. There aren't really two Buddhas. Apart from our own visualizations and higher spiritual perceptions, how do we know about the Buddha except through the human historical Buddha who appeared here 2,500 years ago? All the trans-historical Buddhas and bodhisattvas are extrapolations from that. There certainly is an archetypal, 'metaphysical' dimension, but until we can establish independent contact with it we are dependent upon our knowledge, within the framework of space and time, of the historical Buddha and his teachings, so far as we can make them out.

THE MESSAGE OF THE *SŪTRA*

If one was to study the sūtra *in more detail, what commentaries might be useful?*
Well, various commentaries have been published, but few of them throw much light on the significance of the *sūtra* as a whole. We are still awaiting proper studies of the *sūtra*, studies which take the *sūtra* seriously, both philosophically and spiritually.

I would question, though, whether one really needs much in the way of scholarly commentary. The *sūtra* is not philosophically abstruse.

You can approach it quite straightforwardly, with the help of your general knowledge of Buddhism; you don't need specialist knowledge to understand it. The *sūtra* doesn't contain much doctrine, after all. It is more a question of understanding the message of the *sūtra* as communicated through its overall drama, and its parables, myths, and symbols.

> World-Honored One! It is as if some man goes to an intimate friend's house, gets drunk, and falls asleep. Meanwhile his friend, having to go forth on official duty, ties a priceless jewel within his garment as a present, and departs. The man, being drunk and asleep, knows nothing of it. On arising he travels onward till he reaches some other country, where for food and clothing he expends much labour and effort, and undergoes exceedingly great hardship, and is content even if he can obtain but little. Later, his friend happens to meet him and speaks thus: 'Tut! Sir, how is it you have come to this for the sake of food and clothing? Wishing you to be in comfort and able to satisfy all your five senses, I formerly in such a year and month and on such a day tied a priceless jewel within your garment. Now as of old it is present there and you in ignorance are slaving and worrying to keep yourself alive. How very stupid! Go now and exchange that jewel for what you need and do whatever you will, free from all poverty and shortage.'[147]

The parable of the priceless jewel within the garment, as it may be called, occurs in the eighth chapter of the *Saddharma Puṇḍarīka* or 'White Lotus of the Real Truth' *Sūtra*, one of the most important and influential of all the Buddhist scriptures. This scripture, commonly known as the *White Lotus Sūtra*, opens with the Buddha entering into deep meditation and emitting from between his eyebrows a ray of light that illumines the entire universe. On emerging from this meditation, he explains to his disciples, who are present in large numbers, that truth in its fullness can be understood only by those who are spiritually enlightened. Others must approach it gradually, step by step, through a series of progressive stages. For this reason, he says, he has hitherto confined himself to giving teaching of a more elementary nature. Now, however, the time has come for him to disclose the higher teaching. Now he will reveal the final truth. To many of the disciples this announcement comes as quite a shock. They are convinced that what the Buddha has so far taught them is the whole truth and that they have nothing more to learn. Some of them, indeed, are so convinced of this that they actually withdraw from the assembly, unwilling to hear what the Buddha has to say. Those that remain are, however, in the majority, and it is to them that the Buddha proceeds to reveal the final truth.

He begins by explaining that the different spiritual ideals which he has hitherto taught are only temporary expedients, made necessary by the temperamental and spiritual differences existing among the disciples themselves. In reality there is only one spiritual ideal, the ideal which he himself exemplifies, the ideal of absolute spiritual altruism or Supreme Buddhahood. This ideal, which is the highest ideal, is the ultimate ideal for all the disciples, and in it all lesser ideals therefore eventually merge. These lesser ideals are the different forms of spiritual individualism, to which the disciples who have withdrawn from the assembly still adhere and which they are unwilling to give up. Spiritual individualism is the attitude of being concerned with the attainment of Enlightenment, or salvation, *for oneself alone*, without caring whether others attain Enlightenment or not. Absolute spiritual altruism, on the other hand, is the attitude of being concerned with the attainment of Enlightenment, or salvation, not simply for one's own benefit but for the benefit of all living beings. Such unbounded altruism does not, however, consist in devoting oneself first to one's own spiritual welfare and then to the spiritual welfare of others. Rather does it consist in the spontaneous compassionate activity that manifests when the very distinction between self and others is transcended or when, to speak less metaphysically, one realizes that one's own spiritual development is bound up with that of other people, even as theirs is bound up with one's own.

The Buddha's revelation that in reality there is only one spiritual ideal, the ideal of absolute spiritual altruism, and that this is the ultimate ideal for all, initially meets with a fully positive response from only one member of the assembly. This is Śāriputra, the wisest of the Buddha's disciples, whose only regret is that hitherto he has devoted himself to the lesser ideal of spiritual individualism. As though to console him, the Buddha explains that in a previous existence he had actually dedicated himself to the ideal of absolute spiritual altruism but that, forgetful of this fact, he had in his present existence wrongly imagined spiritual individualism to be the highest ideal. In a future existence, he assures him, he will realize the ideal of absolute spiritual altruism or Supreme Buddhahood and will lead countless other beings to the same lofty realization. This prediction the assembly receives with great rejoicing. Śāriputra then tells the Buddha that twelve hundred disciples who have realized the ideal of spiritual individualism, and who were under the impression that they had nothing more to learn, are greatly perplexed by what they have just heard. Would the Buddha please speak to them and explain the reason for the discrepancy between the old teaching and the new?

In response to Śāriputra's request, the Buddha not only reaffirms the provisional and instrumental nature of his teaching, the sole purpose of which is to lead living beings in the direction of absolute spiritual altruism, but also makes his meaning clear with the help of a lengthy parable, for, he says, 'intelligent people through a parable reach understanding.'[148] This parable is the famous parable of the burning house, according to which the Buddha induces living beings to forsake mundane existence in much the same way that a loving father induces his heedless children to come out of the house that is on fire – that is, by promising to give them the very things of which they happen to be most fond.[149] Such is the effect of the parable that four leading elders realize that it is not too late for them to give up the lesser ideal of spiritual individualism and dedicate themselves to the higher ideal of absolute spiritual altruism, and one of them, the ascetically-minded Mahākāśyapa, explains the joy that they all feel by relating a parable of his own that is, in fact, the Buddhist equivalent of St Luke's parable of the prodigal son.[150] The Buddha then relates five more parables, three of which serve to make the provisional and instrumental nature of his teaching still more clear, while the others are in answer to questions raised by Mahākāśyapa.

By this time the whole assembly is feeling the effect of the Buddha's words, and more and more disciples announce their acceptance of the new teaching. Among them are five hundred disciples who have realized the ideal of spiritual individualism and therefore thought that they had nothing more to learn. Now they have realized their mistake and the Buddha predicts that in a future existence they will all realize the ideal of absolute spiritual altruism or Buddhahood. Overjoyed, they bow down at his feet and like Mahākāśyapa give expression to their feelings in a parable. This parable is the parable of the priceless jewel within the garment, with which we are concerned this morning. Having related the parable, the five hundred 'converted' disciples explain that they themselves are the man who went to his friend's house, got drunk, and fell asleep, that the priceless jewel within their garment is the ideal of absolute spiritual altruism or Buddhahood, and that the friend who tied it there is the Buddha himself. In a previous existence he had taught them the ideal of absolute spiritual altruism, subsequently they had forgotten it, and he has just taught it to them again and reminded them of their original commitment. Now they no longer need trouble themselves with lesser ideals.

Such is the parable of the priceless jewel within the garment in the context of the *White Lotus Sūtra*. But, like most parables, the parable related by the five hundred 'converted' disciples has a more general – even a more universal – significance, both in the context of Buddhist tradition and in the context of the religious experience of mankind. To begin with, the parable taken as a whole is an expression of the overwhelming joy, wonder, thankfulness, and awe we experience on encountering a truth, a reality, that far transcends anything we have previously thought of or felt or imagined. At first, of course, we may shrink from that truth, or that reality, just as the Buddha's disciples did: we may even run away from it; for instinctively we feel that to encounter it will oblige us to give up our most cherished attitudes and beliefs or, at the very least, to modify them drastically. But if we can allow ourselves to encounter the new truth, or the as yet unimagined reality, if we can allow ourselves to accept it and embrace it, then our horizon will expand immeasurably, fresh vistas will open up for us in all directions, and we shall find that we have gained infinitely more than we gave up. Nor is that all. As the parable taken as a whole also makes clear, the new truth, though new, is at the same time strangely familiar. It is as though we have heard it before, known it before, accepted it before. Indeed, we feel that we *have* heard it before, *have* known it before, *have* accepted it before, just as the five hundred 'converted' disciples realize that the ideal of absolute spiritual altruism had in fact been their ideal for many previous existences, even though in their present existence they had, out of forgetfulness, wrongly thought otherwise for a while.

This paradoxical feeling of absolute newness and, at the same time, complete familiarity, is what many Western Buddhists experience, to a greater or a lesser extent, on the occasion of their first contact with Buddhism, whether that contact takes the form of reading a Buddhist book, seeing an image of the Buddha, or paying a visit to a Buddhist spiritual community. They feel not just that they have gained something infinitely precious but that they have *re*gained it. They feel that, after many wanderings, they have not only arrived at last at the gates of a glorious palace but also that, incredible as it seems, they have 'come home'. Some of them seek to account for this feeling of complete familiarity by saying that to them Buddhism represents what they have, in fact, always believed, though without fully realizing it. Others seek to account for it by saying, with varying degrees of conviction, that they must have been Buddhist in a previous existence. However they may account for the feeling, or even if they choose not to account for it at all, such Western Buddhists are naturally astonished when somebody tells them, as somebody occasionally does, even today, that he – or she – is unable to understand how it is possible for one born and brought up in the West, as a member of Western society and in the midst of Western culture, to accept an Eastern religion like Buddhism or, in other words, to accept a religion that is foreign and exotic. But such a thing *is* possible, as daily is becoming more evident, and the reason why it is possible is that the system of spiritual teaching and training that we call Buddhism is, in reality, neither Eastern nor Western, any more than man himself, in the depths of his being, is either Eastern or Western. When, therefore, the so-called Englishman or American or Spaniard accepts the so-called Eastern religion of Buddhism he accepts it, even as he encounters it, on a level where the terms Eastern and Western no longer have any meaning.

If a few words of personal confession may be permitted, this was very much my own experience forty-five years ago when, at the age of sixteen, I had my first real contact with Buddhism. That contact took place when I read two short but exceptionally profound Buddhist scriptures of great historical and spiritual significance. These were the *Diamond Sūtra*, a work belonging to the 'Perfection of Wisdom' corpus, and the *Sūtra of Wei Lang*, a collection of discourses by the first Chinese patriarch of the Chan or Zen school, who is better known as Huineng. Reading these two works and realizing that, although in one sense the truth they taught, or the reality they disclosed, was new to me, in another sense it was not new at all but strangely familiar. I certainly did not feel that I was accepting an Eastern religion, or a religion that was foreign and exotic. Rather I felt that contact with Buddhism was, at the same time, contact with the depths of my own being: that in knowing Buddhism I was knowing myself, and that in knowing myself I was knowing Buddhism.[151]

But from personal confession we must return to the parable of the priceless jewel within the garment, and in particular to the principal motifs or symbols of the parable. There are three of these: (1) the motif of drunkenness or sleep; (2) the motif of the other country; and (3) the motif of the priceless jewel. These are all universal motifs or symbols and, though at present we are concerned with them mainly in their Buddhist form, it would be strange if we were not sometimes reminded, however distantly, of the forms which they assume in other spiritual traditions.

The first motif to appear as the parable unfolds is that of drunkenness or sleep, which is one of the most important motifs in the whole range of Buddhist thought. Drunkenness or sleep, like blindness, represents the state of spiritual *un*awareness or ignorance. It represents a state in which we have no knowledge of any higher truth, or reality, or ideal, and in which we do not, perhaps, acknowledge the theoretical existence of such a truth or even regard it as a possibility. In other words, it represents a state of profound spiritual alienation. This state is, so to speak, the natural condition of man. Here we must not allow ourselves to be misled by an over-literal reading of the parable. In the parable, which of course is a kind of story, the drunkenness and the sleep have a definite point of origin. A man goes to an intimate friend's house, gets drunk, and falls asleep. The actions all take place in time. There is a period before he goes to the friend's house, a period before he gets drunk, a period before he falls asleep, and then there is a period after he has done these things. According to Buddhism, however, there is no point of ultimate origin for the state of spiritual unawareness or ignorance in which we are enthralled. However far back in time we may go, through however many births and deaths and rebirths, we shall never arrive at the point at which unawareness or ignorance began and prior to which 'we' existed in a state of pure awareness or knowledge. No such point can be perceived. Because no such point can be perceived (that is, perceived within the temporal order) the state of unawareness or ignorance is a primordial state, and because it is a primordial state it is spoken of as the natural condition of man.

But though unawareness or ignorance is a natural condition of man, that condition is not necessarily a permanent one. The fact that the ultimate point of origin of the state of unawareness or ignorance cannot be perceived does not mean that the state cannot be transcended. We transcend that state and achieve a state of pure awareness or knowledge when we 'wake up', here and now, to the higher truth, or reality, or ideal, and when we wake up to it – in the existential rather than the theoretical sense – as a result of following a progressive spiritual path that leads us from ethics to concentration and meditation and from concentration and meditation to clear vision or wisdom. Possible though it is to transcend the state of unawareness or ignorance, however, so long as it is *not* transcended there can be no escape from the suffering which is the inevitable concomitant of such a state. This brings us to the motif of the other country to which the man in the parable travels after leaving his friend's house and where 'for food and clothing he expends much labour and effort, and undergoes exceedingly great hardship, and is content even if he can obtain but little.'

The other country represents the objective counterpart of the state of spiritual alienation in which we eventually find ourselves as a result of our spiritual unawareness or ignorance. It represents the kind of world in which we live when we have no knowledge of any higher truth, or reality, or ideal, and do not, perhaps, acknowledge the theoretical existence of such a truth. Since the higher truth is the living water that nourishes the very roots of our being and enables us to grow – another of the *White Lotus Sūtra's* parables likens the Buddha's teaching to the rain – in the absence of that truth our world is a dry and barren place in which, scorched as it is by the heat of the passions, there is hardly any sign of spiritual life.[152] Thus the other country is the Waste Land, the land made desolate by the sickness or infirmity of its king,[153] as well as the 'far country' into which the prodigal son takes his journey, where he wastes his substance with riotous living, and where, when he has spent all, there arises a mighty famine and he begins to be in want.[154] Moreover, the world in which we live when we have no knowledge of any higher truth, or reality, or ideal, is a world in which we devote ourselves to inferior goals and in which, therefore, we experience no deep or lasting satisfaction. In the language of the parable, we expend much labour and effort for food and clothing, undergo exceedingly great hardship, and are content even if we can obtain but little – that is, little in comparison with what we could obtain if we followed the spiritual path and 'woke up' to the higher truth and all that it can give us. This is not to say that in devoting ourselves to our inferior goals we are doing what we really want to do. It is not to say that we are acting from a condition of genuine freedom. Rather do we expend much labour and effort, and undergo the exceeding great hardship, because we are slaves to the compulsion of our own unaware and ignorant desires. For this reason the other country is not only a Waste Land, not only a far country stricken by famine, but also a land of slavery and oppression. In other words the other country is Egypt. It is the Egypt of the biblical story of Israel's bondage and liberation,[155] and it is the Egypt of Gnostic symbolism. It is the land of sorcery into which, in the so-called 'Hymn of the Pearl', the son of the King of the East goes down in order to fetch the One Pearl which lies in the midst of the sea and where the Egyptians cunningly mix drink for him, and give him a taste of their meat, so that he forgets that he is a king's son, and forgets the Pearl.[156]

Since the other country is Egypt, it naturally follows that it is the foreign country; that is, the country that is not simply other than our own, in a neutral sense, but which is actually inimical and hostile to us. Thus the world in which we find ourselves living as a result of our spiritual alienation is a world in which we are foreigners and aliens, and the reason we are foreigners and aliens, even though we may wrongly think of ourselves as actually belonging to that world, is that without knowing it we have in our possession the means of overcoming the alienation and 'waking up' to the higher truth, or reality, or ideal, of achieving a state of pure awareness or knowledge, and of restoring ourselves to a world of spiritual abundance. This brings us to the priceless jewel, the third of the three motifs of the parable with which we are concerned this morning. The priceless jewel represents the higher truth, or reality, or ideal, as this is potentially existent within us. As such it is also the jewel-in-the-lotus of the famous Indo-Tibetan Buddhist mantra;[157] it is the grail of Arthurian legend, whether that grail be a crystal cup, a stone dish, or a magic cauldron; it is the philosopher's stone that transmutes everything into gold. It is also, perhaps, the piece of silver that the woman in the Lucan parable lost and for which she sought diligently until she found it.[158] In the content of the parable of the priceless jewel itself, of course, the priceless jewel represents the higher ideal of absolute spiritual altruism or Buddhahood to which the Buddha's disciples had originally dedicated themselves and which they had forgotten.

As in the case of the motif of drunkenness or sleep, however, we must not allow ourselves to be misled by an over-literal reading of the parable. The fact that the priceless jewel is tied within the man's garment does not mean that the truth, or reality, or ideal, which is potentially existent within us lies just below the surface of consciousness and is immediately accessible. It does not mean that a merely theoretical recognition of the fact that it is possible for us to achieve a state of pure awareness and knowledge is sufficient to make us actually 'wake up' to that state. In the parable itself the man's intimate friend tells him that the priceless jewel that he formerly tied within his garment is still present there. The 'exchanging' of the jewel represents the lengthy process of transforming the truth, or reality, or ideal, as potentially existent within us into that same truth as actually existent in all our thoughts, words, and deeds. It presents the process of following the spiritual path until such time as we succeed in 'waking up' as distinct from merely dreaming about waking up. The exchanging of the priceless jewel thus corresponds to the actual going in quest of the grail by the knights of the Round Table, to the alchemist's actual production of the philosopher's stone, and to the woman's actually lighting the candle and sweeping the house and searching diligently till she finds the lost piece of silver. Without this exchanging, this going in quest, this production, this searching diligently, there can be no doing 'whatever you will, free from all poverty and shortage,' no achievement of the grail, no transmutation of everything into gold, no finding of the lost piece of silver. Thus it is not enough for us simply to tell ourselves that we have the priceless jewel within our garment. We also have to exchange the jewel. It is not enough for us simply to believe that we are spiritually enlightened already, as some modern works on Zen Buddhism, with their ringing declarations of '*Look within; thou art Buddha!*' would appear to suggest. We also have to follow the spiritual path which, leading from ethics to concentration and meditation and from concentration and meditation to clear vision or wisdom, will enable us eventually to achieve a state of pure awareness or knowledge.

But if we must not allow ourselves to be misled by an over-literal reading of the parable of the priceless jewel, neither must we allow ourselves to be confused by an over-literal understanding of its profound modern analogues. In particular, we must beware of the confusion arising from an over-literal understanding of the highly secularized version of the jewel motif that has appeared among us in recent times (say within the last two hundred years) and which forms the basis of a good deal of modern thought, and it is to one aspect of this confusion that I would like to devote a few words before we conclude. According to this secularized version of the jewel motif, man is by nature fundamentally good, in the sense that he has a natural inclination to goodness and health and happiness. Provided we do not understand the terms 'good' and 'goodness' in too superficial and one-sided a manner (that is, in a manner that takes no account of man's distinctively spiritual possibilities), not much harm is done and our secularized version of the jewel motif will still bear some resemblance to its traditional prototype. Confusion arises when from the fact that man is by nature fundamentally good we conclude that it is only circumstances which prevent him from actually being so, particularly circumstances in the form of the social, economic, and political conditions under which he lives. This is to suggest, in effect, that just as in the parable the garment is external to the jewel tied within it, so the factors that prevent man from actually being good are external to him. The truth of the matter is that man comprises both jewel and garment, so to speak, and that – though the parable itself fails to mention this detail – the garment must be untied, that is, the jewel must be removed from the garment or the garment from the jewel before it is even possible for the man in the parable to take the jewel and exchange it for what he needs. The garment within which the priceless jewel is tied is, of course, the unawareness and ignorance that must be overcome before we can achieve the state of pure awareness or knowledge which, in a metaphysical rather than a psychological sense, we are or which, less misleadingly, is us, and we untie the jewel from

Transforming Self and World

THEMES FROM THE SŪTRA OF GOLDEN LIGHT

INTRODUCTION: THE GROWTH OF A MAHĀYĀNA SŪTRA

Most of us carry in our minds what we might call a model of the spiritual life, some image that conjures up what it means for us. Quite possibly we will tend to think in terms of development, growth, opening. We may even see in our mind's eye the unfolding petals of a flower. Perhaps for many of us this is the most helpful way of thinking about the spiritual life. But it is not the only way. We can also see the spiritual life, for example, in terms of transformation.

The word transformation suggests something radical, some fundamental change. Literally it means a change of form. But as a model for the spiritual life it means something much deeper and more thoroughgoing. It signifies a change of consciousness, a total shift in our being, a revolution that affects us from the depths to the heights of our individuality. It describes a *transition* from what is worldly to what is transcendental. It also means a death and a rebirth.

If we are honest with ourselves, if we allow ourselves to think and feel deeply, this is surely what we are looking for: to die and be reborn – but not necessarily in the flesh. What we seek is a withering of the roots of our being and a truly radical rebirth. We are fed up with ourselves as we are, with the self we have been stuck with for so long, perhaps for years upon years. We would like to trade it in for a pristine, brand new self, to emerge like a butterfly from the chrysalis of all our old conditions into an entirely new life of greater freedom and joy, greater awareness and spontaneity.

Not only are we tired of the old *self*. We are tired of the old *world* as well. We want to transform the world, so that it supports our spiritual growth and transformation at every step. We have had enough of political, social, and economic arrangements that do not allow people a decent human life, let alone a life that goes beyond this modest ideal. We are weary of the whole culture of consumerism and possessiveness. We are sometimes tired, too, of the arts within our civilization, when they express the sick mind and the diseased imagination. We want everything to be made new.

This transformation of the self and of the world is what the Buddhist way of life is about. It is also what the *Sūtra of Golden Light*[160] is about, for the golden light is what transforms the self and transforms the world. But where does this light come from? It is not enough to say that it is a spiritual light, for it is more than this. It is, we may say, a *transcendental* light. It is transcendental in the traditional Buddhist sense of the *lokuttara*: that which is beyond the world, beyond the mundane, beyond all that is conditioned. It is therefore without beginning and without end. It does not shine forth from anything – from any particular place, any particular direction – though it may appear to do so, or even be spoken of as doing so. We may call it the light of truth, the light of reality, the light of the Buddha – but even that does not go far enough. It is the light which *is* the truth, *is* reality, *is* the Buddha, and as we examine this text we shall be laying ourselves open to this golden light, for it suffuses the whole of this most popular of all Mahāyāna *sūtras*.

Being a Mahāyāna *sūtra*, the *Sūtra of Golden Light* exemplifies many of the characteristics of Mahāyāna Buddhism – as well as possessing certain special features of its own. The Mahāyāna, which is one of the three major historical forms of Indian Buddhism, is not a particular sect or school of Buddhism, but rather a particular attitude to Buddhism. It arose as a movement of reaction against a narrow interpretation of the letter of the Buddha's teachings, seeking to reconnect with the original spirit of those teachings. This movement has swept through Buddhist history, affecting all aspects of religious, artistic, and even social life. Transcending the immediate historical context, going beyond the reaction which led to its arising, the Mahāyāna has developed a positive spiritual character of its own. Lama Govinda captures this distinctive character in a single phrase: universal perspective.[161]

It is its universal perspective which gives the Mahāyāna its name. Mahāyāna literally means 'great way', and it is so called because it is the way to Enlightenment for a great number of people, in fact for all sentient beings. So the Mahāyāṇa Buddhist doesn't think only in terms of his or her own personal spiritual development. There is no question of gaining Enlightenment for oneself and leaving everybody else to fend for themselves. The Mahāyāna vision is that all men and women can develop spiritually, and that helping them to do so is an intrinsic part of the spiritual life. For this reason, the Mahāyāna stresses the ideal of the bodhisattva. As the word implies (it literally means 'one who is bent on Enlightenment'), the bodhisattva is one who has dedicated himself to the highest spiritual realization. But he is dedicated to it not for his own sake alone, but for that of all living beings whatsoever. He expresses this dedication and determination by taking four great vows:

> However innumerable beings are, I vow to save them.
> However inexhaustible the passions are, I vow to extinguish them.
> However immeasurable the Dharmas are, I vow to master them.
> However incomparable the Buddha-truth is, I vow to attain it.[162]

It may be traditional to speak of the bodhisattva as a person, but if we really try to get a feeling for these vows, we will realize that we cannot think of a bodhisattva in the same sort of way as we think of an ordinary man or woman. We cannot think of a bodhisattva as simply an extraordinary individual. The bodhisattva is not literally a person at all. At least in the more advanced stages of his spiritual career, he transcends individual personality altogether to become what we might call a 'suprapersonal' stream of spiritual energy. But however lofty the spiritual attainment of the bodhisattva may be, Mahāyāna Buddhism encourages absolutely everybody to make that their aim. That is to say, it encourages every single person to co-operate in what it describes as the great work of universal transformation. The bodhisattva ideal is therefore universal in its aim, which is nothing less than supreme Buddhahood; it is universal in its scope, which encompasses all sentient beings; and it is universal in its frame of reference, which is infinite space and boundless time. It is a supremely heroic aspiration.[163]

But, of course, not everybody wants to be a hero. Even among the followers of the Mahāyāna, not everybody wants to be a bodhisattva.

Strange to say, some people are quite reluctant to gain supreme Buddhahood! It is therefore part of the task of the bodhisattva to offer them a helping hand – not to say a crutch or two. To do this the bodhisattva has to assemble a toolkit of what are technically called 'skilful means': an array of methods for helping people spiritually in a way appropriate to their present stage of development, to their temperament, and to their position in life. If the bodhisattva is skilful enough, the recipients of his help may not even notice that they are being helped. In other words, the bodhisattva meets people halfway. He tries to meet them on their own ground, to learn their language. In short, he makes things easy for them – as easy, that is, as is compatible with the objective demands of the spiritual life.

However willing and helpful a bodhisattva may be, he can't magically produce spiritual transformation in you; you have to do it yourself. Whatever the bodhisattva gives you in the way of guidance, encouragement, and inspiration, you need to supply your own active co-operation, even if what you are doing is simply being receptive to his influence.

The bodhisattva does not necessarily do very much – sometimes he helps simply by being around. Nor does he necessarily turn up dressed for the part (as it were), with jewelled headdress and resplendent lotus throne. He may sometimes leave all that behind and appear as just a positive, friendly, sympathetic, warm-hearted, encouraging human being. In the spiritual life we need plenty of encouragement: encouragement not to be afraid of behaving ethically, whatever anyone else may think; encouragement to be generous with our money, our time, and our energy; encouragement to express our feelings of faith and devotion.

In this way, as the bodhisattva learns to meet people halfway, there comes into existence the more popular, even the more ethnic, side of Mahāyāna Buddhism. In the Mahāyāna Buddhist countries of the East, people are encouraged to co-operate in the building of temples and monasteries, to give offerings of food to wandering monks, and to perform simple devotional acts – acts which are simple in form but so meaningful in content – like offering flowers to the Buddha, reciting mantras, and going on pilgrimage to holy places.

Such popular Buddhism is not to be disparaged as a degeneration of the teaching. We can think of it as a kind of bridge: a bridge between ordinary worldly existence and purely spiritual, even transcendental, life. As Buddhism is becoming established in the West, this 'bridge' is taking new forms. Buddhist centres are running arts events which draw on the Western cultural tradition, and putting on activities such as t'ai chi ch'uan, Alexander technique, and yoga classes, as well as establishing businesses such as vegetarian restaurants, all of which give people a means of approach to the Buddhist way of life.

Where popular Mahāyāna Buddhism represents a degeneration of the teaching it does so only because it has become an end in itself, because there have been no bodhisattvas around to remind people what it is all for, and the ultimate goal of supreme Buddhahood has been forgotten. With no one around to remind them why they are doing what they are doing, people tend to start building houses on the bridge instead of using it to cross to the other side.

This is the moral of a little Japanese story about the career of a young monk. Looking ahead to the future, this novice monk thought, 'One day I'm going to be in charge of a temple, and people are going to come along for instruction, so it is very important that I should be on good terms with them. Now what would I be able to do to please them and put them at their ease?' In the end he decided that the best thing to do would be to learn to play the flute. If he could perform some nice music when people came to the temple, it would create a good impression and lead to friendly relations. So he started practising on the flute and – to cut a long story short – in the end he became so engrossed in his music that he forgot all about being a monk. Prematurely adopting 'skilful means' proved his own undoing: he got sidetracked.

So in our Western context, to take the example of a vegetarian restaurant, people might start forgetting that the reason they started running the restaurant in the first place was to offer newcomers a stepping-stone to a Buddhist way of life. They might just settle down into trying to get into the *Good Food Guide*. The only real safeguard against such degeneration is to make sure that all such activities are run by people who are deeply committed to the spiritual life.

While negotiating such pitfalls, Mahāyāna Buddhism has spread very widely indeed, from India to Tibet, China, Japan, and now the West; and as it has done so it has taken in elements from each indigenous culture. We could think of this as an aspect of the bodhisattva's learning to speak the language of the people he tries

to help. This integration with popular culture has developed so abundantly in the East that some modern scholars have been fooled into thinking of the Mahāyāna as an essentially popular movement. But in fact, though the Mahāyāna may be popular, it is also very profound, not just intellectually but spiritually.

For evidence of this, we need only turn to the teachings that centre upon Perfect Wisdom, or – as it is sometimes called – 'the wisdom that has gone beyond', that is to say, gone beyond the mundane, gone to ultimate reality.[164] This ultimate reality to which Perfect Wisdom has gone is known technically in the Mahāyāna as *śūnyatā*, which literally means 'voidness' or 'emptiness'. We should not, however, be misled into imagining some sort of blankness or black hole. *Śūnyatā* is not voidness in the sense of vacuity; it is voidness in the sense of being beyond all concepts, beyond thought, beyond the reach of the rational mind. From the standpoint of ultimate reality, we may say that Perfect Wisdom is the spiritual faculty that intuits *śūnyatā*, and *śūnyatā* is what is intuited by Perfect Wisdom – the one being the subject and the other the object. But from the standpoint of *śūnyatā* – if we can really think of *śūnyatā* as having a standpoint – there is no such distinction. In absolute or ultimate reality there is just one unbroken awareness, undivided by the polarity of subject and object.

It is Perfect Wisdom that makes the bodhisattva a bodhisattva. In realizing *śūnyatā*, he transcends completely the distinction between self and other. Only then, paradoxically, can he help others. The bodhisattva ideal is not a kind of humanitarianism, not even a religious humanitarianism. It is nothing less than the wisdom of the voidness breaking through into the world and functioning in the midst of the affairs of everyday life.

All this emphasis on wisdom does not mean that the Mahāyāna neglects faith and devotion. On the contrary, in Mahāyāna Buddhism devotion is particularly intense, and directed not only to the historical Buddha, Śākyamuni, but also to the ideal Buddha, the universal Buddha, the Buddha who occupies the centre of the Mahāyāna's spiritual universe and appears in a number of different forms or aspects: for instance, Amitābha, the Buddha of Infinite Light, and Vairocana, the Buddha of Sun-like Splendour. Devotees of the Mahāyāna venerate as well the archetypal bodhisattvas: Avalokiteśvara, the Lord who looks down in Compassion; Mañjuśrī, the gentle-voiced one, the Lord of Wisdom;

Samantabhadra, the universally beneficent; Kṣitigarbha, the Earth Womb, who descends into the depths of the states of suffering; and many more. The devotion of the Mahāyāna is directed towards all these great beings.

The *Sūtra of Golden Light* exemplifies many of these characteristics of the Mahāyāna: its universality, its emphasis on the bodhisattva ideal, its spirit of intense devotion, its worship of a plurality of Buddhas and bodhisattvas. It is also, in some ways, a typical *sūtra* (or at least a typical Mahāyāna *sūtra*) – that is, a particular kind of Buddhist scripture. But before we consider what kind of scripture a *sūtra* is, we need to ask a more basic question. What is a scripture? The word literally means simply 'something written down'. But although these days we can go to the bookshop and take our pick of a whole shelf full of Buddhist *sūtras*, it is important to remember that these texts did not start out as written documents at all.

The Buddha himself, the historical Śākyamuni, never wrote anything. It's not even certain that he *could* read and write at all. In his day, writing was not a very respectable occupation. Businessmen used it for keeping their accounts, but the idea of committing anything as sacred as spiritual teachings to writing was simply unthinkable. The Buddha taught, therefore, not by writing spiritual best-sellers, but by talking to people, passing on his teachings through conversation, discussions, and discourses. For their part, his disciples made a point of remembering what he said. Sometimes, indeed, his words were so memorable that no one within earshot could possibly forget them. But even if some disciples did forget, there were others who remembered and in due course passed on the teachings they had heard to their own disciples. In this way the Buddha's teaching was orally transmitted in India for many, many generations, spanning hundreds of years.

Not only did the early disciples remember hundreds and thousands of teachings, they also managed to arrange, edit, and even index them orally, without even beginning to put pen to paper – or rather stylus to palm leaf: surely a tremendous feat. The key figure in this whole extraordinary process was Ānanda, who was the Buddha's cousin and his constant companion for the last twenty years of his life. Wherever the Buddha went, Ānanda went. If the Buddha went for alms, Ānanda would be just a few paces behind him. If the Buddha accepted an invitation, Ānanda was naturally included. And if the Buddha gave a discourse,

Ānanda was present in the audience. For twenty years the Buddha was very rarely to be seen without Ānanda in tow, committing everything his master said to a prodigiously retentive memory.

I must confess to having harboured doubts about Ānanda's superhuman memory, until I actually met someone with comparable powers of recollection, a man who could remember everything he had ever heard me say word for word – together with where I had said it, when, and even why I had said it. This was enough to satisfy me that such an individual as Ānanda is unusual, but no chimera.

It was shortly after the Buddha's death – his *parinirvāṇa* – that Ānanda's gift really came into its own. This was when the Buddha's followers gathered together in a great cave near Rājagṛha in modern Bihar for the purpose of what has since become known as the First Council. But this name for it comes nowhere near evoking the true nature of the occasion. The Sanskrit word used to describe this gathering is *saṅgīti*, which literally means 'a chanting together' or even 'a singing together'. The monks – and there are supposed to have been five hundred of them – chanted or sang together whatever they could remember of the Buddha's teaching. The *saṅgīti* was dominated, however, by Ānanda's contribution to what might be called the collective memory of the spiritual community.[165]

So the words 'Thus have I heard', with which almost every Buddhist scripture begins, represent Ānanda's personal testimony that what follows is a reliable account of what the Enlightened One actually said. They mean that Ānanda had been there, or that if he had not been present the Buddha had repeated it all to him afterwards. They are believed to guarantee the authenticity of that text. 'Thus have I heard at one time' is used like a general imprimatur, so to speak, for the content of any scripture.

The *sūtra* is not, of course, the only kind of Buddhist scripture, although it is perhaps the most important and representative kind. Even during the period of oral transmission, the monks drew up a list of nine forms – increased in the Sarvastivāda school to twelve – that the Dharma as oral communication assumed.[166] These forms appeared later as subdivisions of the canonical literature, but to begin with they were simply different ways in which the Buddha had chosen to speak.

Sometimes, for example – and this may come as a surprise – he chose to speak in verse. This wasn't as difficult as it might sound, because the ancient Indian languages slide much more easily into metre than does modern English. Usually, in fact, the Buddha would break into impromptu verse or *gātha* in response to a question. Occasionally the question would be put in verse, and the Buddha would reply in kind, but sometimes he would even answer a prose question in verse, perhaps because the verse format would make what he had to say easier to memorize. So he would just produce on the spot a little stanza or series of stanzas. This is the origin of one of the best-known of Buddhist scriptures, the *Dhammapada*, as well as of many other texts.

The Buddha didn't always need to be prompted by a question before he would give a teaching. Sometimes he would speak without any prompting at all – or even when there was no one else present. This spontaneous utterance on the part of the Buddha, usually in verse, is known as the *udāna*, meaning literally 'the outward-going breath'. According to ancient Indian tradition there are five different kinds of breath, and the 'outward-going breath', a forcible exhalation, is just one of these. So the Buddha is not being asked a question. No one puts anything to him. He may even be alone. But suddenly there comes the *udāna*. It represents an utterance of the Buddha under tremendous pressure of spiritual emotion. We may say that the Buddha explodes into utterance. He can't keep it to himself – it forces its way out.[167]

Among the other forms of scripture there are the *geya* – teachings given in prose interspersed with verses. Also included in this category are those occasions when the Buddha gave his teaching first in prose, and then repeated it all, sometimes with variations, in verse. There are also the *jātaka* or 'birth stories', in which the Buddha relates incidents from one or another of his previous existences. And there are the *abhūtadharma*, the 'marvellous events', which describe extraordinary occurrences in the Buddha's present life, occurrences which we would regard as magical.

Yet another of these forms of teaching, like *gātha*, *udāna*, *geya*, *jātaka*, and the rest, is *sūtra*. *Sūtra* literally means 'thread'. When we have lost track of what someone is saying, we say we've lost the thread. The 'thread', in other words, is what connects a discourse. A *sūtra*, then, is a connected discourse given by the Buddha – or even a 'lecture' perhaps, if by this is meant something inspirational rather than dry as dust.

When it comes to content, *sūtras* are broadly of two kinds: Hīnayāna *sūtras* and Mahāyāna *sūtras*. The Hīnayāna is the first of the three major historical forms of Buddhism, and it literally means 'little way'. It is not a particular sect or school. The Mahāyāna identified and designated the Hīnayāna as a broad spiritual movement in contradistinction to itself, and coined the term to describe those who, in its view, were concerned predominantly with their own spiritual development, and did not share the Mahāyāna's universal perspective. Just to complete the picture, the third historical form of Buddhism is the Vajrayāna, the way of the diamond or thunderbolt, but the Vajrayāna tradition finds its characteristic expression in what are known as tantras and sādhanas, and produced only two major *sūtras*.

Hīnayāna and Mahāyāna *sūtras* could hardly be more different in character. In the Hīnayāna *sūtras*, or *suttas*, the Buddha's teaching is firmly embedded, not to say embodied, in a specific historical and geographical context: the north-eastern India of the sixth century BCE – the context of the Buddha's own life and times. These *sūtras* are full of references to the contemporary political situation and economic conditions. They also contain details about social customs, currents of religious belief, and philosophical speculations, as well as information about what people wore and what they ate, the crops they grew, the kind of houses they built, their trades and occupations. One of the *sūtras* even lists thirty or forty different games that people played in those days[168] – and there are also references to all sorts of trades and professions. As well as all this social history there is plenty of natural history. The Hīnayāna *sūtras* take place against a backdrop of the great impenetrable forests and the majestic mountain ranges of India, against the rhythm of her various seasons – the hot season, the cold season, the rainy season – and amidst her flora and fauna, amidst all sorts of animals, birds and trees, flowers and insects.

So in the Hīnayāna *sūtras* we are given a detailed and vivid picture of the India that was contemporaneous with Athens under Solon, with the Italy that Pythagoras knew, with the Persia of Zoroaster, and the China of Confucius. We also get a good idea of the kind of people the Buddha taught. Indeed, as the scriptures make clear, there was hardly any kind of person that he didn't teach. We find him addressing wandering monks and ascetics, kings, princes, and ministers, businessmen and farmers, philosophers and robbers, prostitutes and outcasts. He exerted his wise and compassionate influence throughout the northern Indian society of his time.

The Mahāyāna *sūtras*, on the other hand, present us with a very different picture. In many of them we may still be in India – but only just. We could also say that at least in some of them we're still on *Earth* – but only just. Indeed, in some of them we have left the Earth altogether, for some other, higher, heavenly world – we hardly know where, and we hardly care, because it is so beautiful and entrancing. In most of the Mahāyāna *sūtras*, however, the main features of the Indian landscape are still dimly visible. We can still see houses and trees – we can at least see, as though through a radiant mist, a solitary mountain peak. But although we can make out these familiar landmarks, they are all transformed, transfigured, bathed in a supernatural light.

Not only that. As we read or listen to the Mahāyāna scriptures, or rather as we *participate* in them – for that's what it feels like – we become aware of all kinds of extraordinary sensations. Celestial music sounds. Delicate fragrances waft through the air. Sometimes showers of golden blossoms rain down from the sky. And sometimes the scene expands even beyond the transformed landscape to include not just this world, not even just this universe, but thousands upon thousands of worlds, and thousands upon thousands of universes, all with their own Buddhas and bodhisattvas teaching the Dharma.

In the midst of it all, right at the centre of the Mahāyāna *sūtra*, sits the Buddha. He sits on a many-petalled lotus throne supported by a pair of lions, under trees made of all kinds of glittering and resplendent jewels. He is surrounded not just by a few beggarly-looking monks, but by a great host of beings, including many bodhisattvas. From the assembly, and especially from the Buddha, there radiates a great blaze of light. It is this Buddha, seated in the midst of this great blaze of light, who teaches the Mahāyāna *sūtras*. While he teaches, all sorts of marvels occur. The Earth shakes in various ways, flowers rain from the sky, and those listening experience all kinds of spiritual and transcendental insights. The world of the Mahāyāna is a world of light, a world of colour, a world of indescribable beauty and inexpressible joy.

At the same time, it's a very mysterious world. There is something about it that eludes the mind, something awe-inspiring and unfathomable. It is baffling, and yet to experience it gives a feeling of deep happiness and serenity. In the entire spiritual literature of the world there is nothing quite like the atmosphere of the Mahāyāna *sūtras* – they read almost like transcendental science fiction. Probably the nearest Western parallel is to be found in the gnostic sacred books, such as the *Pistis Sophia*;[169] they too are suffused with light and pervaded with a sense of mystery.

In his essay 'Buddhism and Gnosis', Edward Conze has suggested that this parallel may not be coincidental and that Gnosticism may be historically connected with Mahāyāna Buddhism.[170] His arguments are not quite convincing, however; in particular the connection he makes between gnosis and *prajñā*, between the wisdom of Gnosticism and that of Buddhism, seems doubtful. In fact, the distinct differences between gnosis and *prajñā* are quite instructive.[171] While it is difficult to generalize, because Gnosticism is such a broad phenomenon, it would be safe to say that the Gnostics almost always thought of wisdom as the acquisition of knowledge about certain occult mysteries and mythological details. They seem to have had the idea that there were certain great mysteries about the cosmos – so many spheres of existence, so many aeons, and so on – and if you understood all those mysteries, if you had all the right passwords and key words, you had gnosis. For Buddhism, by contrast, wisdom is essentially a metaphysical insight into something which far transcends the myths and occult mysteries with which the Gnostics were concerned.

For example, the Gnostics believed that man was a prisoner – a reasonable enough metaphor for the human condition. But then they believed that the various spheres – the sun, the moon, and the planets – constituted prisons within prisons, each presided over by a particular divinity whose name or password you had to learn in order to become free. Gnostic 'knowledge' was thus a knowledge of certain occult facts, rather than of ultimate reality – *śūnyatā* – in the metaphysical sense.

This suggests that in the Gnostic view the acquisition of knowledge was not a matter of personal spiritual development in the way that Buddhists would see it. For Gnosticism, knowledge simply depends upon approaching someone in the right way, becoming his disciple, and getting him to impart to you certain facts. It involves taking certain mythological structures for literal or, if you like, scientific, fact. It would be like saying that *prajñā* in Buddhism means understanding all the different planes of existence and knowing the names of all the deities who inhabited those planes. But no Buddhist would ever say that. Such knowledge may be part of the Buddhist tradition, but you cannot really develop wisdom until you have realized the true nature of those realms, considered from the highest point of view.

It therefore seems that there is a tremendous difference between what Gnosticism understands by wisdom and what Buddhism understands by it, a difference which is concealed by using the one word 'wisdom' for these two different concepts. However, although Mahāyāna Buddhism and Gnosticism differ in this way, I have felt for a long time that there must be some connection between them – not necessarily a historical one. There is certainly a slight but definite resemblance of spirit. Furthermore, it seems possible to detect the same spirit faintly reflected in later Western literature, in the Arthurian cycle (the earlier pagan-based material, not the later Christian incorporations) and particularly the legend of the Holy Grail – but this is pure conjecture.

The Mahāyāna *sūtras* are classified as either 'early' or 'late', according to whether they were written down and circulated before or after the time of Nāgārjuna. Nāgārjuna was responsible for promulgating on a wide scale the distinctively Mahāyāna teachings, particularly those on the Perfection of Wisdom, and it is fair to say that he is the greatest figure in Mahāyāna Buddhism. He 'flourished' (as scholars usually put it) probably in the second century CE (it is difficult to be certain of dates from this period) and he wrote a number of important works which are still widely and deeply studied today, including the celebrated 'Verses on the Middle Way', the *Madhyamaka-kārikā*.[172] It is because Nāgārjuna quotes from various Mahāyāna *sūtras* that we can be certain that they were in circulation as literary documents by his time. This early group of *sūtras* includes the *Saddharma-puṇḍarīka* or *Lotus Sūtra*,[173] the *Aṣṭasāhasrikā Prajñāpāramitā* or *Perfection of Wisdom in Eight Thousand Lines*,[174] the *Vimalakīrti-nirdeśa* or exposition of Vimalakīrti,[175] the two *Sukhāvatī-vyūha Sūtras*, the *sūtras* on the Array of the Happy Land,[176] and the *Daśabhūmika* or 'Ten Stages of the Bodhisattva's Progress'.[177] The later group of *sūtras* includes works that are just as well known: the large *sūtra* on Perfect Wisdom, the *Diamond Sūtra*, and the *Laṅkāvatāra Sūtra*, as well as the *Nirvāṇa Sūtra* and many others – including the *Sūtra of Golden Light*.

The *Sūtra of Golden Light* appeared in India during the period from the fifth to the eighth century CE, set down in the language known to Western scholars as Buddhist Hybrid Sanskrit. It did not appear all at once, fully formed and complete, at some particular point during those three hundred years. Rather, it emerged as a literary document gradually over that long period – not at all an unusual process of composition for *sūtras*, especially Mahāyāna *sūtras*.

How long the *sūtra* may have existed as an oral teaching before being written down there is no way of knowing, but in spirit at least it goes back to the time of the historical Buddha. He of course wrote nothing at all, and the great accumulation of oral teachings left after his death was arranged, edited, and even elaborated upon by the monks over a period of some four hundred years before so much as one word of it was written down. Even then, the teachings didn't get written down all at once. The whole process of committing the oral tradition to writing went on for a thousand years, from the first century BCE to the tenth century CE. Broadly speaking, the more exoteric teachings were the first to find form as scriptures, while the more esoteric ones remained hidden in the minds of the guardians of the oral tradition for longer, and emerged as scriptures rather later.

So the Buddhist scriptures cannot truthfully be described or judged as literature. They are more like successive literary deposits from the oral tradition. But what is the proof that they really are *Buddhavacana*, the authentic word of the Buddha? How do we know that they weren't just made up? In the case of the Theravāda or Hīnayāna scriptures – which were, incidentally, written down at around the same time as the Mahāyāna ones – we can point to repetitions and stock formulas that suggest a mnemonic element. It is not surprising, though, that the Mahāyāna *sūtras* are not characterized by such elements. The Theravāda has always been concerned with the letter, with verbal accuracy, hence the many repeated passages and formulas of the Pāli canon. By the same token, it is only to be expected that such repetitions are not to be found in the Mahāyāna scriptures, the Mahāyāna tradition being much more concerned to transmit the *spirit* of the Buddha's teachings.

Although the *Sūtra of Golden Light* is a collection of deposits from the oral tradition, those deposits were not necessarily a literal word-for-word record of an oral teaching that already existed in exactly that form. It is much more likely that certain ideas were in circulation in a number of alternative versions, and that when they were written down they were given a 'literary' form. That would be more in accordance with the nature of the Mahāyāna. There is very little direct evidence that this was the case, but that does not really matter. The important point is whether or not one accepts some kind of spiritual continuity between the teaching of the Buddha and the Mahāyāna *sūtras* as we have them today. *Someone* must have produced them. If you maintain that the *Sūtra of Golden Light*, the *Lotus Sūtra*, the Perfection of Wisdom *sūtras*, and all the others have no connection with the Buddha, then you have to posit a whole galaxy of remarkable spiritual personalities who were responsible for producing those *sūtras* – personalities who left no trace, no record of themselves. If the thought, or at least the essential spiritual inspiration, of an extraordinary work like the *Avataṃsaka Sūtra* doesn't go back to the Buddha, then who did produce it?

As we have seen, in the *sūtras* themselves it is the 'eternal Buddha', a glorious mythical figure, who teaches. But the Mahāyāna tradition is, or seems to be, that these *sūtras* were given by the historical Buddha himself. Indeed, some Mahāyāna *sūtras* begin with the Buddha seated on the Vulture's Peak, which was – and is – an actual place in northern India, near Rājagṛha, where the historical Buddha often used to teach. So we have what begins to look like a contradiction here. However, this kind of question – whether the Buddha who taught the *sūtras* was historical or mythological – would not have exercised the ancient Buddhists, whether Theravāda or Mahāyāna, because they did not distinguish between the historical and the mythological in the way we do. It is open to us to believe that the Mahāyāna *sūtras* were not preached by the historical Buddha in the literal sense: that is, in the sense that if we had been around in India in 500BCE, we would have heard the Buddha preaching those *sūtras* in exactly those words. We are at liberty to believe that the *sūtras* were written down after the *parinirvāṇa* of the Buddha by yogis or mystics or meditators who, in their meditation, had heard the archetypal Buddha (the *sambhogakāya*) preaching in that way. But that is not the Mahāyāna tradition.

The scriptures which have come down to us, and which are so widely varying in character, represent different strands of the oral tradition. We could say that the Pāli canon, for example, represents certain elements in the total oral tradition that the Theravādins chose to preserve. There were other elements that they chose to ignore, and this is where the Mahāsāṃghikas come in, because they seem to have preserved traditions which did go back to the Buddha, but which were ignored by or unknown to the Theravādins.[178] So it is not that different schools preserved different versions of the same tradition; it is more that each school preserved certain teachings that it regarded as important, and didn't preserve others.

There is an ancient account that says that the canon of the Mahāsāṃghikas was preserved by both monks and lay people, while that of the Theravāda was the preserve of the monastic community.[179] This perhaps explains the somewhat monastic slant of the whole Pāli Tipiṭaka,[180] a slant which is probably not justified by the total tradition. The fact that the Mahāsāṃghikas preserved more of the non-monastic elements was partly responsible for the more universal teaching of the Mahāyāna.

The literary history of the Mahāyāna *sūtras* in China is quite different from the Indian tradition. The Chinese had a literary culture from the time of Confucius, and they were very critical students of texts. They were well aware of the existence of different readings, and even at an early period made studies of the authenticity of ancient texts. For example, about five hundred years after the time of the Buddha there was a certain Chinese emperor who wanted history to begin with his reign, and ordered a burning of the books.[181] An enormous amount of literature was burned, but some years later, when he was dead, scholars started taking old books out of their hiding places. At that time a lot of forgeries were produced, but Chinese scholars were quite able to deal with the situation, because they were well aware, for instance, that certain words didn't come into existence before certain periods. If they found a text that was ascribed to a writer or teacher of 300BCE, but which contained a word that wasn't in circulation until 100BCE, they would know that it couldn't be genuine. They understood the principles of textual criticism, which means that the *sūtras* produced in China but purporting to have come from India were deliberate literary forgeries.

But the Indians knew nothing about textual criticism. We can therefore take it that *sūtras* produced in India which did not actually go back to the time of the Buddha were written by people who were in touch with some kind of existing tradition, and who did believe that what they were putting into writing was the teaching of the Buddha. They didn't have the literary sophistication of the Chinese.

So, gradually, over the centuries, one *sūtra* after another was committed to writing. Many of them, especially the longer Mahāyāna *sūtras*, were written down not all at once, but in instalments. This is why we may fairly speak of the *growth* of a Mahāyāna *sūtra*. The idea of instalments, however, should in no way be thought to suggest a logical sequence to the *sūtra*, or any purely artistic structure or unity – because, as we have seen, a *sūtra* cannot be approached in the first instance as a work of literature.

More usefully we may, in most Mahāyāna *sūtras*, look for a nucleus – a centre of spiritual energy – which if sufficiently powerful will have attracted to itself fragments from the vast memory bank of floating oral tradition. In the case of the *Sūtra of Golden Light*, this centre of spiritual energy is the famous chapter of Confession (chapter 3 of the text). As Nobel has demonstrated in detail in the introduction to his edition of the *sūtra*, the whole work was built up around this nucleus[182] – or perhaps it would be more accurate to speak of the nucleus as *attracting* other materials from the oral tradition.

There is something very strange about this pivotal chapter of the *Sūtra of Golden Light*. As we have seen, a *sūtra* is meant to be a connected discourse by the Buddha – there are many exceptions to this principle, but it holds good in the main – and yet this most important part of the *sūtra* is not spoken by the Buddha at all. It is not even spoken by a bodhisattva. It is spoken by a drum – a golden drum, and it is spoken in somebody's dream. As you continue to read the *sūtra*, or hear it read, you discover something even more mysterious. Not at first, but gradually, after a while, you realize that there is no question of just sitting back and listening to a definite, specific discourse given by the Buddha – or whoever is speaking. The Buddha, and others in the *sūtra*, are talking *about* the *sūtra*. All manner of marvellous things are happening in it. But then if you start to ask yourself where or what the *sūtra* is, you find there is no locating or identifying it. You are listening to it, people in it are referring to it, praising it ... but *where is the sūtra*? What is it? There seems to be no *sūtra* at all.

It gradually dawns on you that the *sūtra* can only be what is happening in it. It also dawns on you that you are yourself involved in what is happening in it. The *Sūtra of Golden Light* refers to itself not as a particular kind of text or scripture but as 'the profound Buddha region'. What this means is that the *sūtra* is not an item in our own world, but a whole world in itself, a whole spiritual world. In short, it is a *vaipulya sūtra*.

There are in existence several hundred Mahāyāna *sūtras*, some of them in the original Sanskrit, others in both Sanskrit and in Chinese or Tibetan translations, and some only in translation. A number of the most important of these texts are known as *vaipulya sūtras*. *Vaipulya* means 'broad, vast, extensive', and the *vaipulya sūtras* are certainly of a very considerable length, amounting sometimes to a whole thick volume in the English translation. But this is not really what is meant by the term. They are called *vaipulya* because they are broad, vast, and extensive in their scope. Their scope, in fact, is not just one subdivision of the teaching, or one section, or even one aspect, but the total Dharma, although each of the *vaipulya sūtras* sees that total all-inclusive Dharma from its own distinctive angle of vision, and perhaps in terms of the special spiritual needs of a particular kind of spiritual aspirant.[183]

Each of the *vaipulya sūtras* is therefore complete in itself. It can be studied and reflected upon, even practised, without reference to any other formulation of the Dharma, at least so far as the spiritual needs of the student are concerned. If you want to study the *sūtra* from a linguistic or scholastic point of view, that's another matter, but from the spiritual point of view one can confine oneself quite satisfactorily to just that one *vaipulya sūtra*.

The *Sūtra of Golden Light* does not style itself a *vaipulya sūtra* in so many words – the expression '*vaipulya sūtra*' is not part of its official title, as it were – but there is no doubt that this is what it is. To begin with, it is fairly extensive in size, and very extensive indeed in content. Like the other *vaipulya sūtras*, the *Sūtra of Golden Light* is a whole world in itself. As we have just seen, the *sūtra* itself, so to speak, knows this. In the introductory chapter the Buddha says, 'I will make known this *sūtra*, the profound Buddha region, the marvellous mystery of all the Buddhas, for millions of aeons.' In much the same way, in chapter 13, the *sūtra* is spoken of as 'the profound sphere of activity of the Buddha'.

Let us begin this exploration of this profound Buddha region by charting its main outlines, its nineteen chapters:

Chapter 1: An introductory chapter. The Buddha is on the Vulture's Peak (where a great many of the Mahāyāna *sūtras* are delivered) not far from the city of Rājagṛha. Ānanda is also present, not just listening and memorizing, but asking questions to which the Buddha replies, praising the *Sūtra of Golden Light*.

Chapter 2: In Rājagṛha, a bodhisattva called Ruciraketu (which means 'beautiful comet') is worried. He is a bodhisattva, but he has a problem – not a psychological problem, but a spiritual, metaphysical one. He is puzzled as to why the Buddha has such a short life – only eighty years. In answer to his question, four Buddhas appear to him, and as a result of their appearance he comes to understand that the Buddha's life is in fact immeasurable.

Chapter 3: The bodhisattva's dream. Ruciraketu has a dream in which a Brahmin beats a golden drum, and the drum sounds forth a series of beautiful verses of confession. It is these verses that form the nucleus of the whole *sūtra*.

Chapter 4: 'The Abundance of Lotuses'. The Buddha tells of a king who once praised the Buddhas of the past, present, and future. Although we are not explicitly told so, this king is apparently the bodhisattva Ruciraketu in a previous existence.

Chapter 5: 'On Emptiness'. This chapter deals with the subject of *śūnyatā*.

Chapter 6: The longest chapter of the whole *sūtra*, taking up a fifth of its total length. In this, the four great kings, the protectors of the four quarters of the world, promise to protect the *sūtra*, as well as the monks who proclaim it and the kings who promote it.

Chapters 7, 8, and 10: In these chapters three goddesses appear: Sarasvatī, the goddess of learning, Śrī, the goddess of wealth, and Dṛḍhā, the earth goddess. Each goddess also promises to protect the *sūtra*.

Chapter 9: This deals with the maintenance of the names of Buddhas and bodhisattvas, and in it various Buddhas and bodhisattvas are enumerated and saluted, among them several that play a prominent part in other Mahāyāna *sūtras*.

Chapter 11: Saṃjñāya, the general of a class of deities known as *yakṣas*, comes forward and promises to protect the *sūtra*.

Chapter 12: 'On Instruction concerning Divine Kings'. This deals with the ethical, even spiritual, basis of kingship.

Chapter 13: The Buddha describes one of his previous lives, in which, as a king called Susaṃbhava, he invited a monk called Ratnoccaya to expound the *Sūtra of Golden Light*, and also made offerings to the *sūtra* on a rather lavish scale.

Chapter 14: 'On the Refuge of the Yakṣas'. The Buddha addresses Śrī, the goddess of wealth, and explains that those who want to worship the Buddhas of the past, present, and future should listen to the *Sūtra of Golden Light*. He also enumerates a long list of deities who will protect the *sūtra*.

Chapter 15: A chapter of prophecy and prediction. Ten thousand gods come down from heaven into the presence of the Buddha to hear the Dharma. The Buddha predicts that in the infinitely remote future they will all attain Buddhahood through their faith in the *Sūtra of Golden Light.*

Chapter 16: 'On Healing Illness'. This describes how Jalavāhana the merchant's son learned the medical art from his father, and how he travelled throughout India curing people of their illnesses. This chapter gives a lot of information about ancient Indian ideas concerning the origin and treatment of disease, and makes particular reference to the influence on health of food, drink, and the seasons of the year.

Chapter 17: A Jātaka story. Jalavāhana saves ten thousand fish from dying of drought. These fish are eventually reborn as gods, and out of gratitude, they come one night while Jalavāhana is lying asleep and shower him with forty thousand pearl necklaces. This chapter also contains a statement of the law of conditioned co-production.

Chapter 18: Another Jātaka story. In this one, the Buddha, in a previous existence, sacrifices his life to save that of a starving tigress and her five cubs. This is one of the best known of all the Jātaka stories, and here it is related at some length.

Chapter 19: The last chapter, 'On the Praise of all the Tathāgatas'. In this chapter innumerable bodhisattvas sing the praises of a certain Buddha whose name is so long that it takes up almost a whole line of text. The bodhisattva Ruciraketu also praises that same Buddha, as does a goddess who also has a very long name. Then, amid general rejoicing, the *sūtra* concludes.

This, in outline, is the *Sūtra of Golden Light.* Of course, such a swift survey of the 'profound Buddha region' is terribly inadequate. No summary could possibly do justice to the *sūtra*'s spirit of fervent devotion. Every page positively thrills with reverence for the Buddha – and for the *Sūtra of Golden Light* itself. And no summary could capture the *sūtra*'s moments of great literary beauty, including hymns of praise to the Buddha as beautiful as we will find in any Buddhist literature anywhere. But the summary does perhaps do justice to one thing – to the highly composite, not to say miscellaneous, nature of the *sūtra.* When you read the text for the first time, you could be forgiven for thinking that it was a sort of rag-bag – a transcendental rag-bag, to be sure, a rag-bag full of bits and pieces of wonderful, jewelled brocade – but still a rag-bag.

But, despite appearances, the *sūtra* does hang together. It does possess a spiritual unity. Broadly speaking, the nineteen chapters can be classified into three groups. The first 'group' consists of one chapter on its own, the chapter on confession, the original nucleus of the *sūtra*. A second group is formed out of all those chapters in which gods and goddesses come forward and promise to protect the *sūtra*. The third group contains all the remaining chapters, most of which can be regarded as attempts on the part of the *sūtra* to draw into its orbit all the principal Mahāyāna teachings, and all the different kinds of Buddhist scriptures. Chapter 2, for instance, deals with the measure of life of the Tathāgata, which is one of the two major themes of the *Lotus Sūtra*;[184] and chapter 5 is concerned with *śūnyatā*, which is treated at length in the many *sūtras* of Perfect Wisdom.

In this book we shall be concerned mainly with the material contained in the first and second groups, because these chapters contain the *sūtra*'s special, distinctive teaching: transformation of self and transformation of world. The first group, the chapter on confession, involves the transformation of one's individual life through confession and purification. But transformation of self inevitably comes to involve transformation of world, and this is represented by the chapters in which the gods and goddesses promise to protect the *sūtra*. Who these gods and goddesses are, and how their promises represent a transformation of the world, are questions we must leave to be answered in chapters 5, 6, and 7.

Meanwhile, we are still left with the question of what principle of attraction it is that holds the *sūtra* together. What is it that holds transformation of self and transformation of world together? The answer is very simple. This apparently miscellaneous collection of material is held together by the spiritual needs of individuals who want to transform themselves. It is this factor that gives the *sūtra* its spiritual unity.

This principle of attraction is mirrored in the situation in which we find ourselves as western Buddhists. There are now a great number of Buddhist scriptures available to us, but they do not all hold an equal appeal for serious practitioners of the Dharma in the West. Some are much more appealing than others, because they seem much more relevant to our real spiritual needs. It is these that we draw on, these in which we find spiritual nourishment and inspiration, these that we read and study and discuss. In other words, we draw them into our orbit. Simply by virtue of the fact that these texts are drawn into our orbit, they have something in common: us. Each of them in some way meets our spiritual needs. So now we can draw the *Sūtra of Golden Light* into our orbit – or perhaps we could think in terms of allowing ourselves to be drawn into the orbit of the *sūtra*, allowing ourselves to plunge into the heart of the light that transforms both self and world.

PART I
TRANSFORMATION OF SELF

I
THE BODHISATTVA'S DREAM

These days most of us imagine we have so many things to do that we can't afford to spend much of our precious time sitting about reflecting on life. But if we do happen to find time to turn things over in our minds a little more seriously than usual, we may well have to acknowledge certain things about ourselves, things that we may not find altogether pleasant or creditable to accept. And one of the things that on reflection we may be forced to acknowledge is that as human beings we take quite a lot for granted. There are certain things which we know we possess, we know we experience, but the value and significance of which we are totally unaware – so unaware, indeed, that we might as well not possess them at all.

Suppose that when you were a baby, you had been given a pebble to play with, and suppose you kept that pebble and played with it every day, every hour, so that it became as familiar to you as your own hand. You would gradually become so used to the pebble that you would probably not take any particular care of it or attach any particular value to it. You might never realize, in fact, that the 'pebble' was not a pebble at all, but a priceless precious stone.

One of the things we tend to treat as a pebble, instead of the precious stone it really is, is life itself. We fail to understand the significance of the bare fact that we are alive. But it *is* significant. After all, we might just as easily be dead, or never have existed at all. But we do exist. There was, we could say, some unique, unrepeatable combination of circumstances, and here we are. It may have been a billion to one chance, but it has come off. Marvellous to relate, we are alive. We are sitting here. How wonderful!

This is surely what the old Zen monk was celebrating when he cried out 'How wonderful! How miraculous! I draw water and I carry fuel.'[185] He had realized that until then he had taken his ordinary, everyday life for granted, utterly failing to realize its value and significance. Of course, drawing water and carrying fuel are simple, basic human activities. One could hardly imagine even a Zen master being able to say, 'How wonderful! How miraculous! I catch the train to the office in the morning, I watch the television at night.'

Another thing that we take for granted is our 'ordinary' human consciousness, the normal waking state. We take it for granted that we can see and hear. We take it for granted that we can think – those of us who do think. We take it for granted that we can be aware. More often than not, we simply fail to realize the unaccountable singularity of it all.

In the same way, we take sleep for granted – such a wonderful, such a refreshing thing as sleep – unless of course we are unfortunate enough to have to resort to sleeping tablets. We even, most of us, take our dreams for granted. You get bad dreams – this is what our grandmothers used to tell us – if you eat too much cheese at night, and that's all there is to it. Or else – this is another popular theory – dreams are just a jumbled reminiscence of the events of the previous day.

But if you think about it, the dream state is a rather strange thing. In the dream state, the physical sense organs are not functioning, but nonetheless we see, we hear, we even smell and taste. In the dream state we're oblivious to the physical body, but we do seem to have a sort of body. We are free to move about, free to go places – in fact, we have more freedom than we do when we are awake. We can go anywhere, by any method. Sometimes we can even fly.

In dreams we experience a different kind of time, a different kind of space – even a different kind of world. Usually the dream world is a recognizable extension of the world of everyday waking consciousness, but not always. Sometimes it's a completely different world, a world of which we have had no previous experience in any form. It's almost as though we have passed through the dream state into quite another state of consciousness, quite another mode of being – even into a higher state of consciousness, a higher mode of being. To suppose that higher states of consciousness are accessible only from the waking state is pure assumption. It's just another of those things that we take for granted. The fact is that we certainly can have access to these higher states from or through the dream state.

In Buddhism, especially in the Mahāyāna and the Vajrayāna, the value of the dream state is recognized as being twofold. In the first place, it shows us that it is possible to experience a state of consciousness other than the waking state. This is quite an obvious point, but no less profound for that. Secondly, certain dreams show us that we can experience states of consciousness which are not only different from the waking state but higher than it. For this reason, dreams play an important role, sometimes even a crucial role, in the transformation of the individual.

It is a dream that leads directly to the heart of the *Sūtra of Golden Light*, the chapter on confession. At the beginning of the chapter (which is the third one of the *sūtra*) we find the bodhisattva Ruciraketu falling asleep. And while he is asleep he has a wonderful dream. It's what the Native Americans call a 'big dream', a dream of vast archetypal significance. More than that, the dream is a spiritual experience, even a transcendental experience.

In order to begin to understand something of this dream, we need to know at least a little of the dreamer. We need to go back to the previous chapter of the *sūtra*, the chapter at the beginning of which we meet Ruciraketu – his name means 'beautiful comet' – for the first time. The scene is set in the time of the Buddha, in the city of Rājagṛha, which in the Buddha's day was the capital of the kingdom of Māgadha. It is here that Ruciraketu lives and practises Buddhism, for he is a follower of the Mahāyāna. Indeed, he is a very advanced follower, because he is a bodhisattva, which means he has dedicated himself to the attainment of supreme Enlightenment for the sake of all living beings. Not only is he a bodhisattva; according to the text he is quite an advanced bodhisattva. The *sūtra* tells us, for instance, that in previous times he has rendered great service to a previous Buddha, planted great roots of merit (that is to say, performed innumerable skilful actions), and is highly respected, even revered, by hundreds of thousands of millions of Buddhas (such is the cosmic scale of events in Mahāyāna *sūtras*).

But although Ruciraketu is a bodhisattva, and an advanced one at that, although he is revered by all these Buddhas, he has a problem.

It isn't a personal problem or a psychological problem. It's a problem about the Buddha. He simply cannot understand why the Buddha had such a short life. Why did the Buddha live for only eighty years?

We would probably not find this a problem. After all, surely eighty years is a very natural life-span, even for a Buddha. If he had lived to be very much older than that, we might consider that to be a bit of a problem. But not so Ruciraketu. For him, the fact that the Buddha only lived for eighty years is a problem. His reasoning is as follows. In his discourses, the Buddha says that there are certain factors which determine whether one has a long or a short life.[186] In particular, there are two main causes of long life: refraining from killing living beings – that's the first precept[187] of course – and giving away great quantities of food. If you want to live for a long time in your next life, these are the courses of action you must pursue.

We cannot, of course, claim that Ruciraketu's reference point for this information is in the Pāli canon, but that is where several assertions of this kind are to be found. For example, in the *Majjhima Nikāya* several *suttas* describe the different kinds of karma, and the nature of their effects, in some detail.[188] One of the points made is that the results of karma are in keeping with the particular karma or action you have performed. If you are very greedy or selfish, for example, and you are always misappropriating other people's property, you will be poor. In the same way, if you continually take the lives of others, your own life will be taken, or at least shortened. These examples are typical of the Pāli canon, in which the principle is formulated in negative terms rather than in the positive terms which Ruciraketu recalls. None the less, although this is more of a general tendency than something that can be scientifically justified, we are left in no doubt that the karmic effect is in keeping with the nature of the karmic cause.

So Ruciraketu's problem begins with the knowledge that the Buddha refrained from killing living beings for innumerable lifetimes – for many incalculable hundreds of thousands of millions of aeons, according to the text. In all these previous existences the Buddha adhered to the ten skilful actions. Not only that; he also gave away food and all manner of good things. In some of his previous existences he is even said to have gone so far as to sacrifice his own body – his own blood, bones, and marrow – to feed other beings, as when, according to the famous Jātaka story, he fed the starving tigress and her cubs with his own flesh.[189]

Ruciraketu knows that on the basis of his previous actions, the Buddha should have an immeasurably long life. He should live for at least a few million years. But no, the Buddha's measure of life is only a miserable eighty years. So Ruciraketu has a problem, and he's very worried about it, as people usually are when they have a problem. As I have said, we probably wouldn't be bothered by this particular problem – we don't have that sort of faith – but we do have problems of our own. We could even say that there is no spiritual life without problems. Problems, we could say, are a means of development, even a means of transformation.

Problems are not, however, the same as difficulties. Difficulties may seem very big and important when we are assailed by them, but we can settle them simply by using our intelligence and making an effort. Problems, real problems, have to be solved in quite a different way. A problem, as distinct from a difficulty, is something that cannot be solved on its own terms – even while the terms themselves cannot be changed. Strictly speaking, a real problem cannot be solved at all – that's the beauty of it. At the same time, it *must* be solved.

This is quite obviously the case with Ruciraketu's problem. He believes that under the law of karma the performance of certain skilful actions will result in long life. He also believes that the Buddha has performed those actions to an immeasurable extent. At the same time, he knows that the Buddha has only a very short life. So it is impossible for him to change the terms of the problem. He cannot doubt the law of karma, or that the Buddha has performed the appropriate skilful actions; he also cannot deny that the Buddha's life is short. The situation in which he finds himself is both logically absurd and, from a spiritual and psychological point of view, intensely unsatisfactory, uncomfortable, and distressing.

This is the kind of situation we find reflected in the Zen koan; Zen stories are full of these impossible problems. You come into the master's room empty-handed, and the master says, 'What are you carrying?' You say, of course, 'Nothing,' and the master replies, 'Well, put it down then!' If you have no satisfactory response to this, you apparently get thirty blows. There are very famous koans, like 'What is the sound of one hand clapping?' and – arguably the most famous of all, at least in the West – the koan of the goose and the bottle. There is a goose, we are told, in a bottle. Naturally we are never told how it got there. The goose is fully grown; the neck of the bottle is very narrow. The problem is that you have to get the goose out of the bottle without damaging the bird or breaking the glass. In other words, you can't change the terms of the problem.

In Zen monasteries, students sweat over these koans for years. But for us here in the West such koans aren't really koans at all. We may read about them in books or hear about them in lectures, but they're not problems for us. We certainly don't lose any sleep over them. A real koan is something that springs up quite naturally from your own life, your own experience. It's something you can't get rid of, something you're stuck with, something inseparable from your own personality, something that is, in a sense, you – impossible, contradictory you, problematic you. That's the real koan.

This is in fact how koans, or what were later called koans, seem to have originated in the East. They crystallized actual problems arising in the lives of the Zen masters and their disciples. Having found that certain problems focused attention on particular aspects of reality, or constituted points at which it was possible to break through into reality, the masters naturally tended to think that those particular koans, to call them that, might well be useful to their disciples. The master would give his disciple a koan not in an external or mechanical way, but to draw his attention to the particular existential dilemma that the koan represented.

Usually, koans involve a contradiction in logic. They are not just pondering on some deep teaching like 'all things are void'; they involve an element of contradiction and dilemma which you cannot resolve. You are strongly convinced of two different things, but you see that they are inconsistent: if one is true, the other can't be.

An exception to the rule of contradiction is the well-known koan '*mu*', which simply means 'not'. This has a certain universality, because looking at it from a philosophical point of view, '*mu*' denies that anything can be predicated of ultimate reality, and this is what you have to realize. So you reflect on '*mu*' in all sorts of ways, and usually all your reflections are rejected by the master, because they are all intellectual. But eventually, by trying to see that nothing can be predicated of ultimate reality, you do break through at the particular point represented by the '*mu*'; this is what is meant by solving the koan. What you say to the master, although it may not seem to have any logical connection with '*mu*', shows that you have broken through into that dimension.

Since '*mu*' has a place in Zen tradition, somebody working within that tradition will be able to use it – if, that is, they have great faith in the master, so that even if he rejects all their solutions and explanations, they will be able to accept what he says. Apparently when Alan Watts spent a short time with a roshi, he ended up losing his temper with the teacher and saying he had got it all wrong.[190]

These days the tradition of koans has become scarcely more than a matter of routine and formula. In modern Japan you get not only dictionaries of koans with as many as three thousand entries, but also books that provide you with the answers – clear evidence of the degeneration of the koan system. But originally koans did embody life experiences of the kind that I have mentioned, and they can still be useful, if they are used in the traditional way, not just mechanically. It's as though the master needs to manoeuvre the disciple into a position where the koan naturally arises.

This raises the question of the general usefulness to spiritual development of formal structures. There is a pattern to the development of such structures. Someone has a certain spiritual experience which apparently resulted from certain conditions, and on this basis a system is set up that reproduces those conditions, in the hope that this will make it easier for other people to have the same experience. Sometimes this works, and sometimes it doesn't. You have to be careful not to reduce the experience to the conditions in which it took place. Just reproducing the conditions faithfully will not make the experience happen automatically.

So yes, koans have their value if they are used well. We could even reflect on koans that have arisen from Western culture. For instance, we might ponder on Keats' words: 'Beauty is truth, truth beauty.'[191] How can beauty be truth and truth beauty? They are surely quite different things. Surely Keats was talking nonsense! But if you keep on reflecting, you may eventually 'solve' the koan. But how? How do you solve the insoluble? How do you resolve the absurdity, the discomfort of it all? What happens? Let's return to the *Sūtra of Golden Light* to see what happens in Ruciraketu's case.

As Ruciraketu is sitting in his house – because after all he is a householder as well as a bodhisattva – thinking about his problem, something happens. All of a sudden, the house starts to grow. It expands and expands until it is unutterably vast. Not only that – the entire house is transformed into beryl (beryl being a kind of precious stone) and becomes adorned with numerous divine jewels and filled with perfumes. All this, the *sūtra* tells us, is a transformation due to the Tathāgata, the Buddha.[192]

Then something even more wonderful happens. In the house there appear in the four directions four thrones made of divine jewels. On these thrones appear mats made of jewels and fine cotton cloth; and on the mats appear jewel-adorned lotuses. Then on the lotuses appear four Buddhas: Akṣobhya in the east, Ratnaketu in the south, Amitāyus in the west, and Dundubhīśvara in the north. At the same time, the whole city of Rājagṛha, and indeed the whole universe, is filled with light, and all beings in the universe become 'possessed of divine happiness'. The blind can see; the deaf can hear. The mentally disturbed are restored to their senses, the naked are clothed, and the hungry are fed. Disease and deformity disappear. And, the *sūtra* says, on a large scale in the world there is an appearance of miraculous things.

When Ruciraketu sees these four Buddhas, naturally enough he can hardly believe his eyes. Joyful and delighted, he pays homage to them – and in the act of doing so bumps straight into his problem again. He is prompted to recollect the virtues of the historical Buddha, Śākyamuni, and that in turn reminds him of the fact of the Buddha's short life. Once again he is obsessed with his problem.

The four Buddhas seated in the four directions immediately become aware that Ruciraketu's mind is troubled, and, being Buddhas, they also realize what he is thinking, and they all simply tell him that he should not think in this way. The Buddha's life is not limited to eighty years, but is immeasurable, they say. In effect they tell him not to identify the Buddha with his physical body. In effect they tell him that the Buddha is Buddhahood, and that Buddhahood transcends time – hence cannot be measured in terms of time. The Buddha's life is immeasurable not because he lives for an inconceivably long time, but because in the depths of his being he does not live in time at all.

Now innumerable gods and bodhisattvas come together in Ruciraketu's house, and the four Buddhas proclaim the truth of this teaching to them all in a series of verses. There then follows an episode involving a Brahmin called Kauṇḍinya which also demonstrates the

Buddha's length of life. Having had his problem solved, Ruciraketu is extremely happy; the *sūtra* says that he becomes filled with noble bliss. At the same time, innumerable beings develop the will to Enlightenment. The four Buddhas then disappear, and the chapter comes to an end.

So what on earth does all this mean? Well, in a sense it speaks for itself. Above or below or even beyond our rational mind, the *sūtra* does get through; it does manage to speak to us and produce an impression. But it may be difficult for us just to absorb the meaning in this way; our rational mind is also going to want an explanation. Just a few pointers, then, for the rational mind to chew over.

To begin with, Ruciraketu's house and its expansion. The house is everything that belongs to us. It represents our personal framework, our habitual state of consciousness, and its expansion means that when we have a problem, we cannot solve it with our present state of consciousness. The problem, indeed, is in a sense an expression of that state of consciousness. So there must be an expansion of consciousness beyond the problem: not just horizontal expansion into different states of consciousness, but vertical expansion into higher states of consciousness. The house is therefore transformed from wood and stone or brick and plasterwork – or whatever mundane things it's made of – into beryl and other precious stones. Before the transformation it was opaque; now it's translucent, or at least semi-translucent.

In other words, there has been a transformation from ordinary waking consciousness to meditative consciousness. Ruciraketu is now in fact in a state of *dhyāna*.[193] In Buddhism, as in other spiritual traditions, higher states of consciousness are associated with and symbolized by light and jewels. Jewels are colourful, glittering, dazzling, and beautiful, and they therefore fittingly represent a consciousness that is not only higher than the ordinary, but more fascinating and attractive, more beautiful and valuable. It is for the same kind of reason that while ordinary dreams are in black and white, 'big dreams' are in vivid colour. Likewise, in the visualization practices of the Tibetan Buddhist tradition, great importance is attached to the visualization of colour. You visualize not just a Buddha, but a vivid emerald green Buddha, say, or a brilliant red bodhisattva. The colours visualized in this way should be rich and glowing, like those of a stained glass window through which the sun is streaming, only softer and more diaphanous. To employ a more traditional simile, they should be like the colours of the rainbow.

The fact that Ruciraketu is sitting inside his expanded house signifies that he is completely within the higher state of consciousness. His state is reminiscent of the Buddha's simile for the fourth *dhyāna*: a man who has taken a bath on a hot day and sits completely wrapped in a pure white sheet.[194] We also find a parallel in Tibetan Buddhist iconography, in the haloes of coloured light with which Buddhas and bodhisattvas are surrounded. Of course, because paintings are two-dimensional, it appears that the figure is surrounded by a circle of light rather like a rainbow, but in fact the 'halo' is a cross-section of a three-dimensional 'shell' of light. Sometimes the deity is shown sitting not within a series of shells of coloured light, but within tents made of silk of different colours. The general significance is the same, and it comes quite close to that of Ruciraketu sitting inside his expanded and bejewelled house.

The transformation of Ruciraketu's house is ascribed to the power of the Tathāgata (that is, the Buddha), but this is not to be taken at face value. It is not just that the Buddha, the human historical Buddha, has worked a miracle, although a miracle has certainly taken place – as tends to happen in Mahāyāna *sūtras*. But what is the meaning of the miracle? Remember the starting point of it all: Ruciraketu's painful, insoluble problem. When we're in this sort of situation – that a problem has arisen in the context of the spiritual life – what happens?

What happens is that a new factor comes into operation from a deeper level of our being – or a higher level – anyway, a level which we are not conscious of, at least not conscious of as being ours. This new factor is represented by the Buddha. Each of us has, however remotely, the potential to become – to transform ourselves into – a Buddha. Having reached the end of his conscious resources, Ruciraketu has had to call up, or call down, resources of which he is not conscious. The problem is resolved by the intervention of a higher factor, a factor that operates from the unrealized depths or heights of Ruciraketu's own being, and which enables him to rise to a higher level of consciousness.

We could say that the four Buddhas who appear in the house form a mandala, the centre of which Ruciraketu occupies, although he is not yet a Buddha. The appearance of this four-Buddha mandala in the *Sūtra of Golden Light*, prefiguring as it does the Vajrayāna's later development of the mandala of the five Buddhas, seems to suggest a slight Tantric development within the *sūtra*. This is quite possible in view of the fact that as a literary document the *sūtra* is quite a late work, though the original nucleus is a bit older. The names of some of the four Buddhas who appear in the *sūtra* were later standardized in the Vajrayāna tradition. The Buddha who appears in the east keeps the same name – Akṣobhya, the Imperturbable, as does the Buddha of the west, who has the familiar name Amitāyus (Immeasurable Life, a form of Amitābha, Immeasurable Light). But the name of the Buddha of the south, who in the *Sūtra of Golden Light* is called Ratnaketu (Precious Comet or Precious Streamer), was later standardized as Ratnasambhava, the Jewel-Born One. As for the Buddha of the north, he is called Dundubhīśvara, Lord of the Drum, in the *sūtra*, but his name was later standardized as Amoghasiddhi, Unobstructed Success.[195]

The appearance of the four Buddha mandala within the expanded house signifies the appearance within an already heightened state of consciousness of a still higher state of consciousness. Within the meditative state appears the state of contemplation. Within the *dhyāna* or *samādhi*[196] state appears wisdom. Within the context of *śamatha*, calm, arises *vipaśyanā*, insight. Within the context of spiritual experience appears transcendental experience, experience directly connected with ultimate reality. Sparked off by his problem, Ruciraketu has undergone a profound transformation. Furthermore, his transformation is very much an individual matter. It is Ruciraketu's own life that is transformed, his own self, his own consciousness.

So this part of the *sūtra* is mainly concerned with the transformation of self. But there is an objective counterpart to all this. Corresponding to transformation of self, there is transformation of world. This is why we find that the city of Rājagṛha is filled with a great light. The blind see, the deaf hear, and so on. These wonders all serve, as it were, to anticipate the other aspect of transformation: transformation of world.

Then we return to Ruciraketu. The four Buddhas speak to him. Representing different aspects of the higher transcendental awareness, they communicate with him. He is aware of them, as they are of him, and something passes between them – something of the Buddhas' awareness impinges on him. As he experiences flashes of their awareness, his problem is solved on this higher level.

All these miraculous happenings are simply a prelude to the chapter that follows. We may therefore expect something very astonishing indeed to happen next. If we do, we may be momentarily disappointed, because the next chapter, chapter 3, opens with the following words:

'Then indeed the Bodhisattva Ruciraketu slept.' So Ruciraketu has had all these wonderful experiences. His house has expanded, he has seen the four Buddhas, and the Buddhas have spoken to him – and what does he do then but go to sleep.

But we must be on our guard. The dream that Ruciraketu is going to have in this chapter, 'The Bodhisattva's Dream', is no ordinary dream, and his sleep is no ordinary sleep. To understand why he must sleep this extraordinary sleep, we need to go back and have another brief look at the previous chapter. In chapter 2, however wonderful the experiences that Ruciraketu has undergone, his transformation is not complete, and there are various clues which point to this. First, Ruciraketu himself still occupies the centre of the mandala, although he is not yet a Buddha. He only sees the Buddhas. The innermost core of his being, what makes Ruciraketu Ruciraketu, is not yet transformed. Buddhahood, however lucidly he sees it, however sublimely he sees it, however truly he sees it, is still something external to himself. It's still something out there. So although his realization is genuine, it is still a mental realization, still in the realm of mundane consciousness; it has not yet permeated and transformed every aspect of his being. Moreover, even in the midst of the mandala of the four Buddhas, his problem is still with him. True, he now has the solution to it, but so long as you have the solution to a problem, you still have the problem. What you have to do is forget both problem and solution: only then have you really solved your problem. And this is what happens now.

'Then indeed the Bodhisattva Ruciraketu slept.' As I have said, this is no ordinary sleep. It represents the complete erasure, the complete obliteration, the complete blotting out, of the old self, of the old consciousness. In Shakespeare's phrase, it is the sleep of death.[197] But it's not physical death; it's the sleep of spiritual death. It is not the death that comes when we have shuffled off this mortal coil, but the death that comes when we have abandoned all previous conditions. In other words, if we want to develop spiritually, if we want to be completely transformed, as opposed to peripherally transformed, we must die. The *Tibetan Book of the Dead* is famously associated with death, but we may say that the *Sūtra of Golden Light* is also a Book of the Dead. Indeed, every Buddhist scripture is a Book of the Dead, because the whole purpose of any Buddhist scripture is to act as the agent of transformation. That's what it's there for. If we're not prepared to die, we cannot become a bodhisattva. We cannot, in fact, become a Buddhist. The *Tibetan Book of the Dead* is concerned with spiritual death in the context of physical death, but we have to be ready to experience spiritual death at any time. We have to be ready at any time to give up the old life, the old self, to forget the old problems and the old solutions. We have to be ready to make a completely fresh start. Otherwise, we cannot be totally transformed.

So the bodhisattva Ruciraketu slept, and as he slept he had a dream. In his dream he saw, in all directions, innumerable Buddhas seated on thrones of beryl, under trees made of jewels, surrounded by assemblies numbering many hundreds of thousands. In the midst of it all he saw a golden drum, a drum that shone just like the sun in the midday sky, a drum that radiated brilliant golden light throughout the whole of space. A man – a Brahmin – was beating this drum, and as he struck it, it seemed to speak.

Ruciraketu's dream, then, is full of symbolism, symbolism which should give us at least a few hints as to what the dream is all about. On the level of the literal meaning of the *sūtra*, the dream is just a dream, a state of consciousness other than the waking state. But on the level of the real meaning of the *sūtra*, the dream is not just a different state but a higher one, which means that what happens in the dream is to be understood as pertaining to a higher order of reality.

Such dreams are of course the stuff of literary convention in Western culture. Bunyan's *Pilgrim's Progress*, for example, takes place in the context of a dream; so does Langland's *Piers Plowman*; so, come to that, does Lewis Carroll's *Alice's Adventures in Wonderland*. In these cases, as in the *Sūtra of Golden Light*, the dreamer falls asleep when they are not actually tired; they just fall asleep during a pleasant summer afternoon and start dreaming. The dream in these and many other works suggests an entry into some other level of reality.

Dreams in the ordinary sense are produced by the subconscious or the unconscious mind, that is, they represent an influence that operates below the threshold of consciousness. And though Ruciraketu's dream is no ordinary one it still functions in the same way. It represents the working out of his spiritual experiences at a deeper level of his being than the purely mental level. If seeing the mandala of the four Buddhas represents for Ruciraketu the Path of Vision, the dream represents the Path of Transformation.[198] His being is beginning to be completely transformed, and the symbol and centre of that total transformation is the drum, the golden drum which he sees at the beginning of his dream.

Why a drum of all things? We cannot be sure, for after all we are dealing with a dream, but it could be that the image of the drum was sparked off by an interesting detail to do with his vision of the four Buddhas, which is that the name of one of them, Dundubhīśvara, the Buddha of the north, means the Lord (*īśvara*) of the Drum (*dundubhi*). The drum is anyway a very ancient symbol in Buddhism. Shortly after his Enlightenment, when the Buddha declared that he would go to Benares and there proclaim the Dharma, the way he actually put it was that he would beat the drum of the deathless – the drum of Nirvāṇa, the drum of the Absolute.[199]

We may not know quite why the drum appears in Ruciraketu's dream, but we can be sure of one thing – that we cannot assign just one meaning to its appearance. Like all true symbols, it has many meanings, and at the same time it is more than all its meanings. The drum is the absolute, the truth, ultimate reality. I think one has to imagine it as some kind of large suspended kettledrum. It is circular in shape, and in many spiritual traditions the circle or sphere symbolizes perfection (a round jewel, the pearl, for instance, has the same general significance). It is made of gold, and it radiates golden light, the colour gold being the colour of incorruptibility, immortality, eternity.

The drum is also the Buddha: the historical Buddha who proclaims the Dharma even as the drum shines with its golden light, and the eternal Buddha of the Mahāyāna, who is the sun of the spiritual universe. The drum is the Buddha who occupies the centre of the mandala, the missing Buddha, the fifth Buddha. It is also Ruciraketu, the Ruciraketu who is in the process of being completely transformed. And it is the sun, with all the accompanying rich solar imagery of the Indian tradition going back to Vedic times, imagery that is at times reminiscent of the hymns of the so-called heretic Egyptian pharaoh, Akhenaten. Finally, the drum is the *Sūtra of Golden Light* itself, especially the nucleus of the *sūtra*, the verses of confession. All these are elements of the drum's significance, a significance that cannot be confined to words.

There are, of course, other symbols in Ruciraketu's dream. He sees innumerable Buddhas sitting on thrones of beryl underneath radiant jewel trees, and all teaching the Dharma to large assemblies. There is a parallel here with the episode in the previous chapter in which, after

Ruciraketu had seen the mandala of the four Buddhas, the great city of Rājagṛha became filled with light, and many miracles occurred; in other words, the world was transformed. In Ruciraketu's dream, the world is not just transformed, but totally transformed. It becomes a Pure Land, a land in which there are only Buddhas and their disciples, in which everybody is either teaching the Dharma, or listening to the Dharma, or sitting in silence thinking about the Dharma.

More than that, the world in Ruciraketu's dream has been so completely transformed that it is no longer 'world' out there at all. The golden light of the drum fills the whole of space; the innumerable Buddhas and their assemblies also fill the whole of space. The transformed self interpenetrates the transformed world so that there is no self, no world, no subject, no object. The two have become interfused. Indeed, there are several places in the confessional verses where we are unsure whether it is the drum or Ruciraketu speaking, or both or neither.

The third symbol that Ruciraketu sees in his dream is a man, a man with the appearance of a Brahmin beating the drum and calling forth the confessional verses. But what is a Brahmin doing in a bodhisattva's dream? Surely this is rather odd. Well, he is not the kind of Brahmin who may first spring to mind, the kind of zealous Hindu Brahmin who is always cropping up in Buddhist scriptures to argue with the Buddha. In the early days of Buddhism the terms '*brahmin*' and '*bhikkhu*' were practically synonymous. Both, as used by the Buddha, represented the spiritual ideal. In the *Dhammapada*, for instance, we find a 'Brāhmaṇa-vagga', a chapter on the Brahmin, and here the Brahmin stands for the man devoted to the spiritual life, or even for the Enlightened man – just as the *bhikkhu* does.[200] It must be admitted that the Buddha's attempt to 'upgrade' the word '*brahmin*' and dissociate it from its caste significance did in fact fail. Indeed, in this context, as a drum of any size would have to be made of leather, a traditional Brahmin would not touch it, let alone beat it.

But perhaps there is another reason for the presence of the Brahmin in Ruciraketu's dream. Originally, the Brahmin was the priest or shaman of the invading Aryan tribes, and he is therefore a very ancient, arcane figure, a figure that goes right back to the beginning. In the literal sense, to go back to the beginning is to go back in time, but metaphorically, to go back to the beginning is to go out of time altogether. Taken in this sense, the figure of the Brahmin suggests that whatever happens in the dream happens outside time, that the ultimate significance of the dream is transcendental.

It is in the nature of dreams that they conjure up archaic images, and the images they conjure up tend to reflect your cultural background. If as a Western Buddhist you have an archetypal dream, the chances are that you won't dream about a Buddhist temple. You will find yourself in the middle of some beautiful cathedral, because you have been brought up to associate cathedrals with all that is religious and spiritual. That is deeply ingrained in your unconscious mind, even though you are a Buddhist. Maybe your unconscious mind hasn't yet been converted, and still dwells on cathedrals and stained glass windows.

It is probably the same with Ruciraketu. He is a Buddhist, he is a bodhisattva, but because he is an ex-Hindu he has residues of Hinduism and even Brahmanism in his consciousness, which means that his deeper psychological experience is in Hindu terms. As we will see, the *sūtra* exemplifies this throughout by bringing into the sphere of Buddhist teaching quite definitely Hindu figures. It's as though the *sūtra*, and in particular Ruciraketu's dream, represents an attempt to integrate these more archaic attitudes into the Buddhist vision.

The first time I read the *Sūtra of Golden Light*, I pictured the Brahmin as a white-robed man, but when I re-read it, I was surprised to find that there is no mention of the Brahmin as being white-robed. Perhaps I imagined him in white because in India that is the colour that Brahmins traditionally wear, especially for religious ceremonies, and the white-robed figure therefore represents one devoted to spiritual development. I am also reminded of the man wrapped in the white sheet who illustrates the experience of the fourth *dhyāna*. These are purely personal associations, but perhaps they are of some significance.

The Brahmin is not just present in Ruciraketu's dream; he is doing something: beating the drum. In other words, the spiritual devotee takes the initiative. He gathers up his strength, lifts the stick, and strikes. He beats on the drum, he beats on the Absolute. The drum is what in earlier Indian traditions was a solar symbol – that is, the sun as a golden door into a higher world: to open the door, you have to knock. It's rather like what Yeats said of William Blake: 'He beat upon the wall / Till Truth obeyed his call.'[201] The Brahmin beats on the drum, beats on the Absolute – and there's a response. The drum speaks. Reality speaks. The confessional verses come forth.

The golden drum's response takes the form of the celebrated verses of confession which not only make up the greater part of this chapter, but also form the original nucleus of the entire *sūtra*. As one might expect, this being a dream, the verses don't seem to come forth in any particular order. There's no logical sequence. They just flow forth from the golden drum like a great stream of golden light. The golden light is the sound of the drum; the sound of the drum is the golden light. It's what Coleridge called 'a light in sound, a sound-like power in light'.[202] And because they are part of Ruciraketu's dream, both the drum and the golden light *are* Ruciraketu, are *in* Ruciraketu. So it is also Ruciraketu who is speaking – not the old Ruciraketu, but the new Ruciraketu.

Haphazardly as they flow forth, the verses can be divided into ten sections. The first is a prayer, a prayer that by the sound of the drum the world and all living beings may progress. In other words, it's a prayer for the complete transformation of self and world. In the second section we have the drum speaking as Ruciraketu – or Ruciraketu speaking as the drum – and making the bodhisattva vow. He vows to attain supreme Enlightenment for the benefit of all beings, to dedicate himself to the great task of the transformation of self and world. So the influence of the golden light is beginning to make itself felt.

The third section is a lengthy confession of faults. Ruciraketu acknowledges all the unskilful actions which have hitherto prevented him from realizing his ideal, from being a real bodhisattva, from becoming a Buddha. This is followed in the fourth section by a promise to worship the Buddhas in the ten directions; in effect this is a more detailed statement of the bodhisattva vow. Among other things, Ruciraketu undertakes to expound the *Sūtra of Golden Light*, and in particular the confession.

Section five is a second confession of faults, rather shorter than the first, and the sixth is a brief rejoicing in the merits of all beings who perform skilful actions. In the seventh section there is a third confession of faults, the shortest one of all. Then section eight is taken up with praising the Buddhas; here solar imagery is very conspicuous. The Buddha is described as 'the Buddha-sun, removing the obscurity of darkness with his rays of Compassion' and 'a fully Enlightened sun'. 'With meshes of beams full of glory, merit, splendour, and brilliance he stands amid the darkness like the sun in the three worlds.' Section nine contains more aspirations, good wishes, and rejoicing in merits, and the last section declares the advantages of worshipping the Buddha by means of these verses of confession.

From this brief summary we can see that the main subject matter of the verses is the confession of faults, although this is balanced by the bodhisattva vow, verses of praise to the Buddha, and rejoicing in merits. So there is a resemblance between these verses and chapter 2 of Śāntideva's *Bodhicaryāvatāra*, 'Entering the Path of Enlightenment';[203] and what we really have here is a rudimentary and unsystematic but very beautiful sevenfold puja.[204]

2

THE SPIRITUAL SIGNIFICANCE OF CONFESSION

INTRODUCTION

When we hear the word 'confession', those of us with a background in Western culture may well see in our mind's eye the little wooden box with the grille and the hidden priest which is such a central feature of the Roman Catholic church. If we have come close enough to the undesirable aspects of the Catholic confessional, we may associate confession with sin and guilt, punishment and eternal damnation. It may therefore come as a surprise (and perhaps not altogether a welcome one) that confession also occupies a very important place in Buddhist spiritual life. I should hasten to make it clear, therefore, that confession as a Buddhist practice is radically different from Roman Catholic auricular confession, which plays so heavily upon irrational feelings of guilt. Buddhist confession is also very different from the kind of confession valued by modern psychoanalysis. Psychoanalysts may value confession, but they do so very much within a theoretic framework which is – with the possible exception of the Jungian school – secular and humanistic, not to say scientific and rationalistic. The value and significance of confession as understood by psychoanalysis is therefore strictly limited.

But in Buddhism confession has not just a psychological effect, but a profound spiritual significance – as we shall see when we study chapter 3 of the *Sūtra of Golden Light* in detail. But first, why stress that confession – or any other practice – has a *spiritual* significance? The point that some people have made to me in the past is that we should be better off without the word 'spiritual' altogether, because it fulfils no function that is not covered by the word 'psychological'. After all, they say, 'spiritual' experience pertains to the psyche, so we might just as well speak of 'psychological' experience. But to me it seems helpful to draw a sharp distinction between the psychological and the spiritual.

Strictly speaking, 'psychological' means 'that which pertains to or belongs to the *science* of the mind', and when we want to refer to that which pertains to or belongs to the mind (or the psyche) itself, we should, again strictly speaking, use the word 'psychical'. Still, the usage of 'psychological' is well established, and not worth quarrelling with. There are some aspects of the word's use, however, that definitely are worth taking issue with. What we mean by psychological clearly depends on what we mean by psyche. Psyche is 'mind' (or even 'soul' in the popular sense of the term) – but what is 'mind'? As far as most people are concerned, mind is simply that which is different from the body, that which is the seat of thoughts, feelings, and impulses (whether conscious or subconscious): thoughts about work, home, money, politics; feelings of love, hate, jealousy, fear, anxiety; impulses to pursue what is pleasant and avoid what is unpleasant. If you are going to take 'mind' to mean all these things, you are going to tend to take 'psychological' as indicating something belonging to the psyche or mind as you yourself know and experience it.

If we think of Enlightenment as a psychological experience, we are going to tend to think that it is a mental state of a type with which we are already more or less familiar. In other words, we will misunderstand it completely. If, on the other hand, we think of Enlightenment as a spiritual experience – in other words, as an experience of a type with which we are not familiar at all – there is then much less danger of misunderstanding. We will at least register that this is something that does not fall within our present range of experience, something that involves a shift to a higher level of consciousness. According to Buddhist tradition, there are many higher levels of consciousness accessible to us. Above and beyond our everyday consciousness there are, as we have seen, what are called the four *dhyānas*, the four superconscious states of the world of form, each succeeding one higher than the last; beyond them there are what are known as the four formless *dhyānas*; and beyond all of them, there is Nirvāṇa or Enlightenment.

At this point a further distinction is called for. We can define 'spiritual' both in a broad general sense and in a narrow, more specific one. In the broad sense, it refers to all the eight *dhyānas* plus the state of Enlightenment; in the narrower sense it refers only to the dhyānic, not the Nirvāṇic level. If we use the word in this narrower sense, we need a different word to refer to the state of Enlightenment. For this I would suggest the term 'transcendental', which I use as the equivalent of the Sanskrit word *lokuttara* (Pāli *lokuttara*) – literally, 'beyond the world'. So we have three words: psychological, which pertains to ordinary human consciousness; spiritual, which pertains to the higher, dhyānic levels of consciousness; and transcendental, which pertains to Enlightenment, to ultimate reality.

Having rectified our terms in this way, we can no longer use expressions like spiritual practice, spiritual life, spiritual path, and spiritual ideal in a vague, woolly way. Spiritual practice is specifically that practice which is conducive to a state of consciousness higher than that we usually experience, to a dhyānic state, or even, if the word is used in the broader sense, to the state of Enlightenment itself. Spiritual life is the life which is systematically organized to make possible the attainment of higher states of consciousness, and which expresses those higher states. And so on.

To say that confession has a spiritual significance is therefore to say that it has significance for the attainment of higher levels of consciousness, whether the *dhyānas* or the state of Enlightenment itself. Consequently, confession plays a crucial role in the transformation of the individual, in the shift of the centre of gravity from the psychological to the spiritual, and from the spiritual to the transcendental. It is confession in this sense that is expounded in the *Sūtra of Golden Light*, especially in the celebrated verses of confession.

Just to set the scene before we explore the text of the *sūtra* in detail, we will take a look at the history of confession in Buddhism. The *Sūtra of Golden Light* illuminates our understanding of Buddhist confession in a particularly beautiful and comprehensive way, but it is not the first mention of confession as a practice to be found in the scriptures. Confession goes back much further in Buddhist history – back, in fact, to the time of the Buddha.

The history of confession in Buddhism is intimately connected with – believe it or not – the weather. In every country the pattern of life is shaped by the climate. It is the climate that determines when the crops will grow, what kind of housing is needed, what kind of transport will run. Some countries are dark and icebound for part of the year; others have to cope with intense heat and aridity all year round. Everywhere there is some kind of pattern to which life adapts itself.

An aspect of the climate in India that has had a formative effect on life there for thousands upon thousands of years is the rainy season. For three or four months of the year the rain falls solidly and continuously. If you go out in the rain it's like stepping into a warm shower fully clothed; you get completely soaked within minutes, and of course the ground gets so muddy that – if you live out in the countryside – it is difficult to walk very far.

As well as affecting the pattern of social and agricultural life, the rainy season has had its effect on Indian spiritual life, at least so far as its outward expression is concerned. In the Buddha's day, and for centuries afterwards, those of his followers who had given up the household life used to wander from place to place living on alms and teaching the Dharma. But in the rainy season it was impossible to wander about and sleep under trees, as you could do the rest of the year. You needed to find a place to shelter.

At first, the Buddha's followers used to stay in all kinds of places during the rainy season. They might stay in a cave or a wayside shrine devoted to local gods; they might find a shed in somebody's garden or park, or even spend the rainy season in a hollow tree. As time went on, simple buildings were put up for the use of the *bhikkhus* by the lay supporters who continued to live at home.[205] It was these rudimentary shelters that eventually became what we usually refer to as monasteries.

The rainy season increasingly became an opportunity for the monks to spend time together. Some of them remained absorbed in meditation for much of the time, but others took the chance to repeat to each other what they knew of the Buddha's teaching, to preserve the oral tradition. They also used to spend time on more homely tasks – if one can use the word 'homely' in connection with monks – mending and patching their robes, washing and dyeing them.

Come the end of the rainy season, though, they would set off on their wanderings again, either singly or in twos and threes, sometimes even in small bands. The monks wandered on foot from place to place all over north-eastern India. The area they covered was so vast – the

Buddha himself is known to have wandered over an area the equivalent in extent to Great Britain – that they might well go for days and days without seeing any other monk. But twice a month, on the night of the full moon and the night of the new moon, wherever they might find themselves in the course of their wanderings, all the monks in a given area would gather together. There might be as many as a thousand of them, especially if the Buddha was going to be present. They would gather together in a forest clearing in the light of the full moon, and chant together verses in which the Buddha's teaching had been summarized, either by the Buddha himself or by one of his disciples who happened to be poetically gifted. Then, having refreshed their memory of the teaching, they would meditate and reflect on it.

This is what happened during the Buddha's lifetime, as far as we can reconstruct events. But after the Buddha's death, after the *parinirvāṇa*, it seems that a change took place. The *bhikkhus* continued to meet on the nights of the full moon and the new moon, but they no longer meditated or chanted together. Instead, they confessed any offences against the monastic code – by this time comparatively fully schematized – that they had committed since the last meeting.[206] Any transgressions were then dealt with by the assembled chapter of the Order.

Later still, another change took place. The monks confessed their offences not during the actual meeting but before it. They got together in pairs and took it in turns to confess, the senior going first. In the meeting itself the monastic code was simply recited by a single monk appointed for the purpose. The rest of the assembly, having already confessed in private, remained silent.

This kind of confessional meeting is still held in many parts of the Buddhist world today, especially those that follow the Theravādin tradition. Unfortunately the practice has degenerated considerably, at least in some circles, as I discovered for myself as a young monk in Nepal. The occasion was the ordination ceremony of two young novices. Before the ceremony could commence, all the monks present had to purify themselves, and that meant they had to confess. So we all paired off, each pair of monks squatting on their heels face to face and confessing to one another, first the senior monk confessing to the junior, then the junior to the senior. I was quite pleased to discover that we would be confessing to each other in this way, because although I had been ordained for about a year, I hadn't so far had an opportunity to confess any faults. I began to think, 'What have I got to confess? Have I done anything I shouldn't have?' But before I could get very far in my thinking, the monk with whom I was paired started chanting something very rapidly in Pāli. I could make out some of it, but not much because he was chanting so quickly. It only took him about a minute and a half, and then he said, 'Come on. Now you chant.' I said, 'Well, I don't know it by heart', so he said, 'All right, repeat it after me.' He rattled it off and I repeated it phrase for phrase. When I looked up again, all the other monks were standing up already. I was very disappointed.[207]

Although in the Theravādin tradition the confession ceremony which has its roots in the rainy season gatherings has become a formality, this is not the only form of confession practised. For instance, even among Theravādins it does sometimes happen that a monk who feels something weighing on his mind goes and confesses it to his teacher. When you are living under the same roof as your teacher, the practice is that at the end of each day you go to him, bow down, and ask forgiveness for any offences of body, speech, or mind that you may have committed against him in the course of the day. For instance, you may not quite have liked something the teacher said to you, and an angry thought may have flashed across your mind. Well, you've got to confess it that night; you mustn't sleep on it. You've got to bring it out into the open and say, 'This is what happened. I felt angry. I'm sorry, please forgive me.' If the practice is kept up in this way, a positive and open relationship between teacher and pupil is maintained.

In my own case, although I didn't have the opportunity to get to know most of my Tibetan teachers well enough to be able to make a real confession, I was sometimes able to open up to Dhardo Rimpoche, whom I got to know quite well.[208] Once or twice there was something that was making me feel uneasy, and I spoke to him about it. But there wasn't much opportunity for confession, and in any case I didn't think so much in those terms then as I do now. It was one of those things I had to find out for myself.

Ever since the time of the Buddha, confession has been considered important not only for monks, but also for lay people. Take the well-known story of Ajātaśatru, the king of Magadha, who lived in the Buddha's time. Ajātaśatru had become king in a way all too common in those days. He had done it by murdering his father, King Bimbisāra, an old friend and disciple of the Buddha's. Although he had got the kingship he wanted, Ajātaśatru was uneasy in his mind. He couldn't forget what he had done; he could get no rest. One full moon night, after he had been tossing and turning for hours, he just couldn't stand it any longer. He got up to go and see the Buddha, who was staying with his disciples in the middle of the forest. Ajātaśatru went straight to the Buddha and confessed what he had done: evil had overcome him, and he had killed his own father for the sake of the throne. The Buddha heard and accepted Ajātaśatru's confession, and then he gave a teaching. But although Ajātaśatru heard the teaching and was receptive to it, the higher spiritual vision did not arise in him. The Buddha remarked that Ajātaśatru would have attained that vision but for the fact that he had committed that most serious and terrible of offences.[209]

Mahāyāna Buddhism also has its tradition of confession. Indeed, throughout the Buddhist world, verses of confession are chanted as part of devotional practice. In the Mahāyāna tradition such verses – like the ones in the *Sūtra of Golden Light* – are particularly beautiful and elaborate. There are many texts that deal with the practice of confession in detail, and among them the *Sūtra of Golden Light* stands out for its great beauty and its comprehensive treatment of the subject.

We have already seen that the verses spoken by the golden drum, while focusing on the theme of confession, bring in other themes, and in fact take the form, more or less, of a sevenfold puja. A sevenfold puja is a form of worship in which one passes through a sequence of what might be called spiritual moods. First comes recognition of the Buddha, the Enlightened One, and the aspiration to commit oneself to the path of Enlightenment. Then comes confession of all those obstacles that stand between oneself as one is at present and the Enlightened being one aspires to become; then rejoicing in merit, in which one expresses delight at all the skilful actions performed by others. Then comes the request for a teaching, and lastly what is called 'transference of merit', in which one dedicates whatever fruits are borne by one's spiritual efforts to the good of all beings.

This is roughly the form taken by chapter 3 of the *sūtra*, although, the emphasis being on confession, there are three confession sections rather than the usual one, each with a slightly different flavour. Because each section brings out a different aspect of the spiritual significance of confession, we will look at each in some detail. To begin with, though, we will turn to the first utterances of the golden drum, which make clear the context in which confession should be made.

ASPIRATION: THE CONTEXT FOR CONFESSION

We could describe the first section of chapter 3 as a prayer for the progress of all sentient beings. To call it a prayer, however, is a very provisional description. The 'prayer' is just the sound of the drum, the golden light pouring forth from the drum, and more than that, it's the *effect* of the sound and the light – the beneficent effect of that sound and light on all sentient beings:

> By the excellent drum of golden light let the woes in the triple-thousand world be suppressed, the woes in the evil states, the woes in the world of Yama and the woes of poverty here in the threefold world.[210]

The 'evil states' here are those of the beings occupying three of the six realms depicted by the Tibetan wheel of life: the realm of the animals, the realm of the hungry ghosts, and the realm of the hell-beings. Ultimately, of course, you have to get out of all six realms, but these three in particular are the evil states, the 'ill-farings'.

So as yet the aspiration isn't very high. There's just a prayer that these worldly woes may be suppressed. There isn't any reference to the attainment of higher spiritual states.

> And by this resounding of the sound of the drum may all troubles in the world be suppressed, may beings be without fear, free of fear just as great sages are without fear, fearless.[211]

Abhaya or fearlessness is mentioned very often in Buddhism.[212] It is, for example, enumerated as an element in the bodhisattva's practice of *dāna* or giving. Along with material things, culture, life and limb (if necessary), and the supreme gift, the gift of the Buddha's teaching, he is able to impart the gift of fearlessness. By his mere presence the bodhisattva creates confidence and removes people's fear. Certainly freedom from fear is emphasized much more in Buddhism than in Christianity, where we may say fear is positively encouraged: 'The fear of the Lord is the beginning of wisdom.'

I can recall from my own experience one quite vivid instance illustrative of this difference between the two religions. It concerned the death of somebody I knew when I was living in Kalimpong – an elderly Englishwoman who had come out to Kalimpong and become a Buddhist. I came back from Calcutta one day and the first news I got on my return was that Miss Barclay had died, and that there was a dispute about the body. The local Catholic Christians were claiming it and wanting to give it Christian burial, but my students were resisting and saying no, she had become a Buddhist. So I hurried straight to her house and found several local Christians there, plus a number of my students, all Buddhists, and the police.

As I entered, the police inspector said to me, 'Can you tell me what religion this lady followed?' I said, 'Oh yes, she was a Buddhist.' My students said, 'There, we told you so, we told you so!' So the police officer said, 'Ah, but can you prove it?' – and all the Catholics smiled. I said, 'Yes.' The police inspector then said, 'Well, can you produce the proof in the police station tomorrow morning?' 'Yes, certainly.'

We had an organization called the Young Men's Buddhist Association and Miss Barclay had become an associate member. She had signed the application form, and where it said 'Religion' she'd filled in 'Buddhist'. So, to cut a long story short, we claimed the body. We took it from the hospital mortuary back to the YMBA, and, as there was nowhere else, laid it out on the ping-pong table. The funeral had been announced for that afternoon and a lot of people came.

Here we get to the point of the story. Miss Barclay had known quite a few Christians in the area, including missionaries, and they all gathered in the sitting-room; and there were many of my students who had also known her. According to local custom, before someone was cremated you would go and have a last look at them. All my students, who were young Nepalese and Tibetans and Bhutanese, were keen to have a last look at Miss Barclay. She had been a good friend to them; she had often invited them for tea. So they were all going into the games room to take a look: 'Oh yes, she looks OK, quite peaceful....' – that sort of thing.

But when I asked the Christian missionaries and ministers whether they would like to go in and have a look at Miss Barclay, they said, to a man, 'Oh, no thank you!' They clearly had a fear of death, or anything to do with it. Not one of them went in to have a look – they were simply afraid to – but all these quite ordinary Tibetan and Nepalese students went in without any hesitation. You couldn't quite say it was all in a day's work, but they were accustomed to it. It was what happened at home if their grandfather or their great-aunt died. Death was a natural thing, it was a part of life. There was nothing to be afraid of – you all had to die one day, everybody knew that. But these missionaries, even though they were preachers of religion, were obviously afraid.[213]

Whether this was specifically to do with Christianity, or something more to do with modern life in general, it is difficult to say. But certainly there seems to be much more fear of this kind in the minds of people in the West. One shouldn't overstate this, of course; there is fear in everybody, otherwise there would be no need for prayers of this sort, or for bodhisattvas to impart fearlessness. Indeed, the development of fearlessness is central to the practice of Buddhism, especially fearlessness in the face of death.

Very often we don't realize the extent to which we are under the influence of fear and worry and anxiety. Not very many people are completely free from fear, or even free from worry. To be fearless is quite an achievement; in fact, if you are fearless, you are practically Enlightened. By this I don't mean that Enlightenment confers the kind of fearlessness which is simply lack of imagination. I remember once hearing about wartime pilots, and apparently the best of them, the ace fliers, the ones who won decorations, were totally lacking in imagination. They weren't particularly fearless; they just didn't have enough imagination to realize that there was any danger. That isn't true fearlessness. If you are truly fearless, you see the situation clearly, you have no illusions about it, but you don't feel afraid. That is fearlessness as understood by Buddhism. After all, what is fear? You are usually afraid for yourself, or afraid of losing yourself. If you are fearless, therefore, you are practically free from egotism.

The basic fear is, obviously, fear of death, but there are many others. Perhaps surprisingly, a great number of people seem to be afraid of going mad. It seems as though they are already under quite a strain and just a bit more pressure will make them crack. It is noticeable that in the West there is more fear of insane people than you tend to find in India. Here, if someone walked in and started acting the fool, so to speak, we wouldn't quite know how to take it, whereas Indian people wouldn't be embarrassed or put out at all, as long as he didn't do any actual harm. Perhaps this fear of mental illness indicates that in the West one identifies oneself more strongly with the rational part of oneself than people usually do in India, and one therefore tends to have difficulty finding a sense of fellow-feeling with those who have lost their reason.

There is also fear of humiliation. Bunyan's shepherd boy sings, 'He that is down needs fear no fall'[214] – but all too often we *are* afraid of falling, afraid of not being able to live up to what people expect of us. We have a false idea of ourself which we try to live up to, and which other people expect us to live up to, and we feel insecure because we know that we are trying to live up to something false. We feel a sense of strain all the time, because we are afraid of disappointing people's expectations and feeling humiliated as a result.

If you have always thought of yourself as being very clever, and everybody else thinks you're very clever, you feel humiliated if you're made to look a fool because that isn't the image you have of yourself. But if you've got no illusions about yourself and don't try to live up to some unreal image, you're not vulnerable to humiliation in this way. If you've been a fool since the day you were born – and if everybody knows it and you know it too – you're not humiliated by being shown up as a fool. You're just being yourself.

If, as the *sūtra* prays, you become fearless, that is a great spiritual achievement, because it's only the Buddha, the Enlightened one, who is completely fearless. As Buddhism has always attached great importance to the state of fearlessness, it should come as no surprise that the sound of the golden drum has the effect of removing fear.

A solitary retreat, when you spend time alone meditating and reflecting, is very likely to give rise to fear, because it deprives you of the activities and things through which you hide from your basic anxiety. Under more ordinary circumstances, if you start feeling anxious you go and talk to somebody or go to the cinema or do something else to distract yourself. But when you're on solitary retreat you can't do any of those things. There is no escape from anxiety, no escape from fear; you're brought right up against it. There is an element of this in everybody. It's as though it's there all the time, or much of the time, but we usually distract ourselves from it instead of facing it. When we're alone, though, it's a lot more difficult to run away.

If you are able to get away on solitary retreat, you may well find that at first you are keen to keep busy and fill in the day, because you are afraid of getting bored. But as the retreat progresses and you build up a higher level of positivity, you should be able to leave off doing so many things. You find you just don't need that kind of support. After a month or two you could conceivably end up doing nothing at all, and still pass the whole day quite positively – that is, being neither afraid nor empty nor bored nor anything else.

So if you get the chance to go on solitary retreat, or just to spend some time alone, you need to be careful not to use study and meditation to escape from feelings of anxiety. You do objectively need to keep yourself positively occupied, but we should be careful not to do things as defences against the anxiety which arises simply through being alone. It's fine to meditate all the time if it's a spontaneous and natural thing, but not if you are just meditating to keep anxiety at bay. Difficult as it may be, you need to allow yourself to feel afraid. You can't transform the feeling just like that, but if you make sure you are allowing yourself to feel it, it will pass sooner or later. You might find in the end that it is less trouble allowing yourself to feel the anxiety than spending all your time and energy keeping it at bay.

> Just as the great sages who know all in the cycle of existence are endowed with all the noble virtues, so may men be oceans of virtues endowed with the virtues of meditation and the (seven) members of enlightenment.[215]

The seven members – or factors – of Enlightenment are the seven *bodhyaṅgas*: recollection or awareness (*smṛti*), investigation of mental states (*dharma-vicaya*), energy or vigour (*vīrya*), rapture (*prīti*), tension release or bliss (*praśrabdhi*), concentration (*samādhi*), and tranquillity or equanimity (*upekṣā*).[216]

Of course, the factors can't really be divided up quite so neatly. *Vīrya*, for example, although it is listed as a factor (it is also numbered as one of the *pāramitās* or perfections), is needed all along. Without some *vīrya*, some vigour, how can you investigate your mental states, for instance? But all the same, there is a kind of sequence in the factors. First of all you have mindfulness. Then with that mindfulness you examine all your mental states, to see whether they are skilful or unskilful. That is *dharma-vicaya*. Then, having investigated your mental states, you act upon the knowledge gained from the investigation, starting to weed out the unskilful mental states and cultivate the skilful ones. For that you obviously need energy. Not only do you need energy for doing it, but once you have done it, you gain more energy, because the energy that was locked up in the unskilful mental states has been released. The release of energy leads to an experience of *prīti* or rapture – and so on.

The cycle of existence mentioned here is the *nidāna* chain, the wheel of life, and the suggestion is that the great sages have penetrated it through insight into all its aspects.[217] They know it thoroughly, have seen through it completely, and they are at the same time endowed with all the noble virtues.

> And by this resounding of the sound of the drum may all beings possess the voice of Brahma.[218]

Wishing that all beings may possess the voice of Brahmā is in effect to wish that all beings may become Enlightened, because the Buddha is the one who possesses the voice of Brahmā. The Brahmā voice is made up of all possible sounds. Sometimes it's said that it is made up of the sixty-four sounds – there being sixty-four letters in the Sanskrit alphabet – which is to say that it expresses all possible combinations of words and sentences. It says everything, but communicates to each person what they particularly need to hear. To say that the Buddha has the Brahmā voice is therefore to say that when the Buddha speaks, everybody understands in his or her own way.

Take the audience of a talk about Buddhism. Everybody hears the same words, but they each take what they need. One person may say, 'He said something that really impressed me – he said something about the four noble truths.'[219] But someone else may say, 'No, it was all about the life of the Buddha. I really liked that.' No doubt the speaker spoke about both those things, but for one listener it was the four noble truths that registered, while for the other it was what was said about the life of the Buddha.

A talk, of course, has a certain length and includes various different topics, but the Brahmā voice says everything at once, if you can imagine that. It's as though the lecturer had managed to speak about the four noble truths and the life of the Buddha at the same time. The Brahmā voice is the voice from which everybody picks out what they want – or need – to hear. In an ultimate sense we could say that the Buddha doesn't say anything at all, or that everything he says has the same meaning, and that what he says only seems to comprise different things because different people take it differently.

> May they touch the best enlightenment of Buddhahood. May they turn the pure Wheel of the Law. May they remain (living) for inconceivable aeons. May they preach the Law for the welfare of the world. May they destroy impurities, annihilate woes, suppress passion, likewise hatred (and) folly.[220]

This is all pretty straightforward; the essential meaning is again the wish that all living beings may gain Enlightenment. Turning the Wheel of the Law is a reference to the traditional image, the *dharmacakra-pravartana*, the 'setting in motion of the Wheel of the Dharma'.[221] According to some scholars there is some solar symbolism here, the Wheel of the Dharma being the sun-wheel, the sun with its rays.

> May those beings who dwell in an evil state, their limbs alight with blazing fire, hear the sound of the drum. May they take up the refrain: 'Homage be to the Buddha.'[222]

Here we are talking about what we would call hell, although the Buddhist hell differs from the Christian one in that it is not a permanent state. Even beings in hell may make spiritual progress in the long term. These lines express the wish that even beings in such a very unfavourable condition may hear the sound of the drum, in order that they may have some chance to escape from that state, and – eventually – become Enlightened.

> May all beings be mindful of their (former) births during hundreds of births, thousands of millions of births.[223]

First of all, it is worth questioning the point of remembering all one's previous births. Perhaps on the whole it is just as well that we *don't* remember our previous lives. It would probably be such a sordid and sorry tale. We might be terribly discouraged to see ourselves making the same mistakes over and over again. Looking back on the follies of this life is bad enough for some of us. If we peeked back into the previous life and it was no better, and the one before that even worse, and the ten or twelve before that absolutely catastrophic – well, we'd get depressed after the first few hundred. We might start thinking we had no hope. So we are better off, at this stage, only remembering this life – or bits of it. It does seem a merciful providence that wipes the slate clean every time we are reborn so that we can make a fresh start.

But when you have developed these higher spiritual faculties, then it's safe enough to look back and recollect your previous lives. Even if you look back on tens of thousands of wasted lives, it doesn't matter, because at least you're on your way now – you are in fact very near your goal. To say, 'May all beings be mindful of their former births,' is therefore to wish at the same time that all beings may attain a high level of spiritual development, because it is only then that it will be useful or even bearable to recollect all those previous lives.

> Continually mindful of the great sages, let them hear their word, for it is noble. And by this resounding of the noise of the drum may they always obtain a meeting with the Buddhas. May they avoid evil action. May they practise meritorious acts of good.[224]

Being continually mindful of the great sages means recollecting their lives and good qualities, or if they are alive, going to see them and listening to them. In speaking of 'their word' in the singular, the text seems to imply that all the great sages speak one word, that is, that all those who are really great sages give – at least in essence – the same teaching.

> For those men, Asuras, all beings who have desires (and) wishes, may I fulfill them all by this resounding of the noise of the drum.[225]

So here are all these beings who are full of desires and wishes. It's as though the sound of the drum fulfils their real wishes, what they are really after, perhaps even without knowing it. And here we touch upon a fundamental spiritual issue. Often we feel desires for all sorts of things we think we want, but even if we get what we thought we wanted, our desires remain unsatisfied. We experience this, of course, because we are so busy going after things we don't really want. Only too often, when we have had it and enjoyed it – if it was enjoyable – we realize that we didn't really want it after all. We are not really satisfied; we have just been distracted or amused for a while, no more than that. When we think about it, we realize that we could easily have done without it – even have been better off without it.

But when you are in the grip of desire, it's hard to remember all this. When you think you want something, well, you think you want it. You can go through the same procedure time and time again, maybe hundreds of times, before you learn your lesson and accept that you're not going to get what you really want from that thing. It cannot give you real satisfaction – but it's difficult to give up hoping that it might be able to, and trying just once more. 'I'll give it another chance before trying Nirvāṇa!' You really have to wallow in it before you know it's muck.

Even if people tell you that the object of your desire will be a disappointment, and on a rational level you can see that they are right, this still won't help if, deep down, you remain unconvinced. However rational and reasonable the arguments against doing it are, you may well feel compelled to do whatever it is anyway, just to see for yourself.

But, of course, there is really no need to try out everything personally. If somebody tells you that if you put your finger in the fire it will burn, you don't have to test it to see. You might put your finger near enough to get warm, and a bit nearer to get warmer, but that will be enough to convince you. It's a delusion to think that we have to experience personally everything that the Buddha has warned us does not lead in the direction of Nirvāṇa. We just have to take the Buddha's word for it in at least certain areas, and not insist on a personal confirmation of the unsatisfactoriness of every vice.

It isn't even really necessary to experience something of every kind or category of vice. You can group them into one big group called 'worldly pleasures'; if you have had even a taste of one of them, that should be enough to disillusion you about them all. They all come under the same heading; they're all conditioned things, so they don't really differ in any essential respect from one another.

On the other hand, it could be quite dangerous to deprive yourself of all comforts on the basis of a purely rational understanding of the truth, before you have started to get any real satisfaction from practising Buddhism. If you did that, you could well feel so bored and frustrated, and find life so blank and meaningless, that you would be tempted to go to the opposite extreme. You must begin to enjoy being a Buddhist before you give up too much, otherwise you will associate being a Buddhist with a dull, dry, painful, difficult, joyless sort of existence.

This should not, of course, be used as a rationalization for not giving up anything at all. In fact, if you haven't got any enjoyment at all from the Dharma, it might be best to give up a few things and make things really uncomfortable for yourself. That might force the issue. Otherwise you could remain stuck indefinitely, just being mentally occupied with the Dharma, getting no real pleasure from it, and not being willing to give up even small things because you haven't yet started to enjoy the spiritual life. You could stay like that all your life. You might have to do something drastic, take a risk, make yourself really uncomfortable, get thoroughly bored and frustrated. Then you would have to get pleasure from the Dharma because you weren't getting it from anywhere else.

It is tempting to think that the golden light might be somehow reflected in the more refined worldly pleasures, but this is not so at all. It is true that in the case of aesthetic experiences at their very highest, like the music of Bach at its most sublime, you get distant reflections – or perhaps we should say echoes – of the golden light. But the golden light does not actually shine through even the most elevated aesthetic production; and it's not enough just to have a glimpse in the distance in an indirect, remote way. We have to make the experience our own, and this involves a regular, disciplined way of life directed to that end.

In modern times we have got into the habit of sampling experience with no corresponding commitment to what the experience is meant to represent. To take the example of music, we don't usually think of it very seriously. It doesn't involve us in any responsibility towards it; it's just available for us to use and enjoy. We go along to concerts because it's a pleasant sensation. But we could go along and experience them as a revelation which would make a real difference to our lives. It is the nature of the aesthetic experience that you are lifted out of yourself a bit – that's part of its value – and then dropped right back into yourself, virtually the same as you were before. Probably only a musician could listen to music with commitment. The rest of us are more like the so-called religious person who sits at home in the evening with a box of chocolates leafing through the life of Milarepa or the *Parinibbāna Sutta*. It's just an experience in a very superficial, untransforming sense.

We might have a taste of what Bach was trying to convey, but most of us can't become a musician like Bach. In the case of spiritual experience, however, it's different. Something is pointed out to us, or we experience something fleetingly, and then within the spiritual tradition we can make an effort, reproduce that experience within ourselves, and experience it fully. You might never become a Bach, but you can become a Buddha.

Of course, even if it doesn't result in lasting change, aesthetic experience can still be of benefit. If you are weaning yourself off, say, rather gross rock music, then to listen instead to the music of Bach is – at least in my view – very much a step in the right direction. Even if it doesn't reflect the golden light very clearly, it's a light of some kind. At least you are turning from something coarse and crude to something relatively refined, and that prepares the ground for the reception of the golden light.

So the sound of the drum is the giver of true satisfaction. Sometimes mediocre satisfaction blocks the path of true satisfaction; the good is the enemy of the best. We must learn to ask ourselves what we really want, because very often what we think we want is not really our heart's desire. We have got into a habit: we are used to it, we think we can't do without it, we think we enjoy it. But if we stop and think about our experience, we often have to admit that we don't really enjoy the things we usually do. We just don't know what to do instead. We fear that without our habitual activities we would be bored and dull, so we keep on doing them to stave off the boredom.

If you are unhappy, you can go out on the town, dull your perceptions, and pretend to be happy. Alternatively, you can stay where you are, knowing that you are unhappy but at least having some idea where to look for true happiness. Or, at the very least, knowing where you are *not* going to find it. It might sound strange, but in a way the unhappiness you feel is positive because it's simply the discomfort you feel when you are no longer trying to enjoy evanescent satisfactions.

You might perhaps feel, say on a Saturday night when everyone in the world seems to be going out to have a good time, that resisting the pull to join this social stream is somehow disintegrating. By losing touch with the 'social whirl' you feel you are losing touch with your own energy. This is because there is within you something that is in conflict with your more creative energies that responds to that pull. When you surrender to the attraction, all that has happened is that one part of you has triumphed over another with the help of outside forces. That certainly doesn't represent integration. You haven't resolved the conflict; you have just submerged it for the time being. You've temporarily ended the tension within you by yielding to the outside influence.

> For those beings who have taken birth in a fierce hell, their limbs alight with blazing fire, and, without protection and oppressed with grief, wander about, there will be quenching of their fires. Those beings whose woes are fierce and terrible in hells, among ghosts (or) in the world of men, by this resounding of the noise of the drum, may all their woes be suppressed.[226]

Here, if we come right down to earth, the quenching of the fires refers to our experience when we come upon something of a purely spiritual nature. It has the effect of making us realize that all our suffering is unnecessary; we have brought it upon ourselves through our own foolish involvement with certain things. When we realize this, our suffering just ceases.

In his dream, Ruciraketu now not only hears a prayer that by virtue of the drum of golden light all beings may progress; he also actually sees the golden light helping them to progress. In this case the medium really is the message. The prayer of the drum, the prayer of the golden light, is self-fulfilling. As we have seen, the golden drum is the Absolute, the Buddha, as well as being the new Ruciraketu, and also the *sūtra* itself. So what Ruciraketu hears in this opening section is not just a pious wish that all sentient beings may progress. What he hears – and sees – is a sort of cosmic drama, a drama of the effect of the golden light of the transcendental on the darkness of the mundane.

He has in his dream a sort of spiritual vision. He sees that on the one hand there is the golden light, the light of truth, the light of reality; and on the other hand there is the darkness of confusion and bewilderment, the darkness of defilement and passion. And he sees that the darkness is struggling to overcome the light, and the light is struggling to overcome the darkness. He not only hears the prayer that 'the woes in the triple-thousand world may be suppressed' – he sees that in the case of at least some people woes *are* being suppressed. He not only hears the prayer that beings may be without fear; he sees some of them becoming free from fear. In the same way, he sees people gaining

Enlightenment, teaching the Dharma, destroying greed, hatred, and delusion. He sees people paying homage to the Buddha, worshipping the Buddha, recollecting the Buddha, meeting the Buddha, sees them performing skilful actions, sees the fires of hell being quenched, sees all woes being suppressed. In other words, Ruciraketu has a vision of the whole world being transformed. He sees darkness being overcome, and the golden light triumphant.

He, too, feels the effect of the golden light. He, too, wants to be transformed. Not only that, he wants to co-operate with the golden light in its work of transforming the world and helping sentient being to progress. This is his response:

> And may I be for those who are without deliverance, without rescue, without refuge, the deliverer, the refuge, the excellent protector.[227]

In other words, the *bodhicitta*, the will to Enlightenment, arises, and he takes the bodhisattva vow, the vow to attain supreme Enlightenment for the benefit of all sentient beings. The English word 'protector' can be confusing, because it is frequently used to translate two quite different Sanskrit words. When in the sevenfold puja, for example, the Buddhas are referred to as 'protectors', the word translated is *nātha*.[228] On the other hand, the word generally used in connection with the protectors of the four quarters, the four great kings, whom we will come across later in the *sūtra*, is *pāla* – they are the *dharmapālas*. *Nātha* has rather a different significance from *pāla*. For instance, an orphan is called an *anātha* – someone without a protector. So *nātha* could even be translated as 'master'.

Ruciraketu's taking of the bodhisattva vow at this point reminds us that the sense of time in the *sūtra* is all askew. Ruciraketu is introduced to us as a bodhisattva, which implies that he has already taken the bodhisattva vow, but here we find him, or rather the golden drum, taking the vow as though it hadn't been taken before. This shouldn't come as a surprise; after all, this is a dream, and dreams operate on a different timescale from ordinary life.

In fact, Ruciraketu in effect takes the bodhisattva vow again towards the end of the chapter:

> May all beings be such in virtue, appearance, fame, glory, with body adorned with the beautiful major marks (and) decorated with the eighty minor marks. And by this good act, may I ere long become a Buddha in the world; may I preach the Law for the welfare of the world; may I deliver beings oppressed by many woes; may I overcome Māra with his might and with his army; may I turn the Wheel of the excellent Law; may I remain for inconceivable aeons; may I satisfy beings with the water of nectar; may I fulfill the six unrivalled perfections just as they were fulfilled by previous Buddhas; may I smite the impurities; may I destroy woes; may I extinguish passion, likewise hatred (and) folly. And may I be continually mindful of former births for hundreds of births, thousands of millions of births. May I constantly recollect the great sages. May I listen to their speech, for it is noble. And by this good act, may I always find a meeting with the Buddhas; may I utterly avoid evil action; may I practise the good acts, mines of excellence.[229]

This paragraph starts off with an aspiration on behalf of all beings but then it modulates into a sort of bodhisattva vow. There is an important point to be made here. The *bodhicitta*, the will to Enlightenment – or thought of Enlightenment, as it is sometimes (incorrectly) translated – is transcendental. It is not a product of the mundane consciousness. One cannot therefore really speak of 'my *bodhicitta*' or 'your *bodhicitta*'. It is not an individual possession. In fact there is only one *bodhicitta*, just as in reality there is only one bodhisattva and only one Buddha. But the one *bodhicitta* manifests through different individuals, through those that make themselves receptive to it, like light refracting through a prism.

This is what has happened in Ruciraketu's case. He has made himself receptive to the golden light, so that the golden light begins to work through him. In short, he becomes a real bodhisattva. And what a real bodhisattva does is practise the six perfections: generosity, ethics, patience, energy, meditation, and wisdom. He works on himself, and he does his best to help others. But unfortunately, what usually – indeed always – happens next is that he comes up against obstacles within himself, inner resistance. He becomes aware of many weaknesses and faults, of much within him that is actually evil. He becomes aware of the darkness within him, and this darkness resists the influence of the *bodhicitta*, struggles against the golden light. What should the bodhisattva do? What *can* he do? He can confess. He can confess his faults, the evil that is within him. It is Ruciraketu's confession that takes the form of the verses in the *Sūtra of Golden Light*.

Ruciraketu's experience is surely very much our own, even though our experience may be on a lower level and a more restricted scale. We too, perhaps, have seen the workings of the golden light in the world, or at least our corner of it, and we too have wanted to make ourselves receptive to that light, to allow it to work through us. So we too have breathed forth our individual aspirations. We may not have taken the bodhisattva vow, but we have at least resolved to work on ourselves and do our best to help others in whatever way we can. But then we too encounter obstacles within ourselves, inner resistance perhaps far stronger and more terrible than anything Ruciraketu meets. So what can we do? Well, to begin with at least, we too can simply confess.

THE FIRST CONFESSION: THE VICTORY OF THE GOLDEN LIGHT

The word for confession in Sanskrit is *deśanā*, which means 'pointing out', 'indicating', 'explaining', 'expounding' – as in *Dharma deśanā*, which means the pointing out of the Dharma, the explaining of the Dharma. In the same way you get *pāpa deśanā*, the pointing out, the acknowledgement, of faults. *Pāpa* is often translated as 'sin', but I prefer to avoid the word because of its Christian connections. 'Faults', on the other hand, is rather weak. 'Evil' is probably the best translation. *Pāpa deśanā* is a pointing out, a confession, of the evil within us. But none of these expressions really does justice to one's actual spiritual experience at this stage. We need to go into the matter more deeply.

When you come into contact with the golden light, something of it enters into your system. It's a sort of spiritual food – the most concentrated and powerful kind of spiritual food imaginable. More than that, it's a sort of spiritual medicine. When it enters your system, it encounters all sorts of other things you have taken in: greed, hatred, delusion, wrong views.... There ensues a struggle between the golden light and the poison in your system, each trying to throw the other out. Sometimes, unfortunately, the unskilful states win, and succeed in expelling the golden light, which means an end to your spiritual life, at least for the time being. But happily this rarely happens. Once you have really taken in even a little of the golden light, it's very difficult to get rid of: in short, you're stuck with it.

So, does being stuck with the golden light mean that once you have come into contact with the spiritual path you can never fall back? Well, yes and no. It is only once you have entered the Stream that you are irreversibly bound for Enlightenment.[230] Up to that point, any spiritual experience or series of experiences you have is not irreversible, however long it may take to reverse the series.

However, it is probably true to say that once you have attained the level of reflexive consciousness that characterizes a human being, it is unlikely that you will lose it. From a Buddhist point of view, you have perhaps enjoyed reflexive consciousness for a very long time, through many births. What has developed over a long period takes a lot of undoing.

Even in the course of a single lifetime a human being can degenerate greatly through unskilful action – maybe through taking what is not given, or through persistent alcoholism, or even through murder. None the less, however degenerate, that person is still quite recognizably a human being, and reflexive consciousness is still quite clearly there, at least to some extent.

Once you have come into contact with the golden light, as long as your reflexive consciousness persists intact, you can't forget about your experience of that golden light, even though you haven't attained Stream Entry, even though you are not a bodhisattva, and even though in theory you could fall right back to a very low state. In the long run you could, with a great deal of difficulty and as a result of a great deal of unskilful behaviour, shake off the golden light, but it is highly unlikely. None the less there is a sharp distinction between that state and the state of having achieved Stream Entry.

It is of course popularly understood that a human being might be reborn as an animal. Whether we can say that this really happens or not depends very much on what we mean by a human being. If we mean someone who has not only a human body but a fully and genuinely human consciousness, it is extremely unlikely that, after death, that person will be reborn as an animal. But if only a very rudimentary human consciousness has been developed, and if even that has been degraded by unskilful actions so that, at death, that person's mental state is not much higher than an animal's, an animal rebirth would seem not to be impossible.

In Darjeeling years ago I happened to come across a man who kept pigs. He was a Nepalese Buddhist, but he was also a pig-keeper, and he slaughtered pigs for market. He had his piggeries and slaughterhouse just below the place where I was staying, and every night I would hear the pigs screaming. When their throats were cut they emitted a dreadful, long drawn out scream which seemed to go on for minutes together. The pig-keeper spent all his time with those pigs, and he really did look like a pig. He had piggy features, a piggy expression – even a piggy build, with short legs and forearms almost like trotters. I got the impression that he was in close mental rapport with his pigs, and I would find it quite easy to believe that he had been reborn as a pig, especially as in the course of his life he had slaughtered hundreds and thousands of pigs.

So it depends what you mean by a human being. It seems highly unlikely, but it is plausible that in exceptional cases a person could be reborn as an animal, just as one can't help feeling that some animals have got such definitely human qualities that they could easily be reborn as human beings. The idea of humans being reborn as animals may seem to go against the grain of evolution. Having been cast up into the human state, having reached the stage of reflexive consciousness, how could one possibly fall back? But one of the characteristics of reflexive consciousness is that it can work against itself, destroy itself, commit suicide, as it were. For instance, when a man starts drinking to forget, he is deliberately trying to wipe out his truly human nature. It's as though reflexive consciousness has the power to turn round on itself and commit suicide. It's a two-edged weapon.

However, if you are fortunate enough to experience the golden light, then usually the golden light succeeds in throwing out, even throwing up, the poison. This makes it not just a spiritual food or a spiritual medicine, but a spiritual emetic. Once you have taken it, it compels you to vomit up all the evil in your system. It is in this vomiting up of mental and emotional poisons that the confession of evil really consists. It's much more than a verbal acknowledgement; it's an actual revulsion from evil. When we vomit physically, our stomach turns over and there's an upheaval, and it's much the same when we truly confess. There's a spiritual upheaval, and then up comes the poison and we spew it out. This way of putting things is graphic, I know – perhaps even offensive

– but the truth of the matter is that confession can be a painful and unpleasant process, a process in which we may feel that we are spewing up not only the evil that is in us, but our blood and guts as well.

If we are in any doubt about what we should confess, the answer is simple: everything. We need to confess everything that is holding us back, everything that is preventing us from gaining Enlightenment. But this, of course, is by no means easy. There are some things that are very difficult, even impossible, to confess. This is because genuine confession is a powerful thing. Really to confess something is to give it up, not just verbally but in fact. If we are unwilling to confess something, it means that we are unable to give it up. And to the extent that we do not confess the evil within us, the evil we have done, we do not grow. We are hanging on to the past, to our old self, refusing to die.

Ruciraketu's confession is very comprehensive indeed. As far as we can tell, he doesn't leave anything out or hold anything back. There are three verses of confession in the *sūtra*, each with a slightly different emphasis. The first is simply a very full confession of all the evils Ruciraketu may have done. The second brings in the element of forgiveness, and the third adds the idea of evils committed under the influence of various 'oppressions'. Here is the first of the three sections:

> And whatever evil, cruel act was done by me previously, I will confess it all before the Buddhas. Whatever evil I have done by not attending to my parents, by neglecting the Buddhas, by neglecting the good; whatever evil I have done by being drunk with the intoxication of authority or with the intoxication of high birth or by being drunk with the intoxication of tender age; whatever evil I have done, bad thought, bad word, by an act badly done (or) by not perceiving a mishap; whatever evil I have done by the application of foolish reasoning, by a mind dark with ignorance, under the influence of an evil friend or by a mind distracted by impurities, under the compulsion of sport (or) enjoyment, or through the influence of anxiety (or) anger, (or) through the fault of unsatisfied wealth; whatever evil I have done by my associations with ignoble people, by reason of envy (and) greed, (or) by the fault of guile (or) wretchedness; whatever evil I have done through failure to gain the mastery over my desires by reason of fear at the time of approaching troubles; whatever evil I have done through

> the influence of a flighty mind or through the influence of passion (and) anger (or) through being oppressed by hunger and thirst; whatever evil I have done for the sake of drink and food, for the sake of clothing, for a reason involving women, through the various afflictions of impurities; whatever evil of body, tongue and mind, bad action accumulated in threefold manner, I have done, together with similar things, I confess it all. Whatever disrespect I may have shown to Buddhas, doctrines, likewise to Śrāvakas, I confess it all. Whatever disrespect I may have shown toward Pratyekabuddhas or towards Bodhisattvas, I confess it all. (If I have shown disrespect towards those who preach the Good Law or towards other meritorious beings, I confess it all.) If I have unawares continually rejected the Good Law (or shown) disrespect towards my parents, I confess it all. (Whatever evil I have done) through stupidity or from folly or through being full of pride and arrogance, through passion, hatred or delusion, I confess it all.[231]

So this is Ruciraketu's first confession, and it gives a good idea of what is to be confessed. His first statement is:

> whatever evil, cruel act was done by me previously, I will confess it all before the Buddhas.

It is highly significant that the very first evil act that Ruciraketu confesses is cruelty. This is no doubt because cruelty is the behaviour which is most directly opposed to the bodhisattva ideal. If you are cruel, you can't possibly be a bodhisattva, because cruelty is the direct opposite of compassion. One of the words for cruelty is *nirdaya*, which means 'absence of compassion'. So if you want to be a bodhisattva, the first thing you have to confess, the first thing you have to vomit up, is cruelty. Cruel acts are going to obstruct your path more than anything else.

This is why the Mahāyāna is particularly down on all unskilful actions that spring from hatred. Some Mahāyāna *sūtras* go so far as to say that in a sense it doesn't matter if you commit unskilful actions based on greed. At least that shows that you have some affinity for living beings, some inclination towards them. But hatred shows a different attitude altogether. A bodhisattva cannot possibly entertain thoughts of hatred or cruelty. You can be a bodhisattva if you've got a bit of greed left, but you can't be a bodhisattva if you've got even a little bit of hatred left.[232] It is no accident that cruel acts are the very first to be confessed here.

This is perhaps the reason some scriptures say that the bodhisattva should not keep a cat. The cat is supposed to be cruel – that's the Indian idea – because it plays with and torments the mouse before killing it. So Indians regard the cat as a cruel, hard-hearted creature. The cat is said to be the only one of all those present at the time of the Buddha's *parinirvāṇa* who did not weep – apart from the *arhants*, who were Enlightened. All the animals gathered there wept, but the cat just sat there, quite unmoved. So the cat has got rather a bad reputation in Indian myth and legend.[233]

Cruelty is worse than hatred, and hatred is worse than anger. Anger is simply frustrated desire; it's the energy in the desire finding an obstacle and trying to burst through. Anger may be explosive, but it is often very short-lived, and you don't really wish the person who is obstructing you any harm. You just want to break through the obstruction; you don't want to hurt anybody. But when you hate, you have a fixed idea of some definite person or thing obstructing you, and you want to go all out to remove that person or that thing. In fact, if it is a person you feel hatred towards, you don't just want to remove them; you want to harm and injure them because you are so angry with them for having obstructed you. A species of hatred is enmity, which is the sort of vengeful hatred that pursues somebody and won't let go, won't forgive.

You can get angry with someone without ever being in any danger of hating them; you may even like them very much. But you can't hate somebody and at the same time be genuinely fond of them. You can certainly hate somebody and be in love with them – those are two sides of the same coin – but you can't hate a person you've got a genuine liking for. When you're angry with someone it isn't that you want to do them any harm – not intentionally anyway. You just explode because they are getting in your way. Anger can in a sense be quite positive in a way that hatred can never be. The danger is that if you regularly get angry with the same person for the same sort of reason, your anger will eventually consolidate into hatred.

Just as hatred develops out of anger, so enmity is to carry one's hatred beyond the possibility of forgiveness in pursuit of revenge. Cruelty goes a stage further. Cruelty is the inflicting of pain or suffering on someone beyond what is necessary to get them out of the way, and delighting in their suffering. Malice is the enjoyment of inflicting suffering on someone who has done you no harm at all. From the Mahāyāna point of view this is the most unskilful of all possible mental states.

This view is reflected in the general Mahāyāna approach to ethics. For example, when King Aśoka, the great Buddhist ruler of the Mauryan empire, exhorted his people to skilful actions, he always spoke in terms of being gentle, being patient, not giving way to anger. This was, for him, the basis of morality.[234] He never said a word about, for example, sex. In our culture when we think of morality, the first thing that comes into our minds tends to be that we shouldn't do this, and we shouldn't do that. But in Buddhist cultures, if someone is said to be an immoral person, that means that he is rude, unfriendly, harsh in speech, inhospitable, and angry.

> Whatever evil I have done by not attending to my parents ... I confess it all.

After confessing any cruel acts committed, the next thing confessed – even before the confession of neglecting the Buddhas – is evil done 'by not attending to my parents'. If this sequence has any meaning at all, it suggests that not attending to one's parents is quite a serious matter. If you are on bad terms with your parents, it suggests, you can't make much spiritual progress. Your relationship with your parents goes so deep that if it isn't positive, there's a lot in you that isn't positive. This doesn't mean that you have to have a close relationship with your parents or see eye to eye with them. They may see things so differently from you that you may not be able to communicate with them at all. But at least your attitude should be one of good will. If it isn't, that is going to make things difficult for you.

If you feel that your parents are stifling you, if they are not allowing you to grow up, it is essential for you to leave home, literally or metaphorically, and perhaps, on account of your attachment, you cannot but leave with some resentment. But if you really want to develop spiritually, sooner or later you must get over that. Even if your parents never understand what you have done and why, you must cultivate a positive attitude towards them. So long as you feel negative towards them and experience them as being restrictive and oppressive, that is going to get in your way. Our emotions are so bound up with our parents that if we hate them, we may well find it difficult to love anybody, or be capable of much devotion. Gurdjieff used to say, 'A good man always loves his parents.'[235]

I am not advocating the preservation of family life as a stuffy, claustrophobic affair. You need not feel dependent on the warmth of the cosy family group – far from it. From a Buddhist point of view you need to love your parents not just because you are their son or daughter, but because as an individual you are objectively grateful to them for what they have done for you in sponsoring your entry into the world. When Buddhism speaks in terms of a positive attitude towards one's parents, it means something more like *mettā* (loving-kindness) than love in the ordinary sense.[236]

This is true also of Hinduism at its best. A passage in the *Manusmṛti* says that when a son reaches the age of sixteen, his father should no longer treat him as a son but just as a friend. When you are sixteen, you are supposed to be grown up and independent, and you can start relating to your parents as an individual. Ideally your parents will accept you as such. Only then can there be a really positive mutual relationship between parents and children. When the children have grown up and become independent of their parents, and the parents have grown up enough to accept the change and relate to their children as individuals, there can be a very positive relationship. After all, we have known our parents all our lives, and that's a strong basis for a positive relationship.

If your parents have died, or you are not in contact with them, you can at least feel positively towards them, wishing them well wherever they are. If, by contrast, your parents are very much around, and find it difficult to let you go, you can find ways of handling that. If, for example, your mother worries about you excessively, you need not let that get in the way of developing positive feelings towards her. The first thing to recognize is that she is not just a worrying mother; she is a woman who is prone to anxiety. She doesn't just worry about you; she worries about all sorts of things. See her in that light, and you can feel more compassionate towards her.

After all, it is the function of mothers to worry. If our mothers hadn't worried about our material well-being when we were small, we wouldn't be alive now. Like the instinct of the hen to spread her wings over the eggs, it's a basic biological instinct with an obvious survival value for the species. So it is not surprising if your mother fusses and clucks around you – it is in her nature. If you manage to convince her that you have grown up and she doesn't need to worry any more about whether you are eating properly and keeping warm enough, then you can begin to relate to her as another human being. If not, you may just have to accept that she will want to keep fussing over you a bit.

The relationship with one's father may be more problematic, especially for young men, although it may also contain more possibilities. When one is very young, one's father often seems rather a threatening figure. But if a father has himself felt restricted by and dissatisfied with his way of life, he may be pleased that his son is not getting into the same rut. Even if he doesn't manage to say, 'Well done, son. I'm glad you've made more of a success of things than I could,' he may well show that he is pleased with your success – not just your worldly success, but your success in human, even spiritual, terms.

> Whatever evil I have done ... by neglecting the Buddhas, by neglecting the good ... I confess it all.

This is simply the acknowledgement that one has not been worshipping and meditating on the Buddhas, not been listening to their teachings. Neglecting the good is neglecting to cultivate skilful mental states.

> Whatever evil I have done by being drunk with the intoxication of authority or with the intoxication of high birth or by being drunk with the intoxication of tender age ... I confess it all.

The word translated here as 'intoxication' is sometimes translated 'infatuation', and essentially it means pride in the sense of inflation. Take, for example, the intoxication of 'tender age' (or, better, 'youthfulness'). When you are in the full bloom of youth, you can get a bit carried away by the fact that you are young and vigorous, and this can lead you into all sorts of wild and reckless actions. 'Oh, I can get away with it. I'm young. I can stay out drinking all night. I can stand it.' You become rather over-confident, rather inflated, and you tend to look down on or get impatient with those who are elderly, or not as quick and strong as you are. This is the sort of thing meant by the intoxication of tender age.

The intoxication of authority is what we call being 'drunk with power', carried away by the exercise of your own influence. If you are intoxicated by 'high birth', you feel terribly pleased with yourself on account of your breeding, your distinguished background, your old school, your university education, and so on. That intoxication isn't perhaps so common nowadays as it used to be. It has probably been replaced by something else – like celebrity.

You can also be intoxicated by wealth. This brings to mind the fable of the frog and the halfpenny. Once upon a time a frog was hopping along in a field when he found a halfpenny. Overjoyed at finding it, he hid it in his hole, and sat outside the hole puffing and swelling with importance because he was now the proud owner of a halfpenny. As he sat there, an elephant happened to come by. The frog called out, 'Don't you go stepping over my hole! Don't you know who I am? I'm the owner of a halfpenny!' But the elephant didn't even hear the frog. He just went on his way, and stepped over the frog's hole. The frog was so annoyed that he hopped along behind the elephant trying to kick him.[237]

If your mind is intoxicated, this is how ridiculous and reckless you can become. You lose all sense of proportion. A lot of the foolish things we do arise from this sort of inflated idea of ourselves. Just as when you're drunk you feel you can do anything, even stupid, ridiculous, crazy things that you wouldn't normally think of doing, when you're drunk with youth or wealth or social position or power, you behave in a sense just as recklessly and foolishly. You think that because you are young or powerful or well-bred or famous you can get away with it. Intoxication leads to over-confidence; over-confidence leads to over-stretching yourself and making mistakes; and making mistakes leads to a disaster of one kind or another. Most of our unskilful actions are committed not out of deliberate wickedness but because we get so carried away that we start making mistakes – for which, sooner or later, we have to pay. This is what is being confessed here.

> Whatever evil I have done, bad thought, bad word, by an act badly done (or) by not perceiving a mishap; whatever evil I have done by the application of foolish reasoning, by a mind dark with ignorance, under the influence of an evil friend or by a mind distracted by impurities ... I confess it all.

This confession encompasses the well-known classification of body, speech, and mind. 'Not perceiving a mishap' presumably means not perceiving the disastrous consequences that come from unskilful actions. For 'the application of foolish reasoning' we could substitute the modern term 'rationalization'. The evil done 'by a mind dark with ignorance' is clear enough.

But how about evil done 'under the influence of an evil friend'? What might that be? In the *Sigālovāda Sutta* an evil friend is described as one who says, 'Come on, let's go and hear the singing, let's go and join the dancing, let's go and see the girls.'[238] In modern parlance it would be someone urging you to go to a lap dancing club, perhaps.

Then there is evil done 'by a mind distracted by impurities'. This serves to remind us that very few people commit evil out of deliberate wickedness. It's more like foolishness, forgetfulness, unmindfulness. Dr Radhakrishnan said in a lecture that the Buddha thought of people as foolish rather than wicked, ignorant rather than rebellious.[239] Christianity, of course, takes quite a different line.

> Whatever evil I have done … under the compulsion of sport (or) enjoyment … I confess it all.

By 'sport' is really meant play, playing around. Sometimes you're enjoying yourself so much that you start doing something really foolish or even reckless. You get a bit carried away. This sort of thing used to happen sometimes on the first retreats I led in England. In those days, people would either be so 'mindful' that they got stiff and self-conscious, or so spontaneous that they would run riot. My task as leader of the retreat was to keep trying to bring them back to the middle way. At one stage some of the women retreatants lost their mindfulness to such an extent that four or five of them were racing up and down the corridor shrieking aloud.

One of the great problems of the spiritual life is how to keep a sense of enjoyment and positivity while at the same time remaining mindful – but not so mindful that you feel as though you are walking around in a suit of armour. To follow the middle path of being mindful and aware, knowing exactly what you are doing, but at the same time being free and spontaneous and joyful, is the art of the spiritual life.

I remember once going to visit a men's Buddhist community in Norfolk for some kind of celebration. When I got there, however, the atmosphere was far from celebratory – it was quite stiff and joyless, and I wondered what on earth was the matter. I took a walk in the garden and noticed that some tomato plants needed to be staked up with bamboo canes, so I asked a couple of men if they would mind doing that. They said, 'Yes, all right' in a rather dull sort of way, and I left them to it. When I came back ten minutes later, I found them having a 'sword-fight' with two lengths of bamboo – and they looked so happy and joyful, happier than I'd ever seen them before. At the same time, they were clearly allowing themselves to express their aggressiveness. When I reflected on this later, I concluded that they had been being over-mindful, and had not been allowing their more playful sides to emerge.

You learn to draw the line between joy and intoxication when you are able to realize that you are losing your mindfulness. On the other hand, if you become stiff and self-conscious, that's not real mindfulness either. Your awareness has become 'alienated'.[240] Most people tend to begin practising Buddhism by being 'over-mindful' (or rather, falsely mindful), because they usually start off by being completely unmindful. It's as though you have to go to the other extreme for a while and learn to be mindful, and then – not exactly forget about mindfulness, but let go and loosen up a bit. Of course, if you're not careful, you go to extremes again, and need to introduce more mindfulness and awareness. You just have to see which extreme you're tending towards at the moment, and correct the imbalance. The aim is to reach the middle ground where you've got lots of spontaneous, happy energy, but you're mindful at the same time.

Although mindfulness is certainly a key factor in the development of individuality, so is spontaneity. Even 'animal' spontaneity can be turned into a more truly human or even spiritual spontaneity. It's as if there's a certain energy in spontaneity which is refined and made more aware as you become more mindful. Clearly some people need to check their exuberance and high spirits, but others need to get their energies flowing and express themselves more freely. It may be that they need to forget all about mindfulness for a while and let their hair down.

It isn't, of course, that you have spontaneity and mindfulness going on side by side; they are completely blended. It's like the deep absorption of creative activity. When you are painting a picture, for instance, your energy is freely flowing, but at the same time you are aware. You know just what you are doing, but you are not stiff – everything is flowing freely. This is the kind of state I'm talking about, but raised to a much higher pitch of intensity. Sometimes it happens in an emergency. When you've got to do something quickly, all your energy is mobilized, but at the same time you are very aware and alert – you know exactly what you are doing. In a dangerous situation you can act quickly and spontaneously, but very effectively, with full awareness of the total situation.

> Whatever evil I have done by my associations with ignoble people, by reason of envy (and) greed, (or) by the fault of guile (or) wretchedness; whatever evil I have done through failure to gain the mastery over my desires by reason of fear at the time of approaching troubles ... I confess it all.

The first part of this confession is easy to understand; the second may not be quite so obvious. It seems to be drawing attention to the fact that sometimes one is 'unmanned', as the old-fashioned expression has it, by fear at the thought of approaching troubles, and one just loses control over oneself, including control over one's desires.

This frequently happens in wartime. People living under dangerous conditions become a bit reckless. It's as though life isn't as valuable as it used to be; 'Eat, drink, and be merry, for tomorrow you may well be dead.' According to some authorities people's behaviour in wartime has a biological significance. With a lot of people getting killed, nature is interested in replacing them as soon as possible, hence the letting go of conventional moral restraints. It's as if there's an instinctive linking of death with reproduction. Chasing pleasure before battle certainly isn't the result of fearlessness in the face of death. If anything, it's the opposite. In a sense you know that you're going to die, but in another sense you're refusing to face up to it; you're grabbing at life and pleasure almost compulsively right up to the last minute to screen that fact from yourself.

The idea of asking oneself what one would do if one had three months to live may be a cliché, but one's response can be quite revealing. How would you spend the time? Would you go on the booze? Would you go away on solitary retreat? Would you read all those books you've never had time to read? What would you feel like doing? What would be the first thought that came into your head, once you'd got over the initial shock? There is probably something you would regret not being able to do before you die.

> Whatever evil I have done through the influence of a flighty mind or through the influence of passion (and) anger (or) through being oppressed by hunger and thirst; whatever evil I have done for the sake of drink and food, for the sake of clothing, for a reason involving women, through the various afflictions of impurities; whatever evil of body, tongue and mind, bad action accumulated in threefold manner, I have done, together with similar things, I confess it all.

'The influence of a flighty mind' and 'the influence of passion and anger' emphasize once again that one is very unlikely to do evil out of deliberate wickedness. One might think that evil done 'through being oppressed by hunger and thirst' – presumably stealing – need not be confessed because one must get one's food and drink somehow, but perhaps the implication is that one should have worked or begged for food rather than stealing it. The related confession – of evil done 'for the sake of drink and food and clothing' – might be evil committed by way of wrong livelihood. And we can each fill in for ourselves the details of evils done 'for a reason involving women' and 'through the various inflictions of impurities'.

> Whatever disrespect I may have shown to Buddhas, doctrines, likewise to Śrāvakas, I confess it all. Whatever disrespect I may have shown towards Pratyekabuddhas or towards Bodhisattvas, I confess it all. (If I have shown disrespect towards those who preach the Good Law or towards other meritorious beings, I confess it all.)

In a way this is a confession of disrespect to the Three Jewels: Buddha, Dharma, and Sangha – the Sangha (spiritual community) being represented by the *śrāvakas*, the 'hearers'.[241] Showing disrespect to the Buddhas includes not practising their teachings – as well, of course, as being actually disrespectful in their presence if they happen to be alive in your time. Disrespect to doctrines would mean not listening to the teachings or not considering them carefully. In the Indian context to which the *sūtra* refers, disrespect to *śrāvakas* would mean – if you were a householder – things like not providing for the needs of the Buddha's monk disciples, addressing them contemptuously, or telling them to be off when they came on their almsround.

> If I have unawares continually rejected the Good Law (or shown) disrespect towards my parents, I confess it all.

This confession is significant not just because we come back to parents again, but because of this notion of rejecting the Good Law continually. It amounts to a confession of culpable ignorance. You've got the opportunity of hearing and knowing about the Dharma, but you deliberately ignore that opportunity. In a way, therefore, you are – unawares – continually rejecting it.

> (Whatever evil I have done) through stupidity or from folly or through being full of pride and arrogance, through passion, hatred or delusion, I confess it all.

This is the end of the confession. The last three faults confessed are of course *lobha, dveṣa,* and *moha*, the three roots of all unskilful thoughts, words, and deeds.[242]

The noticeable thing about the confession as a whole is that it doesn't list any concrete examples. It seems more concerned with laying down general principles, presumably because individual actions need to be evaluated differently according to circumstances. The general principles given aren't so very abstract, however – they are near enough to actual experience for us to be able to translate them into personally relevant examples under these various headings.

When one is making a confession it is generally best to stick to facts and confess quite specific things – nothing too rarefied or unreal. There is no need to confess the fact that you haven't contemplated Nirvāṇa every day for the last month; that can probably be taken for granted. It would be more useful to confess all the small, mean, sordid things you've done or not done, like getting out of taking your turn with the washing up, that sort of thing. It can be very salutary to experience a kind of disillusionment with yourself, to see that you are not quite the decent person you thought you were. You've got all sorts of mean, nasty little streaks in you. You see that clearly and then confess it, own up to it, bring it out into the open. It is not enough to speak in a pseudo-Jungian way of 'recognizing the shadow side'. You have to feel thoroughly ashamed of it and really want to get rid of it. It is not a rather romantic 'shadow'; it's an unpleasant, smelly stain.

However, as we have seen throughout this passage of the *sūtra*, it is important to remember that for almost all of us, the evil we do is not done out of deliberate wickedness. We do evil through ignorance, or through making a mistake, or under the influence of some basically unskilful mental state. We don't actually set out to do evil.

On the other hand I have very occasionally met people who have said, 'Yes, it's wicked, and I know it's wicked, but I'm going to do it anyway. It's what I want to do.' It's almost as though they are possessed by some demon. They are so caught up in an extreme negative emotion, whether it be hatred or jealousy or the desire for revenge, that they really don't care whether they do evil or not. Such people are comparatively rare, and even more so are those who determine to do evil quite gratuitously.

There is a distinction to be drawn between people who act wickedly in full knowledge that they are doing so and people who do evil things believing that they are in the right. The man who places a bomb in a railway carriage knowing that people are going to be killed or injured by it may genuinely believe that he is not doing evil. He may say that he is fighting for a good cause, fighting for justice. If people have to be killed for the sake of the cause, that's too bad; he regrets it, but it can't be helped. Such a person will not admit that he is doing evil.

We can see a similar if less extreme mental confusion at work in the case of people who eat meat. Many of them wouldn't dream of killing a pig, but they don't hesitate to go out and buy pork chops, even though they know somewhere in their minds that there is a connection between the slaughterhouse and their lunch. Or perhaps a lack of imagination is at work, and they really can't make the connection.

In short, I don't believe that we all have the potential for the worst kind of evil in the same way that we all have the potential for Buddhahood. It is difficult to predict what someone will do or not do under certain conditions, but my feeling is that there are some people who would refuse to do certain things under whatever circumstances.

THE SECOND CONFESSION: FROM GUILT TO OPENNESS

> May the Buddhas watch over me with minds attentive. May they forgive my sin with minds given over to compassion. On account of the evil done by me previously even in hundreds of aeons, I have a troubled mind oppressed with wretchedness, trouble and

> fear. With an unhappy mind I continually fear evil acts. Wherever I go there is no enjoyment for me anywhere. All the Buddhas are compassionate. They remove the fears of all beings. May they forgive my sin and may they deliver me from fear. May the Tathāgatas take away for me the defilement of impurities (and) acts. And may the Buddhas bathe me with the surging waters of compassion. I confess all the evil previously done by me and I confess all my present evil. For the future, I undertake to refrain from all acts evilly done. I do not conceal whatever evil I may have done. The threefold bodily act and the fourfold with the voice, as well as the act in three ways with the mind, all this I confess. What I have done with my body, what I have done with my voice, and what I have thought with my mind, the tenfold act I have done, I confess it all. May I avoid the ten evil acts. May I practise the ten good acts. May I remain in the tenth stage. May I become an excellent Buddha. Whatever evil act I have done bringing an undesired fruit I will confess it all in the presence of the Buddhas.[243]

This may come as a surprise, or even a shock, but the essence of confession is that you confess without any feeling of guilt. In fact, so long as you are experiencing guilt – irrational, neurotic guilt – no genuine confession is possible. You may experience intense regret, you may feel deeply ashamed of what you have done, and angry with yourself for doing it, but if it is real confession, you will not feel guilty.

It isn't easy to say what guilt is; it is perhaps significant that the etymology of the word, which is Anglo-Saxon, is unknown. But this complex phenomenon, so pervasive in Western culture, can be analysed into at least three factors.

First, there's the consciousness of having done wrong, or at least of having done something which somebody else did not want you to do. You may not think it wrong yourself, but the fact that somebody else didn't want you to do it gives you the feeling that you have done something wrong.

Then there is fear of being punished when you are found out, and if you haven't done anything wrong yet, there is the fear of punishment if you were to do it and get caught. The fear of being found out leads to all sorts of complications: secrecy, concealment, deceit, falsehood, hypocrisy, evasiveness, withdrawal, and blocked communication. There is also the acute discomfort and frustration of not being able to do freely what you want to do, to say nothing of the resentment you feel.

But the essential nature of guilt still remains unfathomed. The third factor is perhaps the most telling one of all. The person who does not want you to do something may be someone you love and who loves you, someone to whom you are strongly, possessively, even violently attached, someone on whom you are emotionally dependent, someone without whose love you feel you cannot live. If you do what they don't want you to do, they will not only punish you; in anger they will withdraw their love from you. In other words, they will virtually condemn you to death, the most terrible of all punishments.

So guilt is the painful consciousness of having done, or even having wanted to do, something which will lose us the love of someone on whom we are emotionally dependent. Guilt arises for most of us very early in life, when, of course, the person whose love we are afraid of losing is our mother. All of us have suffered from this to some extent, and some continue to suffer from it in adult life.

As well as feeling guilty in relation to one person, we can feel guilty in relation to the group to which we naturally belong. We tend to seek the approval of the group – our family, our work-place, our society – and we find it difficult to live with its expressed or implied disapproval. Many people will go to almost any lengths to be reconciled to the group. They will say anything required of them, even confessing to crimes they have not committed: this is evident particularly in the political lives of totalitarian states. Sometimes these wretched, unfortunate people even believe their own false confessions. After all, the group must be right. The sort of 'confession' which is made in fear of the disapproval of the group is very different from the kind of confession whose spiritual significance we are considering.

Christianity and the other theistic religions, however, trade heavily on this sense of irrational guilt. According to these religious systems God is a person, a person in whose favour we all need to stay. The religious person loves God, or at least he tries to – and he has been told that God loves him. But there are all sorts of things that God doesn't want him to do, things which in fact make God angry, but which he, the believer, wants to do – or has even done already. So he feels guilty. He feels that because he has offended God, God doesn't love him any more, or even hates him. He may then start hating God, and feel guiltier than ever.

But true individuals confess not because they can't live without the approval of the group, or of mother, or of God, but because they want to develop as individuals. They can never feel guilty, because they are not emotionally dependent on anyone. In the *Sūtra of Golden Light* it is Ruciraketu who represents the true individual – or at least someone who is trying to be a true individual. True individuals are people who have developed reflexive consciousness, who are not only aware, but are aware that they are aware. They are emotionally positive – full of friendliness, joy, compassion, and equanimity – and have a profound and heartfelt faith in the transcendental. Moreover, their energies are not blocked, but free and flowing and unified. They are therefore completely spontaneous, and at the same time completely responsible, aware of the consequences of their actions both for themselves and for others, and act in accordance with that awareness. Above all, perhaps, individuals are not members of the group. They think, feel, and act for themselves, and are in no way emotionally dependent on the group's approval. They confess because they want to get rid of everything that stands between them and the realization of the ideal, not because they want to be received back into the favour of the group.

This is clearly not the basis of confession in, for example, the Roman Catholic church, which encourages people to confess their sins against God's law out of a sense of guilt and fear of punishment. It is drummed into Catholics that if they die with a mortal sin unconfessed and unabsolved, they will go straight to hell forever. Because confession is made to a priest, who represents the group to which they belong (i.e. the church), Catholic believers have incurred, in transgressing God's laws, not only the wrath of God but also the disapproval of the group as represented by the priest. Some people are even more afraid of the priest than they are of God – which puts the priest firmly in control over the believer. This kind of confession may have some element of psychological value – at least it's a bit of a safety valve – but from the Buddhist point of view it has no spiritual significance at all.

In Bombay many years ago I knew an Indian Catholic priest, a middle-aged man who was a great scholar and knew many languages. When I got to know him he was beginning to rebel against the church to which he belonged, the 'Roman racket', as he used to call it. I once happened to meet him on Christmas Day, and noticed that he was looking very upset. I knew him well enough to ask what the matter was, and he told me that he had spent the whole of Christmas Eve hearing people's confessions. 'I feel absolutely sick,' he said. It wasn't that anyone had had anything very terrible – or even very interesting – to confess. It was just the usual catalogue of petty dishonesties and slight impurities. What had sickened him was the atmosphere of fear and guilt with which he had been in contact. He was sickened by people's desperate need to escape punishment and creep back into God's favour, their readiness to grovel and their relief at being let off with a few Paternosters and Ave Marias.

Now you'll never find genuine confession, confession as understood by Buddhism, sickening. On the contrary, you will find it inspiring – because genuine confession is made without any feeling of guilt. Yes, we naturally fear the karmic consequences of our unskilful actions. But those consequences arise naturally as a result of what we have done; they are not meted out by anybody as a kind of punishment. The law of karma is simply a description of the way things happen. Actions have consequences. If you have committed an unskilful action, you will have to suffer the consequences of that action. The law of karma is not administered by the Buddhas. It isn't their business.

So the Buddha, unlike the Christian God, does not sit in judgement over people, does not give out punishments and rewards. Because of the way we have been brought up, we may well approach the Buddha with a fearful, guilty mind, thinking of him as a punitive father figure, but this is completely to misunderstand the nature of Buddhahood. If you fear the Buddhas, you don't really see them as Buddhas at all. The compassion of the Buddha is utterly unwavering. There is no question of asking for forgiveness, still less of grovelling for mercy. The Buddha isn't a sort of God, a father figure who might get angry with you or punish you. You can approach him without any apprehension at all.

This may well be difficult for us to take on board. If we don't think of the Buddha as an ordinary, rather nice human being, we are likely to think of him as God, with all God's attributes – including a tendency to get angry and send people to hell when he is offended. But the Buddha is quite a different kind of character. If we feel guilty, we may not be able to help somehow feeling that the Buddha's attitude towards us has changed, however slightly. Even if we know that he doesn't get angry, we may imagine that he has at least become a bit reserved or a bit distant. It is difficult to realize that whatever we have done, the Buddha's feelings for us do not change one iota. If we happened to meet him, he might speak quite sternly to us, but his attitude to us would essentially be unchanged.

This is very much the flavour of the opening lines of this second verse of confession in the *Sūtra of Golden Light*. Ruciraketu asks the Buddhas to 'watch over me with minds attentive', but this is not to be understood as a call for the Buddhas to pay attention. The Buddhas are there all the time, as it were – their minds are always attentive. What Ruciraketu is really saying is, 'May I remember the Buddhas with an attentive mind,' – reminding himself to be aware of the fact that the Buddhas are watching over him. Similarly, although he asks the Buddhas to 'forgive my sin', this is simply a reminder of the unchanging compassion of the Buddhas.

It isn't the case, on the other hand, that in forgiving us the Buddhas are somehow able to take away the effects of karma. The fact that we confess our evil deeds does not mean that we are going to escape their consequences. Even the Buddha himself had to suffer certain things in his last life as a result of the actions of previous lives.[244] So when in the Vajrasattva mantra one asks for one's karma to be purified, that doesn't literally mean that karma is destroyed. It's more that by virtue of the practice you reach a level on which, although you're experiencing the results of karma, it doesn't really affect you – it doesn't matter any more.

One mustn't think of karma in too mechanical a way. According to some Buddhist *sūtras*, the consequences you reap relate directly to the evil action you have committed – 'an eye for an eye, a tooth for a tooth' – but one cannot really think of karma as though it were an exercise in bookkeeping.[245] I don't think we can literally take it that if you punch somebody on the nose in this life, somebody will punch you on the nose in your next life. In fact, there are some minor karmas which lose their force and never bear fruit at all if they don't have the opportunity to do so within a certain length of time – although you do inevitably reap the consequences of all major karmas.

So, to sum up, when you ask the Buddhas to forgive your faults, you're not asking them to wipe out the consequences of your foolish actions. You know that that would be quite impossible, even for the

Buddhas. When you say, 'May the Buddhas forgive my sin,' you're not begging them to change their minds and stop being angry with you. You are just trying to realize – for your own benefit – that the attitude of the Buddhas hasn't changed towards you, and will never change, whatever you do.

> On account of the evil done by me previously even in hundreds of aeons, I have a troubled mind oppressed with wretchedness, trouble and fear.

While there is no place for irrational guilt, it is equally important that one should not feel comfortable with one's unskilful actions. The *sūtra*'s words here capture how one feels when one has committed unskilful actions that one knows to be unskilful. (Leave aside hundreds of aeons, it could have been last week.) If you have committed an unskilful action you *should* feel guilty – that is, you should feel troubled and even wretched. If someone commits a highly unskilful action, like striking another person, and when taken to task for it, they turn round and say, 'What right have you got to try and make me feel guilty?', this is quite a serious confusion of thought. No one can impose upon you, as a Buddhist, the painful consciousness of having done wrong. But when you do experience such a painful realization, with or without the help of others, then this is a very positive and appropriate thing.

> With an unhappy mind I continually fear evil acts.

This is how you feel if you have really taken on board that actions have consequences – perhaps because you have already started to experience the consequences. Sometimes we fail to confess not through lack of trust but because we don't realize sufficiently strongly that what we have done is unskilful. Very often we have got into such a strong habit of committing certain unskilful actions that our conscience has become rather blunted. The solution is simply – although this is easier said than done – to develop more mindfulness. Say, for instance, you were rather greedy at supper time. Is that something to be confessed? It depends how strongly you feel it. If you think to yourself, 'I was a real pig. Anyone who saw me would have formed a bad impression of what Buddhists are like,' – well, confess it.

We need to develop more and more sensitivity of this kind. It is a matter for concern that some people seem unable to recognize unskilful or even highly unskilful actions. There are quite a few people who aren't particularly bothered about telling a lie, even when it's not a white lie. And some people aren't particularly bothered about not keeping their promises.

> Wherever I go there is no enjoyment for me anywhere.

If your sensibilities are sufficiently acute, this is how you are going to feel. You are conscious of having performed unskilful actions, and perhaps you have already begun to reap the consequences. You know that due to your past bad habits you are in danger of performing even more unskilful actions, and reaping further unpleasant consequences, and this is very much on your mind. You know that there isn't any true enjoyment for you, because there is nowhere to run to escape the consequences of karma. All you can do is confess and make a fresh start.

Hence the next lines of the text:

> All the Buddhas are compassionate. They remove the fears of all beings. May they forgive my sin and may they deliver me from fear.

What is important is not to escape the consequences of your unskilful actions – indeed, that's impossible – but to get rid of your feelings of guilt, fear, and worry. You can do that by confessing. Even though you will go on experiencing the consequences of your previous unskilful actions, it doesn't matter any more. You say, 'All right, never mind. I'm just paying off old debts; I'm not accumulating any new ones. I am going forward now.'

> May the Tathāgatas take away for me the defilement of impurities (and) acts.

This is to be understood in much the same way as the idea of the bodhisattva 'placing' people in the tenth *bhūmi*, the highest stage of transcendental development before becoming a Buddha. Literally speaking it is totally unfeasible; it is to be understood as a rhetorical expression of the bodhisattva's heroic ambition. In a sense the Buddhas are 'taking away our defilements' all the time, but we have to realize that ourselves.

> And may the Buddhas bathe me with the surging waters of compassion. I confess all the evil previously done by me and I confess all my present evil. For the future, I undertake to refrain from all acts evilly done.

This is very important. It is not just a question of confessing what you have done. You have to make a firm resolution to turn over a new leaf, not to commit those unskilful actions any more. This is, of course, roughly what goes on when we make New Year resolutions. The turning of the year is a good time to confess and leave behind the foolish things you have done. You can take the opportunity, perhaps, to write down in black and white all the things you regret having done. You probably haven't done wicked things – most people haven't got the guts for that – but you could write down all the foolish, mean, silly things you did, or were betrayed into doing, or happened to do without thinking. Never mind how many sheets of paper you have to use. Write them all down, burn them, and say, 'May I never do these things again in the coming year. May I stay free from all these things.' You are sure to feel much lighter after doing that. The value of confession as a spiritual practice is that you bring something to light, you objectify it, and to that extent you get rid of it, at least for the time being. If you do it sincerely, you feel cleansed, and lighter than you did before.

Good though the practice of making resolutions is, for a really effective practice of confession we are going to need to make our confessions known to someone else. No, not to an authority figure in a little wooden box. Confession is most effectively made to other individuals, others who are treading the spiritual path as we are. It can of course be made to those who are individuals *par excellence* – the Buddhas and bodhisattvas. In the *sūtra* Ruciraketu confesses in the *presence* of all the Buddhas. But the reason Ruciraketu can confess to the Buddhas is that he can see and hear them. In our own practice we may recite the sevenfold puja and 'confess', as it were, to the Buddha, but we rarely, if ever, have a vivid sense of the Buddha's actual presence. This is not, therefore, confession in the full sense. Full confession means confessing specific offences – including those committed in thought – to others of whose presence we are conscious, and who are conscious of us, others who will hear our confession and accept it.

Furthermore, we need to make our confessions to people on the same spiritual path as ourselves – our spiritual friends or teachers. But why should this be so? Why can't we confess to someone we meet on the bus, or at least to our ordinary friends? There are, broadly speaking, two main reasons. First, we need to confess to people with whom we can be really open; and second, our confession needs to be heard by people who understand its significance for us.

The first of these reasons is highlighted by one of the most important sentences of this passage of the *sūtra*:

> I do not conceal whatever evil I may have done.

We often conceal things not just from other people, but even from ourselves. We don't like to admit that we have done something wrong, that we have made a mistake. It's a form of humiliation to feel that we have not lived up to our image of ourself. Someone once said that when you sit down to write your autobiography, the first thing you become aware of is what you are going to leave out. Almost inevitably you don't tell the whole story. 'Oh no, I'm not going to say that. I'll say everything else, but not that.' To be happy for others to see you exactly as you are, warts and all, is very difficult. Usually there is some little nook or cranny of your character or your life or your past that you don't want anybody to know about. You don't even think about it yourself very much; you hide it even from yourself. Nietzsche said, 'Memory says I did such and such, pride says I couldn't possibly have done it, and pride wins.'[246] Ideally, of course, it should be possible to lead such a life that you can be open with everybody – one's life should ideally be an open book – but most people have at least a few pages, not to say the odd chapter or two, which they would prefer other people not to look at.

It's a strain relating to others with only a part of yourself, keeping back another part that they are never allowed to see. If you never relate to them as a complete, whole person, they don't know who you are, or at least they don't know the whole of you. This doesn't mean that if you have committed a crime you should tell it to everybody – that might be unwise – but certainly there should be a few people with whom you can be completely frank. Assuming you share with them a common spiritual ideal, they will be for you the spiritual community in the full sense. If you don't have friends whom you can trust totally, you are in quite a difficult position.

What prevents many of us from confessing and from being more open generally is the feeling that if other people knew us as we were, then they would no longer accept us. 'If people knew what I was really like, they wouldn't want to have any more to do with me.' But within the context of the spiritual community you are still accepted, even though people may strongly disapprove of what you have done. You may find it difficult to make that distinction – and it may be difficult for your friends in practice – but in principle they will try to retain the same *mettā* for you even though they may be very grieved at what you have done. To be open, you have got to have this kind of confidence in other people's genuine, basic goodwill towards you, which you are convinced will remain unchanged under all circumstances. Even if they tell you off, it will be with basic good will.

Of course, trust – the confidence that people will deal with you from a basis of love rather than from a basis of power – cannot be forced, even in the spiritual community. True confession cannot be the kind of mechanical procedure which goes under the name of confession in so many parts of the Buddhist world. You need to be in close, trustful communication with the person to whom you confess, and you can only trust people if you feel they are not going to hurt you, not going to take advantage of your openness. In a way you need to feel that their attitude towards you is basically like that of the Buddha. Whatever you have done, they are going to forgive you. Their basic attitude towards you is not going to change; they will have the same *mettā* for you even after you have confessed, when they know the worst about you.

The kind of openness developed in a spiritual friendship is of a higher order than that present in ordinary friendship, although openness and freedom of communication on the more ordinary human level does prepare the way for more distinctively spiritual communication. It would be rather surprising if someone went straight from not trusting anybody on the ordinary human level to trusting them in terms of spiritual friendship. You don't usually make that sort of leap unless you have had some quite exceptional, dramatic spiritual experience.

Confession is simply a specific aspect of one's general openness towards people one really trusts. In that sense it is nothing special; it's just a continuation of something one is doing all the time. That doesn't mean that confession is a casual matter. One needs to take the cultivation of openness with people very seriously, and that means taking confession seriously too. In the same spirit of openness, there may be occasions on which you need to point out the faults of your spiritual friend, or they to point out yours. Here, however, one must proceed with great caution. You can't attempt to point out another person's faults unless you are reasonably confident that they trust you, at least to some extent, depending on the seriousness of the matter that you are pointing out.

If you find yourself hesitant about revealing your actions to someone you genuinely believe to be more developed in a spiritual sense than yourself, it is likely to be because you know they will regard your action as unskilful. If you take the plunge, though, you will find that the more evolved the other person is, the more possible it is, in a sense, for you, assuming that you are relatively unevolved, to be open with them.

It takes a long time to become confident enough in another person to be able to confess to them. It also takes a lot of effort. It doesn't happen automatically, even if you spend a lot of time with them; you have to make a definite effort. It comes as quite a relief when you can be genuinely open with somebody, knowing that you don't have to keep up any pretences because you will be accepted for what you are. Your every single action won't be condoned, but *you* will be accepted. It is best to have nothing to confess, nothing to hide, but if we had to wait until we had reached that blameless state before we could be open, most of us would have to wait a very long time. It is the test of real openness, the test of true friendship, that you can be open even though there are unskilful things you would rather not have done. In fact, if you confess, your friend knows that you trust them, and may well become more open with you. If you can't be open with your friend, and your friend can't be open with you, it's not much of a friendship.

But why do we approach confession so cautiously? Why can't we just be open with everybody? The main problem is fear of what people will think. This is odd in a way. After all, they don't have it within their power to do you any harm or damage. Unless you have committed some crime which could land you in prison, why shouldn't everybody know what you've been up to? What does it matter if everybody in the whole city knows that you got drunk the weekend before last? So what?

We may also hold back because of an attitude left over from childhood. As children, when we are just starting to feel more independent, we delight in keeping things from our parents. We think gleefully, 'If they knew, they'd have a fit!' Somehow we feel very clever, as though we have scored over them. That may be fair enough when we are small, but we need to grow out of that sort of attitude. If we feel towards the whole world as a child feels towards its parents, we haven't really grown up yet.

We tend to be very dependent on what people think of us. We want their approval, or at least we want to avoid their disapproval. Ironically enough, the things we can't bring ourselves to be open about are often the things that most people aren't really bothered about anyway. You may sometimes have the experience of trying to tell somebody something about yourself that you think is really awful. You find it excruciatingly difficult to bring it up, but then you notice that they aren't taking much notice of what you are saying because it is so insignificant to them. It simply hasn't registered. You may have imagined that you were going to stop them in their tracks, you may have been waiting for them to gasp in horror, but they just say, 'Oh yes' and start talking about something else. They're not overwhelmed, shocked, or horrified at all. In other words, you have been attaching far too much importance to whatever it was that you did.

I had a friend many years ago who used to say to me, 'If you really knew what I was like, you wouldn't want to have anything to do with me.' This went on for about two years. In the end, when he finally brought himself to confess what it was – it wasn't something he'd done, only something he'd been thinking – I burst out laughing. For two years he'd been convinced that if I knew what he was thinking, I'd never want to speak to him again. It was ridiculous. But this is so often the way we build things up in our minds.

The converse of this is the point we came across earlier: that we need to take our unskilful behaviour sufficiently seriously. And this brings us to the second reason for making our confessions to friends who are on the same spiritual path. Suppose you make your confession to an ordinary friend, a friend who does not share your spiritual ideals. Suppose, for instance, you confess that you got a bit drunk last weekend, or that you haven't meditated for a whole week. An ordinary friend won't be able to understand what those things mean to you, and therefore won't understand your distress. They may even say, with the best of intentions, that you are upsetting yourself unnecessarily. In this case there will be no real communication, and therefore no real confession. You will not have been able to vomit up the evil and get rid of it.

You need to confess to friends who understand what unskilful behaviour is, not just pals who pat you on the back and say, 'That's just the sort of thing everybody does.' Friends of that kind tend to let you off rather lightly, so that your 'confession' doesn't amount to very much. You may not be proud of what you have done, but you may not be very much ashamed of it either. However, even that sort of openness is better than none at all. At least you have got the attitude of opening out, provided you're not just covertly boasting about some rather interesting aspect of your murky past.

If you go to a psychiatrist, or get talking to someone you meet when you're travelling, and end up admitting to certain intimate things – perhaps *because* you are talking to a stranger – that is perhaps a step in the right direction. At least you have said it out loud, and you may be able to go on to make a genuine confession. But it is important to be clear about the difference between admitting to something and truly confessing it. If you confess within the spiritual community, it is quite a different experience. Your spiritual friends will know what you are talking about, and they will be sympathetic with your distress, and genuinely concerned. At the same time they won't be really worried, because there is real communication, and therefore genuine confession, and also therefore real steps being taken to reject the evil that is in you.

When you really aren't sure whether or not you have been unskilful, the solution is easy – consult your spiritual friends. Say, 'Look, what do you think? Have I been unskilful? Give me your opinion.' This is one of the things that spiritual friends are for.

If it feels like a challenge to confess, that's a good thing, because it shows that you are really confessing, not just treating confession as a formality, as it has become in so many parts of the Buddhist world. But if it is too much of a challenge to approach someone and tell them you have something to confess, you could do what I suggested earlier – write your confession down and ceremonially burn it in the context of a puja. That would be halfway between confessing to the Buddha and confessing to a person. You need not even show the piece of paper to anybody: the fact that you have written it down means that you have owned up to what you have done, brought it out into the open as an objective reality. After all, someone might get hold of that piece of paper. You have taken the risk of letting it out.

The ideal time to confess is as soon as you have acted unskilfully, as soon as you are painfully aware of having made an ethical blunder – or as soon as you can get hold of your spiritual friends. The longer you hold back from confessing, the longer you are at a standstill in your spiritual life.

Confession, however, is not something you do once and for all. Moral defeats, unfortunately, are always being suffered, at least in the mind. Until Enlightenment has been attained, there is always some kind of evil or another within us to be got rid of. According to the Mahāyāna tradition, therefore, confession is a part of life. We need to be confessing all the time. Confession, in short, is crucial to the spiritual life.

THE THIRD CONFESSION: THE OPPRESSIONS OF EXISTENCE

We have seen that in his second confession Ruciraketu confesses to committing the ten unskilful acts – three of body, four of speech, and three of mind. The third and last confession adds a new element: the confession of evil heaped up through various oppressions.

> In the oppression of existence (or) through foolish thought, whatever severe evil I have done, in the presence of the Buddha, I confess all this evil. And I confess that evil which has been heaped up by me in the oppression of birth, by the various oppressions of activity due to passion, in the oppression of existence, in the oppression of the world, in the oppression of the fleeting mind, in the oppression of impurities caused by the foolish and stupid, and in the oppression of the arrival of evil friends, in the oppression of fear, in the oppression of passion, in the oppression of hatred and in the oppression of folly and darkness, in the oppression of the opportunity, in the oppression of time, in the oppression of gaining merits, standing in (my) oppression before the Buddha, I confess all this evil.[247]

The word translated as 'oppression' is the Sanskrit *saṃkaṭa*, for which the dictionary gives the following definitions: 'brought together, contracted, closed, narrow, strait, crowded together, dense, impervious, impassable, crowded with, full of; a strait, difficulty, critical condition, danger to or from'. That gives one quite a good idea of what *saṃkaṭa* means, and makes it clear that this term 'oppression', though not bad, is not a fully adequate translation by any means.

The *saṃkaṭas* are those factors by which one is surrounded, which crowd in upon one, which oppress one, which squeeze and limit one. This suggests that there are all sorts of unskilful acts that one performs, as it were, under duress. Our unskilful acts are not those of a free, untrammelled will. If only conditions had been a bit more favourable, we might not have done them at all. There are so many factors in existence which oppress us, making it more likely that we will do something unskilful, and more difficult for us to act skilfully. Circumstances are so often against us. Our surroundings tend almost to compel us to do what is unskilful. Not that that is really any excuse, ultimately, because it is due to our weakness that we feel the oppression *as* oppression. But once again we come back to the point that people are not deliberately wicked; it's more that they are weak and give in to pressure.

The list of oppressions is a long one: existence, birth, bodily activity, the world, the fleeting mind, impurities caused by the foolish, the arrival of evil friends, fear, passion, hatred, folly and darkness, the opportunity, time, gaining merits. The *sūtra* confesses evil committed under the oppression of all these things. So clearly they are not factors that we occasionally encounter and have to resist; they are things that surround us and almost crush us all the time. It's not as though they are just there but don't bother us; they are all around us, hemming us in, breaking in upon us, weighing upon us, and restricting our movements. They are a constant chronic danger, and if we are not conscious of the fact it is because we go along with them to such an extent that there is nothing in us to be oppressed.

The list begins with 'the oppression of existence'. This implies that conditioned existence itself – just being a human being – is pressurizing us to perform unskilful actions. All you have to do is go out for a little walk and you see all sorts of things that cannot but give rise to unskilful thoughts, even unskilful activities, on your part. To be more specific, city life, we could say, is an oppression. In the city, we have to put so much energy into keeping the world at bay – keeping the world from encroaching upon what we have gained already in the way of mindfulness and positivity – that we don't have much left over with which to make real progress. Still, we have to admit that this only happens because something within us has an affinity with these oppressions of the world.

The sense in which 'foolish thought' might become an oppression is fairly obvious. Thoughts are running through our minds involuntarily all the time. We don't deliberately set out to think an unskilful thought; it just pops into our head. We didn't ask it to come, we didn't want it to be there; it just came. This is our experience. We call it 'our' thought, but sometimes it seems as though it is coming from outside, invading us. When we sit to meditate, we try to concentrate our minds, keep them clear and pure, and all these unskilful foolish thoughts keep rushing in and undoing all our best efforts. This is how we feel. And yet we cannot escape the fact that these thoughts are our own; they belong to us.

Then, 'the oppression of birth'. According to some psychologists, birth itself is a traumatic experience. There you are in the womb before birth: warm, relatively quiet, quite comfortable. Then suddenly you are violently squeezed through a narrow aperture, and come out at the other end into a terrible bright light to be seized and plunged into water. This must surely be a very traumatic experience. You are slapped to make you breathe, rubbed with a rough towel, then dressed, tied up, and then you start feeling hungry. This might well be described as the oppression of birth.

But next, in what way might bodily activity be an oppression, or even 'various oppressions'? Well, think about it. You wake up in the morning, you've got to get up and dress yourself, go to the lavatory, brush your teeth, and then you've got to eat. All these are bodily activities which are needed to keep you going. Sometimes there seem to be so many of them that you forget what you are living *for*. As you get older, physical existence becomes more and more of a burden. In the end you can hardly walk, or even get up from a chair without help. You can't get on to a bus without a helping hand. Maybe you can't dress yourself or go to the toilet without help. This is when this oppression really strikes home – although when you are young, you sometimes get a foretaste of it when you are ill. You can't think of very much at all beyond your physical state, your aches and pains, your medicine, and so on.

As for 'the oppression of the world', this could be taken in a narrower sense than the oppression of existence, to mean the whole of social life. Indeed, whatever the specific oppression may be, it is all-pervasive. Take, for instance, 'the arrival of evil friends'. It is not that we occasionally meet an evil friend, someone who is going to try to induce us to perform unskilful actions; we are surrounded by them. Go for a ride on a bus; there they all are. Go to watch a football match; there they all are. We are surrounded by people who are in a sense 'evil friends', in that their influence on us is not a positive, skilful one.

The oppressions of fear, passion, hatred, folly, and darkness we have already touched on in the previous confession sections. But this section continues to add new elements. For example, there's 'the oppression of the opportunity', having to act or make a decision when one may be off guard. And then 'the oppression of time', or as we would say, 'pressure of time', is what so often seems to keep us from skilful action. Certainly under the conditions of modern life we often feel that we don't have enough time to do things properly, or think about what the skilful way to act would be. We act hastily, and the chances are that we act unskilfully.

Even gaining merits, according to the *sūtra*, is an oppression – odd as it may sound. What the *sūtra* is of course pointing to is the danger of getting too attached to our merit. If we think of the spiritual life in terms of acquiring merits too much then it becomes quite oppressive so far as our real spiritual life is concerned. The text doesn't explicitly say so, but I take it that the merits referred to here are of the lower kind, the kind which guarantee you a place in a higher heavenly world after death. I don't see how merits which are dedicated to Enlightenment could be an oppression. Oppression, after all, only arises when you are trying to do something skilful and external factors are getting in the way. Life itself can get in the way, time can get in the way, but merits that are dedicated to Enlightenment surely can't get in the way.

This list draws attention to the fact that there are all sorts of unskilful factors in existence which are always pressing in on us, and from which it is very difficult for us to escape, because we are experiencing them all the time. They never let up. It's as though there is some force at work in the world almost compelling us to do unskilful things against our better judgement and our own wishes. If we are surrounded by these things, sooner or later they are going to have some definite effect. It is not that they give rise to unskilfulness in some mysterious, indirect way. If we are constantly surrounded by evil friends, sooner or later they will have some influence on us. The list is of course selective; all unskilful or unhelpful factors are of this nature.

This is not to suggest that the individual is absolved from responsibility for his behaviour. In confessing the evil you have committed, you accept responsibility for it. It may be understandable when you fail to stand up to the oppressions, but it is your responsibility to stand up to them. If something is not your fault, why should you confess it? There would be no point. The fact that you confess means that you accept responsibility, even though you were strongly tempted. To make a technical distinction, one could say that these oppressions are the occasion of unskilful actions, but not their cause. You are their cause, and therefore the responsibility is yours. Perhaps you are very strongly tempted, but you still have the capacity to resist.

As you become integrated, you don't exactly feel less oppressed, but you feel less pulled around by the oppressions. If you are unintegrated, you are split and divided. When part of you wants to meditate, another part of you doesn't, so if there is any external pressure not to meditate, that can work on you quite easily through the part of you that doesn't want to do it anyway. If you are split, the part of you that is in sympathy with the oppression is vulnerable to its influence.

If you've got a sort of 'traitor within' that is in cahoots with the 'enemy without', you are in a difficult position. In addition to being under pressure from the oppression, you are divided within yourself so that one part of you is putting pressure on another. It is much easier to deal with external pressures when there is no inner conflict. If, for instance, as you go around the city you see advertisements featuring models in scanty attire, but there is nothing within you which is susceptible to that, they can bring as much pressure to bear on you as they like – nothing much will happen. On the other hand, if there is already a traitor lurking within, so to speak, the combined forces of the traitor and the adverts are likely to overwhelm you. If you are divided within yourself you are more likely to succumb to external pressure, but if you are more integrated, you can withstand a corresponding degree of pressure from the environment.

It is a good thing to be aware that there are all sorts of factors in the world that almost oblige us to behave unskilfully. We don't get much co-operation from the world; pressure is brought to bear on us all the time to act in the usual – that is, the unskilful – way. We live in the midst of an oppressive situation and we may feel that we have to block out a lot of things just to survive the day. This is why it is so good to get away on retreat from time to time, to experience the lightness and happiness of feeling that the pressure is off – at least for the time being.

It's a moot point as to whether being aware of oppressions *as* oppressions is really much help. If there's a terrific noise outside while you are trying to meditate, you can certainly become aware of what is happening, but that won't help you to meditate if the noise is still there and you are still being bothered by it.

One could say that it is through having to deal with the oppressions that one becomes strong, but I think there is a point beyond which that doesn't work any more. If you lift weights in the gym, that can certainly strengthen you, but if you are elderly and weak, they may put so much strain on your heart that you drop down dead. It's much the same psychologically. Having to put up with a certain amount is strengthening, but there's a limit to what you can sustain.

From this it follows that you must *know* how much you are able to bear, and if a situation is insupportable, you just have to withdraw from it, if at all possible. For instance, you might be living with someone with a terrible temper. You might be able to handle that for a while, but suppose another person with the same kind of temperament came to live with you as well. You might have to admit that you just couldn't bear to live with two people of that sort – they would just depress you, which wouldn't help you or anybody else. It is better to get out than to go under. We shouldn't be ashamed to admit that our resources are limited. Yes, we need to be strong, but we have to weigh up our own strength and decide what we can reasonably expect from ourselves. Usually we can manage more than we think we can, but we also have to be realistic and not destroy ourselves through false ideas about what we ought to be able to put up with. This is not to say, I should add, that we should necessarily accept our limitations and weaknesses. Sometimes there are certain parts of oneself that shouldn't be indulged or protected.

To sum up, oppression involves some external factor – whether social or psychological – that exerts pressure on us to be unskilful. We need not start feeling sorry for ourselves, but we should recognize quite realistically that by the very fact of living in the world we are up against it. All too often the world, far from co-operating with us in our efforts to be more skilful, almost pushes us in the other direction.

THE EFFECTS OF CONFESSION: PURIFICATION AND REJOICING

The effects of confession should by now be quite clear. When we have truly confessed, we feel cleansed and purified. We feel that we are back on the path, that we can go forward once more. The state in which we find ourselves is beautifully exemplified by the Vajrasattva visualization practice. This is a Vajrayāna practice, but in spirit it is very close to the verses of confession that Ruciraketu hears in his dream.

In the practice you visualize Vajrasattva seated directly above your head on a white lotus throne. He is pure white in colour, like the colour of freshly fallen snow on which the morning sun is shining. He is in the prime of youth, with long flowing black hair, and his expression is smiling and compassionate. In one hand he holds a *vajra* or *dorje*, balancing it against his chest, and in the other he holds a bell, resting on his knee. In his heart you see a deep blue syllable *hūṃ*, and around it, like a garland, the one hundred letters of the mantra of Vajrasattva, also white in colour. The garland of letters revolves in a clockwise direction around the deep blue *hūṃ*, and as they revolve you see drops of pure white nectar oozing from them. This nectar falls down onto the crown of your head in a great stream, through the spinal column and down through all the nerve centres in your system, washing away all evil, washing your whole being absolutely clean. You become pure, transparent, shining, like a crystal vase. Having washed away all the impurities, the nectar accumulates within you, so that little by little you become like a crystal vase full to the brim with pure white curds.

When you have reached that state, you see that the whole sky is filled with pure white lotus flowers edge to edge. Upon each lotus flower is seated a pure white Vajrasattva, and beneath each Vajrasattva is a sentient being, being purified just as you are. You see that you are a pure being in a pure world, a pure being among pure beings. Then you feel that you really have confessed and been forgiven.

Once we have confessed to the Buddhas, it is only natural that we should feel intensely grateful to them for hearing and accepting our confession, and that we should therefore sing their praises as Ruciraketu does in the *Sūtra of Golden Light*.

I worship the Buddhas, who are like oceans of virtues, mountains gleaming with the colour of gold like Sumeru. I go for refuge to those Buddhas and with my head I bow down to all those Buddhas. (Each one is) gold-coloured, shining like pure gold. He has fine eyes, pure and faultless like beryl. He is a mine blazing with glory, splendour, and fame. He is a Buddha-sun removing the obscurity of darkness with his rays of compassion. He is very flawless, very brilliant, with very gleaming limbs. He is a fully enlightened sun. His limbs are as prominent as pure gold. He refreshes as it were the blazing fire of those whose minds are consumed by the fire of impurities with the sage's meshes of moonbeams. His sense organs are beautiful with the thirty-two excellent major marks, his members greatly gleaming with the very brilliant minor marks. With meshes of beams full of glory, merits, splendour, and brilliance he stands amid the darkness like the sun in the three worlds.

Your members resembling silver, crystal or copper, with the various magnificent colours pure as beryl, with meshes of rays manifoldly and variously adorned, coppery red like the dawn, you shine, great sage, like the sun. For one who has fallen into the river of the cycle of existence, in the midst of the flood of disaster, afflicted with anxiety, in the water of death, in the billow of old age, dry up completely with the meshes of rays of the Buddha-sun the ocean of woe, whose current is extremely harsh and cruel.[248]

The whole passage, like so many in other Mahāyāna *sūtras*, gives an impression of inexhaustibility, abundance, and richness, and this is really the whole point of it. It is emphasizing that the Buddha has got far more than just two or three rather monumental and abstract virtues. He is a veritable treasure chest of virtues and merits.

Here the imagery itself – the sun, the mountains, moonbeams, beryl, silver, copper, crystal, dawn, water – is all universal; there's nothing specifically Indian about it. But perhaps the disordered extravagance of it, the lushness, is rather Indian. There isn't much form to all these epithets and comparisons, no arrangement or symmetry. They are heaped on top of one another pell-mell. It may all seem a bit excessive, even alien to us. We may prefer a more 'Zen-like' approach – just one twig of blossom carefully set in a simple vase – but the Indians like to heap up hundreds of flowers all over the place, with no particular arrangement at all. If the Zen-like approach expresses a *real* intensity of stillness and concentration then this may be what we need. But a quiet tasteful restraint – a palette of pastels – is not really a virtue in itself, at least in a devotional context. Better to let ourselves go a bit, be a little less careful even, if by 'careful' we mean being buttoned up and timid.

Of course, the Western tradition is not entirely lacking in this type of prodigality of expression. Thomas Traherne rather lets go of the reins in this way in his *Centuries of Meditations*.[249] So does Shelley in his 'Ode to a Skylark', in which some of the images – for example, comparing the skylark to a high-born maiden in a palace-tower, or a glow-worm – are plainly a little absurd; but I used to teach this poem to students in India, and they loved all these comparisons. English critics usually agree that some of the similes could have been cut to make the poem more compact and unified, but the Indians certainly wouldn't think like that. For them, it could go on as long as it liked.

One could say that this is the difference between the gothic and the neoclassical style. The basic distinction is between a 'heaping-up' style and an 'eliminating' style, and it is exemplified in the Western cultural tradition as well as in Eastern Buddhism. Compare, for example, a Quaker meeting house, so plain and bare and unadorned, and a post-Reformation rococo Catholic church, all odds and ends of tinsel and velvet and lace and plaster and paint, with an effect either effervescent or tawdry. The difference between the Theravāda and the Vajrayāna approach is similar; and they both have their merits. English people tend to shy away from exuberance and profusion, but perhaps that's something we need to overcome.

Of course, it can go too much the other way. Some Tibetan temples get so full of things that they become quite oppressive. So many people have given them so many things – none of which can be thrown away or even given away – that every nook and cranny has an image or a thangka in it, plus umpteen sets of water bowls and umpteen lamps. The temples sometimes look really crowded, especially as things are often put in glass-fronted cases against the wall. It all tends to look a bit museum-like and dusty and moth-eaten. Everything has to be kept because some pious soul has donated it, but sometimes you really wish that you could throw away a few things. I have sometimes thought that

Tibetan Buddhism itself is like that – a bit museum-like. There's too much of it, too many odds and ends in it.

So a middle path is probably needed. Every now and then it's good to go in for a bout of lavish and exuberant munificence, but you can't live with that all the time. And sometimes you feel like being very austere and simple, but you can't live with *that* all the time either. For day-to-day practice, a middle way is probably best. Have your shrine rich, but not cloying, austere but not dull. Festival days are the occasions for real lavishness – spare no expense on decorations and lamps and candles, and really splash out on the flowers.

> I worship the Buddha, whose members shine like gold, whose members gleam with the colour of gold, a mine of knowledge, chief in all three worlds, beautiful, whose members are adorned with very brilliant marks. Just as the water in the ocean is immeasurable, just as the earth is endless with its particles of dust, just as Meru is endless with its stones, just as the sky has an endless limit, so indeed are the Buddha's virtues endless. Even all beings cannot know them. If one should weigh and ponder them for numerous aeons, one could not know the last virtues. The earth with its rocks, mountains and oceans, it is perhaps in aeons possible to count and know, and the water (in the ocean) may perhaps be measured to a hair-point: it is not possible to know the end of the Buddha's virtues.[250]

The Buddha is the one who has reached or realized the Unconditioned, and just as the Unconditioned is not really accessible to thought and cannot be fully expressed, so it is with the Buddha. The Buddha's virtues are immeasurable, inexpressible. There are two ways of trying to get this across. You can either just make the statement 'The Buddha's virtues cannot be expressed,' or you can exhaust your powers of expression trying to describe them, which is what this paragraph in effect does. The second method probably gives a better impression of the inexhaustibility of the Buddha's virtues than the bare logical statement.

In many spiritual traditions there are said to be two main avenues of approach to reality: the negative way and the affirmative way. The negative way consists in denying of the Unconditioned everything that is conditioned. You say of the Unconditioned, 'It isn't this, it isn't that.

It is nothing to do with space, and nothing to do with time. There is no beginning and no end. It is neither light nor darkness, neither good nor evil, neither existence nor non-existence. It's beyond all that.' But the affirmative way consists in saying that the Unconditioned is light – not any ordinary light, but the absolute light, the brightest light, the purest light, the greatest light. Or it says that the Unconditioned is beautiful, but not any ordinary beauty, not any worldly beauty. It is far more beautiful than even the most beautiful thing that we see and experience. It is beauty itself, beauty *sans pareil.*

Both of these, of course, are just ways of seeing things. Strictly speaking we can't think of reality at all, but for practical purposes we have to think about it, and basically there are only these two ways in which we *can* think about it: either by negating with regard to the Unconditioned everything that is conditioned, or by thinking of the Unconditioned in terms of the conditioned at its very height, at its very best, beyond what we ever actually experience within the conditioned.

Well, there is a third way, actually. There is also the approach through paradox, through the forcible juxtaposition of contradictory terms, as when you speak of 'dazzling darkness'. Such contradictions give at least some people some hint of what reality is like. The Buddhist Perfection of Wisdom texts operate through conceptual paradoxes in this way, as well as using the negative approach.

But clearly the *Sūtra of Golden Light* favours the affirmative approach, using images and pictures and lavish descriptions. It contains just one very short chapter on *śūnyatā*, and that is a sort of clumsy version of the Perfection of Wisdom teaching.

The natural consequence of confession is twofold: to rejoice in merits, both one's own and other people's; and to dedicate one's merit to Enlightenment. We get the first hint of this after the second confession:

> Those who in this Jambudvīpa and in other world-spheres do a good act I congratulate on it all. And whatever merit has been gained by me by body, voice or mind, through that merit-root may I touch excellent enlightenment.[251]

Rejoicing in the merits of others gives one strength and inspiration. It also counteracts any tendency to envy and greed because it encourages disinterestedness. You are just as glad if somebody else does a good action as if you had done it yourself. If you manage to cultivate a positive attitude of appreciation, you may feel that in a way you *have* done it yourself.

For some people, rejoicing in the merits of others is not easy. When we think about other people's good qualities, we may even feel quite uncomfortable. The reason for this is that we feel inferior; and we feel inferior because we don't have those good qualities ourselves. This is what riles us. We look at it all in a jaundiced, prejudiced way. Instead of thinking 'Jane is a very kind person,' we start thinking 'She's much kinder than me. She probably thinks she's better than me. What is worse, when other people look at us, *they* probably think she's better than me.' The more we think about it, the more inferior we feel. We may imagine that Jane thinks herself superior to us when the thought has never entered her head. She may even be quite oblivious to our existence. If somebody else's virtue makes them superior to us in a way that makes us feel put down, we are likely to underestimate or depreciate their good qualities, just to keep ourselves, as we see it, on a level with them.

If we have some merits of our own to rejoice in, we may find it easier to rejoice in the merits of others because we feel more on a level with them, but in fact that's just a concession to our weakness. We should be able to rejoice in the merits of others regardless of whether or not we have any merits at all. In fact, the fewer merits we have, the more reason there is to rejoice in the merits of others. If you haven't got any merits of your own, thank goodness somebody has! If there are merits around in the world they should be a natural cause for rejoicing.

The sort of merit the text has in mind is probably the merit that people produce, so to speak, without reference to you personally. But of course even our response to good actions done expressly for our benefit is not necessarily straightforward. Some people rather resist the idea of others doing good to them because they feel it puts them under an obligation. You might be reluctant to borrow a lawn-mower from the people next door, say, because that would mean that you would be under an obligation to lend them something in return. But in trying to avoid being under any obligation you might in the end virtually cut off the relationship altogether. If you have contact with people at all, you simply can't help becoming involved in a network of mutual obligations.

Perhaps when we are unwilling or reluctant to rejoice in other people's merits, we are being a bit too self-conscious. We may need to forget about ourselves and where we stand, and just rejoice in somebody's merits in a quite impersonal way. When the sun is shining, you don't feel jealous of the sun because it has the light and you don't have it. You simply enjoy the sunshine. In the same way, just rejoice that somebody is producing some merits and making the world a brighter and better place. No matter who it is, whether it is you or somebody else, at least those merits are being produced.

After rejoicing in the merits of others, Ruciraketu goes on to dedicate whatever merit he has gained himself to Enlightenment. This dedication is bound up with the 'three aims'. According to some texts there are three possible aims in life. You can wish for well-being in this present life, you can wish for a happy rebirth in some future existence, or you can think in terms of gaining Enlightenment; and you can dedicate your merit to any one of these. To put it simplistically, you can say, 'By virtue of this meritorious act may I be happy and healthy and strong in this life,' or you can say, 'By virtue of this good action may I have a happy heavenly rebirth after I die,' or you can say, 'By virtue of this good action may I gain Enlightenment for the sake of all.' The bodhisattva, of course, does the third, and this is the one that is meant here.

We clearly need to guard against self-consciousness of an unhelpful kind in matters of this sort. Yes, you have an ultimate ideal, and you sincerely wish that whatever good you are doing may not be frittered away but may contribute to the attainment of that ultimate ideal. Clearly, however, you shouldn't do that in a self-conscious way, any more than you should do anything else self-consciously. You don't tell people that you're off to meditate because you want to gain Enlightenment. You just say, 'I think I'll go and meditate.' But in your own mind you are aware that this is the direction in which you are moving, and the goal for the sake of which you are mobilizing all your energies and resources, including the resources represented by your merits. You just wish that if you do have any merits, they may redound to ultimate Enlightenment.

Does it, then, really make any difference what you dedicate your merit to? If you dedicate it to a happy present life, or to a future life, does that make any concrete difference? The traditional Buddhist view is that it does, because your motivation is always the decisive factor. The Chinese Buddhists distinguish between 'pure' merit and 'impure' merit – colloquially they are called 'white merits' and 'red merits', white being the colour of the spirit and red the colour of the earth. The merit of the first and second aims is impure because it is tainted with self-interest, whereas the merit dedicated to the third aim is free of any such taint.

Pure merit tends to be deeper and more powerful than impure merit, inasmuch as it's not that you earn merit as if it were a sort of commodity or income which you can decide to invest either for your own benefit or for the benefit of all. You could say that the returns on an investment of merit for the sake of all are infinitely greater than a personal investment, but it is not quite like that either. Depending on whether you put them into worldly or spiritual things, the merits themselves change, because it's not just merit, it's *you*. Your merits are you.

The idea of a bodhisattva's dedication of merit is above all to help him eliminate any trace of selfishness. He lets go of the idea of working for himself or benefiting himself in this or a future life. He just wants to dedicate whatever resources he has to Enlightenment for the sake of all. In this way he gets rid of all traces of self-seeking.

Usually when we do good we have in the back of our mind somewhere the idea that it will be of some benefit to us personally, in a narrow and individualistic sense. The bodhisattva tries to counteract that natural – and, it should be said, perfectly healthy – tendency by saying, 'Whatever merits I produce, may they not go to my personal advantage in this or a future life. May they help me to gain Enlightenment for the benefit of all, so that I may be of use to everybody.' This helps him to overcome the individualistic attitude represented by the other two dedications, which is of course quite incompatible with the Mahāyāna and the bodhisattva ideal. It guards against our natural tendency to look after number one even in what we like to think of as our spiritual life.

The two strands, rejoicing in the merits of others and dedicating one's own merits to Enlightenment, are brought together after the third confession section:

> Whatever beings here in Jambudvīpa and whatever also in other world-spheres perform various, profound merits, I congratulate them all on this merit. By this my congratulation on their merits (and) by the (merit) obtained (by me) through body, voice or mind, may there be fruitful success for my resolve. May I touch supreme, flawless enlightenment.[252]

This comes just after a long passage of general good wishes. Enjoying spiritual happiness and well-being ourselves, it is only natural that we should rejoice in the spiritual happiness and well-being of others, as Ruciraketu does here. You often have this at the conclusion of a puja or even the conclusion of a Mahāyāna *sūtra*. It's just an expression of good will towards all living beings – that you wish for all of them all good things, both material and spiritual.

> Everywhere in the spheres of all beings may all the woes in the world be extinguished. May those beings whose senses are defective, whose limbs are deficient, all now become complete in senses. May those lying in the (ten) directions who are diseased, powerless, whose body is injured, and who are without protection, all be delivered quickly from their disease, and may they obtain health, strength, and senses. May those beings who are in danger of being threatened or killed by kings, thieves, or scoundrels, who are troubled by hundreds of different fears, may all those beings who are oppressed and suffering be delivered from those hundreds of extreme, very dreadful fears. May those who are beaten, bound and tortured by bonds, and situated in various troubles, distracted by numerous thousands of labours, who have become afflicted by various fears and cruel anxiety, may they all be delivered from their bonds; may the beaten be delivered from the beaters; may the condemned be united with life; and may all those who have come upon troubles become free from fear. May those beings who are oppressed by hunger and thirst obtain a variety of food and drink. And may the blind see the various forms, the deaf hear delightful sounds, the naked obtain various garments, poor beings obtain treasures. And may all beings be blessed with abundant wealth, corn, and various jewels. May the experience of woe harm no one. May all beings be good-looking. May they have beautiful, gracious, auspicious forms and continually have a heap of numerous blessings. As soon as they think of them, may there be for them food and drink as they desire, great abundance, and merits, lutes, drums, (and) pleasant-sounding cymbals, springs, pools, ponds, (and) tanks. As soon as they think of them, may there be for them lotus-ponds of blue and golden lotuses, food and drink, likewise clothing, wealth, gold, ornament of gems and

> pearls, gold, beryl, and various jewels. May there be no sounds of woe anywhere in the world. May there be not one being of opposing mien, and may they all be of noble aspect, creating light for one another. Whatever success there may be in the world of men, may it arise for them at their thought. As soon as they think of them, may all their desires be fulfilled through their merit (and its) fruit. May there rain down three times from the trees perfume, garlands, unguent, clothing, powder, various flowers. May the beings accept them (and) be joyful. May they do honour, inconceivable, to all the Tathāgatas in the ten directions, to the Bodhisattvas, to the Śrāvakas, to the pure, flawless, firm Law. May beings avoid the low states of existence. May they avoid the eight non-opportunities. May they obtain the supreme, chief opportunity. May they always obtain a meeting with Buddhas. May they always be highborn (and) have their treasuries replete with abundant wealth and corn. For numerous aeons may they be thoroughly adorned with beauty, complexion, fame (and) glory. May all women constantly become men, strong, heroic, intelligent, and learned. May they constantly proceed to enlightenment and be active in the six perfections. May they see the Buddhas in the ten directions, comfortably seated under excellent jewelled trees, sitting together on seats of precious beryl. May they hear them expounding the Law. The evil acts obtained by me, what I obtained previously in the oppressions of existences, whatever the evil acts bringing undesired fruits – may they all without remainder be destroyed. May all beings who dwell in the bondage of existence, bound with firm fetters by the fetters of the cycle of existence, be delivered from their bondage by the hands of wisdom. May they be delivered from their woes. May they become Buddhas.[253]

The phrase which jumps out at us here is 'May all women constantly become men.' Women are quite often concerned about what they see as discrimination against women in Buddhism, and they sometimes home in on Buddhist scriptures which seem to suggest that women are being put down. But there is one text that makes the whole matter quite clear. It comes in the passage of the Pāli canon where Mahāprajāpatī comes to the Buddha seeking ordination. At first the Buddha refuses her request. The Buddha's attendant Ānanda, clearly wondering whether

Mahāprajāpatī has been refused ordination because of a lack of spiritual capacity in women, asks the Buddha directly, 'Are women capable of the highest spiritual attainment?' and the Buddha says, 'Yes.'[254]

This, so far as Buddhist tradition is concerned, settled the matter once and for all. No one has ever suggested that the Buddha might not have said it; his words here are absolutely categorical, and all other texts have to be interpreted in their light. This is the basic Buddhist principle – and it is underlined by other Pāli canon texts in which the Buddha emphasized women's capacity to gain Enlightenment.[255]

One might further say that it is only Buddhism, among all the major religions of the world, that has stated categorically that women are capable of the highest spiritual attainment. The question isn't even asked in Christianity. Women can be 'saved'; you can have female saints; but if you start talking in terms of a female 'saviour' – or even of a woman priest in some circles – you run into difficulties. But in Buddhism it has always been said that women are capable of, and have achieved, whatever spiritual attainments men have achieved. There are examples in Buddhist history of women who, whether young or old, have attained Enlightenment, so we know it is possible. The Buddha himself had very accomplished female disciples, so did Milarepa, the Enlightened Tibetan ascetic, and so did Padmasambhava, the great guru of Tibet. In Buddhism women have been able to occupy any spiritual position that men have been able to occupy. There have been not only *bhikkhus* but *bhikkhunīs*, not only male gurus but female gurus. There is nothing in Buddhism to prevent a woman from exercising any spiritual function whatever, and this is the only religion of which one can say that.

So Buddhism has this double attitude. It is very realistic, and at the same time very idealistic. It does say that there are certain disadvantages for women, but on the other hand it says that women can gain Enlightenment, and that whatever spiritual path or function is open to men is also open to women. One has to take both of these together.

The phrase 'May there be not one being of opposing mien, and may they all be of noble aspect, creating light for one another,' is one I haven't come across in any other text. It suggests a sort of creative communication which helps both parties to move forward, each shedding light on the path for the other. It's very much in the spirit of the whole paragraph, which again is rather lavish. The text might just as well have said, 'May all living beings win happiness both mundane and transcendental,' and left it at that, but the Mahāyāna likes to enumerate things very concretely and vividly – which is no doubt much better, at least for the majority of people.

The chapter ends with some final good wishes:

> Whoever worships and praises the Buddhas continually, with mind believing, pure, spotless, by means of this (Confession), which is praised (as a cause of) transfer of merit, and abandons the evil states for sixty aeons, and whoever, men, women, brahmins, warriors, with these celebrated verses, will praise the sage, standing with hands in the gesture of reverence, will recollect (his) births in all existences, will have (his) body adorned with all members and with all senses, (will be) endowed with various merits (and) with virtues, and he will be continually worshipped as a king among men. Such will he be in each place (of birth).
>
> Not under one Buddha have they performed good, nor even under two, nor four, nor five, nor ten, but they in whose ear this Confession enters have performed good under thousands of Buddhas.
>
> So (ends) the third chapter, the Chapter on Confession, in the excellent Suvarṇabhāsa, king of *sūtras*.[256]

So in order to meet with this *sūtra* you must already have accumulated quite a few merits. You must have come into contact with a number of Buddhas – in different lives, because you only get one Buddha at a time. According to tradition the earth could not bear the weight of more than one Buddha at a time.

Again the *sūtra* is typical of the Mahāyāna in going in for lavish praise and rejoicing on a grand scale. Mahāyāna *sūtras* always try to give you an impression of vastness and infinity, multiplicity and abundance. They try to widen your perspective. Perhaps it is only in this way that the compiler of the *sūtra* could express what he really felt; he couldn't do it in a more sober fashion. It must have been very inspiring for the people who took it perfectly literally.

The general impression given by the whole chapter is one of joy and exuberance. It goes with a real swing. Even though there is so much said about faults and evil, the overall impression is very positive. There is nothing morbid about it, no atmosphere of sin and guilt. It is not abstract or abstruse; it states the spiritually obvious in an understandable, straightforward way. It is non-conceptual, direct, and immediate in its appeal. You just have to allow yourself to be carried along by it.

This joy comes across in a number of the Mahāyāna *sūtras*. Everybody is so overjoyed that a Buddha has appeared, that there is the Dharma to be followed, a sangha to make offerings to, stupas to worship. Everybody is overwhelmed with joy, and they think how lucky they are, and how wonderful it all is. It is very pure, colourful, innocent, and child-like, although there is no suggestion of immaturity. This is the traditional atmosphere and spirit of the Mahāyāna. For the average Mahāyāna worshipper, religion has always meant something colourful and joyful, exuberant and happy; and being involved with religion means being generous, outgoing, hospitable, kind, affectionate, welcoming, open, clear, and joyful.

This is the ultimate spiritual significance of confession: to clear away all darkness and evil so that we can experience the freedom and joy of a pure heart and mind. When we have not only seen the golden light at work in the world and been touched by it ourselves, but purified ourselves of the evil within us, the path to ultimate perfection lies clear before us.

PART II
TRANSFORMATION OF WORLD

3
THE PROTECTORS OF THE DHARMA

So far, we have been concerned with the development of the individual, with the transformation by the golden light of the individual self. Now we can begin to make the transition from transformation of self to transformation of world. So – first things first – what is the 'world'? I mean the question not in an abstract or philosophical sense but quite literally. These days we are very used to seeing the world, and the universe, in a particular way. We are so used to 'knowing' about the world in a scientific sense that it is easy to forget that only a few centuries ago the world people 'knew', the pre-Copernican world, was a fundamentally different one. It may still be hard for us to imagine that there could be any other way of seeing the universe than the 'right' way, the scientific way.

But the ancient Indian Buddhists saw the universe quite differently. To see it as they did, we will have to use our imagination. To begin with, imagine space, nothing but space, infinite space, stretching in all directions. Then, as you continue to look, seeing more and more deeply, you will see that diffused throughout that infinity of space is air, air of a deep blue colour. Within that blue air you gradually discern two currents of air, two 'blue winds', blowing in opposite directions, and these winds take the form of two crossed *vajras*, each of which is millions of miles in length.

Now imagine that resting on those two vast crossed *vajras* you can see a great mass of waters, forming a flat disc, and on these waters, towards the edges of the disc, you see four continents or islands, each with two subcontinents. All these continents and subcontinents have bases of solid gold. The eastern continent is called Videha. It is white in colour and shaped like the crescent moon. The southern continent is called Jambudvīpa; it is blue in colour and shaped like the shoulder-blade of a sheep. The western continent, Godānīya, is round, like the sun, and red in colour, and the northern continent, Uttarakuru, is square, and green in colour.

Then, right at the centre of the waters, there towers a great mountain, Mount Meru. It stands 80,000 *yojanas* above the waters (a *yojana* perhaps being something between eight and ten miles) and extends 80,000 *yojanas* below them. It has four faces, rather like a pyramid, and each face is made of a precious substance. The eastern face is of silver, the southern face of lapis lazuli, the western face of ruby, and the northern face of gold. Surrounding Mount Meru is an ocean 80,000 *yojanas* wide and 80,000 *yojanas* deep. Surrounding the ocean is a ring of golden mountains, 40,000 *yojanas* high and 40,000 *yojanas* wide. Then surrounding that is an ocean of the same dimensions. Altogether there are seven circular oceans and seven rings of golden mountains, their dimensions gradually diminishing as one moves outwards, although of course the diameter of the circles they form progressively increases, so that the last ring of golden mountains is only 625 *yojanas* high and 625 *yojanas* wide. Outside this are the waters on which float the four continents and the eight subcontinents. The entire system is enclosed by a great iron wall, the purpose of which is to shut in the light of the sun and the moon and the stars. This wall is said to be 312½ *yojanas* in height, and more than 3½ million *yojanas* in circumference. Outside that great iron wall there is only darkness until another universe is reached.

According to ancient Buddhist tradition there are thousands and millions of such universes throughout space, each with its own Mount Meru, continents, mountains, and oceans – and its own sentient beings and Buddhas. This cosmology would seem to be almost entirely an Indian Buddhist production. The only element which might be Tibetan – apart from a little colouring here and there – might be the blue winds and the two crossed *vajras*. The details are to be found in traditional texts like the *Mahāvyutpatti* – a sort of Sanskrit dictionary compiled to help translators of texts from Sanskrit into Tibetan – and the *Abhidharma-kośa*.[257]

The Indian view of the universe presents, of course, a very different picture of the universe from the modern Western one. However, it has its own validity. I once met a young Tibetan lama who had been studying Western academic subjects and I asked him which he thought was true: the traditional Indo-Tibetan picture of the universe or the modern Western one. He was a very young lama – in fact he was the reincarnation of a very famous Gelugpa lama – but although he was so young, the reply he gave was not only cautious but in my view quite correct. He said, 'The two pictures are useful for different purposes.'

I wouldn't like to comment on the usefulness of the modern Western picture, but there is no doubt about the usefulness of the traditional Buddhist picture, at least so far as its own definite spiritual purposes are concerned. For one thing, it provides the concrete symbolism on which is based a good deal of meditational and devotional practice, especially in the Vajrayāna. One of the most important of all Vajrayāna practices is what is known as the offering of the mandala. 'Mandala' literally means 'circle', and in this context it means the whole circle of conditioned existence as represented in the Buddhist picture of the universe. The practice is quite complex. In the course of your devotions you build up a three-dimensional model of the universe, complete with Mount Meru, the four continents, and so on. (You do this in your imagination, using heaps of rice on a metal tray to symbolize the different elements of the world picture.) This model universe you offer up to the Buddha, or more usually to the guru – especially after receiving teaching or initiation – together with suitable prayers and meditations.[258]

This offering up of the whole universe is a very natural response. After all, you have received the Dharma, something that is infinitely precious, something that is going to transform your whole life – so what are you going to give? It is not a question of giving *in return*; you give because you feel like giving, because you feel so grateful. You want to give everything that you possess, including your own life, your own self. Indeed, you feel that if you were master of the whole universe, you would give that. So this is what you do. It is only by making such an offering that you can express what you feel. For you at that moment the mandala *is* the universe, the universe *is* the mandala.

The traditional Buddhist view of the universe also provides the cosmological background to the Buddha's teaching, and is present, explicitly or implicitly, in the Buddhist scriptures, especially perhaps in the Mahāyāna *sūtras*. In chapter 6 of the *Sūtra of Golden Light*, for example, the Buddha speaks of the 'whole triple-thousand, great-thousand world-sphere, in which there are a hundred million moons, suns, great oceans, [and] Sumerus....'

We have seen something of the 'landscape' of the universe – its mountains, oceans, and islands – but we have not yet been introduced to the beings who inhabit this universe, some of whom will be playing a key role in this chapter of the *sūtra*. We ourselves inhabit Jambudvīpa, the southern continent. Jambudvīpa is the smallest of the continents, only 7,000 *yojanas* in diameter, and according to ancient tradition its inhabitants are rich and prosperous, and perform both skilful and unskilful deeds.

To meet some of the other inhabitants of this universe we need to take a closer look at Mount Meru. The mountain is divided horizontally into eight tiers, four below the waters and four above. The four tiers below the waters contain the hells, which are occupied by various classes of tormented beings, suffering the results of their unskilful actions. The four tiers above the water are inhabited by various classes of demigods: the *yakṣas* (sublime spirits), the *nāgas* (the serpents or dragons), and so on.

Then above Mount Meru are the various heavens of the gods, which begin, according to some accounts, 80,000 *yojanas* above the summit of the mountain. First of all there is the heaven known as the 'Heaven of the Thirty-three' – that is to say the thirty-three gods, the thirty-three Vedic deities. Their king is Indra, who occupies a wonderful palace in the midst of this heaven. Next come the Suyāma gods, and next above them is the heaven of the contented gods, the Tuṣita Heaven. Then there's the heaven of the gods that take delight in their own creations, and then a heaven of gods who take delight in others' creations. So altogether, including the heaven of the four great kings, there are six heavens.

According to Buddhist teaching the whole of conditioned existence is divided into three great planes or levels: the plane of sensuous desire, the plane of pure form, or archetypal form, if you like, and the formless plane. All the heavens mentioned so far fall, like the human realm, within the plane of sensuous desire.

All six heavens of this plane are inhabited by both gods and goddesses, and therefore in each of these heavens there's the possibility of sexual gratification. The higher one ascends, however, the more refined in form that gratification becomes, just as the heavens themselves become progressively more refined the higher one goes. In Indra's heaven, as among human beings, sexual gratification is achieved through copulation, among the Suyāma gods simply by holding hands, among the contented gods by means of a smile, among the gods who delight in their own creations by prolonged gazing, and among the gods who delight in the creations of others, by a mere glance – nothing more.

Above the heavens of sensuous desire with their gods and goddesses are the heavens of the world of pure form. These are inhabited by sixteen or eighteen (accounts vary) classes of Brahma gods. In the first three heavens live gods in the company of Brahmā, gods in Brahmā's retinue, and great Brahma gods. Then in the next three heavens we have the gods of lesser light, the gods of limitless light, and the gods of sonant light (that is, light which is also sound, sound which is also light). Above them are a further three heavens, in which live the gods of lesser purity, the gods of limitless purity, and the gods of radiant purity. Then there are still a further seven (or nine) heavens inhabited by more classes of Brahma gods. The last five of these heavens are collectively known as pure abodes, and here are born all those who on earth have broken all five lower fetters, and attained the path of no return – that is, the path of no further rebirth in the world of human beings, or indeed any realm below the pure abodes.

All the heavens of the plane of pure form are inhabited only by masculine divinities – angels, if you like – and they appear there spontaneously, without any need for the whole business of sexual reproduction. Above the heavens of pure form with their angels are four heavens of the formless plane, inhabited by gods without form.

One can draw correspondences between all these various heavens and the *dhyāna* states experienced in meditation. Each of the groups of heavens of the Brahma gods corresponds to one of the first four *dhyānas*, and the heavens of the formless plane correspond to the four formless *dhyānas*.

To complete our survey of the population of the ancient Buddhist universe, we must come down quite a long way, back to the level of the Heaven of the Thirty-three. In the air at this level is the circle of the eight goddesses: the goddesses of sensuousness, garlands, song, dance, flowers, incense, lamps, and perfumes. These goddesses occupy positions in the eight principal directions of space. They are young and beautiful, and of different colours – white, yellow, red, green, and so on. They all hold in their hands articles corresponding to their natures and their names. Then, immediately outside these goddesses, also suspended in the air in fixed positions, are the seven precious things – the precious wheel, the precious gem, the precious queen, the precious minister, the precious elephant, the precious horse, and the precious steward – plus the vase of treasure. Then, in the innermost circle, immediately around Mount Meru, are the sun, with its chariot drawn by ten horses, the moon, with its chariot drawn by seven horses, the precious umbrella of sovereignty, and the banner of victory. In the centre of it all, in the palace of Indra, is heaped up the entire treasure of gods and men. It's as though in Indra's palace you can find everything that gods and men could possibly desire. In one of the Gospels it is said, 'Where your treasure is, there will your heart be also.'[259] So treasure represents what you desire. And Indra's palace is the place where all your desires are fulfilled – at least your desires up to that level, for there are many heavens and realms above the Heaven of the Thirty-three.

There is just one group of beings in this extraordinary universe that we have not yet met. If we look again at Mount Meru, we will see that there are four figures standing on or near the summit, or perhaps each on a subsidiary peak halfway up the mountain, in each of the four directions. These are the four great kings, the four protectors of the world.

First of all there's Dhṛtarāṣṭra. His name means 'upholder of the land', he is white in colour, and he is the protector of the eastern quarter. He is king of the *gandharvas* (heavenly musicians) and of the *piśācas* (vampires). Then there is Virūḍhaka, whose name means 'growth'. He is yellow in colour, and protects the southern quarter, and he is king of the *pretas* or hungry ghosts and of the *kumbhāṇḍas*. Thirdly there is Virūpākṣa, 'he of the bulging eyes': the protector of the western quarter, he is red in colour, and rules over the *nāgas*, the serpents or dragons, as well as the *pūtanās* or fever-spirits. Finally there is Vaiśravaṇa, whose name means 'greatly learned'. He is green in colour, he is the protector of the northern quarter, and he rules over the *yakṣas* or sublime spirits and the *rākṣasas*, the flesh-eating demons.

All four kings are powerfully built, of defiant mien, and armour-clad. They are often represented in Buddhist art, especially in frescoes inside the vestibules of temples (two on either side of the entrance to the main hall) or in the form of free-standing, often quite gigantic images. And, of course, they appear in the *Sūtra of Golden Light*.

As we have seen, the Buddha is teaching the *sūtra* surrounded by bodhisattvas and many other beings. At the beginning of chapter 6 of the *sūtra* we discover that among these beings are the four great kings. They have apparently been present in the assembly all along, but they have made no contribution to the proceedings until this point. They now rise to their feet, salute the Buddha, and begin to speak. The kings speak a number of times, as does the Buddha – this is the longest chapter of the *sūtra* – but we can get a general sense of their significance by focusing on their opening speech. In this speech, the four kings make two statements and four promises. Firstly, they extol the merits of the *Sūtra of Golden Light*. Secondly, they declare that the *sūtra* nourishes them in – as we shall see – quite a curious and significant fashion. Then they make their four promises: to exercise their sovereignty over the different classes of demigods according to the Dharma, to protect the whole of Jambudvīpa, to protect the monks who proclaim the *sūtra*, and to protect the kings who patronize the monks who proclaim the *sūtra*.

On the subject of the first statement there is just one point I would bring out here. This is that the various grounds upon which the four great kings extol the *sūtra* are of two main kinds: spiritual and worldly. For instance, they extol the *sūtra* because it has been taken care of by multitudes of bodhisattvas and bestows supreme blessings upon all beings: but they also extol it because it repels foreign armies and removes hunger and illness. In effect they are saying it transforms life or self and it transforms the world.

Now for the second statement of the four great kings – that the *Sūtra of Golden Light* nourishes them. What they say is this:

> When, dear Lord, this excellent Suvarṇabhāsa, king of sūtras, is being expounded in detail in the assembly, by merely hearing this Law, and by the nectar juice of the Law, the divine bodies of us four great kings together with our armies and retinues will wax with great might. In our body there will be produced prowess, strength, and energy. Brilliance, glory and splendour will enter our body.[260]

How is it that the mere hearing of the *sūtra* should have this effect on the bodies of the four great kings? What are we meant to understand by 'hearing the *sūtra*'? In order to understand this, we will need to understand more deeply who the four great kings are and what they really represent. There are principally four points to be made.

First, the four great kings occupy the lowest of the heavens of the plane of sensuous desire. They are definitely heavenly beings, but of a very low order, in fact of the lowest order. At the same time they are in touch with the beings that inhabit the earth – not only human beings, but also the various kinds of non-human beings. From the point of view of the world this has decided advantages. The kings occupy an intermediate position, a kind of borderland between the more crude and the more refined, the more chaotic and the more harmonious levels of the plane of sensuous desire. Because they are in direct contact with the earth they are in a position to intervene in its affairs, but because they belong to the heavens, their intervention is sure to be of a positive nature.

The four kings are known as the *lokapālas*, the guardians of the world. In traditional Hīnayāna Buddhism *hiri* and *ottappa* – shame and blame, as they are usually translated – are called the two *lokapālas*, because without them there can be no moral order. This would seem to imply that there is no great difference between the *lokapālas* and the *dharmapālas* of the Vajrayāna tradition – '*dharma*' here having a strong ethical connotation. The Vajrayāna, however – as might be expected – gives a somewhat different slant to things in that it sometimes portrays *dharmapālas* as very fierce, wrathful beings who are in essence Enlightened bodhisattvas. This makes them quite different from the four kings – the *lokapālas* – who are not bodhisattvas but definitely mundane beings, albeit of a very high order.

The second significant aspect of the four great kings is that they are leaders of different hordes of non-human beings. These non-human beings are of many different kinds, of all sorts of shapes and sizes and even colours. Some are very beautiful, or at least capable of assuming beautiful shapes, but most are horribly misshapen and ugly. For example, the *nāgas*, the serpents or dragons, are associated with water and with treasure, and they can make themselves large or small, visible or invisible. They often have a good understanding of the teaching, but they don't practise it. The *yakṣas* are rather terrible, and often of enormous size. The *gandharvas*, the perfume eaters, are so called because they live on perfumes just as human beings live on solid food. They are musicians in the palace of Indra, in the Heaven of the Thirty-three, and are said to be very uxorious.

The *asuras* are fierce, war-like spirits, sometimes compared with the giants of Greek mythology, and they are constantly fighting the gods of the Heaven of the Thirty-three. The male *asuras* are extremely ugly, but the females are very beautiful. The *garuḍas* are enormous, golden-winged creatures like eagles, who feed upon *nāgas*. Then there are the *kiṃnaras*. The name *kiṃnara* means 'What? Is it a man?' and they are so called because they resemble men to some extent, so that when you see one you might not be sure whether it is a man or not. According to some authorities they have horns on their heads; according to others they have men's heads and bird's bodies. Like the *gandharvas*, they are musicians in the palace of Indra – the males sing, the females dance.

There are very many other kinds of non-human beings: vampires, nightmares, ghosts, ghouls, bogles, fever-spirits, and so on. Between them they represent the whole mass of gross, chaotic, turbulent energies that swirl about on this earth plane of ours – energies that can only too easily assume negative and destructive forms. Each of the four great kings rules over a particular group of these non-human beings. In other words, they keep the gross, turbulent, chaotic energies of the earth plane under control. They are not able to transform them, but at least they can prevent them getting too much out of hand.

It is only the four great kings who are in a position to render this kind of service. The gods of the higher heavens couldn't do it. Their energies are so refined that they have no point of contact with *nāgas*, *yakṣas*, *rākṣasas*, and so on – perhaps they are not even aware of their existence. So the four great kings perform a very useful service. They belong to the heavens, but they are in touch with the earth, and they are therefore able to keep the powerful natural energies of the earth under control, and prevent them from having a disruptive effect on the human world.

The third point to be made about the four great kings is that they are protectors of the world, protectors of the four quarters. But what are they protectors against? The kings themselves make this clear in their first speech. Addressing the Buddha, they say, 'We will rout the hordes of Bhūtas, who are pitiless, whose minds are without compassion, who take their glory from others.' *Bhūtas* are evil spirits. They are the forces that are hostile to humanity, inimical to spiritual development, the energies that refuse to accept the control of the four great kings. All the kings can do about them is keep them at bay, keep them out.

It is because they are protectors or guardians in this way that the kings stand on either side of the entrance to the temple, neither inside nor outside, but on the threshold. After all, a temple is not just a building. A temple is an enclosed, sacred space, where sacred, symbolic actions are performed. It is therefore a space that only integrated energies can be allowed to enter. The central position in the temple is occupied by the Buddha or an equivalent figure such as Padmasambhava or Avalokiteśvara, and other positions are occupied by *arhants*, bodhisattvas, spiritual teachers, gods, and goddesses, all harmoniously grouped around the central figure. Even the *nāgas* and *yakṣas* and other non-human beings may have a place. It depends on just one thing: whether they truly worship the Buddha, whether they go for Refuge, whether they place themselves at the service of the Dharma.

One might well ask, of course, how non-human beings like *pretas* and *yakṣas* can possibly place themselves at the service of the Dharma. The answer to this lies in what we make of this kind of symbolism. Let's take an example from rather nearer home: the figure of the Greek god Hermes. Who or what is Hermes? We might say that in Greek mythology he is the messenger of the gods, and that might seem like a satisfactory answer, but it is not really an answer at all. If you read up about Hermes it becomes clear that he was a deeply complex figure with all sorts of aspects, some of them apparently quite contradictory. In order to gain even a little idea of who or what Hermes is or was, you have to comb through the available material very carefully. You have to examine all the hundreds of references to Hermes in the *Iliad* and the *Odyssey* and gradually build up your picture of him. It's simply not enough to say, 'Hermes was the messenger of the gods,' and leave it at that. That could even be quite misleading, in that it might give people the idea that they know all about him.

It's like that with all the mythological figures mentioned in the *Sūtra of Golden Light*. It is not enough just to say, 'The *pretas* are hungry ghosts – so how can hungry ghosts be put at the service of the Dharma?' You have to study the *pretas* – who are they? what are they? – and try to get some understanding of what they are really like. Then perhaps you can begin to see how they can be put at the service of the Dharma.

Let's apply this to the case of the *nāgas* – the dragons or serpents. What might they represent? The protector of the western quarter of the world – that is, *our* quarter – is Virūpākṣa. Virūpākṣa is the leader of, among other classes of non-human beings, the dragons. But what exactly are these dragons? We mustn't confuse them with European dragons, the kind of dragon that was killed by St George. The Buddhist dragon is quite a different kind of creature. According to Buddhist tradition dragons are highly intelligent. They often have a very good understanding of the Dharma, but – and here's the rub – they don't practise it. In particular, they don't observe the precepts. This is perhaps why in Indian Buddhist art dragons are usually represented in serpent form, with big heads, long thin bodies, and no arms or legs. They have no limbs because they don't do anything. They think and understand, but they never practise – they never act upon what they know – so they don't need limbs.

I once read a book written by a Chinese Buddhist monk who, in passing, made the statement that dragons are not as common nowadays as they used to be. I must say, however, that I don't agree with him. I think that, if anything, dragons are more common now, at least in some parts of the world. In the West, dragons are very common indeed. Here there are lots of people who understand the Dharma very well, who know all about *śūnyatā* and Zen, all about the One Mind and the Abhidharma, all about the esoteric Tantric teachings, but who never even think of practising the Dharma. Such dragons – for dragons can take human form – are very common in some Buddhist circles.

In some ways the intellectual dragons of the West are the worst dragons the world has yet seen, because they hardly recognize the authority even of Virūpākṣa. It's as though even that degree of organization has broken down. The *nāgas* have broken away from Virūpākṣa, and perhaps all the other beings and creatures have broken away from their respective guardian kings too. There's a degree of confusion, a degree of chaos, that perhaps has never existed before. Perhaps the most immediately dangerous dragon at large today is represented by the scientific community, in so far as its research and development programmes – that is, the direction of its search for knowledge – are unaffected by ethical considerations. For many members of this enormously influential community, it's as though they have sold themselves to the devil for the sake of professional success, material security, and prestige.

As Buddhists, what we need to do is invoke the help of Virūpākṣa, the protector of the western quarter, to bring our dragons under control. We have to bring our own one-sided intellectual activity under control – by being receptive to the golden light and practising the Dharma. In this way we will bring the *nāgas* within the portals of the temple.

The temple is also a mandala, a harmonious arrangement of psychological, spiritual, and transcendental energies around a common central principle: the principle of Enlightenment. So by bringing the *nāgas* within the portals of the temple, we are also building the mandala. The four great kings are also guardians of the four gates of the mandala. They prevent the entry of any hostile force, any unintegrated energy – that is to say, any energy that is not prepared to align itself, on its own level and in its own way, with the principle of Enlightenment. The four great kings are the guardians of the threshold, a function of great importance. On the one hand they have to keep out the hostile unintegrated forces – otherwise the harmony of the mandala would be disrupted. On the other hand, they have to admit the energies which are integrated and ready to be admitted – otherwise the potential richness of the mandala would be impoverished.

Within the Buddhist tradition there are also other beings who guard the gates of the mandala. These are the four *gaurīs*, the 'fair ones'. They are said to stop people leaving the mandala by means of hooks. From a Western point of view this might sound rather violent, but in Buddhism these hooks are associated with fascination. A 'fascinating woman' can be said to 'hook' men not by violence but just by exerting her charm; and a bodhisattva does the same. The bodhisattva draws us to Enlightenment with beauty, revealing Enlightenment as the truly beautiful. The *gaurī* represents that kind of fascination. For your own good you have to be kept within the mandala, but by the very nature of the situation you can't be kept there by force. So the *gaurīs* would seem to represent the more fascinating aspect of the *lokapālas*, the aspect that makes you want to stay within the mandala rather than leaving it as you might otherwise be tempted to do.

If, say, the mandala is decorated with flowers and looks very beautiful, even though you may not be spiritually drawn to what the mandala represents, at least you like it in there. It's attractive, it's beautiful – and that helps you to stay. That is the *gaurīs* at work with their hooks. The spiritual community is also a mandala. Here too the four great kings have a function. Disruptive energies must be kept out, otherwise the spiritual community will be destroyed, but positive, integrated energies must be welcomed, otherwise the spiritual community will not grow.

The fourth and last point to bear in mind about the four great kings is that they are immensely powerful. This characteristic is well brought out in paintings and images, in which the kings are usually depicted as men a little past the middle of life, and powerfully built, often with enormous bulging muscles. In some ways they resemble the Heracles of Greek mythology, but unlike Heracles they are clad in armour. They represent enormously powerful, positive energies, energies which are not very spiritual or refined but at the same time not quite earthly. Such energies are sometimes described as crude, and crude they certainly are in comparison with the more refined energies of the higher planes. But crude energy is not to be despised – it has an essential part to play in the world. The energy represented by the four great kings is not only enormously powerful, but also extremely free and active. It is not blocked or repressed, but always available to keep turbulent earthly energies under control and repel anti-spiritual forces.

It should now be a little more clear who the four great kings really are, and what they really represent. They represent the forces of balance and harmony in the cosmos, especially in the all-important borderland between the human world and the heavenly world, or, if you like, between the psychological and the spiritual. They represent, indeed, the possibility of transition from the one to the other.

We should also now be in a better position to understand the kings' statement that the *Sūtra of Golden Light* nourishes them. Clearly, this statement is not to be understood in an exclusively literal sense. What nourishes them is the golden light, the light of the transcendental, and they *need* that nourishment. We can understand from this that the positive energies of the cosmos, the energies that make for balance and harmony, however powerful they are, will sooner or later pass over into the opposite and become negative if they are not nourished by the transcendental.

This has important implications. On the level of the individual human life it means that there is no such thing as purely *psychological* positivity in the sense of a positivity whose support comes only from a psychological source. There is no such thing, even, as purely *spiritual* positivity. What, after all, is the criterion of what is positive and what is not? What is skilful and what is not? From a Buddhist point of view, the skilful is something that provides a base for the development of a connection with the transcendental, and what in practice provides a base for the development of the transcendental is the positive. So without that reference to the transcendental, how are you going to determine what is genuinely positive? You have no means of ascertaining the difference between the positive and the merely pleasant, between what is genuinely positive and what simply gives personal satisfaction. You just can't be sure that what seems to you to be positive really is positive without that reference to the transcendental.

There is another consideration to take into account here. Suppose you experience a positive mental state in the ordinary psychological sense; if you have at least a concept of the transcendental, and you know that the positive can provide a basis for the transcendental, you then have an incentive to sustain that experience of the positive. One could go so far as to say that without a reference to the transcendental you have no fundamental reason to develop or sustain positivity.

This means in practice that you need to have a personal connection with someone who has had experience of the transcendental. If you can only refer to it as a memory or an ancient tradition, it loses its sustaining power. This is what happened in the Buddha's day in the case of the Brahmins. Their ancestors had been knowers of Brahma, had attained to Brahma, but by the Buddha's time the Brahmins could refer to no such experience, so they could not sustain the spiritual tradition.

We can look at this in terms of the symbolism of the Tibetan wheel of life, in particular that of the realm of the gods. The gods appear to have a very positive experience of life, but unless they have some awareness of the transcendental, their positivity cannot function as a basis for the realization of the transcendental. According to tradition the gods are simply reaping the reward of previous skilful actions. What sustains their positivity is karma. When their positive karma runs out, so to speak, they will fall from their positive state unless from within it they can envisage the transcendental. But if they do have this vision, then it will provide a basis not just for the realization of the transcendental but also for the extension of their positive experience.

If we accept all this, it follows that we cannot be truly human without going for Refuge. We are human by accident, as it were, or just for a short time; we can't sustain our human state without some reference to the transcendental factor. Our reason for creating the fresh positive karma which will sustain a positive state is ultimately a transcendental reason.

Even after a transcendental experience has ceased to be a living thing and is only a memory, the memory continues to exert some influence for a time. But eventually, if there hasn't been a fresh impulse from or experience of the transcendental, all the positive volitions that have depended on that transcendental factor become weaker and weaker. A society can run on the memory of a vision for a while, but not for long. For instance, over the past hundred years or more many people have ceased to believe in Christianity but have continued to live according to Christian ethics because there was still some momentum left in those ethics. In recent times, though, the momentum has slowed down and many people see no reason to continue to follow Christian ethics.

It is not just that the only true, lasting positivity is that which has its ultimate sanction in the transcendental. Nourished by the transcendental, positivity will be more positive, even on its own level, than it could possibly have been without it. As the four great kings say, 'In our body there will be produced prowess, strength, and energy. Brilliance, glory, and splendour will enter our body.' Here 'body' does not mean body as distinct from mind, but the whole personality, the whole being. In other words, nourished by the golden light, the kings will be greater and more kingly than ever, and they will exercise their distinctive functions more effectively than ever. Similarly, one who goes for Refuge will not only develop spiritually but will also become more of a human being. Distinctively human qualities are nourished by the spiritual, nourished by the transcendental. It is almost possible to say that you can't be a human being unless you go for Refuge. Ultimately it is only the Enlightened human being who is the true human being.

On the level of collective human life, there can be no healthy culture or civilization without some basis in transcendental values, however deeply hidden those values may be. A purely secular culture is really a contradiction in terms – though this certainly does not mean that we in the West are flung back into the arms of orthodox Christianity. There are other alternatives.

Having declared that they are nourished by the Dharma, the four great kings make their four vows. The first, their promise to exercise their sovereignty over the different classes of demigods according to the

Dharma, means that their rule will not be an expression of arbitrary, egoistic will, but will express spiritual power – not their own power but that of the Dharma. They will simply be the channels through which this power is transmitted, through which it reaches the hordes of non-human beings. In becoming such channels they will be all the more truly themselves.

The kings' second promise is to protect the whole of Jambudvīpa, which is the known material world, the human world. The four great kings promise to keep out all hostile forces that threaten to disrupt the fabric of a positive, healthy, human society – that is, a society in which it is possible for the individual to develop. At present the services of the four great kings are very badly needed – in fact, their strength is being strained to the utmost, especially in our western quarter, where hostile forces are trying to break in at a number of points.

Their third promise is to protect the monks who read or recite the *sūtra* and explain its meaning, and to give them their encouragement. Objectively this means that the grosser energies of the cosmos will co-operate with the monks in their work of proclaiming the *sūtra*. Subjectively it means that the monks themselves will integrate their own grosser psychophysical energies so that they can use them for this purpose. After all, one needs a lot of energy to proclaim the Dharma – not only spiritual energy, but sheer physical stamina. This, too, the four great kings promise to give.

Fourthly, they promise to protect kings who patronize the monks who proclaim the *sūtra*. Here 'kings' means governments – social, economic, and political systems that are organized to assist spiritual development. Such 'kings' perform in their respective systems the same function that the four great kings perform in the cosmos at large, and it's only natural, therefore, that the four great kings should protect them. They represent the same spirit on different levels of operation. I will go into this more in the last chapter, which is concerned with the upholders of the moral order.

These four vows, together with the four great kings' commitment to protecting the *sūtra*, mean that, just as the hordes of non-human beings submit themselves to the four great kings, so the kings submit themselves to the golden light. In other words, the earthly energies submit to the heavenly energies, and the heavenly energies submit to the transcendental energies. Thus is the profound principle of spiritual hierarchy introduced. The four great kings, indeed, can even be said to symbolize this principle. They exercise sovereignty over what is below them, while at the same time willingly accepting the sovereignty of what is above them. The kings therefore also represent the principle of world transformation. The world can only be truly transformed if it submits to the golden light, if it is receptive to the golden light – that is, if it organizes itself in such a way as to assist the manifestation of the golden light in the life of the individual.

Having come so far, it is worth exploring in what sense the four great kings can be said to exist. The question hangs, of course, on what one might mean by 'exist'. I have to say that when I was studying this section of the *sūtra* I had the sense that the kings were gathered around me, not so much as separate entities, but more like four clouds joined together. I certainly didn't have the impression that my experience of them was purely subjective. I felt that they did exist in some objective sense, though obviously I can offer no proof of that.

It is perhaps not too far-fetched to think of the four great kings as representing forces of balance and harmony in the cosmos, and as such having a real influence on the world. It does seem to be the case that there is a principle of balance at work in nature, even in the human body. When it becomes ill, the healthy organism has a natural tendency to compensate and heal itself. If an imbalance in the environment is brought about, perhaps by a man-made disaster, there also nature seems to have a tendency to put itself right. Perhaps the four great kings represent that tendency writ large in nature as a whole. They are not separate from nature; they are a part of it, although they do have distinct personalities. They are not standing outside nature and interfering with it like a mechanic tinkering with a car.

There are no obvious counterparts to the four great kings in Western mythology, although King Arthur perhaps comes close. If we disregard the specifically Christian aspects of his mythology, he can still be seen as a king fighting the forces of evil, like the four great kings. Of course, King Arthur is defeated in the end, which the four great kings never are, apparently, so perhaps he doesn't quite do. Another parallel might possibly be drawn with St George, who is at least a legendary figure, in that he doesn't seem to have had a historical existence at all, except in the same kind of remote sense as King Arthur. And then there's the archangel Michael, who is traditionally depicted as fighting with devils.

The only way to invoke the power of the four great kings is to think about them or concentrate on them. My own experience of their presence no doubt happened because I was concentrating intensely on them. They may have mantras – and the Vajrayāna has pujas that include the making of offerings to them – but such practices would only help to invoke them to the degree that one was concentrated and absorbed in the thought of them. The explicit practices would only help one to become concentrated on that basis.

This means that you would have to be *interested* in the four great kings. If you thought of them as no more than a bit of outmoded Tibetan mythology, you certainly wouldn't be able to invoke them. You have to have some feeling for them, just as for any other mythological figure. If you absorbed yourself in material dealing with Hermes you would have a sort of experience of Hermes. It's the same with any archetypal figure, because they all correspond to something in the human psyche. You can contact them through that aspect of the psyche which corresponds to them, but first you have to activate it.

It is not only the four great kings who come forward and promise to protect the *sūtra*. In subsequent chapters, other deities come forward and make similar promises. In particular, three goddesses promise to protect the *sūtra*: Sarasvatī, the goddess of learning, Śrī, the goddess of wealth, and Dṛḍhā, the earth goddess. The promises of the four great kings represent the general principle of the transformation of the world through submission to the golden light, while the promises of the three goddesses represent the working out of that principle in different spheres of human life and activity. What those spheres are, and how that principle works out in them, we shall see in the course of the next three chapters.

If we submit to the golden light, we will be able to transform our own life, our own self, and also co-operate in the transformation of the world. If we do that, in our own small sphere we too shall be one of the protectors of the Dharma.

4
BUDDHISM AND CULTURE

The world is transformed when it becomes wholly receptive to the golden light. By 'the world' in this context I mean the sum total of unenlightened human activities. Agriculture, commerce, the arts, the sciences, medicine, law, government, administration, diplomacy, transport, communication, advertising, entertainment, sport ... all these things together make up the world. They become receptive to the golden light by placing themselves at the service of the spiritual development of the individual. This may of course mean that they have to recognize that they cannot be of any service whatsoever to the individual in his or her spiritual development. In that case they must just quietly abolish themselves: that is the best service they can render.

When all the different activities that make up the world have placed themselves at the service of the spiritual development of the individual, the world will be transformed by the golden light. It will be a world 'fit for individuals to live in', a world that will help individuals to grow.

Of course, to say that all the activities that make up the world should place themselves at the service of the spiritual development of the individual is only a manner of speaking. After all, those activities don't carry on of their own accord; they are carried on by people. It is therefore people who must place themselves at the service of the spiritual development of the individual. Only then will the world be transformed. The vast majority of people have, of course, no intention of doing anything of the sort. They are going to carry on with their particular activities with no reference whatsoever to the golden light and the spiritual development of the individual.

But this does not mean that nothing can be done. The difficulty can be overcome; the world can still be transformed. It can be transformed through teams of spiritually committed individuals taking up different human activities and orienting them in the direction of the golden light in such a way that they conduce to the spiritual development both of those who carry out the activities and those who come into contact with them.

Through becoming involved with as many of these activities as possible, people committed to spiritual development can bring into existence a world within a world. A transformed world within the untransformed world can be brought into being – and gradually expanded.

In exploring the role of the four great kings, we have encountered the general principle of world transformation. We have seen that the world can be transformed only if it becomes receptive to the golden light. From now onwards we shall be concerned with the transformation of specific aspects of the world: culture, the environment, economics, and even politics. The first three of these are represented in the *sūtra* by three goddesses – Sarasvatī, Śrī, and Dṛḍhā, – each of whom comes forward and promises to protect the *sūtra*, thereby placing the department of human activity that she represents at the service of the development of the individual.

The first of these great goddesses to step forward is Sarasvatī. At the beginning of chapter 7 she comes forward, salutes the Buddha, and makes a number of promises relating to the monk who preaches the *Sūtra of Golden Light*. We'll come to what these promises are, but first, who is Sarasvatī?

This is a question we wouldn't have any trouble answering if we happened to be in India, especially if we happened to be there during the five or six weeks after the end of the rainy season. In many parts of India this particular period is known as the 'pujas', and it's so called because at this time a whole series of Hindu religious festivals and celebrations in honour of various Hindu gods and goddesses is held. It's a very festive season: everybody is happy and cheerful, and more friendly than usual. The sky is blue, the sun shines, a gentle breeze blows – it's the most enjoyable season of the whole year. People often take a holiday from work because they just don't feel like working. They buy new clothes, they go to see their friends and relations, they exchange presents, and of course they go, usually in the evening, to worship the various gods and goddesses. In some parts of India, for instance in Bengal, special images are made just for the puja season and installed in temporary shrines in places accessible to the public. In India people go to the pujas rather as in England they go to football matches or bingo, and they go in their tens or even hundreds of thousands. On the occasions of very special festivities, some of which only come around every ten or twelve years, they even go in their millions.

One of the most popular of the gods and goddesses worshipped in the puja season is Sarasvatī. The images of her are usually made of clay, and life-size, sometimes even a little larger than life, and beautifully painted and decorated. The goddess is depicted as a beautiful young woman with long flowing tresses, wearing a brocade Benares sari, usually red with a golden border. She is seated on a white *haṃsa*. *Haṃsa* is usually translated as 'swan' but it's actually a goose. Indian cultural associations with geese are quite different from Western ones; in India the goose is a beautiful, elegant bird that conjures up all sorts of religious associations. So Sarasvatī is seated on a white goose, and she holds a veena – an Indian musical instrument rather like a lute – in her lap.

In India different deities are particularly worshipped by different classes of people. Businessmen, merchants, traders, and shopkeepers worship Ganesha, the elephant-headed god who removes obstacles, and Lakṣmī, the goddess of wealth. Those who go in for physical training – athletes, musclemen, and weightlifters – worship Hanuman, the monkey god, the great devotee of Rama, who is renowned for his physical strength, energy, and enterprise. Women and girls, on the other hand, are particularly fond of Krishna, not so much because he preached the *Bhagavad Gītā* as because he dances at night in the forest with the *gopīs* – the cow-girls, or, more poetically, milkmaids.

Sarasvatī is worshipped in particular by the students. On the eve of her festival her altar is piled high with exercise books and textbooks, pens and pencils, even erasers. In making these offerings the students are invoking Sarasvatī's blessing, and asking for her help in passing the forthcoming examinations, which follow rather too quickly for comfort on the pujas. Sarasvatī is the object of the students' devotion because she is the goddess of learning, of education – in a word, of culture.

The name Sarasvatī does not give us any clue as to her actual function. It means 'abounding in water', sometimes translated even as 'watery'. This is because it is the name, as one might guess, of a river, a river in north-western India. So how did a river come to be transformed into a goddess of learning and culture? As is usually the case in India, this is a very long story. It goes back several thousand years, to the time when the Aryans invaded India. No one really knows where they came from, but they entered India from the north-west, with their horses and chariots, and gradually subdued the original inhabitants of the land, and with these invaders came not only their warriors and rulers, but also their priests, the famous Brahmins.

By this time the Brahmins had developed an elaborate system of ritual and sacrifices. There were sacrifices for every conceivable purpose, every conceivable occasion, and these sacrifices were often performed on the banks of a river. In those days there were no temples. Everything was done in the open air. Being smooth and sandy, with a flat surface for the construction of the altar, a river bank was the ideal place for a sacrifice, and it provided plenty of water for the ritual ablutions to which the Brahmins attached great importance. Moreover, on the banks of the river, perhaps far from human habitation, there was seclusion, there was peace and quiet. The banks of the Sarasvatī were particularly favoured for the celebration of these Vedic sacrifices, so much so that an association grew up between this river and the whole sacrificial system.

A great deal of brahminical culture was based on the sacrificial system, or grew out of it. For example, in the course of the sacrifices, the famous Vedic hymns were recited. These were often of great poetic beauty. There were hymns to the sun and the moon, hymns to the dawn and the winds. There were hymns to the thunder-god Indra, to the heavenly twins and the heavenly horses, and so on. These hymns, which are often very glorious in their language and conception, represent the beginnings of Indian literature. Some may have been composed even before the Aryans entered India. Their language is very archaic, so much so that even by the time they arrived in India it had become quite difficult to understand. This prompted the Brahmins to develop a whole science of etymology called *nirukti*, along with grammar, phonetics, and prosody. The hymns were often chanted to special tunes, so here we have the beginnings of a certain kind of music. Moreover, the altars used in connection with the brahminical sacrifices were very elaborate. They had to be constructed in a certain way, of a certain size and shape – in one case like an eagle with outstretched wings – and even of a certain number of bricks. These exact specifications led, so it is said, to the development of arithmetic and geometry.

So it is safe to say that a great deal of Indian culture – even high Indian culture – was associated with the sacrificial system, and in particular with the banks of the Sarasvatī. By this time the river had 'become' a goddess in her own right. Like all ancient peoples, the ancient Indians identified natural features such as rivers, mountains, and lakes, the sun and the moon, and the earth itself, as deities. They saw them, even experienced them, as gods and goddesses. Quite early in Indian cultural history there appears a river goddess called Sarasvatī who is particularly associated with culture.

But the process of development did not stop there. In the Vedas there are several hymns to an ancient and rather shadowy goddess called Vāc. *Vāc* means 'speech' – not ordinary speech, but speech in the sense of powerful, significant, even creative speech – and incidentally, the fact that the ancient Indians made a goddess out of speech and addressed hymns to her shows that they realized the great importance of human communication. Anyway, in the course of centuries Sarasvatī gradually assumed the attributes of Vāc, so that in a manner of speaking Vāc became absorbed into the goddess Sarasvatī.

It is important to note that Vāc represented speech, the *spoken* word. As yet there was no such thing as writing in India, at least not for religious purposes. Writing was something profane, fit only for keeping records of accounts and so on. Thus the culture of which Sarasvatī became a personification was an orally transmitted culture, with teachings handed down from teacher to pupil by word of mouth. In such a culture, memory is of tremendous importance. If someone's memory fails, knowledge that is of lasting value to the community may be lost. Sarasvatī therefore also became associated with good memory. We can draw a parallel here with the nine muses of ancient Greek mythology. The muses are the personification of various arts and sciences, the companions – some accounts say the daughters – of Apollo, the god of poetry, music, and prophecy. And the mother of the muses is Mnemosyne, whose name means 'memory'. Memory, in other words, is the mother of all the arts and sciences; in all preliterate societies there is no culture without memory.

Of course in India the oral traditions were eventually written down, and when this happened, Sarasvatī became not just a goddess of the spoken word, but also a goddess of literature and scholarship. She also began to be regarded as the wife of the god Brahmā. Brahmā is one of the *trimūrti*, the three principal embodiments of the divine, in Puranic Hinduism: Brahmā the Creator, Viṣṇu the Preserver, and Śiva the Destroyer.

This, then, is the Sarasvatī who is still worshipped in India today, more than a thousand years after all these developments took place. She is the goddess of education and culture, the embodiment of communication, the personification of memory, the patroness of literature both sacred and profane, and the wife of the god Brahmā, the Creator. It is therefore quite interesting that her appearance in chapter 7 of the *sūtra* is the first time she appears in Indian literature.

The question is, what is she doing there? She is clearly a Hindu goddess. What is a Hindu goddess doing in a Mahāyāna Buddhist *sūtra*? How does she come to be there? In chapter 3 we found a Brahmin appearing in Ruciraketu's dream. Now we have a Hindu goddess playing an even more important part in the *sūtra*. What does this mean?

The first thing to remember is that Hinduism is not a universal religion like Buddhism or Christianity or Islam, but an ethnic one like Judaism or Shinto. It is the sum total of the beliefs and practices of the Indian people over a period of 3,000 years. While there are some aspects of Hinduism that are concerned with the spiritual development of the individual, on the whole, like other ethnic religions, Hinduism is much more concerned with the preservation of the group. Sarasvatī therefore represents the cultural heritage of the social group – that is, she represents Indian culture.

But what is 'culture'? It's quite an interesting word. In English its primary meaning is tillage, rearing, production, as in agriculture, horticulture, floriculture, and so on. It then has its applied or derived meanings – as in physical culture, mental culture – so that in the end the word comes to mean something like 'development'. We have the cultured or cultivated person – that is to say, the person who is developed in an all-round manner: physically, mentally, emotionally, and morally.

The Sanskrit equivalent of the English word 'culture' conveys much the same meaning, but with an interesting difference of emphasis. It is *saṃskṛti*, which means 'the perfected' and is contrasted with *prakṛti*, 'the natural'. *Saṃskṛti*, in other words, is the product of human art, while *prakṛti* is the product of nature. We find this difference reflected in the sphere of language. The ancient Indian classical language Sanskrit is the perfected form of language – language which has been regularized, polished, refined – while the language Prakrit is the natural form of language, the vernacular. Sanskrit is spoken by educated, cultured people, while Prakrit is spoken by the uneducated, by the masses. We can see this difference at work in certain classical Indian dramas. The leading characters speak Sanskrit, while the other characters, such as servants, speak Prakrit.

Students of the history of Buddhism may wonder how it was that Buddhist scriptures came to be written down in the polished, cultured Sanskrit rather than the vernacular Prakrit. After all, didn't the Buddha expressly forbid the monks to teach the Dharma in Sanskrit, asking them instead to teach it in the everyday language of ordinary people? Well, the Buddha did say something like that, but the word he used was not *saṃskṛt* but *chandas*.[261] This was what is known as 'Vedic Sanskrit', the language in which the Vedas were composed. It was originally the language spoken by the Aryans, but by the time of the Buddha it was a 'dead' language, as Latin, for example, is today. The Buddha did not want his words to be translated into what was for most people a dead language; he preferred that the Dharma should be available to people in their own language, whatever that was.

Once a religious tradition is embodied in a particular form of language, it tends to remain embodied in that form, due to religious conservatism – religion is always conservative, it would seem. Meanwhile, the ordinary spoken language goes on changing, so that eventually a difference develops between the language of sacred texts, whether oral or written down, and the ordinary, everyday language. This is what happened in the case of Vedic Sanskrit. The Vedas existed in that particular archaic form of the language that couldn't be changed due to the sacredness of the Vedas, but language went on changing. That was how Sanskrit and Prakrit developed, the two being basically the same language – one in a more refined, the other in a less refined, form.

By the time the Mahāyāna *sūtras* came to be written down, Sanskrit – not Vedic Sanskrit but classical Sanskrit – had become a sort of lingua franca that was much more widely understood than Vedic Sanskrit had been in the Buddha's time. The Mahāyāna *sūtras* were written down in Sanskrit simply because it was the language that was most widely understood. There was no departure from principle; the idea throughout was to make the Buddha's teaching accessible to as many people as possible.

The fact that the Buddhist scriptures were translated into Sanskrit didn't mean that they were accessible only to 'educated' people. As I have said, in dramas the more upper-class characters spoke Sanskrit while the servants spoke Prakrit, but they could all understand one another. It's a bit like the difference between standard English and broad Cockney, except that Prakrit was also a literary medium: the Jains, for instance, used Prakrit quite extensively.

All this is perhaps a little beside the point but it does put us in a better position to understand the significance of Sarasvatī's appearance in the *Sūtra of Golden Light*. As we have seen, she represents the culture of the group – specifically Indian culture – but she also represents what that culture itself represents, what *saṃskṛti* represents. She represents human nature in its more developed state, human activities in their more polished and refined forms. We could even say that she represents the cultivated person, the cultivated mind.

I introduced Sarasvatī's appearance in the *Sūtra of Golden Light* by saying that she promises to protect the *sūtra*, but this is not, strictly speaking, quite correct. What she actually promises to protect is the monk who preaches the *sūtra*, who communicates the golden light of the Dharma. And the Dharma – what we call 'Buddhism' – is not an ethnic religion but a universal one, a spiritual teaching addressed to the individual, or the person who is trying to become an individual. The golden light is the light of the transcendental, the light of truth, the light of reality, the light of the Buddha.

For this golden light to be communicated, a language, a medium of communication, is needed, not only literally but metaphorically. That medium of communication has to fulfil two requirements. First of all, obviously enough, it has to be common to both parties. The monk who is preaching the *sūtra* and those to whom he is preaching it have to speak the same language. Secondly, that language has to be sufficiently refined, sufficiently transparent, to communicate at least something of the splendour of the golden light.

The preacher of the Dharma in the *Sūtra of Golden Light* is trying to communicate the golden light to the people of India, and he therefore has to speak the language of Indian culture. Only the language of culture is sufficiently refined to act as the medium of communication for the golden light, and only the language of Indian culture is familiar enough to be intelligible. So this is what the appearance of the great goddess Sarasvatī represents. She stands for the coming together of universal and ethnic religion, the coming together of Buddhism and Indian culture. More specifically, she stands for the coming together of the spiritual ideals of the Mahāyāna and the rich and vital culture of the Indian Gupta period, the period that also produced some of the most distinguished Buddhist art.

Furthermore, in promising to protect the monk who teaches the Dharma, she shows how ethnic culture places itself at the service of universal religion. Although we encounter it here in unusually dramatic form, this is by no means a unique situation. Universal religion, in fact, always speaks the language of ethnic culture, at least to begin with. To begin with, in a sense, there is no other language for it to speak. The Buddha himself spoke the cultural language, or rather languages, of his day. At that time there seem to have been two languages: the language of the Brahmanas and the language of the Śramaṇas; the Vedic language and the non-Vedic or even anti-Vedic language; perhaps even an Aryan language and a non-Aryan language.

As we saw in the last chapter, the *Sūtra of Golden Light* speaks the language of Indian cosmology and mythology. It speaks of rings of golden mountains and circular oceans, gods and goddesses, and various classes of non-human beings. But, of course, Buddhism did not stay confined to India, and as it spread throughout Asia it came into contact with other ethnic cultures, especially with those of Central Asia, China, Japan, and Tibet, and these cultures also placed themselves at the service of the Dharma. Buddhism gradually learned to express itself in terms of Chinese culture, Japanese culture, and so on.

Now the Dharma has come to the West. Individuals of Western origin are coming into contact with the golden light, and even wanting to communicate it to other Westerners. To do this they have to express themselves in terms of Western culture. Buddhism has to learn the language of Western culture. This raises a number of interesting questions. Can Buddhism be separated from Eastern culture? Is an acquaintance with Eastern culture essential for the understanding of Buddhism, or can Western culture place itself at the service of Buddhism? What *is*

Western culture? Can the Dharma be taught without the medium of culture altogether? Before we can answer all these questions, we need to take a more detailed look at chapter 7 of the *sūtra*.

By virtue of its miscellaneous character – miscellaneous even for such a transcendental rag-bag as the *Sūtra of Golden Light* – the seventh chapter is representative of the kind of material that a late Mahāyāna *sūtra* often includes, even though it is quite a short chapter, no longer than five pages in Emmerick's translation. It opens with Sarasvatī saluting the Buddha, and then making various promises. She promises to bestow upon the monk who preaches the Dharma five gifts or blessings.

First of all, Sarasvatī promises to bestow eloquence 'for the sake of adorning the speech of the monk who preaches the Law'. The monk is likely to be a follower of the Mahāyāna, an aspirant to the bodhisattva ideal, and he is naturally going to want to share the Buddha's teaching with as many people as possible. This is going to mean that he must be able to put it across effectively. He needs the power of communication, he needs eloquence, and this is what Sarasvatī gives him. This eloquence is not a matter of textbook rhetoric, not a matter of the tricks of the trade of the professional after-dinner speaker. It is finding easy, natural expression for the genuine feelings of the heart in appropriate thoughts, words, and images.

Secondly, Sarasvatī promises to bestow a good memory. This is clearly necessary for a preacher of the Dharma. There are references in the *sūtra* to its being written down, but memorizing it is still considered to be important, even today in some parts of the Buddhist world. I remember one of my own Tibetan teachers telling me how many pages of scripture he had to memorize each day when he was a novice monk of seven years old. The method of preaching the Dharma in ancient India was rather like a sort of public seminar. The custom was for the monk to recite a few lines of the *sūtra* or other text, and then give his own detailed explanation, perhaps with illustrative stories. In this manner he would make his way through the whole *sūtra* from beginning to end. He might be reciting it and discoursing on it every day for several hours, and in the case of the longer *sūtras* this might go on for several months. Clearly a good memory was needed, and this is what Sarasvatī promises to bestow.

Thirdly, she promises to arrange the substance of the monk's speech so that it is well spoken. The content of Mahāyāna *sūtras* is frequently not only very difficult, but also very disorganized. It is all mixed up and disconnected, even confused. If he is not careful, the monk may get lost, as it were, in the impenetrable jungle of the *sūtra*, and may not perceive its real message. This is certainly the case with the *Sūtra of Golden Light*. It may not be one of the most difficult of the Mahāyāna *sūtras* as regards content, but it is certainly one of the least well arranged, at least in conventional literary terms. So here too Sarasvatī lends a hand, helping the monk to expound the *sūtra* in an orderly, systematic fashion.

To be able to expound the *sūtra* in this fashion, the monk must obviously have an understanding of it, and this is Sarasvatī's fourth gift: great illumination and knowledge. It is not enough for the monk to be able to recite the words of the *sūtra*; he must be able to penetrate its meaning. He must himself be in touch with the golden light, even at one with it. The golden light must shine through him. When he speaks, it must be the golden light speaking – otherwise the *Sūtra of Golden Light* is not truly preached. So the goddess promises to bestow great illumination and knowledge. At this point it becomes clear that she does not represent any merely external agency, because no external agency can give illumination and knowledge. Sarasvatī really represents the monk's own cultured, cultivated consciousness, and the refined, powerful emotions associated with that consciousness, emotions which have now become integrated with the spiritual life and which therefore contribute to the realization of the transcendental.

Fifthly and lastly, Sarasvatī promises to bestow a *dhāraṇī*. A *dhāraṇī* is a sort of magical spell. It is something to be borne in mind, something to be recited. The word comes from the same root as the word Dharma, from the root *dhṛ*, which means 'that which supports or upholds'. The *Sūtra of Golden Light*, as we have already seen, is a late *sūtra*. It was written down in the fourth to eighth centuries CE, and at that time the Mahāyāna was being superseded as it were by the Vajrayāna, or rather by the Mantrayāna, which was the early phase of the Vajrayāna.[262] The goddess's promise of a *dhāraṇī* therefore represents the irruption of the Vajrayāna into the Mahāyāna, or the Mantrayāna into the Pāramitāyāna. It suggests that the preacher of the Dharma needs in his work the special quality associated with the Vajrayāna. He needs something magical, something transcendentally charismatic. He needs to be a kind of Padmasambhava figure; otherwise it is very difficult for him to succeed in his task.

Immediately after Sarasvatī's promises there comes a very curious, indeed a very ethnic passage, which is concerned, believe it or not, with popular magic. Sarasvatī explains how the monk who preaches the Dharma should take a kind of ritual herb bath. The preparation of the bath involves grinding more than thirty different herbs and resins into powder – when a certain constellation is in the ascendant – and then consecrating them one hundred times with a magic spell. Brahminical ideas of ritual purification are clearly reflected here. What we have in this passage, in fact, it seems to me, is a lump of ethnic culture that the *sūtra* has not been able fully to digest.

Examples like this one give us evidence of the way the Mahāyāna absorbed elements of ethnic culture as a skilful means to help communicate the Dharma. A lot of our emotions, including our more refined emotions, are bound up with ethnic culture. As a teacher of Buddhism, one wants to encourage people to integrate these emotions into their practice of the Dharma, and one can do this by absorbing into one's presentation of the Dharma those elements with which people's emotions are tied up. The instance of the herb bath is clearly a case in which the attempt at skilful means doesn't quite work, to the extent that it becomes an unskilful avenue for the infiltration of Hinduism into Buddhism. In such 'undigested lumps' of ethnic culture we can perhaps see the beginning of the end of the Mahāyāna in India. But the principle, or the rationale, behind the incorporation of culture into the Dharma is still valid. It is to engage the emotions fully so that one can live the spiritual life wholeheartedly.

It is not possible, however, to incorporate *all* the emotions in this way. Some emotions are already quite refined, while others, although positive, are very crude. When, for instance, one appreciates a work of fine art, refined emotions are brought into play; whereas if one goes to watch a football match, although the emotions involved are positive ones, they will definitely be of a cruder nature. Only the more refined emotions can be absorbed into one's spiritual life, because only they have been developed to a point where it is possible for them to be absorbed. You can't really, therefore, absorb into the Dharma ethnic elements with which quite crude emotions are associated.

Take, for example, a social event like a party, say a birthday party. People may be very merry – especially if the wine is flowing – and all sorts of emotions will arise. Such an occasion is a sort of ethnic celebration, and it might be quite a positive one, but one can hardly imagine having a party of that sort as an integral part of, say, Wesak, the festival at which we celebrate the Enlightenment of the Buddha. It would be spiritually indigestible, so to speak. Even if it was nominally a part of the Wesak celebration, it would really disrupt things. But an art exhibition or a concert of music could certainly be absorbed into a Wesak celebration if it was in harmony with the spirit of the occasion.

Of course, in absorbing elements of ethnic culture to help communicate the Dharma, one subtly transforms them at the same time. The problem with the ritual herb bath prescribed in the *Sūtra of Golden Light* is that this transformation has somehow not happened. Perhaps it was incorporated in too much of a hurry for it to be properly absorbed.

Sarasvatī goes on to describe how she herself should be worshipped. First of all, one should make a magic circle with cow-dung. It's a very Indian thing, this cow-dung. Their associations as far as cow-dung is concerned are very different from ours. In India, cow-dung is a very holy, sacred thing. So then, having made the magic circle, one should strew it with flowers, and place within it a gold vessel and a silver vessel filled with sweet juice. One should also place within the mandala – for this is what it is, virtually – four men clad in armour. This is all the text says: four men clad in armour. It may be a reference to the four great kings, but the text isn't giving us any clues. We hear little more about the four beautifully adorned maidens who are also, according to the text, to be placed within the circle – except that they are carrying pots. They may perhaps be reminiscent of the offering goddesses, but the text doesn't say so. Various other directions are also given – for example, that the image of Sarasvatī is to be decorated with umbrellas. Again, Indian associations as far as umbrellas are concerned are different from Western ones, and suggest royalty, supremacy, triumph, victory – not just a rainy day. Flags and banners are to be raised; more spells are to be recited. Finally the goddess promises that she herself will be present at the ritual herb bath, and will remove diseases, quarrels, bad dreams, and evil spirits.

All this may seem rather a long way from the golden light. However, Sarasvatī concludes by saying that all that she has said is for the sake of the monks and nuns, laymen and laywomen, who preserve and perpetuate the chief *sūtras*, so that they may gain Enlightenment. The

Buddha congratulates Sarasvatī and praises her for her words concerning spells and medicaments.

Then it is the turn to speak of the Brahmin Kauṇḍinya, whom we have already met in chapter 2. He says:

> Sarasvatī, the great goddess, is worthy of worship, possesses great asceticism, famous in all worlds, a giver of boons, of great virtues.

He then goes on to describe what seems to be a very archaic form of the goddess.

> Dwelling on a peak, beautiful, clad in a grass garment, wearing grass clothing, she stands on one foot.[263]

After this, Kauṇḍinya goes on to give us another, rather different description of her. First he tells us of an occasion on which all the gods assembled and asked the goddess to speak. In reply, she recited a long spell followed by a prayer that one's knowledge might prosper 'in such as textbooks, verses, magic books, doctrinal books, poems'. Then, when he has recounted the goddess's words, Kauṇḍinya goes on to praise Sarasvatī in a beautiful hymn which closes the chapter. Here is the prose translation of the Sanskrit verse hymn, which gives a good description of Sarasvatī in a fully developed Puranic form.

> May all the hordes of Bhūtas hear me. I will praise the goddess, whose face is supremely, extremely beautiful, who among women in the world of gods, Gandharvas, and lords of Asuras, is the supreme, chief, excellent goddess. Sarasvatī by name has members that have piles of adornments of various virtues. Her eyes are broad. She is brilliant in merit. She is full of the virtues of pure knowledge. She is beautiful like a variety of jewels. I will praise her by reason of her distinguished virtues of excellent speech, because she causes excellent, supreme success, because of her famous teaching, because she is a mine of virtues, because she is pure and supreme, because she is brilliant as a lotus, because her eyes are fair and excellent, because her residence is beautiful, because her appearance is beautiful, because she is thoroughly adorned with inconceivable virtues, because she resembles the moon, because

her splendour is pure, because she is a mine of knowledge, because of the superiority of her mindfulness, because she is the best of lionesses, because she is a vehicle for men, because she is adorned with eight arms, because her appearance is like that of the full moon, because of her heartening speech, because of her soft voice, because she is endowed with profound wisdom, because she causes the accomplishment of the best deeds, because she is an excellent being, because she is honoured by the lords of gods and Asuras, because she is praised in all the dwellings of a multitude of gods and Asuras, because she is continually worshipped in the abode of a multitude of Bhūtas.[264]

So if this is Sarasvatī in a fully developed Puranic form, what are we to make of the preceding, clearly more archaic, description? Let's return to the first description of the goddess – that she stands on a peak, on one foot, clad in grass clothing. What can all this possibly mean? Clearly there is some connection with the sacrificial system, or at least with the culture that grew out of that system. But why is the goddess said to dwell on a peak? What is the meaning of her standing on one foot? No doubt there is a meaning, but I must confess that I haven't been able to find it out. I suspect it would require a good deal of research into ancient Indian symbolism, especially Vedic symbolism. Meanwhile, your guess is as good as mine.

The wearing of grass clothing is more explicable. Grass, especially *kuśa* grass and *dūrvā* grass, plays an important part in Brahminical ritual, and it is still widely used in India for religious purposes. Sarasvatī's grass clothing thus shows that there is a definite connection between, on the one hand, this very archaic form of the goddess and, on the other, the brahminical sacrificial system, the culture associated with it, and all that represents. Indeed, the mere mention of these sacred grasses sparks off all sorts of associations in the Indian, especially the orthodox Hindu, mind. Not being familiar with that cultural language, however, the thought of *kuśa* grass is going to leave us cold. So let's consider a parallel example from our own culture.

Take, say, mistletoe. What association does mistletoe spark off in our minds? First of all, of course, we are likely to think of Christmas, and what tradition dictates should happen under the mistletoe![265] But then we may think of the ancient Druids, of oak trees, golden sickles, human sacrifice. We may think of Stonehenge – wrongly, as it happens, because Stonehenge had nothing to do with the Druids. We may think of eisteddfods, Wales, devolution, Welsh dragons, bards, Thomas Gray's ode 'The Bard', Edward I.... For us mistletoe may have all these associations, and many more.

For Indian people it is just the same with *kuśa* grass and *dūrvā* grass. These sacred grasses spark off associations with sacrifices, Brahmins, ancient sages, rishis with long white beards and sacred threads, asceticism, the hermit life, getting away from it all, Vālmīki, the Ramayana, the gods, the Vedas, the Sanskrit language. For the orthodox Hindu, sacred grass will spark off all these associations, and many more. All these associations are bound up with certain very deep emotions. So the fact that Sarasvatī is described as wearing grass clothing not only sparks off associations. It also brings into the *sūtra* the emotions bound up with those associations, and places them at the service of the spiritual development of the individual – at the service, that is, of the golden light. It is therefore of great importance to find what we may call cultural equivalence, to find symbols and images that really speak to us. It is vital that Buddhism should speak the cultural language of the people it is trying to reach.

This brings us back to our questions about the relation between Buddhism and culture, especially Buddhism and Western culture. First, can Buddhism be separated from Eastern culture? Well, not only can it be separated; it *must* be separated, or at least distinguished. Buddhism is not Eastern culture, however beautiful Eastern culture may be. Buddhism is not culture at all. The Dharma is not culture. The golden light is not culture. Culture is only the medium. Unfortunately, many Eastern Buddhists, including those who come to the West hoping to teach, do not understand this. Sometimes they think they are preaching the Dharma when they are only propagating their own national culture, and this causes great confusion in the minds of at least some Buddhists in the West.

Second question: Is an acquaintance with Eastern culture necessary to the understanding of Buddhism? Yes and no. Historically, Buddhism has found expression in terms of Eastern culture, and if we want to approach the Dharma we therefore need to have some acquaintance with Eastern culture, at least to begin with. In the *Sūtra of Golden Light*, for example, the Dharma is expressed very much in terms of

Indian culture, so that unless one has some understanding of Indian culture, the message of the *sūtra* remains more or less inaccessible. An acquaintance with Eastern culture can be dispensed with only if one is in personal contact with a spiritual teacher who does not have to rely on Eastern culture as a medium of communication.

There is, I think, very little purely 'Buddhist' culture. In my view there are very few cultural forms or artefacts which can be said purely to express the spirit of Buddhism. Just because something is labelled 'Buddhist' does not mean that you can call it an expression or even a part of Buddhist culture. At the same time you need, generally speaking, a cultural context of some kind for the practice of Buddhism. So, although a Western Buddhist practising in the West does not have to adopt Eastern culture in principle, until Western Buddhist cultural equivalents have emerged we shall have to use or adapt some elements of Eastern Buddhist culture, for instance in such matters as robes, style of chanting, and iconography. In the East it is probably best for the Western Buddhist to conform completely to the local Buddhist culture – while being careful not to mistake that culture for the Dharma. However, it is becoming less and less necessary for the Western Buddhist to go East at all. Now we have everything we need at home.

Third question – and this is quite a complex one: how can Western culture place itself at the service of Buddhism? Western Buddhists can at least make a start by establishing points of contact with great artists, and other great Western creative figures, who, at least at times and to a limited extent, have made some approach to the Dharma: people like Goethe, Schopenhauer, Nietzsche, Blake, Wordsworth, and even D. H. Lawrence. I certainly hope that one day a Western Buddhist culture will be developed, and there are signs that beginnings are being made. But you can only really hope to create a Western Buddhist culture if you are deeply imbued with the spirit of Buddhism. In a sense, Buddhism comes first and Buddhist culture follows. However, it can work the other way round as well. Involvement with culture in the best sense helps to refine the emotions, and the refinement of the emotions is important, even essential, for one's spiritual development as an individual. The practice of Buddhism and the development of Buddhist culture must go together.

It is possible for the Dharma to be taught without the medium of culture, but only within the context of a close and intense spiritual relationship between teacher and disciple. This whole question of

Buddhism and culture is therefore a very important one. Culture occupies a very important place in our lives, even a very important place in our spiritual development. I can't help wishing that we could have a celebration that would symbolize for us the integration of cultural activity into spiritual life – a Sarasvatī puja of our own, or, even better, a Mañjughoṣa puja. Sarasvatī, after all, represents ethnic culture, but Mañjughoṣa is more universal. He is found all over the Mahāyāna Buddhist world – he was very popular in China and Tibet – and he could perhaps become just as popular in the West. Mañjughoṣa symbolizes the profoundest Wisdom expressed in terms of the most highly developed, most refined culture. He is usually depicted as a beautiful young prince, golden yellow in colour. He sits cross-legged on a blue lotus throne, and wears a headdress of five full-blown blue lotus flowers. In his right hand, which is raised aloft, he wields a flaming sword, the sword of Wisdom, and in his left hand is a book which he holds against his heart. His expression is compassionate and smiling, and the whole figure radiates brilliant golden light.

In popular Tantric Buddhism, certain branches of which had at one time a mania for finding consorts for all archetypal figures, even the Buddha, an effort was made to regard Sarasvatī as the consort of Mañjughoṣa. Of course, in some ways it would be very natural and appropriate to regard Sarasvatī as the consort of Mañjughoṣa: the symbolism would refer to ethnic culture (represented by Sarasvatī) as being receptive to universal culture (represented by Mañjughoṣa). It ties up very neatly. But I am rather unwilling to give any prominence to *yab-yum* forms – these conjoint male-female Buddha or bodhisattva forms – because people in the West have a tendency to take them as justifying a romanticization, not to say glorification, of the ordinary sexual couple, the mutually dependent male and female human being. To most people, an image of male and female bodhisattvas together communicates the message that it is not just OK but even of spiritual benefit to have a spouse. They may think that as husband and wife, or boyfriend and girlfriend, they somehow exemplify the wisdom and compassion of the Buddhas – which is not, to put it mildly, usually the case. It would definitely not be skilful means to encourage that sort of fatuous inflation.

As it happens, despite the best efforts of the Tantra, the *yab-yum* form of Mañjughoṣa has never been popularized, perhaps because he was so firmly established iconographically as a single, solitary male bodhisattva figure. Mañjughoṣa remains eternally without a consort: single, celibate, perfect. There's no need, therefore, to have a personification of culture as a separate being. In the person of Mañjughoṣa, culture has been fully assimilated, fully absorbed. Culture is, if you like, represented by the ornaments that sparkle on the golden body of Mañjughoṣa. Ultimately, in other words, the golden light transcends culture.

5
NATURE, MAN, AND ENLIGHTENMENT

In the last two chapters we have been particularly concerned with the theme of protection. First the four great kings came forward and promised to protect the *sūtra*, and then the great goddess Sarasvatī promised to protect the monk who preached the *sūtra*. In this chapter we are still concerned with the theme of protection; indeed, we are concerned with the promise of another goddess to protect the *sūtra*. The goddess who *should* now come forward is Śrī, the goddess of wealth and prosperity, because in the *sūtra*, the chapter on Śrī follows immediately after the chapter on Sarasvatī. However, in this chapter, for the purposes of explication, we are introducing Dṛḍhā, the earth goddess, and keeping back Śrī for our next chapter, when we deal with Buddhist economics. No disrespect to the *sūtra* is intended, of course.

The last chapter was concerned with the great goddess Sarasvatī and her promise to protect the monk who preaches the *sūtra*, but said nothing at all about the monk himself. He remained simply an anonymous figure whom the goddess promised to protect. In this chapter I want to give quite a full introduction to Dṛḍhā, the earth goddess, but also to say something about the monk who preaches the *sūtra*, the monk who is the medium for the transmission of the golden light. I will also say just a little about the golden light itself.

So we shall be concerned in the first place with Dṛḍhā, the earth goddess; secondly, with the monk who preaches the *sūtra*; and thirdly, with the golden light. Or, in the terms of the chapter's title, we will be concerned with nature, man, and Enlightenment; but we won't deal with them in that order. We will look first at Dṛḍhā, the earth goddess or Mother Nature, then at the golden light or Enlightenment, and finally at the monk who preaches the *sūtra* – that is, we will look at man.

To begin with, we need to take a look at the opening words of the chapter on Dṛḍhā. It is an abrupt beginning: 'Then indeed the earth-goddess Dṛḍhā spoke thus to the Lord,' – that is to say, to the Buddha. In fact, chapter 8, the chapter on Śrī, begins in exactly the same way. But chapter 7, the chapter on Sarasvatī, opens in a noticeably different manner. It begins:

> Then indeed Sarasvatī, the great goddess, covered one shoulder with her robe, placed her right knee on the ground, made the gesture of reverence in the direction of the Lord and spoke thus to the Lord.[266]

The difference is that Śrī, the goddess of wealth, and Dṛḍhā, the earth goddess, do not salute the Buddha before speaking, but Sarasvatī does, as do the four great kings and Saṃjñāya, the great general of the *yakṣas* who appears in chapter 11. This difference perhaps signifies that Śrī and Dṛḍhā are naturally less amenable to the influence of the golden light than is Sarasvatī: in other words, that it is more difficult to transform the world of economics and the world of nature than it is to transform the world of culture. This may sound rather far-fetched, but there is surely meaning to be discovered in many of the minor details of the *sūtra*.

Although she dispenses with the salutation, Dṛḍhā nonetheless makes her promise, and it is a long and beautiful one. First of all she promises to be present wherever the *sūtra* is expounded. Not only that; she says she will go up to the Dharma seat – the seat on which the monk who is preaching the *sūtra* is sitting – with her invisible subtle body, and lean with her head upon the soles of the feet of the monk who is preaching the Dharma. We are not told this, but the monk is presumably seated cross-legged on one of those rather high, throne-like Dharma seats, very nearly the height of a man, such as are still used today, or were at least used until recently, in Tibet. We are apparently to imagine the goddess going up to this throne, bowing her head slightly, and placing it against the soles of the monk's feet. It could be, of course, that the monk is to be imagined sitting in European fashion as though in a chair, in which case the goddess would stand placing her head directly beneath his feet. She's not present in her gross physical body, so she doesn't have to stand on the surface of the earth.

In either case, this scene is reminiscent of a well-known episode from the life of the Buddha, an episode that occurred shortly before he gained full Enlightenment. The Buddha-to-be – Siddhartha as he still was then – had seated himself on the *vajrāsana*, the diamond throne, which is the seat on which all Buddhas sit when they gain Enlightenment, and which is regarded in Buddhist tradition as the symbolic centre of the universe. There Siddhartha seated himself. He knew that his hour had come, that he was going to attain Enlightenment that very night, so he seated himself on that spot, at the centre of the universe, on the diamond seat. No sooner had he done so than Māra, the evil one, appeared. Māra had been dogging Siddhartha from the very moment that he left home, trying to find a way into his mind. On this occasion he challenged him, saying, 'What right have you got to sit where all the Buddhas of the past have sat?' – as if to say, 'Why are you so sure that you are going to gain Enlightenment?' Siddhartha replied that he had the right to sit there because he had practised the *pāramitās*, the perfections – generosity, ethics, patience, energy, meditation, wisdom – not in just one lifetime, but in many; not even in hundreds but in thousands, in tens of thousands of lives. He was now ready, he said, to gain Enlightenment. He had the right to take his seat on the diamond throne.

So Māra said, 'It's all very well to talk like that. It's all very well to make these claims that you've practised the *pāramitās*, but who saw you? Who saw you doing all these wonderful things? Who is your witness?' and Siddhartha said, 'The earth is my witness. All these deeds of mine have been performed on the face of the earth, so the earth goddess has witnessed them.' Then Siddhartha tapped the earth with the tips of the fingers of his right hand, and at once the earth goddess rose up out of the depths of the earth, and she said, 'Yes, I have seen it all. I have seen him practising all these *pāramitās*. He is truly worthy to take his seat on the diamond throne.'

This scene is often depicted in Buddhist art. The earth goddess, as she rises up, is usually depicted as a beautiful woman of mature appearance, not particularly young without being actually old. She is golden brown or dark green in colour, and she is usually represented with only the upper half of her body emerged from the earth, just like Mother Erda in Wagner's *Ring*. Her hands are clasped in salutation. Just occasionally she is depicted as standing beside or beneath the *vajrāsana*, with her head placed against the soles of the Buddha's feet, just as the earth goddess is described in the *Sūtra of Golden Light* in relation to the monk who preaches the *sūtra*. But however she is depicted or described, the significance is clear: the earth goddess is subordinated to the Buddha, and subordinated to the monk who preaches the *sūtra*.

This point is emphasized further by the symbolism of head and feet. According to the ancient Indians, including the ancient Indian Buddhists, the head was the noblest, most worthy part of the whole body. The Sanskrit for 'head' is *uttama aṅga*, which means the superior limb or superior member. The feet, on the other hand, are the most ignoble and unworthy part, because in ancient India people went barefoot, and their feet were often very dirty. If you wanted to show respect for someone, you placed your head in contact with their feet; in other words, you subordinated what was highest in you to what was lowest in them. If they were truly superior to you this would be the only way in which real contact between you could be established, the only way in which you could make yourself truly receptive to whatever they had to give.

We find the same kind of symbolism in the meditation practices in which one visualizes the bodhisattva or Buddha Vajrasattva seated above one's head; or when one visualizes the lineage of gurus seated, one on top of another, above one's head. One makes oneself receptive to their spiritual influence by aligning oneself with them vertically. It is still the custom in India to touch the feet of holy men with one's fingers and then touch one's own head; the idea is that you take dust from their feet and place it on your head. Many Indians show respect not only to holy men but to parents, elders, and even secular teachers in the same way. In the Buddhist countries of the East we find much the same custom, the only difference being that in the Theravāda countries there is no physical contact. What happens is that the lay people salute the monks, and the monks salute the senior monks, their own teachers, by kneeling down and touching the ground in front of their feet with their own forehead. The principle is just the same.

In India and the Buddhist countries of the East there are a number of other customs connected with heads and feet. For instance, you should never touch the head of someone whom you regard as superior to yourself, and above all, of course, you should never touch his head with your feet. This would be regarded as a reversal of the natural order of things. In the same way, you should never sit with your feet stretched out pointing in the direction of anyone whom you consider superior – not in the direction, for instance, of a Buddha image, especially in the shrine-room. Such behaviour would be considered grossly disrespectful and insensitive.

Having promised to lean with her head against the soles of the feet of the monk who is preaching the Dharma, the earth goddess goes on to make further promises. She promises that she will feed on the nectar juice of the Dharma – that is to say, she will derive spiritual nourishment from the Dharma, from the golden light. She promises that she will do homage, that she will rejoice, that she will increase the savour of the earth. She will make the earth stronger so that trees, flowers, fruits, and crops will be made stronger – not only stronger but tastier, more beautiful, and more abundant. Not only that; the fact that the fruits that the earth produces are tastier, more beautiful, and more abundant will affect the people who live on them. Their longevity, their strength, their complexion, and the power of their senses will be increased, and they will then perform the numerous hundreds of thousands of activities appropriate to the earth. They will be devoted; they will be thorough; they will do acts that have to be done with power. Thus the whole of Jambudvīpa will become peaceful and prosperous. People will be happy and their thoughts will then turn to the *Sūtra of Golden Light*. They will approach members of the spiritual community with a pure mind, and ask them to expound the *sūtra*.

When the *sūtra* is being expounded, Dṛḍhā herself, together with her retinue, will become stronger and more powerful. The words she uses are almost the same as those used by the four great kings. She says, 'In our body there will be produced great power, fortitude, and strength. Brilliance, glory, and fortune will enter our body.' She will be satisfied, she says, with the nectar juice of the Dharma, and the earth will increase its savour, will become stronger. People who are dependent on the earth will increase and grow, and they will experience various pleasures and enjoyments. For all these reasons, says Dṛḍhā, everybody should be grateful to the earth, and to the earth goddess who has made all these things possible. She wishes that they may listen to the *sūtra* respectfully, and then talk about it, rejoicing that they have heard the Dharma, that they have acquired merit, that they have pleased the Buddhas. They will also rejoice that they have escaped rebirth in lower states. They will not be reborn in hell, in the world of Yāma, nor as an animal, nor among the hungry ghosts. They will rejoice, Dṛḍhā says, that they are assured of rebirth among gods and men. Not only that; the goddess hopes that, after hearing the *sūtra*, people will tell their friends and neighbours whatever they remember of its teaching. When they do this, the earth will become stronger; people will become stronger, they will be blessed, they will have great wealth and enjoyment, but they will be devoted to liberality, to *dāna*, and they will have faith in the Three Jewels.

The goddess's promise makes a sort of circular movement. First the *Sūtra of Golden Light* is preached, and this nourishes the earth goddess. So nourished, she increases the savour and strength of the earth, and the people who live on the earth therefore become stronger and more prosperous. Because they are stronger and more prosperous, they become happy; because they are happy, they want to hear the *sūtra* preached. When the *sūtra* is preached, the goddess is nourished; when the goddess is nourished, she makes the earth stronger; and the whole process is repeated once again.

It is not surprising that the goddess's promise should follow this circular pattern. After all, she is the earth goddess. She is nature; she is even Mother Nature – and nature's activity is essentially cyclical. The earth goddess therefore represents change, mutability, especially cyclical change. She represents the cyclical process of action and reaction between opposites. She is conditioned existence. She is *saṃsāra*. She is the wheel of life.

However, we are going a little too fast. We are not yet finished with Dṛḍhā's promise. You will probably have noticed that in the course of her promise the goddess repeats the circular pattern three times, each time on a slightly higher level. At the end of the first repetition, people listen to the *Sūtra of Golden Light*, at the end of the second, they tell others about it, and at the end of the third, they develop faith in the Three Jewels. In other words, the circular movement is not completely circular: the circle is trying to become a spiral. In a sense, it *is* a spiral, but it is not a true spiral. On the true spiral, the true Spiral Path, when we pass the Point of No Return, when we achieve Stream Entry, progress is irreversible. On the circle, the wheel of life, there is no progress; that is, no permanent spiritual progress, no transcendental progress. But in between the circle and the spiral comes the section of the path with which we are now concerned. On that section, spiritual progress does take place, but that progress is not irreversible. We can still fall back into the circle, into a state in which we simply go round and round without making any progress at all.

In chapter 7 Sarasvatī promises that the monks, nuns, laymen, and laywomen who hold the chief *sūtras*, including the *Sūtra of Golden Light*, will escape from the cycle of existence, but here the goddess Dṛḍhā makes no such promise. She can only promise that beings will escape rebirth in the lower realms, that they will be reborn among gods and men, that they will have faith in the Three Jewels. She can't even promise that they will go for Refuge. The earth goddess, in other words, has her limitations. Nature can only take us so far.

This is borne out by the remainder of the chapter. After Dṛḍhā has made her promise, the Buddha speaks. He says that those who hear even a single verse of the *Sūtra of Golden Light* will be reborn among the group of the thirty-three gods, and other groups of gods. Those who show honour to the *sūtra* will be reborn in heavenly palaces made of the seven jewels. They will be reborn seven times in each palace, and they will experience inconceivable heavenly blessings.

Dṛḍhā then speaks again. She repeats her promise, she prays that beings may continue to hear the *sūtra* and experience inconceivable divine and human pleasures. Finally she prays that they may awaken to supreme perfect Enlightenment. But this is only a prayer; it is not a promise. It is a prayer which she sees as being fulfilled in the infinitely remote future. From the standpoint of the natural order, Enlightenment is seen as a far-off divine event, not a practicable possibility here and now. With this prayer, the chapter on the earth goddess Dṛḍhā concludes.

The earth goddess in the *sūtra* is rather a shadowy figure. There is no description of Dṛḍhā, there is no hymn of praise to her as there is to the great goddess Sarasvatī – and indeed the great goddess Śrī in the previous chapter. She remains shadowy, amorphous, unrecognized. In modern Hindu India it is much the same. Sarasvatī is a highly popular goddess, worshipped all over India, especially by scholars, writers, and students. Śrī or Lakṣmī is, if anything, even more popular, and even more widely worshipped: by all householders, and especially by shopkeepers, businessmen, financiers, and speculators in stocks and shares. Other goddesses are also worshipped. There is Durgā, the ten-armed slayer of the buffalo demon. There's Kālī, the Black One, she who dances on the prostrate corpse of her husband, she who wears a garland of freshly-severed heads, whose red tongue hangs out, and whose mouth drips with blood. There is also Sitala, the dreaded goddess of smallpox. All these goddesses are worshipped by millions of people in India; they all have their shrines, their images, and their priests. But Dṛḍhā is not worshipped. She has no shrine, no image, no priests.

The omission, however, is more apparent than real. In a simple sense, all goddesses are earth goddesses, just as all gods are sky gods. If you step down from Unity, so to speak, and taking that as the ultimate principle, you have a primordial dualism – which is to be found in most ancient philosophies, religions, and systems of mythology. Reducing this dualism to its simplest terms – as in, for example, ancient Egyptian mythology – you have the earth and the sky. The earth is represented by various goddesses, the sky by various gods.

One can, of course, think of individual figures who seem to be exceptions to this basic rule. Pluto, for instance, is the god of the underworld – but I don't think he can be seen as a god of the earth in the same way that Dṛḍhā is a goddess of the earth. He is a god, and he lives underground and rules over Hades, but that doesn't make him the masculine equivalent of an earth goddess. Demeter is an earth goddess, but she lives on the surface of the earth. In other words, living underground is not synonymous with being an earth god or goddess. As for Neptune, the god of the sea, he doesn't give the impression of being a masculine counterpart of an earth goddess. He is much more akin to his brother Jupiter, who rules the kingdom of the air.

One could say of Pallas Athene that she is not an earth mother figure because of her close association with Zeus. She was born from the head of Zeus, according to Greek mythology (she had no mother at all) so in a way she is an extension of Zeus's own personality, and she has a number of masculine attributes. A scholar once compared her to Mañjuśrī, the Bodhisattva of Wisdom, saying that, like Pallas Athene, Mañjuśrī was all intellect and chastity – hardly characteristics of the earth goddess. But if Athene is the exception, she is the exception that proves the rule; although technically feminine, she doesn't have any of the usual attributes of the earth goddesses.

Dṛḍhā is perhaps the original Indian earth goddess, not to say earth mother, before her various functions became differentiated. She is parallelled to some extent at least by similar figures in other cultures:

by Rhea and Demeter in ancient Greece, by Isis and Hathor in Egypt, by Ishtar in Babylonia, by Diana of the Ephesians, and by Erda or Hertha in northern Europe. But we can find a closer parallel, perhaps, in the various anonymous neolithic figures, the so-called neolithic Venuses, figures with enormous breasts, buttocks, and wombs, but only rudimentary heads. Like them, perhaps, Dṛḍhā represents the primitive reality behind the more sophisticated appearance represented by some of the other goddesses.

Be that as it may, Dṛḍhā is not only a more shadowy figure than Sarasvatī or Śrī; she is also much less human. I have said that the three goddesses represent three different areas of human activity, and that their promises to protect the *sūtra* represent transformations of these areas achieved through placing them at the service of the golden light. In the case of Dṛḍhā, however, this is only partly true. Her promise to protect the preacher of the *sūtra* therefore has a somewhat different and more complex significance. Those human energies which are part of nature can be placed at the service of the golden light – they can be transformed. But nature herself cannot be placed at the service of the golden light. Nature herself cannot be transformed. All that we can transform is our attitude to nature, and that is sufficient.

I am going to look at our attitude to nature under three headings. First of all, our use of nature – that is to say, of natural resources and the environment – secondly, the appreciation of nature or enjoyment of nature, and thirdly, the understanding of nature.

'Use of nature' means use of natural resources; nowadays we hear a great deal about this. We are being warned that certain natural resources are finite, and that we are using them up at an alarming rate and in a most wasteful fashion. As Buddhists, those who try to follow the Dharma, we should be very aware of this. We should try to use everything of natural origin very carefully indeed, and, moreover, use as little of it as is possible, and in the best possible way – that is to say, for the benefit, the true benefit, of self and others. The same principle applies to our use of the natural environment. We shouldn't destroy it or spoil it in any way, as, for instance, through pollution; and above all, we should think carefully before bringing about irreversible changes.

All this has become the commonplace of informed and responsible thinking, and there is no need for me to elaborate. I am only concerned to underline the general principle involved: that the right use of nature is part of the spiritual life. I would, however, like to make specific mention of one particular misuse of nature that is of special interest to all Buddhists: the pollution, the desecration even, of the environment by noise. Nowadays there is far too much noise. This is especially the case in big cities, but even little villages are not exempt. Even there, aircraft rip through the air and thirty-tonne articulated lorries thunder through the tiny main streets. Under such circumstances, life becomes very difficult, and in particular meditation becomes very difficult. So Buddhists should be particularly aware of such problems, and should do whatever they can to reduce noise, even giving active support to organizations working to this end.

The second aspect of our attitude to nature I want to consider is the appreciation or enjoyment of nature in an aesthetic, even contemplative, sense. Here there is no question of using nature, or doing anything with it. You simply look at nature, simply appreciate it for its own sake – whether you are looking at a mountain or the vast expanse of the sea, a tiny flower or even just a grain of sand. This sort of appreciation of nature is comparatively new in the West. In England, for instance, it became general only with the romantic poets, especially with Wordsworth and Coleridge. Their time, of course, was the time of the industrial revolution, when there was a great upsurge of utilitarianism, when nature began to be used – and misused – more than ever before in history. Perhaps the emphasis the romantic poets gave to the appreciation of natural beauty was necessary to restore the balance – and that emphasis is still needed, especially by those who are trying to develop spiritually. There is no need to idealize or romanticize nature, much less to sentimentalize it as even Wordsworth sometimes did, but there is no doubt that the appreciation of nature, especially of great natural beauty, can play an important part in the spiritual life. It can have a very soothing, tranquillizing effect, even a restorative effect, as we find when we go away on retreat in the country, or even just for a walk in the park on a fine afternoon.

The third area I want to mention is the understanding of nature. The kind of understanding I mean is not scientific or even philosophical, but essentially a spiritual understanding which consists in seeing nature as she really is. Nature is seasonal, nature is cyclic, and nature is therefore *saṃsāra*.[267] Nature is the wheel of life: not as a static picture painted on a wall, but as a living, perpetually recurring process.

In the West we are accustomed to thinking of everything as having a definite beginning. Even nature itself, even mundane existence itself, we think, must have a beginning in time, or at least a beginning with time. Christians, for instance, have believed for centuries that the universe had a definite beginning, when God created it out of nothing. In fact they have pinned this event down to a definite date. They used to assert with some confidence that the world was created in 4004 BCE, although this date has since been revised.

But this idea that there was a beginning, that the world was created at a certain time, is not the Buddhist view. It is axiomatic to Buddhism that *saṃsāra* has no beginning, or rather, no perceptible beginning – the operative word here being perceptible. Where there is a perceiving subject there is an object – that is, there is a world. The subject, therefore, cannot perceive the beginning of the world. It can only go back and back in time indefinitely. It can perceive a relative beginning and a relative end, but not an absolute beginning or an absolute end. It can perceive the beginning of a particular universe, but before that it will perceive another universe; before that, another, and so on. According to Buddhist teaching, universes evolve over a period of many, many millions of years, from a subtle state to a gross state, and when they reach the height of their development the opposite process sets in – that is to say, involution from a gross state to a subtle state – and this also takes many, many millions of years. Thus there are periods of expansion and periods of contraction. There are breathings in and breathings out of the cosmos, just like the breathing in and out of the human body, except that these cosmic inhalations and expirations take millions of years. *Saṃsāra* is cyclic; conditioned existence is cyclic.

But we must be careful not to become too abstract or remote. After all, we are still dealing with nature. In fact, we are dealing with the earth goddess. The earth is not only cyclic, or seasonal. It is also cold and dark; it has no heat or light of its own. It receives them from outside itself, from the principle which is not only opposite to the earth, but higher than the earth. In terms of the earth, this higher principle is heaven. In terms of nature, it is Enlightenment. In terms of the changing, it is the unchanging. In terms of the conditioned, it is the Unconditioned. In terms of the mundane, it is the transcendental. In terms of *saṃsāra*, it is Nirvāṇa. In terms of darkness, it is light. In terms of Dṛḍhā, the earth goddess, it is the golden light, the light of truth, the light of reality, the light of the Buddha, the light which *is* the truth, *is* reality, *is* the Buddha. It is this principle that the Buddha refers to in the *Udāna* when he says, 'There is, monks, an unborn, an unbecome, an unmade, an uncompounded. If, monks, there were not here this unborn, unbecome, unmade, uncompounded, there would not here be an escape from the born, the become, the made, the compounded. But because there is an unborn, an unbecome, an unmade, an uncompounded, therefore there is an escape from the born, the become, the made, the compounded.'[268]

We thus have two principles: the compounded and the uncompounded, the conditioned and the Unconditioned, *saṃsāra* and Nirvāṇa; or, in the terms of this chapter of the *sūtra*, nature and Enlightenment, Dṛḍhā the earth goddess and the golden light. These two principles are separate and independent, at least within the subject–object framework. The one cannot be derived from the other, or reduced to the other. *Saṃsāra* is without perceptible beginning in time. There is no point, therefore, at which it is connected with Nirvāṇa as its effect. Nirvāṇa is beyond time altogether, just as it is beyond space, so there is no point in time at which it is connected with *saṃsāra* as its cause. Spiritual life consists in making the transition from one principle to the other, from *saṃsāra* to Nirvāṇa, from nature to Enlightenment, from the conditioned to the Unconditioned. It consists in abandoning the ignoble quest for the noble quest, *anariyapariyesanā* for *ariyapariyesanā*. To quote the words of the historical Buddha, Śākyamuni, again, it consists in the conditioned pursuing the Unconditioned, not the conditioned pursuing the conditioned.[269]

But who is it that makes the transition? Who is it that achieves the noble quest? It is man. It is the monk who is the preacher of the *Sūtra of Golden Light*. As we have seen, this monk is an anonymous figure. In three chapters of the *sūtra* a goddess comes forward and promises to protect him, but nothing whatever is said about him – at least, not in these chapters. It's as though he is simply a hook on which the goddesses hang their promises. However, something is said about him in chapter 13, the chapter on Susaṃbhava – or rather, something is said about *a* preacher of the *sūtra*, a monk called Ratnoccaya. (Ratnoccaya, incidentally, means 'jewel heap' or 'precious accumulation'.) In this chapter, the Buddha himself is speaking, and he tells the story of one of his previous lives. He says that there was once a king called Susaṃbhava, which means 'happily born' or 'born of happiness', and he was the ruler of all four continents.

And one night Susaṃbhava had a dream in which he saw the monk Ratnoccaya shining in the midst of the sun. Apparently he was brighter even than the sun, and he was expounding the *Sūtra of Golden Light*. On waking up from his dream, feeling extremely happy, the king went to see the Buddha's disciples and enquired after Ratnoccaya. Ratnoccaya, at that time, was elsewhere, sitting in a cave, studying and reflecting on the *Sūtra of Golden Light*. So the disciples took King Susaṃbhava to Ratnoccaya. The king fell down and worshipped Ratnoccaya's feet, and invited him to expound the *sūtra*; and Ratnoccaya agreed to do so. The king very joyfully made all the appropriate preparations and Ratnoccaya expounded the *sūtra*. The king, needless to say, was greatly impressed, greatly moved – so much so that he shed tears of joy. Indeed, he was so moved that he presented all his possessions – which included, we are told, the four continents filled with jewels – to the Order of Ratnaśikhin, who was the Buddha at that time. Having told the story, the Buddha, Śākyamuni, then reveals that he himself was Susaṃbhava, and that the Buddha Akṣobhya was Ratnoccaya.

So here something at least is said about the preacher of the *sūtra*, or at least *a* preacher of the *sūtra*, and what is said underlines one particular point. The preacher of the *sūtra* is always a monk, a *bhikṣu*. All three goddesses promise to protect the monk who preaches the *sūtra*. This raises two questions. What is a monk? And why should a monk in particular be the preacher of the *sūtra*?

We must remember that the *Sūtra of Golden Light* is a Mahāyāna *sūtra*, and the Mahāyāna invariably attaches more importance to the spirit than the letter of the Buddha's teaching (although this does not mean that it ignores or neglects the letter). In the same spirit, it attaches more importance to the realities of the spiritual life than to the appearances. For the Mahāyāna, therefore, the monk is not just one who observes certain minor disciplinary precepts, who shaves his head and wears a yellow robe, although he may of course do these things. The monk, according to the Mahāyāna, is one who is totally committed to the spiritual life, to the noble quest for the Unconditioned, not just for his own sake but for the sake of all living beings. The Mahāyāna monk is therefore a bodhisattva, at least in intention, even if the *bodhicitta* has not actually arisen.

Now only a free man can commit himself. You cannot be totally committed unless you are free from all mundane ties and responsibilities.

The two biggest mundane responsibilities, so far as a man at least is concerned, are, first, a wife and family, and second, wage-earning work; the two, of course, usually go together. The monk, therefore, is celibate, unmarried; he has no wife, no children, no family responsibilities. The English word 'monk' means one who is on his own, one who is single, solitary, alone. But this does not necessarily mean that the monk is a hermit. He may in fact live as a member of a spiritual community, even a monastic community. The idea that as a monk he is alone refers to the fact that he does not belong to any group that is held together by purely mundane ties of blood, emotional dependence, or common worldly interests. Within the spiritual community, one can be alone and one can be with others. Within the group, however, one is neither alone nor with others.

Also, the monk has no worldly occupation. He doesn't work for a living. He doesn't make anything, he doesn't produce anything, he doesn't earn anything. Economically speaking, he is a parasite. He is a glorious spiritual parasite, because he depends for food and clothing on others, as we shall be seeing in the next chapter.

I am, of course, using the word 'parasite' here ironically, and you may be wondering how realistic it might be to think of being a 'glorious spiritual parasite' in modern Western society. These days it is not actually possible to think in terms of being a parasite in the sense of living off the State; even when you are on unemployment benefit you are obliged to 'work' at looking for work. It is even more difficult to be a spiritual parasite, let alone a glorious spiritual parasite. A spiritual parasite, glorious or otherwise, is someone who is not making any direct economic contribution to society, but who is nonetheless supported by society.

This brings in the whole question of wages and payment and exchange. The Buddhist spiritual ideal is to give what you can on whatever level, without thinking in terms of *quid pro quo*, of payment of any kind, of taking what you need 'in return', but giving whatever you can, whether your gifts are material, cultural, or spiritual. It isn't a Buddhist ideal literally to be a spiritual parasite if by that one means someone who only takes and never gives. But there is certainly no taking and giving in terms of a sort of bartering – i.e. if you give me so much material support, I'll give you so much spiritual guidance. A spiritual parasite in a Buddhist sense would be someone who takes from society what he needs for his material support without necessarily giving anything material in return, but nonetheless quite genuinely giving what he can in other ways, and not simply as a rationalization for allowing himself to be supported.

The monk is one who leads a purely spiritual life, who is totally committed to a spiritual life, who has no worldly ties or responsibilities. The monk therefore lives what some of the old Christian writers called the angelic life. Monks live as it were in heaven. They live like angels. In heaven there is neither marriage nor giving in marriage, neither ploughing nor sowing nor reaping.[270] The monastic life is therefore the happy life. I can testify to this from my own experience and observation, at least so far as Buddhist monks are concerned (I can't answer for the others). In fact, I have no hesitation in saying that the monastic life is the best and happiest of all lives. In India I not only lived as a monk myself, I had contact with monks of many different schools and many different nationalities – Theravādin monks and Mahāyāna monks, Zen monks, Nichiren monks, Gelugpa monks, Nyingmapa monks. Some were Sinhalese, some were Burmese; there were Thais, Vietnamese, Cambodians, Laotians, Chinese, Tibetans, and Nepalese, and they were all noticeably happier than the lay people, even than the Buddhist lay people. The lay people were happy enough, but the Buddhist monks were even happier.

Now this may seem odd. After all, the lay people had wives, children, jobs, money, cars, all conceivable pleasures and enjoyments. But it is true to say that more often than not they looked relatively miserable. The monks, on the other hand, usually had none of these things. Most monks that I knew owned little more than their robes, their begging-bowl, and a few books; maybe a fountain pen or the odd camera. Many of them took no solid food after midday at all, contenting themselves with a cup of tea. Some of them were so strict that they didn't even take milk in their tea. Yet they were all remarkably happy, contented, and friendly. It was really a joy to be with them.

So this is what a monk is – a real monk, not just someone who has formally received monastic ordination. A monk is one who is totally committed to the spiritual life, who has no worldly ties or responsibilities, who is celibate, that is to say unmarried, without wife and children, who does not work for a living, who is supported by others, who receives food and clothing and so on from others. Moreover, the monk is one who leads an angelic life, who is happy. In other words, the monk is one who has made the transition from the conditioned to the Unconditioned, from *saṃsāra* to Nirvāṇa, from nature to Enlightenment, or one who is very definitely in the process of making that transition. The monk is one who has at least set out on the noble quest.

I may seem to be presenting an idealized picture of the monastic life. In fact, because in my interpretation of the *sūtra* the monk stands for man, just as Dṛḍhā stands for nature, and the golden light for Enlightenment, what I am really presenting is an idealized picture of man. The monk only happens to be a monk. He is primarily man, man as committed to the spiritual life, man as going for Refuge.

Of course, I have taken 'monk' in the true sense, not just as someone who has formally received a certain ordination and is therefore a monk in the technical sense. There are many monks in the East who do not come up to the ideal because although they have been formally ordained, they are not really committed to the Three Jewels, to the ideal of Enlightenment. Perhaps it is rather misleading that the monk in the *sūtra* is called a monk, and the people who are wearing yellow robes but not living up to the ideals of Buddhism are also called monks. This is just an accident of history.

Having said all that, it is not easy to make the transition from the conditioned to the Unconditioned. It is not easy to leave *saṃsāra* behind, however miserable it is. It is not easy to give up the world. After all, *saṃsāra* is not only outside us, the world is not only outside us, it is also within us. Man is a being with a dual nature. On the one hand, he is the child of earth; on the other, he is the offspring of heaven. He is part of nature, but at the same time he transcends nature. He feels the gravitational pull of the conditioned; he also feels the gravitational pull of the Unconditioned. So man is a being in conflict, in conflict with himself, in conflict within himself. We may even go so far as to say that man is a battleground of opposing forces. There is a great battle taking place in every human being, the forces of nature fighting with the forces of Enlightenment, Dṛḍhā the earth goddess with the golden light.

The monk is one in whom the conflict has been resolved, the battle has been won. His natural energies have submitted to the golden light, are completely at the service of the golden light. In Christian phraseology, he has overcome the world.[271] It should be obvious now why the monk is the preacher of the *Sūtra of Golden Light*, and why the earth goddess places her head against the soles of his feet. Only one who has identified himself with the golden light can be the preacher of the *Sūtra of Golden Light*. The monk has made the transition from the conditioned to the Unconditioned, from *saṃsāra* to Nirvāṇa, from nature to Enlightenment, or is in the process of making it. He has identified himself with the golden light, become as it were one with the golden light, at least to some extent, so he is able to be the preacher of the *sūtra*. Ultimately, of course, it is the Buddha himself who is the preacher of the *sūtra*, and therefore the Buddha himself who is protected.

Nowadays, unfortunately, the earth goddess has got out of control. Nature has got out of control; and by this I mean not nature outside man, except in so far as this has been disturbed by man himself, but nature inside man, the natural human energies. Today the conditioned pursues the conditioned relentlessly. Hardly anyone pursues the Unconditioned; the emphasis is almost exclusively on material values. But if civilization is not to collapse, if mankind is not to destroy itself, there must be a much stronger emphasis on spiritual values. There must be a revival of spiritual life, and by 'spiritual life' I mean real spiritual life, not just the old conventional religiosity, which we have, or should have, outgrown. What we need, in fact, is an uncompromising assertion of the monastic ideal in the truest and best sense.

6
BUDDHIST ECONOMICS

The chapter on Śrī, chapter 8, is quite short, consisting of fewer than three pages in Emmerick's translation, and Śrī's promise takes up only a part of it.[272] But the length of her promise is no indication of its impact. She doesn't promise simply to protect the monk who is the preacher of the *sūtra*; she is much more specific, and promises much more, than that. As we have seen, she doesn't even begin by saluting the Buddha. She comes straight out with her promises. She says that she will give the monk, first, zeal; second, garments; third, begging-bowl; fourth, bed and seat; and fifth, medicines – plus, she says, other excellent equipment. She also makes it clear why she is going to give these gifts. She will give them, she says, so that the preacher of the Dharma may be provided with every equipment, so that he may have no lack, so that he may be sound in mind, so that he may pass night and day with a happy mind, so that he may examine the words and letters of the *sūtra*, so that he may perpetuate them for the sake of all living beings, and so that all living beings may eventually awaken to full, perfect Enlightenment.

So, first of all, who is the great goddess Śrī? We have seen that the goddess Sarasvatī is widely worshipped by modern Hindus, especially by scholars, writers, students, and anybody who has anything to do with learning. In the same way, the goddess Śrī is still worshipped in India today; in fact, she is worshipped even more widely than Sarasvatī. Śrī is worshipped in practically every Hindu home, usually under the name of Lakṣmī. It is easy enough to understand what she represents. The word *śrī* means 'prosperity', and *lakṣmī* means 'luck' or 'good fortune'. The prosperity which is meant here, of course, is material prosperity, and the good fortune is good fortune in the worldly sense – the kind of good fortune that causes you to win the National Lottery, not the kind that causes you to find a copy of *Buddhism for Today* lying on a seat in the bus.

So the goddess represents material prosperity, material success. The modern Hindu Lakṣmī is depicted more or less like the modern Hindu Sarasvatī: in other words, as a beautiful young woman with long, flowing, glossy black hair, dressed in a crimson sari with a golden border. Lakṣmī, however, is more definitely represented as a young married woman. She wears the red *tilaka* of the married woman on her forehead, and perhaps also the red powder called *kum-kum* in the parting of her hair, as well as various items of jewellery: necklaces, bracelets, anklets, earrings, and, of course, nose ring or nose stud. The South Indian Lakṣmī especially is adorned in this sort of way. Sarasvatī is generally dressed much more simply, as befits a goddess of learning. Lakṣmī is seated not on a goose, as Sarasvatī is, but on an enormous lotus flower, usually pink or white, and sometimes she holds a lotus flower in her hand.

There are many images of Lakṣmī in the temples, and often they have more than one pair of arms. Lakṣmī usually stands beside her consort, who is the god Viṣṇu, the second member of the Hindu *trimūrti*. It is clearly appropriate for Viṣṇu the preserver and Lakṣmī the goddess of wealth and prosperity to be regarded as being 'married' to each other, and sometimes they are jointly referred to as Lakṣmī-Nārāyaṇa – Nārāyaṇa being another name for Viṣṇu. In New Delhi there is a famous and colossal Lakṣmī-Nārāyaṇa temple. It was renovated by a modern Hindu multi-millionaire, in fact a multi-multi-multi-millionaire, G. D. Birla, one of the wealthiest men that India has produced in modern times (so he had good reason to be devoted to Lakṣmī). He was a well-known businessman who was the principal financial supporter of Mahatma Gandhi and the Congress Party in the days before Indian independence. It was he who made the famous remark, 'It costs me two thousand rupees a day to keep Bapu (that is, Mahatma Gandhi) living in poverty.'

As one might expect, the goddess Lakṣmī is much worshipped by members of the business fraternity in India. Every Hindu shopkeeper has a brightly coloured image or picture of the goddess in his shop, as well as an image of Ganesha, the elephant-headed god who removes obstacles. The orthodox Hindu businessman worships these images every day – in the sense that he lights sticks of incense and waves lights in front of their pictures or images. Every Hindu shop has a safe in the corner, or at least a big, strong iron box, and you will find the image or picture of Lakṣmī placed immediately above the safe, or sometimes even inside it. You see Hindu shopkeepers opening the safe first thing in the morning, and as they do so they worship the image or picture of Lakṣmī inside the safe, so that you could say that they are quite literally worshipping riches; they really do worship money. Even the account books are bound in a traditional red because that is the colour of Lakṣmī's sari.

Images or pictures of Lakṣmī are also found in the home, for obvious reasons; Lakṣmī is probably the most popular household deity in India. There is not much religious feeling attached to her; she is just generally believed to bring good luck and prosperity. A good wife, incidentally, is called a '*lakṣmī*'. If a woman is cheerful and industrious, if she is a good cook, housekeeper, and mother, and if her husband's affairs prosper, then his friends will say to him, 'Your wife is a real Lakṣmī,' or, 'The goddess of fortune has surely come to your house,' – in other words, your wife has brought you good luck. But I'm sorry to say that there is a darker side to the picture. If the husband's affairs go wrong, or if he dies prematurely, then his relations will say that it was his wife's fault, that she brought him bad luck. Generally speaking, however, the married woman, especially the young married woman with children, is regarded as a bringer of good luck. If, when you are leaving the house in the morning, whether to go to work or do something else, the first person that you see is a married woman – and in India you always know if a woman is married or not, because married women wear the red mark on the forehead – you will have good luck during the day. But if the first person you see is a monk, you will have bad luck, because the monk represents the negation of worldly prosperity and success. This belief prevails so strongly that there are some Hindus, especially some orthodox Brahmins, who, on meeting a monk of any kind first thing in the morning, just turn back and go home again. They don't even attempt to do anything that day; they say they know it won't be successful. They have met that monk, and he has completely destroyed their good luck for the whole day.

This is, of course, the Hindu point of view, and Hinduism, being an ethnic religion, stresses group values and worldly prosperity. The Buddhist point of view is quite different. I won't go so far as to say that according to the Buddhist point of view it is unlucky to meet a married woman in the morning, but it is certainly regarded as auspicious to meet a monk – auspicious, that is, from a spiritual point of view.

There are many legends concerning the goddess Lakṣmī, one of which concerns her birth. It is said that the gods one day decided to churn the great cosmic ocean of milk. So they uprooted Mount Meru to use as their churning stick, and took Ananta the cosmic serpent as a rope to wind round Mount Meru, and then some of the gods and goddesses pulled one end of the rope, some pulled the other, and as they pulled back and forth, they churned this cosmic ocean of milk. And out of it all sorts of marvellous things were produced, just like butter. First of all, up came the cow of plenty. Next to appear was the wish-fulfilling tree, the tree that fulfils all desires; you have only to touch it and wish, and at once your wish is granted. Then there came the heavenly elephant, the elephant that goes as fast as the wind and has six tusks. Then there came up the goddess Lakṣmī; this is how she was born. But after her there came up a pot full of poison, poison strong enough to kill all the beings in the universe.

Of course, everybody wanted to take the good things that had come up – the gods especially wanted to take the goddess Lakṣmī – but nobody wanted the poison. In the end Viṣṇu took Lakṣmī and married her, and as for the poison, it was swallowed by the god Shiva. That, at least, is what happened according to the Hindus. According to the Buddhists, it was the bodhisattva Avalokiteśvara who swallowed the poison. But whether it was Shiva or Avalokiteśvara who swallowed it, it did neither of them any harm because it went no further than their throat. But each of their throats turned deep blue – which is why they are both known as Nīlakaṇṭha, 'the blue-throated one'.

The poison here represents the suffering of the world, *duḥkha*, which Avalokiteśvara swallows out of wisdom and compassion. The emphasis in the Buddhist version, and probably in the Hindu one too, is on the bodhisattva or the god intervening to take upon himself the sufferings of the world. But of course that can't be taken literally. He can only show you – out of wisdom and compassion – how to swallow the poison yourself, how to deal with suffering yourself. It is not that he literally swallows the pain which you would otherwise have experienced. As we churn the ocean of *saṃsāra* – and this is what most of us are doing most of the time – all sorts of beautiful and delightful things come up which everybody wants, but sooner or later the pot of poison comes up. Nobody else, strictly speaking, can swallow the poison for us, but they can show us how to swallow it, in other words, how to face our own suffering, and eventually transcend it. In a sense, we each have to be our own Avalokiteśvara.

It is sometimes said that the myth of the blue-throated Avalokiteśvara came from the Hindu myth about Shiva, but it is not impossible that it might be the other way round. There is no doubt that in ancient India – we are not even sure exactly when – there was a whole floating mass of myth and legend and folklore which wasn't really the property of any particular religion. All the religions which we now call Hinduism, Buddhism, Jainism, and so on, dipped into this pool, as it were, and drew upon these stories, myths, parables, proverbs, and sayings, adapting them to their own purposes.

However, to leave these old stories and turn back to chapter 8 of the *sūtra*, we probably now have a fairly clear idea of what the modern Hindu goddess Lakṣmī represents. She is worldly prosperity, she is wealth and riches, especially in their more domestic aspect. We could perhaps say that she is affluence or even that she is economics. In the *sūtra* she promises to give the monk who preaches the Dharma zeal, garments, begging-bowl, bed, seat, medicines, and other excellent equipment. She does this, as we have seen, so that he can preach the *sūtra* properly and so that all beings can benefit.

This means that wealth and riches are placed at the service of the monk who is the preacher of the *sūtra*, and thus at the service of the Dharma, the golden light. So Śrī represents wealth and riches devoted to spiritual ends. The difference between the Hindu goddess Lakṣmī and the Buddhist goddess Śrī is that Lakṣmī represents wealth and riches devoted to worldly ends, and Śrī represents wealth and riches devoted to spiritual ends. Lakṣmī is economics in general, but Śrī is Buddhist economics, which is of course the title of this chapter.

Before I go any further, I have a confession to make. This title is not original. As you may have guessed, I borrowed it from E. F. Schumacher, the author of *Small is Beautiful*, a book which all Buddhists should read. In the chapter of this book called 'Buddhist Economics', Schumacher's point of departure is exactly the same as my own. The chapter opens with the following statement:

'Right livelihood is one of the requirements of the Buddha's Noble Eightfold Path. It is clear, therefore, that there must be such a thing as Buddhist economics.'

Schumacher goes on to explore the implications of this statement within a predominantly modern, non-traditional context, whereas in this book we are concerned with Buddhist economics within a predominantly traditional, spiritual context, within the context of the *Sūtra of Golden Light*. Nevertheless, I find myself fundamentally in agreement with Schumacher's approach; his thinking, it seems to me, is very much along the right lines. I am glad that his book has received so much attention, and I hope it will continue to receive it. I hope also that more and more people will act on his recommendations. In short, to put it in Buddhist terms, I rejoice in Schumacher's merits.

I also rejoice in the great goddess Śrī's merits, and in the promise that she makes. The fundamental nature of her promise is really very simple – so simple that we might easily overlook it. Fundamentally, the great goddess Śrī's promise is a promise to give. What does she promise to give? Virtually everything – everything, that is, that is necessary to support the spiritual life: food, clothing, residence, and medicine. You don't really need anything more than that. So we can say that Buddhist economics is the economics of giving. We can even go further than that and say that the Buddhist life is the life of giving. To the extent that we possess, to that extent we must give – material things, at least, if we can't give anything more than that. If there is no giving, there is no spiritual life.

We can see this very clearly in the case of the bodhisattva, the ideal Buddhist of the Mahāyāna, the one who is committed to the attainment of *bodhi* – Enlightenment – not just for his own sake but for that of all sentient beings. A bodhisattva practises six *pāramitās* or transcendental virtues;[273] and the first of these is *dāna* or giving. *Dāna* can be of many different kinds, because there are all sorts of things that can be given to all sorts of people in all sorts of ways.

The practice of *dāna* is widespread in all Buddhist countries, whether they practise according to the Theravāda, the Mahāyāna, or any other school. In those countries, the Dharma and those practising and preaching it are supported on a scale that we in the West can hardly imagine. Nowhere is this more so – or rather *was* this more so – than in Tibet as it existed until 1950, or to some extent even until 1959.

I remember in this connection a conversation I had in Kalimpong many years ago – it must have been in the early 1950s – with a Tibetan student called Aggen Chototsang who was learning English with me. He was about thirty years old, and he was a native of eastern Tibet; in fact, he was a Khamba. The Khambas have a reputation for being fierce and warlike to the point of being both aggressive and undisciplined, but also for being very good Buddhists. Aggen was one of five brothers, and they were all traders. He was short and stocky, and very straightforward, very direct. I am sorry to say that he was killed about ten years later fighting the Chinese in eastern Tibet. I hope he had a good rebirth, even though he died fighting. Anyway, Aggen once told me how he and his brothers spent their income. They divided whatever money they had made by the end of the year into three parts. Then they gave one third for Dharma purposes: for repairing monasteries, providing food and clothing for monks, printing copies of sacred texts, sponsoring religious ceremonies, commissioning images and paintings of Buddhas and bodhisattvas, and so on. They spent another third on pleasure: this consisted, regrettably, mainly of drinking and gambling, especially gambling – though not smoking. The old-fashioned Tibetans regarded smoking as much worse than drinking. The third part was devoted to household expenses, as well as being reinvested in the business. According to Aggen, this was the general practice in Kham; every family gave one third of their income for the Dharma – which is really something for Buddhists everywhere to live up to. We generally think that we are giving quite a lot if we give a tenth of our income, but by Khamba standards this would be comparative meanness.

The goddess Śrī promises to give the monk who is the preacher of the *sūtra* such things as food, clothing, bed, and seat; in other words, what she gives, she gives in kind, not cash. This is the traditional practice which is still widespread in some parts of the Buddhist world, though less so now than it used to be. I lived in this way myself for a couple of years – not in a Buddhist country but in India. I didn't keep any money at all, not even in the bank. I didn't handle money, didn't touch it, and I didn't accept money if it was offered to me. I found that this arrangement simplified life greatly. There were lots of things that I simply did not have to think about, because I didn't have any money.

I later discovered, however, that it was only possible to live like this while I was concerned exclusively with my personal spiritual practice. I couldn't sustain that lifestyle when I started to engage in organizing Buddhist activities. For that I needed money, even in India. If this was the position even in India, it is much more the position here in the West. It is still possible even here to invite the monk who is the preacher of the *sūtra* for a meal; it is still possible to present him with a pair of socks or a small country house. But if you want to support the Dharma to any great extent, it means giving money; in fact, it means giving quite a lot of money.

People's attitude to money is rather strange. This is perhaps not surprising: money itself is a strange, protean thing. One could almost say that money is everything except money. Money is life, money is power, money is prestige, money is success, money is security, money is pleasure, money is love. After all, with money we can buy love, or anything we want – or at least we think we can. The strangest thing about people's attitude to money is perhaps their reluctance to part with it. In the West this is true even of some Buddhists. They seem to think that there is somehow something wrong in giving money for Dharma work. This reluctance probably has something to do with our basic attitude towards money. We tend to think of it as something dirty and disgusting, something that decent people have as little to do with as possible, at least in public. The expression 'filthy lucre' probably reflects our basic attitude towards money – and in the West some Buddhists tend to share this attitude. They think of the Dharma as something that is very pure, and has to be kept pure. How do you keep the Dharma pure? Well, one way is to keep your dirty, disgusting money as far away from it as possible.

But this is certainly not the traditional attitude. The traditional attitude is that money – money that you've acquired by ethical means, in accordance with the principles of Right Livelihood – is good, wholesome stuff, and the best thing you can do with it is to give it for Dharma work. You could say that money is like manure: it smells a bit sometimes, but it's good, clean, wholesome stuff really. We need not be squeamish about handling it, or about giving it away. As Sir Francis Bacon said four centuries ago, 'Money is like muck, not good except it be spread.'[274]

So if you have any of this muck, you want to spread it around, especially in the direction of the Dharma. The Salvation Army used to have a slogan: 'Give until it hurts.' But surely this is quite wrong;

surely this reflects a typically Christian attitude. It makes us think of the spiritual life as something essentially painful, and prompts an attitude to giving like the one most of us have towards going to the dentist. We put it off for as long as possible because we think it is going to hurt. (It is an attitude that requires the recipient of one's giving to be truly miserable as well.) But in fact giving doesn't hurt at all. In fact, the more you give, the happier, lighter, and freer you will feel. So we should leave others to work their way up to giving in whatever way they can. As Buddhists we should say, 'Give till you swoon with joy.'

Giving, I should add, does not mean paying. When I first began to run Buddhist activities in England, I found that people were very reluctant to give for the sake of the Dharma, even though they assured me that they were benefiting from it. They were, however, quite ready to pay – for lectures, yoga classes, retreats, and so on. I used to wonder why this was so, and eventually came to certain tentative conclusions which seemed to shed at least some light on the matter.

When you pay, you buy. What you buy, you own. And when you own something, it's yours, it's for you, so you don't mind paying – even paying for the Dharma. When you give, however, you give away. Money given is money lost. What you give away is no longer yours, it's not for you, so you are reluctant to give, even for the sake of the Dharma. This whole mental attitude is quite a miserable one, and I have noticed that people who can get rid of it are decidedly happier.

Now for the things that the great goddess Śrī promises to give the monk who is the preacher of the *sūtra*. First of all, she promises to give him zeal, which implies both enthusiasm and energy. But how does this goddess come to be giving zeal? Surely she is essentially a goddess of wealth and riches. How does she come to be giving a psychological or even spiritual quality like zeal? Has she not stepped a little out of line? Has she not gone beyond her proper jurisdiction?

Not really. She gives zeal not directly but indirectly, by giving the other things: garments, begging-bowl, bed, and so on. The monk needs to be able to devote all his energies to the spiritual life, to preaching the *Sūtra of Golden Light*. If he had to bother about food and clothing, that would take up some of his energy, so food and clothing have to be provided, and this is what the great goddess Śrī does. By giving the monk food and clothing, she enables him to devote all his energies to preaching the *sūtra*. After all, the monk has not only given up the responsibility of supporting a wife and family; he has also given up the responsibility of supporting himself, and this is widely recognized in most Buddhist countries. This is especially the case in Theravāda countries, where, as I know from my own experience, a monk is not permitted to cook for himself, or even to make himself a cup of tea. Everything is provided for him, everything is done for him.

There is, though, another side to the coin. The monk has to devote all his energies to the Dharma, and all means *all* – not an easy thing for anybody to do. He may devote himself to Buddhist activities such as preaching the *Sūtra of Golden Light*, or to meditation, or to a combination of the two, but in one way or another all his energies are devoted to the Dharma, and it is the goddess Śrī who makes this possible. In other words, it is Buddhist economics – the economics of giving – that makes this possible.

Secondly, Śrī gives the monk the gift of garments. It is interesting – and very much in accordance with the original spirit of Buddhism – that the translator renders it 'garments', not 'robes'. In the Buddha's day, monks (as we call them now) wore ordinary dress: one piece of cloth round the waist, another piece draped under the right arm and over the left shoulder, and a third cloth of double or treble thickness which served several purposes – it could be worn as a shawl during the day, used as a blanket at night, and folded to make a sort of cushion. Some monks stitched a number of small pieces of cloth together to make one large piece, and this later became general practice.

The only real difference between the monk's dress and that of the layman was in the colour. The layman's dress was white; the monk's dress was dyed – or rather discoloured – a sort of yellowish-brown, a bit like khaki. The reason for this discoloration was twofold. If the cloth looked rather dirty rather than clean and white, it would be much less likely to be stolen; and it also made the monk easy to recognize. If people saw someone wearing this discoloured cloth, they knew that here was someone who needed to be supported. The monk's dress was not a robe, if by robe we mean something gorgeous and ceremonial, not to say theatrical, though in the course of time it tended to become so. So the goddess Śrī gives the monk who is the preacher of the *sūtra* garments, in other words, ordinary clothes.

Thirdly, Śrī gives the monk a begging-bowl. The Sanskrit word for monk is *bhikṣu*, and a *bhikṣu* is usually explained as one who lives upon *bhikṣā* or almsfood – food that has been begged. *Pātra* means bowl – or rather, 'bowl' is used to translate *pātra* – and it can be of earthenware or wood or iron, so the *bhikṣāpātra* is the bowl in which almsfood is collected and out of which it is eaten. The begging-bowl is one of the traditional eight requisites of the monk, the eight things that you are given when you are ordained as a monk. (The others are the three garments – the inner, the outer, and the upper – one girdle or belt, one water strainer, one razor, and one needle and thread.)

The general practice was that the monk went out early in the morning, and went from door to door without missing out any house – that is, without picking and choosing where he would be best received and fed. At each house he received a small quantity of cooked food, and when his bowl was full, or when he had collected enough, he stopped and returned to his monastery or wherever he happened to be staying. When he got back he would offer some of the food to his teacher, and perhaps also share it with fellow disciples. The rest of the day he spent meditating, studying, teaching, and so on. If he happened to be travelling, after collecting his food he would retire to a secluded spot, perhaps to a grove of trees, where he would eat the food, rest, and meditate, before resuming his journey.

Monks are also allowed to accept invitations to eat food at the houses of the laity, and the laity can bring food to the monastery, but in either case the food is deposited in the bowl and the monk eats from it. The bowl is also used for fetching water, and for drinking from, so it is clearly a very useful piece of equipment. A well-known ancient text says that the monk with his bowl and his three garments is like a bird with its two wings; equipped with these, he can go freely wherever he pleases.[275]

It is interesting to note that the goddess does not promise to supply the monk with food, but with a begging-bowl. We could, of course, say that the begging-bowl stands for food, and this is true, but perhaps there is another explanation. The monk begs food, or at least collects it. He is dependent for food on others, but not only that: he is dependent on others even for the very means by which he begs food – the begging-bowl. He doesn't even provide his own bowl; even that has to be given to him. In other words, he is totally dependent on others for his worldly requirements, and left totally free to devote all his energies to the Dharma, in this case to preaching the *sūtra*.

Fourthly, Śrī gives a bed or seat. The word used is *sayanāsana*: not so much bed or seat in the sense of big, heavy items of furniture, but something more like a place to sleep, a place to sit, or somewhere to stand. We mustn't forget that the monk was originally a wanderer. There was no question of his being permanently settled in the monastery; that came later. In the course of his wanderings, all that he needed was a place to stay, either just for a single night or for a few days. It could be at the foot of a shady tree, or in a summer house in somebody's private park, or in a cave. In the last chapter we found the monk Ratnoccaya sitting in a cave, studying and reflecting on the *Sūtra of Golden Light*. This is what the goddess promises to supply, whether in the form of a tree, a hut, or a cave: she promises to supply somewhere to stay.

Fifthly and lastly, the goddess promises to give medicines. In the Buddha's time these were comparatively simple. A medicine that is frequently mentioned in Pāli texts is gallnuts dissolved in cow's urine, which was regarded as a sort of panacea for the sick monk.[276] I have never tried it myself, but I have known monks who had great faith in it. There was one Sinhalese monk in particular who strongly recommended it to me in my early days as a monk, saying that it would cure me of all my complaints. This was the monk who – as I have recorded in my volume of memoirs, *The Rainbow Road* – urged me to stop writing poetry and turn out more articles on Buddhist philosophy.[277] I'm afraid I have not been able to follow his advice: I haven't yet tried gallnuts dissolved in cow's urine, and I still occasionally write poetry. He must be turning in his stupa.

However, to return to the medicines, whether it is gallnuts in cow's urine or the latest miracle drug, the principle is the same: there is no objection to the monk's receiving medical treatment. There is, in fact, a chapter on curing illness in the *sūtra* itself. Medical treatment, whether of the monk or anybody else, should, however, be in accordance with spiritual principles, and with the laws of nature. To tell whether or not treatment is 'in accordance with spiritual principles' one has to look at both the purpose of the treatment and its nature. The purpose of medical treatment is ultimately to restore one's health so that one can use that health and energy to lead a spiritual life. And the nature of the treatment shouldn't be unethical or violate any spiritual principle. I have serious doubts, for example, about experimenting with animals.

It is not in accordance with spiritual principles to have recourse to medical treatment which is dependent upon the suffering of other living beings.

Another issue is whether or not some treatments take away pain at the expense of mental clarity. Obviously mental clarity isn't something to be sacrificed lightly, but there is no point in suffering if you don't really need to. One should only refuse pain-killers if their use has implications that are worse than the pain itself. We experience enough pain anyway from time to time – toothache, stomach-ache, and so on. We don't need to be reminded of what that kind of suffering is like.

The general point here is that you are not necessarily any nearer to insight into the truth of suffering because you are experiencing suffering. You can even have insight into the truth of suffering while you are in a state of happiness. Experiencing suffering as such doesn't teach you anything. People who have suffered quite a lot can very quickly forget it, if they have had no insight into the truth of suffering.

Often when people are dying, they are given increasing doses of morphine, and this might seem to be at odds with the Tibetan teachings about dying with mental clarity. But if the pain is clouding your awareness as much as the drug is, it's really six of one and half-a-dozen of the other. You have to try to find the fine point of balance where you are not taking so much of the drug that you have no mindfulness left, but not taking so little that the pain is clouding your mind just as much as the drug would have done. That may be a very fine point of balance, and in some sad cases it may not be possible to find it. You have no choice, really. The pain clouds your awareness and so does the drug. For most people it is just not possible to bear the pain and remain mindful, still less turn their thoughts to the Buddha, Dharma, and Sangha.

Some people say that if you are in pain it is the result of your karma, and you shouldn't really interfere with that process. But you don't *know* whether it's the result of your karma. It may be, but it may not – you normally don't know unless you have some very special insight. The practical test is usually said to be that if all means of relieving your condition fail, you can fall back on the explanation of karma; but if your pain can be relieved by drugs, presumably it isn't due to karma, because drugs would not defeat karma. Even if the illness was due to karma, you could argue that it was due to subsequent good karma that drugs were available to treat it.

In saying that medical treatment should also be in accordance with the laws of nature, I mean that it should not be merely palliative. It should do more than just patch people up. Some people lead unhealthy lives and as a result suffer from all sorts of ailments which they expect the doctor to cure while they continue to live in an unhealthy way. If you lead a healthy life, you will be healthy; the way to be healthy is to lead a healthy life. So medical treatment should not simply enable you to carry on leading an unhealthy life; it should encourage you to live a healthy life.

I am not just advocating naturopathy or nature cures here. If an ordinary doctor says to a patient, 'You've just got to cut down on the meat and eat fewer eggs. It's no use my just giving you pills. You should take more exercise and cut down on alcohol,' – *that* is giving medical treatment in accordance with the laws of life and nature.

So these are the five things that Śrī promises to give the monk who is the preacher of the *sūtra*: zeal, garments, begging-bowl, bed and seat, and medicines. The last four correspond to a well-known list which is to be found in many ancient Buddhist texts, a list of four things that the monk has the right to expect from the Buddhist laity: food, clothing, shelter, and medicine. These four represent the indispensable minimum required to support life; in other words, the monk has the right to expect from the laity only what is necessary, no more.

This brings us to the question of the relation between the monk and the laity. In the Buddhist East the lay people accept full responsibility for supplying all the material needs of the monk, and they do this very happily. They are very happy to be able to make it possible for the monk to devote all his time and energy to the spiritual life because they believe that this is for everybody's benefit. In fact, they believe that by supporting the monk they are laying up for themselves a stock of merit which will help them to have a better rebirth, and even contribute to their material prosperity in this life. Some lay people, it must be admitted, support the monk simply for the sake of the merit. But even though they may not have much understanding of the spiritual life, they do have a firm belief in the superior virtue of the monk and in the meritoriousness of supporting him.

In the modern West the monk cannot expect to be supported in this way or for this kind of reason, certainly not by the general public; perhaps not even by the lay Buddhist public. It is becoming difficult for monks to be supported in this way even in the East. Some other way must be found to provide for the material needs of the full-timer – that is to say, one who is devoting all his or her time and energy to the Dharma. This is why the development of Right Livelihood businesses is such a crucial aspect of the establishment of Buddhism in the West.[278]

After the great goddess Śrī has made her promise, the chapter continues with, evidently, the Buddha Śākyamuni speaking, although we are not actually told so. He tells of a previous Buddha, a Buddha under whom the goddess Śrī planted, as the text says, a merit root – in other words, under whom she performed skilful actions, actions which have presumably led to her being reborn as the goddess Śrī. He says that this Buddha should be ceremonially worshipped with perfumes, flowers, and incense, and that he should be worshipped by the power of the great goddess Śrī. Śrī herself, he says, should also be worshipped with perfumes, flowers, and incense, as well as by the sprinkling of various juices. In this way one will acquire 'a great heap of corn'.

The Buddha then quotes a rather interesting verse (at least, we can assume it is still the Buddha speaking).

> The earth's savour grows in the earth. The deities rejoice continually. The deities of the fruits, crops, shrubs, bushes, and trees make the crops grow in brilliant condition.[279]

There are two things to notice here. According to the verse, fruits, crops, and so on do not grow as a result only of material factors. Psychical factors – referred to here as *devas* or deities – are also involved. Only a few years ago, people in the West would have dismissed such a notion as utter nonsense, a relic of ancient pre-scientific, animistic superstition. But now Western people, even scientists, are not so sure. They are now considering the matter rather more carefully.

The second thing to notice is that in this passage the great goddess Śrī becomes a sort of goddess of agriculture, even a goddess of corn. This illustrates something I said in the last chapter – that in a sense all goddesses are earth goddesses. In Śrī's case, the connection is particularly clear. After all, the most primitive form of wealth, next to cattle, is corn or grain. The Sanskrit word for riches (*dhana*) and for corn or grain (*dhānā*) is almost the same, because a wealthy man was a man who had a lot of grain in his storehouse.

The remainder of this chapter of the *sūtra* consists mainly in directions for the ceremonial worship of Śrī as the goddess of riches, even as the goddess of corn or grain – and various magic spells are provided for the purpose as well. The worship is to be carried out mainly by lay people. They should perform meritorious actions, repeat magic spells over a period of seven years, observe the full moon and new moon days – by keeping the eight moral precepts – and worship all the Buddhas in the morning and in the evening with flowers, perfumes, and incense. And they should do this for the sake of their own Enlightenment and that of all beings. If one does all this, all one's wishes will be fulfilled, the great goddess Śrī will appear, and one's abode will be replete with gold, jewels, and wealth. One will – in short – be blessed with a supply of every blessing.

Clearly this kind of practice is more appropriate for lay people than for monks. Nevertheless, it seems that monks also worshipped the great goddess Śrī. The text says that one who performs worship makes his house – or his monastery or forest retreat – pure. Later, the text says:

> In that house, village, city, settlement, monastery or forest retreat, no one at all will cause deficiency.[280]

So it appears that monks were worshipping the great goddess Śrī at the time that the *sūtra* was committed to writing – that is to say, monks performed magical ceremonies for the acquisition of wealth. This would seem inconsistent with the first part of the chapter, in which the great goddess Śrī promises to supply the monk with everything that he needs anyway. We could regard this passage as evidence of some degeneration, as evidence of the fact that some of the monks, at least, hankered after worldly things. This is one interpretation. Alternatively, we could perhaps regard it as pointing in the direction of the future, to a time when monks would no longer be able to rely for support on the laity in the traditional way.

Be that as it may, the chapter on Śrī clearly falls into two parts. In the first part, the great goddess Śrī promises to give the monk who is the preacher of the *sūtra* everything he needs. Here we have Buddhist economics in its purest form, the economics of giving. Worldly wealth, worldly riches, are dedicated to purely spiritual ends, placed at the service of the golden light. In the second part of the chapter we are more concerned with the great goddess Śrī herself – more concerned, indeed, with wealth itself. Despite the reference to Enlightenment in this part of the chapter, it seems that wealth and riches are tending to become ends in themselves. In the first part of the chapter we encounter the Buddhist goddess Śrī, but in the second part we really encounter the Hindu goddess Lakṣmī. Śrī represents Buddhist economics; Lakṣmī represents economics in general. Śrī represents wealth devoted to spiritual ends; Lakṣmī represents wealth simply collected and accumulated. Śrī is the bare necessities of life; Lakṣmī is abundance, even opulence.

This ceremonial worship of Śrī, or Lakṣmī, does raise one topic of fundamental importance: the subject of the production of wealth. It is all very well to talk about giving money, but where is it going to come from? Before you can give it away you've got to have it, and before you can have it you've got to produce it. So how is this to be done? How is wealth to be produced?

The second part of the chapter on Śrī tells us this quite clearly. It says wealth is produced by worship of the great goddess Śrī, or rather of Lakṣmī. But can we really accept this? We may need money for our Buddhist activities, but do we really believe that it will come if we perform the ceremonial worship of Lakṣmī, even if we perform it for seven years? I don't wish to deny the importance of the psychological factor in the creation of wealth, even the psychic factor; it might help – it certainly wouldn't do any harm – but I don't think it would be the really decisive factor. Hindus, of course, believe very much in worship – not so much in the sense of devotion for the sake of purely spiritual ends, but in magical worship, worship for the sake of bringing about some worldly objective. If you want to pass your exams, the Hindu would say, worship Sarasvatī; if you want to remove obstacles, worship Ganesha; if you want success in battle, worship Kārttikeya; if you want wealth, worship Lakṣmī. We also find this attitude reflected in this chapter of the *sūtra*. But it does not really belong to Buddhism. It belongs more to Indian culture, and we need not therefore consider ourselves to be bound by it.

So if wealth is not produced by worship, what is it produced by? It is produced by work, by the application of human energy – your energy and my energy. Of course, there is work and work. There is work which is not in accordance with the principles of Right Livelihood, and there is work which is. Most people are only too familiar with the first kind:

work which is concerned with the production of harmful or frivolous things, work which is boring, repetitive, and non-creative, work which is done under conditions that are unfavourable to personal development, and in the company of people who are indifferent or even hostile to spiritual life. But there is an alternative: work done for the sake of the Dharma, not for the sake of a wage or one's own creature comforts. It is done so that the wealth produced or acquired can be given to the Dharma, and it is ideally done with others similarly committed to the spiritual life.

Of course, efforts are being made in the direction of more ethical work practices even within the capitalist system. There is now some ethical stockbroking: companies that advertise themselves as guaranteeing that any money you invest won't go into arms dealing, tobacco, or any other unethical enterprise. This would suggest that some non-capitalist ideology must have got a toehold; usually capitalists want to make money at any price, regardless of ethical considerations. So ethical investment is at least a step in the right direction, even though it is a modification of the system rather than a replacement of it by something more ethical and idealistic.

But I am doubtful as to whether there is an alternative economic system that can supply us with consumer goods in the way and to the extent that the capitalist system does. People tend to assume that we could change from the capitalist system to some other ethically more desirable one and still have the consumer goodies coming in just as before. I personally rather doubt that. I don't even know that one could come up with a viable alternative, but if there *were* an alternative, I think it would be at the expense of at least some of the consumer goodies. It would therefore be an alternative that most people would not be prepared to contemplate – at least, not without a great deal of education, perhaps over a period of centuries.

To give a crude example, suppose everybody did go back to the land and grow their own food. To do that they would probably have to give up their cars and televisions, and most people simply wouldn't be prepared to do that. There is a price to be paid if you want to introduce a more ethical system, and I doubt whether most people would be prepared to pay that price. So we have to be prepared to live in a capitalist world without partaking in capitalist values, practices, and objectives.

I regard the co-operative structure as being opposed to the capitalist one, and that is one reason I favour it. But it is not at all easy to apply. In a team-based Right Livelihood situation, as distinct from a business of the ordinary capitalist type, there is an equal sharing of responsibility – or rather, everybody has responsibility to the measure of their understanding and experience of the business. This principle gives rise to a lot of difficulty, because for various reasons people don't find it easy to co-operate with each other in the way that is essential if the business is to work. Some people *want* to be bosses, although the co-op structure doesn't really allow for that, and others *want* to be told what to do rather than taking a share of the responsibility. These opposite tendencies both detract from the application of the co-operative principle. It is important, therefore, to be realistic about what setting up a Right Livelihood business involves. People sometimes get starry-eyed about how easy and lovely it will be just because you are all working together, but it isn't really as simple as that. However, it is well worth making the effort and having faith in the co-operative principles – that you take what you need and give what you can.

A Buddhist team-based Right Livelihood project has three aims. First, it aims to provide its workers with a means of support – that is, it aims to provide for their needs: not just their need for food, clothing, and shelter, but also their need to go on retreat, buy Dharma books, and so on. Secondly, it aims to provide a working situation that is conducive to spiritual progress. This means that it functions, within that particular economic context, as a sort of spiritual community, inasmuch as its workers are friends with one another and share the ideals of the project. In short, it should provide the people working within it with an experience of *kalyāṇa mitratā*, spiritual friendship. The third aim is to help finance Buddhist activities: Buddhist centres, publications, and so on. To be considered fully successful, the Right Livelihood business needs to fulfil all these three objectives.

If it does so, Right Livelihood becomes a spiritual practice in itself. It becomes what the Hindus call *niṣkāma-karma yoga*, unselfish action practised as a means of self-development. Buddhist economics is not only an economics of giving; it is also an economics of the right acquisition of wealth, the right creation of wealth, and it is this that will help us transform the world.

7
THE MORAL ORDER AND ITS UPHOLDERS

In the course of this commentary I have not been able to deal exhaustively with the theme of transformation of self and world in the *Sūtra of Golden Light*. I have only been able to draw a rough sketch – and the sketch is not complete. There are quite a few areas of human life and activity still untransformed, and it is with one of these that we will be concerned in this concluding chapter, in which I propose to examine chapter 12 of the *sūtra*, 'On Instruction concerning Divine Kings'.

The chapter opens with a salutation to a Buddha who has already appeared in the chapter on Śrī. The Buddha Śākyamuni is also saluted, as well as the goddesses Śrī and Sarasvatī. We are then introduced to two kings, King Balendraketu and his son King Ruciraketu. (We are not told whether this Ruciraketu is the same as the bodhisattva Ruciraketu whom we encountered in chapters 2 and 3.)

At the beginning of chapter 12, King Ruciraketu has just been consecrated or, as we would say, crowned. In other words, he has just been installed as king, presumably by his father. This was apparently the custom in ancient India: each king consecrated his successor and then retired. More often than not he went off into the woods and mountains and became a hermit, passing the rest of his days in contemplation. But before he left, the old king would naturally give the new, young king, some good advice, and this is what we find King Balendraketu doing. He tells his son, King Ruciraketu, that there is a textbook for kings called 'Instruction concerning Divine Kings'. He further says that his father, King

Varendraketu, explained it to him when he himself was consecrated, and he adds that for 20,000 years he has exercised sovereignty according to its teaching (in those days they lived much longer, apparently). It is now his intention to explain that textbook to Ruciraketu.

But first he relates how the textbook came into existence. Once upon a time, he says, the divine kings held a meeting. They met on a great mountain called Vajrākara. Brahmā, the teacher of the gods, was present, and so were the four world-protectors, the four great kings. Now we have already met the four great kings – but do we recognize Brahmā, the teacher of the gods?

In the *sūtra* as a whole there are, as we have seen, many examples of Hindu mythology being incorporated into the structure of Buddhist thought and spiritual practice. We have noticed, for instance, that Sarasvatī and Śrī have very definite 'Hindu' features – ethnic Indian features, we might say. It is much the same here. Here it is Brahmā in his originally Vedic or semi-Vedic character who is introduced, not a *brahma* such as we encounter in, say, the Pāli scriptures.

In Buddhist cosmology, as we saw in chapter 4, *brahmas* occupy the heavens of the *rūpaloka*, which correspond to the four *dhyānas*, so they are more or less spiritual beings; but the Brahmā of Hindu mythology is a rather different kind of figure. He is conceived of, especially within the Vedic context, as a sort of chaplain or spiritual adviser (the term is *purohit*) to the gods. It is in this capacity that he appears in this chapter. One must therefore dissociate him from the more refined and spiritual Buddhist associations of the term '*brahma*'. Neither should he be confused with the Brahmā of Puranic Hindu mythology, who is a creator god. In the earlier Vedic mythology with which we are involved here, Brahmā is often conceived of as the Brahmin *par excellence*. If the gods, especially Indra, are archetypal rulers, then Brahmā is a sort of archetypal Brahmin adviser to them. So it is quite appropriate that Brahmā gives the instructions concerning divine kings.

Again the question arises as to whether the emergence of these Hindu mythological figures represents a sign of corruption – the Hindu world encroaching on the Buddhist world – or a brave attempt to go out into the Hindu world on behalf of the Buddhists. There is a thin dividing line, really. Yes, you can go out into the world and speak the world's language, and try to express through it your particular spiritual message. But you have to be careful that the world doesn't overcome you, that the medium doesn't become the message. Perhaps one could argue that there was a point at which Buddhism overbalanced and incorporated so much of popular Hindu belief and practice that the spiritual message of Buddhism was eventually swamped and lost sight of. It is perhaps not really possible to say whether this happened in the case of the *Sūtra of Golden Light*, and for us in the West it is an abstract question; there is little danger of our being overwhelmed by Hindu mythology, although modern Indian Buddhists might be very suspicious of any attempt to express Buddhist truths in this sort of language. In the West it is much more the attitudes, beliefs, myths, and legends of Christianity against which we have to be on our guard.

Anyway, it is definitely the Brahmā of the Vedic tradition who advises the four great kings on this occasion. They begin by asking him a series of questions:

> You, Brahma, are a venerable teacher among the gods, you are lord of the gods. Solve our problems. Remove our doubt. Why is a king, though born among men, called 'divine'? And for what reason is a king called a 'divine son'? If he is born here in the world of men, he should become king, but how will a god exercise kingship among men?[281]

Apparently it was the ancient Indian custom to address kings as '*deva*', much as we say, 'Your Majesty'. *Deva*, of course, means god with a small G – a divine being, a divine one – and this is the usage we find in the Pāli Buddhist texts. The Buddha himself, for instance, addresses King Bimbisāra as '*deva*', though translators usually render this as 'your majesty', which rather obscures the point. So the four great kings are asking why the king is addressed in this fashion. After all, he is to all appearances a man. Why is he addressed as a divine being? The rest of the chapter consists of Brahmā's reply to this question, which is very interesting, not only for what he says but also for the terms in which he says it.

In the course of his reply he uses, in fact, two kinds of terms, even two languages, which we can call the mythic and the conceptual, or the mythic and the rational. This serves as a reminder of the general situation in the midst of which Buddhism arose. Very broadly speaking, the age in which the Buddha lived was an age of transition from old values to new values, from the ethnic to the universal, from the group to the individual. The group spoke, as it were, the language of myth, while the individual spoke the language of concepts, the language of reason. As far as the existing records show, the Buddha himself spoke the language of reason. Later, individuals in the Buddhist tradition learned to speak the language of myth and adapt it to their own higher spiritual purposes, but that is another story. As a literary document, Brahmā's speech, or the chapter in which Brahmā's speech is embedded, belongs to a period 1,000 years later than that of the Buddha, but it reflects very clearly the process of transition from the old to the new, from Vedic Hinduism to Buddhism. Brahmā therefore gives, in effect, two replies to the four great kings, or rather, he gives the same reply twice in two different languages: firstly the language of myth, and secondly the language of concepts, or even the language of doctrine.

Brahmā says first of all that, having been asked, he will speak, for the good and the welfare of all beings, of the origin of kings born in the abode of men, and explain how they become kings in their territories. So first we have the more mythic explanation. Brahmā says:

> Under the blessing of the divine kings, he will enter the womb of his mother. Having first been blessed by the gods, he afterwards enters her womb. Although as king he is born and dies in the world of men, yet since he comes from the gods he is called a divine son. The Thirty-three divine kings have given a portion to the king, saying 'You are our son, a lord of men magically created by all the gods'.[282]

So here Brahmā makes four statements. They are not logically consistent, but this doesn't really matter, because we are concerned here with myth. The first statement is that the king comes to this earth from the world of the gods. He is, as it were, a god incarnate. Secondly: before entering the womb of his future mother, he is blessed by the divine kings, and by the gods. Thirdly: the thirty-three divine kings have each given a portion of themselves to the king; in other words, the king is fashioned, as it were, from their substance. Fourthly: the king has been magically created; presumably this means that the king possesses what is called an illusory body, a body that, like a mirage, is perceived by people but does not really exist in the sense of having any real empirical existence.

Inconsistent though they may be, these four statements all clearly convey one thing, which is that the king is not an ordinary man. There is something divine about him; he is indeed a divinity. This belief, strange as it may sound to us, was widespread at a certain period of ancient history, and indeed traces of it are found even in modern times, even in England. The belief that the king was a sort of divine being was particularly strong in ancient Egypt, in Sumeria, and, in a somewhat different form, in China; it was certainly strong at one time in India. But by the Buddha's day it had already begun to decline. A more rational justification of the nature and function of kingship was needed, and it is this that Brahmā now proceeds to offer.

Continuing his speech, Brahmā says:

> For the sake of suppressing what is unlawful, a destroyer of evil deeds, he would establish beings in good activity in order to send them to the abode of the gods. Whether the lord of men (is) a man or a god, a Gandharva, a Rākṣasa, an untouchable, he removes evil deeds. The king is the parent of those who do good deeds. The king has been blessed by the gods as one who exibits (their) fruition and fruit. The king has been blessed by the gods as belonging to the present world to show the fruition and fruit of deeds well done and of deeds ill done. For when a king overlooks an evil deed in his territory and does not inflict appropriate punishment on the evil person, in the neglect of evil deeds lawlessness grows greatly, wicked acts and quarrels arise in great number in the realm.[283]

Before going on we need to be sure we know who these gods or *devas* really are in this context. In the Vedas, the most ancient Hindu sacred books (or what were later written down as books), the *devas* are, on the whole, personifications of natural phenomena. There is, for instance, Sūrya the sun god, there is Indra the god of rain and violent thunderstorm, there is Uṣas the goddess of the dawn, and Agni the god of fire, particularly the sacrificial fire. There are also the *maruts* or wind gods. All these are personifications of natural phenomena. Later on, there arose gods of a different kind, gods that personified ethical and spiritual qualities, gods like Mitra and Varuṇa; even deities that personified human activities and functions, like the goddess Vāc, whom we met in the chapter on Buddhism and culture.

When we meet some of these gods a few hundred years later, in the Buddhist scriptures, we find that a great change has taken place. The gods are no longer personifications of natural phenomena, no longer to be feared or propitiated. They are beings like ourselves, only happier, more powerful, and much longer lived. So what has happened? What has brought about this change? What has in fact happened is that a new idea has been introduced: the law of karma, or, if you like, an extension of the law of karma. It is not always realized that the law of karma was not known to the most ancient Aryans. It is briefly referred to in one of the most ancient pre-Buddhist Upaniṣads, but only as an esoteric teaching. It is with Buddhism, and perhaps Jainism too, that karma is placed in the forefront of the teaching and described in a full and detailed manner.

The law of karma is the operation on one level of the still more comprehensive law of conditionality, which applies to all conditioned existence whatsoever. The law of karma applies to all sentient existence. It applies wherever there is consciousness, wherever there is mind and will. Briefly stated, it says that skilful action produces happiness and unskilful action produces suffering. Skilful actions are those that are free from greed, hatred, and delusion and are, on the contrary, accompanied by contentment, friendliness, and wisdom. Unskilful actions are those that are accompanied by, and spring from, greed, hatred, and delusion.

Traditionally, the law of karma is envisaged as operating not just within the context of the present life, but over a whole series of lives; in other words, the law of karma, traditionally speaking, is bound up with the fact of rebirth. Because the law of karma operates at all levels of conditioned existence, a human being can be reborn as a god as a result of performing skilful actions while on earth; and conversely a god can be reborn as a human being. We can also be reborn as *asuras*, infernal beings, hungry ghosts, and so on. According to the popular version of the teaching, human beings can even be reborn as animals as a result of performing unskilful actions. All this is depicted in the well-known Tibetan wheel of life.

We are now in a better position to understand Brahmā's second, more rational, explanation of why kings are addressed as '*deva*'. We'll take it sentence by sentence. First of all, Brahmā says:

> For the sake of suppressing what is unlawful, a destroyer of evil deeds, he would establish beings in good activity in order to send them to the abode of the gods.

As we have already seen, the king has come from heaven; the king is a god reborn on earth as a man. This is common ground to both of Brahmā's explanations, the mythical and the rational. In the mythical account, however, there is no explanation of how the god became a god. No explanation, in fact, is needed. A god is a personification of natural phenomena.

In the rational account, however, an explanation is needed, and this explanation is given within the framework provided by the law of karma. A god has become what he is as a result of skilful actions. Originally he was a man, but having performed an extraordinary number of skilful actions, he was reborn after death in a higher heavenly world as what we call a *deva*, a god. In that higher heavenly world he enjoys great happiness and power, and he lives for a very long time, even for thousands of years. But eventually the karma that caused him to be reborn as a god is exhausted, and he is reborn again on earth. However, as a secondary result of all his skilful actions, he is not reborn as an ordinary man. He is reborn as a very prominent man, a leading man, a king.

All this is common ground to all forms of Buddhism; there is no school that would not accept it, although they might place varying degrees of emphasis upon it. But the whole idea suggests a rather idealized view of kingship; it suggests that the institution of kingship is such that it has a definite moral basis, and is an extremely happy state. It would have to be so in order to be the reward, as it were, of skilful deeds. So kings could be said to be gods reborn only where the institution of kingship exists in an ideal form.

Put it this way. Suppose you were to be reborn in the family of one of the Caesars, say Caligula or Nero. That would hardly be a blessing – it would be more of a disaster. So kingship as such cannot be the reward of virtuous deeds, and therefore it is not necessarily the case that kings have been *devas* in their previous existences. It would seem to depend upon the nature of kingship at the time into which they were born. If one happened to be born into a royal family that represented or embodied an ideal conception of kingship, in a time of peace and prosperity, that could conceivably be the result of skilful actions performed in the past, and you could conceivably have been a *deva* in your previous existence. But if you were born into a royal family that simply exercised power, that had no moral basis or standards, in a time of war and conflict, even conflict within that royal family itself, with the possibility of being murdered or assassinated at an early age, or living in terror for decade after decade – well, clearly that would not be the result of any skilful actions you had performed.

So it would seem that Brahmā is speaking of quite an ideal state of affairs, of kingship in the ideal sense, and of what one might describe as cosmically normal conditions. It also appears that, at the time of which Brahmā is speaking, and presumably at the time the *sūtra* was composed or written down, kingship was hereditary, whereas in modern times rulers are often elected, or even seize power in the case of military dictators. Brahmā's statement cannot be taken as implying that present-day rulers are gods reborn. They could well be *asuras* reborn, or – even worse – *pretas*.

Of course, one cannot infer from this that rulers born into unfavourable circumstances have done so necessarily because they have committed unskilful deeds in former lives. This raises a general question: can the innocent suffer? Take the case, say, of the Dalai Lamas. The ninth, tenth, and eleventh Dalai Lamas died, or were murdered, very young. It could be that the particular being who was identified as the Dalai Lama in each of these cases was not in fact the incarnation of the bodhisattva Avalokiteśvara, but some other unfortunate being whose unskilful actions had caused him to be born into that particular family and selected in that particular way. On the other hand, it could be that he was indeed the real Dalai Lama, but that Avalokiteśvara's efforts on behalf of the Tibetan people were simply cut short by people who were hungry for power themselves. There are those two possibilities – but which of them applies to the case of any particular Dalai Lama we probably have no way of knowing. The popular Indian Buddhist attitude seems to be that the good man is always successful, because he has so much *puṇya* to his credit that no real misfortune can happen to him, but one has to question that.[284] A bodhisattva, after all, is willing to take risks.

The Indian attitude, including the Indian Buddhist attitude, can be one of rather superficial optimism. Traditional Buddhism sometimes doesn't give sufficient weight to the fact that a person who is genuinely innocent and doesn't have a lot of unskilful karma to his credit – or rather debit – can suffer as the result of other people's unskilful actions. Perhaps there is too great a tendency – not so much in Buddhism, but in Indian thought in general – to assume that if anything unpleasant befalls you, you must have deserved it. This would seem to reduce everything that befalls you to your karma, to your own previous skilful or unskilful actions. But that is not really the Buddhist teaching.

To the best of my knowledge the teaching of the five *niyamas* – which shows that there are four other levels on which conditionality operates besides the karmic level – doesn't appear in Buddhism outside the Theravāda.[285] Even in the Theravāda itself it appears not in the canon but in the commentarial literature, as a sort of systematization of the teaching contained in the canon. One of the most important places in which it appears is Buddhaghosa's commentary on the *Dhamma-saṅgaṇī*, the first book of the *Abhidhamma Piṭaka*. It doesn't seem to have reached Tibetan Buddhism or the Sarvastivāda. The consequence is that in Tibetan Buddhism, and in the Mahāyāna generally, there is a tendency to think that everything that happens to you is a result of your own personal past karma, although the teaching of the five *niyamas* makes it clear that that is not the case.

No one school of Buddhism has got the whole Buddhist teaching, although there are useful teachings to be found in all the schools. So if you confine yourself to Tibetan Buddhist and Sarvastivādin sources, for example, you don't come across the teaching of the five *niyamas*, and that is a serious loss which can cause serious misunderstanding. Broadly speaking, no one school of Buddhism can concern itself with all possible aspects. Some things are bound to get left out, and others are bound to be emphasized. This makes it important to have as wide an acquaintance as one can with all the different forms of Buddhism. It may even be that relevant points are missed by the Buddhist tradition as a whole, for various perhaps historical reasons. Perhaps we can take a point from Plato or Schopenhauer or Shelley that is useful to us, but does not occur in the Buddhist tradition. It probably won't be a major point, but even minor points can be very useful at a comparatively early stage of one's spiritual development.

So we can say that Indian Buddhism didn't seem to be sufficiently aware that such a thing as tragedy was possible. It is perhaps an insight that has been contributed by the West. You might think that if someone was born with an accumulation of merit, he would be able to guide his life away from adverse events, and that is certainly the case – but there are limits. Sometimes other people, for unskilful reasons, are determined to do you some harm or injury. The fact that you yourself have always been skilful or are highly intelligent will not necessarily enable you to evade that. You may be able to maintain a positive mental or emotional attitude, but externally you may be defeated, or even killed, despite all the *puṇya* you have accumulated. Traditional Indian thought, including Buddhist thought to some extent, doesn't take that sufficiently into consideration. It always wants a happy ending. This attitude seems to be embedded in the Indian attitude to life, which is why in India they have got drama but not tragedy. There is always a happy ending, even if in order to produce it a god has to appear and restore all the dead bodies to life. It's a bit like the Book of Job, which comes very near to being a tragedy, but swerves away at the last minute. After all Job's sufferings God gives him back everything he has lost tenfold – as though having ten more sons and ten more daughters could compensate you for the sons and daughters that you have lost; as though the tragedy, the suffering, could be wiped out.[286]

King Bimbisāra in the Pāli canon may have lost his kingdom – but his story is no real tragedy. After all, he was a Stream Entrant, possibly an *anāgāmi*, so being deprived of his kingdom was no great loss from his point of view.[287] A man who has attained Stream Entry cannot possibly be regarded as having failed in life, regardless of what has happened to him externally. If Oedipus or King Lear had gained Stream Entry, there would have been no tragedy, whatever other disasters may have befallen them.

So when Brahmā says that a king has been a *deva* in his previous life, we have to ask ourselves what he is really saying, what kind of conception of kingship he is referring to. In some ways it doesn't seem very much in accordance with the kind of Western conception of kingship implied by Shakespeare's idea that 'uneasy lies the head that wears a crown'.[288] On the other hand, another of Shakespeare's characters says, 'There's such divinity doth hedge a king.'[289] Shakespeare's historical plays certainly seem to involve the assumption that there is something divine about kingship. In the British coronation ceremony, which goes back to medieval times, the sovereign is ordained as a clerk in holy orders, and anointed with consecrated oil. Especially in Stuart times, the king was regarded as God's representative on earth. King Charles I asserted this principle very strongly at the time of his trial – that he was responsible only to God, not to his subjects. That was his basic principle, and he never budged from it: 'A subject and a sovereign are clean different things.'[290]

There was also the belief, right down to the time of Queen Anne, that the sovereign had healing power. There was a disease called scrofula which was known as the 'king's evil', because people believed that the king (or queen) could heal it by touching the afflicted person. Charles II, it is estimated, touched about 200,000 people in the course of his reign. As a child Dr Johnson was touched by Queen Anne for this purpose – one of the last people in England to be touched in that way. It was believed that this power – which is supposed to have descended from Edward the Confessor through all the English sovereigns – died out with the Stuarts, because the Hanoverians were a collateral branch and therefore hadn't inherited that power. There are even now some remnants of the belief in divine kingship in the case of the English monarchy. It is quite interesting how much fuss was made over Princess Diana's shaking hands with victims of AIDS.

Although it is a commonplace within Buddhist tradition that the king was a *deva* in his previous life, the *Sūtra of Golden Light* has a further point of its own to make. As a result of his past history – we could even say his previous positive conditioning – the king has a natural inclination towards skilful actions. He performs skilful actions himself, and he encourages others to perform them. Not only that; as king, he suppresses what is unlawful, what is against the moral order. He destroys evil deeds. He establishes beings in skilful, meritorious activities.

He does this, we are told, so that as a result of such activities beings may be reborn in the world of the gods: that is to say, in the world from which he himself has come. This brings to mind a parallel with the *Bhagavad Gītā* which no one seems to have remarked on before. The *Bhagavad Gītā* is a dialogue between Krishna and Arjuna which forms part of the great Hindu epic, the *Mahābhārata*. The *Gītā* consists of eighteen chapters, and in chapter 4, Sri Krishna explains to Arjuna that both of them have been born many times before. The difference is that he, Krishna, remembers his previous lives, while Arjuna does not. Krishna then says, 'When righteousness declines, when unrighteousness increases, then I appear for the protection of the good. For the destruction of the wicked, for the establishment of Dharma, I am born age after age.' This is perhaps, at least in India, the most famous verse in the entire *Bhagavad Gītā*.[291] It is the foundation of Hindu *avatāravāda*, the belief in the successive descents, or, as we might say, incarnations, of God – God with a capital G.

But there are two important differences between this text and the *Sūtra of Golden Light*. In the *Bhagavad Gītā* it's the Supreme Being himself who descends as Rama, Krishna, and so on; and he descends of his own free will. But in Buddhism, of course, there is no supreme being. The descent takes place within the framework of conditioned existence – from a higher to a lower plane of conditioned existence, from heaven to earth – and it takes place under the law of karma. Brahmā speaks of the king as the 'destroyer of evil deeds'. Sri Krishna, however, speaks of himself as coming 'for the destruction of the wicked'.

Continuing with his explanation of why kings are addressed as '*deva*', Brahmā says:

> Whether the lord of men (is) a man or a god, a Gandharva, a Rākṣasa, an untouchable, he removes evil deeds.

'He' could refer to the king, because in the previous sentence, Brahmā has been talking about the king – 'he [i.e. the king] would establish beings in good activity'. So the sentence might mean that the king discourages all classes of sentient beings from performing unskilful actions. However, it's more likely that the sentence is a sort of interjection, so that 'he removes evil deeds' is to be understood more as 'one removes evil deeds'. In other words, it doesn't matter what class of beings one belongs to, what position in society one occupies, whether one is a man or a god: one can still perform skilful actions and evil deeds, and one has the possibility of a higher heavenly rebirth. Understood in this way, the sentence is an affirmation of the basis upon which Brahmā's rational explanation of the nature and function of kingship rests. In other words, it is an affirmation of the law of karma.

But it is also possible to understand the sentence in another way. We could take it that it doesn't matter what the king's origin is, what caste he belongs to by birth. The main thing is that he removes evil deeds. If he does that, he is a king. This, of course, is very much in accordance with the general spirit of Buddhism as a universal religion, and in direct contrast to orthodox Hinduism, according to which only one who belongs by birth to the Kṣatriya caste can be king, just as only one who belongs to the Brahmin caste by birth can teach.

The next sentence is very short:

> The king is the parent of those who do good deeds.

This means that those who do good deeds have nothing to fear from the king; he will look after them and protect them. More than that: by encouraging people to perform good deeds, he stands in a parental relation to them, morally speaking. I will have something more to say about the parental function in a more literal sense later on.

The next two sentences say practically the same thing in different words, so we will take them together. Brahmā says:

> The king has been blessed by the gods as one who exhibits (their) fruition and fruit. The king has been blessed by the gods as belonging to the present world to show the fruition and fruit of deeds well done and of deeds ill done.[292]

These sentences comprise the essence of Brahmā's whole speech, the essence of the 'Instruction concerning Divine Kings', the essence of King Balendraketu's advice to his son King Ruciraketu. The matter is expressed still more clearly later on in Brahmā's speech, when he says:

> He is called king because he acts in various ways in order to demonstrate the fruition and fruit of acts that are well done or ill done.[293]

This means that the social order should mirror the law of karma. Under the law of karma, skilful actions result in happiness, and unskilful actions result in suffering. It should be the same within the social order: skilful actions should be encouraged, and unskilful actions should be punished. In other words, the social order should be a moral order, and the upholder of that moral order is the king. Each king is responsible for upholding it in his own territory.

The moral order works according to a very simple principle, one which is even more simple and fundamental in a sense than the law of karma. *Actions have consequences.* We often forget this. We tend to do things on the spur of the moment, without thinking. We don't realize that what we are doing will have consequences – perhaps even very serious consequences – both for ourselves and for others. To act without thinking of the consequences of one's actions is irresponsibility; to act bearing in mind the consequences of one's actions is responsibility. To the extent that one acts responsibly, one is an individual; to the extent that one acts without responsibility, one is not an individual. So if one wants to become an individual, one must learn to act responsibly. One must remember that actions have consequences; one must be mindful of the law of karma; one should understand why the social order should be a moral order.

But why *should* the social order be a moral order? I have already answered this question to some extent. If the social order is a moral order, then it is a training ground, as it were, in skilful actions. If we perform skilful actions we will accumulate merit, and if we accumulate merit we will be reborn in a happy heavenly state – that is, as a god. So if the social order really *is* a moral order, if the king does his duty – if, in other words, he does not overlook any evil deed – and if his subjects observe the moral order and perform skilful actions, the result will be that they will all be reborn as gods, and the ranks of the gods will be strengthened.

This is of great significance. There is a constant battle going on in the universe between the gods and the *asuras*, between the positive and the negative forces within the conditioned, within *saṃsāra*. Sometimes the gods are victorious, but sometimes the *asuras* win the day. The gods, therefore, have a vested interest, as it were, in human beings performing skilful actions, because such human beings will be reborn as gods and the ranks of the gods will be strengthened. They will be then more likely to overcome the *asuras*. So the traditional Buddhist point of view is that the maintenance of the moral order on earth is of cosmic significance, because it helps to keep the balance in favour of the positive, even the spiritual, forces in the universe.

As we saw in the chapter on 'The Spiritual Significance of Confession', the spiritual is not the same thing as the transcendental. We should not, therefore, confuse this battle between the gods and the *asuras* with the conflict between the golden light and the darkness, the conflict between Enlightenment and nature. The first is a battle within the conditioned, but the second is the much more serious and radical conflict between the Unconditioned and the conditioned; or rather, between the Unconditioned and the negative part of the conditioned. The positive part of the conditioned is on the side of the Unconditioned, as it were. The gods are on the side of the Buddha; skilful actions are on the side of Enlightenment; the ethical is on the side of the transcendental; *śīla* and *samādhi* are on the side of *prajñā*; the moral order is on the side of the spiritual community.

However, I am going too far too fast. Let's go back to the responsible individual, the individual who performs skilful actions, or rather, let us go back to individuals in the plural. The moral order can be described as a network of ethically responsible individuals, people who act responsibly towards themselves and towards one another – people, that is to say, who try to do what is truly best for themselves and others. This creates a society in which everyone acts in an ethically responsible manner, a society which is totally a moral order, which clearly, faithfully, and fully reflects the law of karma. Perhaps no human society – certainly no large human society – has ever been a completely moral order. But, large or small, all human societies are moral orders to some extent.

The moral order obliges us to act in an ethically responsible manner, to perform skilful actions, to pay some heed to the law of karma. In other words, it obliges us to develop as individuals. The social order should be a moral order because ultimately it helps people to develop spiritually. We cannot develop without becoming ethical individuals, without developing some sense of responsibility towards ourselves and others. But it is very difficult to be an ethical individual in an unethical society, so society must help the individual; society must be a moral order. In other words, it must reflect the operation of the law of karma.

Now the first human society with which we come into contact when we enter this world is, of course, the family. The family is not just a biological unit; it should also be a moral order. It should reflect the larger moral order of society, just as society itself should reflect the ideal moral order which is the law of karma. The upholders of the moral order within the family are, obviously, the parents. Parents are divine kings on a small scale. They educate their children in the observance of moral norms. They teach them that actions have consequences. It's not just a question of socializing your children; you have to give them some understanding, however rudimentary, of the law of karma, some training, however elementary, in the performance of skilful action. This will help the child to become later on a true member of a society which is also a moral order, and will help him or her to develop as an individual.

In the Pāli scriptures we find the Buddha himself doing this very thing. We are told that one day when he was out walking, maybe going for alms, the Buddha passed a group of small boys. As small boys will, whether in India or England or anywhere else – they were tormenting something. They had found a crow that had broken its wing, and they were tormenting it. So the Buddha went up to them and asked them whether they would like to be treated like that. So they replied no, of course not. The Buddha then said, well, if they would not like to be treated like that themselves, why treat others like that? The crow doesn't like it any more than they would. Hearing it put like that, the boys understood, and let the crow go free.[294]

It is well known that children need to know where they stand, what they can and cannot do, what actions will meet with approval and what actions will get them into trouble. If the parents laugh when the child is naughty one day, but get angry with him the next day for just the same kind of naughtiness, the child will become confused and even anxious, because he just doesn't know what to do. It is much the same with adults. We need to feel that certain actions will definitely be followed by certain consequences. We need to exist within an order; best of all, to exist within a moral order, although, psychologically speaking at least, almost any order is probably better than no order at all.

So what happens when the moral order breaks down? What happens when 'the king overlooks an evil deed', when an evil deed is not followed by its appropriate result? To find this out, we must go back to chapter 12 of the *sūtra*, back to Brahmā's speech. This is his picture of a society which is not a moral order, and which is therefore not a society at all. I will just quote enough to give an idea of what happens when the moral order of society collapses.

Brahmā says:

> When a king overlooks an evil deed in his territory and does not inflict appropriate punishment on the evil person, in the neglect of evil deeds lawlessness grows greatly, wicked acts and quarrels arise in great number in the realm. The chief gods are wrathful in the dwellings of the Thirty-three when a king overlooks an evil

deed in his territory. His territory is smitten with dreadful, most terrible acts of wickedness, and his realm is destroyed on the arrival of a foreign army, his enjoyments and houses. Whoever has accumulated wealth, by various evil acts they deprive one another of them. If he does not perform the duty on account of which he has kingship, he destroys his own realm, just as the lord of elephants (tramples) on a lotus-pool. Unfavourable winds will blow; unfavourable showers of rain (will fall); unfavourable (will be) planets and asterisms, likewise moon and sun. Crop, flower, fruit, and seed will not ripen in due season. Famine will arise where the king is neglectful. Unhappy in mind will the gods be in their dwellings when the king overlooks an evil deed in his territory. All the kings of the gods will say to one another: 'Unlawful is this king, for he supports the side of the lawless.' This king will ere long anger the gods. Through the anger of the gods his territory will perish. There will be destruction by the weapon and lawlessness in that territory. Wicked acts, quarrels, diseases will arise. The lords of the gods will be angry. The gods will ignore him. His realm will be ruined. The king will come to grief. He will find himself separated from his loved ones, from brother or son, separated from his beloved wife. Or his daughter will die. There will be showers of meteors, likewise mock suns. Fear of foreign armies and famine will increase greatly. His beloved minister will die and also his beloved elephant. As soon as they have died, his beloved horses and female camels will likewise (die). They will carry off one another's house, enjoyments, wealth. In every district they will slay one another with arms. In the territories there will be disputes, quarrels, evil acts. An evil demon will enter the realm. There will be severe disease. After that the venerable will become lawless. His ministers and attendants will become lawless. After that there will be respect for the lawless person and there will be constantly oppression of law-abiding beings. Through honour for lawless people and in the case of oppression of the law-abiding, three things will go wild there: asterisms, water, and winds. Three things perish when there is acceptance of lawless people: the savour, essence, and strength of the Good Law, the strength of beings, and the savour of the earth. (Where there is) honour for untruthful people and dishonour for truthful people, there will be there three things:

famine, thunderbolt, and death (by plague). After that there will be no savour or strength in fruit or crop. Many beings will become ill in those territories. Large sweet fruits in those territories will become small, bitter, and sharp. Play, laughter, and pleasure, things previously enjoyable, will become feeble and unenjoyable, fraught with hundreds of troubles. The savour of the moist essence of crops and fruits will disappear. Thus they will not satisfy the body, the senses, or the elements. Beings will become of bad complexion, of very little strength, and very weak. Having eaten much food they will not attain satiety. After that they will get no strength, prowess or energy. Beings in those territories will become without prowess. Beings will become disease-ridden, oppressed by various illnesses. There will arise evil demons, asterisms, and various Rākṣasas. A king would be lawless if he stood on the side of lawlessness: the three spheres, the circle of the whole triple world are harmed. Numerous such evils arise in those territories when a king is partisan and overlooks an evil act. (If) he overlooks an evil act, a king does not exercise his kingship according to the duty for which he was consecrated by the lords of the gods.[295]

The picture that Brahmā paints is a grim and terrible one. It is also a picture that is not entirely unfamiliar. Certain features of it we recognize only too well, because we ourselves are living today in a society that is not a moral order. The moral order has not broken down equally everywhere, but it has broken down to a great extent in many parts of the world, and in many areas of human life. This is not to say that large numbers of people have all at once become deliberately wicked. People are probably much the same as they always were, but the situation has changed.

To begin with, the spiritual values on which the moral order was traditionally based are no longer so widely accepted. Science and technology seem to have made them irrelevant. In some parts of the world, in some societies, those values have indeed been openly attacked and overtly rejected, and even where that has not happened, spiritual values are not really important to significant numbers of people. The moral order of society therefore has no real, solid foundation. It continues only out of force of habit, as it were, and that cannot go on for very long. Then, corporate life has become not only larger but also more impersonal. Sometimes it is very difficult to find out who is responsible for what, who has done what. Things just happen – even things that have a strong effect on us personally. We cannot trace them back to anyone in particular. Nobody accepts responsibility. They are nobody's actions. This is particularly true of government departments, as well as of large businesses.

Social life, life as a member of a human society, has become very complex, like an enormous Persian carpet, but one without a pattern – just thousands and thousands of threads running in all directions, making it impossible to see where any particular thread begins and ends. Thousands upon thousands of events are happening in society, but it is difficult to trace any one event through its entire course, to know what has caused what. Very often we don't even know whether a particular factor in the situation is cause or effect.

The result of all this is that we feel we are living in a world where actions do not have consequences; where certain causes are not invariably followed by certain effects – at least, not in the human world. We feel that we are living in a society that is not an intelligible moral order. We feel that there is not much point in performing skilful actions, that it doesn't matter what you do, because actions seem to have no real moral consequences, at least none that one can either experience or observe. We thus cease to be ethically responsible, and to that extent we cease to be individuals; not only cease to develop, but even deteriorate. Not only that; we feel that we do not count personally. We feel that society at large takes no notice of us, doesn't take us into account, doesn't listen to what we say even when we can say it. Consequently we feel frustrated, powerless, and resentful.

So how can the moral order of society be restored? We no longer have any kings in the old sense, so we cannot exhort them to uphold the moral order as Brahmā does. What are we to do? Well, there is only one thing we can do. We ourselves have to become the upholders of the moral order, to the extent that we can within our own sphere of influence. We ourselves have to become divine kings. Those who are true individuals or who are trying to develop individuality have to get together, have to establish an ethical order on a small scale among themselves, a smaller moral order within the larger non-moral order. And within that smaller moral order we have to behave responsibly towards ourselves and to one another, strengthen our sense of ethical responsibility, and increase our awareness of the law of karma. To the extent that we can do this, we will become individuals, and when we become individuals, we will be able to act more effectively in the larger world, to act with ethical responsibility. The moral order to which we belong will give us the strength to do this.

This moral order is what I call the positive group. It is not the spiritual community, but it is the basis on which the spiritual community can be established. It doesn't represent the transformation of the world any more than the development of a sense of ethical responsibility represents the transformation of the individual self, but it is the basis of that transformation, just as the development of a sense of ethical responsibility is the basis for the transformation of self.

Within a spiritual community, within a Buddhist order, there can be no question of law and punishment, because law and punishment are based at least to some extent on the power mode, and by its very nature a spiritual community is based on the love mode. One member of the order cannot punish another, because that would mean invoking the power mode. In any case, if a member of the order behaves in such a way that punishment is necessary, he or she is to that extent no longer a member of the order. Suppose, to take an extreme example, he or she commits a murder. Because they have broken a precept to such a disastrous extent, they cease to be a member of the order. There would be no question of their being punished by the order; they would simply have placed themselves beyond the pale of the order. The order wouldn't even punish them by expelling them; they would automatically expel themselves, and the order would recognize that.

But suppose a member of the order somehow succeeded to political power. Then the question of law and punishment would arise. One would have to consider the extent to which an order member could exercise political power; in other words to what extent they could function in the power mode. I would suggest that one can operate in the power mode in the world so long as that power mode is based on and controlled by the love mode – as when, for example, you forcibly restrain a child from doing something that would be harmful for the child. What form punishment would take if a member of the spiritual community happened to be in a position of power it is difficult to say; it seems remote from the present reality, but it might have to be considered one day.

There are, of course, 'Buddhist states' that have laws and punishments, but these do not always spring from Buddhist principles. In Burma, for example, it seems that they base themselves on the laws of Manu to a great extent. Usually what has happened is that the influence of Buddhism has modified laws and punishments to some extent, rather than introducing a system of laws and punishments based on Buddhist principles.

One has to regard the extent to which a spiritual community can exercise political power as an open question. Traditionally, except in Tibet, the view has been that the spiritual community, especially if it is in the form of a monastic order, should exercise influence rather than power – but one could argue that that is a shirking of responsibility.

Dr Ambedkar, the great Indian statesman who championed the cause of the people who used to be called Untouchables and eventually led them in converting to Buddhism, has discussed the question of whether a society can be kept in order by force.[296] His conclusion is that obviously it can't. There needs to be some generally accepted moral principle which will hold society together and maintain order. You can perhaps keep an anti-social minority under control by force, but you can't keep the majority of people under control by force – at least not for long – so a moral basis is needed. Perhaps the spiritual community would be better occupied in trying to strengthen the moral basis of society than in taking on political power and having direct responsibility for dealing with the anti-social minority by methods that are in accordance with the power mode rather than the love mode.

The spiritually committed can never really give up hope on anyone. You can't think, 'There are people who are simply not spiritual, and need a kind of law distinct from that which operates within the spiritual community.' On the other hand, you need to be open to the possibility that even those people who in the long run would be amenable to the love mode, can only be dealt with in the short term in accordance with the power mode. The fact that you forcibly prevent the child from running into the street doesn't mean that you give up all hope that one day he will be a rational human being. But it seems to me that the law and order problems experienced by many countries today are mainly attributable to the fact that the moral order has broken down for many people, and there are certain moral sanctions which they no longer accept or recognize.

Despite his fearful warning of what happens when the king overlooks an evil deed in his territory, when he fails to uphold the moral order, Brahmā's reply to the questions of the four great kings ends on a positive note, with a description of what will happen if the king *does* uphold the moral order. He says that the gods will be joyful. Asterisms, moon, and sun will move properly, the winds blow at the proper time, rains fall at the proper time, and the abode of gods become full of immortals and sons of immortals. The realm will become full of plenty. The king will become famous, and he will easily protect his subjects.

I want to end this exploration of the *Sūtra of Golden Light* on a positive note too. The crucial thing is this: there is only one way of transforming one's own self and the world, and that is by making them receptive to the golden light, the light of the transcendental. It is only this light that can really transform. In the words of the *sūtra* itself:

> By the exposition of the Suvarṇaprabhāsa [the golden light] may the ocean of evil be dried up for me; may the ocean of acts be destroyed for me; may the ocean of impurities be destroyed for me; may the ocean of merit be filled for me; may the ocean of knowledge be purified for me. By the excellent splendour of flawless knowledge may I become the ocean of all virtues. Filled with jewel-like virtues, with the virtues of enlightenment, by the power of the Suvarṇaprabhāsa and its Confession, may there be for me splendour of merits; may the splendour of enlightenment be pure for me. By the excellent splendour of flawless knowledge may there be splendour of body for me. By the shining of the splendour of my merit may I become distinguished in the whole triple world. Continually endowed with the power of merit, a deliverer from the ocean of woe, and like a sea of all blessing, may I proceed to enlightenment in a future aeon.[297]

Both now and in the years to come, may this be the aspiration of us all.

The Inconceivable Emancipation

THEMES FROM THE VIMALAKĪRTI-NIRDEŚA

I

THE MAGIC OF A MAHĀYĀNA SŪTRA

Nearly all of us share a particular perception of our own lives which we know to be essentially false. This perception is that our lives tend to be characterized by a certain sameness. We spend our time doing much the same sort of things, day after day, even year after year. However much we try to introduce variety, interest, and excitement into our lives, we settle into routines; patterns of one kind or another develop; at the very least we all have to perform all sorts of ordinary human functions – getting dressed, eating, defecating, sleeping – day after day. And we have a sense that our experience of the things we do every day or every week is just the same every time. Of course we know that this is not really the case. We may be washing up the same dishes every day, but we don't wash them in exactly the same circumstances. Each time we wash the dishes is a unique, unrepeatable occasion. Every time we meet a friend – even if we see them every day – it is really for the first time. Every moment of our lives is unique.

Unfortunately, it is all too easy to forget this. We tend to feel that we are doing the same old things in the same old way, day in, day out. Routine and habit seem to drive all the freshness and spontaneity out of life. This can happen not just in our everyday, ordinary lives, but in our spiritual lives as well. Spiritual life is all about change, development, growth. We know that every time we meditate, for instance, it is a completely new experience. We know that it is not even just a question of every time. There is only ever just one time. Each experience, by its very nature, is unrepeatable. This perception of the uniqueness of our experience is what in the Buddhist tradition is known as 'beginner's mind'. But if we are honest we have to admit that we don't always experience this beginner's mind, that our spiritual practice can feel just as flat, dull, and stale as everything else.

If we are beset by this kind of spiritual ennui, it is vital that we shake it off, that we get completely away from any feeling that life – even spiritual life – is dull and boring. From time to time we need to let go of what seems ordinary, safe, comprehensible, and allow ourselves to experience – at least in imagination – some other universe, some other dimension of being, some other system of things. The answer, we may find, is to enter, from time to time, the mysterious world of a Mahāyāna *sūtra*. We can, if we choose, take a plunge into the unfamiliar, extraordinary – even bizarre – world of a work like the *Vimalakīrti-nirdeśa*, a world where all the familiar landmarks are removed, a world where we may feel that we are being turned completely upside-down.

The *Vimalakīrti-nirdeśa* contains pieces of straightforward doctrinal exposition which touch upon some of the most profound philosophical themes of Buddhism. It also contains passages of lavish description, including descriptions of all sorts of magical feats and happenings. It contains poetry, even poetry in the formal sense of the term. It contains elements of biography and autobiography and reminiscence, and even episodes of high drama – together with quite a bit of humour. Altogether it is an exuberant and complex work, surprisingly so when one considers how short it is. It consists of only fourteen quite brief chapters – the English translation is just about one hundred pages. It is no longer than a long short story, yet it brings together quite a number of very important themes.

Before we take our first step into this rich and strange world, a few words of explanation about the origin of the text are probably in order. It is, to begin with, a Mahāyāna text. The Sanskrit word *mahāyāna* means simply 'the great way' (*mahā*, 'great', and *yāna*, 'way'). So the Mahāyāna is that form of Buddhism which sets no limit whatever upon the spiritual potential of the individual. It encourages all living beings without exception to aim at the highest conceivable – even the highest inconceivable – goal of the spiritual life: supreme perfect Enlightenment.

One who aims at this supreme perfect Enlightenment not only for their own sake but for the benefit of all beings is known as a bodhisattva, a being (*sattva*) dedicated to Awakening (*bodhi*). To put it very simply, you could say that for the Mahāyāna the bodhisattva is the ideal Buddhist. It's what every Buddhist would like to become. And you become a bodhisattva by developing in yourself those qualities which will give rise to what is called the *bodhicitta*: the urge or will to Enlightenment. The path of the bodhisattva begins when you take the four great vows:

> However innumerable beings are, I vow to save them;
> However inexhaustible the passions are, I vow to extinguish them;
> However immeasurable the Dharmas are, I vow to master them;
> However incomparable the Buddha-truth is, I vow to attain it.[298]

These magnificent, awe-inspiring vows may seem like a tall order, to say the least. What we have to understand here is that there is not really any question of our ordinary limited self taking these vows as though it were making them part of itself. It is more that, in taking the vows, the ordinary self opens itself up to the forces of Wisdom and Compassion which they represent, allowing itself to be inspired and transformed by them, allowing Wisdom and Compassion to work through it. So these four great vows express the essential spirit of the tradition out of which this *sūtra* emerged.

The word *sūtra* means simply 'thread', especially in the sense of a connecting thread. In the Buddhist context, *sūtras* are a particular type or class of Buddhist canonical text, so called because they usually deal with a number of different topics in a more or less connected fashion. So prominent is this class of text within the Buddhist canon that the '*sūtras*' have become almost synonymous with what in the West we tend to call the Buddhist scriptures.

However, it is a little misleading to think of these texts as 'scriptures'. The word 'scripture' literally means something written down, but the *sūtras* were not originally preserved in written form. The Buddha himself, as far as we know, never wrote anything at all. As he travelled around north-eastern India, meeting people and teaching them, he communicated entirely by means of the spoken word. He communicated the Dharma orally, face to face, directly – as much of it as his listeners could assimilate, as much of it as they could bear.

And those who came into contact with him remembered what he had said. Sometimes it made a tremendous impression upon them, sometimes it brought about a turning point in their lives, so how could they forget it? It was burned into their hearts, into their minds, into their very being. And as they put the teachings into practice, they absorbed them, became one with them, learned them by heart. In time the Buddha's followers attracted their own disciples, and taught them in the same way – by word of mouth. Their disciples in turn carried on the oral tradition, and in this way the Buddha's teaching was handed down orally in India for several centuries, until it was eventually committed to writing – not all at once, but bit by bit over several hundred years. It is this oral tradition – in written form – which constitutes Buddhist canonical literature. Some *sūtras* are still extant in the original Pāli or Sanskrit languages in which they were first written down, but others are known to us only through ancient Chinese and Tibetan translations.

Broadly speaking, then, a Mahāyāna *sūtra* is a canonical text in which the Buddha is represented as teaching, directly or indirectly, the bodhisattva ideal, the ideal of supreme perfect Enlightenment for the benefit of all living beings. There are hundreds, perhaps thousands, of Mahāyāna *sūtras* in existence: the *Perfection of Wisdom sūtras*, which include the well-known *Diamond Sūtra* and *Heart Sūtra*, the *White Lotus Sūtra*, the *Sūtra of Golden Light*, and many others.

The *Vimalakīrti-nirdeśa*, although a Mahāyāna text, cannot really be counted among these *sūtras*, inasmuch as it is not quite a *sūtra* in the usual sense. In Sanskrit it is not actually called a *sūtra* at all, and in the Chinese translations it is called a *jing*. *Jing* is the usual translation of '*sūtra*' in Chinese, but the term originally meant 'classic' in the literary sense. The Sanskrit title of the work is simply *Vimalakīrti-nirdeśa*, which means 'the teaching' – or exposition or instruction – 'of Vimalakīrti'. Vimalakīrti's name means something like 'Stainless Glory', 'Immaculate Fame', or 'Pure Repute', and he is represented as a Buddhist layman living in the northern Indian city of Vaiśālī at the time of the Buddha.

The point is that it is Vimalakīrti who does most of the teaching in this work, not the Buddha (that is, Śākyamuni Buddha) himself. If a *sūtra* is defined as a discourse by the Buddha, there are clear grounds for not giving this title to the *Vimalakīrti-nirdeśa*. However, Śākyamuni does appear in the text at several points, especially the beginning and the end, he does teach, and he does as it were adopt the work at the end. Perhaps, therefore, there is another reason for dispensing with the term *sūtra*. Perhaps it is that '*sūtra*', like 'scripture', suggests something spiritually authoritative. In fact, of course, it does no such thing: 'spiritually authoritative' is really a contradiction in terms. The Buddhist scriptures – as we call them in English – do not, like the Bible, constitute some infallible revelation from God. They are a record of the life and teaching of a supremely and perfectly Enlightened human being, a human being who was the living embodiment of absolute Wisdom and infinite Compassion. None the less, some people probably do read a *sūtra* as though it *were* Holy Writ, and feel that they have no choice but to accept whatever the Buddha says in it, whether they like it or not; and such a projection of authority may create in them some resistance to the *sūtra*'s message.

But if a particular text is not actually labelled a *sūtra*, we can avoid the mistake of regarding it as 'spiritually authoritative'. We can read it, in fact, more or less as we would read any other work of the imagination – a novel, a poem, or a short story. If we can read Buddhist texts as literature rather than dogma, as poetry rather than scientific fact or philosophical truth, we may perhaps be more open to their spiritual message. We may even allow ourselves to be captivated – at least a little – by their atmosphere and their magic. (Conversely – this is just a thought – we might try reading works of imagination as though they were *sūtras*, and in this way open ourselves to their real spiritual content. Such a thought suggests a more profound conception of the imagination than we usually have.)

What I am getting at is that *sūtras* can be approached as sources of inspiration and enjoyment, not as texts that you have to slog your way through because you happen to be a Buddhist. You may have to put in some additional study and reflection – it may take some time and many readings to understand a *sūtra* deeply and really appreciate it – but some phrases or images may affect you quite powerfully straight away. It is true that we may well feel more at home with Western literature. Most of it is easier to read because it has been written by unenlightened people like ourselves – with all sorts of little glimmers of insight here and there – and it deals generally with ordinary human predicaments with which we can easily identify. But human frailty is not the only possible subject for literature; it is certainly not always the most inspiring and uplifting one. We can also read literature which takes us away from our ordinary human life and its frailties. And this is what the Mahāyāna *sūtras* are all about – to take us away from the ordinary, to give us a taste of the magical.

Obviously it is difficult to rise to that level of experience, so it's going to be difficult to read *sūtras*, just as it is to read some of the great works of Western literature. Any work of literature has an effect commensurate with the effort one makes to understand it. It is really a matter of getting into the habit of stretching oneself a bit. If you have a strong enough desire to understand, you will make the effort. This is why translations like Robert A. F. Thurman's version of the *Vimalakīrti-nirdeśa* are so valuable. If the language is beautiful, you can read and enjoy a text even though you don't fully understand it. It is as though the beauty of the language has its own value. One can read and enjoy the Authorized Version of the Bible, for instance, without believing a word of it. The Authorized Version was gradually shaped out of several earlier translations; no doubt more attractive versions of the Mahāyāna *sūtras* will emerge in a similar way.

We know that the *Vimalakīrti-nirdeśa* is one of the older Mahāyāna *sūtras*, but we do not know when it was first written down, because the Indian scribes did not date their work. They were not historically and chronologically minded. With the Chinese, however, it was another matter. When they translated Buddhist texts from Sanskrit into Chinese, they recorded not only the name of the translator, together with that of whoever assisted him and the place where he was working, but also the day of the week and the month and the year when he started, and the precise date when he finished as well. The *Vimalakīrti-nirdeśa* must have been a very popular text in China because in the course of the centuries some seven Chinese translations were made, among them versions by Kumārajīva and Xuanzang, the two greatest translators of Buddhist texts to appear in the entire practically two-thousand-year history of Chinese Buddhism.

Kumārajīva's version is remarkable, as are all his versions of Buddhist texts, especially of Mahāyāna *sūtras*, for its fidelity to the spirit of the original and its great literary beauty. Xuanzang's version, on the other hand, is impressive in its scholarly accuracy and precision. Kumārajīva's version has always been by far the more popular of the two. One complete Tibetan translation is also extant, as well as fragments of translations in various Central Asian languages. The original Sanskrit text of the *Vimalakīrti-nirdeśa* has unfortunately been lost apart from a few short passages which are quoted in Indian Buddhist writings of a later period, for instance Śāntideva's *Śikṣā-samuccaya* and Kamalaśīla's *Bhāvanā-krama*.

In recent times the *Vimalakīrti-nirdeśa* has been translated into a number of modern languages, both Eastern and Western. There are several versions in English, three of which are at present available. We thus have plenty of material in English for the study of this very important text, one of the most fascinating, readable, and inspiring of all Mahāyāna *sūtras*.

The three English versions current are by Charles Luk, Étienne Lamotte (his French translation having been rendered into English by Sara Boin), and Robert Thurman. Luk's version, based on Kumārajīva, is perhaps the most traditional of the three, in the strict sense of the term 'traditional'. Lamotte's, based on the Tibetan version and on Xuanzang, is the most scholarly in the academic sense. Thurman's version, the most recent, based mainly on the Tibetan, comes somewhere in between and I would say above these two. It is both traditional and scholarly in the best sense of these terms, but at the same time scholarship has been subordinated to the needs of spiritual understanding. Thurman has also taken great pains with the literary style. The result is almost a model version of an English translation of a Mahāyāna *sūtra*: traditional, scholarly, and also very readable – a rare combination of qualities, as you will know only too well if you have ploughed your way through more indigestible English translations of Buddhist texts. Reading Thurman's version of the *Vimalakīrti-nirdeśa* is not only a spiritual experience but also a literary one. It is this translation, for the most part, that I will be using as my source text.

The *Vimalakīrti-nirdeśa* has several alternative titles, the most important of which is *Acintya-vimokṣa*, the 'inconceivable emancipation'. It is in terms of emancipation that the goal of the spiritual life has been envisaged in Buddhism from the most ancient times down to the present day: emancipation from craving, from hatred, from delusion, from all that conditions and confines us, from all that distorts our deepest creativity, from all that prevents us from becoming Enlightened. This experience of spiritual emancipation, of absolute liberation, of total freedom, is what the Buddha's teaching is all about, and what essentially it has always been all about.

Vimokṣa is one of a whole group of similar terms very prominent in early Buddhism. In addition to *vimokṣa* and *mokṣa* (Pāli: *vimokkha* and *mokkha*), there are also *vimukti* and *mukti* (Pāli: *vimutti* and *mutti*). (The prefix *vi-* acts as an emphatic in Pāli and Sanskrit.) They all have the same general sense of emancipation, liberation, or freedom, and they are words which occur over and over again in Pāli and Sanskrit texts.

In a well-known passage in the *Udāna*, the 'Verses of Uplift', the Buddha says that just as, wherever you take the water from, the mighty ocean has but one taste, the taste of salt, in the same way his teaching – whether you take the four noble truths, the Noble Eightfold Path, the six *pāramitās*, conditioned co-production, *śūnyatā*, or whatever – has but one taste: the taste of freedom.[299]

According to another well-known formula, there are four stages of spiritual development: morality, or uprightness; concentration and meditation, or higher consciousness; transcendental wisdom, or insight into reality; and emancipation. (Here again the term used is *vimutti*.)

Vimutti is also the penultimate stage of the Spiral Path, the spiritual path described in terms of the twelve positive links. Here freedom arises in dependence upon dispassion, a state of complete spiritual serenity or imperturbability. Dispassion in turn arises in dependence upon disentanglement from worldly concerns, which is itself consequent upon the attainment of 'knowledge and vision of things as they really are'. In terms of the Spiral Path, therefore, freedom is again consequent upon Insight.[300]

Sometimes freedom is spoken of as being twofold. *Ceto-vimukti* is the emancipation of the heart, complete freedom from all subjective, emotional, and psychological biases. *Prajñā-vimukti* is the emancipation that comes from wisdom: freedom from all wrong views, all ignorance, all opinions. This twin freedom, of heart and mind, is the summit of human experience.

Then there is the teaching of the eight *vimokṣas*, the eight emancipations or 'releases'. These represent successively more refined levels of meditative experience, a movement from the realm of the senses, the *kāmaloka*, to the *rūpaloka*, the realm of form, or the archetypal realm, and eventually the *arūpaloka*, the 'formless realm'. The first emancipation is achieved when craving for this or that sense object arises and you reflect on the unattractive or repulsive aspects of that particular object. And when you continue to reflect on the unattractiveness of that object and thus craving does not arise, that's the second emancipation. The third emancipation is reached by way of more and more intense appreciation of the purity and beauty of the state of non-craving. Then fourthly, there's emancipation by way of the experience of the infinity of space, the experience of there being no obstruction, no hindrance, no limit in any direction whatsoever. Fifthly, there's emancipation by way of the experience of the infinity of consciousness. There's no limit to the mind, no limit to the higher consciousness. It can go on and on, like light, as far as it pleases. It need never stop; it has no boundaries, no limits. This is the fifth emancipation. And then sixthly, there's emancipation by way of the experience of 'no-thing-ness'. There's no experience that 'this is this and that is that'; those hard outlines are as it were dissolved. At the same time, paradoxically, you see things more distinctly, clearly, and vividly than ever, but not as separate, isolated, mutually exclusive things, whether material, mental, or spiritual. And then seventhly, there's emancipation by way of the experience of neither perception nor non-perception. There's no object in the ordinary sense and therefore no subject in the ordinary sense, so there's no subject–object duality in the ordinary sense. You have begun to transcend that sort of division. It isn't completely transcended by any means – in fact it hasn't yet been transcended at all – but you no longer see things so rigidly in terms of a subject here and an object, or a world of objects, out there. This is the seventh emancipation. And then eighthly comes the emancipation by way of the perfect cessation of all suffering, the perfect cessation of the purely conditioned, reactive mind, and the release of total creativity: in other words, Enlightenment. The fourth to seventh emancipations correspond to the four *arūpa* (formless) *dhyānas*, and the eighth emancipation corresponds to Enlightenment itself.[301]

Yet another way of describing emancipation is in terms of the three *vimokṣa-mukhas*, or doors to emancipation (also known as the three *samādhis*). These are three different approaches to the realization of the Unconditioned. According to Buddhist tradition, conditioned, mundane existence has three primary characteristics: that is, it is unsatisfactory, impermanent, and insubstantial. Having developed the profound wisdom which penetrates one of these three characteristics – so that you really *see* the unsatisfactoriness, impermanence, and insubstantiality of things – you attain the corresponding emancipation, which gives you a way in, a doorway, to the Unconditioned.[302]

These are just some of the ways in which the Buddhist tradition has expressed the dimension of spiritual experience which it calls *vimokṣa*. But *acintya* means 'inconceivable' or 'unthinkable'; it also suggests 'inexpressible', even 'ungraspable'. The *acintya-vimokṣa* or 'inconceivable emancipation' is an emancipation which is particular to the Buddhas and irreversible bodhisattvas, and that is really all we can say about it. Because it is inconceivable, it is also inexpressible.

We can go further than that. We can say that *all* emancipations, to the extent that they are emancipations, are inconceivable. Indeed, emancipation is always emancipation *from* something – the term has no meaning except in relation to a previous state of bondage or imprisonment. And when we have always been in a particular state we cannot really imagine what emancipation from it is like. Indeed, when we have always been in a state of imprisonment, we cannot really get any sense of how imprisoned we are. We may even think that we are not imprisoned at all. We realize the extent to which we were imprisoned only when we have attained release from that imprisonment. If we cannot understand how imprisoned we are, by this and by that, we have little chance of being able to imagine what the state of emancipation from that imprisonment would be like. It is simply inconceivable to us.

We often speak of higher spiritual experience – or even Nirvāṇa – as if we knew all about it. But we don't. In fact, we don't really know anything about it at all. We cannot even conceive of it. And it is important to remember this. It means that as we progress in the spiritual life, we are going forward into the unknown. Commitment to the spiritual life is commitment to the unknown. Emancipation, spiritual emancipation, is always emancipation from the known; and the attainment of emancipation is always attainment of the unknown, the unpredictable, the unforeseen, even the unforeseeable. Every emancipation is therefore inconceivable.

But the inconceivable emancipation of the Buddhas and bodhisattvas is inconceivable – according to the Mahāyāna – in a special and deeper sense. The Mahāyāna, like the Hīnayāna, sees existence not statically, but dynamically; not in terms of entities, but in terms of processes; not in terms of fixed solid unchanging 'things', but in terms of what are called *dharmas* – an untranslatable term which means something like 'phenomena'. According to the Mahāyāna – and this is where it differs from the Hīnayāna – these *dharmas* are in the ultimate sense neither existent nor non-existent. 'Existent' and 'non-existent' are only ideas of our own mind. Because they are neither existent nor non-existent, they naturally neither appear nor disappear. Suffering, for instance, doesn't really appear, and it doesn't really disappear.[303]

Dharmas are thus peaceful from the beginning, and by nature completely – to coin a rather ungainly word – 'Nirvanized'. We are accustomed to thinking of Nirvāṇa – Enlightenment – as a noun, as representing a state rather than a process, but it does appear in a verbal form in both Pāli and Sanskrit. Obviously a verb describes action, and action takes place in time, but 'Nirvanization' is not a process taking place in time. It represents the fact that all *dharmas* are in a state of not being affected in reality by either arising or ceasing. But this does not mean that Enlightenment is something static. In short, we really have no words for this state of affairs.

Moreover, because *dharmas* are neither existent nor non-existent, they have no separate characteristics by which they can be distinguished or recognized. Because they have no separate characteristics, they are inconceivable and inexpressible. All *dharmas* are therefore the same – or rather, to avoid giving any impression that Buddhism teaches some sort of monism – not-different. Buddhism does not teach that all the phenomena of existence are reducible to one, whether to one absolute being, like the Brahman of the Vedantic tradition or the 'substance' of Spinoza, or to one matter. Buddhism therefore speaks in terms of 'not-different' or 'not-two' (the Sanskrit is *advaya*) rather than 'the same' or 'one'. We need to avoid any suggestion that the concept of sameness is being reified.[304] Indeed, for the Mahāyāna there can be no question of the reification of any of these terms. Yes, all *dharmas* are 'void of self-nature', as it is expressed; but this voidness is not itself an entity. Voidness is also void.

It is not, I need hardly say, easy to understand this. The inconceivable emancipation really is inconceivable. Not only that. The bodhisattva sees that existence itself is inconceivable. It is not just that we don't know anything about higher spiritual experiences or Nirvāṇa; we don't really know anything about anything at all. It's not that we don't know very much, or that we don't know it very well. This statement is to be taken quite literally: we don't know anything about anything.

But, of course, we think we know, and on that basis we build up all sorts of thought-constructions, all sorts of ideas, attitudes, views, and philosophies. But according to the Mahāyāna these are nothing but delusions. We don't really know anything about anything. And this is something to reflect on from time to time. We are usually so sure that we know what's what. But just take a stone in your hand and feel it, just look at a flower or a tree, and you will see that they are inconceivable. A human being too is inconceivable – staggeringly inconceivable. And, of course, a Buddha, an Enlightened human being, is utterly inconceivable; a bodhisattva is inconceivable; Buddhism is inconceivable.

So here we have a paradox. The Dharma reveals the nature of existence – but if the nature of existence is inconceivable and not to be fathomed by thought, it cannot be uttered in words. Not only can we not *know* anything about anything; we cannot really *say* anything about anything. If the Buddhas and bodhisattvas see existence as inconceivable and the Dharma as inexpressible, how is it possible for them to say anything about it? How is the Dharma to be taught?

With this question we begin to get quite close to the strange world of the *Vimalakīrti-nirdeśa*. Even the Buddhas and bodhisattvas cannot really teach the Dharma in words; instead they demonstrate it through action, and in particular through magical action. According to Buddhist tradition, the Buddhas and bodhisattvas possess all sorts of magical powers. They can move things from place to place, create things, transform themselves into the likeness of anything they wish. Moreover, they can do all this on a cosmic scale. They can move whole universes, and play with space and time.

In chapter 5 of the *Vimalakīrti-nirdeśa*, for example, Vimalakīrti prepares for the visit of Mañjuśrī (the bodhisattva of Wisdom) and a great crowd of various beings by magically causing the contents of his house to vanish. When the visitors arrive, nothing is to be seen except Vimalakīrti lying on his bed, apparently ill. In the next chapter he has thirty-two-hundred-thousand lion-thrones transported from a distant Buddha-land so that everyone can sit down, and his house enlarges itself to accommodate them all.

In chapter 10 Vimalakīrti miraculously enables the company to see yet another of the many far-away Buddha-lands. All Buddha-lands have their own particular characteristics; in this one, everything is composed of fragrances, including the food, some of which is brought back by a messenger magically emanated by Vimalakīrti for the purpose. A single vessel of this food proves sufficient to feed everyone present, including the ninety million bodhisattvas who have accompanied it from whence it came. There is even some left over.

There are many more such happenings throughout the *Vimalakīrti-nirdeśa*. But why on earth does Vimalakīrti do this sort of thing? Why should he make his immediate surroundings invisible and far-distant Buddha-lands visible? Why should he go to the trouble of shifting lion-thrones and magical foodstuffs around? Why bother? All this 'materializing' begins to sound like the stuff of transcendental science fiction.

The simple answer is that in the world of the *Vimalakīrti-nirdeśa*, such magical acts are regarded as being demonstrations of the Dharma. After each magical occurrence the text tells us that many thousands or even hundreds of thousands of beings attain some higher state of spiritual insight, usually 'the spirit of unexcelled, perfect enlightenment' – that is, the *bodhicitta*. Their spiritual vision has been broadened and deepened by these magical acts. In chapter 6 Vimalakīrti explicitly states that the ability to perform such acts is an aspect of the inconceivable emancipation. The bodhisattvas who live in this emancipation, he says, thoroughly realize the relativity of space and time. They can put Mount Sumeru into a mustard seed without shrinking the one or enlarging the other. They can place all living beings in the palm of their hand. They can make a week seem like an age and an age like a week. They have the magical power to transform anyone into anyone and anything into anything.

The *Vimalakīrti-nirdeśa* is not alone among Mahāyāna texts in its attribution of a philosophical significance to magic. In the Mahāyāna, existence itself is frequently compared to a magic show.[305] But how does this square with the Buddha's well-known admonition to his disciples that they should positively refrain from performing miracles?[306] How can magical acts be regarded as demonstrations of the Dharma?

Magic was very popular in India in ancient times, as I believe it still is today. It seems that the Indians have always been rather good at it. Imagine, for example, a wandering magician walking into a village in ancient India one morning. (Perhaps he has left his magic carpet round the corner.) As he arrives, a drum starts to beat, and people begin to gather round, eager and expectant, waiting for something to happen. It's natural to be curious about such things. If a magician came down the street at this very minute, you would probably drop the book and go out to have a look – and rightly so, because you can read a book any old time, but you don't see a magical display every day of the week. In the ancient Indian village, the magician would no doubt start off by doing something quite routine, quite ordinary, the kind of thing that magicians are expected to do. He conjures up, let's say, an elephant. He repeats a certain mantra and instantly, in front of everybody, an elephant appears. There it calmly stands, as large as life: bulky body, flapping ears, waving trunk. People can see it, hear it, perhaps smell it, perhaps even touch it – or think that they can touch it. Maybe some people in the audience even get frightened and run away.

In the modern West we would probably call this a collective hallucination. But the Mahāyāna would point out that the elephant perceived by all those villagers is neither absolutely unreal nor absolutely non-existent. After all, you cannot easily deny the testimony of your own eyes. Everybody in the village knows perfectly well what an elephant looks like – and they have all seen one standing in front of them. Furthermore, it has had an effect, because some people have run away. But at the same time it is not absolutely real, not absolutely existent. The magician made it appear, and sooner or later he will make it disappear.[307]

According to the Mahāyāna, ordinary existence as we experience it is just like this. The *dharmas* are just like this. They are neither existent nor non-existent – not in absolute terms – so they cannot be said really to appear or really to disappear. They are just like the magical illusion. Existence is just like a great collective hallucination. The Mahāyāna also compares it to a dream, an echo, a mirage, a reflection, a ball of foam, and so on.[308] The point of all these comparisons is not that something which is not really there is perceived to exist, but rather that what is perceived to exist is not absolutely existent. Phenomenal existence arises in dependence on causes and conditions, so it is neither absolutely real nor absolutely unreal. 'Absolutely real' here means that which does not arise in dependence on causes and conditions. In terms of the older Buddhist texts, it is what is usually translated as 'the Unconditioned' – the *asaṃskṛta*, literally 'the incomposite', that which is not put together.

But even if everything is in a sense like a magical illusion, we still have to engage with it, because we consider it to be real. When the magician conjures up the elephant, people perceive it and even become frightened enough to run away. Their fright is a real experience – at least relatively real – and something has to be done about it. So the fact that your relative experience is, in a sense, illusory, doesn't mean that you ignore it. You experience it as real, just as the people who perceive the illusory elephant perceive it as real. They don't know that it is illusory. They don't know that their perception has arisen in dependence on the complex of causes and conditions (represented by the magician). Only when they see that there is no elephant there, absolutely existent in its own right, but only a phenomenon that has arisen in dependence on the volition of the magician, can they cease to act as though the elephant were real.

Continuing the traditional Buddhist line of thought, if you were Enlightened, you would perceive the elephant, but you would know that what you were perceiving was a magical illusion, so you would not react to it as you would if you were not Enlightened. Even if it charged towards you, you would know that nothing was going to happen, that it was only an illusion, so you would not try to get out of the way, or experience any fear.

But, to take this illustration a little further, if you were Enlightened and you saw a real elephant charging towards you, you would get out of the way, because you would know that your physical body was on the same level of existence as the elephant's. Even though both are illusory in the metaphysical sense, both are physical bodies. They exist within and belong to the same order of reality, and within that order of reality they can affect each other. But you would still not experience fear, because your mind would be attuned not to relative reality but to absolute reality.

In a sense, whether you are Enlightened or not, you see the same object, but you interpret it differently. For instance, things are impermanent, and it is obviously inappropriate to be attached to things that are impermanent. None the less, we do become attached; despite the fact that we 'know' that something is impermanent, we treat it as though it is permanent. And if you see or experience an illusion as an absolute reality and treat it accordingly, that gives rise to unskilful mental states. But if you were Enlightened, you would be fully aware of its impermanence, and would treat it as such.

Using the terms 'illusion' or 'illusory' when discussing Buddhism can create a lot of misunderstanding. The illustration of the magically-produced elephant is an illusion only when it is considered metaphysically, not in terms of ordinary human experience. There is an objective difference between an elephant that is actually an elephant and an elephant that is only an illusory elephant. This is where Mahāyāna Buddhism differs from the Hinduism of the Advaita Vedānta. Vedāntins would use the same illustration to try to show that the elephant conjured up by the magician doesn't exist in reality *at all*. For the Advaita Vedānta, the whole of phenomenal existence is like that; only ultimate reality exists.

Some Vedāntins might regard this as an unfair presentation of Śankara's teaching, but many Indian philosophers, including Sri Aurobindo, have taken it to be his actual view – a view which Buddhism would regard as being one-sided. We can see the difference in the positions of the two religions if we consider their usage of the term *māyā*, illusion. In the Advaita Vedānta, *māyā* indicates that which doesn't have any existence at all, but is pure illusion. But in Buddhism it indicates that which has a relative but not an absolute existence. And, of course, Buddhism goes further and says that, in the last analysis, there is no distinction between the relative and the absolute. It is not that the relative is merged into the absolute in a one-sided manner, as in the Advaita Vedānta; both 'relative' and 'absolute' are equally applicable and equally inapplicable to ultimate reality.[309]

So the Mahāyāna does not doubt or question our experience. It is not trying to tell us that nothing exists at all. What it questions is the ultimate validity of the conceptual constructions which we superimpose upon it. Where we go wrong is in interpreting our experience in terms of fixed, solid, unchanging things. This is why the *Vimalakīrti-nirdeśa*, and the Mahāyāna in general, regard magical acts as being demonstrations of the Dharma: because these acts are themselves an illustration of what existence is really like.

It is this magical atmosphere in which the events of the *Vimalakīrti-nirdeśa* unfold. One could spend a lifetime exploring the text and contemplating the vision it presents, but here we will be looking at just a few of its themes. To get an idea of the context in which these themes appear, however, we will begin with a brief survey of the whole work.

Although, as we have seen, the text is not strictly speaking a *sūtra*, it opens in typical Mahāyāna *sūtra* fashion, with the Buddha, surrounded by a great assembly of disciples, giving a teaching. On this occasion he is staying in Āmrapālī's Park,[310] on the outskirts of the city of Vaiśālī – Vaiśālī being where the historical Buddha gave a great many of his teachings. And the great assembly surrounding him is made up of all sorts of beings: *arhants*, bodhisattvas, as well as Brahmās, and various non-human beings – gods and deities of all kinds – besides monks and nuns, laymen and laywomen.

Just as the Buddha is about to start teaching, the bodhisattva Ratnākara arrives from Vaiśālī to visit him, accompanied by no fewer than five hundred Licchavi youths – that is, young men of the tribe whose capital was Vaiśālī – and each of these youths carries with him an umbrella or parasol. These are not to shield them from sun or rain: in ancient India parasols were not just utilitarian, but symbolized sovereignty, or even spiritual sovereignty. And like so many things in Mahāyāna *sūtras*, these parasols are made of the seven precious substances – gold, pearl, and so on. The Licchavi youths offer these five hundred parasols to the Buddha, and with his magical power he transforms them all into a single enormous precious canopy which covers the entire billion-world galaxy. In this precious canopy every single world and every single being within the galaxy is reflected. After praising the Buddha in a very beautiful hymn, Ratnākara asks him to explain how a bodhisattva creates and purifies a Buddha-land. We will be going into the Buddha's reply in our Chapter 2, 'Building the Buddha-land'.

In the second chapter of the text, the scene shifts to the city of Vaiśālī and we meet Vimalakīrti himself. He is a great bodhisattva, even a Buddha, but he lives just like an ordinary layman. He lives at home, seems to have a family, seems to have a job, seems to be like other people. But all this is simply his 'skilful means'. He outwardly adapts himself to people so that he can approach them and teach them the Dharma. And as part of his skilful means, he falls sick – or appears to fall sick. As a result, all sorts of people come to visit him, and he takes the opportunity of teaching them the Dharma. This will be the subject of our Chapter 3, 'On Being "All Things to All Men"'.

In chapters 3 and 4 of the text, we move back to Āmrapālī's Park, where the Buddha airs the suggestion that someone should call on Vimalakīrti and ask him how he is. He asks first the *arhants*, beginning with Śāriputra, and then the bodhisattvas, beginning with Maitreya. But they are all strangely reluctant to meet Vimalakīrti. They have, it seems, encountered him before, and, *arhants* or bodhisattvas though they are, he has treated them all to a very rough time: that is to say, he has ruthlessly exposed the inadequacies of their approach to the Dharma.

We will be going into this in our Chapter 4, 'The Transcendental Critique of Religion'.

In the next chapter of the *Vimalakīrti-nirdeśa*, someone finally agrees to visit Vimalakīrti. Mañjuśrī, the bodhisattva of Wisdom, says he will go, and together with many of those in the assembly he sets out for Vaiśālī. When he arrives at Vimalakīrti's house, he immediately enters into a vigorous dialogue with Vimalakīrti on the nature of emptiness and liberation. Each tries to give the other a real dialectical hammering, but they are very evenly matched.

Once this little transcendental sparring match is over, Mañjuśrī comes to the point and asks Vimalakīrti why he is sick. Vimalakīrti's reply to this question has become very famous. He says that he is sick because beings are sick; his sickness has arisen from great Compassion. He also explains at some length how a 'sick' bodhisattva should control his mind. Here and in later chapters, we find Mañjuśrī, a mythical figure, and Vimalakīrti, a historical personality, juxtaposed: myth and history face to face. This will be our theme in Chapter 5, 'History Versus Myth in Humanity's Quest For Meaning'.

Chapter 6 of the text deals, as we have seen, with the inconceivable emancipation itself. By his magical power, Vimalakīrti transports thirty-two-hundred-thousand thrones from the Buddha-land of the Buddha Merupradīparāja, which is innumerable Buddha-lands away in the eastern direction. All these thrones, which are apparently miles and miles high, are quite comfortably accommodated in Vimalakīrti's house – a magical feat that demonstrates the relativity of space. Space is only a concept, just as time is only a concept. Vimalakīrti then describes various other magical feats which the bodhisattva who lives in the inconceivable emancipation is capable of performing.

In chapter 7 Vimalakīrti explains in response to a question from Mañjuśrī how a bodhisattva should regard all beings. At this point, a goddess who lives in Vimalakīrti's house showers the whole assembly with heavenly flowers. The flowers that land on the bodhisattvas touch them and fall to the ground, but those which land on the *arhants* stick to them. Śāriputra tries, unsuccessfully, to brush them off; monks are not supposed to wear flowers. A dialogue ensues between Śāriputra and the goddess in which she demonstrates her deep understanding of the Dharma and explains the wonderful characteristics of Vimalakīrti's house.

In chapter 8 Vimalakīrti explains how to attain the qualities of a Buddha. For his part, Mañjuśrī then explains what the true family of the Buddha consists in. They both speak in highly paradoxical terms. After this, one of the bodhisattvas present enquires after Vimalakīrti's family. In India people always want to know all the personal details: who your father is, who your mother is, where they live, whether you are married, how many children you have, and so on, and so on. Vimalakīrti's reply to this questioning is in the form of a series of beautiful verses – indeed, one of the most beautiful passages in the whole work. He says that the bodhisattva's mother is the Perfection of Wisdom. The Perfection of Wisdom gives birth to him, nurtures and nourishes him. His father is Skilful Means. His wife is Delight in the Dharma. His daughters are Love and Compassion, and his sons are Righteousness and Truth. As for his home, that is meditation on the meaning of the Void. Vimalakīrti continues in this way for forty or fifty verses.

Chapter 9 deals with the question of non-duality. Vimalakīrti asks all the bodhisattvas present to explain their ideas about non-duality, which, in turn, they do. They then ask Mañjuśrī what his explanation of non-duality is. They have all spoken well, he says, but their explanations fall short in that they are all dualistic, whereas non-duality cannot be expressed at all. This statement of Mañjuśrī's is very profound, but he does not get the last word ... or rather he does. When he has spoken, he asks Vimalakīrti for his own explanation of non-duality – whereupon Vimalakīrti remains completely silent. This is the famous 'thunder-like silence' of Vimalakīrti. When we come to this incident in our sixth chapter, 'The Way of Non-duality', however, we will find at least something to say.

In chapter 10 of the text we come relatively down to earth. Śāriputra starts worrying about when everybody will be having lunch. After all, monks are not supposed to eat after twelve o'clock. (If you have never been a monk, you won't know how important this is.) Vimalakīrti knows what Śāriputra is thinking; he has that magical power too. And it is here that he conjures up a beautiful young bodhisattva, golden in colour, whom he sends off to a Buddha-land called 'Fragrant with all Fragrances' to get some food. This bodhisattva returns with a bowl containing fragrant ambrosia, and with him come ninety million other bodhisattvas who all somehow manage to squeeze into Vimalakīrti's house. The ambrosia, strange to say, provides more than enough to feed the whole assembly. In response to a question from Vimalakīrti, the bodhisattvas who have just arrived say that the Buddha of their Buddha-land does not teach the Dharma by means of sound and language. He teaches it by means of perfumes. This will be the subject of our seventh chapter, 'The Mystery of Human Communication'.

In chapter 11 of the text we return to Āmrapālī's Park, where the Buddha is teaching all those disciples who did not accompany Mañjuśrī on his visit to Vimalakīrti. While he is teaching, the whole park suddenly gets larger, and everything in it is tinged with a beautiful golden hue. We get the feeling that something is about to happen – and it does. No sooner has the Buddha told Ānanda that Vimalakīrti and Mañjuśrī are coming from Vaiśālī with their retinue than they all arrive. The Buddha proceeds to give a teaching, explaining that different Buddhas teach the Dharma in different ways, yet their Enlightenment and their spiritual realizations are all the same. He also speaks at length on the Emancipation called 'the Destructible and the Indestructible'.

In chapter 12, after Vimalakīrti has explained his perception of the Buddha, Śāriputra wants to know where Vimalakīrti comes from. He is told that the great bodhisattva comes from Abhirati – 'Great Delight' – the Buddha-land of the Buddha Akṣobhya in the eastern direction. The next thing is that everyone wants to see this marvellous land, so the Buddha asks Vimalakīrti to show it to them and, magically, Vimalakīrti does so.

In chapter 13 Indra, the king of the gods, praises the teaching of the inconceivable emancipation and promises to protect the Dharma. The Buddha then relates how he himself practised the Dharma in a previous existence, following teachings he received from the Buddha of those days, Bhaiṣajyarāja. Among these is the teaching of the four reliances: that one should rely on the meaning of the Dharma, not on the literal expression; on Wisdom, not on ordinary consciousness; on ultimate teachings, not on provisional teachings; and on principles, not on personalities. We will be going into these four reliances in our eighth chapter, 'The Criteria for the Spiritual Life'.

In chapter 14 of the text the Buddha entrusts this teaching of supreme Enlightenment to Maitreya, the future Buddha. Maitreya promises to protect and promote the Dharma, especially the present exposition, which he will ensure is widely taught, copied, talked about, remembered, and understood. All the bodhisattvas promise likewise, and so do the four great kings, the guardians of the four quarters of the universe. Ānanda, who thinks of everything, asks by what name this exposition of the Dharma is to be known. The Buddha tells him that it is to be called the Vimalakīrti-nirdeśa, and amid general happiness and rejoicing, the text closes. Everybody is overjoyed, uplifted, transformed; everybody has advanced on the path through hearing these wonderful things.

2
BUILDING THE BUDDHA-LAND

According to ancient Buddhist cosmology, space is infinite. And this infinite space is occupied by an infinite number of world systems, each existing on three planes: a plane of sensuous desire, a plane of pure form, and a formless plane. A thousand such world systems make up one small universe; a thousand small universes make up one middling universe; and a thousand middling universes make up one great universe. We could go on, but this should be enough to establish an overall cosmological scale of things.[311]

If the beings living in a great universe are fortunate, they may – whether they know it or not – also be living in a Buddha-land. A Buddha-land is the sphere of spiritual influence of one particular Buddha, one supremely, perfectly Enlightened being who is responsible for the spiritual welfare of all the living beings in all the world systems within that great universe, or even within several great universes. So not only do we have an infinity of world systems; we have also this idea of an infinity of Buddhas – or at least, if that sounds too outrageous, a plurality, a very considerable plurality, of Buddhas.

Not all great universes are fortunate enough to have a Buddha responsible for them. A Buddha is not some sort of god. He starts off as an ordinary human being, just like anybody else. What makes him extraordinary is his commitment to the spiritual life. He takes the bodhisattva vow, and follows the bodhisattva path for thousands upon thousands of lives, pursuing his spiritual career within the world systems of the particular great universe for which he will one day have spiritual responsibility. In the course of his bodhisattva career he comes into contact with an enormous number of living beings, whom he helps to the best of his ability. And eventually, after many, many lives of spiritual endeavour as a bodhisattva, he becomes, in his last lifetime, a Buddha.

The Mahāyāna tradition draws a distinction between a Buddha's sphere of knowledge, which is coterminous with the whole of conditioned existence, and his sphere of influence, his Buddha-land, which is held to be limited to one or more great universes. A Buddha's knowledge is unlimited because it is an inner realization, not dependent on or manifested through any particular form, however subtle or refined. But his influence on other beings who are by definition not on the same level has to be exerted through a particular form, a particular medium – and that medium is limited. A human historical Buddha – a *nirmāṇakāya* Buddha in the language of the Mahāyāna – has a physical body and physical senses, and his influence is communicated through those. The fact that he is embodied in that way limits his influence.

It is not always clear, however, whether the Buddha whose influence extends over so many worlds in the Mahāyāna *sūtras* is a *nirmāṇakāya* Buddha (a historical Buddha) or a *sambhogakāya* Buddha (an archetypal Buddha), or a Buddha somewhere between the two. What *is* clear is that a Buddha whose influence extends over many, many worlds is not as limited in his influence as a *nirmāṇakāya* Buddha in the narrowest sense – that is, a human historical Buddha. But however far the Buddha's influence extends, it has a limit, because it proceeds from a Buddha who is limited – limited, that is, with regard to his outward form, whether that outward form belongs to a lower or a higher level. It is only the *dharmakāya* which is unlimited, and it is therefore only on the level of the *dharmakāya* that a Buddha's knowledge has no limit. When the Buddha wants to communicate, when he wants to influence beings, he has to come down a step or two, in order to communicate through his human or archetypal personality with the beings on those lower levels. It is usually said that the *sambhogakāya* is that aspect of the Buddha which communicates with the bodhisattvas, but it is sometimes said that the *sambhogakāya* has two levels: on one level the Buddha communicates with advanced bodhisattvas, and on the other he communicates with other Buddhas. If you think in terms of other Buddhas, there is division, there is limitation; but if all those divisions and limitations are removed there is only the *dharmakāya*.[312] On that level there is no question of communication, there is no question of influencing. There is only a non-dual knowledge or intuition. Because in respect of his supreme, perfect Enlightenment one Buddha does not differ from another; in a sense all Buddha-lands are one Buddha-land.

The Mahāyāna does, however, distinguish between two kinds of Buddha-land: pure and impure. An impure Buddha-land is one in which all six realms of sentient existence are found: the realms of the gods, human beings, *āsuras* or anti-gods, hungry ghosts, tormented beings, and animals. In an impure Buddha-land the basic necessities of life – food, clothing, and shelter – are hard to obtain. It is difficult to hear the Dharma, and difficult to come into contact with Buddhas and bodhisattvas. In short, it is a place where conditions are not at all conducive to spiritual development, where it is difficult for living beings to evolve towards Enlightenment. Our own Buddha-land, in which our Buddha gained Enlightenment, is – and no doubt this will come as no surprise – an impure Buddha-land. It is described in the Mahāyāna *sūtras* as a dirty, disagreeable, dangerous place, and bodhisattvas belonging to other Buddha-lands are warned to be very careful when passing through it.

A pure Buddha-land is, of course, the exact opposite. Apart from Buddhas and bodhisattvas, it contains only gods and human beings. Food, clothing, and shelter appear spontaneously, without anyone having to work to produce them. The sound of the Dharma is everywhere, and everywhere you can come into contact with Buddhas and bodhisattvas. Conditions are perfectly conducive to spiritual development. It's a land where it's easy to follow the path to Enlightenment. The best-known example of a pure Buddha-land is Sukhāvatī, the 'Happy Land' or 'Land of Bliss', which is the Buddha-land of Amitābha, the Buddha of Infinite Light. There are lengthy descriptions of its great beauty in the three 'Pure Land' *sūtras*, which describe it entirely in terms of flashing jewels, brilliant lights, lotus flowers, music, and perfume. In the midst of Sukhāvatī the Buddha Amitābha, golden in colour (he is elsewhere depicted as a red figure), sits on a magnificent lotus-throne, flanked by his two chief bodhisattvas, Avalokiteśvara and Mahāsthāmaprāpta. Beings appear in Sukhāvatī, as they do in other Pure Lands, by way of apparitional birth or spontaneous appearance, not as a result of sexual union. And having appeared, they have nothing to do but enjoy being in the presence of Amitābha and his bodhisattvas, listen to his teaching, and develop spiritually in accordance with it.[313]

The distinction between pure and impure Buddha-lands is not, however, absolute. It is possible for a Buddha to transform an impure Buddhaland into a pure Buddha-land, and vice versa. Purifying a Buddha-land is, in fact, equivalent to building one. Of course, one might well ask why a Buddha should want to transform a pure Buddha-land into an impure one. One answer is that, as we shall see when we come to look at the first chapter of the *Vimalakīrti-nirdeśa*, people find it very difficult to live in a pure Buddha-land. Alternatively, it might be that a pure Buddha-land would be less helpful spiritually to people who need to mature than an impure one. The Buddha might 'create' an impure Buddha-land because that suits certain people better.

Both the question and the answers are based on the assumption that a Buddha literally creates a Buddha-land, whether pure or impure – which we shall find is not the whole truth. But if one thinks in terms of the Buddha transforming a pure Buddha-land into an impure one, it can be only as a skilful means for the sake of those beings who are not able to benefit for one reason or another from a perfectly pure Buddha-land. At the same time – and again, this is a point which will receive dramatic demonstration in the opening chapter of our text – it is said that in the ultimate sense all Buddha-lands are pure. The Buddhas see them as pure even if ordinary beings do not. It is also possible for a bodhisattva to create a pure Buddha-land in the midst of an impure Buddha-land. Vimalakīrti's house as described in chapter 7 of the *Vimalakīrti-nirdeśa* is a pure Buddha-land of this sort.

A Buddha-land is also known as a 'Buddha-field' (*buddha-kṣetra* in Sanskrit). A field is, of course, something in which seeds are planted and grow, so the suggestion is that living beings, the inhabitants of the *kṣetra*, are like plants to be cultivated, and that the Buddha is, so to speak, a great cosmic gardener. Indeed, the Mahāyāna texts repeatedly describe the Buddhas and bodhisattvas as 'maturing' or 'ripening' living beings – assisting them gradually, step by step, to spiritual perfection.

This sort of imagery is found very early in the history of Buddhism. Shortly after his Enlightenment, 'our' Buddha, Śākyamuni, had a vision of all people being just like lotus flowers at various stages of development: some sunk deep in the mud, others just beginning to rise up from it; some just buds, others half-open blossoms, and still others almost completely open.[314] Similarly in the *White Lotus Sūtra* the Buddha is compared to the sun, shining down on all beings alike, and his Dharma or teaching to the rain. Living beings are of course like the trees, shrubs, and other plants, and when the rain falls and the sun shines, they all grow and flourish in their own way.[315] The idea of the Buddha-land or Buddha-field uses the same kind of horticultural imagery.

The building and purifying of the Buddha-land is the main theme of the first chapter of the *Vimalakīrti-nirdeśa*. The chapter begins, as we have seen, in Āmrapālī's garden, the park which Āmrapālī, the erstwhile courtesan, donated, towards the end of her life, to the Buddha and his disciples. The text tells us that the Buddha was staying there with a great gathering of his disciples. There were eight thousand monks – all in their yellow robes, shaven-headed, and presumably with their begging-bowls ready. All of them were *arhants*, that is, they had gained Enlightenment on their own individual account. In traditional Buddhist art the *arhant* is usually represented as a wrinkled old man bowed down with age, sometimes with a staff. In addition, there were thirty-two thousand bodhisattvas, who are, by contrast, traditionally depicted as beautiful young princes, sixteen years of age. More than fifty of these bodhisattvas – including Mañjuśrī and Maitreya – are mentioned by name.

There were also many thousands of gods ('Brahmās, Śakras, Lokapālas, devas') and what we would regard as mythological beings and beasts of different kinds ('nāgas, yakṣas, gandharvas, asuras, garuḍas, kiṃnaras, and mahoragas') as well as ordinary monks, nuns, laymen, and laywomen. So, we are told, 'surrounded and venerated by these multitudes of many hundreds of thousands of living beings', and towering over them 'just as Sumeru, the king of mountains, looms high over the oceans', the Buddha 'shone, radiated, and glittered as he sat upon his magnificent lion-throne'.[316] So this is the marvellous, extraordinary setting for the whole work – the Buddha preparing to teach the Dharma in the midst of this fantastic assembly.

But before he can get started, he is interrupted by the arrival of the bodhisattva Ratnākara coming from Vaiśālī, just a little way distant. He is accompanied by no fewer than five hundred Licchavi youths – the Licchavis being the tribe of people whose capital was Vaiśālī – each carrying a parasol made of the seven precious substances. In Mahāyāna *sūtras* things are often made of these seven precious substances, usually enumerated as gold, silver, pearl, sapphire, ruby, emerald, and diamond (the list varies slightly in different texts).

As soon as they arrive, the youths salute the Buddha, and then, carrying their five hundred precious parasols, they walk round him seven times, keeping him all the time on their right – an ancient Indian way of showing respect often mentioned in the Buddhist texts. Having circumambulated the Buddha in this way, they offer their parasols to him, and by his magical power he proceeds to transform those five hundred parasols into a single precious canopy so enormous that it covers the entire billion-world galaxy. We are told that the contents of the billion-world galaxy are reflected in the interior of this canopy, so that all those present can look up into it and see limitless suns, moons, and stars, limitless heavenly realms, limitless Mount Sumerus, limitless oceans and rivers, limitless villages and cities, limitless people – and limitless Buddhas teaching the Dharma. The voices of all these Buddhas teaching can be distinctly heard echoing in the interior of the canopy. Naturally, the assembly is astonished and delighted at this extraordinary vision, and they all bow down before the Buddha.

Without suggesting that there is some allegorical, point-by-point interpretation of this sequence of events to be attempted, we can perhaps lay down a few pointers as to their significance. The five hundred parasols borne aloft, so brilliant and so colourful, surely represent the spiritual aspirations of those five hundred Licchavi youths – in particular their urge or will towards supreme perfect Enlightenment for the benefit of all beings. In other words, the parasols represent the arisen *bodhicitta*.

There are five hundred youths, and therefore five hundred parasols; so you might imagine that there would be five hundred *bodhicittas*. But the fact that the parasols are all offered to the Buddha shows us that the spiritual aspirations of the youths all have one and the same object: supreme perfect Enlightenment, as represented by the Buddha himself as he sits there. This shared aspiration acts as a unifying force. It means that their aspirations tend to converge, even to unite, to become one single aspiration. This is why the Buddha transforms the parasols into a single canopy.

But what is that one single aspiration? What does the great canopy represent? As long as we don't take the expression too literally, as long as we take it poetically rather than dogmatically, we can think of it as representing what may be called the 'cosmic *bodhicitta*'. And just as the entire billion-world galaxy is reflected in the canopy, the cosmic *bodhicitta* is aware of, and responsive to, the needs of all sentient beings. It is not collective; at the same time it is not individual in the ordinary sense. It belongs to a mysterious category for which we have as yet no word, a category which also includes the expression 'spiritual community'. This is the possible significance of this incident at a very high level, but we can also explain it in more ordinary terms. It could signify that to the extent that our spiritual aspirations have a common object, they will be united; and to the extent that they are united, they will be a force for good in the world.

After the offering of the parasols, the bodhisattva Ratnākara praises the Buddha in a series of beautiful verses: a *stuti*, or 'praising', or what we might call in English a 'hymn'. It is intensely joyful and devotional, full of admiration and reverence for the Buddha; but at the same time – and this is one of the extraordinary features of these Mahāyāna hymns, in fact of the Mahāyāna generally – it is profoundly philosophical in content. It starts like this:

> Pure are your eyes, broad and beautiful,
> like the petals of a blue lotus.
> Pure is your thought, having discovered
> the supreme transcendence of all trances.
> Immeasurable is the ocean of your virtues,
> the accumulation of your good deeds.
> You affirm the path of peace.
> O Great Ascetic, obeisance to you![317]

Then later we come to a verse which summarizes the philosophical paradox at the heart of the *sūtra*. Ratnākara says:

> All these things arise dependently, from causes,
> Yet they are neither existent nor nonexistent.
> Therein is neither ego, nor experiencer, nor doer,
> Yet no action, good or evil, loses its effects.
> Such is your teaching.[318]

At the conclusion of this hymn, Ratnākara asks the Buddha a question on behalf of the five hundred Licchavi youths who have accompanied him. Having taken the bodhisattva vow, they want the Buddha to explain to them the purification of the Buddha-field of the bodhisattvas. In other words, Ratnākara wants to know, and they want to know, how to set about building a Buddha-land.

The Buddha is quite pleased with this question, and he answers at some length. He says, to begin with:

> Noble sons, a buddha-field of bodhisattvas is a field of living beings. Why so? A bodhisattva embraces a buddha-field to the same extent that he causes the development of living beings. He embraces a buddha-field to the same extent that living beings become disciplined. He embraces a buddha-field to the same extent that, through entrance into a buddha-field, living beings are introduced to the buddha-gnosis. He embraces a buddha-field to the same extent that, through entrance into that buddha-field, living beings increase their holy spiritual faculties. Why so? Noble son, a buddha-field of bodhisattvas springs from the aims of living beings.
>
> For example, Ratnākara, should one wish to build in empty space, one might go ahead in spite of the fact that it is not possible to build or to adorn anything in empty space. In just the same way, should a bodhisattva, who knows full well that all things are like empty space, wish to build a buddha-field in order to develop living beings, he might go ahead, in spite of the fact that it is not possible to build or to adorn a buddha-field in empty space.[319]

He goes on to say that a bodhisattva's Buddha-field is a field of positive thought, a field of high resolve, a field of virtuous application, a field of the six perfections, a field of the four immeasurables, a field of the thirty-seven aids to Enlightenment, a field of the ten precepts, and so on. And he concludes by saying of a bodhisattva:

> His virtuous application is tantamount to his high resolve, his high resolve is tantamount to his determination, his determination is tantamount to his practice, his practice is tantamount to his total dedication, his total dedication is tantamount to his liberative technique, his liberative technique is tantamount to his development of living beings, and his development of living beings is tantamount to the purity of his buddha-field.

> The purity of his buddha-field reflects the purity of living beings; the purity of the living beings reflects the purity of his gnosis; the purity of his gnosis reflects the purity of his doctrine; the purity of his doctrine reflects the purity of his transcendental practice; and the purity of his transcendental practice reflects the purity of his own mind.[320]

At this point Śāriputra, one of the Buddha's chief disciples, who is present in the assembly, is troubled by a thought. Why should the Buddha's own Buddha-field be so impure? He even wonders whether it is because the Buddha's mind was impure when he created it. Reading his mind, the Buddha tells him that, just as the blind cannot see the sun and moon, however brightly they shine, so some beings cannot see the splendour of his Buddha-land due to their 'spiritual blindness', their ignorance. The Buddha-land is pure, but Śāriputra cannot see it.

The great god Śikhin then joins in the conversation, asserting that he himself sees the Buddha-land as equal in magnificence to the highest heavenly realms. Śāriputra replies that he sees it

> with its highs and lows, its thorns, its precipices, its peaks, and its abysses, as if it were entirely filled with ordure.

Śikhin replies:

> The fact that you see such a buddha-field as this as if it were so impure, reverend Śāriputra, is a sure sign that there are highs and lows in your mind and that your positive thought in regard to the buddha-gnosis is not pure either.

As if to settle the matter, the Buddha touches the earth with his big toe, whereupon the whole universe is seen as a mass of sparkling jewels, and the entire assembly, including Śāriputra, perceive themselves to be seated on thrones of jewelled lotuses.[321]

The Buddha explains to Śāriputra that his Buddha-field is always as pure as it now appears,

> but the Tathāgata makes it appear to be spoiled by many faults, in order to bring about the maturity of inferior living beings.

Furthermore, he says that

> living beings born in the same buddha-field see the splendor of the virtues of the buddha-fields of the Buddhas according to their own degrees of purity.

These two statements are, of course, contradictory. Do people see the purity or impurity of a Buddha-field because of how the Buddha makes it appear, or according to their own degree of purity? Both, the text would have us believe. In a way this contradiction runs throughout this particular aspect of the Mahāyāna. In the first case the Buddha-field objectively seems impure, and there is apparently no variation between the perceptions of the different beings who reside in it. To the extent that it is real as a creation, it really is an impure land. If it was unequivocally the case that the Pure Land consisted of the perception of the beings in it, that would imply that the Buddha creates the perceptions of other beings, which he does not. If he did, that would deprive them of all freedom and spiritual autonomy, whereas the implication of the second statement is that they have their own perceptions, which are not created by the Buddha.

It is a sort of koan, perhaps intentionally so. We should not try to explain the contradiction away; we need to meet it head on and admit that there is a contradiction. We should reflect on it and meditate on it from both points of view, and see whether that meditation results in a flash of Insight which enables us to reconcile the opposites, to rise above the contradiction. It may feel rather unsatisfactory not to be able to answer the question, but in fact it is deeply satisfying to find a real contradiction in a Mahāyāna text, a contradiction which cannot be resolved just by looking up one or two words in the *Buddhist Hybrid Sanskrit Dictionary*, but has to be meditated upon.

Having demonstrated the purity of the apparently 'impure' Buddha-field, the Buddha then returns the Buddha-field to its 'usual' state. As a result of all that has happened, the spiritual vision of large numbers of living beings is purified, and they attain varying degrees of realization. And so the first chapter ends.

It is possible that this chapter was originally a short separate work incorporated into the *Vimalakīrti-nirdeśa* at some point in its development. No more is heard of Ratnākara; and Vimalakīrti himself first appears at the beginning of the next chapter. Be that as it may, the chapter certainly constitutes an appropriate prologue to the main body of the text, setting the scene with its wonderful imagery and poetry, and its elements of magic and devotion.[322]

It also forms the background to the theme of the Buddha-land, which we will now consider in more detail. We have already seen what a Buddha-land is in terms of traditional Indian Buddhist cosmology. And we have also seen that the Buddha-land does not just appear. It is brought into being – built, even – by the bodhisattva, who in the course of his own spiritual evolution sets up the ideal environment for the leading of the spiritual life. It is the bodhisattva who 'purifies' the Buddha-land, as the text has it. Of course, a Buddha can create a Pure Land too, but generally it is a bodhisattva who does so; and he does so in fulfilment of his vow to attain supreme perfect Enlightenment for the benefit of all living beings.

I have been referring to the bodhisattva in the singular, but the text in fact suggests at several points that it is the bodhisattvas – plural – who purify the Buddha-land. So why is this? Can a bodhisattva not manage to build a Buddha-land on his own? Well, according to the Mahāyāna, an advanced bodhisattva is quite capable of purifying or building the Buddha-land single-handed, just as a magician is capable of creating a magical elephant through his own power. But what would be the use? Yes, you can create a Buddha-land and give people a glimpse of it. You may even be able to keep them in it for a little while. But you cannot keep them there indefinitely – not even if you are a bodhisattva. This is because they are not going to co-operate, they are not going to want to stay there indefinitely, or even for very long, because they will not feel at home there. They are not ready for it.

There's a little Indian story that illustrates this point, and it will perhaps bring us down to earth somewhat, but never mind. The story is about a woman who sold fish. She lived in a small village on the banks of a big Indian river, and every week she took her fish to the market in a big basket. Now, one week, for some reason or other, it took her rather a long time to sell all her fish. She decided that rather than make her way back to the village so late at night, she had better stay in town. Fortunately she found a flower shop still open, and the flower-seller was sympathetic to her plight and said she could spend the night in his shop. Indian flower shops don't sell cut flowers in bunches as Western ones do; they sell sweet-smelling garlands, and little bunches of sweet-scented flowers for the ladies to put in their hair. The fish seller lay down to sleep among all those sweet-smelling flowers, but she tossed and turned, and couldn't get to sleep. She couldn't bear the scent of the flowers – they were so sweet, so beautiful. In the end, she got her old fish basket, which of course smelled strongly of fish, and put it right next to her, right by her nose. And after that, she slept quite soundly.

We might laugh at the fish-seller's plight, but we ourselves are in much the same position. She felt uncomfortable in the flower shop among all those sweet-smelling flowers; but we would feel no less uncomfortable in the Pure Land. We could manage a short visit, perhaps a weekend, but eventually we would want to introduce some equivalent of her smelly old fish basket into the Pure Land. We would want to bring along some physical or mental distraction – perhaps our television, our motorbike, our record collection, our lover, or our office files. Then we would feel more comfortable, more at home. But then, of course, the Pure Land would no longer be the Pure Land.

So the bodhisattva cannot keep people in the Buddha-land against their will. In any case, that would be a contradiction in terms, because the spiritual life is essentially the autonomous life, the free life, the emancipated life. So what is the bodhisattva to do? He cannot create a Buddhaland by magical power and then hold people in it – at least, not for very long. They will soon start getting uncomfortable, and then – no more Buddha-land.

The answer is that the Buddha-land has to be a joint creation. It has to be built by a number of people – bodhisattvas and would-be bodhisattvas – working together. One of them may be more advanced than the others, may have more vision, may even be the first to attain Enlightenment and then help the others to take that final step. But all must be inspired by the same ideal, the ideal of supreme perfect Enlightenment for the benefit of all beings. They all therefore follow the bodhisattva path, follow it for thousands of lives – and all follow it together. This is a truly wonderful conception: the whole spiritual community being reborn together as a spiritual community, living and working together, helping one another, life after life, until the Buddha-land is established.

There is some reflection of this idea in the Pāli Jātaka stories, in which the Buddha's disciples – Ānanda, Yaśodharā, Sāriputta, Mahākassapa, even Devadatta – are represented as having been associated with him in many previous existences. On a more mundane level, a remarkable book was published in England a few years ago telling the story of a group of Cathars in southern France in the thirteenth century who were said to have been reborn during the Napoleonic wars, and again in the present century in Cornwall. In all these different lives they have been in personal contact with one another, and have tried to help one another in their development.[323]

But why does the bodhisattva – why do the bodhisattvas – build the Buddha-land? It would be easy to answer this question along straightforward traditional lines. We could say that the bodhisattva wants to help others by providing them with an ideal environment in which to develop spiritually. This is quite correct as far as it goes, but it only raises a further question. Why should the bodhisattva be concerned with others at all?

To answer this we have to go a little deeper. Should we devote ourselves to our own emancipation or to helping others? This question is crucial to the spiritual life. In the context of Buddhism it amounts to asking whether we should follow the *arhant* ideal or the bodhisattva ideal – envisaging these two ideals in their extreme, even mutually exclusive, forms.

In its extreme form, the *arhant* ideal is to gain emancipation for oneself alone without bothering too much about other people. The bodhisattva ideal, on the contrary, is to help others to become free without bothering too much about oneself. But the two ideals are not as contradictory as they may seem. Indeed, they cannot really be separated. You cannot really help yourself without helping others, and you cannot really help others without helping yourself.

We are social beings. (I won't say '*essentially* social beings' as this could be misunderstood to suggest that we have to have a 'social life'.) It is impossible to cut yourself off from other people for any length of time, even though you may cut yourself off from physical contact with them. You influence them; they influence you. If you develop emotional positivity, imagination, and insight within yourself, that has its effect on others; and if you work for others, give to others, sacrifice yourself for them, that has its effect on you.

So we cannot really separate helping ourselves from helping others, certainly not in the spiritual sphere. The *arhant* ideal and the bodhisattva ideal are inseparable. Carried to their logical conclusion, each includes the other. The bodhisattvas build the Buddha-land because they have no alternative. If you want to evolve spiritually, you have to evolve in free association with others. Blake says: 'Mutual forgiveness of each vice: Such are the gates of paradise.'[324] Similarly – though less poetically – we could say: 'Mutual helpfulness in leading the spiritual life: such is the foundation of the Buddha-land.'

And what do the bodhisattvas use to build the Buddha-land? The Buddha himself answers this question in his reply to Ratnākara: 'A buddha-field of bodhisattvas is a field of living beings.' In other words, a Buddha-land is built with living beings – that is, with living beings who want to evolve. As Hakuin says in his 'Song of Meditation': 'Outside living beings, no Buddhas.'[325] No living beings, no Buddha-land. In short, if you want to build a Buddha-land, you need people. In a sense, in fact, people are all that you need. It doesn't matter if you don't have buildings or money. If you have got people, you have got everything. And if you haven't got people, you haven't got anything.

This is true not only in building the Buddha-land, but at all levels of the spiritual life. If you want to have a spiritual community or a spiritual movement, you need people. If you want to hold a retreat or give a talk on Buddhism, you need people. It is not enough to have the facilities, not enough to have the teacher or the speaker. You need people – people who want to become true individuals, people who want to evolve.

At the same time, we should not take this metaphor too literally. The bodhisattva is not a sort of spiritual bricklayer, fitting people neatly into place with the aid of a bit of compassion for cement. People are not passive; people are not inert; people are not things. A bodhisattva can build the Buddha-land with people only with their co-operation – and co-operation means communication. So there is no question of the bodhisattvas literally building the Buddha-land with other people. In helping to build the Buddha-land, the 'other people' are themselves aspiring bodhisattvas – so the bodhisattvas really build the Buddha-land with themselves.

As to how the bodhisattvas build the Buddha-land, the Buddha answers this question too, when he says that a bodhisattva's Buddha-field is a field of positive thought, a field of high resolve, a field of virtuous application, a field of the six perfections, a field of the four immeasurables (friendliness, compassion, joy, and equanimity), a field of the ten precepts, and so on. Bodhisattvas build a Buddha-field to the extent that they develop themselves spiritually, to the extent that they practise the Dharma for the benefit of all. They purify a Buddha-field to the extent that they purify their own minds. Notice that the Buddha speaks of *a* bodhisattva here. This reminds us that the Dharma is to be practised by each of us individually, even though we practise in spiritual fellowship with others who are also practising. The Buddha-land is built by the bodhisattvas' united but individual practice of the Dharma.

We have seen that the Buddha-land is the ideal environment – envisaged on a cosmic scale – for the leading of the spiritual life. It is built by the united spiritual efforts of the bodhisattvas, and they build it because, if they want to be bodhisattvas at all, they have no choice. The spiritual development of one of them involves the spiritual development of all, and vice versa. The bodhisattvas build the Buddha-land with their own lives and by means of their individual practice of the Dharma within a context of spiritual fellowship.

But in a way this doesn't help us very much. It only leads to an even bigger question: what has all this to do with us? All the magic and splendour, all the deep metaphysical ideas, all the colour of this Mahāyāna *sūtra*: what has it to do with us? What have we to do with building the Buddha-land? A Buddha-land is, after all, something we can hardly imagine. It is built mainly by advanced bodhisattvas, beings we can hardly imagine, by means of a practice of the Dharma we can hardly imagine. So what has it all got to do with us?

To answer this question we have to come right down to earth. Or rather, we have only to come some way down to earth, because the question may be addressed, at least indirectly, by considering a field of human activity which, we may say, mediates between the world of higher spiritual values and mundane, everyday existence. This is the field of art and creativity.

One often hears people saying – sometimes apologetically, sometimes defiantly, sometimes wistfully, sometimes ironically – 'I'm not very creative.' What they usually mean by this is that they cannot paint pictures, write poetry, compose music, or throw pots. Artistic creativity seems to be in vogue these days; everyone is supposed to be creative. But what do we mean by being creative? Is it just a matter of being able to paint pictures?

Creativity involves a distinction between subject and object. On the one hand there is you, the artist; on the other, the material out of which you create your work of art, as well as the 'idea' in accordance with which you create it, an idea that may be more or less conscious. And the 'material' out of which the artist creates may be of several kinds. There's the obvious physical stuff out of which a work is made – clay, paint, sound, language, or whatever. Then there's the involvement of the artist's own person: the voice, the physical body, the mental and emotional states. And other people also become 'artistic material', either as merely passive material for the artist's creativity (like a sculptor's model), or actively co-operating with it, themselves creative in relation to the artist's creativity (like an orchestra or a cast of actors). In the latter case, there is no absolute distinction between the artist and the 'material' – the people – from which they create.

Generally we experience ourselves as subjects in relation to the 'object' of the whole external world in the broadest sense. But we are not passive in relation to the external world. We do not merely register impressions. The world impinges on us, and we also impinge on the world, on our own environment, or a part of it. We impinge on our own selves, on ourselves considered as objects to ourselves (that is, considered reflexively), and we also impinge on other people. Not only do we impinge on the world; we affect it in various ways. We alter it, we arrange it, we *re*-arrange it – at least to some extent, however slight. And not only that. There is a pattern to the way in which we impinge on the world. We don't impinge on it at random, but in accordance with a certain idea, a certain pattern, image, gestalt, or myth, within ourselves – even, we could say, a pattern which *is* ourselves.

It is rare for us consciously to realize this, but what it means is that our relationship with the world is essentially creative. We are creating all the time. Creativity is not limited to the exercise of the fine arts; everyone is creative. It is only a question of the quality of our creativity – greater or lesser success, greater or lesser clarity, greater or lesser positivity. We are creative when we speak, when we decorate a room, when we write a letter. This is the basic principle of what we may call 'applied Zen' – Zen applied to the art of living itself.

Zen is a well-known example of the application of spiritual realization to various otherwise mundane activities in such a way as to bring them into harmony with that realization. In this way, Zen is applied to architecture, to landscape gardening, to archery or swordsmanship, to flower arrangement, and to everyday manners and customs. The Zen approach, in which the human subject is creative in relation to its object, is akin to the building of the Buddha-land, in that it transforms various aspects of the world.

The extent to which it is possible to bring about such a transformation will depend on all sorts of factors: the material resources that are available to you, the nature of the environment, the degree of co-operation that you get from other people, and so on. Suppose, for instance, you want to apply the principle of Zen to the surrounding landscape. It doesn't depend just on your own personal inspiration or realization; you need the co-operation of other people, because they have as much responsibility for the environment as you. But in principle there is no reason why it shouldn't be possible to express your creativity in this large-scale way. It depends not only on how deep your meditation practice is, but on other quite mundane factors, even on worldly power. In the past, kings and emperors who have been sympathetic to Chan or Zen have been able to order the construction of many Zen-type gardens and buildings.

It is not, either, that your creativity always needs to take a particular kind of formal expression, but it always takes *some* kind of formal expression. The expression has to take a particular form, whether it be that of painting or poetry, architecture or landscape gardening, archery or flower arranging. If you don't have the power to construct a Zen temple, you can at least paint your room, or even just tidy it up. The way you eat your food, the way you set out your dishes, even the way you do the washing-up – all these can be the application of Zen to the art of living.

Art is a particularly appropriate analogy for the creation of a Buddha-land because it involves giving a harmonious external embodiment to an idea, which is what, in a very much higher sense, a Buddha or a bodhisattva does when he sets about building a Buddha-land. A Buddha-land is a sort of work of art. But the principle operates in everyone's life all the time, not just in the life of the artist, because all the time we all have an influence on our environment; we interact with the world, and that interaction can be negative and destructive or positive and creative. It is the positive, creative kind of interaction with the world to which especially we give the name 'art'.

Another close analogy to building a Buddha-land is the 'art' of statesmanship. The laying down of laws which make possible the development of a positive and harmonious society is certainly one of the arts in the broader sense in which we have defined the term. The lawgiver impinges on the world in accordance with a certain idea, a certain pattern, which he usually quite consciously realizes. One could therefore regard great statesmen and leaders as being essentially creative or as exercising a specifically creative function.

In most cases throughout history 'the masses' have been relatively passive, and their leaders have just issued orders sanctioned by force and fear. These situations have not therefore given the statesmen the opportunity to practise the highest form of such creativity. You could practise this only if you could enlist people's willing co-operation in the formation and enactment of laws and the creation of the kind of society that those laws made possible. Statesmen – whether individually or collectively – can certainly change society. Whether they change it positively or in a genuinely creative manner, is, of course, quite a different question. But we could speak of Zen and the art of statesmanship.

In Buddhist tradition, the *cakravartin-rāja*, the 'wheel-turning king', is ranked second only to the Buddha. Had the Buddha himself not decided to become a Buddha, tradition has it that he would have become a *cakravartin-rāja*. We are told quite specifically that the principal function of a *cakravartin-rāja* is to create or maintain a society in which the ten *akuśala-dharmas* are banished and the practice of the ten *kuśala-dharmas* (ten precepts) is encouraged. We could say that the Buddha works on a restricted section of society, primarily on the Sangha; but the *cakravartin-rāja* works on society as a whole – without of course being Enlightened in the way that the Buddha is.

We should not, however, confuse the essentially mundane activity of the *cakravartin-rāja* with, say, Amitābha's creation of Sukhāvatī. At the very least, Sukhāvatī is a transfigured material world, whereas the world of the *cakravartin-rāja* is definitely the ordinary, workaday world of society, economics, politics, ethics, and so on: the world of government in the ordinary sense. But the ruler performs essentially the same function, or engages in essentially the same type of activity, as the artist. His task may be more difficult, because he is having to deal with human beings rather than inert materials. It is comparatively easy to manipulate pigments and marble and words; but to create a particular kind of society by organizing the activities of human beings without restricting their freedom is extremely difficult. In fact, you would have to be something of a saint to succeed. People sometimes complain about organizations and the state without really considering what a difficult task government must be.

Ideally, of course, there would be no need for government, because we would all take responsibility for ourselves. If our relation to the world is essentially creative, the notable conclusion that follows is that the world – *our* world – is our creation. We create the world we live in. There is no question, therefore, of whether or not we should be creative, of whether or not we should create a world. We have no choice. The only choice we have is what kind of world we create.

The Tibetan wheel of life depicts six realms of existence which illustrate the kinds of worlds we can create for ourselves. We can create a world of the gods, a world of refined, sensuous, intellectual, aesthetic, but rather selfish, self-indulgent pleasure; or a world of human beings, a world of ordinary domestic, civic, political, and cultural obligations and activities. We can create a world of *āsuras* or anti-gods, a world of jealousy, excessive sexual polarization, over-aggressiveness, ruthless competition, and overt or covert conflict; or a world of hungry ghosts, a world of neurotic craving, intense possessiveness, and relationships characterized by extreme emotional dependence. We can create a world of tormented beings, a world of pain and suffering, of intense physical and mental distress; or a world of animals, a world of straightforward food, sex, and sleep.

But we need not feel bound to choose any of these worlds. There is another option open to us. Turning our back on the wheel of life altogether, we can begin to tread the Spiral Path that leads to Enlightenment. We can devote ourselves to developing as individuals, to the bodhisattva ideal. And in so doing, we choose to create another kind of world. In other words, we devote ourselves, directly or indirectly, to building the Buddha-land.

3
ON BEING 'ALL THINGS TO ALL MEN'

Over the past nearly four hundred years, the Authorized Version of the Bible has had a great influence on the English language, and many people still relish its turn of phrase. Being 'all things to all men' is an expression taken from the New Testament, from one of the letters of the apostle Paul to the Christians of the various cities he visited in the course of his travels. In several of these epistles, Paul refers to problems or disputes within those early Christian communities. Reading between the lines of his first letter to the Corinthians, one gets the impression that he feels he has to defend himself against some criticism. We find him saying, apparently by way of justification, that he has made himself every man's servant, to win over as many people as possible. To win over the Jews he has become like a Jew; to win over the Gentiles, the heathen, he has become like a Gentile. In short, he says, he has become 'all things to all men, that I might by all means save some'.[326] His strategy, in other words, is to relate to everybody on their own terms.

Being 'all things to all men' is what the bodhisattva Vimalakīrti excels at. The second chapter of the *Vimalakīrti-nirdeśa* introduces him to us:

> He was liberated through the transcendence of wisdom. Having integrated his realization with skill in liberative technique, he was expert in knowing the thoughts and actions of living beings. Knowing the strength or weakness of their faculties, and

being gifted with unrivaled eloquence, he taught the Dharma appropriately to each. Having applied himself energetically to the Mahāyāna, he understood it and accomplished his tasks with great finesse. He lived with the deportment of a Buddha, and his superior intelligence was as wide as an ocean. He was praised, honored, and commended by all the Buddhas and was respected by Indra, Brahmā, and all the Lokapālas. In order to develop living beings with his skill in liberative technique, he lived in the great city of Vaiśālī.[327]

The text goes on to describe Vimalakīrti's practice of the six *pāramitās*, the six 'perfections' of the bodhisattva: generosity, morality, patience, vigour, meditation, and wisdom:

His wealth was inexhaustible for the purpose of sustaining the poor and the helpless. He observed a pure morality in order to protect the immoral. He maintained tolerance and self-control in order to reconcile beings who were angry, cruel, violent, and brutal. He blazed with energy in order to inspire people who were lazy. He maintained concentration, mindfulness, and meditation in order to sustain the mentally troubled. He attained decisive wisdom in order to sustain the foolish.

We are then given a vivid picture of his way of life:

He wore the white clothes of the layman, yet lived impeccably like a religious devotee. He lived at home, but remained aloof from the realm of desire, the realm of pure matter, and the immaterial realm. He had a son, a wife, and female attendants, yet always maintained continence. He appeared to be surrounded by servants, yet lived in solitude. He appeared to be adorned with ornaments, yet always was endowed with the auspicious signs and marks. He seemed to eat and drink, yet always took nourishment from the taste of meditation. He made his appearance at the fields of sports and in the casinos, but his aim was always to mature those people who were attached to games and gambling. He visited the fashionable heterodox teachers, yet always kept unswerving loyalty to the Buddha. He understood the mundane and transcendental sciences and esoteric practices, yet always took pleasure in the delights of the Dharma. He mixed in all crowds, yet was respected as foremost of all.

In order to be in harmony with people, he associated with elders, with those of middle age, and with the young, yet always spoke in harmony with the Dharma. He engaged in all sorts of businesses, yet had no interest in profit or possessions. To train living beings, he would appear at crossroads and on street corners, and to protect them he participated in government. To turn people away from the Hīnayāna and to engage them in the Mahāyāna, he appeared among listeners and teachers of the Dharma. To develop children, he visited all the schools. To demonstrate the evils of desire, he even entered the brothels. To establish drunkards in correct mindfulness, he entered all the cabarets.[328]

So as he went about living his life in the great city of Vaiśālī, Vimalakīrti met everybody at their own level, in their own environment, and on their own ground. This is why I would suggest that Vimalakīrti was 'all things to all men'. This quality of being able to relate to people on their own terms is technically known as *upāya-kauśalya*, 'skilful means' or, as here, 'liberative technique', and the Mahāyāna attached such great importance to it that it came to be considered the seventh *pāramitā*, a seventh perfection for the bodhisattva to cultivate as well as the usual six.[329]

But why does Mahāyāna Buddhism hold skilful means in such high regard? To answer this, we need to consider again the situation of a bodhisattva creating a Buddha-land. We have seen that a bodhisattva may magically create a Pure Land – either literally or metaphorically – but even a bodhisattva cannot force people to stay in it if they do not feel at home there. The Pure Land has to be a joint creation, built by a number of bodhisattvas working together, a community of people inspired by the same ideal, the ideal of supreme perfect Enlightenment for the benefit of all.

Similarly, the bodhisattva, however sincere and well-intentioned, is not going to get very far if he approaches everybody in the same way or speaks to everybody in the same language – least of all if he tries to speak to them as a bodhisattva. People, as we realize more and more the older we get, are very diverse indeed. We all have our different backgrounds, our different conditioning. We have our different ways of looking at things, our different attitudes. We live in different circumstances, and we pursue different occupations and interests. We have different tastes and prejudices, and even different virtues.

To be effective – and a bodhisattva who is not effective is not a bodhisattva at all – the bodhisattva has to take all this into account. To communicate with people, you have to speak to them in their own language, literally and metaphorically. More than that: to be able to speak to them at all, you first have to establish contact with them. And to do that, you have to appear like one of them. You have to be 'all things to all men'. Vimalakīrti exemplifies this to a greater degree than any other figure in Mahāyāna Buddhist literature, with the possible exception of the Buddha himself. He appears among businessmen as a businessman; among government officials as a government official; among warriors as a warrior. Above all, he appears among laymen as a layman. Vimalakīrti's status as a layman has, however, led to some serious misunderstandings, which we will be looking at later in this chapter.

In reality, of course, he is quite different from other people; he is an advanced bodhisattva. But he doesn't make a point of being different; he doesn't insist on it. He doesn't appear among people proclaiming that he is an advanced bodhisattva, wearing his bodhisattva gear. He doesn't always have to appear nodding his three heads or waving his four arms, although this is very often the sort of thing people expect. They think that someone who is spiritually advanced will appear different from others in an obvious, striking, even peculiar or eccentric way.

Many years ago in Calcutta I got to know a religiously-minded Bengali lady. One day she told me that when she was a little girl, about seven or eight, her mother took her to see the 'Holy Mother', Sarada Devi. Sarada Devi was the consort of the famous Bengali mystic Sri Ramakrishna. She outlived him by many years, and was believed to be a very spiritually advanced person in her own right. My friend's mother told her that they were going to see a real *devi*. Now, in Indian languages the term *devi* generally means 'a lady', but it can also mean 'a goddess' or 'a spiritual woman'. So the little girl got very excited. She had heard and read so much about *devis*, but so far she had only seen images of them in the temples. Now she was going to see a real goddess at last, and she was looking forward to seeing a larger than life figure, probably breathing fire, and almost certainly having at least eight arms. When they got home from the visit, however, she complained bitterly to her mother. She said, 'You told me that we were going to see a real goddess, but all we saw was a little old lady in a white sari!'

Like the little girl, we are often unable to appreciate the fact that someone is spiritually advanced if they look more or less like anyone else. But this is how the bodhisattva appears. At the same time, just as he doesn't make a point of being different, he doesn't make a point of being like other people either. He doesn't act 'ordinary' in a self-conscious way. He is not like a liberal Christian clergyman who takes off his dog-collar, goes along to the local pub, and tries to behave like 'one of the lads'. The bodhisattva doesn't go around earnestly assuring people that he is just like everybody else.

The bodhisattva is simply himself. On the one hand, he doesn't behave in a special bodhisattva-like manner; on the other hand, he doesn't pretend to be ordinary. He *is* ordinary; but at the same time, he *is* a bodhisattva. He is himself. And because he can be himself, he can approach people and communicate with them in a natural, unselfconscious way.

The bodhisattva does not use a special technique – not even a 'liberative technique', which is how Thurman translates *upāya-kauśalya*. In his notes, Thurman says that he has chosen the word 'technique' in preference to the more usual 'method' or 'means' because it has a stronger connotation of efficacy in our technological world. This may be so, but I can't help wondering whether it connotes the right sort of efficacy in this particular context. It makes it sound as though the bodhisattva has some sort of trick up his sleeve, or as though he tries to 'win friends and influence people' in a rather slick, artificial way. Even the words 'method' and 'means' have that sort of connotation to some extent. But *upāya-kauśalya* is essentially a matter of being able to be with people, of empathizing with them, encouraging them to be open with you and to you. This is why the Mahāyāna attaches great importance to skilful means.

The Hīnayāna does not emphasize skilful means in quite this way;[330] although we can see the Buddha exercising this virtue in various ways – for instance, with Kisā Gotamī[331] – it is not named as such till we come to the Mahāyāna.

Skilful means, as the Mahāyāna sees it, has a broader meaning, in fact, than simply acting in a way that encourages people to be open with you. It can even include actions which appear to be unethical but which are in fact highly ethical on account of the underlying motivation; indeed, such actions could be said to be examples *par excellence* of *upāya-kauśalya*, because you are being so very skilful that you use even an apparently unethical action to fulfil a spiritual purpose.

This, of course, does not take account of what third parties might think of what you are doing. What makes the *upāya-kauśalya* skilful is its effect on the person towards whom it is directed. If it fulfils its purpose in an apparently unethical manner, it is more skilful than ever. But the bodhisattva has to take into account all the sentient beings in the environment, so he does have to consider the possible effects of his skilful means on observers. Having done this, he may decide to go ahead with the apparently unethical action for the benefit of the person towards whom it is directed, or he may not. But whatever he does, it will be a skilful means. He may, through supernormal powers, be able to make his action invisible to those who are not directly involved with it.

In the parable of the burning house in the *White Lotus Sūtra*, we find that the Buddha appears to feel he has to justify his action in promising the children three different kinds of cart when he knew that he was only going to give them one kind. He has to explain that he has not really told a lie. The reason he has to spell it out is that at the time the *White Lotus Sūtra* was produced, the term *upāya-kauśalya* apparently had an ambiguous meaning; perhaps the specifically Mahāyānic sense of the term had not been definitely established. This is speculation; but certainly in that parable the Buddha appears very conscious of the fact that his skilful means could be regarded as just ordinary trickery.[332] But eventually *upāya-kauśalya* came to mean skilful means in a purely spiritual sense.

Sometimes people use the term 'skilful means' as a rationalization for unskilful behaviour; this is of course to be avoided. We should use the term *upāya-kauśalya* only when we are talking about *upāya-kauśalya*, not when we are talking about our own weaknesses or mistakes. For instance, if in the course of discussion you become very angry with someone and lose your temper, you may say afterwards 'I'm sure it did him good – so I guess that was just my skilful means.' But really you are fooling yourself. We should be careful not to use the expression 'skilful means' as a euphemism for tricky behaviour; that debases the whole idea.

Very often disciples rationalize the dubious activities of their spiritual teachers in this way, and insist on regarding questionable behaviour on the part of the so-called teacher as being his 'skilful means'. They do this, presumably, because they need to keep up their 'faith' in their teacher. They say 'he could not have been angry' because they need to believe that he could not possibly ever get angry. One does find, particularly among some Western followers of Tibetan Buddhism, this very rigid belief – one can't call it faith in the real sense – in the integrity of their teachers which they are just not prepared to question or examine at all.

Traditionally, Mahāyāna Buddhism holds that the practice of skilful means consists essentially in three things: first of all, the four *saṃgrahavastus* or 'elements of conversion'; secondly, the four *pratisaṃvids* or 'analytical knowledges'; and thirdly, the *dhāraṇīs* or 'magical formulas'. We will go into each of these in turn; between them, they give a good idea of what skilful means is really about.

1. THE FOUR *SAṂGRAHAVASTUS* OR 'ELEMENTS OF CONVERSION'

'Elements of conversion' is the usual translation, but Thurman has suggested an alternative that brings out the real meaning of the term: 'means of unification'. Unification here is the unification of the spiritual community, or, as Thurman explains it, 'the four ways in which a bodhisattva forms a group of people united by their common aim of practising the Dharma'.[333] The point here is that the bodhisattva's aim in using skilful means – in being himself the skilful means – is not just to lead people to Enlightenment individually, but to enlist their co-operation in building the Buddha-land for the benefit of all.

(a) *Dāna*: 'Giving' or 'Generosity'

The first means of unification is that most basic of Buddhist virtues, *dāna* or giving. It is perhaps surprising to find *dāna* included as part of the seventh *pāramitā*; after all, it has a whole *pāramitā* to itself – *dāna* is the first *pāramitā*. But here it has a special function. In this context it is a means of establishing positive contact between people, of creating spiritual friendship, of helping to form a spiritual community.

We usually think of *dāna* in a more utilitarian way; we tend to give people something because they need it. But *dāna* in this context is not quite like that; at least, not in a narrow sense. You give people things because you like them, because you want to be spiritual friends with them, because you want to form a spiritual community with them.

Not, of course, that you give in a calculating way, to bring about those particular results. The whole process is completely natural, completely spontaneous. By giving someone a present, you give expression to your special awareness of them, your positive feeling towards them, your special concern for them. Giving is in fact a form of communication.

We could even say, as a general principle, that a spiritual community is characterized by the constant exchange of presents among its members. The exchange of presents strengthens the spiritual community. It is, indeed, a natural expression of the life of the spiritual community. These gifts are not given 'in return' for anything. You just naturally feel like giving to one another, and you express that feeling by the giving of gifts.

(b) *Priya-vāditā*: 'Loving Speech'

The second means of unification is another familiar quality among all those that the Buddhist seeks to develop: *priya-vāditā* or *priya-vacana* is enumerated as an aspect of Perfect Speech, the third limb of the Noble Eightfold Path.[334] *Priya* can also be rendered as 'affectionate', 'pleasing', or 'pleasant'. The bodhisattva establishes contact with people by speaking to them in an emotionally positive – that is, kindly – manner. Affectionate speech is therefore the rule within the spiritual community, among those who are engaged in building the Buddha-land. A bodhisattva is not afraid of giving expression to affection for others, or of letting other people know that he likes them. He is not even afraid of telling them to their face that he likes them – just in case there is any doubt about it. After all, some people find it difficult to believe that anybody actually likes them. It may even come as quite a shock. But it's important to understand what is really meant by affectionate speech. It doesn't necessarily involve going around addressing everybody as 'dear' or 'darling'. There's nothing wrong with terms of endearment as such – but I remember hearing a snippet from some drama on the radio and an American character saying, 'I'm going to kill you right now, darling.'

The word *priya* usually means 'love' or 'affection' in quite an ordinary sense. But here *priya-vāditā* is being practised by the bodhisattva as a means of helping to create the spiritual community, as an aspect of the seventh *pāramitā*, *upāya*. And the *pāramitā* which precedes *upāya* is *prajñā*, wisdom. It follows that for the bodhisattva 'loving speech' is an expression of transcendental wisdom. The love to which the bodhisattva gives verbal expression is not just love in the ordinary sense. It is not ordinary human affection or friendliness, still less sexual attraction or sentimentality or even plain gregariousness. In this context, love is an expression of spiritual insight, of the bodhisattva's delighted awareness of people's spiritual potential.

(c) *Artha-caryā*: 'Beneficial Activity'

The third means of unification is *artha-caryā*. *Artha-caryā* can be translated as 'beneficial activity' – that is, activity for the benefit of others – but it literally means 'doing good'. This is not at all to suggest that the bodhisattva is some kind of professional 'do-gooder', doing to people what he thinks will be good for them. Once again we have to look at the context. *Artha-caryā* doesn't mean doing merely what is of benefit in an ordinary, everyday, worldly sense. It means doing whatever helps people spiritually, whatever helps them to attain higher and ever higher levels of being and consciousness. The bodhisattva practises beneficial activity by sharing with people his own experience of the Dharma, sharing with them – in a word – himself.

This is not a matter of teaching the Dharma in the way that you might teach history or arithmetic. It is not simply a question of imparting information, although that may be involved. The bodhisattva teaches people by encouraging them to grow and develop. It has been said that inspiration is the single most important factor in the whole of the spiritual life. You may have all the information you need, you may have all the facilities and opportunities, but if you don't have inspiration, you are not going to get very far. So the bodhisattva benefits people by inspiring them, by sparking them off; by communicating to them the emotional positivity, the creativity, and the excitement, the sheer adventure, of the spiritual life. The bodhisattva is like a candle which lights thousands upon thousands of other candles – after which they go on burning on their own fuel. Not only that: all of them in their turn light thousands upon thousands of other candles.

(d) *Samānārthata*: 'Exemplification'

The fourth means of unification is exemplification. In other words, the bodhisattva's behaviour is consistent with his teaching. His teaching is the Dharma and his behaviour exemplifies his teaching. In a time-honoured phrase, he practises what he preaches (except, of course, that he doesn't preach). The bodhisattva is the living embodiment of all the qualities that he encourages others to develop. He inspires people to lead the spiritual life because he himself is inspired.

Here a difficulty arises – not so much for the bodhisattva, but for those of us who are still trying to become bodhisattvas. We may have a vision of the ideal, a vision of spiritual perfection, even a vision of the Buddha-land, but we cannot live up to it. Sometimes, in fact, we fall very far short of it indeed. We sincerely believe in it, we are inspired by it, but we find it very difficult to transform our lives in accordance with it. In other words, we come up against that well-known divide between the Path of Vision and the Path of Transformation.[335]

But the discrepancy we feel between our vision and our ability to live in accordance with it need not prevent us from trying to communicate that vision. All that we really have to communicate – all that we *can* communicate – is ourselves. The key is simply to be as honest as possible. We can feel free to talk as much as we like about our vision and our efforts to transform ourselves in accordance with it. We can rejoice in our successes and, if necessary, confess our failures. We need not be afraid to be honest; we need not hold back because our practice is 'not good enough'.

In any case, the Buddhist vision is not of some fixed and finite goal. It is a vision of constant transformation, of ever-increasing creativity with no perceptible limit. When we exemplify our vision, this is what we really exemplify. Exemplification does not mean embodying a particular static point in the process of spiritual development, however high that point may be. It means embodying the process of spiritual development itself, to however limited an extent. What is going to come across is that, whatever point we have reached so far, we are truly making an effort to evolve.

2. THE FOUR *PRATISAṂVIDS* OR 'ANALYTICAL KNOWLEDGES'

The four *pratisaṃvids* are the second group of qualities in which the practice of skilful means consists. Like the *saṃgrahavastus*, they were taken over by the Mahāyāna from the Hīnayāna, and in taking them over the Mahāyāna modified their meaning in accordance with its own rather more altruistic outlook.[336] 'Knowledges' is not really a very satisfactory translation, as one of these four items is not a knowledge in the ordinary sense at all, and 'infallible penetrations', another often-used translation, does not help us much either. We can only really get some idea of the nature of the *pratisaṃvids* by going into them a little.

(a) *Dharma-pratisaṃvid:* 'Analytical Knowledge of Phenomena'

We need not take the idea of 'knowledge of phenomena' too seriously; another possible translation is 'analytical knowledge of principles'. It consists in the realization of the truth or the reality of things independent of any words or conceptual formulations. This is possible only if one has gone beyond words and conceptual formulations, only if one is personally in contact with the truth and reality of things.

According to the *Daśabhūmika Sūtra*, *dharma-pratisaṃvid* includes knowledge of how the different paths or *yānas* of the Buddhist tradition merge together.[337] Essentially the *yānas* are formulations of the Buddha's teachings in accordance with the needs of different kinds of people; in other words, the *yānas* themselves are skilful means. They all eventually meet together in one *yāna* because they are all concerned in one way or another with the same thing, with the spiritual development of the individual. The more individuals develop, the more they realize their unity with one another; and the more they realize their unity with one another, the more they realize that they are all following the same path. This idea of the *ekayāna*, the 'one way', is one of the fundamental teachings of another important Mahāyāna text, the *White Lotus Sūtra*.[338]

(b) *Artha-pratisaṃvid*: 'Analytical Knowledge of Meaning'

One might think that realization of the truth or reality of things is a considerable achievement – but it is not enough for the bodhisattva. The four analytical knowledges are all part of the seventh *pāramitā*, the perfection of skilful means; so the bodhisattva is going to want to communicate the truth or reality of things to other people, in the interests of their growth and development.

And if you want to communicate, you need a medium of communication. To begin with, you need a common rational framework. In Buddhism this is provided by the conceptual formulations of the teachings: the four noble truths, the Noble Eightfold Path, the five spiritual faculties, and so on. In other words, it is provided by what may be called the philosophy of Buddhism. (It is also provided by the various things which the bodhisattva creates by means of his magical power, but we are not concerned with that aspect of the matter at present.) Thus *artha-pratisaṃvid* consists in knowledge of the conceptual formulations of the teaching, not just on their own conceptual level, nor for their own sake, but as a medium for communicating the truth or reality of things, a medium for communicating spiritual values.

(c) *Nirukti-pratisaṃvid*: 'Analytical Knowledge of Etymology'

Surely this is a rather strange, not to say academic, accomplishment for a bodhisattva to bother acquiring – a knowledge of the origin and derivation of words? Well, not really. We have seen that knowledge of the truth and reality of things is not enough. We have seen that the bodhisattva wants to communicate, so he needs the 'analytical knowledge of meaning', that is, knowledge of the meaning of the conceptual formulations of the teaching. But even this is not enough. The bodhisattva needs to be able to give expression to his understanding of those conceptual formulations in words – and for that, he must know precisely what the words mean.

Only too often our communication is limited by our vagueness about the meaning of the words we use. We tend to fall back on a limited number of expressions which constant repetition has rendered almost meaningless. Speaking in clichés is really little better than grunting or squeaking. We therefore need to know what words mean – not just in the dictionary sense, although that is not to be despised. Just as concepts need to be related back to the experience of reality which they formulate, so words need to be related back to the concepts of which they are the expression. And it is in this that the bodhisattva's analytical knowledge of etymology essentially consists. The bodhisattva is never misled by words. He is never carried away by words. He never gets lost in words. He uses words to express concepts, clear concepts, just as he uses concepts to formulate spiritual experiences, spiritual realities.

Nirukti-pratisaṃvid also includes knowledge of such things as linguistics, public speaking, and literary composition, all of which are traditionally associated with the figure of Mañjuśrī or Mañjughoṣa, the Bodhisattva of Wisdom. In fact, he is the embodiment of all four analytical knowledges. The colophon of the Mañjughoṣa Stuti Sādhana ends with these words: 'And through this [practice] may all living beings gain power in the *jñāna* of the four *pratisaṃvids*.' We could hardly find a clearer emphasis of the importance of the four *pratisaṃvids* to the bodhisattva's practice of skilful means.

(d) *Pratibhāna-pratisaṃvid*: 'Analytical Knowledge of Courage'

You may have personal experience of the truth and reality of things, at least to some extent. You may have conceptual formulations of that experience clearly in your mind. You may even have the words with which to express those conceptual formulations. But all that is not enough. There is still something else you need if you are going to communicate effectively: courage. It is not enough to know the words. You must be able to find them – and the courage to say them – at the very moment they are needed. You need boldness, promptitude, wit. The words – and the courage – are no use a week or a day or even an hour later. It may be poor memory that prevents us from finding the right words when we need them, but often it is simply lack of confidence in ourselves and in what we have to communicate. So as part of *upāya-pāramitā* the bodhisattva also cultivates the 'analytical knowledge' of courage, the courage to speak out when necessary.

It is perhaps sobering to consider the contrast between the bodhisattva's practice of the *pratisaṃvids* and our own efforts in this area. To begin with, most of us have little or no experience of the truth or reality of things. And our conceptual formulations, our ideas, are more often than not vague, confused, and unsystematic. On top of that, our command of language may well be weak, inadequate, clumsy, and halting. And finally we often lack courage and boldness of speech – except perhaps when we are ignorant of what we are talking about. So it is hardly surprising that we find it hard to communicate.

Disappointingly, some of these very shortcomings can be discovered where one might least expect to find them: on the back covers of Charles Luk's and Robert Thurman's translations of the *Vimalakīrti-nirdeśa*. Both of these 'blurbs' – a very expressive and appropriate word – betray fundamental misunderstandings about Vimalakīrti's status as a layman.

The back cover of the American edition of Luk's translation tells us that the text is 'particularly applicable to Western Buddhist students because it expounds the practice that a layman may follow'. When I first saw this sentence, I could hardly believe my eyes. Is being able to teach the Dharma to such *arhants* as Śāriputra and Mahāmaudgalyāyana and such bodhisattvas as Maitreya part of 'the practice that a layman may follow'? Is bringing thirty-two thousand lion-thrones from a distant Buddha-land and accommodating them all in one small house part of 'the practice that a layman may follow'? Vimalakīrti discourses about Wisdom and Compassion with Mañjuśrī, reveals other universes, emanates a golden bodhisattva, and transports thousands of beings into the presence of the Buddha. Is all this part of 'the practice that a layman may follow'? One wonders what sort of layman the blurb writer had in mind.

And on the back cover of Thurman's translation we find something almost as bad. Here the blurb says, among other things, 'His [Vimalakīrti's] message is particularly appealing to our secular age, because he was a man of the world, not a monk or saint.' One would have thought that if Vimalakīrti's message appealed to our secular age, that would be a sure sign that it had been misunderstood.

There is so much confusion of thought in these two short sentences that it is hard to know where to begin to sort it out. The first claims that the *Vimalakīrti-nirdeśa* 'expounds the practice that a layman may follow', the second that Vimalakīrti 'was a man of the world'. The reasoning, such as it is, seems to be as follows. Vimalakīrti was a layman. Therefore Vimalakīrti 'was a man of the world'. Therefore Vimalakīrti's teaching expounds 'the practice a layman may follow'. Therefore Vimalakīrti's message 'is particularly appealing to our secular age'.

But Vimalakīrti was *not* a layman: that is the whole point. Vimalakīrti lived like a layman, *appeared* to be a layman, but that was only his skilful means. In reality he was an advanced bodhisattva. As the text says: 'He wore the white clothes of a layman, yet lived impeccably like a religious devotee. He lived at home, but remained aloof from the realm of desire, the realm of pure matter, and the immaterial realm. He had a son, a wife, and female attendants, yet always maintained continence. He appeared to be surrounded by servants, yet lived in solitude.'

It is easy enough to see how the whole misunderstanding has arisen. The blurb writers simply did not reflect on the real meaning of the words they used. They did not realize that the terms 'layman' and 'man of the world' mean one thing when applied to Vimalakīrti, who was a layman only in a formal technical sense, but quite another when applied to the sort of real lay people who might buy and read an English translation of the text.

To say that Vimalakīrti's teaching 'expounds the practice a layman may follow' is to imply that the layperson who wishes to practise the spiritual life does not have to give anything up. He or she can just carry on living at home with their partner, children, job, car, dog, cat, television, and mortgage. The crux of the matter, the underlying mental confusion, is the view that you don't really have to change. According to this view, you can practise the sublimest teaching of the Mahāyāna without giving up anything, without changing in any way. You can practise it staying at home as an ordinary layman, a 'man of the world'. Why? Because Vimalakīrti was an ordinary layman, Vimalakīrti was 'a man of the world'....

But Vimalakīrti's own teaching to 'ordinary laymen' carries quite the opposite implication. As we have seen, he has created the opportunity to speak to a whole crowd of laymen by appearing to be ill as a skilful means, and thousands of people have come to enquire after his health. According to the text, the king himself is among the visitors, as well as government officials, lords, young men and women, townsfolk and country folk, aristocrats, and businessmen – a real cross-section of lay society. And Vimalakīrti's teaching to all these people is not that they should stay at home and carry on just as before. Instead, he strikes right at the heart of the matter, right at the one thing that we are most unwilling to give up: the physical body. Giving up the physical body means death; it means the loss of all the pleasures that we enjoy through the senses. Towards the end of chapter 2, Vimalakīrti declares:

> Friends, this body is so impermanent, fragile, unworthy of confidence, and feeble. It is so insubstantial, perishable, short-lived, painful, filled with diseases, and subject to changes. Thus, my friends, as this body is only a vessel of many sicknesses, wise men do not rely on it. This body is like a ball of foam, unable to bear any pressure. It is like a water bubble, not remaining very long. It is like a mirage, born from the appetites of the passions. It is like the trunk of the plantain tree, having no core. Alas! This body is like a machine, a nexus of bones

> and tendons. It is like a magical illusion, consisting of falsifications. It is like a dream, being an unreal vision. It is like a reflection, being the image of former actions. It is like an echo, being dependent on conditioning. It is like a cloud, being characterized by turbulence and dissolution. It is like a flash of lightning, being unstable, and decaying every moment. The body is ownerless, being the product of a variety of conditions.
>
> This body is inert, like the earth; selfless, like water; lifeless, like fire; impersonal, like the wind; and nonsubstantial, like space. This body is unreal, being a collocation of the four main elements. It is void, not existing as self or as self-possessed. It is inanimate, being like grass, trees, walls, clods of earth, and hallucinations. It is insensate, being driven like a windmill. It is filthy, being an agglomeration of pus and excrement. It is false, being fated to be broken and destroyed, in spite of being anointed and massaged. It is afflicted by the four hundred and four diseases. It is like an ancient well, constantly overwhelmed by old age. Its duration is never certain – certain only is its end in death. This body is a combination of aggregates, elements, and sense-media, which are comparable to murderers, poisonous snakes, and an empty town, respectively. Therefore, you should be revulsed by such a body. You should despair of it and should arouse your admiration for the body of the Tathāgata.[339]

So much for the mortal, human body. Now for a different sort of body, the embodiment of the highest spiritual ideal:

> Friends, the body of a Tathāgata is the body of Dharma, born of gnosis. The body of a Tathāgata is born of the stores of merit and wisdom. It is born of morality, of meditation, of wisdom, of the liberations, and of the knowledge and vision of liberation. It is born of love, compassion, joy, and impartiality. It is born of charity, discipline, and self-control. It is born of the path of ten virtues. It is born of patience and gentleness. It is born of the roots of virtue planted by solid efforts. It is born of the concentrations, the liberations, the meditations, and the absorptions. It is born of learning, wisdom, and liberative technique. It is born of the thirty-seven aids to enlightenment. It is born of mental quiescence

and transcendental analysis. It is born of the ten powers, the four fearlessnesses, and the eighteen special qualities. It is born of all the transcendences. It is born from sciences and superknowledges. It is born of the abandonment of all evil qualities, and of the collection of all good qualities. It is born of truth. It is born of reality. It is born of conscious awareness.

> Friends, the body of a Tathāgata is born of innumerable good works. Toward such a body you should turn your aspirations, and, in order to eliminate the sicknesses of the passions of all living beings, you should conceive the spirit of unexcelled, perfect enlightenment.[340]

Such, then, is the true nature of Vimalakīrti's advice to 'laymen'. It is not exactly an exhortation to go home and put your feet up. Vimalakīrti the layman cannot meaningfully be a model for members of the Sangha, either individually or collectively, for the simple reason that he is, we are told, a fully Enlightened bodhisattva who simply appears as a householder as a skilful means. Before you can behave like Vimalakīrti, you have got to be a Buddha. His external lifestyle can only be a model inasmuch as it shows that you can pursue the spiritual path under a certain set of conditions. But commitment to that Path in principle must precede following it in that particular way. In other words, commitment must precede lifestyle. You don't imitate Vimalakīrti simply by living as a layman, because Vimalakīrti was not just anybody living as a layman. What made Vimalakīrti what he was was not his lifestyle, but his spiritual attainment – so to imitate him, you have to imitate his spiritual attainment.

According to the Pāli scriptures the Buddha started off as an ordinary human being who gained Enlightenment by his own efforts. So we can follow in the Buddha's footsteps even though we may not do exactly the things the Buddha did. And to follow – or imitate – the Buddha means, first of all, gaining Enlightenment. But Vimalakīrti is presented to us as being a Buddha already. His human life represents not an effort to gain Enlightenment, but rather an approach by a Buddha to other human beings purely as a skilful means. Vimalakīrti may act in a certain way which appears to us as ethical, but he does not act in that way to attain Buddhahood, because he has already attained it. He is acting in that way as a skilful means. So if we want to imitate Vimalakīrti, we have to imitate the actions he performs as a skilful means; and we can't do that unless we have gained Buddhahood first.

Imitating Vimalakīrti, in short, means imitating Vimalakīrti. It doesn't mean imitating what Vimalakīrti does without being Vimalakīrti, without being a Buddha. In the strict Mahāyāna sense, skilful means is an expression of Enlightenment, not something that the ordinary person can engage in. What we *can* infer from the example of Vimalakīrti is that commitment to practice – effort in the direction of Enlightenment – is primary, and lifestyle is secondary. Being a monk or nun does not automatically guarantee you spiritual progress, and being a layperson need not be a handicap. This is not to say, of course, that lifestyle is unimportant; one's way of life should be both an expression of one's commitment to spiritual practice and a support to it.

This is not how the whole Buddhist tradition views this matter, of course. What is sometimes known as the 'monastic–lay split' crops up again and again in Buddhist history, with some traditions giving more 'status' to those who lead a 'monastic' life than to 'laymen' – regardless, sometimes, of who is the more faithful practitioner of the Dharma. In the Tibetan tradition, however, there are Dharma practitioners and teachers following different lifestyles: some of them happen to be lay people, and others happen to be monks or nuns. For instance, Milarepa's teacher Marpa was a married householder, and his disciple Gampopa was a monk, while Milarepa himself was an itinerant yogi. In the Vajrayāna there is not the dichotomy between monk follower and lay follower that is found in the Hīnayāna and even to some extent in the Mahāyāna. Practising the teachings and achieving the fruits of that practice is not seen as dependent on following a particular lifestyle. Some of the most prominent Nyingmapa lamas of recent times have been married. The Gelugpas, on the other hand, are essentially monastic. In the Triratna Buddhist Order we also regard commitment to practice as primary and lifestyle as secondary. So we also do not emphasize a difference between monks and laity.

3. THE *DHĀRAṆĪS* OR 'MAGICAL FORMULAS'

Now we come to the third aspect of the skilful means practised by the bodhisattva. Traditionally, a *dhāraṇī* is a sort of protective mantra – or at least it is on its way to being a mantra. Historically speaking, mantras would appear to be a further evolution of *dhāraṇīs*. *Dhāraṇīs* are usually much longer – some go on for pages – and their conceptual content is often quite considerable. Mantras, by contrast, are almost always short, often have a minimum of conceptual content, and are usually connected with a particular Buddha or bodhisattva in a way that a *dhāraṇī* is not. The *dhāraṇī* seems on the whole to have been used in a purely magical way, whereas a mantra is often repeated as an aid to concentration, and therefore becomes a part of meditation practice in a way that a *dhāraṇī* rarely does.

A *dhāraṇī* has some sort of magical power or potency; it brings about results. It is usually given to the bodhisattva by a friendly deity, and it is supposed to protect him from any danger he may encounter in the course of his work. There is no reason why we should not take this traditional explanation quite literally. But more broadly, we may also see the *dhāraṇīs* as giving a touch of magic, a touch of the inconceivable, a hint of something beyond words, beyond thoughts. Inasmuch as 'spiritual experience' takes place within the dualistic subject–object framework, the *dhāraṇī* can even be said to give a touch of something beyond spiritual experience. And this touch of magic is indispensable to the bodhisattva's practice of skilful means. This kind of skilful means is less accessible to us than the others; the use of *dhāraṇīs* as skilful means is a mysterious and subtle business, and one would really have to be a bodhisattva to see how it works.

All the ways of practising skilful means we have explored are specific aspects of the bodhisattva's interaction with other people. But the practice of skilful means is broader than this. Indeed, the whole of the Dharma is a skilful means, the greatest of all skilful means. And we can define the Dharma as whatever helps us to grow, whatever conduces to our spiritual development. But even the Dharma cannot be a skilful means in the abstract. You can't find it in a book. A skilful means is a skilful means only to the extent that it is practised, only to the extent that it is lived out.

So if we want the Buddha's discovery of the truth of things to be more widely known, we ourselves must become a skilful means. We must communicate our vision of what men and women can become, and make every effort to transform ourselves in the light of that vision. If we are generous and open in our dealings with people, if we speak to them kindly and affectionately, if we succeed in inspiring them, in sparking them off, and if we show that we ourselves are at least making an effort to evolve, we will be practising skilful means. And if we have some experience of the truth and reality of things, if we think clearly, if we express ourselves adequately, and if we are full of courage and self confidence, we will be able to communicate our vision to others. Above all, our actions and our communication need a little touch of magic, a touch of the inconceivable, a touch of that which is beyond words. Then, and only then, we shall truly be able to be 'all things to all men'.

4

THE TRANSCENDENTAL CRITIQUE OF RELIGION

Once our basic needs for food, clothing, shelter, and leisure have been met, what do we need more than anything else in life? What is our essential need as human beings? Surely it is freedom. The real meaning of human life is to develop our distinctively human characteristics: awareness, emotional positivity, responsibility for ourselves and others, and creativity. But we cannot develop, we cannot grow, unless we have space – both literally and metaphorically – to grow into. We need freedom: freedom from all that restricts us, both outside us and within us, freedom from our own conditioning, even freedom from our old self.

And what helps us to be free – apart from our own efforts – is, or at least is considered to be, religion. We have seen that in Buddhism the spiritual life is frequently described in terms of freedom, but Buddhism is not alone in this. The followers of other religions, at least the universal religions, would probably also say that their religion stands for the freedom of the individual. The Christian might quote from the New Testament the words: 'You shall know the truth, and the truth shall set you free.'[341]

But if we consider what it is that stops us from becoming free – apart from our own sloth and torpor, laziness, neglect, forgetfulness, and so on – we encounter a tremendous paradox. Strangely enough, religion, rather than helping us to become spiritually free, only too often helps to keep us enslaved, and even adds further shackles to our chains. To many people, the very idea that religion has anything to do with freedom sounds like an absurd contradiction in terms. Some people, and I must confess that I am among them, feel uncomfortable using – in a sense being obliged to use – the word 'religion' at all.

We find it so difficult to associate religion with freedom – we in the West, that is – not because of what religion is in principle, but rather because of its historical record. Take, for example, the record of Christianity over the last sixteen hundred years, since it was declared the official religion of the Roman Empire. It is fairly obvious that we cannot develop as individuals unless we are free at least to think for ourselves. But organized Christianity – certainly in the form of its major churches – has hardly ever allowed the individual that freedom. People in Christian countries have been obliged to think as the Church thought, to toe the theological line – or face the consequences. Even today, what the Church calls blasphemy is still a criminal offence in Britain.[342]

Not only has organized Christianity refused to allow individuals to think for themselves. It has made them think in ways actually detrimental, actually inimical, to their own personal development. It has made them think of themselves as miserable sinners, as weak and powerless, made them think that being independent and taking the initiative is wrong, if not positively sinful.

So what went wrong? How is it that religion has become not a liberator but a jailer? The short answer is that religion has become an end in itself. The forms which religion takes – doctrines, rituals, institutions, rules – have all become ends in themselves. It has been forgotten that religion is a means to an end – that end being the individual's development from ignorance to Enlightenment, from mundane consciousness to transcendental consciousness.

What are we to do in this situation? We need to grow, we need to become free, and we need something to help us do so. If we agree to call that thing 'religion', how are we to make sure that religion does not become a means of enslaving or stultifying, even of crushing, the individual? We need something that will constantly remind us of the limitations of religion, something that will constantly remind us that religion is only a means to an end. In other words, we need a transcendental critique of religion. And in chapters 3 and 4 of the *Vimalakīrti-nirdeśa* we find such a critique. In Thurman's translation these chapters are entitled 'The Disciples' Reluctance to Visit Vimalakīrti' and 'The Reluctance of the Bodhisattvas'.

We have already learned that, out of his skilful means, out of his great Compassion, Vimalakīrti has fallen sick. Many people have come to visit him and enquire after his health, and he has taken the opportunity of teaching them the Dharma. At the beginning of chapter 3, we find Vimalakīrti at home, in his own room, lying on his bed. And as he lies there, a thought passes through his mind – or perhaps, as he is an advanced bodhisattva, we should say that he allows a thought to pass through his mind. He thinks:

> I am sick, lying on my bed in pain, yet the Tathāgata, the saint, the perfectly accomplished Buddha, does not consider me or take pity upon me, and sends no one to inquire after my illness.

The Buddha, meanwhile, is in Āmrapālī's garden on the outskirts of the city of Vaiśālī teaching the great assembly of *arhants*, bodhisattvas, and others. And as he sits there teaching, the Buddha becomes aware of the thought passing through Vimalakīrti's mind. It's as though the two of them are playing a sort of game. After all, Vimalakīrti is not really sick in the ordinary sense, and presumably the Buddha knows that, but he seems quite happy to play his part in the game, quite willing to 'play ball'.

So what is his next move? Knowing the thought that is passing through Vimalakīrti's mind, the Buddha says: 'Śāriputra,' – in the Mahāyāna *sūtras* it always seems to be poor old Śāriputra who gets singled out – 'go to inquire after the illness of Vimalakīrti.' Or, as we would say, 'Please go and enquire after his health' – an interesting difference of idiom.

Śāriputra is one of the two leading disciples of the Buddha, the other being Mahāmaudgalyāyana. He is an *arhant*, so he has gained individual emancipation, he is liberated at least from the ordinary passions. But what does he say? He says, 'I am reluctant to go', or, more literally, 'I am not very keen on going.' He does not actually refuse – after all, it is the Buddha who is asking him to go – but he would much rather not, and he explains why. One day, he says, he was sitting at the foot of a tree in the forest – as good monks were supposed to do in ancient India – absorbed in contemplation, when Vimalakīrti happened to pass by. 'That is not the way to absorb yourself in contemplation,' he told Śāriputra. And he proceeded to explain what absorption in contemplation really was. His explanation was so profound that Śāriputra was left dumbfounded, and quite unable to reply. This is why he is unwilling to go and ask Vimalakīrti about his illness. He has had some experience of Vimalakīrti before, and he is not very keen on encountering him again.

The Buddha tries again. He asks Mahāmaudgalyāyana to go. But, strange to say, Mahāmaudgalyāyana is also reluctant. It seems that he too has been rebuked by Vimalakīrti. One day, when he was teaching the Dharma to some householders, Vimalakīrti came along and told him how it should really be done – and Mahāmaudgalyāyana was also left dumbfounded by his remarks.

In this way, the Buddha asks ten of the leading *arhant* disciples to go. He asks Mahākāśyapa, Subhūti, Pūrṇa, Kātyāyana, Aniruddha, Upāli, Rāhula, even Ānanda. But, one and all, they are reluctant to go; they have all had some previous experience of dear old Vimalakīrti. He has exposed the spiritual shortcomings of them all. In doing so, he has exposed, in fact, as we shall see, the spiritual shortcomings of the Hīnayāna when its teachings are taken literally, taken as ends in themselves.

So the Buddha turns to the bodhisattvas who are also in the great assembly. (One gets the impression that he is rather enjoying this little game.) He asks Maitreya to go and enquire about Vimalakīrti's illness. Maitreya is of course the future Buddha, who at present resides in the Tuṣita *devaloka*, the 'contented' heaven, waiting for the time when he will be reborn on earth for his last life, in which he will himself gain supreme perfect Enlightenment as a Buddha. But even he, even Maitreya, would rather not go. He too has already encountered Vimalakīrti.

One day, he says, while he was speaking with the gods of the Tuṣita heaven, Vimalakīrti turned up, and said:

> Maitreya, the Buddha has prophesied that after one more birth you will attain supreme perfect Enlightenment. But what is the nature of that birth? Is it past, present, or future?

And he went on to show, with great dialectical skill, that it could not be any of these. He showed that the very notion of birth – and also the notion of birthlessness – is self-contradictory. He showed that in reality there is no such thing as the attainment of Enlightenment – in fact, no such thing as Enlightenment at all. He even showed that there is no such thing as Maitreya, no such thing as a future Buddha. Maitreya was rendered speechless. He too is therefore reluctant to go to Vimalakīrti and enquire about his illness.

The Buddha next asks Prabhāvyūha; but Prabhāvyūha has had a similar experience. One day he just happened to meet Vimalakīrti, who asked him where he was coming from – an innocent enough question. Prabhāvyūha replied that he was coming from the *bodhimaṇḍa*, the 'place of Enlightenment'. In other words, he was coming from Bodh Gaya, where the Buddha gained supreme perfect Enlightenment, and in particular from the *vajrāsana*, the diamond throne, the place where the Buddha sat under the bodhi tree. That was where he was coming from, he said. Vimalakīrti thereupon explained to him at some length that the *bodhimaṇḍa* is not really a place at all but a state of mind, something from which there is no question of a bodhisattva coming, because he is in it all the time. Everything a bodhisattva does is an expression of it. Not unnaturally, Prabhāvyūha too was rendered speechless, and thus he also is reluctant to visit Vimalakīrti. He does not want another dose of the same medicine.

The Buddha asks two more of the great bodhisattvas – Jagatīṃdhara and Sudatta – to go, but for similar reasons they too are reluctant. In the end the Buddha asks Mañjuśrī, the Bodhisattva of Wisdom – but that is another story, and what happens we will see in the next chapter. The point here is that Vimalakīrti has exposed the spiritual shortcomings of Maitreya and the other bodhisattvas. He has, in other words, exposed the spiritual shortcomings of the Mahāyāna taken literally, taken as an end in itself.

It is fairly obvious what Vimalakīrti represents here, but not so easy to put it into words. We could say that Vimalakīrti represents truth or reality itself devoid of all concepts. That will do provided we don't take it too literally, provided we don't let it roll off the tongue too glibly. We could say that Vimalakīrti represents the actual Enlightenment experience. For what happens when our partial spiritual experiences are brought into contact with truth or reality? What happens when the means to Enlightenment – our rituals, our doctrines, our institutions, our rules – are brought into contact with the Enlightenment experience?

What happens is that their limitations are revealed. And this can be a very painful and traumatic experience indeed – painful and traumatic, that is, for those who identify themselves with their own partial spiritual experiences, and derive their emotional security from that identification.

Vimalakīrti is like a high-voltage current of electricity. You touch him at your peril – except that you don't touch him; he comes along and touches you. In traditional terms, Vimalakīrti is like a great *vajra*, a great thunderbolt or diamond. He is powerful, he is incisive, and at the same time he is brilliant and scintillating. He bursts through all your defences, all your limitations. He destroys what you are so that you are free to become what you can be.

Vimalakīrti's effect on people reminds me of the main character in a film I saw some years ago: Pasolini's *Theorem*. In this film, in a very brief space of time, this one person has a tremendous impact on the lives of those who encounter him. He is a young salesman who spends the weekend with a middle-class Italian family. (He has some business with the father of the family, who is the head of an industrial concern.) The family consists of father, mother, grown-up son, grown-up daughter, and not-so-young maidservant, and in the course of the weekend the young man manages to have affairs with all of them. The rest of the film shows the dramatic results of their contact with him. The mother becomes a nymphomaniac. The daughter has a nervous breakdown; we see her being taken away in an ambulance to a mental hospital. The son, an artist, destroys all his paintings. The maidservant becomes a nun and works miracles. In the last scene the father is seen walking through a crowded railway station slowly taking off his clothes. The critics, I remember, had a field day discussing the meaning of this film, especially what the young man represented. Some said that he was a sort of Christ figure, others that he symbolized reality – and some thought he was just being himself.

In these two chapters of the *Vimalakīrti-nirdeśa*, the irruption of Vimalakīrti into the lives of the disciples and the bodhisattvas happens on a much higher level, and has a much more positive effect – but it is still devastating. The impact of reality in any form has a shattering effect on anyone's life. Each of the disciples and bodhisattvas concerned is left dumbfounded. Thurman comments: 'He' – the disciple or the bodhisattva – 'is overwhelmed and speechless, yet intuitively recognizes the rightness of Vimalakīrti's statements. He can neither accept them and put them into practice nor reject them outright.'[343]

This is perhaps something that we too may experience on our own level of development. When our *kalyāṇa mitra*, our 'good friend', points out something about our own character that we have not noticed before, or something about the Dharma that is new to us, to begin with we may feel simply stunned. We have to recognize the truth of what is being said but, initially at least, we are quite unable to do anything about it. It takes time to adjust to new knowledge and put it into practice.

So it is not surprising that the disciples and the bodhisattvas are 'not very keen' on going to meet Vimalakīrti. It is not surprising that the partial experience should be reluctant to encounter the total experience, that the means to Enlightenment should be reluctant to encounter Enlightenment itself. The experience is too painful, too traumatic. But although it may be painful, or even traumatic, it is highly positive. The purpose of Vimalakīrti's strictures is not to humiliate the disciples and the bodhisattvas. He is not just 'putting them down'. His purpose is to help them to move on from their present partial experience, their present relatively limited outlook. (It is only *relatively* limited because they are, after all, *arhants* and bodhisattvas.)

We also need to bear in mind that Vimalakīrti's behaviour here exemplifies the skilful means of an advanced bodhisattva. When we ourselves feel the need to criticize someone's behaviour, we need to make sure that we are doing so from a positive basis. We should certainly be careful not to upset people for the sake of it. At the same time, we should not hold back from speaking the truth simply because people may find it upsetting. If you can put your point effectively in a gentle way, that is clearly best. But very often a point does not get across to people unless it has some edge. They may be so closed to any views other than their own that a dignified, objective, and emotionally neutral statement of your point of view has little effect, in which case you may have to express yourself more trenchantly. And unfortunately it is not always possible to make a point without making a personal criticism of someone. If their views stem directly from their character, and you are criticizing those views, you can hardly help criticizing their character too. The purpose of criticism is to help someone grow and develop. Therefore, the rule of thumb is to upset people as little as possible, while still saying what you feel must be said.

In the same way, the purpose of the transcendental critique of religion is not to destroy religion, but rather to restore it to its true function, which is to be a means to an end, a means to the spiritual development of the individual. All that is destroyed is religion as an end in itself. The transcendental critique of religion is therefore essential to the very existence of religion. It must accompany it all the time. It is important to understand this; it's important to understand it in detail. So let us look a little more closely at the encounters of some of the Buddha's disciples, Pūrṇa, Upāli, Rāhula, and Ānanda, and the bodhisattva Jagatīṃdhara, with Vimalakīrti.

First, the disciple Pūrṇa. Pūrṇa was teaching the Hīnayāna doctrine to some young monks in the forest when Vimalakīrti came along. And Vimalakīrti said that Pūrṇa was teaching the monks wrongly, because they were capable of following the Mahāyāna, which was a higher teaching. Now, Vimalakīrti was not criticizing Pūrṇa simply for teaching the Hīnayāna instead of the Mahāyāna. After all, as we have seen, he was quite capable of exposing the limitations of the Mahāyāna too, considered as an end in itself. He was criticizing Pūrṇa for teaching the Dharma mechanically, without looking to see what the spiritual needs of the young monks really were. He said:

> Reverend Pūrṇa, first concentrate yourself, regard the minds of these young *bhikṣus*, and then teach them the Dharma! Do not put rotten food into a jeweled bowl! First understand the inclination of these monks, and do not confuse priceless sapphires with glass beads!
>
> Reverend Pūrṇa, without examining the spiritual faculties of living beings, do not presume upon the one-sidedness of their faculties; do not wound those who are without wounds; do not impose a narrow path upon those who aspire to a great path; do not try to pour the great ocean into the hoof-print of an ox; do not try to put Mount Sumeru into a grain of mustard; do not confuse the brilliance of the sun with the light of a glowworm; and do not expose those who admire the roar of a lion to the howl of a jackal![344]

As a result of listening to Vimalakīrti's critique, Pūrṇa realized:

> The disciples, who do not know the thoughts or the inclinations of others, are not able to teach the Dharma to anyone.

This is a pretty strong statement. Vimalakīrti is criticizing Pūrṇa for not being in real communication with the people he is teaching. Pūrṇa seems to have a fixed idea about the Dharma, to think that it consists in *this* particular teaching and *that* particular conceptual formulation; and this is what he conveys to the people he teaches, regardless of whether or not it will actually help them to develop.

Some Eastern Buddhist teachers tend to do this when they come to the West. They have learned about the Dharma in the East and they think that all they have to do is repeat it in the West. But to communicate the Dharma effectively, you need to be aware of the spiritual needs of the people you are teaching – and this takes time. Vimalakīrti is not criticizing Pūrṇa for teaching the Dharma; he is criticizing him for teaching it in the wrong way, for regarding the teaching of the Dharma as an end in itself.

I found myself teaching the Dharma 'in the wrong way' in India some years ago. I was asked to lecture regularly on full moon days at a certain Buddhist hall in Calcutta. A lot of people, in fact hundreds of people, mostly Bengali Buddhists, used to come, but I soon realized that they had not come to listen to the Dharma. They saw the occasion as a social gathering, and there would always be quite a lot of noise, shouting and talking, going on. What they actually wanted was a monk just talking quietly away in the corner, lending a faint air of religiosity to the proceedings. My suspicions were confirmed when I eventually complained to the head monk about the behaviour of the audience (although they weren't really an *audience* because they weren't listening). He said, 'It doesn't matter if nobody can hear what you're saying; we just want you to lecture on the Dharma.' A lecture on the Dharma had become part of the social ritual. Someone had to be seen to be giving it, but it didn't matter whether or not anybody could hear or understand what was being said. The whole thing had become quite meaningless. So I had actually been asked to teach the Dharma 'in the wrong way'. This is an example – rather an extreme one – of the sort of thing that Vimalakīrti is getting at.

Now for Upāli's encounter with Vimalakīrti. Among all the Buddha's disciples, Upāli was the great expert in the Vinaya or monastic law, and it was because of this expertise that one day he was approached by two monks. They had committed some offence against the monastic rule, and, ashamed to appear before the Buddha, they went instead to Upāli and asked him to remove their anxieties by accepting their confession and witnessing their promise not to commit the offence again – that being the regular monastic procedure. Upāli agreed, and into the bargain gave them what the text calls a 'religious discourse'.

At this point Vimalakīrti came along and said that Upāli was only making matters worse. He said:

> Reverend Upāli, do not aggravate further the sins of these two monks. Without perplexing them, relieve their remorse. Reverend Upāli, sin is not to be apprehended within, or without, or between the two. Why? The Buddha has said, 'Living beings are afflicted by the passions of thought, and they are purified by the purification of thought.'[345]

He went on to say quite a lot more of a metaphysical nature, but this passage is enough for our present purpose. What is Vimalakīrti getting at? Why does he say that Upāli is only making matters worse? What does he mean by saying that there is no such thing as sin? Let us look at the situation. The two monks have committed an offence – that is, they have broken a rule. But why was the rule laid down in the first place? It was laid down to help the individual – in this case the individual monk – to grow spiritually. Having broken the rule, the two monks have put an obstacle in the way of their spiritual development. They have perhaps even regressed. So Upāli should not be concerned simply with the fact that they have broken the rule; that would be to treat the rule as an end in itself. His main concern, Vimalakīrti is implying, should be to get them back on the right path.

Belief in 'sin' is nothing but a stumbling block which arises out of treating rules as ends in themselves. When we break them, 'sin' comes into existence, and we waste time worrying about how to get rid of it instead of getting on with the task of our individual development. This is of course an essentially Christian predicament. If you believe in God, and the laws or commandments he is said to have laid down, what happens if you break one of those rules? 'Sin' comes into existence, and you feel guilt and fear of punishment. And when this happens, you need someone to save you from the consequences of your sin: a saviour. All this is what is known as 'religion' in the West. In fact, the situation is even more complicated, because sin came into existence before we were even born, when Adam and Eve disobeyed God and ate of the tree of the knowledge of good and evil. According to the Christian tradition, sin is our inheritance; we are born into sin. This is the predicament of the Christian, as well as that of the ex-Christian who is not aware that past indoctrination is still having an effect. It is to avoid such a predicament that we need to be aware of the danger of regarding rules as ends in themselves. This is why Vimalakīrti takes Upāli so firmly to task.

Vimalakīrti says that there is no such thing as sin. He says:

> Sin is not to be apprehended within, or without, or between the two.

In other words, sin is a mere concept, a mere word. Consider the effect of doing something unskilful. It will in most cases have affected someone else, and it is important that one should regret that. But this is only part of it. The action will also have had the effect of hindering one's own spiritual progress. If you have something of which to repent, your urge to develop has weakened, at least to some degree, and it needs to be revitalized. The two things – repentance for what you have done and renewal of your inspiration – are closely interlinked.

Vimalakīrti is simply making the point that your concern should go beyond your failures. Yes, you do have to repent unskilful acts, you have to resolve to do better, you have to experience remorse. But you must also make sure that you revive your original inspiration; because it was due to the flagging of that inspiration that you committed the unskilful action in the first place. So you have to deal with the unskilful action itself – and possibly with its consequences – but within the context of reviving your inspiration. The two are not alternatives; you really need to do both. In fact, one might say that you can genuinely repent only if there is a genuine revival of your inspiration.

So the first thing you have to do is try to understand what you have done. Then you cultivate a sense of regret that you have done it, especially if it has involved injury to another person. Thirdly, you resolve not to do that particular thing again. And fourthly, you take steps to ensure that in future you do what is right. 'Sin' does not come into it at all. That's why Vimalakīrti quotes the Buddha as saying:

> Living beings are afflicted by the passions of thought, and they are purified by the purification of thought.

As to the steps you take to modify your behaviour in future, here you must tread carefully. It is probably not helpful, for example, to think in terms of penances. It is important to remember that you are not punishing yourself. 'Discipline' is probably a better word to use in a Buddhist context. For example, suppose you became aware that your behaviour was unskilful with regard to food – that you were greedy – and you therefore decided to limit your intake of food. That would be an attempt to retrain yourself, to modify your behaviour based on your understanding. It would not be a punishment for eating too much.

The term penance, as ordinarily used, seems to mean something halfway between a punishment and a discipline. A penance is intended to 'pay for', 'make up for', what one has done. For example, a Catholic may be given the penance of, say, reciting ten 'Hail Marys' – quite a mild penance for some small sin – and it is presumably intended to inspire the penitent with thoughts of the Virgin Mary so that they don't commit that sin again. But if it is taken as a sort of spiritual bookkeeping, it probably doesn't contribute all that much to spiritual development. Often people know in advance what sort of penance they will get if they commit a particular sin; they know that they will do the penance and then they will be 'quits'. You then get a cycle of unskilful action – penance – unskilful action – penance – and so on. In the end you hardly remember which came first. You can even end up thinking in terms of having permission to do something unskilful because you have done the penance, in which case there will be no real modification of your behaviour or mental attitude. Penance has spiritual value only when it is seen not as a sort of punishment but as a discipline, intelligently imposed upon oneself in order to check certain unskilful attitudes and develop more skilful ones.

One has to be careful not to put oneself through a kind of aversion therapy, in which one instils an unconscious reaction or revulsion against a particular course of action. Clearly this sort of counter-conditioning can have no spiritual value, and probably no ethical value either. It results in 'ethical' behaviour through the most basic motivation: fear of pain if one does otherwise. One must guard against conditioning oneself in a particular way without properly understanding what is happening and without genuinely changing one's attitude.

Next we come to Vimalakīrti's encounter with Rāhula. Rāhula was, of course, the Buddha's son, and he had become his grandfather's heir after his father had left home and gone forth. So in going forth himself, Rāhula renounced not only the world, but also the throne.[346] And when a number of Licchavi youths asked him why he had renounced the kingdom, he outlined for them the benefits and virtues of renouncing the world. But as he was getting into his stride, Vimalakīrti came along and said that Rāhula was explaining the matter all wrong. He said:

> Renunciation is itself the very absence of virtues and benefits. Reverend Rāhula, one may speak of benefits and virtues in regard to compounded things, but renunciation is uncompounded, and there can be no question of benefits and virtues in regard to the uncompounded.[347]

Renunciation – leaving the world – is essentially a spiritual activity. It is not a matter of *gaining* – even gaining benefits and virtues – but of growing. However, the young men still do not understand. They say:

> We have heard the Tathāgata [the Buddha] declare that one should not renounce the world without the permission of one's parents.

They are still thinking in formal terms: in terms of a formal leaving of the world, in terms of becoming a monk in a literal or technical sense. Vimalakīrti returns to his point more emphatically than ever. He says:

> Young men, you should cultivate yourselves intensively to conceive the spirit of unexcelled, perfect enlightenment. That in itself will be your renunciation and high ordination!

Renunciation consists in the development of the *bodhicitta*, in Going for Refuge to the Three Jewels. 'Leaving the world' and 'becoming a monk' are not ends in themselves. Vimalakīrti is not saying that these forms of renunciation are unnecessary. He is saying that the outer action is of value only to the extent that it is the expression of an inner attitude. You are not a monk simply because you are wearing a yellow robe.

Now we come to the story of Ānanda's meeting with Vimalakīrti. Ānanda was the Buddha's personal attendant and companion for the last twenty years of the Buddha's life. Naturally he was in close contact with the Buddha, and sometimes we get the impression that he was quite attached to him as a person. One day, it seems, the Buddha was unwell and needed some milk to help him recover. So Ānanda took his begging-bowl and went to the mansion of a great Brahmin family to beg for some. Vimalakīrti turned up and asked Ānanda what he was doing there so early in the morning, and Ānanda said:

> The body of the Lord manifests some indisposition, and he needs some milk. Therefore, I have come to fetch some.[348]

Vimalakīrti then proceeded to scold Ānanda for saying such a thing:

> Reverend Ānanda, the Tathāgatas have the body of the Dharma – not a body that is sustained by material food. The Tathāgatas have a transcendental body that has transcended all mundane qualities.... Reverend Ānanda, to believe there can be illness in such a body is irrational and unseemly!

The gist of Vimalakīrti's reply is that the Buddha should not be identified with his physical body, but with the *dharmakāya*, the body of truth, the body of reality. The physical body – even that of the Buddha – is not an end in itself, but a means to Enlightenment. When you have seen the physical body of the Buddha, you should not think you have seen the Buddha himself. The Buddha is essentially the Enlightened mind.

Hearing this, Ānanda felt ashamed that he had misunderstood the Dharma in this way. But a voice from the sky spoke, telling Ānanda not to be ashamed. After all, the Buddha does in a sense have a body, at least for a while. The voice said:

> Since the Buddha has appeared during the time of the five corruptions, he disciplines human beings by acting lowly and humble.

The suggestion is that the Buddha's illness, like that of Vimalakīrti, is skilful means; so Ānanda should go and get the milk.

The bodhisattva Jagatīṃdhara's encounter with Vimalakīrti happened as he was receiving an unexpected and extraordinary visit at home one day: a visit from Māra, the evil one.[349] Māra did not come as Māra, of course – Māra never does! He came disguised as Indra, the king of the gods, and accompanied by twelve thousand heavenly maidens, all singing and playing music. What a scene they must have presented: the glorious figure of the king of the gods – as he seemed to be – in a blaze of light, decked with jewels; the twelve thousand heavenly maidens, no doubt looking very elegant in all sorts of silken drapery, with their hair floating down their backs; and all of them singing and playing wonderful music. (Imagine perhaps a highly trained choir of twelve thousand singing Monteverdi's 'Vespers'.) Then Māra, as Indra, saluted Jagatīṃdhara very meekly and humbly, even going to the extreme of touching the bodhisattva's feet with his head, before standing respectfully to one side.

Jagatīṃdhara was completely taken in by this – as one usually is by Māra's disguises. He rose to the occasion and delivered a little sermon – I think we can call it that – suitable for a god: a sermon on impermanence. Māra appeared to be deeply moved and, to show gratitude, asked Jagatīṃdhara to accept the twelve thousand divine maidens as his servants. But Jagatīṃdhara was not a complete fool. He declined the offer, saying that heavenly maidens were not suitable servants for someone like himself who had taken up the spiritual life.

At this point Vimalakīrti entered on the scene and exposed what was going on. He said to Jagatīṃdhara:

> Noble son, do not think that this is Indra! This is not Indra but the evil Māra, who has come to ridicule you.[350]

And to Māra he said that since Jagatīṃdhara was unable to accept the divine maidens, he, Vimalakīrti, would give them a home.

Even the disciples and bodhisattvas were reluctant to meet Vimalakīrti, so you can guess how Māra felt. He was absolutely terrified. He tried to make a quick getaway, but it was no use. In the end he had to hand over all twelve thousand heavenly maidens – who were of course really Māra's daughters in disguise. And Vimalakīrti set about teaching the heavenly maidens to practise the Dharma. In the end he taught them to develop the *bodhicitta*, the will to supreme Enlightenment for the benefit of all beings. Even that is not the end of the story. Māra later tried to get his daughters back, but they returned to him inspired by the Dharma and ready to inspire others.

So what does all this mean? Māra's daughters, the heavenly maidens, represent the emotions, the passions, in their relatively crude and unrefined forms. Obviously one who has taken up the spiritual life should not succumb to them, but should have them well under control. This stage of development is represented by Jagatīṃdhara, whose name, significantly perhaps, means 'Ruler of the World'.

But control, conscious control, is not the last word in the spiritual life. Rejection is not enough. Asceticism is not an end in itself. After all, the emotions have to be converted; they have to be transformed; they have to contribute their energies to the spiritual life. It is this stage that is represented by Vimalakīrti.

According to Thurman there is a definitely Tantric element in the *Vimalakīrti-nirdeśa*, especially in this passage. This may well be so, but we should be careful not to misunderstand this possibility. We need to avoid falling into the trap of thinking that we are accepting Māra's daughters as Vimalakīrti did when we are really only succumbing to them like an ordinary person. The stage represented by Jagatīṃdhara is one that most of us will be in for a very long time – assuming we can reach it, that is. But in the long run, it is not an end in itself; it is only a means to an end.

Having taken a closer look at the encounters of some of the disciples and bodhisattvas with Vimalakīrti, we should now be quite clear about the main point. As Vimalakīrti's 'transcendental critique' serves to remind us, the Hīnayāna is a means to an end. The Mahāyāna is a means to an end. Buddhism is a means to an end. Religion is a means to an end. And that end is the spiritual development of the individual.

This critique has always been part of Buddhism. The Buddha said, 'I teach the Dharma under the figure of a raft.'[351] In other words, just as a raft is useful for getting you across the water, but you wouldn't carry it with you once you had reached dry land, so the Buddha's teaching is useful for carrying us across the waters of *saṃsāra*, but we will have no need for it when we have reached the other shore of Enlightenment. This sort of emphasis is particularly strong in the Mahāyāna, and strongest of all, perhaps, in Zen. You get Japanese and Chinese pictures of the Sixth Patriarch tearing up the *Diamond Sūtra*. There is the story of the travelling monk who needed fuel because he was cold, and chopped up the wooden Buddha images in the temple at which he was staying. And there is the master who famously said to his disciple, 'If you meet the Buddha on the road, kill him!'

These are all rather extreme, rather bizarre ways of underlining the same message: that Buddhism is only a means to an end. It is because

Buddhism has always been aware of the difference between means and ends that down the centuries it has remained spiritually alive. For the same reason, it has not on the whole been dogmatic or intolerant. It has never persecuted the followers of other religions, and the followers of one form of Buddhism have rarely persecuted the followers of another.

Other religions, it must frankly be said, are not really on a par with Buddhism in this respect. They do not always help the individual to become free. They do not really see themselves as a means to an end in the way that Buddhism does. The theistic religions are especially hampered in this respect. They have no critique of religion, whether transcendental or otherwise; they have no self-critique. It is therefore necessary that we apply the Buddhist critique to them, that we get Vimalakīrti to come along. And when we do this, we find only too often that other religions are not in fact means to the development of the individual at all. The critique perforce turns into a criticism.

Some people think that one should not criticize religions other than one's own, or even that one should not criticize religion at all. But such criticism is essential in revealing obstacles to one's development as an individual. It is only by means of a critique that we can ensure that the means to the development of the individual remains a means and does not harden into an end in itself.

We should therefore apply this critique, even this criticism, to everything that presents itself to us as religion. We should apply it to Christianity, apply it to Buddhism, apply it to the Hīnayāna, apply it to the Mahāyāna, apply it to the Vajrayāna. It is perhaps impressive that the *Vimalakīrti-nirdeśa*, a Mahāyāna text, shows up the imperfections of bodhisattvas. This does not happen in any of the other well-known Mahāyāna *sūtras*; perhaps it is one of the distinctive functions of the *Vimalakīrti-nirdeśa* to reveal the bodhisattvas' shortcomings. Of course, the bodhisattvas whose behaviour Vimalakīrti criticizes are not apparently archetypal bodhisattvas; perhaps they are novice bodhisattvas. And, as we shall see, Mañjuśrī, *the* archetypal bodhisattva, is shown as being almost perfect.

We need, of course, to make sure that we apply our critique appropriately; sometimes it is more appropriate to express appreciation. A guiding principle might be to apply the critique first and foremost to oneself. If we all applied this transcendental critique to our own spiritual practice, there would hardly be any need for a transcendental critique of religion in general, or of our own religion in particular. We must be careful not to knock away the very ladder by which we are climbing – not, at least, until we are ready to do without it. We need to apply the critique to whatever practices we undertake – whether it is meditation or devotional practice, reading books or attending lectures, living in a community or working in a Right Livelihood business. We need to stay alive to the crucial question: is it helping me to develop? We should never allow any of these things to become ends in themselves; they are all means to an end. If we can remember this, we ourselves will be living embodiments of the reality of religion, and at the same time living embodiments of the transcendental critique of religion. Religion will then help us to become free. And then perhaps we will have at least a foretaste of the inconceivable emancipation.

5
HISTORY VERSUS MYTH IN HUMANITY'S QUEST FOR MEANING

In 1956, the year in which the Buddhist world celebrated the two-thousand-five-hundredth anniversary of the Buddha's Enlightenment, I found myself in New Delhi at the invitation of the Indian government, along with other 'eminent Buddhists from the border areas', as the government was pleased to style us. I suppose they had in mind a picture of aboriginal Buddhists turning up from the jungles of Assam and West Bengal – and actually we did look a very motley bunch, in robes of all shades of red and orange and yellow.

Of all the celebrations and speeches and events that went on, the most interesting from my point of view was an exhibition of Asian Buddhist art. At that time it was probably one of the biggest such exhibitions ever mounted anywhere in the world, and all the different Buddhist countries – Japan, Cambodia, Thailand, Bhutan, Tibet, and so on – had their own sections. After the Indian section, which was vast, the biggest and perhaps the most important collection was that organized by the People's Republic of China. (This was still in the palmy days of Indo-Chinese friendship, before the 1962 border war.)

Some of the Chinese exhibits were magnificent – I had never seen anything like them. And I remember one especially: a full scale copy of an ancient mural painting which occupied the whole of one wall. It dated, as far as I remember, from the T'ang Dynasty, or perhaps even earlier, and it depicted a number of figures, all more or less life-size. But there were two of these figures, occupying the centre of the picture, that particularly stood out. To the left, under a jewelled canopy, a beautiful young man was seated on a magnificent lotus-throne. He was clad in all manner of silks and jewels, and surrounded by standing yellow-robed figures. From the position of his hands and fingers – his *mudrā* – he seemed to be saying something to the other main figure, who was seated to the right within a sort of curtained pavilion. This was a very old man. His face was covered with tiny wrinkles and he had a long, white, rather wispy beard. He wore a blue-grey robe, the traditional robe of the Chinese scholar – though this was, as we shall see, artistic licence – and he was surrounded by more standing figures in white robes. From the position of his hands and fingers he seemed to be replying to the young man. The two figures were, of course, Mañjuśrī, the Bodhisattva of Wisdom, on the left, and Vimalakīrti, the wise elder of Vaiśālī, on the right. The painting illustrates the famous meeting between them which is described at the beginning of chapter 5 of the *Vimalakīrti-nirdeśa*: 'The Consolation of the Invalid'.[352]

As we saw in the last chapter, all the *arhants* and bodhisattvas present in the Buddha's assembly were reluctant to go to enquire after Vimalakīrti's health. This was because each and every one of them had had a painful, perhaps even rather embarrassing, encounter with Vimalakīrti which had exposed the limitations of their particular approach to the Dharma. We will take up the story at the beginning of chapter 5, at which point Mañjuśrī has just agreed to visit the invalid. He is fully aware of the difficulties and dangers of the undertaking. He knows that if you come into contact with such a powerful current of spiritual electricity as Vimalakīrti, you may get a shock. But he says:

> Although he cannot be withstood by someone of my feeble defences, still, sustained by the grace of the Buddha, I will go to him and will converse with him as well as I can.[353]

The word translated here as 'grace' is the Sanskrit word *adhiṣṭhāna*, which certainly does not mean 'grace' in the Christian sense. 'Grace' here is the non-dualistic influence of the Buddha's transcendental experience of Enlightenment as that influence appears within the framework of the dualism of subject and object. Because in reality there is no such dualistic split, this influence cannot really be said to have an external source, but it *appears* to have one.

You could see *adhiṣṭhāna* as a powerful influence emanating from a powerful spiritual source, an influence which can have a radically transforming effect on you if you open yourself up to it. But it is not automatic – which is why 'grace' is not really an adequate translation. It is not exactly that you have to earn it, but it certainly is related to your capacity to receive it. Even on an ordinary level, if you experience goodwill coming from another person, that will have an effect on you. Your state of consciousness will be altered to some degree, and you will respond on that basis. In the same way on a higher level, if you can experience goodwill coming from a person who has some spiritual realization, even some insight into the nature of reality, presumably that will have an even greater effect on you. In fact, *adhiṣṭhāna* is flowing from the Buddhas and bodhisattvas all the time, just as light and heat are constantly radiating from the sun. And you will be benefited by it to the extent that you are receptive to it.

In Tibetan, *adhiṣṭhāna* is translated as *chin lab*, which literally means 'power-wave'. *Chin* also has connotations of 'majesty' and 'splendour'. We tend to understand the word 'power' in a purely secular sense, but the power of the transcendental is more like power in the sense of love: a powerful expression of *mettā*. Perhaps one could speak of a 'love-wave', or even a 'blessing' with a great deal of strength behind it.

Adhiṣṭhāna is something that seems to come from above rather than arising from below; it is something that is 'given' to one. It is like artistic inspiration. Usually inspiration is spoken of coming up from the depths. But sometimes it seems to come down from some higher power: after hearing the first performance of his oratorio 'The Creation', Haydn is said to have murmured: 'It came from above.'[354] So *adhiṣṭhāna* is perhaps analogous to the artist's invocation of the Muses, where one addresses oneself to higher powers and asks for their blessing.

This raises the question of the nature of effort in the spiritual life. We need, it seems, to make the effort to be receptive, but this may sound like a contradiction in terms. Is it possible to invoke the Muses so vigorously that you can't hear them singing? Take the example of playing in an orchestra: you are making a tremendous effort, but at the same time you are being receptive. Are the two things really so antithetical? Do you have to stop doing everything in order to be receptive? Or take the art of writing: you can be making a very intense effort, but at the same time you do feel receptive; something is flowing into you.

The problem seems to be that we make the wrong kind of effort. This happens when you try to appropriate a higher experience as something to be incorporated into your existing being, when what you should be doing is incorporating your existing being into the experience in such a way that your existing being is transformed. This effort, which is really just wilful exertion, is an attempt to retain the experience within the existing structure of your being, without allowing it to change you. Until Enlightenment is attained, there will always be a conflict between appropriating and experiencing, between incorporating and surrendering. It is no good thinking that all effort is wilful effort, and therefore to be avoided. The solution to the problem of wilfulness is not simply to take things easy.

It may be that the effort you make is not distributed over a broad enough spectrum of interests, so that your spiritual life becomes rather one-sided, and you lose your motivation. If you are working in a Right Livelihood business, you may need to make an effort, even a great effort, to apply yourself to the work; but at the same time you need to make effort in meditation, in spiritual friendships, and so on. It is not that you have been placing too much stress on effort, but that the effort is not distributed sufficiently widely. There are two ways of solving this problem. You can either make some provision, in the course of every day or over a week or a month, for all your requirements or interests to be met; or else you can spend a few weeks, even a few months, concentrating on one, then a few weeks or months concentrating on another, and so on. Either way, over the period of, say, a year, all your requirements would be met.

However, Mañjuśrī does not have any such problems when he makes the effort to visit Vimalakīrti on his sick-bed, because he is 'sustained by the grace of the Buddha'. What Mañjuśrī means by *adhiṣṭhāna* is that he is not going to see Vimalakīrti under his own steam, as it were. He is not going to embark on the visit with any fixed idea; he is going to deal with the situation spontaneously – which means that he is not even going with a fixed idea of 'acting spontaneously'.

When Mañjuśrī says he will go and see Vimalakīrti, everybody in the assembly – except, of course, the Buddha, who just sits there smiling through it all – gets tremendously excited. They think that if these two come together there will be a wonderful discussion, a real clash as between two cymbals, out of which something truly profound and illuminating will emerge.

So eight thousand – a quarter – of the bodhisattvas and five hundred – one-sixteenth – of the *arhants* decide to accompany Mañjuśrī on his visit. (No doubt these numbers have some significance.) Many hundreds of thousands of gods and goddesses also decide to go, so a great retinue accompanies Mañjuśrī on his journey to the city of Vaiśālī. Fully aware of their approach, Vimalakīrti exercises his magical power and makes everything around him disappear. The house itself, all his attendants, all the furniture, the seats, the couches – everything vanishes. All that can be seen is old Vimalakīrti himself, lying on his couch, suspended in mid-air.

At this point Mañjuśrī arrives. It would not be quite accurate to say that he enters, because there is no door to enter by, and no floor to walk on, but no doubt Mañjuśrī, being the Bodhisattva of Wisdom, manages to overcome that little problem. On seeing him, Vimalakīrti takes the initiative, calling out:

> Welcome, Mañjuśrī! You are very welcome! There you are, without any coming. You appear, without any seeing. You are heard, without any hearing.[355]

Mañjuśrī is not at all disconcerted by this style of greeting; he is quite equal to the occasion. He replies

> Householder, it is as you say. Who comes, finally comes not. Who goes, finally goes not. Why? Who comes is not known to come. Who goes is not known to go. Who appears is finally not to be seen.

Then, having answered Vimalakīrti in his own terms, Mañjuśrī goes on quite coolly to carry out his purpose and ask Vimalakīrti about his sickness. He tells Vimalakīrti that the Buddha has been enquiring after him, and finally he says:

> Householder, whence came this sickness of yours? How long will it continue? How does it stand? How can it be alleviated?

These questions take the form of the standard polite Indian enquiries. But Vimalakīrti's reply is not at all standard, and it constitutes one of the most famous and impressive passages in the whole of the *Vimalakīrti-nirdeśa*. He says:

> Mañjuśrī, my sickness comes from ignorance and the thirst for existence and it will last as long as do the sicknesses of all living beings. Were all living beings to be free from sickness, I also would not be sick. Why? Mañjuśrī, for the bodhisattva, the world consists only of living beings, and sickness is inherent in living in the world. Were all living beings free of sickness, the bodhisattva also would be free of sickness. For example, Mañjuśrī, when the only son of a merchant is sick, both his parents become sick on account of the sickness of their son. And the parents will suffer as long as that only son does not recover from his sickness. Just so, Mañjuśrī, the bodhisattva loves all living beings as if each were his only child. He becomes sick when they are sick and is cured when they are cured. You ask me, Mañjuśrī, whence comes my sickness; the sicknesses of the bodhisattvas arise from great compassion.[356]

This is Vimalakīrti's reply, and his words resound throughout the history of Mahāyāna Buddhism. But what he is talking about – the bodhisattva's experience of *mahākaruṇā*, great Compassion – does present us with an intractable mystery. For us bliss and pain are essentially incompatible. So how does a being who under all circumstances experiences the bliss of liberation also experience the suffering that Vimalakīrti describes? We could say that it is an aspect of experiencing Wisdom and Compassion, *prajñā* and *karuṇā*, as non-different; that is, it is an aspect of the bodhisattva's compassionate response to suffering as being not different from the same bodhisattva's profound realization of the emptiness of all things, including living beings and their suffering (and the profound realization itself, of course). We could say that it is an aspect of being in Nirvāṇa and *saṃsāra* at the same time. If that is possible, presumably it is possible to experience the bliss of emancipation at the same time that one suffers with beings through great Compassion.

However, we are still in the realm of theory. Perhaps we can find a mundane, if rather faint, analogy for the experience of *mahākaruṇā* in the way we are able to remain fully absorbed in doing something – like playing a strenuous game – while at the same time receiving some painful knocks. Up to a certain point we don't really notice the pain – or rather we don't take notice of it. It is there, we feel it, but it is very much at the periphery of our consciousness because we are so absorbed in the game and finding it so enjoyable. Perhaps it is not even enjoyment; we are just so caught up in the game that we don't really think about whether we are enjoying it or not.

The bodhisattva really feels *for* beings rather than suffering *with* them. He certainly doesn't suffer in the same way, or in the same sense, that they do. This is because he is Enlightened, and their suffering is due to their being unenlightened. His 'suffering' is a sympathy rather than an actual experience of suffering. And just as it is impossible actually to experience the toothache that another person experiences, however sympathetic you are, so the bodhisattva can never experience the suffering of not being Enlightened.

The bodhisattva's suffering is, in Tennyson's words, a 'painless sympathy with pain',[357] which in a way involves a pain of its own. And this pain is very different, both in quality and in degree, from the kind of sympathy that we might feel. To some people, indeed, a bodhisattva's sympathy might not seem like sympathy at all, inasmuch as it would not be an indulgent kind of sympathy.

Vimalakīrti's account of the sickness which arises from great Compassion is all very sublime, very deep, very true, very heartfelt – but Mañjuśrī is not satisfied. He is not going to let it rest there. So more brisk dialectical exchanges between Mañjuśrī and Vimalakīrti follow, in the course of which Vimalakīrti becomes very paradoxical indeed.

After this, in reply to another question from Mañjuśrī, Vimalakīrti explains how a bodhisattva should console another bodhisattva who is sick. He also explains, at great length, how a sick bodhisattva should control his mind, and this is followed by a long passage about the nature of the 'domain' of the bodhisattva. Among Vimalakīrti's many descriptions of this domain, there is this rather baffling specification:

> Where one seeks the gnosis of omniscience, yet does not attain this gnosis at the wrong time, there is the domain of the bodhisattva. Where one knows the Four Holy Truths, yet does not realize those truths at the wrong time, there is the domain of the bodhisattva.[358]

What might this mean? How can there possibly be a wrong time for the realization of the four noble truths, a wrong time for Enlightenment?

The 'wrong time' to 'attain this gnosis' is when the realization is sufficient to gain Arhantship, but not sufficient to gain full Enlightenment. If there is a real distinction between *samyak sambodhi*, supreme Enlightenment, and Arhantship, then you need more wisdom to gain *samyak sambodhi* than to attain Arhantship. And if you are a bodhisattva, you want to gain *samyak sambodhi*, so you don't develop the gnosis of omniscience as a basis for becoming 'merely' an *arhant*. Of course, the whole distinction between *samyak sambodhi* and Arhantship is an artificial one, inasmuch as it is a function of the historical development of the Mahāyāna. But there is a general point to it which holds good: one shouldn't settle down in a partial experience of Enlightenment, even though it may be a genuine experience of Enlightenment so far as it goes. To the extent that there is anything further to realize, one must continue to make an effort. Even the Buddha's Enlightenment was not final; he didn't settle down in a state of realization which thereafter remained the same.

There can't literally be a wrong time for Enlightenment; but there is the possibility that one will settle down in and take as ultimate an experience – whether of 'omniscience' or of the Four Truths – which is in fact only partial. The real mistake is to imagine that Enlightenment represents a sort of conclusion to one's development. If you don't make this mistake then even if you do attain some kind of gnosis, you won't make the mistake of resting on your laurels. You won't think you're Enlightened when you're not. This is what the text is really getting at. And the effect of the whole discourse is such that in eight thousand of those listening to Vimalakīrti the *bodhicitta*, 'the spirit of unexcelled, perfect enlightenment' as the text calls it, is awakened.

So the meeting between Vimalakīrti and Mañjuśrī has a dramatic effect; and it continues to do so over the next four chapters of the *Vimalakīrti-nirdeśa*. In fact, their confrontation is one of the main features of the whole work, and it is this that I want now to explore at greater length: the figures of Mañjuśrī and Vimalakīrti, facing each other just as I saw them in that ancient Chinese mural in 1956.

This meeting is more than a confrontation. It is a vigorous dialectical exchange in which neither bodhisattva spares the other. In a sense each is out to win, to defeat the other – but not in an egoistic way. Each is testing the other, just as a potter tests an earthenware pot to see whether it is cracked. In this confrontation each experiences or tests the other;

at the same time, each experiences or tests himself in contact with the other. Each experiences the truth, the reality, of the situation.

The contest between them therefore takes place within a context that is completely positive. Blake says 'Opposition is true friendship.'[359] Friendship, especially spiritual friendship, is not sentimental and indulgent. It is vigorous, challenging, demanding, bracing, invigorating, stimulating – like a cold shower, not a warm bath. In the last chapter we saw Vimalakīrti offering this kind of vigorous friendship to the various *arhants* and bodhisattvas. They were not quite able to stand up to it – it was rather too much for them – but Mañjuśrī is equal to the challenge. The two are in fact more or less evenly matched – so they can be friends.

Nietzsche takes Blake's *aperçu* even further, saying that one's enemies are really one's friends. The greater the enemy, the better the friend. Towards the end of chapter 6 of the *Vimalakīrti-nirdeśa* Vimalakīrti himself says much the same thing in his own way. Mahākāśyapa, one of the *arhants*, has just exclaimed:

> What could the entire host of Māras [the evil ones] ever do to one who is devoted to this inconceivable liberation?

To which Vimalakīrti replies:

> Reverend Mahākāśyapa [they are always very polite to each other in these Mahāyāna texts], the Māras who play the devil in the innumerable universes of the ten directions are all bodhisattvas dwelling in the inconceivable liberation, who are playing the devil in order to develop living beings through their skill in liberative technique. Reverend Mahākāśyapa, all the miserable beggars who come to the bodhisattvas of the innumerable universes of the ten directions to ask for a hand, a foot, an ear, a nose, some blood [they do all these things in the Jātaka stories], muscles, bones, marrow, an eye, a torso, a head, a limb, a member, a throne, a kingdom, a country, a wife, a son, a daughter, a slave, a slave-girl, a horse, an elephant, a chariot, a cart, gold, silver, jewels, pearls, conches, crystal, coral, beryl, treasures, food, drink, elixirs, and clothes – these demanding beggars are usually bodhisattvas living in the inconceivable liberation who, through their skill in liberative technique, wish to test and thus demonstrate the firmness of the high resolve of the bodhisattvas.

Why? Reverend Mahākāśyapa, the bodhisattvas demonstrate that firmness by means of terrible austerities. Ordinary persons have no power to be thus demanding of bodhisattvas, unless they are granted the opportunity. They are not capable of killing and depriving in that manner without being freely given the chance.

Reverend Mahākāśyapa, just as a glowworm cannot eclipse the light of the sun, so, reverend Mahākāśyapa, it is not possible without special allowance that an ordinary person can thus attack and deprive a bodhisattva. Reverend Mahākāśyapa, just as a donkey could not muster an attack on a wild elephant, even so, reverend Mahākāśyapa, one who is not himself a bodhisattva cannot harass a bodhisattva. Only one who is himself a bodhisattva can harass another bodhisattva.... Reverend Mahākāśyapa, such is the introduction to the power of the knowledge of liberative technique of the bodhisattvas who live in the inconceivable liberation.[360]

In the last chapter we saw how Indra, the king of the gods, approached the bodhisattva Jagatīṃdhara and offered him twelve thousand heavenly maidens, which Jagatīṃdhara refused – and how Vimalakīrti came along and said that it was not Indra at all but Māra, the evil one. But in the light of this passage it seems we can go even further than that. Yes, 'Indra' was Māra. But – and this is a question we must put aside as simply a subject for reflection – who was Māra?

The positive aspects of confrontation explain why Vimalakīrti and Mañjuśrī represent what I have called history *versus* myth in our quest for meaning. But what do I mean by our quest for meaning? And we might well ask – as modern scholars, critics, and philosophers have asked – what 'meaning' means in any case. It is not even altogether self-evident what we mean by 'history' and 'myth'. And how does history oppose myth? We shall be going into these questions, but we shall not be going into them very systematically or directly. We shall simply be bringing out some of the implications of the scene depicted in that mural painting. The painting itself is the real answer, the direct answer; that is, the answers are to be sought and found in terms of vision and imagination.

Let us start with the figure of Vimalakīrti. First of all, he is an old man. He has a long white wispy beard, even long white wispy eyebrows, and a puckered, wrinkled, but cheerful and humorous old face. It is quite obvious that he is subject to the process of time – as are we all, even though we might not be wrinkled and white-haired (with or without the wispy beard) – yet.

Not only is Vimalakīrti subject to time, he also lives at a particular point in time. He lives at the time of the Buddha, which according to modern scholarship is the sixth century BCE. He's also subject to space. He lives in a particular part of the world, in the great Indian mercantile city of Vaiśālī. He lives in a particular part of the city, in a particular house (even though at the beginning of chapter 5 he makes it disappear). He has a particular personal identity. He is known by a particular name and belongs to a particular social group. He follows a particular occupation (being apparently engaged in some sort of business), and has, or appears to have, a wife and children. Vimalakīrti thus has a historical personality, a historical existence, an existence which is specific, concrete, contingent, an existence which is determined by time, space, and causality. Vimalakīrti therefore represents historical reality. This does not necessarily mean, incidentally, that he actually existed; this is indeed a matter for dispute among modern Western scholars. What it means is that Vimalakīrti is depicted in the *Vimalakīrti-nirdeśa* as a historical personality.

Mañjuśrī, on the other hand, is a young man. In fact, he is eternally young; that is, he is not subject to the process of time, he does not live at any particular point in time. Nor is he subject to space. He doesn't live in any part of the world. (Chinese Buddhists did try to locate him on Mount Wutai, one of the five sacred mountains of Buddhist China, but their attempt was not very successful.) However, while he is not bound to any particular time or place, he can *appear* at any time and in any place. Moreover, while Mañjuśrī has a particular personal identity, it is not a mundane identity. His name is a no-name. He doesn't belong to any particular group, doesn't follow any particular occupation. He just does, as occasion arises, whatever is necessary to help living beings develop. And he certainly doesn't have even the semblance of a wife and children.

Mañjuśrī thus has no historical existence. He is not a historical personality. He has an existence which in a manner of speaking is specific and concrete, but which is not contingent, not determined by time, space, or causality. He has what may be called a transcendental existence, a glorified individuality, as his physical appearance suggests. He is not only young but extremely beautiful; he is clad in silks and jewels, and his entire body is surrounded by an aura of brilliant golden light. Mañjuśrī therefore represents supra-historical or archetypal reality; he represents myth. Myth, that is, understood loosely, rather than in any literal sense of the word. In fact, the word does not really have a literal sense. In recent times a whole industry has been set up to explain the meaning of ancient myths; but myths cannot really be explained or understood in a conceptual sense. The meaning of myths, of myth in general, has to be felt, experienced, enacted – lived.

If you take a myth in the modern, sophisticated sense, it has its effect on you, but if you are able to believe that the myth is literally true, it has a much greater effect. For instance, if you are a Christian and you believe that the resurrection of Christ has a deep symbolical significance, even though he didn't literally rise from the dead, the resurrection is a very meaningful symbol for you. But if as an orthodox Christian you believe that Christ literally rose from the dead because he was the son of God and he had that power inherent in him, your belief will have much deeper foundations, or at least you will be more strongly motivated. The nature of our approach to 'myth' is one of the basic questions that have to be faced nowadays, not only by Christians but by Buddhists as well.

For Buddhists, however, it is not such a key issue, because in Buddhism, especially early Buddhism, the taking of myth as literal truth doesn't occupy such an important place. If you read, for example, that the Buddha walked up and down in the air emitting water and fire at the same time, you can believe that quite literally and no doubt find it inspiring.[361] But taking that myth – if it is a myth – literally doesn't occupy the kind of central place in Buddhism that belief in the resurrection of Christ occupies in Christianity. There is no doubt, however, that if you are able to take myth as being literally true, you are likely to practise your religion more zealously and energetically. Of course, such literal belief can go to the undesirable extreme of fanatical fundamentalism. But in avoiding that, perhaps we need to take care not to fall into too sophisticated or rational an approach to myth. The whole point about the realm of myth is that it is a realm not of clearly defined meanings, but of undefined, even indefinable meanings. To this realm also belong such things as symbols, archetypal images, the imagination itself, and poetry.

But just where does Mañjuśrī come from? Where does myth come from? We need be in no doubt about Vimalakīrti's origin; like Gautama the Buddha, he is represented as a historical personality playing his part on the stage of history. But the figure of Mañjuśrī requires some explanation. He is not found in the Pāli scriptures. How did he get into Buddhism? How did he get into the pages of the *Vimalakīrti-nirdeśa*? How did he get into the Buddha's assembly?

We can begin to answer this question by reaching back to the Pāli scriptures, which are the records of the Buddha's teaching kept by the Theravāda or 'School of Elders', one of the earliest schools of Buddhism. Although these scriptures were not written down until several hundred years after the Buddha's *parinirvāṇa*, the oldest parts of them undoubtedly reflect, at least to some extent, the conditions under which Gautama the Buddha lived and taught, and the form that his teachings assumed. We find in them a great deal of information about the political situation, social conditions, economic life, manners and customs, religious beliefs and superstitions prevalent in the India of the Buddha's time. They are in fact our main source of information about northern India during this period. The result is that in the Pāli scriptures we find the Dharma deeply embedded in its historical context, even overlaid to some extent by that context. We find a Buddhism that is a historical phenomenon; a Buddhism determined by time, space, and causality; a Buddhism that exists and expresses itself in terms of historical reality, but which is also obscured and concealed by that historical reality.

Like the figure of Vimalakīrti, the Buddhism of the Pāli scriptures belongs to the realm of historical rather than archetypal reality. It is true that some elements of myth are found in the Pāli scriptures, but these are found in a rudimentary though still very beautiful form, mainly in parables and extended similes. By contrast, the elements of historical reality found in the Mahāyāna *sūtras* occupy a distinctly subordinate place. For instance, in the *Vimalakīrti-nirdeśa* we find ourselves in Āmrapālī's Garden and in the city of Vaiśālī, but into this realm of homely historical reality there irrupts the realm of archetypal, even spiritual, reality. Or, to put it another way, the realm of homely historical reality is made to open up in all directions into the realm of archetypal reality, as when Vimalakīrti or the Buddha performs a miracle or puts on a display of magical power.

The origins of the Mahāyāna *sūtras* lie partly in the dissatisfaction of some early Buddhists with the Pāli scriptures. They were not satisfied with the expression of Buddhism in terms of historical reality. They were not interested – as nowadays we only too often are interested – in Buddhism as a historical phenomenon. The notion of history in the modern sense was in any case probably quite unknown to them. For them, the Dharma really was *sanātana*, eternal. They wanted to free it from its historical context, to emancipate it from the limitations of a merely historical existence.

They were interested, we could say, in what the Buddha said rather than in the historical conditions under which he said it. They were committed to the Dharma as a living spiritual reality. Consequently, they tended to forget the historical situation in which the Buddha lived and taught. It didn't seem very important to them. Instead, they concentrated more and more on the Buddha as a purely spiritual personality, and on the Dharma as a purely spiritual truth whose deeper implications they sought to bring out.

Thus they sought not only to emancipate the Dharma from the limitations of history, but also to universalize it, to reformulate it in such a way as to make it applicable not just to the people of northern India in the sixth century BCE, but to all living beings throughout time and throughout space. This was, of course, implicit in the Dharma as the Buddha taught it. He taught it, after all, *bahujana hitāya, bahujana sukhāya*, 'for the welfare and happiness of many people'.[362] But the forebears of the Mahāyānists felt that the universal quality of Buddhism needed to be made more explicit. This dehistoricizing, universalizing, idealizing tendency was one aspect of the development of what later came to be known as the Mahāyāna, which eventually found expression in the Mahāyāna scriptures.

Another element the Mahāyānists brought to the teachings was a love of adornment and decoration. A friend of mine once remarked, 'That which we love, we adorn.' If this is true, the Mahāyāna scriptures show us how very much those who originated them must have loved the Dharma, because they adorned it magnificently. They set it in an ideal, archetypal realm, flashing with light and glowing with all the colours of the rainbow, a realm where everything was made of jewels, and the air was filled with music and perfume. In short, they transferred the Dharma from the realm of historical reality to the realm of spiritual reality, from the realm of history to the realm of what I have called myth.

We can see this process most clearly, perhaps, in the development of the figure of the Buddha himself. In the Pāli scriptures the Buddha appears as a wandering religious mendicant. The texts describe him as 'shaven-headed', but we must not imagine him with a shiny pate; his head and chin were probably covered in a heavy stubble. His 'robes' were not the bright, carefully laundered garb of the modern *bhikkhu*, but ochre-coloured rags. He carried a wooden or metal begging-bowl. From a distance he must have been indistinguishable from the thousands of other wandering ascetics who thronged India in his time – and still do today. The Pāli scriptures themselves describe occasions on which the Buddha was not recognized by other people, even by *bhikkhus* at close quarters.

But it is impossible to mistake the Buddha of the Mahāyāna for anyone else. As he appears in the Mahāyāna scriptures, he is seated on a lofty, elaborate, jewelled throne with a canopy of jewels suspended, glittering, above his head. The begging-bowl in his lap appears to be carved from a solid block of lapis-lazuli or emerald, and a brilliant golden light radiates from his head and body. He teaches the Dharma not just for a few hours, or a few years, or the span of a human life, but for age upon age without pause. He teaches it in a purely spiritual or archetypal realm, to hundreds of thousands, even millions, of living beings. Some of these beings – like *arhants* such as Ānanda – are figures familiar to us from the Pāli scriptures, but others are not familiar to us at all. And among these unfamiliar figures are the bodhisattvas, including, of course, Mañjuśrī.

So if you read the Pāli scriptures and then the Mahāyāna scriptures – say two or three volumes of each, enough to give you a taste of them – you will notice that you get something from the Mahāyāna scriptures that is completely missing from the Pāli texts. This is not by any means to dismiss the unique historical and spiritual importance of the Pāli scriptures. They give us a vivid and deeply moving picture of the life and teaching career of the human historical Buddha. They contain all the basic spiritual principles and practices from which all the subsequent forms of Buddhism developed. They are rich in content and full of inspiration. We cannot possibly dispense with the Pāli scriptures; as Buddhists, we are enormously indebted to them. Humanity, in fact, is indebted to them. They cannot be praised enough and we cannot be sufficiently grateful for them.

They do not, however, contain everything that everybody needs. There is an element missing, and it is this element that we find in the Mahāyāna scriptures. Reading the Mahāyāna scriptures, we are emancipated from the contingent and the determinate, from time, space, and causality, from historical reality. We experience archetypal reality, myth, the realm of undefined meanings. In technical terms, we encounter the *sambhogakāya*. That is, we encounter the Buddhas and bodhisattvas of the Mahāyāna in their archetypal forms. Through this experience we contact something within us of which we were not previously aware. Something is sparked off that even the Pāli scriptures were unable to spark off. And this happens because the realm of archetypal reality, of myth, of undefined meanings, corresponds to something within us.

According to the *Tibetan Book of the Dead*, we experience this realm directly when we die. In the intermediate state between death and rebirth we experience all sorts of visions, including visions of Buddhas and bodhisattvas in both their peaceful and their wrathful forms. And the Buddhist tradition tells us not to be afraid, but to recognize all these visions, all these Buddhas and bodhisattvas, as our own thought forms, as phenomena of our own true mind. If we can do this, we attain liberation on the spot.

As a writer, one inevitably notices a difference in feeling between the experience of composing passages of conceptual prose and the experience of writing something more creative, more inspired or poetic. It is this kind of shift we feel when we make the transition from the prose of the Pāli scriptures to the poetry of the Mahāyāna scriptures, the transition from history to myth on a grand scale.

Unfortunately, some people cannot make this transition. Take the well-known case of Charles Darwin. As a young man Darwin loved poetry and literature, especially Shakespeare, but for the greater part of his life he immersed himself in scientific research. When as an old man he tried to get back to Shakespeare, he found to his dismay that poetry held no meaning for him any more; he had lost his capacity to enjoy it. In the course of his years, even decades, of scientific research a whole side of him had withered and died.[363] Much the same happened to John Stuart Mill, at least for part of his life. Even as a small boy his favourite subjects were logic and political economy; and as he grew older he found that he became more and more cut off from poetry. It is not just that he was cut off from poetry in the literary sense; he was – to put it rather poetically – cut off from the poetry of life.

Today we are all exposed to this sort of danger. We all suffer from this sort of deprivation, at least to some extent. We have been suffering from it, in fact, since the Industrial Revolution, at the beginning of which William Blake warned against the loss of what he called 'the divine vision'. He criticized Bacon, Newton, and Locke so vigorously because he felt that they tended to limit humanity to the realm of historical reality, the realm of time, space, and causality.[364] In his own literary and visual creative work Blake, of course, was not limited in this way. In his Prophetic Books especially he explores the deeper levels of human experience. Blake's profound concern with archetypal forces and forms must explain why he continues to hold such a great fascination for so many people today.

Our desire to contact the realm of the archetypal also explains the popularity of tales of myth and fantasy, whether traditional, like the stories of King Arthur, or modern, like *The Lord of the Rings* and some forms of science fiction. Such works explore facets of humanity's quest for meaning, and in reading them we are trying, perhaps unconsciously, to break out of the prison of merely historical reality, seeking to experience a deeper meaning to our existence.

Meaning is not a thing that you can grasp by looking in a dictionary. Meaning must be meaning *for you*, something that you personally experience. Our quest for meaning is therefore our quest for ourselves, our quest for the totality, the wholeness, of our own being. On one level we belong to the realm of historical reality; but on another, we belong to the realm of spiritual reality. The Mahāyāna scriptures reveal this world to us. So does myth; so does poetry. And they reveal it to us not as something external to ourselves, but as our own world, as a world in which we ourselves actually live, usually without knowing it.

It was a maxim of the Neoplatonists that the eye could not behold the sun unless it had within its nature something sun-like, something akin to the sun.[365] Similarly, we can experience the archetypal realm only because we ourselves are, on another level, archetypal beings. If we really allow ourselves to become absorbed in a Mahāyāna *sūtra*, we become part of it. We join the great assembly and experience ourselves right in the midst of it, taking part in the events of the *sūtra* as they unfold.

But although we can make the transition to the realm of archetypal reality, this does not mean that we leave the realm of historical reality behind. We cannot – must not – opt for myth and discard history. We need both – because we exist in both realms. We exist in them both all the time, whether or not we are aware of it. And of course a lot of the time we are not aware of it. Our relation to the archetypal realm is analogous to our relation to the dream state. When we are asleep and dreaming, we exist, one might say, in the dream realm, and we have all sorts of experiences. When we wake up, we are no longer in the dream state, but the emotions we experienced while we were dreaming continue. It's just like an underground river that we descend into from time to time through a hole in the ground. Just as the river is flowing all the time, so there is continuity between dreams. You can even have a dream, wake up, and then fall asleep again and continue with the same dream, as though it has been going on all the time.

So in a sense we are living in that dream realm all the time. And we can extend that to the realm of archetypal experience. Just as a very strong dream continues to have its effect when we have woken up, so the archetypal realm continues to affect us, whether or not we are conscious of it. There is no question, therefore, of our literally passing from one realm to the other. They do not even exist side by side. In the mural painting Vimalakīrti and Mañjuśrī *confront* one another in a vigorous encounter. This is history *versus* myth – and what we have to do is bring them together. There has to be a sort of 'marriage' between Vimalakīrti and Mañjuśrī. We have to realize that Vimalakīrti *is* Mañjuśrī, and Mañjuśrī *is* Vimalakīrti. Time is eternity; eternity is time. *Rūpa* is *śūnyatā*; *śūnyatā* is *rūpa*. If we can realize that, then history and myth will have played their part in humanity's quest for meaning; and that quest for meaning – our quest for ourselves – will be complete.

6
THE WAY OF NON-DUALITY

So Mañjuśrī and Vimalakīrti confront each other in Vimalakīrti's 'empty' house in Vaiśālī. In front of an audience of thousands upon thousands of bodhisattvas, *arhants*, gods, and goddesses, they discourse profoundly on the sickness of bodhisattvas and living beings, on the nature of emptiness, and on the domain of the bodhisattvas, where all extremes, all dualities, are transcended. The entire company is spellbound by their eloquence. In fact, in eight thousand gods and goddesses the *bodhicitta* – the will towards supreme perfect Enlightenment for the sake of all living beings – is awakened.

And yet, at the beginning of chapter 6, 'The Inconceivable Liberation', our friend Śāriputra has a problem. There is now an immense crowd in Vimalakīrti's house – but all the furniture has disappeared. Where is everybody going to sit? After all, Śāriputra is perhaps thinking, according to ancient Indian etiquette, no guest of whatever kind should be kept standing. Bodhisattvas and *arhants* should certainly not have to remain standing while Vimalakīrti is lying on his couch, even though he is sick.

As we know, Vimalakīrti has the disconcerting faculty of telepathy. Knowing Śāriputra's thoughts, he puts to him a rather pointed question:

> Reverend Śāriputra, did you come here for the sake of the Dharma? Or did you come here for the sake of a chair?

Well, you can imagine Śāriputra's feelings! He very humbly replies:

> I came for the sake of the Dharma, not for the sake of a chair.

But Vimalakīrti continues, saying:

> Reverend Śāriputra, he who is interested in the Dharma is not interested even in his own body, much less in a chair.[366]

And, no doubt to Śāriputra's great embarrassment, he presses the point home, carrying on in this vein for several paragraphs.

But Vimalakīrti's initial question gives us quite enough to think about. We may be tempted to smile at poor old Śāriputra. Here we have a great assembly of bodhisattvas, *arhants*, and all sorts of extraordinary beings. The wise elder Vimalakīrti and Mañjuśrī, the Bodhisattva of Wisdom himself, have just had a discussion of tremendous spiritual significance. Everybody has been highly delighted and uplifted by it, and they are all wondering what is going to happen next. And Śāriputra starts worrying about chairs....

But if we find Śāriputra's behaviour a source of amusement, we should also be able to look to our own behaviour for further amusement, because this little incident warns us against a danger to which we are all liable – the danger of getting sidetracked. Say we attend a meditation class, or a lecture on the Dharma, or perhaps even go away on retreat into the depths of the countryside. We may get quite deeply absorbed in our meditation, or engaged in the lecture, or immersed in the retreat experience – but sooner or later our attention wanders. We start wondering when the tea and biscuits are going to appear, or whether a certain attractive person we saw last week will be there, or whether the central heating is going to be turned up.

We might well ask ourselves the kind of question that Vimalakīrti asked Śāriputra. 'Did I come for the sake of the Dharma or did I come for the sake of the tea and biscuits?' 'Did I come for the sake of the Dharma or for the sake of seeing that attractive person?' 'Did I come for the sake of the Dharma or for the sake of the central heating?' There is nothing easier than to get sidetracked in this way, to succumb to the gravitational pull of the conditioned. We have a deeply ingrained tendency to be over-concerned with the mundane, the trivial, the everyday, at the expense of our spiritual development: in a word, to be over-concerned with comfort.

Before we move on, it is worth bearing in mind that the Śāriputra who appears in the *Vimalakīrti-nirdeśa* is not the same figure as the relatively historical Śāriputra (or rather Sāriputta) that we encounter in the pages of the Pāli scriptures. Historically, Śāriputra was one of the two most prominent disciples of the Buddha Śākyamuni (the other being Mahāmaudgalyāyana) and he was renowned as the wisest teacher of the Dharma after the Buddha himself. But in the Mahāyāna *sūtras* he came to represent the narrow, rather literalistic attitude that had developed in some Buddhist circles, and which the Mahāyāna tried to correct. We should therefore bear in mind that the *Vimalakīrti-nirdeśa* uses the figure of Śāriputra, both here and in several other places, in an imaginative rather than a historically factual manner. As Thurman puts it, perhaps rather crudely, he is used as a 'fall guy' to express the limited Hīnayāna view so that it can then be exposed by the Buddha, or by Vimalakīrti or some other bodhisattva. He also seems liable, as in this particular instance, to be prey to petty and mundane anxieties.

So Śāriputra is worried about chairs. All right, Vimalakīrti gives him chairs: thirty-two-hundred-thousand of them. And they are not ordinary chairs, but lion-thrones, brought by Vimalakīrti's magical power from a distant Buddha-land in the eastern direction, whence, according to Mañjuśrī, the best lion-thrones come. And all these thrones fit into Vimalakīrti's house without crowding; it seems to grow to accommodate them. And not only the house needs to grow. All the thrones are thirty-four-hundred-thousand leagues high, and the visitors have to be helped to enlarge their own bodies so that they can take advantage of these unusual seating arrangements. Perhaps not surprisingly, the *arhants* have more difficulty than the bodhisattvas, but this is soon overcome. Śāriputra remarks how astonishing the whole business is, and this gives Vimalakīrti the opportunity to explain the inconceivable emancipation, the state of emancipation in which a bodhisattva – through comprehending fully the relativity of space and time – can bring about all sorts of magical transformations.

In chapter 7, entitled 'The Goddess', Śāriputra is in trouble again. First of all though, Mañjuśrī asks Vimalakīrti how a bodhisattva should regard all living beings, and Vimalakīrti replies in a series of beautiful similes which illustrate how a bodhisattva should regard beings in order to realize that they are ultimately selfless or insubstantial. They are like the reflection of the moon in water, the sound of an echo, a flash of lightning, a face in the mirror, and so on. But if a bodhisattva considers all beings in this way, Mañjuśrī wants to know, how does he generate love towards them? And Vimalakīrti speaks very movingly about the nature of the loving kindness, the *mettā*, that the bodhisattva feels. After this poetic exchange, there follows another vigorous dialectical debate between the two bodhisattvas.

At this point a certain goddess appears. She lives, apparently, in Vimalakīrti's house and she is so delighted with the teaching she has been hearing that she showers the whole assembly – the *arhants*, the bodhisattvas, everybody – with flowers. In the case of the *arhants* – who being monks are not supposed to decorate themselves – the flowers become uncharacteristically and embarrassingly sticky. Despite his best efforts to brush them off, Śāriputra remains spectacularly adorned.

The goddess explains that the flowers do not stick to the bodies of the bodhisattvas because they – the bodhisattvas – have no attachment to discriminative views and thought-constructions. This leads to an exchange of views in which Śāriputra, as usual, comes off worst, and is at one point completely lost for words. A little later on he finds himself still more embarrassed when, to make a point about the relativity of manifesting as a man or as a woman, the goddess causes him to undergo a change of sex. First of all he changes from male to female, which is bad enough in his opinion, and then from female back to male, which is even worse. I am making fun of Śāriputra here, but the point is that undergoing a sex change from male to female really should have alerted him to the relativity of gender. But instead of becoming androgynous as a result of this experience, he remains within the dichotomy of gender – so when he returns to his original gender, he still hasn't really learned anything.

This incident has rather a modern ring to it, of course, in an era when having a 'sex change' in a literal sense is possible. From a spiritual point of view, I doubt very much whether having a sex change would help anyone to transcend the dichotomy of gender; those who have had such an operation often seem to have the experience of feeling trapped by it. Such changes represent alternation, not integration. Spiritually speaking, what is important is for a man to incorporate the so-called feminine psychological qualities, and for a woman to incorporate the so-called masculine ones – in addition to those proper to one's own physical-cum-psychological gender. This would be true androgyny, for which there could never be an operation. The surgeons might be able to make someone a hermaphrodite, but they could never make anyone genuinely androgynous.

Śāriputra's double 'sex change' happens in the space of a few minutes; and the chapter ends with Vimalakīrti praising the goddess as an irreversible bodhisattva. Chapter 8 is entitled 'The Family of the Tathāgatas' – that is, the family of the Buddhas. Replying to yet another question from Mañjuśrī, Vimalakīrti explains, in his usual highly paradoxical fashion, how the bodhisattva follows 'the way to attain the qualities of the Buddha'. Vimalakīrti himself then puts a question to Mañjuśrī, asking him what is meant by the expression 'family of the Tathāgatas'. Mañjuśrī's response is also highly paradoxical, and it is praised at some length by Mahākāśyapa.

Following this discussion of families, a bodhisattva called Sarvarūpasaṃdarśana ('Universal Manifestation') then asks Vimalakīrti a whole string of questions about his own family:

> Householder, where are your father and mother, your children, your wife,

– remember that Vimalakīrti is lying there on his couch and nobody else can be seen –

> your servants, your maids, your laborers, and your attendants? Where are your friends, your relatives, and your kinsmen? Where are your servants, your horses, your elephants, your chariots, your bodyguards, and your bearers?[367]

Vimalakīrti replies to this typically Indian enquiry in a long series of beautiful verses, over forty of them. They last until the end of the chapter and comprise the longest verse passage in the *Vimalakīrti-nirdeśa*. Here, just to give a taste of them, are the first twelve:

Of the true bodhisattvas,
  The mother is the transcendence of wisdom,
The father is the skill in liberative technique;
  The Leaders are born of such parents.

Their wife is the joy in the Dharma,
  Love and compassion are their daughters,
The Dharma and the truth are their sons;
  And their home is deep thought on the meaning of voidness.

All the passions are their disciples,
  Controlled at will.
Their friends are the aids to enlightenment;
  Thereby they realize supreme enlightenment.

Their companions, ever with them,
  Are the six transcendences.
Their consorts are the means of unification,
  Their music is the teaching of the Dharma.

The incantations make their garden,
  Which blossoms with the flowers of the factors of
    enlightenment,
With trees of the great wealth of the Dharma,
  And fruits of the gnosis of liberation.

Their pool consists of the eight liberations,
  Filled with the water of concentration,
Covered with the lotuses of the seven purities –
  Who bathes therein becomes immaculate.

Their bearers are the six superknowledges,
  Their vehicle is the unexcelled Mahāyāna,
Their driver is the spirit of enlightenment,
  And their path is the eightfold peace.

Their ornaments are the auspicious signs,
  And the eighty marks;

Their garland is virtuous aspiration,
And their clothing is good conscience and consideration.

Their wealth is the holy Dharma,
And their business is its teaching,
Their great income is pure practice,
And it is dedicated to the supreme enlightenment.

Their bed consists of the four contemplations,
And its spread is the pure livelihood,
And their awakening consists of gnosis,
Which is constant learning and meditation.

Their food is the ambrosia of the teachings,
And their drink is the juice of liberation.
Their bath is pure aspiration,
And morality their unguent and perfume.

Having conquered the enemy passions,
They are the invincible heroes.
Having subdued the four Māras,
They raise their standard on the field of enlightenment.[368]

In this way we come to chapter 9, 'The Dharma Door of Non-Duality'. The structure of this chapter is very simple. Vimalakīrti asks the bodhisattvas a question, to which thirty-one of them in turn give answers. The same question is then put by the bodhisattvas to Mañjuśrī, and by Mañjuśrī to Vimalakīrti, and each of them answers it in his own way. The question Vimalakīrti asks is 'Please explain how the bodhisattvas enter the Dharma-door of non-duality.'

Now, what kind of question is this? To begin with, what is meant by the expression 'Dharma-door'? It is a term which occurs frequently in Mahāyāna texts – *dharma-mukha* is the Sanskrit expression. In this context, *dharma* has its usual meaning – the teaching or the doctrine of the Buddha – and *mukha* is 'door', 'entrance', 'opening', or 'mouth'. The Dharma is a door in the sense that it is a means of access to the ultimate truth, to the experience of Enlightenment. But a door, any door, has a twofold function. It can open into something, but it can also shut something out. In the same way, the Dharma is a means of entrance into ultimate truth when it is approached as a means to an end, but it shuts you out from ultimate truth when it is taken as an end in itself. If you regard it as an end in itself, the door – or what should have been the door – becomes just part of the wall. You may even forget that it was ever meant for going through. Furthermore, the word Dharma itself has a double meaning. As well as meaning the teaching or doctrine, it also means the truth or reality indicated by that teaching or doctrine. So the Dharma is the door to the Dharma: the Dharma as teaching is the door to the Dharma as reality – provided it is not taken as an end in itself.

To return to Vimalakīrti's question: How do the bodhisattvas enter the Dharma-door of non-duality? What *is* the bodhisattva's Dharma-door of non-duality? The Dharma as teaching or doctrine is expressed in concepts, and every concept you can think of has an opposite. If there is truth, there must be falsehood. If there is brightness, there must be darkness. The Dharma is therefore always expressed, whether explicitly or implicitly, in terms of pairs of opposites – that is, in terms of duality. The Yogācāra, a philosophical school of Mahāyāna Buddhism, offers a reason for this. It says that concepts are the creation of the *kliṣṭā-mano-vijñāna* or 'defiled-mind-consciousness', which sees everything, even reality itself, in terms of pairs of opposites.[369] But in the experience of reality, all duality is transcended, even the duality between duality and non-duality. Reality is *advaya*, non-dual. In reality, duality is not obliterated – one is not left with a blank featureless unity – for there can be no question of obliterating something which in reality does not exist.

We ourselves are creatures of duality. Our consciousness is dualistic; our experience is dualistic; our thoughts, words, and deeds are dualistic; our understanding and practice of the Dharma is dualistic. The Dharma itself is expressed in terms of concepts which are pairs of opposites: skilful and unskilful; mundane and transcendental; conditioned and unconditioned; bondage and liberation; defilement and purity. We have to use dualistic expressions as a means of realizing non-dual reality; we have no alternative. And in fact it works because in reality there is no absolute duality between duality and non-duality. If this were not true, no emancipation would be possible.

But how in practice can we realize non-duality by means of the dualistic? This is what Vimalakīrti is getting at in his question to the bodhisattvas. How do the bodhisattvas make a dualistic Dharma function in a non-dualistic way? Being themselves riddled with dualism, how do they follow the way of non-duality?

It's a good question, and the bodhisattvas, one by one, set about answering it. Each bodhisattva, speaking from his own point of view, states a pair of opposites, a duality, and then shows how, by means of the contradictions inherent in it, that duality can be transcended in terms of itself.

For example, the bodhisattva Bhadrajyotis says:

> 'Distraction' and 'attention' are two. When there is no distraction, there will be no attention, no mentation, and no mental intensity. Thus, the absence of mental intensity is the entrance into nonduality.[370]

This is Thurman's translation. Lamotte's version makes the meaning a little clearer: 'Distraction and attention are two. If there is no distraction, there is neither attention nor reflection nor interest. This absence of interest is the entry into non-duality.'[371]

The word used for distraction is *vikṣepa*, which means distraction in the sense of floundering: the floundering, the tossing, the wandering of the mind. And the word for attention is *manana* in the sense of 'paying attention'. We could also perhaps render the word as 'concentration' but it is not quite the same thing. *Manana* is more like what makes concentration possible.

This pair of opposites is experienced especially within the context of meditation, as anybody who practises meditation knows very well. What usually happens is that we begin by paying attention to our object of concentration – breath, mantra, whatever it may be. But after a while the mind gets restless. It feels uncomfortable and starts to wander. Sooner or later we become aware of what has happened – what *is* happening – and we start paying attention again. In this way we oscillate between the two: distraction and attention, distraction and attention. This is how our meditation proceeds.

If we are to learn to concentrate in meditation, we will have to find the doorway to non-duality. We have to question the very terms of the situation – or rather, question the absoluteness of those terms. We have to realize that it is not enough to try to sustain attention by means of a forcible act of will. If distractions persistently arise when we are meditating, we have not understood ourselves deeply enough. There are psychological factors at work within us of which we are not conscious. We need, therefore, to become conscious of them, to take them into consideration – in a word, to become more integrated. When we are more integrated, the different elements of our being will no longer be in conflict with one another, and we will no longer have to oscillate between them, because they will all pull in the same direction.

So in the case of distraction and attention, integration is the entry into non-duality. Integration within the context of meditation practice is not synonymous with the experience of non-duality in the highest sense, but it is certainly a step in that direction. This does not mean that we should never try to concentrate, never try to get rid of distractions. That may be necessary as a provisional measure – in fact, it almost certainly will be. And some meditation practices – the mindfulness of breathing, for example – have an integrating effect. But in the long run the opposition between distraction and attention which plagues so much of our meditation practice can only be resolved if we become more psychologically and emotionally integrated.

Let's take another example. The bodhisattva Subāhu declares:

> 'Bodhisattva-spirit' and 'disciple-spirit' are two. When both are seen to resemble an illusory spirit, there is no bodhisattva-spirit, nor any disciple-spirit. Thus, the sameness of natures of spirits is the entrance into nonduality.[372]

Here, 'spirit' does not mean 'ghost'. It translates the Sanskrit *citta* and means something like 'mental attitude'. Again, Lamotte's translation is clearer: 'Bodhisattva mind and Listener mind are two. If it is seen that these two minds are the same as an illusionary mind, there is neither Bodhisattva mind nor Listener mind. This sameness of the mark of minds is the entry into non-duality.'[373]

'Illusory spirit' or 'illusionary mind' (*māyā-citta* in Sanskrit) is not a mind that is absolutely non-existent, but rather a mind that, like the magical show, cannot be defined in terms of existence or non-existence. It is a relatively real mind which has a relatively real existence, and which sees things in a relatively real way. It corresponds roughly to the *kliṣṭā-mano-vijñāna* or 'defiled-mind consciousness' of the Yogācāra, which sees things in terms of pairs of mutually exclusive opposites: self and other, good and bad, pure and impure, and so on.[374]

One of these pairs of apparent opposites is gaining emancipation for oneself alone, or gaining emancipation for others. If the illusory mind identifies itself with the latter, it becomes the bodhisattva-mind; if it identifies itself with the former, it becomes the *śrāvaka*-mind, the listener- or disciple-mind. But this distinction is ultimately unreal. You cannot progress spiritually yourself without paying attention to the needs of others, without developing friendliness and compassion. And you cannot help others to progress spiritually unless you have made some progress yourself.

Bodhisattva-mind and disciple-mind, bodhisattva ideal and *arhant* ideal, are not mutually exclusive. The Mahāyāna and the Hīnayāna are not mutually exclusive. Both are products of the illusory, relative, dualistic mind, and both represent attempts on the part of this mind to apprehend the nature of the non-dual spiritual ideal. If we understand the limitations of that mind, we will understand the limitations of bodhisattva-mind and disciple-mind considered as mutually exclusive. The realization that bodhisattva-mind and disciple-mind are both the same as illusory mind is the Dharma-door to non-duality. When we use terms like 'bodhisattva ideal' and '*arhant* ideal' we must realize that they have only a relative validity. They are not ends in themselves; their function is simply to help us grow.

Next, we'll examine a reply concerned with the concept of sin. The bodhisattva Siṃha says:

> 'Sinfulness' and 'sinlessness' are two. By means of the diamond-like wisdom that pierces to the quick, not to be bound or liberated is the entrance into nonduality.[375]

The word translated as 'sinfulness' is *sāvadya*. Lamotte translates it as 'blame', which is more literal. So, who blames us? Who says we are sinful? It could be the group; it could be an individual. Let's say it is the group. When we are blamed by the group, especially our own group, the group to which we feel we belong, we feel very wretched and miserable indeed. We may be ready to do almost anything to recapture the group's approval; we are completely at its mercy. The opposites here are praise and blame – we swing between elation when we are not blamed and wretchedness when we are. The situation becomes even worse when God comes into it. Then we may be found not just blameable but actually sinful. But we won't go into all that now – it is too horrible even to think about. What we need to do is find out how to escape the oscillation between praise and blame. The door to non-duality in this case is the development of transcendental individuality, an individuality which is not at the mercy of the group, which is in a sense indifferent to the opinion of the group.

It is difficult enough to develop ordinary individuality. Transcendental individuality can be developed only by means of Wisdom, the transcendental wisdom that cuts like a diamond, that sees through the power of the group. Ordinary mundane wisdom is not enough. The impact of the group on the individual is strong and persistent, and we cannot help weakening, even giving in, sometimes. Only transcendental individuality is strong enough to resist the pressure, to remain unaffected by the group's opinion. This is quite a sobering thought. It means that until we have entered the Stream[376] – for only then does transcendental individuality begin to develop – we shall continue to swing between praise and blame, between elation and wretchedness, at least to some extent.

No doubt other, more metaphysical interpretations of Siṃha's declaration are possible, but this one seems particularly appropriate to us. And we need not be afraid to place our own interpretations on traditional texts. When told that a rival saint had interpreted a passage in the Bible differently from himself, Saint Augustine apparently said calmly, 'The more interpretations the better.' This has always been the view of the Buddhist tradition towards its scriptures: the more interpretations the better. (I might note in passing, however, that this has not always or even usually been the view of the Christian tradition, where differences in interpretation have frequently been the cause of very bitter, even vicious, disputes and persecution.)

To take a fourth and last example, let's look at the declaration of the bodhisattva Śāntendriya. He says:

> It is dualistic to say 'Buddha', 'Dharma', and 'Sangha'. The Dharma is itself the nature of the Buddha, the Sangha is itself the nature of the Dharma, and all of them are uncompounded [or, as it is more usually expressed, Unconditioned]. The uncompounded

is infinite space, and the processes of all things are equivalent to infinite space. Adjustment to this is the entrance into nonduality.[377]

Here we have two pairs of opposites: Buddha and Dharma, Dharma and Sangha. Dharma, the term the two pairs have in common, is here to be taken in the more metaphysical sense: not the Buddha's teaching as expressed in words and concepts, but the ultimate reality of which that teaching is the expression and towards which it points. By virtue of his Enlightenment experience the Buddha is the living embodiment of the Dharma in this sense; so, as Śāntendriya declares, there is no duality between Dharma and Buddha.

We find something similar in the case of the Sangha – that is, the Ārya-Saṅgha, the spiritual community of bodhisattvas, *arhants*, non-returners, once-returners, and Stream Entrants. All of them are following the transcendental path, so all of them stand in some relation to the Unconditioned, some nearer, some further away. In some cases they have actually reached it. This means that in principle there is no duality between the Dharma and the Sangha. And if there is no difference between the Buddha and the Dharma, and no difference between the Dharma and the Sangha, there can be no difference between the Buddha and the Sangha. All three essentially *are* the Unconditioned. The Dharma is the Unconditioned itself; the Buddha is the Unconditioned as fully realized by the individual; and the Sangha is the Unconditioned in process of realization.

So in the case of the two pairs of opposites which make up the Three Jewels, the entry into non-duality is the realization that the Buddha, the Dharma, and the Sangha are essentially Unconditioned. So long as we see them as conditioned, we see them as three, but when we see them as Unconditioned, we see them as one. From this point of view, when we go for Refuge to the Three Jewels, we commit ourselves not to three different things, but to one Unconditioned non-dual ultimate Reality.

Now all this may sound rather metaphysical, not to say abstract – although these four examples are among the simpler, less metaphysical of the bodhisattvas' replies to Vimalakīrti's question. But the general drift is clear enough. Dualities, pairs of opposites – including those pairs of opposites which are the doctrinal categories of Buddhism itself – are created by the mind. One enters the Dharma-door of non-duality when one realizes that all pairs of opposites are created by the mind and that they are therefore not ultimately valid. They are not ends in themselves but means to an end, means to the spiritual development of the individual. Moreover, any pair of opposites whatsoever can be a Dharma-door to non-duality. Duality itself is the means to non-duality, because the duality between duality and non-duality is not ultimate.

This is still, it must be admitted, very much in the realm of the metaphysical. But we can apply the same principle on a much more down-to-earth level, and come up with our own dualities. Here are a few to begin with. They are certainly not so sublime as those of the *Vimalakīrti-nirdeśa*, but no doubt they come somewhat closer to our own experience and as such they may be more useful. They may not carry us as far into the depths of non-duality, but at least they will help us move in that direction from where we are now.

> Masculine and feminine are two; individuality is the entrance into non-duality.
> Organizer and organized are two; co-operation is the entrance into non-duality.
> Teacher and taught are two; communication is the entrance into non-duality.
> God and man are two; blasphemy is the entrance into non-duality.
> Male and female are two; celibacy is the entrance into non-duality.
> Individual and group are two; the spiritual community is the entrance into non-duality.

These are just a few suggestions; no doubt there are many more such dualities to be reflected on. But it is possible to go even further than seeking the entrance to non-duality in any pair of opposites, as Mañjuśrī's reply to Vimalakīrti's question shows. He says:

> Good sirs, you have all spoken well. Nevertheless, all your explanations are themselves dualistic. To know no one teaching, to express nothing, to say nothing, to explain nothing, to announce nothing, to indicate nothing, and to designate nothing – that is the entrance into non-duality.[378]

Mañjuśrī means that the bodhisattvas' explanations are dualistic because they are all expressed in terms of concepts, which are essentially dualistic. We cannot explain the bodhisattva's entry into non-duality by means of concepts; to explain it, we have to give up concepts altogether. We cannot, therefore, rely on words to explain non-duality. The only thing we can do is remain completely silent.

But to explain this, Mañjuśrī himself has resorted to speech. He has *said* that silence is the bodhisattva's entry into non-duality. So Mañjuśrī's explanation itself is not entirely free from duality. There is still one more step to be taken – and Vimalakīrti takes it.

> Then, the crown prince Mañjuśrī said to the Licchavi Vimalakīrti, 'We have all given our own teachings, noble sir. Now, may you elucidate the teaching of the entrance into the principle of non-duality!'
>
> Thereupon, the Licchavi Vimalakīrti kept his silence, saying nothing at all.[379]

Vimalakīrti remains completely silent. He puts into actual practice what Mañjuśrī has only expressed in terms of concepts. This is the famous 'thunder-like' silence of Vimalakīrti, the silence that is more powerful, more expressive, than any words. And it represents not only the climax of the chapter, but surely the climax of the entire *Vimalakīrti-nirdeśa*.

But is not Vimalakīrti's reply also dualistic? Speech and silence are opposites. To explain the bodhisattva's entry into non-duality in terms of silence is therefore surely as dualistic as explaining it in terms of speech. What is the entry into non-duality here? The answer is that Vimalakīrti does not have a concept of silence. He acts spontaneously according to the circumstances. That is why his silence here is meaningful. After all, there is silence and silence. In chapters 3 and 4 the *arhants* and bodhisattvas were reduced to silence when they encountered Vimalakīrti. In chapter 8 Śāriputra was reduced to silence by the goddess. But theirs was the silence of stupefaction. Vimalakīrti's is the silence of understanding, the silence of Enlightenment.

Vimalakīrti uses silence, but he has no concept of using it. He uses it as a means to an end, to communicate, but he also uses speech whenever necessary. He does not stick to silence. In fact, in the course of the *Vimalakīrti-nirdeśa* he says rather a lot. And speech and silence are not his only means of communication. He communicates also through marvellous magical displays. The means of communication are, in fact, infinite, as we shall see in the next chapter.

7
THE MYSTERY OF HUMAN COMMUNICATION

What can possibly follow Vimalakīrti's thunder-like silence? One might think that almost anything, however sublime, however impressive, would be an anti-climax. But as it turns out, it is not really so difficult to follow – not, at least, for Śāriputra. At the beginning of chapter 10 we find him worrying again. The text says:

> Thereupon, the venerable Śāriputra thought to himself, 'If these great bodhisattvas do not adjourn before noontime, when are they going to eat?'[380]

A short while ago, he was worrying about chairs. Now he is worrying about lunch.

But why is he so concerned that they should eat before noon? Well, Śāriputra is a monk, and according to the Hīnayāna Vinaya, the monastic law, monks are supposed to finish eating by noon. If they haven't managed to have a meal by then, they just have to wait until the following morning. Even then, they are not permitted to eat until they can clearly distinguish the lines on their own hand by means of natural light.[381]

This rule is still observed in many parts of the Buddhist world. I followed it myself for several years when I lived in India, and there is quite a lot I could say about what some monks used rather irreverently to call 'the twelve o'clock business'. Monks are generally dependent for food on the laity. I often noticed that if lunch had not made its appearance by 11.30am – or even 10.30 – some of my fellow monks became very uneasy. A few started worrying about lunch as soon as breakfast was over. And some would get up at the crack of dawn so that they could have an enormous breakfast, then go back to bed and have a second breakfast later, and still have time for lunch before twelve o'clock. In a famous passage Buddhaghosa declares that someone is a 'one-mealer' even if they eat ten meals, provided they eat them all before noon.[382] This is the Theravāda at its most ridiculously formalistic.

What I do take seriously is the principle of moderation in eating – and you could practise this by eating only in the evening as effectively as by eating only in the morning. The Sufis apparently try to observe a perpetual Ramadan, eating only after dark. But you could eat ten times a day and still be practising moderate eating, if you ate just a small quantity. The important thing is to eat mindfully, and eat only what is really necessary for health and strength.

It is a good thing to have a definite framework of behaviour, definite guidelines, especially when one is young, and it is even a good thing to be quite strict in observing those guidelines. An old Brahmin lawyer I used to know in India, a very rigid, orthodox old man, was fond of saying, 'A disciplined life gives strength,' and this is true. In the case of this old man, he derived his strength from following the brahminical rules, with some of which I would violently disagree because they involved the strict observance of the caste system. But they did make him into a very strong character, because he believed that he was following a divinely inspired way of life.

But following a system of discipline doesn't necessarily have any spiritual value at all. You develop a kind of strength in the army, in which you are governed by a certain ethos and have to observe certain rules. And even the 'rules' of Buddhism, the guidelines which you find in the traditional Vinaya Piṭaka, are not necessarily helpful to us now. The principle behind all of them is probably still valid, but it may require a different application, a different expression. It might be a useful exercise to go through all the Vinaya rules systematically, examining each rule to see what principle is involved, how it was applied or formulated in the Buddha's day, whether that formulation still applies, and, if not, what fresh formulation of that principle might be helpful.

Some Theravādins would argue that one should continue to observe the rules out of faith in the Buddha. This sort of attitude cannot be disregarded altogether, but one could argue that it could not be the result of faith, because the Buddha encouraged his followers to think for themselves. The value of observing rules is not to be underestimated, but one has to give careful thought to what rules one does observe and why; one should not be inflexible about it.

It is no good trying to defend the Vinaya rules by saying, 'If it was good enough for the Buddha, it's good enough for me.' We shouldn't just accept the tradition unthinkingly. It's a question of finding a middle way. You can't go it alone, relying in a one-sided, individualistic way on your own judgement, your own opinion; you need to consult with those who are wiser and more experienced than yourself. On the other hand, you don't want to submit unquestioningly to authority. It is not easy to follow this middle path, but we have to try. There has to be a place for faith and there has to be a place for healthy scepticism. It is very easy to go from one extreme to the other, rather than searching for the middle way. But if we are going to accept some authority unquestioningly, why bother with Buddhism? Why not just go and join the Catholic Church, which is so much closer to us in culture? Why give ourselves the trouble of going to the East and setting up an infallible authority there? And on the other hand, if you're going to be a thoroughgoing sceptic, why bother with Buddhism at all? Go and be a humanist, go and be an agnostic. Buddhism is a middle way between the extreme of authoritarianism and the extreme of individualistic thinking for oneself.

Whether or not Śāriputra is going to extremes, here we find him getting sidetracked once again. And once again Vimalakīrti takes him to task. He knows what Śāriputra is thinking, of course, and he says:

> Reverend Śāriputra, the Tathāgata has taught the eight liberations. You should concentrate on those liberations, listening to the Dharma with a mind free of preoccupations with material things. Just wait a minute, reverend Śāriputra, and you will eat such food as you have never before tasted.

Vimalakīrti then puts himself into a state of deep concentration and exerts his magical power. As a result, the whole assembly is enabled to see a far distant Buddha-land. There are, as we have seen, an infinite number of Buddha-lands or Pure Lands, each with its own characteristics. And here, in chapter 10, 'The Feast Brought by the Emanated Incarnation', we find ourselves introduced to another one. Like so many places and people in the Buddhist scriptures, it has rather a long name – Sarvagandhasugandhā, which means 'Sweetly Fragrant with All Fragrances' or 'Sweetly Perfumed with All Perfumes' – and it is to be found in the zenith, the upward direction, infinitely distant from our own wretched, impure Buddha-land. The text says that it is 'beyond as many buddha-fields as there are sands in forty-two Ganges rivers'. That kind of distance takes quite a bit of imagining.

This Buddha-land is presided over by the Buddha Sugandhakūṭa, which means 'Heap of Fragrance' or 'Mountain of Perfume'. The trees emit a wonderful fragrance, which, we are told, 'far surpasses all the fragrances, human and divine, of all the buddha-fields of the ten directions'. Even the names of *arhant* and *pratyekabuddha* are unheard of here. The Buddha Sugandhakūṭa teaches the Dharma to an assembly consisting exclusively of bodhisattvas. All the houses, the avenues, the parks, and the palaces are made not of brick and stone, not of marble, not even of jewels, as they often are in the Mahāyāna *sūtras*, but of perfume. And the fragrance of the food eaten by the bodhisattvas in that Pure Land pervades and permeates innumerable universes.

So, through Vimalakīrti's magical power, the whole assembly is enabled to 'see' – or rather experience – this Pure Land Sarvagandhasugandhā, which consists entirely of perfumes. And just at the moment that it is revealed to them, the Buddha Sugandhakūṭa and his bodhisattvas sit down to a meal. (Apparently it is lunch-time there too.) The meal is served by a class of deities called Gandhavyūhāhāra ('Gloriously Perfumed'), all of whom are devoted to the Mahāyāna.

Vimalakīrti asks the assembly gathered in his invisible house if anyone would like to go to that Buddha-land and bring back some food. But, rather strangely, nobody is willing to go. The reason is that they have all been restrained from offering to make the journey by the supernatural power of Mañjuśrī, the Bodhisattva of Wisdom. Luk's translation here is 'All the bodhisattvas remained silent as Mañjuśrī was noted for his supernatural power,' while according to Thurman no one volunteered because they were restrained by Mañjuśrī's magical power, and Lamotte says 'Through the supernatural intervention (*adhiṣṭhāna*) of Mañjuśrī ... all the bodhisattvas kept silent.' It seems quite clear that the original must be 'because of Mañjuśrī's supernatural power'. One translator takes that to mean that Mañjuśrī actually intervened with his supernatural power, while the other interprets it that Mañjuśrī had the reputation of possessing such power. Incidentally, Lamotte's assertion that Mañjuśrī's supernatural intervention, as he renders it, is equivalent to *adhiṣṭhāna* is not quite right; it's more like the Sanskrit *ṛddhi*, supernatural power.

The point here is that Mañjuśrī wants to give Vimalakīrti an opportunity to show what he is capable of. He doesn't want the other bodhisattvas present to make an exhibition of their own blundering efforts to go to this other Buddha-land, so he prevents them from volunteering so that they can see what Vimalakīrti can do. This seems to me to be the sense of the text. If Mañjuśrī is 'restraining' the bodhisattvas in some way, it can only be as a skilful means; it cannot be for any selfish motive.

Vimalakīrti obligingly takes this opportunity to perform a magical feat. By means of his magical power, he emanates an incarnation bodhisattva of youthful appearance, adorned with all sorts of auspicious marks and signs, and so beautiful that he outshines the whole assembly. Vimalakīrti directs the emanated incarnation to go to the Pure Land 'Sweetly Perfumed with All Perfumes', bow down before the Buddha Sugandhakūṭa, and say that Vimalakīrti asks for the remains of his meal, because with those remains Vimalakīrti 'will accomplish the Buddha-work in the universe called Sahā'. Sahā ('Suffering' or 'Tribulation') is, of course, our own world.

And so the emanated incarnation goes to that distant Buddha-land, is given the food in a perfumed vessel, and, in a fraction of a second, returns with it to Vimalakīrti. And that is not all he returns with. He is accompanied by ninety million bodhisattvas, who have been given leave to come by Sugaṇḍhakuṭā. Vimalakīrti, of course, makes room for all of them in his house. This time he doesn't bother bringing in more thrones from elsewhere; he just creates them out of thin air.

The fragrance of the food brought back spreads throughout the entire great city of Vaiśālī and beyond – spreads, in fact, throughout a hundred universes. Noticing the fragrance of this wonderful perfume, everybody in Vaiśālī is amazed, and filled with joy and elation. They feel purified by the perfume, cleansed in body and mind. And they all come flocking to Vimalakīrti's house, where they too sit down, all eighty-four thousand of them. The gods too, we are told, are attracted by the perfume, and they also turn up at Vimalakīrti's house. And everybody in this now truly vast assembly is then given a portion of the food to eat.

As he distributes the food, Vimalakīrti says:

> Reverends, eat of the food of the Tathāgata! It is ambrosia perfumed by the great compassion. But do not fix your minds in narrow-minded attitudes, lest you be unable to receive its gift.[383]

Once everyone has been fed – so many tens of millions of beings – there is just as much food as before. And having eaten, everybody present is completely satisfied. They all experience a deep spiritual bliss, and a wonderful perfume emanates from the pores of their skin.

Vimalakīrti then asks the bodhisattvas who have recently arrived how the Buddha Sugandhakūṭa teaches his Dharma. They tell him:

> The Tathāgata [the Buddha of that Buddha-land] does not teach the Dharma by means of sound and language. He disciplines the bodhisattvas only by means of perfumes. At the foot of each perfume-tree sits a bodhisattva, and the trees emit perfumes like this one. From the moment they smell that perfume, the bodhisattvas attain the concentration called 'source of all bodhisattva-virtues'. From the moment they attain that concentration, all the bodhisattva-virtues are produced in them.

The bodhisattvas then return Vimalakīrti's question, asking him how the Buddha Śākyamuni, 'our' Buddha, teaches the Dharma in our world. And Vimalakīrti replies:

> Good sirs, these living beings here are hard to discipline. Therefore, he teaches them with discourses appropriate for the disciplining of the wild and uncivilized. How does he discipline the wild and uncivilized? What discourses are appropriate? Here they are:
>
> This is hell. This is the animal world. This is the world of the lord of death. These are the adversities. These are the rebirths with crippled faculties. These are physical misdeeds, and these are the retributions for physical misdeeds. These are verbal misdeeds, and these are the retributions for verbal misdeeds.

These are mental misdeeds, and these are the retributions for mental misdeeds. This is killing. This is stealing. This is sexual misconduct. This is lying. This is backbiting. This is harsh speech. This is frivolous speech. This is covetousness. This is malice. This is false view. These are their retributions. This is miserliness, and this is its effect. This is immorality. This is hatred. This is sloth. This is the fruit of sloth. This is false wisdom and this is the fruit of false wisdom. These are the transgressions of the precepts. This is the vow of personal liberation. This should be done and that should not be done. This is proper and that should be abandoned. This is an obscuration and that is without obscuration. This is sin and that rises above sin. This is the path and that is the wrong path. This is virtue and that is evil. This is blameworthy and that is blameless. This is defiled and that is immaculate. This is mundane and that is transcendental. This is compounded and that is uncompounded. This is passion and that is purification. This is life and that is liberation.

Thus, by means of these varied explanations of the Dharma, the Buddha trains the minds of those living beings who are just like wild horses. Just as wild horses or wild elephants will not be tamed unless the goad pierces them to the marrow, so living beings who are wild and hard to civilize are disciplined only by means of discourses about all kinds of miseries.[384]

Most of this is straightforward, not to say blunt. There is just one aspect of it that may require a little explanation. Vimalakīrti says that the Buddha teaches that 'this is false wisdom and this is the fruit of false wisdom'. 'False wisdom' is a very misleading translation, making it sound as though there are two kinds of wisdom, one true and one false. The Sanskrit word here is *dausprajña*, and this corresponds to the Pāli *duppañña*, a term which occurs several times in the *Dhammapada*, and is usually translated 'evil understanding'.[385] One could say that *duppañña* and *micchā-diṭṭhi*, 'false view', are roughly synonymous, but that *micchā-diṭṭhi* is a much more precise technical term. A *micchā-diṭṭhi* is a certain definite point of view which is wrong. *Dupañña* is just the general state of having an evil or wrong understanding, an understanding clouded by unskilful mental factors. One could say that *micchā-diṭṭhi* is *dupañña* articulated into specific philosophical positions which are mistaken. So *prajñā* is being used here in its more general sense of 'understanding'. *Prajñā* in the highest sense could not possibly be false.

Conditions in this very impure Buddha-land are such, Vimalakīrti says, that bodhisattvas who work here have to have very strong compassion and determination – much stronger, in fact, than that of bodhisattvas in Buddha-lands such as Sarvagandhasugandhā. Such bodhisattvas accomplish, therefore, correspondingly greater benefits for living beings. Then, after a few more exchanges between the visiting bodhisattvas and Vimalakīrti about the practices and qualities that a bodhisattva in this Buddha-land needs, the chapter ends.

There is a great deal that could be said about all these incidents and the figures involved in them. By this I do not mean that there are a lot of specific points that could be made in the ordinary discursive way. It is more that if you allow your mind to dwell upon this particular episode, a number of different facets and aspects of its significance disclose themselves. You could investigate, for instance, why the emanation bodhisattva bows down when he arrives in that other Pure Land. Why does Vimalakīrti ask for the remains of the meal, and why does Sugandhakūṭa comply with his request? What does the meal itself signify? What does the ambrosia or *amṛta*, the nectar of immortality of which the food consists, represent? Is there some meaningful connection to be made between the vessel in which the food is contained and the Holy Grail? And why is the food it contains not depleted, even though millions of beings have been fed? There is plenty of scope for imaginative reflection here.

We will focus, however, on just one topic. We have heard that the Tathāgata Sugandhakūṭa teaches his Dharma, 'disciplines' the bodhisattvas, not through sound and language but through perfumes. Perfumes are his medium of communication. This may seem to us very bizarre, but what a nice way of being disciplined!

Like the other physical senses, the sense-consciousness of smell arises through the contact of sense-organ and sense-object. But in the case of the sense of smell, rather curiously, there is less direct contact between the two than there is between the eye and shapes and colours, or the ear and sounds. In the case of the sense of smell there is a kind of intermediary. A rose in a distant garden emits millions of tiny invisible particles; some of them enter our nostrils and come into contact with the olfactory nerve endings; and we 'smell' the rose.

Scent, or perfume, is an extremely subtle thing. We can't see it, we can't hear it, but it is very definitely there. Almost everybody can distinguish a 'good' smell from a 'bad' smell, a perfume from a stink, but smell very often affects us on an almost unconscious level and can therefore be used to create a mood or feeling. This has led to the manufacture of all sorts of artificial odours which are used in various ways. They are used in social life, when we want to make ourselves more attractive – or at least less offensive – to other people. They are also used in religious life to create a particular kind of atmosphere – many religions, for example, use particular kinds of incense in connection with certain ceremonies and observances – which suggests a definite connection between certain odours and certain mental and emotional states.

The sense of smell is the least well developed of all our senses. In this respect we are very different from certain other animals. In dogs, for instance, the sense of smell is very highly developed, more so indeed than their other senses. It is said that dogs experience, and therefore live in, quite a different world from human beings: a world of odours. When the dog puts its nose outside the door, it experiences hundreds of different smells coming from all directions, all quite vivid and distinct one from another, and all meaning something. Some human beings, of course, have a more acute sense of smell than others, but certainly not as acute as that of dogs and other animals.

Perfume can therefore be said to be a symbol for something very subtle and delicate; something that is quite intangible, yet definitely there; something that can be perceived and that can have certain effects on us, even from a distance. According to the Mahāyāna, the subtlest of all influences is the influence of the Buddhas and bodhisattvas, the influence of Enlightenment, the influence of great Compassion. It is not easily perceived, yet in a sense it is always present, like radio waves in the air. Great Compassion is not just an individual emotion, at however high a level. It is a transcendental emanation of reality itself, of the reality with which the Buddhas and great bodhisattvas are at one. In the mythic language of the *Vimalakīrti-nirdeśa*, this reality is *amṛta*, which literally means 'deathless'. It is what the Greeks called ambrosia, the nectar of immortality. And this ambrosia is perfumed. Vimalakīrti says to Śāriputra and the great disciples:

Reverends, eat of the food of the Tathāgata! It is ambrosia perfumed by the great compassion.

In the Pure Land 'Sweetly Perfumed with all Perfumes' Sugandhakūṭa and the bodhisattvas regularly feast on this ambrosia. They feast on reality, they are nourished by it, and they are therefore pervaded by its influence, by the perfume of compassion. In fact, the whole of that Pure Land is pervaded by it. Everything there is made of it, made of Compassion. 'In that universe, all the houses, the avenues, the parks, and the palaces are made of various perfumes.' It is a universe of purely spiritual, purely transcendental influences. Power in the sense of force does not exist there, in however subtle a form. In this way we may descry something of the meaning of what is going on when Vimalakīrti has the ambrosia brought from Sugandhakūṭa's Pure Land, when its fragrance pervades the entire great city of Vaiśālī, and when it permeates and pervades one hundred universes. And we can begin to see the nature of its effect on the people of Vaiśālī and the gods and goddesses.

We find this same symbolism in an important and historically influential text of Far Eastern Buddhism: *The Awakening of Faith in the Mahāyāna*. Mahāyāna here refers not just to a particular form of Buddhism; it means something like 'Great Principle'. This work is not a *sūtra* – it is not represented as being a discourse by the Buddha – but a *śāstra*, a text attributed to a great Buddhist teacher, in this case Aśvaghoṣa. It survives only in Chinese translation, and according to some scholars it was actually composed in China. It speaks of ultimate reality as *tathatā* or *bhūta-tathatā*. *Tathatā* means simply 'suchness'. *Bhūta-tathatā* means 'the suchness of things'. Ultimate reality is 'such as it is'; it can't be described. If you ask what reality is, the only possible answer is that it is 'such as it is'. All that you can say about reality is that it is characterized by 'suchness' or 'such-as-it-is-ness'.

This ultimate reality is spoken of in *The Awakening of Faith in the Mahāyāna* as 'perfuming' conditioned existence. Something of reality 'rubs off', so to speak, onto conditioned existence. A few infinitesimally tiny 'particles' are 'transmitted', and we can therefore perceive ultimate reality, however faintly, in the midst of conditioned existence. And, perceiving it, we can strive towards it.[386]

Not only does ultimate reality 'perfume' conditioned existence. According to *The Awakening of Faith in the Mahāyāna*, conditioned existence 'perfumes' (if that is the right word) ultimate reality. And ultimate reality's response is to manifest Compassion. This is a very profound conception – but it gives us some idea of the appropriateness of perfume as a symbol for great Compassion, whose influence is so very subtle and delicate.

Practising meditation gives one at least a limited sense of this kind of influence. A time comes when you begin to sense something which you cannot describe or define. It doesn't come under any mundane category, yet at the same time there is nothing vague or cloudy about it. It is intensely vivid, intensely real, like the perfume of some unknown flower. We might say that it is the perfume of the thousand-petalled lotus itself, the lotus that blooms in the Pure Land.

Two things follow from the fact that we can have this kind of experience. First, just as we can perceive odours only because we have a sense of smell and a nose, in the same way we can perceive the subtle perfume of ultimate reality only because we have within us a kind of transcendental sense, something that has an affinity with the transcendental, something to which the 'particles' of the transcendental can be transmitted. This is what the Mahāyāna in a general way calls the *tathāgata-dhātu*, the element of Buddhahood. Secondly, this transcendental sense of ours can be developed, can be made more sensitive and more refined, to the extent that eventually it can tell us where the perfume is coming from and which direction we have to take to find its source.

We have seen that in the Buddha-land called 'Sweetly Perfumed with all Perfumes' Sugandhakūṭa communicates the Dharma by means of perfume. This is not really such a strange idea as it may at first seem. In fact, we know from our own experience that perfume or odour is a means of communication. Everything and every place has its own distinctive odour. When I visited New Zealand, for example, I noticed the distinctive spicy smell of the countryside, the 'bush': very sweet, yet at the same time sharp and refreshing, even stimulating – and very different from anything that one can experience in England.

People also have an odour. Here we begin to tread on rather delicate ground – this is something that we are not supposed to talk about. A person's odour is not just due to hygiene and cosmetics. It is affected, for instance, by the type of food you eat. A vegetarian smells quite different from a meat-eater. My vegetarian friends in India say that sometimes they cannot bear being too near Westerners because of the smell – the smell, they believe, of the meat they have eaten.

Women smell different from men; children smell different from adults; and very young people smell different from very old people. People who come from one part of the world smell different from people who come from another. Dogs can recognize these distinctive natural odours, but most humans cannot – although they can certainly develop the capacity, and some so-called 'primitive' peoples have it, at least to some extent. It seems quite likely that all human beings originally had this power, but most of us have subsequently lost it, especially once we started living in settled communities, away from such close contact with nature. But one smell that many people can still recognize is what we might call the smell of death. When someone is dying of illness or old age, they give off a distinctive smell which can be perceived even by people whose sense of smell has been blunted by civilized living.

Smell has its part to play in communication. The most important factor in any communication is the emotional state of the people engaged in it; and emotional states produce all sorts of physical reactions, including glandular secretions which each have their own odour. We speak, for instance, of 'the smell of fear' or 'the smell of anxiety'. We do not often have occasion to speak about the odours of more positive emotions, probably because they are less powerfully and pungently developed. It is, however, well known that a perfume similar to that of roses or jasmine is sometimes perceived in a room where someone is meditating – not only by the meditator, but also by other people present.

Whether or not we are conscious of it, smell is very much part of our response to other people. So, although we tend to assume that communication is possible only through words, we should not really be surprised to learn that in the Buddha-land of Sugandhakūṭa, perfume is the means of communicating the Dharma. Of course, we may object that rarefied communication by perfume is all very well between Buddhas and bodhisattvas at a transcendental level, but has little relevance to what goes on between ordinary human beings. But Buddhas and bodhisattvas are human beings too. They may be Enlightened or partially Enlightened, but their communication, however rarefied, is still a form of human communication, and as such it can be developed by us too.

The important point is that words and language are not the only medium of communication; many others are possible. We find this emphasized in the next chapter of the *Vimalakīrti-nirdeśa*, chapter 11, which is called 'Lesson of the Destructible and the Indestructible'. At the beginning of this chapter there is a change of scene. We are no longer in the vast throne-filled mansion that Vimalakīrti's house has by now become, but back in Āmrapālī's Park with the Buddha, who is teaching the Dharma to the rest of the assembly. And as he teaches, the park becomes larger and larger. Not only that; the entire assembly is suffused with a beautiful golden light.

Ānanda is rather surprised by this, and asks the Buddha what it may mean. The Buddha replies that it means that Vimalakīrti and Mañjuśrī are on their way with a great multitude – and a few seconds later they all arrive. In fact, Vimalakīrti magically transports the entire assembly, thrones and all, on the palm of his right hand. When they have arrived, saluted the Buddha, and taken their thrones, Ānanda remarks on the strong scent of perfume which suddenly pervades the air. The Buddha tells him that it is emanating from the pores of all the bodhisattvas. Śāriputra hastens to add that it is emanating from the pores of the *arhants* too – and he explains to Ānanda how it has come about. After exchanging a few remarks with Vimalakīrti about the perfume and the food, and about how the perfume emanates from the bodies of all who have partaken of this food, Ānanda then says to the Buddha:

> Lord, it is wonderful that this food accomplishes the work of the Buddha!

And, in a very important passage, the Buddha replies:

> So it is, Ānanda! It is as you say, Ānanda! There are buddha-fields that accomplish the buddha-work by means of bodhisattvas; those that do so by means of lights; those that do so by means of the tree of enlightenment; those that do so by means of the physical beauty and the marks of the Tathāgata; those that do so by means of religious robes; those that do so by means of food; those that do so by means of water; those that do so by means of gardens; those that do so by means of palaces; those that do so by means of mansions; those that do so by means of magical incarnations; those that do so by means of empty space; those that do so by means of lights in the sky. Why is it so, Ānanda? Because by

> these various means, living beings become disciplined. Similarly, Ānanda, there are buddha-fields that accomplish the buddha-work by means of teaching living beings words, definitions, and examples, such as 'dreams', 'images', the 'reflection of the moon in water', 'echoes', 'illusions', and 'mirages'; and those that accomplish the buddha-work by making words understandable. Also, Ānanda, there are utterly pure buddha-fields that accomplish the buddha-work for living beings without speech, by silence, inexpressibility, and unteachability. Ānanda, among all the activities, enjoyments, and practices of the Buddhas, there are none that do not accomplish the buddha-work, because all discipline living beings. Finally, Ānanda, the Buddhas accomplish the buddha-work by means of the four Māras and all the eighty-four thousand types of passion that afflict living beings.[387]

In this passage the Buddha goes much further than we have gone so far. He says that there are *many* alternative means of communication, many means to 'accomplish the buddha-work', to teach the Dharma. It is possible, he says, to communicate by means of bodhisattvas – perhaps Vimalakīrti did this when he sent the golden emanation bodhisattva to visit Sugandhakūṭa. Vimalakīrti has also communicated by various other means: through the food that was brought back, and through silence. It is also possible, the Buddha says, to communicate by means of the bodhi tree. This makes me think of examples of early Indian Buddhist art which do not represent the human figure of the Buddha, but just show the bodhi tree as a symbol of the Buddha's presence. And there is even the possibility, apparently, of communicating by means of 'lights in the sky'. Naturally, some people will take this to be a reference to UFOs, which are said to be an attempt on the part of extra-terrestrial beings to communicate with people on earth.

Be that as it may, we do need to be reminded of these alternative means of communication, because we tend to depend too much on words and language. (This tendency is perhaps not quite so pronounced in Asia and Africa as it is in the West.) Only too often we feel that we have not really expressed ourselves unless we have put it all into words, unless we have spelled everything out in full verbal detail. Educated people are particularly prone to this. Of course, we have already seen how important it is for the bodhisattva to express himself clearly and correctly: we need to be articulate. But we should not think that when we have put something into words, whatever it is has necessarily been fully expressed. There are alternative ways of communicating.

In fact, we do not rely entirely on words, even though we may think we do. When you compare a written transcription of a seminar with a tape-recording, for example, the written version seems to have a dimension missing. Listening to the tape, you hear not only the words but also the way in which they were used – the tone, the pace, the pitch, the volume – all of which contribute to what the speakers wanted to say. If the seminar was video-taped, you would get an even better impression of what the participants wanted to communicate, because you would have not only words and sounds, but also gestures, expressions, and so on. In the Buddhist scriptures, of course, we have only the words of the Buddha. Something of the context is often given, but we do not have his tone of voice or the look with which he said something. We do not have the Buddha himself saying it. We have only the words – and this surely makes a big difference.

In exploring 'alternative' means of communication, we are not simply seeking to exchange one means for another. Different means of communication allow us to communicate different things. It has been said that when we learn a new language, we acquire a new soul. It is certainly true that we can say things that we could not say before, as I know from my own experience. There are some things that I can say in Hindi that I can't say in English. The words may be translatable, but somehow they fail to convey the entire meaning, all the nuances and connotations. And some languages are more suitable for certain purposes than others. When asked what language he usually spoke, Charles V, the Holy Roman Emperor in the sixteenth century, is supposed to have replied that when he spoke with his courtiers, he spoke in French; when he spoke to his mistress, he spoke in Italian; when he spoke to God – that is, when he said his prayers – he spoke in Spanish; and when he spoke to his horse, he spoke in German.

The same applies to alternative means of communication. With them we can say things that we could not say before. It is not simply that they enable us to say the same things in a different way; with them we can say different things. It's like having an additional sense through which more of the universe is revealed. It is well known that our physical perceptions are very limited: the eye perceives only a certain spectrum of colours; the ear perceives only a narrow range of sounds; and the nose perceives only a very few odours. The same applies to our mental perceptions, the perceptions of our ordinary conscious mind. They too are very limited, and in any case they function entirely within the distorting overall framework of the subject–object relationship.

It is important, therefore, that we acquire new senses and new means of communication. The more means of communication we have at our disposal, the better. So let us learn to communicate in terms of perfumes. Let us learn to communicate in terms of silence. Let us learn to communicate in terms of 'lights in the sky'. It is important that we very much enlarge the total range of our being and consciousness. The mystery of human communication is perhaps even greater than we had supposed.

8

THE FOUR GREAT RELIANCES: CRITERIA FOR THE SPIRITUAL LIFE

Throughout north-eastern India, where the Buddha lived and taught, there are scattered a number of places that have special associations with events in the Buddha's life. There is Bodh Gaya, where he gained Enlightenment; Sarnath, where he first taught the Dharma; Śrāvasti, where he spent many rainy seasons and gave many teachings; and Kuśinagara, where he finally passed away between the twin sal trees.

All these holy places have their own atmospheres, and their own ways of commemorating the Buddha. But although they are so different, the sacred sites have one thing in common: they all have stupas. A stupa is a reliquary, a dome-shaped structure which contains – or supposedly contains – a body relic of the Buddha or one of his disciples: a tiny fragment of bone or ash. The Indian ones are made of brick faced with stone, and they are often quite enormous.[388]

In the course of the centuries the stupas at the sacred sites have been neglected, and some have even been plundered for their materials. As late as the eighteenth century, for instance, bricks were taken from one of the great stupas at Sarnath to build a market-place in the city of Varanasi. Today many of the stupas are little more than heaps of rubble. But even those that are relatively undamaged, or have been restored to some extent, have a desolate, uncared-for look. After all, the Archaeological Department's responsibility is just to restore them – not to decorate them or make them beautiful. It is true that among the many tourists and sightseers, increasing numbers of pilgrims now visit the major sites. Even so, these places are a sad and feeble shadow of what they were one or two thousand years ago.

In those days, all the stupas would have been intact, and they would have been entirely covered with stone, much of it elaborately carved. Moreover, each stupa would have been beautifully decorated with multitudes of coloured flags and banners, and all sorts of streamers, some of them made of gold or silver plates hinged together, just as one sees in Nepal even today. Each stupa would have been hung with strings of pearls and festoons of flowers. At night one would have seen hundreds of tiny oil lamps burning in all the niches. And on the four sides of the stupa – north, south, east, and west – gateways of sweet-smelling Indian flowers would have been set up.

Above all, around the stupas there would have been thousands upon thousands of pilgrims, all dressed in garments of spotless white. They would not have been aimlessly milling around, gaping at the stupa like tourists. They would have been circumambulating it: walking round and round it, keeping it on their right as a sign of respect. They would have processed around it, perhaps eight or ten abreast, carrying in their hands trays containing all sorts of offerings: flowers, lights and lamps, sticks of lighted incense. And as they marched round and round, they would have chanted the Refuges and Precepts, and all sorts of devotional verses in praise of the Buddha and the great bodhisattvas. Accompanying the chanting there would have been the sound of drums and other musical instruments. Altogether it must have been a truly wonderful spectacle, especially when the sun shone down on it all from a clear blue sky.

This sort of observance, which was very popular with Buddhists in ancient India, is usually known as 'stupa worship'. But this is not quite correct. The devotees were not really worshipping the structure of brick and stone, however beautiful it was. They were worshipping the body relics of the Buddha, enshrined within the stupa, and thus worshipping the Buddha. This sort of worship, known as *āmisa-pūja* or 'worship with material things', has, of course, its counterpart – with greater or lesser degrees of splendour – in all religious traditions.

But in chapter 13 of the *Vimalakīrti-nirdeśa* – which, together with chapter 14, Thurman entitles simply 'Epilogue' – a fundamental question arises. Is there not a better way of worshipping the Buddha? It is in the course of the answer to this question that we come across the four great reliances as criteria for the spiritual life. But although it is in chapter 13 that this question is asked directly, we get some hint of it in the previous chapter: 'Vision of the Universe of Abhirati and the Tathāgata Akṣobhya'.

The vision of the title is the main event of the chapter, and it comes about when Śāriputra asks the Buddha in which Buddha-land Vimalakīrti died before being reborn in this, our world. The Buddha tells Śāriputra to ask Vimalakīrti himself – but Vimalakīrti, perhaps predictably, is rather unhelpful, becoming very metaphysical and paradoxical. So the Buddha comes to Śāriputra's rescue. He says that Vimalakīrti comes from the presence of the Buddha Akṣobhya in the universe Abhirati, and has been reborn in this Sahā universe, this universe of suffering and tribulation, not as a result of his past karma, but voluntarily. He has come here to purify living beings and to make the light of wisdom shine in the midst of the darkness of the passions. Having heard this, everybody present in the great assembly wants to see Abhirati; so Vimalakīrti, at the Buddha's request, shows it to them by means of his magical power.

The hint we are looking for – as to a better way of worshipping the Buddha – comes in a little exchange between the Buddha and Vimalakīrti at the beginning of the chapter. The Buddha asks Vimalakīrti:

> Noble son, when you would see the Tathāgata [the Buddha], how do you view him?

And Vimalakīrti replies:

> Lord, when I would see the Tathāgata, I view him by not seeing any Tathāgata. Why? I see him as not born from the past, not passing on to the future, and not abiding in the present time. Why? He is the essence which is the reality of matter, but he is not matter. He is the essence which is the reality of sensation, but he is not sensation. He is the essence which is the reality of intellect, but he is not intellect. He is the essence which is the reality of motivation, yet he is not motivation. He is the essence which is the reality of consciousness, yet he is not consciousness. Like the element of space, he does not abide in any of the four elements. Transcending the scope of eye, ear, nose, tongue, body, and mind, he is not produced in the six sense-media.

He is not involved in the three worlds, is free of the three defilements, is associated with the triple liberation, is endowed with the three knowledges, and has truly attained the unattainable.

The Tathāgata has reached the extreme of detachment in regard to all things, yet he is not a reality-limit. He abides in ultimate reality, yet there is no relationship between it and him. He is not produced from causes, nor does he depend on conditions. He is not without any characteristic, nor has he any characteristic. He has no single nature nor any diversity of natures. He is not a conception, not a mental construction, nor is he a nonconception. He is neither the other shore, nor this shore, nor that between. He is neither here, nor there, nor anywhere else. He is neither this nor that. He cannot be discovered by consciousness, nor is he inherent in consciousness. He is neither darkness nor light. He is neither name nor sign. He is neither weak nor strong. He lives in no country or direction. He is neither good nor evil. He is neither compounded nor uncompounded. He cannot be explained as having any meaning whatsoever.

The Tathāgata is neither generosity nor avarice, neither morality nor immorality, neither tolerance nor malice, neither effort nor sloth, neither concentration nor distraction, neither wisdom nor foolishness. He is inexpressible. He is neither truth nor falsehood; neither escape from the world nor failure to escape from the world; neither cause of involvement in the world nor not a cause of involvement in the world; he is the cessation of all theory and all practice. He is neither a field of merit nor not a field of merit; he is neither worthy of offerings nor unworthy of offerings. He is not an object, and cannot be contacted. He is not a whole, nor a conglomeration. He surpasses all calculations. He is utterly unequaled, yet equal to the ultimate reality of things. He is matchless, especially in effort. He surpasses all measure. He does not go, does not stay, does not pass beyond. He is neither seen, heard, distinguished, nor known. He is without any complexity, having attained the equanimity of omniscient gnosis. Equal towards all things, he does not discriminate between them. He is without reproach, without excess, without corruption, without conception, and without intellectualization. He is without activity, without birth, without occurrence, without origin, without production, and without nonproduction. He is without fear and without subconsciousness; without sorrow, without joy, and without strain. No verbal teaching can express him.

Such is the body of the Tathāgata and thus should he be seen. Who sees thus, truly sees. Who sees otherwise, sees falsely.[389]

In other words, the Buddha is to be identified with his spiritual essence. He is to be identified with what makes him a Buddha: with his Enlightenment, with his realization of the nature of ultimate reality. So worship of the Buddha must go far beyond the worship of his body relics enshrined in a stupa. Not that stupa worship is wrong – it helps to develop devotional feeling – but the body relics are not the Buddha. The Buddha, in fact, is not to be identified with his material body at all – not even during his lifetime.

So, if it is good to develop devotional feelings, but worship of body relics is not enough, what should be worshipped? This is the opening theme of the next chapter of the text, chapter 13. Here we are again concerned with the question of previous incarnations, including those of the Buddha Śākyamuni himself. At the beginning of the chapter we find Śakra, more usually known as Indra, the king of the gods, coming forward. He says that he has never before heard such a wonderful teaching as this *Vimalakīrti-nirdeśa* and he praises it at length. He also promises to protect it. (From all this, incidentally, we can gather that the text is beginning to come to an end.)

Approving of what Śakra says, the Buddha asks him to imagine that the whole great universe is full of Buddhas, as full of Buddhas as it is of plants, bushes, grass, and trees. Suppose, he says, these Buddhas passed away into *parinirvāṇa*, or – in ordinary parlance – suppose they died. And suppose somebody erected marvellous stupas for each and every one of them, stupas made entirely of precious stones, each stupa as large as a world. Suppose that devotee spent a whole aeon or more worshipping all those stupas with flowers, perfumes, and music. They would certainly gain much merit. But, the Buddha continues, if someone were to accept, recite, and understand deeply the exposition of Dharma called 'Instruction in the Inconceivable Emancipation', their merits would be far greater. Why? Because the Enlightenment of the Buddhas arises from the Dharma, so one truly honours the Buddhas not by material offerings, but by honouring the Dharma.

This may be clear enough, but how does one go about 'Dharma worship'? What is Dharma worship? The Buddha answers this question by way of further instruction to Śakra, in the course of which he refers to events of the remote past. Once upon a time, the Buddha says (the text doesn't actually say 'once upon a time', but there is that sort of feeling to the story coming up), there was a Buddha called Bhaiṣajyarāja, 'King of Healing' or 'Medicine King'. He lived an inconceivably long time ago and his lifespan was twenty short aeons. He had a retinue of thirty-six million billion disciples, that is, followers of the Hīnayāna, and also a retinue of twelve million billion bodhisattvas, or followers of the Mahāyāna. At the same time, there lived a universal monarch called Ratnacchattra, 'Precious Umbrella' or 'Precious Parasol', and he had a thousand sons. This king and his sons were very devoted to the Buddha Bhaiṣajyarāja. They all worshipped him by making many offerings of material things, and they continued to do so for ten whole aeons.

But there was one prince – the odd man out or, we might say, the individual – who was not satisfied with this sort of thing. We might even go so far as to say that he was fed up with it all. His name was Candracchattra, 'Lunar Umbrella' or 'Lunar Parasol'. Retiring into solitude, Candracchattra thought to himself, 'Is there not another mode of worship, even better and more noble than this?' And he got an answer. The gods spoke to him from the sky, and they said, 'Good man, the supreme worship is the Dharma-worship.' Whether or not Candracchattra was at all taken aback by this occurrence the text doesn't tell us, but he asked the gods what this 'Dharma-worship' might be, and they replied, 'Go to the Tathāgata Bhaiṣajyarāja, and he will tell you.'

So Candracchattra duly went to see Bhaiṣajyarāja, and put to him the same question: 'What is Dharma-worship?' And Bhaiṣajyarāja replied:

> Noble son, the Dharma-worship is that worship rendered to the discourses taught by the Tathāgata. These discourses are deep and profound in illumination. They do not conform to the mundane and are difficult to understand and difficult to see and difficult to realize. They are subtle, precise, and ultimately incomprehensible. As Scriptures, they are collected in the canon of the bodhisattvas, stamped with the insignia of the king of incantations and teachings. They reveal the irreversible wheel of Dharma, arising from the six

transcendences, cleansed of any false notions. They are endowed with all the aids to enlightenment and embody the seven factors of enlightenment. They introduce living beings to the great compassion and teach them the great love. They eliminate all the convictions of the Māras, and they manifest relativity.

They contain the message of selflessness, living-beinglessness, lifelessness, personlessness, voidness, signlessness, wishlessness, nonperformance, nonproduction, and nonoccurrence.

They make possible the attainment of the seat of enlightenment and set in motion the wheel of the Dharma. They are approved and praised by the chiefs of the gods, nāgas, *yakṣas*, gandharvas, āsuras, garuḍas, kiṃnaras, and mahoragas. They preserve unbroken the heritage of the holy Dharma, contain the treasury of the Dharma, and represent the summit of the Dharma-worship. They are upheld by all holy beings and teach all the bodhisattva practices. They induce the unmistaken understanding of the Dharma in its ultimate sense. They certify that all things are impermanent, miserable, selfless, and peaceful, thus epitomizing the Dharma. They cause the abandonment of avarice, immorality, malice, laziness, forgetfulness, foolishness, and jealousy, as well as bad convictions, adherence to objects, and all opposition. They are praised by all the Buddhas. They are the medicines for the tendencies of mundane life, and they authentically manifest the great happiness of liberation. To teach correctly, to uphold, to investigate, and to understand such Scriptures, thus incorporating into one's own life the holy Dharma – that is the 'Dharma-worship'.

Furthermore, noble son, the Dharma-worship consists of determining the Dharma according to the Dharma; applying the Dharma according to the Dharma; being in harmony with relativity; being free of extremist convictions; attaining the tolerance of ultimate birthlessness and nonoccurrence of all things; realizing selflessness and living-beinglessness; refraining from struggle about causes and conditions, without quarreling, or disputing; not being possessive; being free of egoism; relying on the meaning and not the literal expression; relying on gnosis and not on consciousness; relying on the ultimate teachings definitive in meaning and not insisting on the superficial teachings interpretable in meaning; relying on reality and not insisting on

> opinions derived from personal authorities; realizing correctly the reality of the Buddha; realizing the ultimate absence of any fundamental consciousness; and overcoming the habit of clinging to an ultimate ground. Finally, attaining peace by stopping everything from ignorance to old age, death, sorrow, lamentation, misery, anxiety, and trouble, and realizing that living beings know no end to their views concerning these twelve links of dependent origination; then, noble son, when you do not hold to any view at all, it is called the unexcelled Dharma-worship.[390]

So this is Bhaiṣajyarāja's explanation of Dharma worship – and when Candracchattra heard it, he was overwhelmed by a profound transcendental experience. Vowing to devote himself to the Dharma and to attain Supreme Enlightenment, without delay he went forth from home into the homeless life.

Having told the story, the Buddha proceeds to identify the characters in it for Śakra's benefit. He says that King Ratnacchattra was none other than the Buddha Ratnarcis, as he afterwards became, and his thousand sons are the thousand bodhisattvas of the present aeon. And Prince Candracchattra was the Buddha Śākyamuni himself in a previous life.

So, as this story shows, there *is* a better way of worshipping the Buddha than by making offerings of material things, and it is known as Dharma worship. And the first thing that Bhaiṣajyarāja mentions as constituting Dharma worship is 'determining the Dharma according to the Dharma; applying the Dharma according to the Dharma' – or, as Lamotte translates it, 'understanding the Law according to the Law.'

'Determining the Dharma according to the Dharma' implies *not* determining the Dharma in terms of that which is not the Dharma. For us in the West this means not trying to understand the Dharma – whether consciously, unconsciously, or semi-consciously – in accordance with Christian beliefs, or modern secularist, humanist, rationalist, or scientific modes of thought, or 'new age' philosophies. The Dharma is to be determined and understood in accordance with the Dharma. To determine it or understand it in accordance with anything else is to falsify it, distort it, and betray it.

In the same way, Dharma worship consists of *applying* the Dharma according to the Dharma. If you try to break off a bit of the Dharma, to take some Buddhist teaching and apply it according to, say, Christian ideas, it just won't work – that is, it won't work as the Dharma. There is no such thing as 'Christian Zen', for example. The Dharma is to be applied according to the Dharma.

Nowadays we hear a great deal of talk about the spiritual life: about 'growth', about 'personal development', even about meditation. But these terms are often used rather vaguely and superficially; few people have a clear idea of what they really mean. And if you don't know what such terms mean, you lay yourself open to what can only be called exploitation. If someone comes along – from the East or, even more likely, from California – and they set up their spiritual shop, advertising this or that technique of personal development, this or that brand of meditation, or even some quite bizarre teaching, and charging quite a lot of money, it seems there is no way of knowing clearly what you would be letting yourself in for if you got involved with them. Without clear criteria to apply, you may get involved with a reasonably positive group or you may get psychologically damaged by a cynical racket – but you won't be able to make *real* spiritual progress. If you have no criteria to apply, you have no way of telling.

So we need criteria for the spiritual life – and such criteria we find in the four great reliances which Bhaiṣajyarāja cites in the *Vimalakīrti-nirdeśa*. The word 'reliance' here translates the Sanskrit term *pratisāraṇa*. *Sāraṇa* means 'refuge', and *prati* is a preposition meaning in this context something like 'about' or 'connected with'. When you rely on something or someone, you entrust yourself to it or to them; you take refuge in it or in them. *Pratisāraṇa* is probably a little stronger in meaning than our word 'reliance', so it is appropriate to call them the 'four *great* reliances' – and this also serves to emphasize their intrinsic importance.

Thurman translates the reliances in the following way: (1) relying on the meaning and not the literal expression; (2) relying on gnosis and not on consciousness; (3) relying on the ultimate teachings definitive in meaning and not insisting on the superficial teachings interpretable in meaning; (4) relying on reality and not insisting on opinions derived from personal authorities.

These four great reliances are not unique to this text, but are to be encountered in many others. For some reason or other, in the *Vimalakīrti-nirdeśa* they are not enumerated in the usual order, but we will look at them in the order in which they are usually presented because this makes them rather more intelligible. I will also change the translation somewhat – Thurman's translation paraphrases a little[391] – and I will put the reliances in the more usual preceptive or admonitory form. Thus we get:

(1) One should rely on the Dharma, not on any person; (2) one should rely on the meaning, not the expression; (3) one should rely on the discourses of explicit meaning, not on the discourses of implicit meaning; (4) one should rely on transcendental awareness, not on discriminative consciousness.

1. ONE SHOULD RELY ON THE DHARMA, NOT ON ANY PERSON

The word for 'person' used in this first reliance is *pudgala*, which could also be rendered 'individual'. *Dharma*, of course, means 'the teaching of the Buddha'. So, 'one should rely on the teaching of the Buddha, not on any individual'. At first sight, this is rather a strong statement. Does it mean that one should not rely upon one's teachers or spiritual friends? Is it advocating that we should simply read books about Buddhism without having any contact with Buddhists – as some people in fact do?

Certainly not. What this reliance is really getting at is that one should rely on someone only to the extent that they embody the Dharma – not represent it or symbolize it, but *embody* it. The Dharma does not exist in the abstract. There is no such thing as friendliness; there are only friendly people. There is no such thing as joy; there are only joyful people. There is no such thing as meditation; there are only people who meditate. There is no such thing as wisdom; there are only people who are wise. We could even say that there is no such thing as Enlightenment, but only people who are Enlightened. An abstract Dharma is a non-existent Dharma. The Dharma does not really exist in the *sūtras*. It does not really exist in books. It exists only to the extent that it is practised and realized in the lives of individual human beings.

So relying on the Dharma, not on any person, does not mean abandoning the living Dharma, the Dharma as actually realized by individuals, for the sake of the dead Dharma, the words of the Dharma as preserved in books. We are not being advised to give up on the spiritual community and shut ourselves up in the library, or be self-sufficient in an individualistic way. Still less should we take this as a directive to rely on our own limited subjective understanding of the words of the scriptures. What it does mean, in a word, is that we should not rely on authority.

But what is authority? First, a distinction needs to be drawn between natural authority and artificial authority. An appreciation of spiritual hierarchy, a reverence for those more developed than oneself, is crucial to a healthy spiritual life, and this we could call a response to natural authority. It is artificial authority, spiritual triumphalism, upon which we should never rely. Let's return to the example of the mystic guru. Suppose some new spiritual teacher is expected in town – perhaps from the East, from mystic Tibet, exotic Japan, or maybe from mysterious India – or, indeed, from California. Before he or she arrives, posters and leaflets are plastered all over town. You hear, usually from some devotee speaking with bated breath, that this is a very great teacher indeed, a very great guru – in fact, the rumour is that he is Enlightened. Depending on the tradition to which he belongs, you may be told that he is an incarnation of God, *the* incarnation of God, or just plain God – or you may be told that he is the umpteenth reincarnation of some great spiritual personality of the past, or the head of a huge organization with thousands, even millions, of followers who are in possession of all sorts of wonderful, esoteric spiritual secrets.

Eventually the great guru arrives, and a big meeting is organized to receive him. You don't get anywhere near him, of course, although you may catch a glimpse of him from a distance. Then you see him sitting up at the front of the hall, on a throne or surrounded by a halo of electric light bulbs. Next, you hear what he has to say. It is pretty platitudinous, but you are terribly impressed. You believe every word, accept every word, hang upon every word – after all, you have been told that this is an Enlightened master – or even God – speaking. After a few days, he flies on to the next capital city and another big reception. And in his wake a local group is started, advertising his particular technique of 'personal development' or meditation, and you enrol yourself as a disciple – all on the strength of an illusion.

This is perhaps rather an exaggerated story – but it is not exaggerated very much. Such things have happened, and they will keep on happening as long as people continue to rely on a person, not on the Dharma. This is not at all to suggest that there are no genuine spiritual teachers coming to the West – and those who come should be given proper respect. But real spiritual teachers do not make claims about themselves, and they do not allow claims to be made on their behalf. They are not out to impress; they are not after power. Anybody who does make such extravagant claims is not a spiritual teacher but a politician. This needs to be stated strongly because in some quarters there are signs that the great Eastern spiritual traditions are being turned into nothing less than a racket, signs that people are being exploited because they are insecure, because they want to be told what to do by some authority figure.

This first reliance comes, therefore, as a timely warning. One should rely not on claims, not on authority, not on power, but on the Dharma – the Dharma as actually embodied in the lives of spiritual friends with whom one is in real contact and communication. It is spiritual friendship that helps us practise the Dharma, not glamorous but distant spiritual superstars.

This emphasis on contact with the living Dharma, with people who are practising Buddhism, does not mean that we can forget all about the study of the Dharma as presented in the scriptures. The scriptures are the record of the spiritual experiences, insights, discoveries, and realizations of the Buddha and his disciples down the ages, and studying them is a tremendously valuable source of inspiration. But the scriptures are best studied with the help and companionship of spiritual friends. By virtue of their own spiritual experience they will be able to bring the words of the scriptures to life. They will, as Bhaiṣajyarāja puts it, 'determine the Dharma according to the Dharma'; that is, they will explain the Dharma according to the Dharma, not according to preconceived ideas that have nothing to do with the Dharma, or according to their own subjective emotional states.

2. ONE SHOULD RELY ON THE MEANING, NOT ON THE EXPRESSION

The second of the four great reliances is advising us to rely on the meaning, not on the expression. In other words, whether we are considering the scriptures themselves or what our spiritual friends have to say about the scriptures, we need to make sure that we are being sensitive to the spirit – not just the letter – of what is being said.

The word translated as 'meaning' is *artha*, but the word rendered as 'expression', *vyañjana*, is rather more difficult to explain. In this context it means something like 'a manifestation or expression of meaning in words'. Such an expression can never be more than approximate; in fact, it demonstrates that words have their limitations – even though within those limitations they can usually do far more than we think they can. We don't find Shakespeare, for instance, complaining about the limitations of language, even though he had more to express than most people. None the less, we cannot understand what someone is saying – or even what the Buddha is saying – if we pay more attention to the way they are talking than to what they are trying to say.

This often crops up in the course of ordinary communication. You may be trying to tell somebody something, but you find, at first to your surprise, and eventually to your annoyance, that they keep picking you up on phrases, figures of speech, even individual words, in a quite unreasonable way. In the end it dawns on you that they are trying to trip you up with words because they don't really want to understand what you are trying to say. They don't really want to communicate, so they are listening to your expression, not your meaning.

Communication is possible only on a basis of openness and receptivity. This means really wanting to understand what the other person is trying to say. The important thing is to pay attention to *them*, to be aware of *them*, because the meaning is after all their meaning. So one should rely on the meaning, not on the expression; on the spirit, not on the letter. This applies to ordinary day-to-day communication, to one's communication with one's spiritual friends, and also to one's study of the scriptures. One should rely on the meaning of the Dharma, not on its expression in words and phrases. Otherwise one is in danger of becoming a mere scholar of Buddhism, someone who may have the letter of the Dharma at their fingertips, but who does not come within a million miles of its spirit.

3. ONE SHOULD RELY ON THE DISCOURSES OF EXPLICIT MEANING, NOT ON THE DISCOURSES OF IMPLICIT MEANING

With this third reliance we become just a little technical. 'Discourses' translates the word *sūtras* – that is, discourses delivered by the Buddha, discourses on the Dharma. It is these discourses, of course, which make up the greater part of the Buddhist scriptures. They are very numerous – they are traditionally said to comprise eighty-four thousand *dharma skandhas* or categories of teachings – and they are also very varied, in form, in content, and in other ways. In some cases their meaning is quite obvious; in others, some interpretation is needed.

We can get an idea of this distinction from two simple examples from the *Dhammapada*. Verse 5 of the *Dhammapada* says, 'Enmity does not cease by enmity at any time; it ceases only by non-enmity.' This is sometimes translated, 'Hatred never ceases by hatred; it ceases only by love.' Now, the meaning of this verse is quite clear; it would seem to need no interpretation, because it does not seem open to any misunderstanding. It would not be possible, for instance, to interpret the verse as meaning that enmity does cease by means of enmity. One could not interpret it as meaning that violence or war is justified, or that there could be a 'war to end all wars'. The meaning of the verse is quite unambiguous; it means exactly what it says.

But another verse from the *Dhammapada*, verse 294, says, 'Having killed mother and father, the brahmana goes blameless.' What about this verse? Does it mean what it says? Well, it is clear enough what it seems to mean, but we can hardly leave it at that. It needs interpretation, and this is what, elsewhere, the Buddha himself gives. He says that 'mother' is craving, and 'father' is ignorance; they are called 'mother' and 'father' because they are the root of *saṃsāra*, the root of conditioned existence. To cut this root is to put an end to *saṃsāra*. That is why one who kills 'mother and father' 'goes blameless'.

So here we have the two kinds of discourse: those that do not require any interpretation and those that do: discourses of explicit meaning, as they are called, and discourses of implicit meaning. The Sanskrit is *nītārtha* and *neyārtha*, or *nītārtha* and *anītārtha*. It is important to be clear about this distinction, and the third great reliance depends upon it. One should rely on the discourses of explicit meaning, not on the discourses of implicit meaning, because the meaning of the former is clear, obvious, and unambiguous, needing no interpretation.

Not only that. Discourses of implicit meaning should be interpreted in accordance with discourses of explicit meaning. The discourses of explicit meaning, in other words, represent or embody the criterion. Your interpretations can be as fanciful and far-fetched as you like. You can bring out all sorts of strange, unexpected and outlandish ideas from *sūtras* of implicit meaning. This is perfectly legitimate and valid. But what you bring out must not contradict the discourses of explicit meaning.

We can apply this principle to the *Vimalakīrti-nirdeśa* itself. How do the passages in it that deal with all sorts of magical events stand in relation to this third great reliance? There are two points to be made. Firstly, the meaning of these passages is not rational or scientific, but poetic, imaginative, mythic. As such, it makes its own non-rational appeal. The distinction between explicit meaning and implicit meaning applies mainly to discourses of a more discursive nature. But secondly, if these passages are interpreted or translated, so to speak, from the poetic to the rational mode of expression, then the rational expression must not contradict the discourses of explicit meaning.

4. ONE SHOULD RELY ON TRANSCENDENTAL AWARENESS, NOT ON DISCRIMINATIVE CONSCIOUSNESS

The Sanskrit words used in this fourth great reliance, *jñāna* and *vijñāna*, are both derived from the root *jñā*, 'to know'. *Jñāna* is pure knowledge, pure awareness, knowledge without any subject or object. It is knowledge which does not know anything and does not belong to anybody. I have therefore rendered it 'transcendental awareness'. It is what Edward Conze, describing emptiness, calls the 'clear non-dual Shine'.[392]

Vijñāna is divided knowledge, divided awareness, knowledge which is divided between subject and object, whether it is between sense organs and sense objects, or between mind and mental objects, or between ego-self and world. It is knowledge which takes place within the subject–object framework and which is therefore limited, or even distorted, by that framework. I have therefore rendered *vijñāna* as 'discriminative consciousness'.

The depth psychology of the Yogācāra enumerates eight *vijñānas*: the five sense-consciousnesses, the mind-consciousness (*mano-vijñāna*), the soiled mind-consciousness (*kliṣṭa-mano-vijñāna*), and the relative store-consciousness (*ālaya-vijñāna*). The work of the spiritual life is to transform these eight *vijñānas*, these eight discriminative consciousnesses, into the five *jñānas*, the five transcendental awarenesses or 'wisdoms' which are symbolized by the five Buddhas of the mandala.[393] There are the Buddhas of the four directions: Amoghasiddhi (the all-accomplishing wisdom), Akṣobhya (the mirror-like wisdom), Ratnasambhava (the wisdom of equality or sameness), and Amitābha (the all-distinguishing wisdom). And the wisdoms of these four Buddhas are all aspects of the wisdom of the *dharmadhātu*, which sees the entire universe as fully pervaded by or as manifesting reality. This fifth *jñāna* is symbolized by Vairocana, the Buddha of the centre of the mandala. But this is all rather technical.

The main point is that the Dharma can be truly, deeply understood only by means of transcendental awareness. It cannot be understood by means of discriminative consciousness. We should therefore rely on transcendental awareness. But that is easier said than done. Before we can rely on transcendental awareness, we must *have* transcendental awareness. And if we don't have it, we must develop it by one means or another.

And one of the means by which a transcendental awareness can be awakened is through the study and exploration of a strange and magical text like the *Vimalakīrti-nirdeśa*. Our explorations here have been, of course, very far from adding up to a complete and systematic exposition of the text. We have looked at only a few of the hundreds of possible themes, taken only a few drops from the ocean. It remains for us to plunge into the ocean itself – the ocean of the *Vimalakīrti-nirdeśa*, the ocean of the inconceivable emancipation.

NOTES

FOREWORD

1 Jaan Kaplinski, 'Poetry' from *Four Poems* (1985) translated by the author with Sam Hamill and Riina Tamm.

THE DRAMA OF COSMIC ENLIGHTENMENT

CHAPTER 1

2 '[Buddhas] know all the different phenomena in all worlds, interrelated in Indra's net.' Thomas Cleary (trans.), *Flower Ornament Sūtra* (*Avataṃsaka Sūtra*), Shambhala Publications, Boston 1993, p. 925.

3 This is very much the language of the *Avataṃsaka Sūtra*, in which the enlightening being Universal Good avers that 'In every single atom/ Are all things of all places and times'. In the same sequence of verses, the bodhisattva warns, however, that 'If sentient beings should hear of this,/ They'd go mad in confusion.' See Thomas Cleary (trans.), *The Flower Ornament Scripture*, Shambhala Publications, Boston 1993, p. 959. Later on in the text, Vairocana's tower is described by the pilgrim Sudhana as 'the abode of those with unobstructed eyes/ Who perceive infinite lands, buddhas, beings,/ And ages, in a single point.' See Cleary, ibid., p. 1459.

4 These are the famous first lines of William Blake's *Auguries of Innocence*, a 132-line poem probably composed in the early years of the nineteenth century and found in what is called the Pickering Manuscript; the poem was not published until 1863.

5 Sangharakshita's series of lectures on the 'Higher Evolution of Man' can be heard and transcripts read at www.freebuddhistaudio.com; the lectures are also included in *Complete Works*, vol. 12. See also Sangharakshita, *The Bodhisattva: Evolution and Self-Transcendence* (*Complete Works*, vol. 4).

6 See, for example, Dhammapala's commentary, the *Cariyāpiṭaka Aṭṭhakathā*, in Bhikkhu Bodhi (trans.), *The Discourse on the All-Embracing Net of Views: The Brahmajāla Sutta and Its Commentaries*, Buddhist Publication Society, Kandy 1978, pp. 289–96 and pp. 322–3. See also Gampopa, *The Jewel Ornament of Liberation*, Snow Lion Publications, Ithaca NY 1998, pp. 185–9.

7

> Behold, I do not give lectures
> or a little charity,
> When I give I give myself.

Walt Whitman, 'Song of Myself', section 40, in *Leaves of Grass*.

8 The words 'reverence for life' ('Ehrfurcht vor dem Leben') came to Albert Schweitzer in 1915 when he was on a journey in Africa, and became central to his philosophy. He wrote in his autobiography, *Out of My Life and Thought*, 'Lost in thought, I sat on the deck of the barge, struggling to find the elementary and universal concept of the ethical that I had not discovered in any philosophy. I covered sheet after sheet with disconnected sentences merely to concentrate on the problem. Two days passed. Late on the third day, at the very moment when, at sunset, we were making our way through a herd of hippopotamuses, there flashed upon my mind, unforeseen and unsought, the phrase: "Reverence for Life". The iron door had yielded. The path in the thicket had become visible. Now I had found my way to the principle in which affirmation of the world and ethics are joined together!'

9 The five precepts are practised in all schools of Buddhism, and are enumerated many times in the Pāli canon, for example, *Aṅguttara Nikāya* 5.179 (iii.212); see Bhikkhu Bodhi (trans.), *Numerical Discourses of the Buddha*, Wisdom Publications, Boston 2012, p. 792; or E. M. Hare, *The Book of the Gradual Sayings*, vol. iii, Pali Text Society, Oxford 1995, ch. 18, 'The Lay Disciple', p. 155.

10 This phrase, 'energy in pursuit of the good', is Sangharakshita's favoured translation of a phrase from Śāntideva's *Bodhicāryāvatāra*, chapter 7, 'The Perfection of Vigour', verse 2: 'What is vigour? The endeavour to do what is skilful.'

11 The four exertions spell out specifically the practice of

the sixth limb of the Noble Eightfold Path, Perfect Effort. For more about the practice, see chapter 6 of Sangharakshita, *The Buddha's Noble Eightfold Path* (*Complete Works*, vol. 1). Canonical references include *Saṃyutta Nikāya* v.197–9; see Bhikkhu Bodhi (trans.), *The Connected Discourses of the Buddha*, Wisdom Publications, Boston 2000, pp. 1671–2; or F. L. Woodward (trans.), *Book of the Kindred Sayings*, part 5, Pali Text Society, Oxford 1989, pp. 219–20; and the *Saṅgīti Sutta*, *Dīgha Nikāya* 33 (iii.221); see M. Walshe (trans.), *The Long Discourses of the Buddha,* Wisdom Publications, Boston 1995, p. 487; or T. W. Rhys Davids (trans.), *Dialogues of the Buddha*, part 3, Pali Text Society, Oxford 1991, p. 215.

12 The three levels of wisdom are enumerated in, for example, the *Saṅgīti Sutta*, *Dīgha Nikāya* 33 (iii.219); see M. Walshe (trans.), *The Long Discourses of the Buddha,* Wisdom Publications, Boston 1995, p. 486; or T. W. Rhys Davids (trans.), *Dialogues of the Buddha*, part 3, Pali Text Society, Oxford 1991, p. 212.

13 These are the three 'marks of conditioned existence' (*lakṣaṇas*, Pāli *lakkhanas*), which are enumerated and discussed in many places in the Pāli canon. For example, *Saṃyutta Nikāya* 22 (iii.20–4); see Bhikkhu Bodhi (trans.), *The Connected Discourses of the Buddha*, Wisdom Publications, Boston 2000, pp. 867–71; or F. L. Woodward (trans.), *Book of the Kindred Sayings*, part 3, Pali Text Society, Oxford 1989, pp. 19–23. See also *Udāna* iii.10 in John Ireland (trans.), *The Udāna and the Itivuttaka*, Buddhist Publication Society, Kandy 1997, p. 49. The *locus classicus* is *Dhammapada* 277–9. Sangharakshita discusses these in chapter 11, 'The Nature of Existence', of *The Three Jewels*, Windhorse Publications, Birmingham 1998, pp. 72–84 (*Complete Works*, vol. 2).

14 According to the Prajñāparamitā teaching, emptiness or *śūnyatā* has four levels. See Sangharakshita, *A Survey of Buddhism*, Windhorse Publications, Birmingham 2001, pp. 345–6 (in the chapter on 'The Scriptures of Perfect Wisdom') for a description of meditation on these four 'levels' (*Complete Works,* vol. 1).

15 For a further description of the six *pāramitās*, see, for example, the section called 'The Six Perfections' in Sangharakshita's *Survey of Buddhism,* Windhorse Publications, Birmingham 2001, pp. 466–90 (*Complete Works*, vol. 1).

16 The parable of the raft is told in sections 13 and 14 of the *Alagaddūpama Sutta*, *Majjhima Nikāya* 22 (i.134–5);

Bhikkhu Ñāṇamoli and Bhikkhu Bodhi (trans.), *The Middle Length Discourses of the Buddha*, Wisdom Publications, Boston 1995, pp. 228–9; or I. B. Horner (trans.), *Middle Length Sayings*, vol. i, Pali Text Society, Oxford 1957, pp. 173–4. For the parable of the blind men and the elephant, see *Udāna* 6.4 (*Paṭhamanānātitthiya Sutta*), in John D. Ireland (trans.), *The Udāna and the Itivuttaka*, Buddhist Publication Society, Kandy 2007, pp. 81–4. And the parable of the ever-smouldering anthill is found in the *Vammika Sutta*, *Majjhima Nikāya* 23 (i.143–5): see Bhikkhu Ñāṇamoli and Bhikkhu Bodhi (trans.), *The Middle Length Discourses of the Buddha*, Wisdom Publications, Boston 1995, pp. 237–9, or I. B. Horner (trans.), *Middle Length Sayings*, vol. i, Pali Text Society, London 1967, pp. 183–6.

17 For an outline of these Abhidharma works, see chapter 7, 'The Fundamental Abhidharma' in Sangharakshita, *The Eternal Legacy*, Windhorse Publications, Birmingham 2006, pp. 62–85 (*Complete Works*, vol. 14).

18 In his introduction to the *Comprehensive Manual of Abhidhamma* (Buddhist Publication Society Pariyatta Editions, Unalaska WA 1999, p. 6), Bhikkhu Bodhi says

> The Abhidhamma takes no account of the personal inclinations and cognitive capacities of the listeners; it makes no concessions to particular pragmatic requirements. It reveals the architectonics of actuality in an abstract, formalistic manner utterly devoid of literary embellishments and pedagogical expedients. Thus the Abhidhamma method is described as the *nippariyāya-dhammadesanā*, the literal or unembellished discourse on the Dhamma. This difference in technique between the two methods also influences their respective terminologies. In the Suttas the Buddha regularly makes use of conventional language (*voharavacana*) and accepts conventional truth (*sammutisacca*), truth expressed in terms of entities that do not possess ontological ultimacy but can still be legitimately referred to them. Thus in the Suttas the Buddha speaks of 'I' and 'you', of 'man' and 'woman', of living beings, persons, and even self as though they were concrete realities. The Abhidhamma method of exposition, however, rigorously restricts itself to terms that are valid from the standpoint of ultimate truth

(*paramatthasacca*): dhammas, their characteristics, their functions, and their relations. Thus in the Abhidhamma all such conceptual entities provisionally accepted in the Suttas for purposes of meaningful communication are resolved into their ontological ultimates, into bare mental and material phenomena that are impermanent, conditioned, and dependently arisen, empty of any abiding self or substance.

19 The *Laṅkāvatāra Sūtra* has been translated into English by D. T. Suzuki, published by Motilal Banarsidass, Delhi 1999.

20 The *Avataṃsaka Sūtra* is available in English as Thomas Cleary (trans.), *The Flower Ornament Scripture*, Shambhala Publications, Boston 1993.

21 The *Vimalakīrti-nirdeśa* is available in several English translations; the one on which the commentary in this volume is based is Robert A. Thurman (trans.), *The Holy Teaching of Vimalakīrti*, Pennsylvania State University Press, University Park and London 1976.

22 The *Lalitavistara Sūtra* is published as Gwendolyn Bays (trans.), *The Voice of the Buddha*, Dharma Publishing, Berkeley 1983.

23 The Pure Land *sūtras* are described in chapter 11 of Sangharakshita, *The Eternal Legacy*, Windhorse Publications, Birmingham 2006, pp. 155–67 (*Complete Works*, vol. 14). See also Ratnaguna and Śraddhāpa, *Great Faith, Great Wisdom*, Windhorse Publications, Cambridge 2016.

CHAPTER 1 Q&A

24 It was Dr Edward Conze who termed *pratītya-samutpāda* 'conditioned co-production'; see, for example, his introduction to his translation of *The Large Sutra on Perfect Wisdom*, University of California Press, Berkeley 1984, p. 14. This fundamental Buddhist doctrine is expressed in the Pāli canon (at *Majjhima Nikāya* i.32) thus: 'This being, that becomes, from the arising of this, that arises; this not becoming, that does not become; from the ceasing of this, that ceases.' See Bhikkhu Ñāṇamoli and Bhikkhu Bodhi (trans.), *The Middle Length Discourses of the Buddha*, Wisdom Publications, Boston 1995, p. 655; or I. B. Horner (trans.), *Middle Length Sayings*, vol. ii, Pali Text Society, London 1967, p. 229. In other words, all things arise and cease in dependence on conditions. For a detailed introduction to the *pratītya-samutpāda* doctrine, see Sangharakshita, *A Survey of Buddhism*, chapter 1, section 11, 'The Essence of Enlightenment', Windhorse Publications, Birmingham 2001,

pp. 110–9 (*Complete Works*, vol. 1).

25 Sangharakshita describes this development in chapter 3, section 8, 'The Scriptures of Buddhist Idealism', in *A Survey of Buddhism*, Windhorse Publications, Birmingham 2001, pp. 389–95 (*Complete Works*, vol. 1).

26 See D. T. Suzuki, *The Essence of Buddhism*, Buddhist Society, London 1957, p. 51; also D. T. Suzuki, *On Indian Mahāyāna Buddhism*, Harper and Row, New York, Evanston and London 1968, pp. 156–7.

27 The *Avataṃsaka Sūtra* is available in English as Thomas Cleary (trans.), *The Flower Ornament Scripture*, Shambhala Publications, Boston 1993.

28 This is in verse 77 of the apocryphal *Gospel of Thomas*.

29 One of the most famous of these was the thirteenth-century Persian poet Rumi, among whose many verses about the Beloved is:

> In truth everything and everyone
> Is a shadow of the Beloved,
> And our seeking is His seeking
> And our words are His words…
> We search for Him here and there, while looking right at Him.
> Sitting by His side, we ask:
> 'O Beloved, where is the Beloved?'

30 *Stanford Encyclopaedia of Philosophy*: The *Parmenides* is, quite possibly, the most enigmatic of Plato's dialogues. The dialogue recounts an almost certainly fictitious conversation between a venerable Parmenides (the Eleatic Monist) and a youthful Socrates, followed by a dizzying array of interconnected arguments presented by Parmenides to a young and compliant interlocutor named 'Aristotle' (not the philosopher, but rather a man who became one of the Thirty Tyrants after Athens' surrender to Sparta at the conclusion of the Peloponnesian War). Most commentators agree that Socrates articulates a version of the theory of forms defended by his much older namesake in the dialogues of Plato's middle period, that Parmenides mounts a number of potentially devastating challenges to this theory, and that these challenges are followed by a piece of intellectual 'gymnastics' consisting of eight strings of arguments (deductions) that are in some way designed to help us see how to protect the theory of forms against the challenges. Beyond this, there is precious little scholarly consensus. Commentators disagree about the proper way to reconstruct Parmenides' challenges, about the overall logical

structure of the Deductions, about the main subject of the Deductions, about the function of the Deductions in relation to the challenges, and about the final philosophical moral of the dialogue as a whole. The *Parmenides* inspired the metaphysical and mystical theories of the later Neoplatonists (notably Plotinus and later, Proclus), who saw in the Deductions the key to the hierarchical ontological structure of the universe.

31 A famous quotation from the Smaragdine Tablet, an ancient alchemical document ascribed to Hermes Tresmegistus, states the 'Hermetic correspondence' between higher and lower levels of reality: 'That which is above is like that which is below and that which is below is like that which is above, to accomplish the miracles of one thing.'

32 Insight here is used in the specific sense of insight into Reality. In the formulation of spiritual progress known as the twelve positive *nidānas* (links), the stage at which transcendental insight arises is called 'seeing things as they really are'. In the Buddhist tradition, specific meditation practices (*vipaśyāna* practices) have been developed to bring about the arising of insight, or rather to strengthen the insights we all have in the course of our lives, particularly at times when we are experiencing grief, contemplating great beauty, or absorbed in thought. These experiences, recollected in meditation, have a cumulative effect until, like adding grains to a weighing scale, the balance tips, and transcendental insight arises. The arising of insight in this sense coincides with the point of Stream Entry as described in the early Buddhist tradition, and it carries the same sense of irreversibilty. When insight has arisen in the full sense, one is consistently able to live on the basis of 'seeing things as they really are'.

33 'Selfishness is simply unwillingness to face new experiences.' Sangharakshita, *The Religion of Art*, Windhorse Publications, Cambridge 2010, p. 94 (*Complete Works*, vol. 26).

34 Beyond a certain point on the spiritual path, one's practice has sufficient momentum to guarantee that one will continue to progress towards Enlightenment; there is no further danger of falling back. This point was called by the Buddha 'Stream Entry', and someone who has reached it is thus a 'Stream Entrant'. For more on Stream Entry, see, for example, chapter 6, 'The Gravitational Pull and the Point of No Return' in Sangharakshita, *What is the Dharma?*, Windhorse Publications, Birmingham 1998 (*Complete Works*,

vol. 3). Among the many references to Stream Entry in the Pāli canon, the *Saṃyutta Nikāya* has a whole section devoted to the subject. See Bhikkhu Bodhi (trans.), *The Connected Discourses of the Buddha,* Wisdom Publications, Boston 2000, pp. 1788–1837; or F. L. Woodward (trans.), *Kindred Sayings*, part 5, Pali Text Society, Oxford 1979, pp. 296–351.

35 This is a reference to the *trikāya* doctrine, the doctrine of the three bodies of the Buddha: the human, historical Buddha, the archetypal Buddha, and the Buddha principle. For an account of the development of this doctrine, see, for example, chapter 5, 'Philosophical Interpretations', in Sangharakshita, *The Three Jewels*, Windhorse Publications, Birmingham 1998, pp. 33–40 (*Complete Works*, vol. 2).

36 It was the Buddha himself who first exemplified fearlessness in meditation. This is described in the *Bhayabherava Sutta* of the *Majjhima Nikāya* 4 (i.22); see Bhikkhu Ñāṇamoli and Bhikkhu Bodhi (trans.), *The Middle Length Discourses of the Buddha*, Wisdom Publications, Boston 1995, p. 102–7; or I. B. Horner (trans.), *Middle Length Sayings*, vol. i, Pali Text Society, Oxford 1957, pp. 21–30. The Buddha describes staying in fearful places:

> And while I dwelt there, a wild animal would come up to me, or a peacock would knock off a branch, or the wind would rustle the leaves. I thought: 'What now if this is the fear and dread coming?' I thought: 'Why do I dwell always expecting fear and dread? What if I subdue that fear and dread while keeping the same posture that I am in when it comes upon me?

The Vajrayāna cremation ground practices mentioned here are described in chapter 8, 'The Cremation Ground and the Celestial Maidens', in Sangharakshita, *Creative Symbols of Tantric Buddhism*, Windhorse Publications, Birmingham 2002 (*Complete Works*, vol. 13).

CHAPTER 2

37 For example, the *Sekha Sutta, Majjhima Nikāya* 53. There are other texts in which, a disciple having spoken, the Buddha is consulted later and gives his blessing to what was said; for example, *Cūḷavedalla Sutta, Majjhima Nikāya* 44.

38 The Prakrit languages of India were essentially vernacular dialects; *prakrit* literally means 'natural', as opposed to *sanskrit*, which means 'refined' or 'put together'. There is scholarly controversy over the relationship of Pāli, the language in which

the Buddha's teachings were passed on orally and eventually written down, to the dialect of Magadha, the area of India in which the Buddha lived and taught. Paiśāci was thought by early grammarians to have been a purely literary language grouped with the Prakrit languages but never having been spoken. And it is said that when the Prakrit languages were formalized and written down, they came to be called Apabhraṃśa.

39 Bunnō Katō and Soothill's translation of the *White Lotus Sūtra* was further revised, and published by Kosei Publishing, Tokyo, in 1975, together with the preceding and succeeding *sūtras*, as *The Threefold Lotus Sutra*. Several more translations of the *sūtra* have now been published, for example a version translated by Burton Watson and published by Columbia University Press, and a translation by Gene Reeves published by Wisdom Publications.

40 'This very body the Buddha' is a line from a famous sequence of verses, the *Song of Meditation*, by Hakuin. Hakuin Ekaku was a Japanese Zen master who lived from 1686 to 1768. He is credited with reviving the Rinzai school of Zen and with the koan 'What is the sound of one hand clapping?' He is also famous for his inspiring writings, of which the *Song of Meditation* is among the best loved, and for his calligraphy and painting.

41 The Vulture's Peak (Gṛdhrakūṭa) is near the Bihari town of Rajgir (Rājagṛha), which was the ancient capital city of the Magadha kings and is famous for its hot springs. Today it is possible to take a cable car up to a Japanese peace pagoda built on top of the hill, but pilgrims usually walk up the path to a smaller peak which is said to be where the historical Buddha gave his teachings.

42 See Francesca Fremantle and Chogyam Trungpa (trans.), *The Tibetan Book of the Dead*, Shambhala Publications, Boston and London, p. 41.

43 Oliver Cromwell, Letter to the General Assembly of the Church of Scotland, 3 August 1650.

44 For a fuller account of these three *yānas*, see chapter 2, section 3, 'The Three Vehicles', in Sangharakshita, *A Survey of Buddhism*, Windhorse Publications, Birmingham 2001, pp. 241–9 (*Complete Works*, vol. 1).

45 This is a paraphrase of the story. For the parable as told in the *sūtra*, see Bunnō Katō and W. E. Soothill (trans.), *The Threefold Lotus Sutra*, Kosei Publishing, Tokyo, 1975, pp. 162–9.

46 Ibid., pp. 231–6.

CHAPTER 2 Q&A

47 *Karuṇā-Puṇḍarīka*, edited with introduction and notes by Isshi Yamada, School of Oriental and African Studies, London 1968.

48 Sangharakshita, *The Eternal Legacy*, Windhorse Publications, Birmingham 2006, p. 89 (*Complete Works*, vol. 14).

49 The *Lalitavistara Sūtra* has been published in two volumes as Gwendolyn Bays (trans.), *The Voice of the Buddha*, Dharma Publishing, Berkeley 1983.

50 The restriction given by the Vinaya is 'Whatsoever Bhikkhu shall cause one not received into the higher grade of the Order to recite the Dhamma clause by clause – that is a *paccittīya* [offence]'. Vinaya Piṭaka iv.15; See T. W. Rhys Davids and Hermann Oldenberg (trans.), *Vinaya Texts*, part 1, Motilal Banarsidass, Delhi 1974, p. 32.

51 See Bunnō Katō and W. E. Soothill (trans.), *The Threefold Lotus Sutra*, Kosei Publishing, Tokyo, 1975, p. 107.

52 *Buddhavacana* literally means 'Buddha speech'. It is sometimes used in a narrow sense to refer to words literally spoken by the Buddha, or words spoken by one of the Buddha's disciples which the Buddha declared to be true, but the term is capable of a wider interpretation. 'If we mean by Buddha simply the state of Supreme Enlightenment by whomsoever experienced, then by *Buddhavacana* is to be understood any expression, or better reflection, of this transcendental state in the medium of human speech.' Sangharakshita, *The Eternal Legacy*, Windhorse Publications, Birmingham 2006, p. 1 (*Complete Works*, vol. 14).

53 Isaac Williams, *Reserve in Communicating Religious Knowledge*, Oxford 1841.

54 For example, in a paper on 'Buddhism in Iran', Mehrak Golestani says that 'Iranian influence is found in the figure of the Buddha Amitabha; the way he is so closely related to eternal light and endless life is very similar to the Iranian Time God, Zurvan. Scholars agree that this notion of Iranian influence is certainly possible especially during the formative phase of Central Asia when Iranian and Indian concepts came into close contact.' In this paper, published online by the Circle of Ancient Iranian Studies, Golestani is careful to point out that the area he is concerned with is 'not the region of modern day Iran, rather the area of Central Asia inhabited by Iranian people from roughly 500 BCE onwards. This would include modern day Iran, Tajikistan, Uzbekistan, Afghanistan, as well as parts of North-West Pakistan and India.' According

to Pāli records, Iranians of this area are said to have met the Buddha and returned home to build temples dedicated to him, and the area was further influenced by Buddhism during the time of Emperor Aśoka. The development of Mahāyāna Buddhism, he says, is closely associated with the Kushan rule and in particular the development of Gandharan Buddhist art, an amalgamation of Greek, Iranian, and Indian influences.

55 See *Mahāsudassana Sutta*, *Dīgha Nikāya* 17 (ii.180–1), in T. W. and C. A. F. Rhys Davids (trans.), *Dialogues of the Buddha*, part 2, Pali Text Society, Luzac, London 1971, p. 201; or M. Walshe (trans.), *The Long Discourses of the Buddha*, Wisdom Publications, Boston 1995, pp. 283–4.

56 Nichiren, the founder of the Japanese sect bearing his name, lived in the thirteenth century CE. One of his three principal teachings – the 'Three Great Secrets' – was the 'wonderful truth of the *Lotus Sūtra*'. He termed the mantra *namu myōhō renge kyō* ('homage to the Lotus of the Good Law') a summation of the *Lotus Sūtra*, and his followers adopted the incantation. Today there are almost forty subsects of Nichiren's adherents, chief of which is the Nichiren Shoshu.

57 The *trikāya* doctrine is the doctrine of the three bodies of the Buddha: the human, historical Buddha, the archetypal Buddha, and the Buddha principle. For an account of the development of this doctrine see, for example, chapter 5, 'Philosophical Interpretations', in Sangharakshita, *The Three Jewels*, Windhorse Publications, Birmingham 1998, pp. 33–40 (*Complete Works*, vol. 2).

58 See *Bṛhadāraṇyaka Upaniṣad*, chapter 1, section 4.

59 Going for Refuge to the Three Jewels – the Buddha, the Dharma, and the Saṅgha – is the expression traditionally used to refer to the commitment of any Buddhist, whether monastic or lay, to the Buddhist path. It is axiomatic to Sangharakshita's teaching that this wholehearted commitment comes first, the way one chooses to live being an expression of that commitment. 'Commitment is primary; lifestyle is secondary.' Thus, while members of the Triratna Buddhist Order have a whole range of lifestyles, they all receive the same ordination. For an account of the development of Sangharakshita's thinking on Going for Refuge, see Sangharakshita, *The History of My Going for Refuge*, Windhorse Publications, Glasgow 1988 (*Complete Works*, vol. 2).

60 *Saṃyutta Nikāya* iv.251; see Bhikkhu Bodhi (trans.), *The Connected Discourses of the*

Buddha, Wisdom Publications, Boston 2000, p. 1294; or F. L. Woodward (trans.), *The Book of the Kindred Sayings*, vol. iv, Pali Text Society, London 1956, p. 170. The Pāli words *lobha, dosa*, and *moha* translate as greed, hatred, and delusion.

61 For Mrs Rhys Davids' reference to the twelve positive *nidānas*, see C. A. F. Rhys Davids (trans.), *The Book of the Kindred Sayings*, vol. ii, Pali Text Society, London 1952, pp.viii–ix. For an account of the positive *nidānas*, see chapter 7, 'The Spiral Path', in Sangharakshita, *What is the Dharma?*, Windhorse Publications, Birmingham 1998, pp. 105–26 (*Complete Works*, vol. 3).

62 F. L. Woodward (trans.), *Itivuttaka, The Minor Anthologies of the Pāli Canon*, part 2, Pali Text Society, London 1985.

CHAPTER 3

63 For the parable in the *sūtra*, see Bunnō Katō and W. E. Soothill (trans.), *The Threefold Lotus Sutra*, Kosei Publishing, Tokyo, 1975, pp. 85–109.

64 Vinaya Piṭaka i.34; see I. B. Horner (trans.), *The Book of the Discipline*, part 4, Pali Text Society, London 1982, p. 45; and *Saṃyutta Nikāya* iv.19–20; see F. L. Woodward (trans.), *The Book of the Kindred Sayings*, part 4, Pali Text Society, London 1980, p. 10, or Bhikkhu Bodhi (trans.), *The Connected Discourses of the Buddha*, Wisdom Publications, Boston 2000, p. 1143.

65 For an account of the Tibetan wheel of life, see chapter 1 of Sangharakshita, *Creative Symbols of Tantric Buddhism*, Windhorse Publications, Birmingham 2002 (*Complete Works*, vol. 13).

66 The story of Krishna's flute is told in the *Srimad-Bhāgavata*. See Radhakamal Mukerjee, *The Lord of the Autumn Moons*, Asia Publishing House, Bombay 1957, pp. 97–102.

67 *The Voice of the Silence* is the title of a book of verses, many of which are of Mahāyāna Buddhist character, composed by H. P. Blavatsky on the basis of an original Tibetan text and published in 1889. See also Sangharakshita's essay, 'Paradox and Poetry in The Voice of the Silence' in *The Religion of Art*, Windhorse Publications, Cambridge 2010, pp. 171–97 (*Complete Works*, vol. 26).

68 It was the Mahāyāna that placed special emphasis on this quality, as an aspect of the Bodhisattva's practice. Indeed, when the list of six perfections (*pāramitās*) practised by the bodhisattva was extended to ten, *upāya kauśalya pāramitā* was counted as the seventh perfection, explained by Har Dayal in *The Bodhisattva Doctrine in Buddhist Sanskrit Literature* (Motilal, Kegan Paul, London 1932, p. 248) as

'skilfulness or wisdom in the choice or adoption of the means or expedients for converting others or helping them'. For more about this, see chapter 4, section 6 of Sangharakshita, *A Survey of Buddhism* (*Complete Works*, vol. 1).

69 For a fuller account of these three *yānas*, see chapter 2, section 3, 'The Three Vehicles', in Sangharakshita, *A Survey of Buddhism*, Windhorse Publications, Birmingham 2001, pp. 241–9 (*Complete Works*, vol. 1).

70 'There is a book, who runs may read, / Which heavenly truth imparts': John Keble (1792–1866), *The Christian Year: Septuagesima*.

71 Here 'universalism' refers to the view that all religious teachings are equally true and lead equally to salvation. This sense of the term has nothing to do with the usage of the term Universalism within a specifically Christian context. Although Buddhism is not 'universalist', it is universal, in that its teachings are addressed and applicable not to one section of humanity only, but to all people whatsoever.

72 Arnold offered a definition of God as 'that stream of tendency by which all things seek to fulfil the law of their being'. The phrase 'stream of tendency' is apparently borrowed from William Wordsworth, who wrote in his long autobiographical poem *The Prelude* of 'the mighty stream of tendency / Uttering, for elevation of our thought, / A clear sonorous voice' (*Prelude* 9:88–90).

CHAPTER 3 Q&A

73 Bunnō Katō and W. E. Soothill (trans.), *The Threefold Lotus Sutra*, Kosei Publishing, Tokyo, 1975, p. 80.

74 Ibid. p. 82 and p. 135.

75 This is a reference to the third of the 'ten fetters' that bind us to the wheel of life and which are progressively 'broken' in the course of the spiritual life. (At the point of Stream Entry the first three fetters have been broken.) 'Grasping ethical rules and religious observances as ends in themselves' is the traditional version of the third fetter; in *The Taste of Freedom* (Windhorse Publications, Glasgow 1990), Sangharakshita terms it 'superficiality', and recommends 'commitment' as its antidote. The ten fetters are enumerated in, for example, the *Sangīti Sutta*, *Dīgha Nikāya* 33 (iii.234); see M. Walshe (trans.), *The Long Discourses of the Buddha*, Wisdom Publications, Boston 1995, p. 495; or T. W. Rhys Davids (trans.), *Dialogues of the Buddha*, part 3, Pali Text Society, Oxford 1991, p. 225. See also *Mahāvagga* 179–180, *Saṃyutta Nikāya,* (v.61); Bhikkhu Bodhi (trans.), *The Connected Discourses of the*

Buddha, Wisdom Publications, Boston 2000, p. 1565; or F. L. Woodward (trans.), *Kindred Sayings*, part 5, Pali Text Society, Oxford 1979, p. 49.

76 Bunnō Katō and W. E. Soothill (trans.), *The Threefold Lotus Sutra*, Kosei Publishing, Tokyo, 1975, p. 88.

77 Ibid. p. 70.

78 The five orders of conditionality, or *niyamas*, are enumerated by Buddhaghosa in his commentary on the *Dhammasaṅgaṇi*, the first book of the Abhidhamma Piṭaka, vol. ii. Pe Maung Tin (trans.), *The Expositor*, ch. 10, ed. C. A. F. Rhys Davids, Pali Text Society, London 1921, p. 360; also in Buddhaghosa's commentary on the *Dīgha Nikāya*, ed. W. Stede, Pali Text Society 1920, p. 360 (not available in English translation). Sangharakshita's source is C. A. F. Rhys Davids, *Buddhism: a Study of the Buddhist Norm*, Williams and Norgate, London 1912, pp. 118–9. For Sangharakshita's account of them, see, for example, Sangharakshita, *The Three Jewels*, Windhorse Publications, Birmingham 1998, pp. 62–3 (*Complete Works*, vol. 3).

79 Bunnō Katō and W. E. Soothill (trans.), *The Threefold Lotus Sutra*, Kosei Publishing, Tokyo, 1975, p. 70.

CHAPTER 4

80 Sophocles, *Antigone*, 322.

81 For the parable in the *sūtra*, see Bunnō Katō and W. E. Soothill (trans.), *The Threefold Lotus Sutra*, Kosei Publishing, Tokyo, 1975, pp. 110–25.

82 Luke 15:11–32.

83 For a translation of the 'Hymn of the Pearl', see, for example, Hans Jonas, *The Gnostic Religion*, Beacon Press, Boston 1958, pp. 113–16.

84 The parable of the poisoned arrow is told in the *Cūḷamālunkya Sutta*, *Majjhima Nikāya* 63 (i.427–32); see Bhikkhu Ñāṇamoli and Bhikkhu Bodhi (trans.), *The Middle Length Discourses of the Buddha*, Wisdom Publications, Boston 1995, pp. 533–6; or I. B. Horner (trans.), *Middle Length Sayings*, vol. ii, Pali Text Society, Oxford 1957, p. 99.

85 See Abraham Maslow, *Towards a Psychology of Being*, Van Nostrand Reinhold, New York 1968, pp. 21–60.

86 See Francesca Fremantle and Chogyam Trungpa (trans.), *The Tibetan Book of the Dead*, Shambhala Publications, Boston and London, p. 37.

87 T. S. Eliot, 'Burnt Norton', part 1, in *Four Quartets*.

88 Matthew 6:21.

CHAPTER 4 Q&A

89 *Dīgha Nikāya* 27 (iii.83–97); see M. Walshe (trans.), *The Long Discourses of the Buddha*, Wisdom Publications,

Boston 1995, pp. 407–15; or T. W. and C. A. F. Rhys Davids (trans.), *Dialogues of the Buddha*, part 3, Pali Text Society, London 1957, pp. 77–94.

90 This is a reference to the two modes of conditionality. In the cyclical mode, in dependence upon feeling, craving arises, and the cycle continues, as symbolized by the twelve images around the edge of the Tibetan Wheel of Life. However, there is another possibility. In dependence upon feeling can arise awareness of *duḥkha*: that is, suffering, or unsatisfactoriness. In dependence upon that, faith can arise, and thus a sequence of ever more positive mental states can be experienced; this is the 'spiral path'. These two sets of links are the two sets of twelve *nidānas*, and there is a meditation practice in which one specifically reflects on these two sequences, one cyclical, the other spiral. For a detailed account, see Sangharakshita, *What is the Dharma?*, chapters 2 and 7 ('The Dynamics of Being' and 'The Spiral Path') in *Complete Works* vol. 3, pp. 182–204 and pp. 258–79.

91 Bunnō Katō and W. E. Soothill (trans.), *The Threefold Lotus Sutra*, Kosei Publishing, Tokyo, 1975, p. 297.

92 One might cite Charles Dickens' *Dombey and Son*: 'Those three words [i.e. *Dombey and Son*] conveyed the one idea of Mr Dombey's life.' The destructive tragedy of Emily Brontë's *Wuthering Heights* stems partly from Mr Earnshaw's favouritism of the adopted Heathcliff over his own son Hindley; and there is equally destructive tension between Philip Wakem and his father in George Eliot's *Mill on the Floss*.

93 See Lama Anagarika Govinda, *Foundations of Tibetan Mysticism*, Century Hutchinson, London 1987, p. 123.

94 The heavenly realms are listed in, for example, the *Sāleyyaka Sutta*, *Majjhima Nikāya* 41 (i.289); see Bhikkhu Ñāṇamoli and Bhikkhu Bodhi (trans.), *The Middle Length Discourses of the Buddha*, Wisdom Publications, Boston 1995, p. 384; or I. B. Horner (trans.), *Middle Length Sayings*, vol. 1, Pali Text Society, Oxford 1957, p. 348. Note that it is not the realms themselves but their inhabitants, the gods, who are described as having ever greater brilliance, from the gods of Limited Radiance to the gods of Immeasurable Radiance, Streaming Radiance. and so on.

CHAPTER 5

95 W. E. Soothill (trans.), *The Lotus of the Wonderful Law*, Curzon, London 1987, pp. 125–8.

96 The Buddha's vision of humanity like a bed of lotuses is described at *Saṃyutta*

Nikāya i.138; see Bhikkhu Bodhi (trans.), *The Connected Discourses of the Buddha*, Wisdom Publications, Boston 2000, p. 233; or C. A. F. Rhys Davids (trans.), *The Book of the Kindred Sayings*, part 1, Pali Text Society, Oxford 1989, p. 174; also Vinaya Piṭaka i.6; see I. B. Horner (trans.), *The Book of the Discipline*, Part 4, Pali Text Society, London 1982, p. 9.

97 For a detailed exposition of this way of seeing the Noble Eightfold Path, see Sangharakshita, *The Buddha's Noble Eightfold Path*, Windhorse Publications, Birmingham 2007, especially pp. 138–9 (*Complete Works*, vol. 1).

98 See H. Kern (trans), *Saddharma Puṇḍarīka*, Sacred Books of the East series, vol. xxi, Clarendon Press, Oxford 1963, p. 128.

99 Each of the archetypal Buddhas in the mandala of the Five Buddhas is associated with the sun at a particular time of the day: Akṣobhya with the dawn, Amoghasiddhi – mysteriously – with the sun at midnight, and so on. Apart from Vairocana, the Buddha of the mandala with the best known association with sun imagery is Amitābha, whose name means 'Infinite Light'. He is associated with the setting sun, with the West, and he is therefore represented iconographically as being a rich deep red colour. For more about the mandala of the Five Buddhas, see, for example, chapter 8, 'The Five Buddhas, "Male" and "Female"', in Sangharakshita, *Creative Symbols of Tantric Buddhism*, Windhorse Publications, Birmingham 2002 (*Complete Works*, vol. 13).

100 *Aṅguttara Nikāya* 10.21 (v.33): 'The Lion: This, monks, is a name for the Tathāgata, the Arahant, the Fully Enlightened One. When, monks, the Tathāgata expounds the Dhamma in an assembly, that is his lion's roar.' See Bhikkhu Bodhi (trans.), *The Numerical Discourses of the Buddha*, Wisdom Publications, Boston 2012, p. 1362; or F. L. Woodward (trans.), *The Book of the Gradual Sayings*, vol. v, Pali Text Society, Oxford 1972, pp. 23–4. But would the Buddha ever literally have heard a lion roar? Quite possibly. The Asiatic lion formerly occurred in south-eastern Europe, the Black Sea basin, Caucasus, Mesopotamia, and much of India. Lions are depicted on top of some Aśoka pillars, for example the one at Sarnath.

CHAPTER 5 Q&A

101 This is the sixth of the eight qualities of the great ocean described by the Buddha in the *Uposatha Sutta*, *Udāna* 5.5. See John D. Ireland (trans.), *The Udāna and the Itivuttaka*, Buddhist Publication Society,

Kandy 2007, p. 68. See also Sangharakshita's talk 'The Taste of Freedom' (*Complete Works*, vol. 11).

102 There is no satisfactory equivalent for the Pāli *mettā* in English, but it is usually translated 'loving kindness'. This positive emotion is cultivated systematically in a specific meditation practice, the *mettā bhāvanā*, in the final stage of which the meditator develops *mettā* towards all living beings. For Sangharakshita's detailed commentary, see *Living with Kindness*, Windhorse Publications, Birmingham 2004 (*Complete Works*, vol. 15).

103 Lama Anagarika Govinda, *Foundations of Tibetan Mysticism*, Century Hutchinson, London 1987, pp. 133–5.

CHAPTER 6

104 See the *Mahāparinibbāna Sutta* section 5.11, *Dīgha Nikāya* 16 (ii.143); M. Walshe (trans.), *The Long Discourses of the Buddha,* Wisdom Publications, Boston 1995, p. 264; or T. W. Rhys Davids (trans.), *Dialogues of the Buddha*, part 2, Pali Text Society, Oxford 1977, pp. 155–6.

105 *Mahāparinibbāna Sutta* sections 6.24–7, *Dīgha Nikāya* 16 (ii.164–6); see M. Walshe (trans.), *The Long Discourses of the Buddha,* Wisdom Publications, Boston 1995, pp. 275–7; or T. W. Rhys Davids (trans.), *Dialogues of the Buddha*, part 2, Pali Text Society, Oxford 1977, pp. 187–90.

106 See Lobsang P. Lhalungpa (trans.), *The Life of Milarepa*, Dutton, New York 1977, pp. 184–5.

107 For details of the source of this tradition, see Reginald Ray, *Buddhist Saints in India*, Oxford University Press, Oxford 1994, p. 326.

108 See S. Z. Aung and C. A. F. Rhys Davids (trans.), *Points of Controversy (Kathā-vatthu)*, Pali Text Society, London 1915, p. 312.

109 See John S. Strong (trans.), *The Legend of King Aśoka (Aśokāvadāna)*, Princeton University Press, Princeton 1983, pp. 219–20.

110 See H. Kern (trans.), *Saddharma Puṇḍarīka*, Sacred Books of the East, vol. xxi, Clarendon Press, Oxford 1963, pp. 227–8.

111 For more on *ākāśa*, see Lama Anagarika Govinda, *Foundations of Tibetan Mysticism*, Century Hutchinson, London 1987, pp. 137–8.

112 This association of the elements of the stupa with colours and shapes is part of the traditions of Tibet, China, and Japan. Lama Anagarika Govinda mentions it in *Psycho-Cosmic Symbolism of the Buddhist Stupa*, Dharma Publishing, Emeryville

1976, pp. 91–2, and gives a lengthy description in his *Foundations of Tibetan Mysticism*, Hutchinson, London 1987, pp. 181–6. (There is a useful diagram on p. 184.) In his essay 'Tantric Buddhism and Chinese Thought in East Asia', Fabio Rambelli says that the stupa is described thus in a Chinese text called 'Ritual of the Secret Dhāraṇīs of the Three Sindhis for the Destruction of Hell, the Transformation of Karmic Hindrances, and the Liberations from the Three Conditioned Worlds'; Rambelli says that the ideas and practices of this text circulated in China in the ninth and tenth centuries CE, and became influential in Japan from the twelfth century. See chapter 21 of David Gordon White (ed.), *Tantra in Practice*, Motilal Banarsidass, Delhi 2001, p. 366ff.

CHAPTER 6 Q&A

113 See *Dhammapada*, chapters 25 and 26.

114 *Mahāparinibbāna Sutta* section 6.27, *Dīgha Nikāya* 16 (ii.167–8); M. Walshe (trans.), *The Long Discourses of the Buddha*, Wisdom Publications, Boston 1995, p. 277; or T. W. Rhys Davids (trans.), *Dialogues of the Buddha*, part 2, Pali Text Society, Oxford 1977, p. 190.

115 *Mahāparinibbāna Sutta* section 5.10, *Dīgha Nikāya* 16 (ii.143); M. Walshe (trans.), *The Long Discourses of the Buddha*, Wisdom Publications, Boston 1995, p. 264; or T. W. Rhys Davids (trans.), *Dialogues of the Buddha*, part 2, Pali Text Society, Oxford 1977, pp. 155–6.

116 See, for example, J. J. Jones (trans.), *Mahāvastu*, vol. ii, Luzac, London 1952, pp. 331ff.; and J. J. Jones (trans.), *Mahāvastu*, vol. iii, Luzac, London 1956, p. 297.

117 The *Jātaka* stories are a collection of folk tales which describe the heroic acts of the Buddha-to-be in former lives. Some of them depict him in human form, others in the form of an animal or bird. See *The Eternal Legacy*, Windhorse Publications, Birmingham 2006, pp. 51ff. (*Complete Works*, vol. 14). The Pāli tradition has preserved a vast collection of *Jātakas* now published in English translation by the Pali Text Society in three volumes edited by Professor E. B. Cowell (London 1981). The Sanskrit tradition has its own series of *Jātaka* stories, the *Jātakamālas*, 'Garlands of Birth Stories', the most famous of which is that by the poet Āryaśūra, who lived in around the fourth century CE.

118 The *dhyānas* are the levels of higher consciousness identified by the Buddha. They are most often experienced in meditation, though the

lower *dhyānas* may occur in other circumstances. There are four '*dhyānas* of the world of form' (*rūpa dhyānas*) and four 'formless *dhyānas*' (*arūpa dhyānas*); the sphere of infinite space and the sphere of infinite consciousness are the first and second *arūpa dhyānas*. For more about the *dhyānas*, see chapter 7, 'On the Threshold of Enlightenment', in Sangharakshita, *The Bodhisattva Ideal*, Windhorse Publications, Birmingham 1999, pp. 155–63 (*Complete Works*, vol. 4); and Sangharakshita, *The Purpose and Practice of Buddhist Meditation*, Ibis Publications, Ledbury 2012, pp. 231–82 (*Complete Works*, vol. 5).

119 In meditation, *vitarka* and *vicāra* – 'initial thought' and 'applied thought' – are two of the five factors present in the experience of the first *dhyāna*. These five factors are enumerated by the Buddha in the *Anupada Sutta*, *Majjhima Nikāya* 111 (i.25–9); see Bhikkhu Ñāṇamoli and Bhikkhu Bodhi (trans.), *The Middle Length Discourses of the Buddha*, Wisdom Publications, Boston 1995, p. 899; or I. B. Horner (trans.), *Middle Length Sayings*, vol. iii, Pali Text Society, London 1959, p. 78. At *Visuddhimagga* 142–3, Buddhaghosa says, 'applied thought is like the hand that grips firmly and sustained thought is like the hand that rubs, when one grips a tarnished metal dish firmly with one hand and rubs it with powder and oil and a woollen pad with the other hand.' Bhikkhu Ñāṇamoli (trans.), *The Path of Purification*, fourth edition, Buddhist Publication Society, Colombo 2010, p. 137.

120 See Lama Anagarika Govinda, *Foundations of Tibetan Mysticism*, Century Hutchinson, London 1987, p. 184.

121 For an account of the *pāramitās*, see p. 8.

CHAPTER 7

122 See chapter 4, section 6, 'The Ten Perfections and the Ten Stages', in Sangharakshita, *A Survey of Buddhism*, Windhorse Publications, Birmingham 2001, pp. 490–9 (*Complete Works*, vol. 1).

123 *Padme* isn't a locative but a vocative, so a literal translation is simply 'jewel lotus'. Donald Lopez devotes an entire chapter of *Prisoners of Shangri-la* (University of Chicago Press, 1999) to a discussion of how this mantra has been misconstrued in the West.

124 See Bunnō Katō et al. (trans.), *The Threefold Lotus Sutra*, Kosei Publishing, Tokyo 1995, p. 177.

125 Jung terms the emergence of true individuality 'the individuation of the self'; this

is the sense of 'self' that is meant here, not the Vedantic idea of a fixed, unchanging self, which is completely un-Buddhistic.

126 For more on the complex term *bodhicitta*, see chapter 2, 'The Awakening of the Bodhi Heart', in Sangharakshita, *The Bodhisattva Ideal*, Windhorse Publications, Birmingham 1999, pp. 31–58 (*Complete Works*, vol. 4).

127 See Vessantara, *Female Deities in Buddhism*, Windhorse Publications, Birmingham 2003, pp. 19–20.

128 For more on Avalokiteśvara, see Vessantara, *A Guide to the Bodhisattvas*, Windhorse Publications, Birmingham 2008, pp. 13–24; and on Guanyin, see Vessantara, *Female Deities in Buddhism*, Windhorse Publications, Birmingham 2003, pp. 101–9.

129 Bunnō Katō et al. (trans.), *The Threefold Lotus Sutra*, Kosei Publishing, Tokyo 1975, pp. 323–6.

130 For more about the mandala of the Five Buddhas see, for example, chapter 8, 'The Five Buddhas, "Male" and "Female"', in Sangharakshita, *Creative Symbols of Tantric Buddhism*, Windhorse Publications, Birmingham 2002 (*Complete Works*, vol. 13).

CHAPTER 7 Q&A

131 'We can hardly classify the Dharmas into "Sudden" and "Gradual," But some men will attain enlightenment much quicker than others.' *The Sūtra of Hui Neng*, trans. Wong Mou-lam, Shambhala Publications, Berkeley 1973, p. 33.

132 This was part of a speech given by Dr Ambedkar in Bombay on 24 May 1956. See Dhananjay Keer, *Dr Ambedkar: Life and Mission*, Popular Prakashan, Bombay 1981, p. 493.

133 For example, the *Vimalakīrti-nirdeśa* describes the universe Sarvagandhasugandhā, where the Tathāgata named Sugandhakūṭa teaches the Dharma by means of perfumes. See R. A. F. Thurman (trans.), *The Holy Teaching of Vimalakīrti*, Pennsylvania State University Press, University Park and London 1976, p. 81; see also *The Inconceivable Emancipation*, p. 559 above.

134 See G. W. F. Hegel, *The Philosophy of Mind*, trans. W. Wallace and A.V. Miller, Oxford 1971.

135 As one of the five *skandhas*, the five 'aggregates' which, according to Buddhism, make up psychophysical existence, *vijñāna* is consciousness through the five physical senses and through the mind at various levels. In chapter 4 of *The Meaning of Conversion in Buddhism*, Sangharakshita says, '*Vijñāna* is usually translated as

"consciousness", but that is not exactly accurate. The prefix *vi-* means "to divide" or "to discriminate", and *jñāna* means "knowledge" or "awareness", so we can translate *vijñāna* as "discriminating awareness". *Vijñāna* therefore refers to awareness of an object not just in a pure mirror-like way but in a way which discriminates the object as being of a particular type and belonging to a particular class, species, or whatever.' *Jñāna* or *prajñā* means 'wisdom' or simply 'awareness', the wisdom that arises when one sees that each of the *skandhas*, including *vijñāna*, is empty of separate existence. The arising of this wisdom represents the transformation of bare awareness into spiritual understanding. See Sangharakshita, *The Meaning of Conversion in Buddhism*, Windhorse Publications, Birmingham 1994, pp. 66–71 (*Complete Works* vol. 2).

136 The three levels of wisdom are enumerated in, for example, the *Saṅgīti Sutta*, *Dīgha Nikāya* 33 (iii.219); see *The Long Discourses of the Buddha*, Wisdom Publications, Boston 1995, p. 486; or T. W. Rhys Davids (trans.), *Dialogues of the Buddha*, part 3, Pali Text Society, Oxford 1991, p. 212.

CHAPTER 8

137 Gandhāra Buddhist art was developed in what is now north-west Pakistan and east Afghanistan between the first century BCE and the seventh century CE. The Gandhāra region was a crossroads of cultural influences. During the reign of King Aśoka (third century BCE) it was the scene of much Buddhist activity, and in the first century the region (now part of the Kushān empire) maintained contacts with Rome, hence the Graeco-Roman origin of the Gandhāra style. In its interpretation of Buddhist legends the Gandhāra school represented the Buddha with a youthful Apollo-like face, and dressed in garments like those seen on Roman Imperial statues.

138 The parable of the poisoned arrow is told in the *Cūḷamālunkya Sutta*, *Majjhima Nikāya* 63 (i.427–32). see Bhikkhu Ñāṇamoli and Bhikkhu Bodhi (trans.), *The Middle Length Discourses of the Buddha*, Wisdom Publications, Boston 1995, p. 533–6; or I. B. Horner (trans.), *Middle Length Sayings*, vol. ii, Pali Text Society, Oxford 1957, p. 99.

139 Buddhaghosa, *Visuddhimagga* 573: 'The ordinary man is like a madman' (*ummattako viya hi puthujjano*); see Bhikkhu Ñāṇamoli, *The Path of Purification*, Buddhist

Publication Society, Kandy 1991, p. 591.

140 W. Liebenthal (trans.), *The Sūtra of the Lord of Healing (Bhaiṣajyagūru Vaiḍūryaprabha Tathāgata)*, Peiping 1936.

141 See Bunnō Katō and W. E. Soothill (trans.), *The Threefold Lotus Sutra*, Kosei Publishing, Tokyo, 1975, pp. 303–11.

142 The monk in the famous photograph was Thích Quảng Đức, who was 66 years old at the time of his self-immolation on 11 June 1963. David Halberstam, a *New York Times* journalist who witnessed the event, wrote (in *The Making of a Quagmire*, Random House, New York 1965), 'I was to see that sight again, but once was enough. Flames were coming from a human being; his body was slowly withering and shriveling up, his head blackening and charring. In the air was the smell of burning human flesh; human beings burn surprisingly quickly. Behind me I could hear the sobbing of the Vietnamese who were now gathering. I was too shocked to cry, too confused to take notes or ask questions, too bewildered to even think.... As he burned he never moved a muscle, never uttered a sound, his outward composure in sharp contrast to the wailing people around him.'

143 This was published as Maha Sthavira Sangharakshita, *Flame in Darkness*, Triratna Grantha Mala, Pune 1980, and later as Sangharakshita, *Anagarika Dharmapala: A Biographical Sketch* by Ibis Publications, Ledbury 2013 (*Complete Works*, vol. 8).

144 For the parable as told in the *sūtra*, see Bunnō Katō and W. E. Soothill (trans.), *The Threefold Lotus Sutra*, Kosei Publishing, Tokyo, 1975, pp. 252–6.

CHAPTER 8 Q&A

145 Ibid., p. 307.

146 G. I. Gurdjieff, born around 1870 in what is now Armenia, travelled widely in Africa and Asia seeking the truth, and in 1912 began teaching in Moscow a way of life that aimed at awakening through direct experience; he called it the 'Fourth Way'. He settled near Fontainebleau in France with a group of followers, and in a question-and-answer session in December 1941 he said, 'One needs fire. Without fire, there will never be anything. This fire is suffering, voluntary suffering, without which it is impossible to create anything. One must prepare, must know what will make one suffer and when it is there, make use of it. Only you can prepare, only you know what makes you suffer, makes the fire which cooks, cements, crystallizes, *does*.'

147 See Bunnō Katō et al. (trans.), *The Threefold Lotus Sutra*, Kosei Publishing, Tokyo 1995, p. 177.

148 Ibid., p. 85.

149 Ibid., pp. 86–109.

150 Ibid., pp. 111–25.

151 See Sangharakshita, *The Rainbow Road*, Windhorse Publications, Birmingham 1997, p. 80 (*Complete Works*, vol. 20).

152 See Bunnō Katō et al. (trans.), *The Threefold Lotus Sutra*, Kosei Publishing, Tokyo 1995, pp. 126-34.

153 The legend of the Fisher King and the land made infertile by the king's affliction first appeared in Arthurian legend and is today best known through T. S. Eliot's poem *The Waste Land*.

154 Luke 15:13 (Authorized Version).

155 This is the story told in Exodus.

156 For a translation of the 'Hymn of the Pearl', see, for example, Hans Jonas, *The Gnostic Religion*, Beacon Press, Boston 1958, pp. 113–16.

157 This is the mantra *oṃ maṇi padme hūṃ*. See chapter 7, 'The Jewel in the Lotus', in *The Drama of Cosmic Enlightenment*, pp. 165 ff. above.

158 Luke 15:8–10.

159 'The Priceless Jewel' was delivered as a sermon in the chapel of King's College, Cambridge, on the morning of Sunday 15 July 1987, to a congregation consisting mainly of American tourists who had come, presumably, to hear the famous choir rather than to listen to a Buddhist discourse of instruction. Sangharakshita gave the sermon at the invitation of the chaplain, the Rev. Stephen Coles, who conducted the service.

TRANSFORMING SELF AND WORLD

INTRODUCTION

160 R. E. Emmerick (trans.), *The Sūtra of Golden Light* (*Suvarṇabhāsottamasūtra*), Pali Text Society, third edition, Oxford 2001. All references are to this edition.

161 See Lama Govinda, 'The Universal Attitude of the Mahayana and the Bodhisattva Ideal', chapter 7 of *Foundations of Tibetan Mysticism*, Rider, London 1969, pp. 40–3.

162 These four lines expressing the Bodhisattva vow are recited throughout the Mahāyāna Buddhist world. This particular version is given in, for example, D. T. Suzuki, *A Manual of Zen Buddhism*, Rider, London 1974, p. 14.

163 For a fuller exposition of the Bodhisattva ideal, see Sangharakshita, *A Survey of Buddhism*, Windhorse Publications, 2001, pp. 437ff. (*Complete Works*, vol. 1); also Sangharakshita, *The Bodhisattva Ideal*, Windhorse Publications, Birmingham 1999, pp. 31–58 (*Complete Works*, vol. 4).

164 For a detailed exploration of the Perfection of Wisdom, see Sangharakshita, *Wisdom Beyond Words*, Birmingham 2000 (*Complete Works*, vol. 14).

165 For the story of the *saṅgīti*, see Vinaya Piṭaka ii.284–93; I. B. Horner (trans.), *The Book of the Discipline*, part 5, Pali Text Society, Oxford 1992, pp. 393–406.

166 For details of these nine forms, and the three added by the Sarvastivāda school, see Sangharakshita, *The Eternal Legacy*, Windhorse Publications, Birmingham 2006, pp. 13–5 (*Complete Works*, vol. 14).

167 A collection of these 'breathed-out' utterances is part of the *Khuddaka Nikāya* of the Sutta Piṭaka, and several English translations are available, for example John D. Ireland (trans.), *The Udāna and the Itivuttaka*, Buddhist Publication Society, Kandy 2007.

168 For a list of sports and games, see sections 1.13 and 1.14 of the *Brahmajāla Sutta, Dīgha Nikāya* 1 (i.7); M. Walshe (trans.), *The Long Discourses of the Buddha,* Wisdom Publications, Boston 1995, p. 70; or T. W. Rhys Davids, *Dialogues of the Buddha*, part 1, Pali Text Society, Oxford 1977, pp. 9–11. Another intriguing list of games is given at Vinaya Piṭaka iii.180; I. B. Horner (trans.), *The Book of the Discipline*, part 1, Pali Text Society, London 1982, pp. 316–8.

169 Gnosticism is a religious movement of Eastern origin which penetrates early Christianity and gave rise to a variety of sects who claimed spiritual knowledge. They developed the figure of Sophia to explain how the divine principle of light came into contact with darkness. See, for example, Tobias Churton, *The Gnostics*, Weidenfeld and Nicholson, London 1987.

170 This idea was developed by Edward Conze in his paper 'Buddhism and Gnosis' presented to the Origins of Gnosticism colloquium of Messina, 13–18 April 1966. Conze says in the preface to *Thirty Years of Buddhist Studies* (Bruno Cassirer, London 1967, p. xi) that 'the July issue of *Numen* 1967 contains my final views on the striking similarity between Buddhism and Gnosis'.

171 *Prajñā* is the direct intuitive apprehension of the real nature of things. This can be brought about, according

to Buddhist tradition, in three stages: (1) listening to the Buddha's teachings, (2) reflecting upon them, (3) meditating upon them. For an account of these three stages see Sangharakshita, *What is the Dharma?*, Windhorse Publications, 1998, pp. 148–50 (*Complete Works*, vol. 3). The three levels of wisdom are enumerated in, for example, section 1.10 (43) of the *Saṅgīti Sutta*, *Dīgha Nikāya* 33 (iii.219); see M. Walshe (trans.), *The Long Discourses of the Buddha*, Wisdom Publications, Boston 1995, p. 486; or T. W. Rhys Davids (trans.), *Dialogues of the Buddha*, part 3, Pali Text Society, Oxford 1991, p. 212.

172 This is available in various English translations; for example, Mark Siderits and Shōryū Katsura (trans.), *Nāgārjuna's Middle Way*, Wisdom Publications, Boston 2013.

173 This *sūtra* is available in several translations. For a commentary on the *sūtra*, see Sangharakshita, *The Drama of Cosmic Enlightenment*, in this volume.

174 E. Conze (trans.), *The Perfection of Wisdom in Eight Thousand Lines and its Verse Summary*, Four Seasons Foundation, 1983.

175 R. A. F. Thurman (trans.), *The Holy Teaching of Vimalakīrti*, Pennsylvania State University Press, University Park and London 1976. For Sangharakshita's commentary, see *The Inconceivable Emancipation* in this volume.

176 For original texts, see the *Larger Sukhāvatī-vyūha*, *Smaller Sukhāvatī-vyūha*, and *Amitayur-dhyāna Sūtras* in E. B. Powell (ed.), *Buddhist Mahāyāna Texts*, Dover Publications, New York 1969. For a survey of the Pure Land literature see Sangharakshita, *The Eternal Legacy*, Windhorse Publications, Birmingham 2006, chapter 11 (*Complete Works*, vol. 14); and for information on Pure Land thought see Sangharakshita, *A Survey of Buddhism*, chapter 3, section 7, Windhorse Publications, Birmingham 2001 (*Complete Works*, vol. 1). Ratnaguna provides a commentary on the three principal Pure Land *sūtras* in Ratnaguna and Śraddhāpa, *Great Faith, Great Wisdom*, Windhorse Publications, Cambridge 2016.

177 The *Daśabhūmika Sūtra* appears as the 26th chapter of Thomas Cleary (trans.), *The Flower Ornament Scripture* (*Avataṃsaka Sūtra*), Shambhala Publications, Boston 1993, pp. 695–811.

178 A major development of Mahāsaṅghika teaching, which dates from c.120 BCE, was the doctrine of the *lokuttaravāda*, or 'supramundane' Buddha, *lokuttara* meaning literally 'beyond the world', in contrast

to 'worldly or unliberated' (*laukika*).

179 This was the account of the seventh-century Chinese scholar-pilgrim Xuanzang. For details, see Étienne Lamotte, *History of Indian Buddhism*, trans. Sara Webb-Boin, Peters Press, Louvain Paris 1988, p. 286.

180 *Tipiṭaka* (Pāli) means 'three baskets' and refers to the earliest collections of the Buddha's words. These are the Vinaya Piṭaka, Sutta Piṭaka, and Abhidhamma Piṭaka. Together they make up the canonical writings used in the Theravāda school of Buddhism.

181 This was Qin Shi Huang, the First Emperor of a unified China, who ruled from 246 BCE to 210 BCE, and in whose tomb were placed the figures of the Terracotta Army.

182 See R. E. Emmerick (trans.), *The Sūtra of Golden Light*, Pali Text Society, third edition, Oxford 2001, p. ix; and for details of Johannes Nobel's German translations, see Emmerick, p. xiii.

183 For more about *vaipulya sūtras*, see Sangharakshita, *The Eternal Legacy*, Windhorse Publications, Birmingham 2006, pp. 87 (*Complete Works*, vol. 14).

184 The eternal life of the Tathāgata is, for example, the theme of chapter 16 of the *Lotus Sūtra*; see Bunnō Katō et al. (trans.), *The Threefold Lotus Sutra*, Kosei Publishing, Tokyo 1975, pp. 249–56. See also Sangharakshita, *The Drama of Cosmic Enlightenment*, p. 165 in this volume.

CHAPTER 1

185 This famous verse is attributed to Pang Yun (also called Hōkoji), a lay disciple of the eighth century; see, for example, D. T. Suzuki, *Essays in Zen Buddhism*, Rider, London 1958, p. 319.

186 For example, see the story of Suppavāsā at *Aṅguttara Nikāya* ii.62–3; see Bhikkhu Bodhi (trans.), *Numerical Discourses of the Buddha*, Wisdom Publications, Boston 2012, pp. 446–7; or E. M. Hare, *The Book of the Gradual Sayings*, vol. ii, Pali Text Society, Oxford 1995, pp. 71–2.

187 The five precepts are the most fundamental set of Buddhist ethical guidelines. Put in negative terms they involve working to refrain from (1) harming living beings, (2) taking the not-given, (3) sexual misconduct, (4) untruthfulness, and (5) dulling the mind with intoxicants. Positively they mean striving to develop (1) loving-kindness, (2) generosity, (3) contentment, (4) truthfulness, and (5) awareness. For more information, see chapter 3 of Sangharakshita, *The Noble Eightfold Path* (*Complete

Works, vol. 1). The five precepts are enumerated many times in the Pāli canon, for example, *Aṅguttara Nikāya* 5.179 (iii.212): see Bhikkhu Bodhi (trans.), *Numerical Discourses of the Buddha*, Wisdom Publications, Boston 2012, p. 792; or E. M. Hare, *The Book of the Gradual Sayings*, vol. iii, Pali Text Society, Oxford 1995, ch. 18, 'The Lay Disciple', p. 155.

188 For example, see the *Cūḷakammavibhaṅga Sutta*, *Majjhima Nikāya* 135 (iii.203–6); Bhikkhu Ñāṇamoli and Bhikkhu Bodhi (trans.), *The Middle Length Discourses of the Buddha*, Wisdom Publications, Boston 1995, pp. 1053–7; or I. B. Horner (trans.), *Middle Length Sayings*, vol. iii, Pali Text Society, London 1967, pp. 248–53.

189 For the *Sūtra of Golden Light*'s version of the story of the starving tigress, see R. E. Emmerick (trans.), *The Sūtra of Golden Light*, Pali Text Society, third edition, Oxford 2001, pp. 93–6. The story is not preserved in the Pāli *Jātaka* tradition, but is the first story in Aryaśūra's Sanskrit *Jātakamālā* ('garland of birth stories'); for a translation, see for example Peter Khoroche (trans.), *Once the Buddha Was a Monkey: Arya Śūra's Jātakamālā*, University of Chicago Press, Chicago 1989.

190 Alan Watts (1915–1973) did a great deal to bring the ideas and practice of Zen to the West through his many books, the first of which, *The Spirit of Zen*, was published in 1936. The incident referred to here is described in his biography: 'After some eight or nine months of study Watts lost his temper in sanzen, shouting at his teacher that he was right. "No, you're not right," Sokei-an replied. That was the end of formal Zen.' Monica Furlong, *Genuine Fake: a Biography of Alan Watts*, Heinemann, London 1986, pp. 69–70.

191 From Keats, 'Ode on a Grecian Urn', 1820, stanza 5.

192 Tathāgata is a title of the Buddha. It can mean 'one thus gone' or 'one thus come'. A Buddha goes from the world through wisdom – seeing its illusory nature. He comes into it through compassion – in order to teach living beings how to put an end to suffering.

193 The *dhyānas* are the levels of higher consciousness identified by the Buddha. They are most often experienced in meditation, though the lower *dhyānas* may occur in other circumstances.

194 This simile for the fourth *dhyāna* is given in many places in the Pāli canon, for example, section 18 of the *Mahā-Assapura Sutta*, *Majjhima Nikāya* 39 (i.279); see Bhikkhu Ñāṇamoli and Bhikkhu Bodhi (trans.), *The Middle Length Discourses of the Buddha*, Wisdom Publications, Boston

1995, p. 369; or I. B. Horner (trans.), *Middle Length Sayings*, vol. i, Pali Text Society, Oxford 1957, p. 332.

195 For more about the mandala of the five Buddhas, see, for example, chapter 8, 'The Mandala of the Five Buddhas', in Sangharakshita, *Creative Symbols of Tantric Buddhism*, Windhorse Publications, Birmingham 2002 (*Complete Works*, vol. 13).

196 *Samādhi* (literally the state of being firmly fixed or established) is a state of deep and concentrated meditation. In terms of the spiral path, in dependence upon *samādhi* arises 'knowledge and vision of things as they really are' i.e. transcendental insight.

197 For in that sleep of death
what dreams may come,
When we have shuffled off
this mortal coil,
Must give us pause.

Hamlet, III. i.

198 This is a reference to that most basic Buddhist teaching, the Noble Eightfold Path. According to the Buddha, one begins by traversing the mundane eightfold path – starting with right view, which leads to the progressive development of the remaining seven stages: right resolve, right speech, right action, right livelihood, right effort, right awareness, and right *samādhi*. In the course of spiritual practice one gradually refines each area of one's life until transcendental insight is attained. It is then that one begins to tread the transcendental eightfold path, which is divided into the Path of Vision and the Path of Transformation. The Path of Vision corresponds to the arising of Perfect Vision, the transcendental counterpart of right view, while the Path of Transformation comprises the perfection of each of the other seven stages of the path – right resolve becomes Perfect Emotion, right speech becomes Perfect Speech, and so on. When all eight stages have been perfected, full Enlightenment is attained. See chapter 1, Sangharakshita, *The Buddha's Noble Eightfold Path*, Windhorse Publications, Birmingham 2007 (*Complete Works*, vol. 1).

199 This famous metaphor comes from the *Ariyapariyesanā Sutta, Majjhima Nikāya* 26 (i.171); see Bhikkhu Ñāṇamoli and Bhikkhu Bodhi (trans.), *The Middle Length Discourses of the Buddha*, Wisdom Publications, Boston 1995, p. 263; or I. B. Horner (trans.), *Middle Length Sayings*, vol. i, Pali Text Society, London 1967, p. 215. When the Buddha was on his way to give his first teaching, the Buddha met a man called Upāka, and it was to him that he said, 'I go now to the city of Kasi/ To set in motion the Wheel of

Dhamma./ In a world that has become blind/ I go to beat the drum of the Deathless.'

200 Chapter 26 of the *Dhammapada*. For Sangharakshita's translation, see *Dhammapada*, Windhorse Publications, Cambridge 2014 (*Complete Works*, vol. 15).

201
> Grant me an old man's frenzy,
> Myself must I remake
> Till I am Timon and Lear
> Or that William Blake
> Who beat upon the wall
> Till Truth obeyed his call;

W. B. Yeats, 'An Acre of Grass', 1936.

202
> Oh! the one life within us and abroad,
> Which meets all motion and becomes its soul,
> A light in sound, a sound-like power in light,
> Rhythm in all thought, and joyance everywhere.

Coleridge, 'The Eolian Harp', 1796, lines 27–9.

203 Published in several editions under different titles. One of the most thorough, with a commentary, is Kate Crosby and Andrew Skilton (trans.), *The Bodhicaryāvatāra*, Windhorse Publications, Birmingham 2002.

204 A Buddhist puja (devotional worship) is a ceremony of recitation and chanting before the Buddha image. This is a demonstration of devotion in the sense of reverence for the ideal of Enlightenment. Regular practice of puja refines one's emotional positivity, breaking through habitual self-centredness and isolation, and leading to an empathy with all life. The sevenfold puja is a traditional Mahāyāna form much practised in the Triratna Buddhist Community; see *Puja*, Windhorse Publications, Birmingham 1999, pp. 7–32.

CHAPTER 2

205 *Bhikkhu* (Pāli) means monk, or one who goes for alms. The Sanskrit is *bhikṣu*.

206 Comprising volumes iii and iv of the Vinaya Piṭaka, the *Suttavibhaṅga* sets out the basic rules of conduct for *bhikkhus* and *bhikkhunīs* (the *patimokkha*) and the occasions on which they were established; see I. B. Horner (trans.), *Book of the Discipline*, parts 1–3, Pali Text Society, London. Volumes i and ii (parts 4 and 5 of the Pali Text Society edition) elaborate on the ethical behaviour expected of the monastic sangha, and also include various other material including many stories of the Buddha's life.

207 See also Sangharakshita's memoir, *Facing Mount Kanchenjunga*, Windhorse Publications, Glasgow 1991, p. 324 (*Complete Works*, vol. 21).

208 Dhardo Rimpoche was an eminent Tibetan lama

of the Gelugpa tradition. Sangharakshita, who met him in Kalimpong in 1953, and received the Bodhisattva ordination from him, described him as 'perhaps embodying the Bodhisattva ideal to a greater extent than anybody I had met' in *The History of My Going For Refuge*, Windhorse Publications, 1988, p. 89 (*Complete Works*, vol. 2). See Suvajra, *The Wheel and the Diamond: The Life of Dhardo Tulku*, Windhorse Publications, Sheffield 1991; and Sara Hagel (ed.), *Dhardo Rimpoche: A Celebration*, Windhorse Publications, Birmingham 2000; also Sangharakshita, *Precious Teachers*, Windhorse Publications, Birmingham 2007 (*Complete Works*, vol. 22). The Dhardo Rimpoche whom Sangharakshita knew in Kalimpong was the thirteenth of that name and died in 1990; the fourteenth Dhardo Rimpoche was born in 1991 and received his monastic education in South India.

209 For the story of Ajātaśatru's visit to see the Buddha and his confession (at the end of the *sutta*), see *Sāmaññaphala Sutta*, *Dīgha Nikāya* 2 (i.47–86); M. Walshe (trans.), *The Long Discourses of the Buddha*, Wisdom Publications, Boston 1995, pp. 91–109; or T. W. Rhys Davids (trans.), *Dialogues of the Buddha*, part 1, Pali Text Society, Oxford 1977, pp. 65–94.

210 R. E. Emmerick (trans.), *The Sūtra of Golden Light*, Pali Text Society, third edition, Oxford 2001, p. 9.

211 Ibid.

212 It was the Buddha himself who first exemplified fearlessnes in meditation. This is described in the *Bhayabherava Sutta*, *Majjhima Nikāya* 4 (i.22); see Bhikkhu Ñāṇamoli and Bhikkhu Bodhi (trans.), *The Middle Length Discourses of the Buddha*, Wisdom Publications, Boston 1995, p. 102–7; or I. B. Horner (trans.), *Middle Length Sayings*, vol. i, Pali Text Society, Oxford 1957, pp. 21–30.

213 This story is told in more detail in chapter 6, 'Assam Idyll', of Sangharakshita's volume of memoirs *In the Sign of the Golden Wheel*, Windhorse Publications, Birmingham 1996 (*Complete Works*, vol. 22).

214 This is the first line of the shepherd boy's 'Song in the Valley of Humiliation', from part 2 of John Bunyan's *Pilgrim's Progress*.

215 R. E. Emmerick (trans.), *The Sūtra of Golden Light*, Pali Text Society, third edition, Oxford 2001, p. 9.

216 For an account of the seven *bodhyaṅgas*, see Sangharakshita, 'Mind – Reactive and Creative', in *Buddha Mind*, Windhorse Publications, Birmingham

2001, pp. 55–61 (*Complete Works*, vol. 11).

217 The *nidāna* chain is made up of the twelve links of conditioned co-production which represent the application of the general Buddhist principle of conditionality to the process of rebirth. See, for example, chapter 1, section 13, 'Conditioned Co-production and the Twelve Links', in Sangharakshita, *A Survey of Buddhism*, Windhorse Publications, Birmingham 2001, pp. 128–37 (*Complete Works*, vol. 1).

218 R. E. Emmerick (trans.), *The Sūtra of Golden Light*, Pali Text Society, third edition, Oxford 2001, p. 9.

219 According to the Pāli canon, the four noble truths were set out by the Buddha in one of the first teachings he gave after his Enlightenment; see *Dhammacakkappavattana Sutta, Saṃyutta Nikāya* 56.11 (v.421); see Bhikkhu Bodhi (trans.), *The Connected Discourses of the Buddha*, Wisdom Publications, Boston 2000, p. 1844; or F. L. Woodward (trans.), *Book of the Kindred Sayings*, part 5, Pali Text Society, Oxford 1989, p. 357.

The four noble truths are (1) the truth of the existence of suffering, (2) the truth of the cause of suffering, which is egotistical desire and craving, (3) the truth of the cessation of suffering, which is the cessation of egotistical desire, and (4) the truth of the way to the cessation of suffering, which is the Noble Eightfold Path.

220 R. E. Emmerick (trans.), *The Sūtra of Golden Light*, Pali Text Society, third edition, Oxford 2001, pp. 9–10.

221 This image occurs in one of the accounts of the Buddha's first teaching, in the 'Turning the Wheel of the Dharma' or *Dhammacakkappavattana Sutta, Saṃyutta Nikāya* 56.11 (v.421); see Bhikkhu Bodhi (trans.), *The Connected Discourses of the Buddha*, Wisdom Publications, Boston 2000, p. 1844; or F. L. Woodward (trans.), *Book of the Kindred Sayings*, part 5, Pali Text Society, Oxford 1989, p. 357.

222 R. E. Emmerick (trans.), *The Sūtra of Golden Light*, Pali Text Society, third edition, Oxford 2001, p. 10.

223 Ibid.

224 Ibid.

225 Ibid.

226 Ibid.

227 Ibid.

228 The third verse of the Sevenfold Puja based on Śāntideva's *Bodhicaryāvatāra* – which is used in the devotional practice of the Triratna Buddhist Community – begins:

> This very day
> I go for my refuge
> To the powerful protectors,
> Whose purpose is to guard
> the universe.

229 R. E. Emmerick (trans.), *The Sūtra of Golden Light*, Pali Text Society, third edition, Oxford 2001, pp. 14–15.

230 A Stream Entrant is someone who has developed a degree of insight sufficient to attain to the first stage of the transcendental path, thereby breaking the first three of the ten fetters, i.e. fixed self-view, doubt or lack of commitment, and dependence on ethical rules and religious observances as ends in themselves. Traditionally, once one has gained Stream Entry, progress towards the goal of full Enlightenment is irreversible. Among the many references to Stream Entry in the Pāli canon, the *Saṃyutta Nikāya* has a whole section devoted to the subject. See Bhikkhu Bodhi (trans.), *The Connected Discourses of the Buddha,* Wisdom Publications, Boston 2000, pp. 1788–837; or F. L. Woodward (trans.), *Kindred Sayings*, part 5, Pali Text Society, Oxford 1979, pp. 296–351.

231 R. E. Emmerick (trans.), *The Sūtra of Golden Light*, Pali Text Society, third edition, Oxford 2001, pp. 10–11.

232

> If while practising the Mahayana a Bodhisattva continues to break precepts out of desire for kappas as numerous as the sands of the Ganges, his offence is still minor. If a Bodhisattva breaks precepts out of hatred, even just once, his offence is very serious. Why? Because a Bodhisattva who breaks precepts out of desire (still) holds sentient beings in his embrace, whereas a Bodhisattva who breaks precepts out of hatred forsakes beings altogether.... If he breaks precepts out of hatred, it is a grave offence, a gross fault, a serious, degenerate act, which causes tremendous hindrances to the Buddha-Dharma.

Upāli-paripṛccha Sūtra, in Garma C. C. Chang, *A Treasury of Mahāyāna Sūtras: Selections from the Mahāratnakūṭa Sūtra,* Penn State University Press 1983, p. 270.

233 This legend is a key element of a children's story set in Japan, *The Cat who went to Heaven*, written by Elizabeth Coatsworth in the 1930s and now published by Aladdin Paperbacks, Simon and Schuster, New York 2008.

234 Born c. 300 BCE, Aśoka became by succession an emperor of the Mauryan dynasty in India. After waging a dreadfully destructive war and conquering Kalinga, he became sick of violence and began to practise the Buddha's teachings and encourage their practice throughout his empire. We know what he advocated through written records and also through the edicts carved

onto rocks and stone pillars in many places throughout India and beyond. For example, in the first of the Kalinga Rock Edicts, Aśoka advises the judicial officers of the city of Tosali how to treat prisoners:

> While being completely law-abiding, some people are imprisoned, treated harshly and even killed without cause so that many people suffer. Therefore your aim should be to act with impartiality. It is because of these things – envy, anger, cruelty, hate, indifference, laziness or tiredness – that such a thing does not happen. Therefore your aim should be: 'May these things not be in me.' And the root of this is non-anger and patience.

And the seventh Pillar Edict states

> Noble deeds of Dhamma and the practice of Dhamma consist of having kindness, generosity, truthfulness, purity, gentleness and goodness increase among the people.

235 G. I. Gurdjieff (1866–1949) was a Russian mystic, philosopher, and spiritual teacher. On the wall of the Study House at the Prieuré des Basses Loges near Fontainebleau, where Gurdjieff established the Institute of Harmonious Development of Man, are inscribed thirty-eight aphorisms, of which the eleventh is 'A true sign of a good man is if he loves his father and mother.'

236 There is no satisfactory equivalent for the Pāli *mettā* in English, but it is usually translated 'loving-kindness'. This positive emotion is cultivated systematically in a specific meditation practice, the *mettā bhāvanā*, in the final stage of which the meditator develops *mettā* towards all living beings. For a detailed account of *mettā*, see Sangharakshita, *Living with Kindness*, Windhorse Publications, Birmingham 2004 (*Complete Works*, vol. 15).

237 This story was told by the Vedanta sage Sri Ramakrishna; see the section called 'Maya creates upadhis' in the *Gospel of Sri Ramakrishna*.

238 This is in effect what is said in section 14 of the *Sigālaka Sutta*, *Dīgha Nikāya* 31 (iii.184); see M. Walshe (trans.), *The Long Discourses of the Buddha*, Wisdom Publications, Boston 1995, p. 463; or T. W. Rhys Davids (trans.), *Dialogues of the Buddha*, part 3, Pali Text Society, Oxford 1991, pp. 176–7.

239

> Serenity of spirit and love for all sentient creation are enjoined by the Buddha. He does not speak of sin, but only of ignorance and foolishness which could be

cured by enlightenment and sympathy.

Dr S. Radhakrishnan, *Gautama the Buddha*, Hind Kitabs, Bombay 1946, p. 29.

240 For an account of alienated awareness, see chapter 10, 'The Integrated Individual' of *What is the Sangha?* (*Complete Works* vol. 3), especially pp. 487–8.

241 The word *śrāvaka* (Sanskrit; the Pāli equivalent is *sāvaka*) literally means 'hearer' and is used to refer to a disciple of the Buddha, whether monastic or lay, male or female, who has gone for Refuge to the Three Jewels.

242 *Saṃyutta Nikāya* iv.251; see Bhikkhu Bodhi (trans.), *The Connected Discourses of the Buddha*, Wisdom Publications, Boston 2000, p. 1294; or F. L. Woodward (trans.), *The Book of the Kindred Sayings*, vol. iv, Pali Text Society, London 1956, p. 170. The Pāli words *lobha, dosa* (Sanskrit *devṣa*), and *moha* translate as greed, hatred, and delusion.

243 R. E. Emmerick (trans.), *The Sūtra of Golden Light*, Pali Text Society, third edition, Oxford 2001, pp. 12–13.

244 The example often cited is the occasion when the Buddha's cousin Devadatta tried to kill him by dropping a boulder on him. See Vinaya Piṭaka ii.193 (*Cullavagga* 7.9) in I. B. Horner (trans.), *The Book of the Discipline*, part 5, Pali Text Society, Oxford 1992, p. 271. The attempt failed, but the Buddha's foot was injured, and he explained that this was the karmic consequence of his trying to kill his step-brother in a previous life. In *Jātaka Stories in Theravāda Buddhism* (Routledge, London 2016, pp. 27–8), Naomi Appleton mentions a set of twelve *Jātakas* that are said to explain the suffering the Buddha experienced after his awakening, although, as she goes on to explain, this is a controversial explanation which is contradicted by other texts.

245 See, for example, the *Cūḷakammavibhaṅga Sutta*, *Majjhima Nikāya* 135 (iii.203–6); Bhikkhu Ñāṇamoli and Bhikkhu Bodhi (trans.), *The Middle Length Discourses of the Buddha*, Wisdom Publications, Boston 1995, pp. 1053–7; or I. B. Horner (trans.), *Middle Length Sayings*, vol. iii, Pali Text Society, London 1967, pp. 248–53.

246 'I have done that', says my memory. 'I cannot have done that' – says my pride, and remains adamant. At last – memory yields.

Friedrich Nietzsche, *Beyond Good and Evil*, trans. R. J. Hollingdale, Penguin, 2003, p. 91.

247 R. E. Emmerick (trans.), *The Sūtra of Golden Light*, Pali

Text Society, third edition, Oxford 2001, p. 13.

248 Ibid., pp. 13–14.

249 Thomas Traherne was a Herefordshire priest in the seventeenth century who wrote ecstatic mystical prose and verse. His literary work was obscure until discovered (some of it quite by chance, one book being on the point of being burned on a bonfire, not having been recognized for what it was) in the twentieth century. *Centuries of Meditation* is among several of his works now in print.

250 R. E. Emmerick (trans.), *The Sūtra of Golden Light*, Pali Text Society, third edition, Oxford 2001, p. 14.

251 Ibid., p. 13.

252 Ibid., p. 17.

253 Ibid., pp. 15–17.

254 Vinaya Piṭaka ii.253ff., e.g. I. B. Horner (trans.), *The Book of the Discipline*, part 5, Pali Text Society, Oxford 1992, pp. 352–5.

255 For example, see section 14 of the *Naḷakapāna Sutta*, *Majjhima Nikāya* 68 (i.466); Bhikkhu Ñāṇamoli and Bhikkhu Bodhi (trans.), *The Middle Length Discourses of the Buddha*, Wisdom Publications, Boston 1995, p. 569; or I. B. Horner (trans.), *Middle Length Sayings*, vol. ii, Pali Text Society, London 1967, p. 139.

256 R. E. Emmerick (trans.), *The Sūtra of Golden Light*, Pali Text Society, third edition, Oxford 2001, pp. 17–18.

CHAPTER 3

257 The first English translation of the *Mahāvyutpatti* was made by the pioneering Hungarian Tibetologist Sándor Kőrösi Csoma (1784–1842). The work is now available in Richard Mahoney et al. (eds.), *Tibetan and Sanskrit Terms: Mahāvyutpatti and Yogācārabhūmi*, Indica et Buddhica, Oxford (New Zealand) 2004. For the *Abhidharmakośa*'s description of the universe, written in Sanskrit by Vasubandhu, see Vasubandhu, *Abhidharmakośabhāṣyam*, vol. ii, trans. Leo M. Pruden, Asian Humanities Press, Berkeley 1991, pp. 451ff.

258 For more information, see chapter 6, 'Offerings and Self-Sacrifice', in Sangharakshita, *Creative Symbols of Tantric Buddhism*, Windhorse Publications, Birmingham 2002 (*Complete Works*, vol. 13).

259 Matthew 6:21.

260 R. E. Emmerick (trans.), *The Sūtra of Golden Light*, Pali Text Society, third edition, Oxford 2001, p. 24.

CHAPTER 4

261 Two monks [it is related] of fine cultivated language and fine eloquent speech, came to the Buddha and said: 'Lord, here monks of various names, clan-names, races [or castes]

and families are corrupting the Buddha's words by repeating them in their own dialects. Let us put them into Vedic (*chandaso aropema*).' The Lord rebuked them: 'Deluded men! How can you say this? This will not lead to the conversion of the unconverted.'... And he delivered a sermon and commanded all the monks: 'You are not to put the Buddha's words into Vedic. Whosoever does so shall be guilty of an offence. I authorize you, monks, to learn the Buddha's words each in his own dialect (*sakāya niruttiyā*).'

Vinaya Piṭaka ii.139 (*Cullavaga* 5.33). This translation is by Franklin Edgerton in *Buddhist Hybrid Sanskrit Language and Literature*, Benares 1965, p. 5; see also I. B. Horner (trans.), *The Book of the Discipline*, part 5, Pali Text Society, Oxford 1992, pp. 193–4.

262 The term Mantrayāna seems to have owed its origin to the necessity of distinguishing that branch of the Mahāyāna which advocated the repetition of the mantras as the principal means to Enlightenment from that which continued to emphasize the practice of the *pāramitās*.

Sangharakshita, *A Survey of Buddhism*, Windhorse Publications, Birmingham 2001, p. 424 (*Complete Works*, vol. 1).

263 R. E. Emmerick (trans.), *The Sūtra of Golden Light*, Pali Text Society, third edition, Oxford 2001, p. 47.

264 Ibid., p. 48–9.

265 Mistletoe is a plant with pale green leaves and white waxy berries like pearls; it is a parasite (i.e. gets its nutrients from other plants) and is especially seen growing from the branches of apple trees. In British tradition it is associated with the Christmas season, and what happens under the mistletoe at that time is kissing.

CHAPTER 5

266 R. E. Emmerick (trans.), *The Sūtra of Golden Light*, Pali Text Society, third edition, Oxford 2001, pp. 44–5.

267 The term *saṃsāra*, literally 'perpetual wandering' (Nyanatiloka, *Buddhist Dictionary*, Frewin and Co., Colombo 1970) has been in use in the Indian tradition from very early times, from the Vedas onwards, and is key to Hinduism and Jainism as well as Buddhism. Briefly, it is the cyclic round of birth and death, marked by suffering and frustration, which can only be brought to an end by the attainment of Enlightenment. In the *Assu Sutta* of the *Saṃyutta Nikāya* (ii.179) the Buddha asks the monks:

> Bhikkhus, this saṃsāra is without discoverable beginning. A first point is not discerned of beings roaming and wandering on hindered by ignorance and fettered by craving. What do you think, bhikkhus, which is more: the stream of tears that you have shed as you roamed and wandered on through this long course, weeping and wailing because of being united with the disagreeable and separated from what is agreeable – this or the water in the four great oceans?

Bhikkhu Bodhi (trans.), *The Connected Discourses of the Buddha*, Wisdom Publications, Boston 2000, pp. 652–3.

268 *Udāna* 8.3; see F. L. Woodward (trans.), *Minor Anthologies of the Pali Canon*, part 2, Pali Text Society, London 1987, p. 98.

269 See section 13 of the *Ariyapariyesanā Sutta, Majjhima Nikāya* 26 (i.163); Bhikkhu Ñāṇamoli and Bhikkhu Bodhi (trans.), *The Middle Length Discourses of the Buddha*, Wisdom Publications, Boston 1995, p. 256; or I. B. Horner (trans.), *Middle Length Sayings*, vol. i, Pali Text Society, London 1967, p. 206.

270 These statements are a mixture of quotations from the New Testament: Luke 20:34–6:

> And Jesus answering said unto them, The children of this world marry, and are given in marriage. But they which shall be accounted worthy to obtain that world, and the resurrection from the dead, neither marry, nor are given in marriage. Neither can they die any more: for they are equal unto the angels; and are the children of God, being the children of the resurrection'; Matthew 6:26: 'Look at the birds of the air; they do not sow or reap or store away in barns, and yet your heavenly Father feeds them. Are you not much more valuable than they?

and Matthew 22:30:

> At the resurrection people will neither marry nor be given in marriage; they will be like the angels in heaven.

271 John 16:33.

272 R. E. Emmerick (trans.), *The Sūtra of Golden Light*, Pali Text Society, third edition, Oxford 2001, pp.49–52.

273 For a further description of the six *pāramitās*, see, for example, the section on 'The Six Perfections' in Sangharakshita, *A Survey of Buddhism*, Windhorse Publications, Birmingham 2001, pp. 466–90 (*Complete Works*, vol. 1).

CHAPTER 6

274 Francis Bacon, in the essay 'Of Seditions and Troubles' (1625).

275 Section 66 of the *Sāmaññaphala Sutta*, *Dīgha*

Nikāya 2 (i.71); M. Walshe (trans.), *The Long Discourses of the Buddha*, Wisdom Publications, Boston 1995, p. 101; or T. W. Rhys Davids (trans.), *Dialogues of the Buddha*, part 1, Pali Text Society, London 1977, p. 81.

276 Buddhaghosa says at *Visuddhimagga* 24, 'It is proper for an ascetic to cure himself with putrid urine and broken gall nuts.' See Bhikkhu Ñāṇamoli (trans.), *The Path of Purification*, Buddhist Publication Society, Kandy 1991, p. 27; or Pe Maung Tin (trans.), *The Path of Purity*, Pali Text Society, London 1975, p. 29. Another name for 'gall nut' is myrobalan, which incidentally is the fruit that the Medicine Buddha of Mahāyāna Buddhism, Bhaiṣajyarāja or Bhaiṣajyaguru, is depicted as holding. (See chapter 8, 'The Archetype of the Divine Healer', in *The Drama of Cosmic Enlightenment*, above.)

277 Sangharakshita, *The Rainbow Road*, Windhorse Publications, Birmingham 1997, p. 436 (*Complete Works*, vol. 20).

278 Right Livelihood is the fifth limb of the Noble Eightfold Path. It is of crucial importance that those who wish to develop spiritually attend to their means of livelihood. See chapter 5 of Sangharakshita, *The Buddha's Noble Eightfold Path*, Windhorse Publications, 2007 (*Complete Works*, vol. 1).

279 R. E. Emmerick (trans.), *The Sūtra of Golden Light*, Pali Text Society, third edition, Oxford 2001, p. 50.

280 Ibid., p. 52.

CHAPTER 7

281 Ibid., p. 60.

282 Ibid., p. 61.

283 Ibid.

284 *Puṇya* is spiritual merit.

285 From Sangharakshita, *What is the Dharma?*, chapter 10 (*Complete Works*, vol. 3):

> The Buddha identified five orders of conditionality, five *niyamas*, as Buddhaghosa subsequently called them: physical inorganic; physical organic (i.e. biological); psychological; karmic; and transcendental. Unless one has the insight of a Buddha, one cannot be sure which *niyamas* have brought about what particular effect. The example usually given is that of a fever. If one gets a fever, it may be a chill caused by a sudden change in temperature; or one may have caught a viral infection; or perhaps one has succumbed to illness as a result of some kind of mental strain; or it may have been caused by an unskilful action committed in the past; or it may even be the effect on one's

system of transcendental insight. Thus the same end result may have been brought about by something physical, something biological, something psychological, something karmic, or something transcendental – or a combination of two or more of these.

The five orders of conditionality or *niyamas* are enumerated by Buddhaghosa in his commentary on the *Dhammasaṅgaṇi*, the first book of the Abhidhamma Piṭaka, vol ii. Pe Maung Tin (trans.), *The Expositor*, ch. 10, ed. C. A. F. Rhys Davids, Pali Text Society, London 1921. p. 360; also in his commentary on the *Dīgha Nikāya*, ed. W. Stede, Pali Text Society 1920, p. 360 (not available in English translation). Another of Sangharakshita's sources is C. A. F. Rhys Davids, *Buddhism: A Study of the Buddhist Norm*, Williams and Norgate, London 1912, pp. 118–9.

286 Job 42:12.

287 The story of King Bimbisāra's first meeting with the Buddha is told in the *Pabbajjā Sutta* of the *Sutta-Nipāta* (Curzon Press, London 1983, pp. 46–7), in which the young King Bimbisāra sees Siddhartha, who hasn't yet become the Buddha, approaching. He sends one of his men to ask where the Buddha is going, and then visits him on Vulture's Peak. So their connection dated from those days, even before the Buddha's Enlightenment, and they were in contact from time to time. There are quite a number of *suttas* in the Pāli canon and the commentaries which mention different meetings between the Buddha and Bimbisāra. Intriguingly, in the *Janavasabha Sutta*, *Dīgha Nikāya* 18 (ii.205), Bimbisāra appears having been reborn as a *yakkha* called Janavasabha. He declares that he is a Stream Entrant ('For a long time I have known myself to be exempt from the states of woe') and says that he now aspires to become a once-returner. See M. Walshe (trans.), *The Long Discourses of the Buddha*, Wisdom Publications, Boston 1995, p. 293; or T. W. Rhys Davids (trans.), *Dialogues of the Buddha*, part 2, Pali Text Society, London 1977, p. 240. Although various episodes in the Pāli canon hint at the sad story of the king's death at the hands of his son Ajātasattu, this story is told in most detail in the Mahāyāna Pure Land *sūtras*, especially the one known as *Guān Jīng*, the 'Visualization Sūtra' or 'Meditation Sūtra', in which account Bimbisāra, although languishing in the dungeon into which his son

has cast him, becomes a non-returner, an *anāgāmi*, 'naturally and spontaneously'; see F. Max Müller (ed.), *Buddhist Mahayana Sutras*, Oxford 1894, p. 167. For reflections on this text and King Bimbisāra's role in the story, see Sangharakshita, *The Eternal Legacy*, Windhorse Publications, Birmingham 2006, p. 161 (*Complete Works* vol. 14); and Ratnaguna and Śraddhāpa, *Great Faith, Great Wisdom*, Windhorse Publications, Cambridge 2016, pp. 188–90.

288 The king says this in *Henry IV*, III. i.

289 Claudius says this in *Hamlet*, IV. v.

290 This statement was part of the speech King Charles I made before his execution.

291 *Bhagavad Gītā*, chapter 4, verse 8.

292 R. E. Emmerick (trans.), *The Sūtra of Golden Light*, Pali Text Society, third edition, Oxford 2001, p. 61.

293 Ibid., p. 64.

294 At *Udāna* 5.4, the Buddha tells this story and draws from it exactly this moral, though in that story the boys are tormenting some fish, not a crow. See John D. Ireland (trans.), *The Udāna and the Itivuttaka*, Buddhist Publication Society 2007, p. 66.

295 R. E. Emmerick (trans.), *The Sūtra of Golden Light*, Pali Text Society, third edition, Oxford 2001, p. 61–4.

296 In his article on 'Buddha and the Future of his Religion', written in 1950, Dr Ambedkar wrote, 'Society must have either the sanction of law or the sanction of morality to hold it together. Without either, society must go to pieces.' In Dr Babasaheb Ambedkar, *Writings and Speeches*, vol. xvii (part 2), Education Department, Government of Maharashtra 2003, p. 104.

297 R. E. Emmerick (trans.), *The Sūtra of Golden Light*, Pali Text Society, third edition, Oxford 2001, pp. 20–1.

THE INCONCEIVABLE EMANCIPATION

CHAPTER 1

298 These four lines expressing the bodhisattva vow are recited throughout the Mahāyāna Buddhist world. This particular version is given in, for example, D. T. Suzuki, *A Manual of Zen Buddhism*, Buddha Dharma Education Association, 1935, p. 3.

299 This is the sixth of the eight qualities of the great ocean described by the Buddha in the *Uposatha Sutta*, *Udāna* 5.5. See John D. Ireland (trans.), *The Udāna and the Itivuttaka*, Buddhist Publication Society,

Kandy 2007, p. 68. See also Sangharakshita's talk 'The Taste of Freedom' (*Complete Works*, vol. 11).

300 For a detailed exposition of the spiral path, see, for example, Sangharakshita, *The Three Jewels*, Windhorse Publications, Birmingham 1998, chapter 13 (*Complete Works*, vol. 2).

301 For an enumeration of the eight *vimokṣas*, see Robert A. F. Thurman (trans.), *The Holy Teaching of Vimalakīrti*, Pennsylvania State University Press, University Park and London 1976, p. 153.

302 For more about the 'entrances to liberation', see chapter 14, 'The Goal', in Sangharakshita, *The Three Jewels*, Windhorse Publications, Birmingham 1998 (*Complete Works*, vol. 2).

303 For a fuller explanation, see Sangharakshita, *Wisdom Beyond Words*, Windhorse Publications, Birmingham 2000, pp. 29ff. (*Complete Works*, vol. 14), where the statement 'in *śūnyatā* no *dharmas* exist' is discussed.

304 For more on *advaya*, see Sangharakshita, *A Survey of Buddhism,* Windhorse Publications, Birmingham 2001, p. 301 (*Complete Works*, vol. 1).

305 As in, for example, verse 32a of the *Diamond Sūtra*, in Edward Conze (trans.), *Buddhist Wisdom Books*, Allen & Unwin, London 1958, pp. 68ff.

306 See sections 4–7 of the *Kevaddha Sutta*, *Dīgha Nikāya* 11 (i.215); M. Walshe (trans.), *The Long Discourses of the Buddha*, Wisdom Publications, Boston 1995, pp. 175–6; or T. W. Rhys Davids (trans.), *Dialogues of the Buddha*, part 1, Pali Text Society, London 1977, p. 279.

307 For the metaphor of the illusory elephant, see stanzas 27–30 of Vasubandhu's *Trisvabhāvanirdeśa*, a significant treatise written by the Yogācāra master Vasubandhu, consisting of thirty-eight stanzas explaining the concept of the three natures (*trisvabhāva*) or three distinguishing characteristics (*trilakśaṇa*). See Vasubandhu, *Trisvabhāvanirdeśa*, trans. Sujitkumar Mukhopadhyaya, Visvabharati, Calcutta 1939.

308 The most famous use of these images expressive of the ephemeral nature of things is found in this verse, from section 32 of the *Diamond Sūtra*, here translated by Edward Conze:

> As stars, a fault of vision, as a lamp,
> A mock show, dew drops, or a bubble,
> A dream, a lightning flash, or cloud,
> So should one view what is conditioned.

309 For more on this, see Sangharakshita, *Wisdom Beyond Words*, Birmingham

2000, pp. 262–3 (*Complete Works*, vol. 14).

310 According to early Buddhist accounts, Āmrapālī (Sanskrit) or Ambapālī (Pāli) was a 'courtesan' of the Buddha's time who gave the Buddha and his followers a mango grove in which they often gathered, and which was the setting for the *Ambapālī Sutta*, *Saṃyutta Nikāya* 47, in which the Buddha describes the four aspects of mindfulness. The story of Ambapālī and how she met the Buddha is told at Vinaya Piṭaka i.231–3 (*Mahāvagga* 6.30); see I. B. Horner (trans.), *The Book of the Discipline*, part 4, Pali Text Society, London 1982, pp. 315–8; also sections 2.14 to 2.19 of the *Mahāparinibbāna Sutta*, *Dīgha Nikāya* 16 (ii.95–7); see M. Walshe (trans.), *The Long Discourses of the Buddha*, Wisdom Publications, Boston 1995, pp. 242–4; or T. W. Rhys Davids (trans.), *Dialogues of the Buddha*, part 2, Pali Text Society, Oxford 1991, pp. 102–5. Her mango grove, now a park, suitably transformed in Mahāyāna fashion, is the setting for the *Vimalakīrti-nirdeśa*.

CHAPTER 2

311 More information on ancient Indian Buddhist cosmology can be found in Randy Kloetzli, *Buddhist Cosmology*, Motilal Banarsidass, Delhi 1983, and also chapter 4, 'The Cosmic Refuge Tree and the Archetypal Guru', in Sangharakshita, *Creative Symbols of Tantric Buddhism*, Windhorse Publications, Birmingham 2002 (*Complete Works*, vol. 13).

312 For an account of the Mahāyāna *trikāya* doctrine see, for example, section 6, chapter 2, Sangharakshita, *A Survey of Buddhism*, Windhorse Publications, Birmingham 2001, pp. 282–97 (*Complete Works*, vol. 1).

313 For original texts, see the *Larger Sukhāvatī-vyūha*, *Smaller Sukhāvatī-vyūha*, and the *Amitayur-dhyāna-sūtra* in *Buddhist Mahāyāna Texts*, ed. E. B. Powell, Dover Publications, New York 1969. For a survey of the Pure Land literature see Sangharakshita, *The Eternal Legacy*, Windhorse Publications, Birmingham 2006, chapter 11 (*Complete Works*, vol. 14); and for information on Pure Land thought see Sangharakshita, *A Survey of Buddhism*, chapter 3, section 7, Windhorse Publications, Birmingham 2001 (*Complete Works*, vol. 1). Ratnaguna provides a commentary on the three principal Pure Land *sūtras* in Ratnaguna and Śraddhāpa, *Great Faith, Great Wisdom*, Windhorse Publications, Cambridge 2016.

314 Section 21 of the *Ariyapariyesanā Sutta*, *Majjhima Nikāya* 26 (i.169);

see Bhikkhu Ñāṇamoli and Bhikkhu Bodhi (trans.), *The Middle Length Discourses of the Buddha*, Wisdom Publications, Boston 1995, p. 261; or I. B. Horner (trans.), *Middle Length Sayings*, vol. i, Pali Text Society, London 1967, p. 212.

315 See W. E. Soothill (trans.), *The Lotus of the Wonderful Law*, Curzon, London 1987, pp. 125–8; and chapter 5, 'Symbols of Life and Growth' of *The Drama of Cosmic Enlightenment*, pp. 116 ff. in this volume.

316 R. A. F. Thurman (trans.), *The Holy Teaching of Vimalakīrti*, Pennsylvania State University Press, University Park and London 1976, p. 12.

317 Ibid., p. 13.

318 Ibid.

319 Ibid., pp. 15–16.

320 Ibid., pp. 17–18.

321 Compare this incident with what happens in H. V. Guenther (trans.), *The Life and Teachings of Naropa*, Oxford University Press, Oxford 1963, p. 105, where Marpa offers all his gold in the form of a mandala to Naropa, but Naropa rejects it: 'Naropa handed the gold back and said: "I do not need it; all that is here is gold," and touching the ground with his big toe turned it all into gold.'

322 Sangharakshita discusses the connection between this chapter and the rest of the *Vimalakīrti-nirdeśa* in *The Eternal Legacy*, Windhorse Publications, Birmingham 2006, p. 148 (*Complete Works*, vol. 14).

323 The book was Arthur Guirdham's *The Great Heresy*, Neville Spearman, Jersey 1977. It is reviewed by Sangharakshita in *Alternative Traditions*, Windhorse Publications, Glasgow 1986, pp. 16–22 (*Complete Works*, vol. 13).

324 From Blake's Prologue to 'For the Sexes: The Gates of Paradise,' in *Complete Writings*, Oxford University Press, Oxford 1966, p. 761.

325 Hakuin was a Japanese Zen master who lived in the eighteenth century, and his 'Song of Meditation' is much loved. The translation quoted here is from Trevor Leggett, *First Zen Reader*, Charles E. Tuttle, Tokyo 1960, pp. 67–8.

CHAPTER 3

326 I Corinthians 9:22.

327 R. A. F. Thurman (trans.), *The Holy Teaching of Vimalakīrti*, Pennsylvania State University Press, University Park and London 1976, p. 20.

328 Ibid., pp. 20–1.

329 In some Mahāyāna texts ten perfections are enumerated. In addition to the usual six, the extra four are: skilful means (*upāya-kauśalya*), vow (*praṇidhāna*), power (*bala*), and knowledge (*jñāna*). See chapter 4, section 6, 'The Ten Perfections and the Ten Stages',

in Sangharakshita, *A Survey of Buddhism*, Windhorse Publications, Birmingham 2001, pp. 490–9 (*Complete Works*, vol. 1).

330 The term *upāya-kauśalya* (in its Pāli equivalent, *upāya-kosalla)* occurs seldom in the Pāli canon, but does appear, for example, in the *Saṅgīti Sutta*, *Dīgha Nikāya* 33 (iii.220), as one of 'three skills'; here it is translated (by Walshe) as 'means to progress'. See M. Walshe (trans.), *The Long Discourses of the Buddha,* Wisdom Publications, Boston 1995, p. 486; or T. W. Rhys Davids (trans.), *Dialogues of the Buddha*, part 3, Pali Text Society, Oxford 1991, p. 214.

331 For the story of Kisā Gotamī see C. A. F. Rhys Davids and K. R. Norman (trans.), *Poems of Early Buddhist Nuns* (*Therīgātha*), Pali Text Society, Oxford 1989, p. 88. Sangharakshita tells the story in chapter 12 of *What is the Dharma?*, Windhorse Publications, Birmingham 2000 (*Complete Works*, vol. 3).

332 See chapter 3 of *The Drama of Cosmic Enlightenment* above, p. 74.

333 R. A. F. Thurman (trans.), *The Holy Teaching of Vimalakīrti*, Pennsylvania State University Press, University Park and London 1976, p. 150.

334 See Sangharakshita, *The Buddha's Noble Eightfold Path*, Windhorse Publications, Birmingham 2007, chapter 3 (*Complete Works*, vol. 1).

335 For more discussion, see the beginning of chapter 2, 'Perfect Emotion', in Sangharakshita, *The Buddha's Noble Eightfold Path*, Windhorse Publications, 2007 (*Complete Works*, vol. 1), in which context Sangharakshita says, 'For most of us the central problem of the spiritual life is to find emotional equivalents for our intellectual understanding.'

336 The Pāli form of the word is *paṭisambhidā*, and a whole book of the Pāli Tipiṭaka is dedicated to the subject: the *Paṭisambhidāmagga*, the twelfth book of the *Khuddaka Nikāya*. This has been translated by Bhikkhu Ñāṇamoli and published as *The Path of Discrimination* (Pali Text Society, London 1982). In his introduction to the text, A. K. Warder explains that the term does not occur in the *Majjhima*, *Dīgha*, or *Saṃyutta Nikāyas*, but is found in the *Aṅguttara Nikāya*, which scholars think is a slightly later text. Among other interesting observations, Warder quotes the *Aṅguttara Nikāya* (ii.139) as saying that 'it is impossible that there should be "exhaustion" from the point of view of "meanings" (*attha*) or "expressions" (*vyañjana*) in one endowed with the four discriminations'. Warder goes on to say that 'this implies

that they represent a certain power of understanding or marshalling words and meanings. Sāriputta realized the four discriminations after his "entrance" into the Community and could thus explain any doubts…' (*The Path of Discrimination*, p. viii). It also suggests a degree of altruism in the person endowed with these discriminations.

337 The *Daśabhūmika Sūtra* is included as the 26th book of the *Avatamsaka Sutra*. In Thomas Cleary's translation, *dharma-pratisaṃvid* is translated as 'specific knowledge of principles'. The relevant section says that by specific knowledge of principles enlightening beings know 'the variety of entries into the One Vehicle'. See Thomas Cleary, *The Flower Ornament Scripture*, Shambhala, Boston & London 1993, p. 781.

338 See Sangharakshita, *The Drama of Cosmic Enlightenment*, p. 41 above.

339 R. A. F. Thurman (trans.), *The Holy Teaching of Vimalakīrti*, Pennsylvania State University Press, University Park and London 1976, p. 22.

340 Ibid., pp. 22–3.

CHAPTER 4

341 John 8:32.

342 The UK blasphemy law was repealed in 2008.

343 R. A. F. Thurman (trans.), *The Holy Teaching of Vimalakīrti*, Pennsylvania State University Press, University Park and London 1976, p. 115.

344 Ibid., p. 28.

345 R. A. F. Thurman (trans.), *The Holy Teaching of Vimalakīrti*, Pennsylvania State University Press, University Park and London 1976, p. 30.

346 Rāhula's story is told in the *Dhammapada* commentary, published as Eugene Watson Burlingame (ed.), *Buddhist Legends*, Luzac, London 1969, part 1, pp. 219–20. See also Vinaya Piṭaka i.82 (*Mahāvagga* 1.54); I. B. Horner (trans.), *The Book of the Discipline*, part 4, Pali Text Society, Oxford 1992, pp. 103–4.

347 R. A. F. Thurman (trans.), *The Holy Teaching of Vimalakīrti*, Pennsylvania State University Press, University Park and London 1976, p. 31.

348 Ibid., p. 32.

349 Māra is in a sense a 'devil' figure, but unlike the Satan of Christianity, he has no real power. In practical terms it is perhaps most useful to think of him as personifying whatever gets in the way of one's spiritual progress. For a more detailed account of the significance of Māra, see chapter 1, 'The Buddha's Victory', in Sangharakshita, *The Buddha's Victory*, Windhorse Publications, Glasgow 1991, pp. 21–9 (*Complete Works*, vol. 11).

350 R. A. F. Thurman (trans.), *The Holy Teaching of Vimalakīrti*,

Pennsylvania State University Press, University Park and London 1976, p. 37.

351 See sections 13 and 14 of the *Alagaddūpama Sutta*, *Majjhima Nikāya* 22 (i.134–5); Bhikkhu Ñāṇamoli and Bhikkhu Bodhi (trans.), *The Middle Length Discourses of the Buddha*, Wisdom Publications, Boston 1995, pp. 228–9; or I. B. Horner (trans.), *Middle Length Sayings*, vol. i, Pali Text Society, Oxford 1957, pp. 173–4.

CHAPTER 5

352 This mural is found in Cave 103 of the Mogao Caves, the 'Thousand-Buddha Caves', at Dunhuang, China, now a UNESCO world heritage site. UNESCO's website:

> Carved into the cliffs above the Dachuan River, the Mogao Caves south-east of the Dunhuang oasis, Gansu Province, comprise the largest, most richly endowed, and longest used treasure house of Buddhist art in the world. It was first constructed in 366 AD and represents the great achievement of Buddhist art from the fourth to the fourteenth century. 492 caves are presently preserved, housing about 45,000 square meters of murals and more than 2,000 painted sculptures.

353 R. A. F. Thurman (trans.), *The Holy Teaching of Vimalakīrti*, Pennsylvania State University Press, University Park and London 1976, p. 42.

354 The last performance of *The Creation* Joseph Haydn attended was on 27 March 1808, just a year before he died: the aged and ill composer was carried in with great honour on an armchair. According to one account, the audience broke into spontaneous applause at the coming of 'light' and Haydn, in a typical gesture, weakly pointed upwards and said, 'Not from me – everything comes from up there!'

355 R. A. F. Thurman (trans.), *The Holy Teaching of Vimalakīrti*, Pennsylvania State University Press, University Park and London 1976, p. 43.

356 Ibid.

357 Alfred Lord Tennyson, *In Memoriam*, lines 87–8:

> Can'st thou feel for me
> Some painless sympathy
> with pain?'

358 R. A. F. Thurman (trans.), *The Holy Teaching of Vimalakīrti*, Pennsylvania State University Press, University Park and London 1976, p. 48.

359 'Opposition is true friendship' is the caption of Blake's illustration of a sea serpent writhing in the waves; see p. 20 of his original manuscript of *The Marriage of Heaven and Hell*. (This comes

at the end of the section of the work called 'A Memorable Fancy'.)

360 R. A. F. Thurman (trans.), *The Holy Teaching of Vimalakīrti*, Pennsylvania State University Press, University Park and London 1976, p. 55.

361 For an account of what is called the 'Great Miracle', see Eugene Watson Burlingame (ed.), *Buddhist Legends*, part 3, Luzac, London 1969, pp. 45–7.

362 This was the phrase the Buddha used when he exhorted his first disciples to go out and teach the Dharma 'for the welfare of the many'. See Vinaya Piṭaka i.21 (*Mahāvagga* 1.11), in I. B. Horner (trans.), *The Book of the Discipline*, part 4, Pali Text Society, Oxford 1996, p. 28.

363 I have said that in one respect my mind has changed during the last twenty or thirty years. Up to the age of thirty, or beyond it, poetry of many kinds, such as the works of Milton, Gray, Byron, Wordsworth, Coleridge, and Shelley, gave me great pleasure, and even as a schoolboy I took intense delight in Shakespeare, especially in the historical plays. I have also said that formerly pictures gave me considerable, and music very great, delight. But now for many years I cannot endure to read a line of poetry: I have tried lately to read Shakespeare, and found it so intolerably dull that it nauseated me. I have also almost lost my taste for pictures or music. Music generally sets me thinking too energetically on what I have been at work on, instead of giving me pleasure.... This curious and lamentable loss of the higher aesthetic tastes is all the odder, as books on history, biographies, and travels (independently of any scientific facts which they may contain), and essays on all sorts of subjects interest me as much as ever they did. My mind seems to have become a kind of machine for grinding general laws out of large collections of facts, but why this should have caused the atrophy of that part of the brain alone, on which the higher tastes depend, I cannot conceive. A man with a mind more highly organized or better constituted than mine, would not, I suppose, have thus suffered; and if I had to live my life again, I would have made a rule to read some poetry and listen to some music at least once every week; for perhaps the parts of my brain now atrophied would thus have been kept active through use. The loss of these tastes is a loss of happiness, and may possibly be injurious to the intellect, and more probably to the moral character, by

enfeebling the emotional part of our nature.

Charles Darwin, *Recollections of the Development of my Mind and Character*, 1887.

364 Turning his back to the Divine Vision, his Spectrous
Chaos before his face appeard: an Unformed Memory.
Then spoke the Spectrous Chaos to Albion darkning cold
From the back & loins where dwell the Spectrous Dead
I am your Rational Power O Albion & that Human Form
You call Divine, is but a Worm seventy inches long.

William Blake, *Jerusalem*, plate 29

O Divine Spirit sustain me on thy wings! That
I may awake Albion from His long & cold repose.
For Bacon & Newton sheathd in dismal steel, their terrors hang
Like iron scourges over Albion, Reasonings like vast Serpents
Infold around my limbs, bruising my minute articulations

I turn my eyes to the Schools & Universities of Europe
And there behold the Loom of Locke whose Woof rages dire
Washd by the Water-wheels of Newton: black the cloth
In heavy wreathes folds over every Nation; cruel Works
Of many Wheels I View, wheel without wheel, with cogs tyrannic
Moving by compulsion each other.'

William Blake, *Jerusalem*, Plate 15.

365 Never did eye see sun unless it had first become sunlike, and never can the Soul have vision of the First Beauty unless itself be beautiful.

Plotinus, *The Enneads*, I.vi.9, trans. Stephen MacKenna, Penguin 1991, p. 55.

CHAPTER 6

366 R. A. F. Thurman (trans.), *The Holy Teaching of Vimalakīrti*, Pennsylvania State University Press, University Park and London 1976, p. 50.

367 Ibid., p. 66.

368 Ibid., p. 67.

369 For more about the *kliṣṭa-mano-vijñāna*, see chapter 4, 'The Turning About in the Deepest Seat of Consciousness', in Sangharakshita, *The Meaning of Conversion in Buddhism*, Windhorse Publications, Birmingham 1994 (*Complete Works*, vol. 2).

370 R. A. F. Thurman (trans.), *The Holy Teaching of Vimalakīrti*, Pennsylvania State University Press, University Park and London 1976, p. 73.

371 Étienne Lamotte (trans.), *The Teaching of Vimalakīrti*

(*L'Enseignement de Vimalakīrti*), rendered into English by Sara Boin, Pali Text Society, London 1976, p. 190.

372 R. A. F. Thurman (trans.), *The Holy Teaching of Vimalakīrti*, Pennsylvania State University Press, University Park and London 1976, p. 73.

373 Étienne Lamotte (trans.), *The Teaching of Vimalakīrti* (*L'Enseignement de Vimalakīrti*), rendered into English by Sara Boin, Pali Text Society, London 1976, p. 190.

374 On the Yogācāra generally, see Sangharakshita, *A Survey of Buddhism*, Windhorse Publications, Birmingham 2001, pp. 387–412 (*Complete Works*, vol. 1). On the eight kinds of discriminating consciousness, see Sangharakshita, *The Meaning of Conversion in Buddhism*, Windhorse Publications, Birmingham 1994, pp. 66–72 (*Complete Works*, vol. 2).

375 R. A. F. Thurman (trans.), *The Holy Teaching of Vimalakīrti*, Pennsylvania State University Press, University Park and London 1976, p. 74.

376 The Stream Entrant is someone who has developed a degree of transcendental insight sufficient to attain to the first stage of the transcendental path, thereby breaking the first three of the ten fetters, i.e. fixed self-view, doubt or lack of commitment, and dependence on ethical rules and religious observances as ends in themselves. Traditionally, once one has gained Stream Entry, progress towards the goal of full Enlightenment is irreversible. Among the many references to Stream Entry in the Pāli canon, the *Saṃyutta Nikāya* has a whole section devoted to the subject. See Bhikkhu Bodhi (trans.), *The Connected Discourses of the Buddha,* Wisdom Publications, Boston 2000, pp. 1788–837; or F. L. Woodward (trans.), *Kindred Sayings*, part 5, Pali Text Society, Oxford 1979, pp. 296–351.

377 R. A. F. Thurman (trans.), *The Holy Teaching of Vimalakīrti*, Pennsylvania State University Press, University Park and London 1976, p. 75.

378 Ibid., p. 77.

379 Ibid., p. 77.

CHAPTER 7

380 Ibid., p. 78.

381 The Vinaya specifies undertaking the training principle of not eating at 'the wrong time'; this is the sixth of the *uposatha*, the eight precepts listed in, for example, the *Uposatha Sutta* (*Aṅguttara Nikāya* iv.248), and traditionally practised by the monastic community at all times and by the lay community on festival days. This phrase 'the wrong time' is applied in the Vinaya to many different activities, and key to the specific understanding of

what skilful practice involves is the definition of when the day starts: hence the specification that the day officially begins when one can see the lines on the palms of one's hands.

382 Buddhaghosa doesn't specify ten meals (or any other number) but states at *Visuddhimagga* 70–1 in a section called 'One-Sessioner's Practice' that an eating session counts as one meal so long as the diner has not got up from his seat. Buddhaghosa further says that there are three grades of this practice: if you observe it strictly, you will eat only the food that you have laid your hand upon, 'whether it be little or much', while if you are a medium practitioner you will continue eating until everything in your bowl has been consumed, and if you practise 'mildly' or 'softly', you may continue eating until you get up from your seat. See Bhikkhu Ñāṇamoli (trans.), *The Path of Purification*, Buddhist Publication Society, Kandy 1991, pp. 69–70; or Pe Maung Tin (trans.), *The Path of Purity*, Pali Text Society, London 1975, pp. 78–9.

383 R. A. F. Thurman (trans.), *The Holy Teaching of Vimalakīrti*, Pennsylvania State University Press, University Park and London 1976, p. 81.

384 Ibid., p. 82.

385 See *Dhammapada* verses 26, 111, 140, 164, and 355.

386
> Clothes in the world certainly have no scent in themselves, but if a man permeates them with perfumes, then they come to have a scent. It is just the same with the case we are speaking of. The pure state of Suchness certainly has no defilement, but if it is permeated by ignorance, then the marks of defilement appear on it. The defiled state of ignorance is indeed devoid of any purifying force, but if it is permeated by Suchness, then it will come to have a purifying influence.

Aśvaghoṣa, *The Awakening of Faith in the Mahāyāna*, trans. Yoshiko S. Hakeda, Columbia University Press, New York 1967, p. 56.

387 R. A. F. Thurman (trans.), *The Holy Teaching of Vimalakīrti*, Pennsylvania State University Press, University Park and London 1976, p. 86.

CHAPTER 8

388 For more information on stupas see chapter 2, 'The Tantric Stupa', in Sangharakshita, *Creative Symbols of Tantric Buddhism*, Windhorse Publications, Birmingham 2002 (*Complete Works*, vol. 13); also chapter 6, 'Five Element Symbolism and the Stupa', in Sangharakshita, *The Drama of Cosmic Enlightenment*,

pp. 139 ff. in this volume; and Lama Anagarika Govinda, *Psycho-cosmic Symbolism of the Buddhist Stupa*, Dharma, Emeryville California 1976.

389 R. A. F. Thurman (trans.), *The Holy Teaching of Vimalakīrti*, Pennsylvania State University Press, University Park and London 1976, pp. 91–2.

390 Ibid., pp. 98–9.

391 Ibid., p. 150, for his remarks on the four reliances.

392 Edward Conze, *Buddhist Meditation*, George Allen & Unwin, London 1956, p. 136.

393 For more on the eight *vijñānas,* see chapter 4, 'The Turning About in the Deepest Seat of Consciousness', in Sangharakshita, *The Meaning of Conversion in Buddhism*, Windhorse Publications, Birmingham 1994 (*Complete Works*, vol. 2).

SOURCES

THE DRAMA OF COSMIC ENLIGHTENMENT

The chapters are edited from the transcripts of a series of eight lectures, 'Parables, Myths, and Symbols of Mahāyāna Buddhism in the White Lotus Sūtra', given in London in 1971. The question and answer sessions that follow each chapter are from a study seminar held at Padmaloka retreat centre in 1985. The book was originally published by Windhorse Publications in 1993.

THE PRICELESS JEWEL

This is an edited version of the transcript of a lecture, or perhaps one might call it a sermon, given in King's College Chapel, Cambridge, on the morning of Sunday 15 July 1987. It was originally published in the collection of essays and addresses called *The Priceless Jewel* (Windhorse Publications, Glasgow 1993).

TRANSFORMING SELF AND WORLD

This commentary is based on a series of eight lectures, 'Transformation of Life and World in the Sūtra of Golden Light', given in 1976, augmented by points from a study seminar held in 1987.

Chapter 2, 'The Spiritual Significance of Confession', has been further augmented by material from a study seminar, 'Confession –

from the Sūtra of Golden Light', held in Sukhavati community, above the London Buddhist Centre, in December 1976.

The book was originally published by Windhorse Publications in 1995, and a revised edition was published in 2008.

THE INCONCEIVABLE EMANCIPATION

The series of eight lectures on which this commentary is based was given in London in 1979, here supplemented by points from a study seminar held at Padmaloka retreat centre in 1987. The book was originally published by Windhorse Publications in 1995.

Verbatim transcripts of all lectures and seminars are available at www.freebuddhistaudio.com.

INDEX

discriminative 581–2
painful experience and 202
symbols for lack of 170
transcendental 261, 576, 581–2
āyurveda 193

Bach, J.S. 285–6
Bacon, Francis 402, 619n
bahujana hitāya 530, 629n
Bahuśrutīyas 30
Balendraketu 414, 426
bardo 532
beauty 257
beneficial activity, *see artha-caryā*
begging bowl 142, 395, 405, 408, 531
beginner's mind 440
Beowulf 85
Bhadrajyotis 543
Bhagavad Gītā 361, 424
Bhagavan 192
Bhaiṣajyaguru 193ff
Bhaiṣajyarāja 193ff, 205, 458, 572
bhāvana-krāma 445
bhikkhus 30, 31, 153, 265, 272–3, 531; *see also bhikṣus*
bhikśāpātra 405
bhikṣus/bhikṣuṇīs 65, 106, 390, 405, 408, 611n; *see also bhikkhu*, monks
bhūmis 150, 167
Bhūtas 349
Bible 22, 33, 86, 444, 479, 546
Bihar 5
Bimbisāra, King 274, 423, 621n
birth
apparitional 169, 462
into caste 426
contradictory notion 502
and death, cycle of 71, 163
in hell 287
intoxication of high birth 293, 299
previous 282–3, 289, 291, 336
not in vain 130
oppression of 319, 321
stories 235; *see also Jātaka* stories
Blake, William 4, 11, 100, 266, 473
Auguries of Innocence 23, 583n
as bridge from our own tradition 22, 23–4
on forgiveness 473, 625n
on friendship 525, 628n
Prophetic Books 533
vision compared to *Gaṇḍhavyūha Sūtra* 23
warning of loss of divine vision 533, 629–30n
blessings 50, 179, 180, 333 347, 361, 368, 410, 417, 519
blame 545–6, 557
bliss 11, 102, 280, 556
of liberation 522
noble 259
Bodh Gaya 48, 503, 567
bodhi 7, 63, 400
bodhi tree 15, 48, 156, 564
Bodhicaryāvatāra 268, 611n, 613n
bodhicitta 174–5, 289–90, 390, 441, 451, 465, 602n
absolute and relative 58
and renunciation 511
cosmic 465–6
bodhimaṇḍa 503
bodhisattva 7, 25, 47, 167, 253
and *arhant*, contrast between 7, 14, 25–6
archetypal 121, 167, 232–3, 515
attitude 29
behaving as 187
buddha-fields of 467, 473
career of 39; *see also bhūmis*
of Compassion 176; *see also* Avalokiteśvara
definition of 441
of *dharmakāya* 167
historical and archetypal 167
ideal 29, 41, 54, 67, 74, 126, 229, 234, 368, 442, 472, 545, 606n, 612n
irreversible 47, 48, 50, 198, 448, 539
like a candle 487
mind 545
monk as 390
practice of *pāramitās* 8–12, 400
suffering and 523
urge to Enlightenment of 24; *see also bodhicitta*
vows 179, 229, 267, 441, 460, 605n
of Wisdom, *see* Mañjuśrī
bodhisattvayāna 41, 74
bodhyaṅgas, seven 280, 612n
bodies, three, *see trikāya*
body
astral 136
chakras 135
giving up 493
illusory 417
not absolutely discrete 135
physical 70, 135, 136, 160, 200, 252, 512
nature of 493–4
relics 158–9, 567–8, 571
stupa correlated with human 148

Buddhist
art, *see* art, Buddhist
cosmology 341–2, 344, 460, 624n
economics 400ff
ideal 441
literature, canonical, *see* scriptures, *sūtras*
practices, danger of losing connection with 114
scriptures not infallible revelation 443
states 434
vision 20, 137
vocabulary 60
way of life 228
bullock carts 69, 74
bumpa 150
burial mound 141, 148
Burma 15, 143, 434
burning house, *see* parable, of burning house
business, right livelihood, *see* right livelihood

cakravartin-rāja 477
Calcutta 9
call of Truth 72–3
Candracchattra 572, 574
canonical literature, Buddhist 442
capitalism 94
Carroll, Lewis 263
cat 295
Cathars 472
Catherine, Saint 158
causality xii, 527, 529, 532–3
celebrations, *see* festivals
cessation of suffering 192, 447
cessation of unskilfulness 63
ceto-vimukti 446
chairs 536
Chaityavādins 154, 155
chakras, *see* psychic centres
chandali 121
chandas 365
change
external and internal 122–3
fear of 109–10
Charles I, King 424, 622n
Charles II, King 424
Charles V 565
Chen, Mr 135–6
China 15, 18, 35, 84, 150, 156, 178, 194, 197, 205, 236, 242, 376, 418
Chinese
art 18, 25, 46, 517–8
language 15
sutras 52, 242
translation of texts 444
chorten 150, 157, 165; *see also* stupa
Chototsang, Aggen 401
chin lab 519
Christ, *see* Jesus
Christianity 92, 112, 127, 177, 182
and Buddhism, difference between 90, 276–7, 282, 300, 309, 528
and freedom 500
decline of in West 137
cintāmaṇi 174–5
citta 544
clairaudience/clairvoyance 11
collective unconscious 5
Coleridge, Samuel Taylor 267, 387, 611n
comfort 170, 201, 207, 213, 271, 284–5, 321, 471, 536–7
commitment 216, 285, 448, 460, 495, 496, 595n, 614n, 631n, 665
precedes lifestyle 495, 593n
communication 10, 53, 318, 473, 486, 551ff, 587n; *see also* speech
blocked 307
of the bodhisattva 10
creative 335
of the Dharma 506, 548
energy of 135
of Enlightened mind 33, 53–4
goddess of 363–4
of golden light 366–7
limited by vagueness 490
through magic 550
medium of 489–90
non-verbal 565
by perfume 561–2
power of 368
and trust 315, 579
Communists 82
communities, single-sex 25
compassion 14–15, 99, 177–8, 181, 294, 522–3
bodhisattvas of, *see* Avalokiteśvara and Tāra
of the Buddha 305–6, 309–10, 312–3
perfume as symbol of 561
of Vimalakīrti 456, 501
compassionate activity 214
compounded and uncompounded 389
concentration 11, 23, 136, 219, 280, 446, 497, 543; *see also samādhi*
concepts, language of 15–16, 17, 68
conceptual thinking
danger of 112
inadequacy of 21

disrespect 294, 303–4
distraction, mental or emotional 79, 207, 284, 293, 300, 471, 536, 543–4, 553
diversity 20–1, 23, 40
Divine Comedy 86
Divine Healer 189ff
divine kings, *see* four great kings
doctrine, feeling versus 66, 130
Doṇa 153
dorje, *see vajra*
dosa 63, 594n
dragons, *see nāgas*
Dṛḍhā 245, 358, 360, 378ff, 386, 388, 389, 393
dreams 191, 204–5, 252–3, 259, 452
  interpretation 204–6
  as other level of reality 263, 266
  in *Sūtra of Golden Light* 245
  role in transformation of individual 253
  twofold value in Mahāyāna and Vajrayāna 253
drugs 10, 407
drum 243ff
  as solar symbol 266
  golden 243, 264, 279, 287–8
  of the deathless 264, 610n
drunkard and jewel, parable of, *see* parables
drunken state 299, 317
  symbolism of 170–1, 218, 221, 223
dualism
  primordial 385
  transition to Insight 112
dualities 112, 535, 542–5, 547–9
duality 541ff
  mind-created 112–3, 547
  primordial 385
  of subject and object 518
  transcending 447
duḥkha 11, 398; *see also* suffering
Dundubhīśvara 258, 261, 264
Durgā 384
dveṣa 304

earth 144–7
  as symbol of material world 163
  element 144
  characteristics of 388
  goddess 378ff, 388, 393–4, 409; *see also* Dṛḍhā
eating 510, 551–2, 631–2n
economics 399ff
ecumenism 422
education and culture, giving 8
Edward the Confessor 424
effort 61, 80, 135, 202, 286, 495
  nature of in spiritual life 519–20
  need to distribute widely enough 520
  escape from 79
  Perfect 585n
  wilful 520, 544
ego 24–5, 27–8, 74, 97, 466, 581, 613n
Egypt 91, 170, 189
Egyptian
  deities 189
  mythology 112, 159–60, 385
eight requisites 405
eightfold path, *see* Noble Eightfold Path
ekarasa 125
ekayāna 41, 489
elements
  and five Buddhas 147
  as symbols, 147
  compared to different kinds of people 146
  five 144ff, 160
  six 160
  stupa and five 144, 599n
elephant 87, 299, 398, 430, 526, 557
  illusory 452–4, 470, 623n
  parable of blind men and 16, 586n
eloquence 168, 185–6, 368, 480, 535
emanations, magical 65
emancipation 446, 448; *see also* freedom, *vimokṣas*, *vimukti*
  bondage, in relation to 448
  description of 445
  experience of 126
  of heart 446
  inconceivability of 448
  individual 67, 99, 472, 501, 545
  twofold 446
emotional positivity 280, 300, 353–5, 472, 487, 499, 611n
emotions
  and spiritual quest 101
  importance of engaging 129, 370
  language of 15
  negative 10, 41, 67, 76, 97, 99, 200
  positive, development of 10, 25
  primitive 102
  unblocking 134
emptiness, *see śūnyatā*
  of concepts 12
encouragement 25, 49, 109, 199, 230, 356, 488
  of friends 109
enemies 55, 286, 525

energies 134–5
creative 137
flowering of 134
mental 145
psychic 11
energy, 229, 230, 281; *see also vīrya*
of anger as frustrated desire 295
at psychic centres 132
blocked 144, 145
expansion of 145
flowing 301–2
mana 159
potential 121
primordial 145
release of 134, 301
spiritual, nucleus of in Mahāyāna *sūtras* 243
suprapersonal 229, 357, 435
enjoyment
importance of 285
and mindfulness 300–1
and monastic life 392
and nature 382–3, 387
'no enjoyment for me anywhere' 306, 312
of *sūtras* 443–4
Enlightened
consciousness 33, 37, 120, 126
disciples 54
privately 40
Enlightenment 19, 43, 67, 90, 96, 120, 123, 140, 151, 440, 576; *see also nirvāṇa*, Reality
and fall 100
as a process 449
as bird with two wings 15
as total creativity 447
aspects of 167, 193
Buddhas 156
cosmic process of 67
earth goddess bears witness to 380–1
eternal 49, 58
factors of 540, 573; *see also bodhyaṅgas*
light of 131
nature of 174–5
nothing to do with time 93
objective dimension of 12
partial experience of 524
potential symbolised 180
prediction to 168
private 74
speed of attainment 183
spiritual not psychological experience 270
subjective dimension of 12
thought of 289; *see also bodhicitta*
universally recognized goal 80
urge/will to 7, 24, 175; *see also bodhicitta*
enmity 295, 579–80
environment 181, 323, 360
ideal for spiritual life 470–1, 472, 474
imbalance in 357
impinging on 475–6
use of resources 386–7
Epidaurus 192, 204
eradication of negative emotions 41, 63, 67
Erda 380
escapism 78–9
Essence of Buddhism, The 22
Eternal Legacy, The 52
eternalism 84
eternity and time 18, 140, 199, 203, 534
ether (space) 144, 145, 146, 151; *see also ākāśa*
ethics 10, 56, 219, 222, 296, 355; *see also pāramitās*, precepts, *śīla*
need for encouragement to practise 230
ethnic
culture 367, 370–1, 376
practice 142
religion 77, 182, 364, 366–7, 398
values, transition to universal 417
enthusiasm 403
etymology 362, 490
symbolic 166
evil 289–90, 292–4, 300, 302–5, 319, 336–7, 429–31
friends 299–300, 322–3
result of ignorance 305
understanding 557
evil states 276
evolution 5, 24, 76, 79
evolution
higher, *see* Higher Evolution
lower 149, 163, 175
spiritual 148
evolutionary process 78
exemplification 487–8
exertions, four, *see* four right efforts
existence
bondage of 334
conditioned 69, 71, 343–4, 383, 388, 419, 425, 560

friendship 525; *see also* spiritual friendship

games 18, 68, 74, 236, 480, 501–2, 606n
Gampopa 496
gandharvas 346, 348–9, 464
Gaṇḍhavyūha Sūtra 17, 23
Gandhavyūāhāra 554
Gandhi, Mahatma 396
Ganesha 361, 397
garbha 150
garuḍas 349, 464, 573
gātha 235
gaurīs 352
Gelugpas 496
gender 538
generosity, *see* giving
George, Saint 357
geya 235
ghosts 68, 70, 349, 544
 hungry, *see* hungry ghosts
giving 8–9, 12, 230, 343, 392
 Buddhist economics as 400
 different to paying 403
 five kinds of 8
 as *saṃgrahavastu* 485–6
 yourself 8
gnosis 238, 468, 494, 523–4, 570, 573, 575
Gnostic gospel 22
Gnosticism 22, 170, 91, 238–9, 606n
God 25, 56, 307–8
god realm 70, 109, 169, 345, 346, 354, 384, 429, 462, 465, 468, 478, 597n
Godānīya 342
goddesses
 earth goddess 378ff, 388, 393–4, 409
 Dṛḍhā 245, 358, 360, 378ff, 386, 388, 389, 393
 Sarasvatī 245, 358, 360ff, 379, 384, 386, 395, 396, 411, 415
  worship of 371
 Śrī 245, 358, 360, 378–9, 384–6, 395ff, 414–5
 in Vimalakīrti's house 456, 537–9
gods, *see devas*
 Greek 85, 103, 182, 190–1, 350, 353, 363, 385
Going for Refuge 63, 179, 207, 354, 355, 393, 511, 593n, 656
going through the motions 82–3
golden drum, *see* drum
golden light 228
 not reflected in worldly pleasures 285
 as emetic 292
 as food 290
 as suprapersonal force 357
good physician, parable of, *see* parable
goose
 and bottle 255–6
 symbolism 361
Govinda, Lama 107, 134, 161–2, 228, 605n
grace 518–9
gradual and sudden method 171–2
grass, symbolism of 373
Great Physician 192
Great Way, *see* Mahāyāna
Greeks, ancient 85, 103, 190, 204, 559
group, the 24–5
 age of transition to individual from 417
 blame of 545
 guilt in relation to 307
 monk does not belong to 391
 preservation of in Hinduism 364
 positive 433
Guanyin 178
guardian
 angel 110–2
 deities 167
 of the world, *see lokapālas*
Guenther, H. V. 166
guilt 83, 90, 269, 306–9, 311–2, 336, 508
Gurdjieff, G. I. 206, 297, 604n
Guru Granth Sahib 59
gurus 171–2, 179–81, 183–4, 335, 343, 577
 yoga 381

habit 55, 89, 109, 259, 285–6, 311–2, 431, 439, 444, 574, 611n
Hakuin 473, 591n, 623n, 625n
Hamlet 86, 610n, 622n
haṃsa 361
Hanuman 361
hardship 171, 206–7
harmikā 148–51, 161–2
harmony 92, 481, 573
 of cosmos 352–3, 357
 of speech 10
hatred 28, 294–5, 580, 614n
 of self 201
Haydn, Joseph 519
head, symbolism of 381
healer, divine 190
 the Buddha as 192–3
healing 190–4, 198–9, 424
health 184, 190–2, 222, 246, 333, 406, 493, 501

karma 254, 309, 419–20, 425–8
as *puṇya devatā* 111
effects occluded 432
law of 13, 255, 309, 419–20, 425–8, 423–3
literalism and 310
misunderstood in Mahāyāna and Tibetan Buddhism 422
pain and 407
positive, insufficient without vision of transcendental 354
results of 254
Kārttikeya 411
karuṇā 522; *see also* compassion
Karuṇā Puṇḍarīka Sūtra 51, 592n
Kashmir 35
Kathā-vatthu 143, 154
Katō, Bunnō 36
Kauṇḍinya 258, 372
kāyas, three, see trikāya doctrine
Keats, John 138, 257, 609n
Keble, John 75
Kern, Hendrik 36
Khambas 401
kiṃnaras 349
king, wheel-turning 477
kings, four great, *see* four great kings
Kisā Gotami 483, 626n
kliṣta-mano-vijñāna 542, 544, 581, 630n
koans 92, 255–7, 469
Koran 108
Krishna 73, 361, 424–5
kṣānti 10–12, 164
basis for ethics 296
ksetra 463
Kṣitigarbha 233
Kuanyin, *see* Guanyin
Kumārajīva 35, 444–5
kuṇḍalinī 121
kunta 150
kusa grass 373
Kuśinagara 567

laity 65, 142, 496
and preservation of Dharma 242
not handicapped 496
and monastics 63, 405, 408
practice of 154
lakṣaṇas 11, 585n
Lakṣmī 361, 384, 395–9, 411
Lalitavistara Sūtra 18, 33, 53, 587n
Lamotte, Étienne 445
Langland, William 263
language 15, 60, 110, 137, 162, 230, 231, 442, 444
of Buddhism 62
of concepts 15–16, 417
dependence on 564
developing indigenous Buddhist 137
effect of different 565
of images 15–16, 18
of immanence 61, 62, 111
in metaphorical sense 15, 366
limitations of 578–9
literal and metaphorical 482
of myth and symbol 17
mythic and conceptual/rational 416
of potentiality 61, 111
of reason 417
Sanskrit and Prakrit 365, 590n
secular, of poet and artist 138
symbolic 69
Tibetan 106
traditional Buddhist 138
translation of Dharma into local 15, 374, 618n
use of by the Buddha 60, 265, 417
Laṅkāvatāra Sūtra 17, 239, 587n
law
cosmic 84
of gravity, Dharma compared to 84
of karma, *see* karma
liberation, spirit of 126
liberative technique, *see* skilful means
Licchavi youths xiv, 455, 464–5, 466, 511
life
balance of effort in 520
as battle 86
Buddhist way of 228
and darkness 287
eternal 49, 150, 198
everyday 21, 47, 188, 232, 252, 476
as journey 86
preciousness of 251, 302
refraining from taking 9
social 228, 322, 432, 472, 559
spiritual, models of 227
upward tendency of 99
lifestyle 402, 495–6
light
in iconography 260
interpenetrating 50
symbol of higher states of consciousness 259
transcendental 228, 366, 388
of Truth 96
limitations, working with our 324, 503–4

Mañjuśrī 17, 39, 47, 167, 232, 385, 450, 456, 457, 490, 492, 503, 515, 518ff
embodiment of all four *pratisaṃvids* 491
mano-vijñāna 581
mantra 166ff, 180, 182–3, 496–7
of Avalokiteśvara 176
etymology 166
visualized 135
Mantrayāna 369, 618n
Manu 434
Manusmṛti 297
Mao, Chairman 166
Māra 48, 81–2, 380, 512–14, 525–6, 564, 573, 627n
as bodhisattva 525
daughters of 513
Marpa 496
maruts 418
masculine 12
and feminine 548
qualities 164
principle 148
Maslow, Abraham 94, 596
material things, giving 8
materialism 351, 394
matted-hair ascetics 70
Maudgalyāyana 156
Maurya empire 143
māyā 454; *see also* illusion
māyā-citta 544
meals 552, 631n
meaning 533, 578
explicit and implicit 579ff
undefined xiii, 532
meat eating 305
medhī 150
medicine 190, 193–4, 199–200, 395, 400, 406
Chinese 193–4
the Dharma as 201
golden light as 290–2
and monks 408
Tibetan 194
Medicine Buddha 193, 620n
Medicine King 572
meditation 576
and reactive patterns of behaviour 114
as *pāramitā, see samādhi*
distraction in 543
on symbols 179
perfume in 561
seen as dangerous 128
teaching 43
memory 34, 234, 243, 273, 355, 363–4, 368–9
phenomenal 36–7
merits 107, 322, 253, 336, 423, 427, 620n
dedication of 180, 267, 275, 329, 331
from honouring Dharma 571
lay people and 408
oppression of 320, 322
and personality 132
pure and impure 331–2
rejoicing in 267–8, 275
three aims in dedicating 331
Meru, Mount 342–4, 346, 398
Merupradīparāja 456
metaphor 85
language of 16
taken literally 133
mettā 134, 297, 315, 519, 538, 599n
mettā bhāvanā 135, 299n
micchā-diṭṭhi 557
Michael, archangel 357
middle way, the 195, 300–301, 328, 553
Milarepa 141, 335, 496
Mill, John Stuart 532
Milton, John 86
mind 270
bodhisattva and *śrāvaka* 545
illusionary 544
reactive 447
unconscious 70, 263, 266
mindfulness, 280
as ethical precept 10
excessive 301
four foundations of 14
of breathing 544
with spontaneity and joy 300
miracles 19, 260, 265, 504, 529
mirror, one way 110
mistakes 282–3
mistletoe 373, 618n
Mnemosyne 363
moha 63, 304, 594n
mokṣa 446
monastic-lay split 496
monasticism 65, 392
monasteries 272
money 172, 397, 401ff; *see also* wealth
Mongolia 15
monks 390; *see also bhikkhu, bhikṣus*
Monkey 86
moon 148
appearance of Sarasvatī 373
divinity 189–90
gathering at full 273

morality, *see śīla*
mother
as symbol of material world 163
relationship with 102
mu 256
mūdra, lotus 179
mukha 541
mukti 446
Mūlasarvāstivāda 30
mummifying 159
muses 363, 519
music 73, 77, 190, 231, 285–6, 362–3, 371, 530, 540
listening to 285–6
musician 146, 285–6, 346, 349
mutual interpenetration 22, 50
doctrine of 20–1, 23, 61
and Hermetic idea, 'as above, so below' 23–4
and *śūnyatā* 21
mystic 4, 98, 146
myth
allegorical interpretations of 102, 103
of the Fall 100–2
and history both needed 534
has to be lived 328
literal belief in 528
not graspable in conceptual terms 105, 528
of return journey xii, 42, 86ff, 120
and symbol, language of 16
mythological figures 192, 350, 358 415, 464
mythology, Western 357

nāgas 344, 346, 348, 349, 350, 351–2
kings 16–7
princess 65
Nāgārjuna 16–17, 239
Nārāyaṇa 396
nātha 288
nature 383, 384, 386ff
appreciation of 387
right use of 386–7
understanding of 387
need, subjective 94
negative emotions, eradication of 41, 98
neither perception nor non-perception 447
Nietzsche, Fredrich 314, 525, 616n
Neoplatonists 103, 533, 589n, 630n
Nepal 3, 35, 148, 157, 273, 568
Neptune 385
Never Direct, bodhisattva 49–50
New Zealand 561
neyārtha 580
Nichiren 59, 593n
nidāna chain 14, 281
nidānas, twelve positive 64, 446, 589n, 594n
Nīlakaṇṭha 398
nirdaya 294
nirdeśa 442
nirmāṇakāya 77, 461; *see also trikāya*
nirukti 362
nirukti-pratisaṃvid 490
Nirvāṇa 11, 36, 38, 39, 122, 192, 448; *see also samyak sambodhi*, Enlightenment, Reality
as process 449
Hīnayāna 43
negative definition of *nibbāna* 63
positive and negative aspect of 63–4
psychological sense of 43
niśkāma-karma-yoga 413
nītārtha 580
niyamas, *see* five *niyamas*
Nobel, Johannes 243
Noble Eightfold Path 14, 122–3, 172, 446, 486, 585n, 598n, 610n
noble truths, *see* four noble truths
noise 324, 387
non-conceptual 104, 377
non-duality 457, 462, 518, 541ff, 581; *see also advaya*
non-human beings 38, 65, 348–51, 356, 367, 453
non-returner 423, 622n
'no-thing-ness' 447
nuns 14, 46–7, 196, 197, 205, 496, 626n
Nyingmapa 496

ocean 16–17, 125–6, 328, 342, 446, 506, 598n, 619n, 622n
Odyssey 86
offerings 59, 70, 230
to the Buddha 571, 574
of food
to the four great kings 358
goddesses 371
mandala 343
parasols 466
sacrifice of oneself 195–6, 198, 205
to Sarasvatī 361
to stupas 142, 195
Old Testament 143
oṃ 176, 186
oṃ āḥ hūṃ 135

lower 384
of mundane consciousness 262
of myth 528
need to realize true nature of 238
of senses 446
six, in wheel of life 276, 462, 478
of spiritual reality 531, 533
in two simultaneously xiv, 534
of undefined meanings xiii, 532
reason xiii, 4, 129, 148, 279, 417
rebirth 282–3, 419, 571, 613n
as an animal 291–2
cycle of 71, 163
in a god realm 331, 420, 425
and karma 419
positive 383, 384, 408
in Pure Land 18
spiritual 70–1, 180, 227
together 471
receptivity 10–11, 61, 150, 579
adhiṣṭhāna and 519
effort and 519
reflection 187, 443, 558
reflexive consciousness 291–2
Reformation, attitude during 82
regret 41, 215, 302, 305, 313, 509
regular steps, path of 56
reification 84, 133, 449
rejoicing 333, 336, 459
in merits 267, 268, 275, 329–31, 332
relationships, neurotic and dependent 25
relativity
of concepts 12
of gender 538
of space and time 451, 456, 537
reliances, *see* four great reliances
relics 158
of Buddha 141
of Milarepa 141
return of 156
worship of 143, 154, 568
religion 128
as wake-up shout 170
become an end in itself 500
conventional 79
freedom and 499
decline of 185
dualistic stage 112
ethnic 77, 182, 364, 366–7, 367
and secular 138
transcendental critique of 500ff
universal 12, 77, 162, 364, 366–7, 425
Religion of Art, The 24
reminiscence, Platonic doctrine of 61
remorse 509
Renaissance 128
resolutions 313
responsibility
failure to accept 432
family 403–4
individual 25, 323
to preserve the *White Lotus Sūtra* 47
sharing 413, 476
for the world 478
renunciation 493, 511
retreats 25
solitary 207, 279–80, 302
return journey
emotional appeal of 101–2
myth of xii, 42, 86ff, 120
outside time 92
Rhys Davids, Mrs 64
right livelihood, *see* livelihood
Ring Cycle 380
rituals 128
as ends in themselves 83
robes 142, 272, 375, 393, 531
Roman Catholics 55
rosary 166, 180
routine, daily 207
Ruciraketu xiii, 245–6, 253–5, 258–60, 262–7, 290, 293, 364
rules 12–13, 30, 346, 385, 503, 505, 508–9, 551–3
rūpa dhyānas 601n; *see also dhyānas*
rūpakāya 60–1
rūpaloka 415, 446

sacrifice 191, 195, 198, 206, 246, 254, 362, 374, 472
Ṣaḍakṣarī 178
saddharma 51
translation of 32
Saddharma Puṇḍarīka, see White Lotus Sutra
sādhanas 236, 491
sage 146–7
great 276, 280–1, 283, 289, 326
Sahā-world 45–6, 48, 50, 555, 569
saints 7, 26
Śākyamuni 5, 45, 49, 66, 151, 232; *see also* Buddha, Siddhartha, *Tathāgata*
Buddhas emanating from 65
vision of lotuses 463, 597n
previous life 50, 574
Śākyan clan 5
samādhi 11–12, 261, 280, 428, 447
levels of meaning 11

samādhis, three 447
samānārthata 487–8
Samantabhadra 233
śamatha 261
sambhogakāya 27, 52, 53, 61, 77, 241, 461, 532; *see also trikāya* doctrine
sameness 439, 449, 544, 581
saṃgrahavastus 485
Samjñāya 379
saṃkaṭa 320
saṃsāra 100, 383, 387–9, 393–4, 399, 514, 522, 580, 618–9n
  within us 393
saṃskṛti 364
samyak sambodhi 324
sanātana 530
Sanchi 155–6
Sangha 477, 547; *see also* spiritual community, Three Jewels
  disrespect to 303
saṅgīti 234, 606n
Śankara 454
Śantideva 445
Sanskrit 32, 34, 44, 52, 84, 140, 145, 165, 192, 342, 365
  Buddhist Hybrid 35
  pure 35
  Vedic 365
Śāntendriya 546
Śāntideva 268
Sarasvatī 245, 358, 360ff, 379, 384, 386, 395, 396, 411, 415
  worship of 371
Sāriputta/Śāriputra 63
  representative of narrow views 81–2, 537
  in the *Vimalakīrti–nirdeśa* 455, 456, 468, 501–2, 569
    as a figure of fun 535–7, 538–9, 551, 553
    interactions with the goddess 456, 537–9
  in the *White Lotus Sutra* 41, 68, 81, 83, 86, 215
Sarnath 576
sāraṇa 575
Sarvagandhasugandhā 554, 602n
Sarvarūpasaṃdarśana 539
sāvadya 545
Śikhin 468
Sarada Devi 482
śarīras 158–9
Sarvastivāda 30
śāstra 560
scent 632; *see also* perfume
Schumacher, E. F. 399
Schweitzer, Albert 9
science 15, 67, 193, 431
science fiction 37, 237, 451, 533
scriptures 233, 578; *see also sūtras*
  best studied with spiritual friends 578
  Buddhist, not infallible 443
  Sikh 59
sectarianism 76, 127
secular
  culture 355
  spirituality 137
  contrasted with religious 138
seeing, different way of 184
self-visualization 187
self-conscious 7, 24
self-immolation 195–6, 197
self
  alienation of higher and lower 91–2, 94, 95, 98
  development by unselfish action 413
  disillusionment with 304
  guarding function of higher 110
  lower and higher 95, 110
  old 228, 262–3, 293, 499
  pricelessness of contact with true 173
  seen as unchanged in journey myth 122
  transformed, interpenetration of transformed world 265
  true, in Jungian sense 173
self/other distinction, transcended 232
serpent 121, 177, 190; *see also nāgas*
servant, and master relationship 105–6
Set 190
seven precious things 44, 168, 169, 346, 455, 464
sex change 538–9
sexual couple, glorification of 376
sexual misconduct, abstaining from 10
shadow 304
Shakespeare, William 86, 104, 262, 423, 532, 578
Shelley, P. B. 327
Shiva/Śiva 71, 364, 398
sickness, of Vimalakīrti, *see* Vimalakīrti
Siddhartha 5, 380; *see also* Buddha, Śākyamuni, *Tathāgata*
siddhāsana 121
Sigālovāda Sutta 300
Sikhism 58–9
Śikṣā-samuccaya 445
śīla 9, 12; *see also* ethics
silence xiv, 73, 203, 549, 551, 564, 566
Siṃha 545

as source of inspiration and enjoyment 443
as work of literature 57, 243
Sūtra of Golden Light
composite nature of 246
confession in, *see* confession
ethnic culture in 370
Hindu mythology in 266, 415
inclusion of principal Mahāyāna teachings 247
origin of 239
outline of 244–6
spiritual unity of 247
Tantric development within 260, 369
as *vaipulya sūtra*, *see vaipulya*
Sūtra of Hui Neng 183, 602n
suttas, Pāli 33, 54, 57
Suvarṇabhāsa, see Sūtra of Golden Light
Suzuki, D. T. 22
symbols
bodhi tree 564
drum 264
experienced, not intellectually understood 189
fire 70
head and feet 381
how to meditate on 179
jewel 26, 169–71, 213, 218, 220–3
journey 122–3
life and growth 120
need to feel 126
not defined 189
plants 122, 123
servant and son 105
separation of father and son as 91
shape, sound and light 167
solar 175
universal 124
symbolic language 69
symbolism 41
inconsistencies in 162
and literalism 107–9
shared with Hindus and Jains 134

tactful means 83; *see also* skilful means
t'ai chi 231
Tantras 182, 236
Tantric Buddhism 124, 163, 178, 376
Tāra 178
taste of freedom 125, 446, 595n, 299n
Tathāgata 124, 246–7, 258, 260, 494–5, 511–12, 556, 569–72, 608n, 609n; *see also* Buddha, Śākyamuni, Siddhartha
tathāgata-dhātu 561
tathatā 560
teacher
claims of spiritual 578
function of 25
teachings
danger of hearing prematurely 56
degeneration of 231
misinterpreted 76
telepathy 11
television 79, 252, 412, 471, 493
temperament, difference of 76
temples 142, 156–7, 230, 266, 327, 346, 350, 352, 362, 476, 593n
temporal terminology 101
temptation 103, 105, 158
Tennyson, Alfred Lord 523, 628n
Thailand 15
theism 72
Theorem 504
Theravāda 15, 20, 28–30, 77, 126, 240–2, 422
compared to Vajrayāna 327
formalism of 552
literalism of 60
now more proselytizing 28
Theravādins 16, 63
thirst 294, 303, 333
Thomas, Saint 91
Thoth 189, 190
three bodies, *see trikāya*
Three Jewels 175, 383–4, 393, 511
disrespect to 303
interrelation of 547
represented in shrine room 59
three *kāyas* 61
three *lakṣaṇas* 447, 585n, 623n
three levels of wisdom 11, 186, 585n, 607n
three marks of conditioned existence, *see lakṣaṇas*
three natures 452, 623n
three planes/levels of existence xiv, 344
three vehicles 74
Threefold Lotus Sūtra 52, 591n
threefold way 56, 219, 222
Thurman, Robert 444, 445, 607n
'Thus have I heard' 36–7, 234
Tibet 15, 139, 156, 165–7, 193–4, 367, 376, 379
Tibetan
Buddhism 29, 71, 121, 135
iconography 260
lifestyle in 496
language 15
temples 327

Vulture's Peak 38, 49, 241, 244, 591n
vyañjana 578
Vyāsa 85

Wagner, Richard 380
Waste Land, the 219, 605n
Watts, Alan 257
wealth 411; *see also* money
Western
  culture 257, 263, 367–8, 374–5
    at the service of Buddhism 375, 422
  monastic orders 106
  mythology 357
  philosophy 5
  cultural tradition 231
wheel of life, Tibetan 71, 276, 281, 354, 419, 594n, 597n
Wheel of the Law 156, 282, 613n
wheel-rolling king 477
  parable of 47
wheel-turning gesture 124
White Lotus of Compassion Sūtra 51
White Lotus Sūtra 18, 239, 489
  commentaries on 208
  compared to Pāli canon 59–60
  consequences of disparaging 54
  date as literary document 34
  history of 35
  how to approach 209
  illustration of 35
  influence in Vietnam 197
  merits of preaching 49
  message of 208–9
  non-rational response to 104
  preaching of 46
  preservation of 47
  Pure Land of 184
  qualities of protectors of 47
  raising one to a higher level of experience 66
  recited, copied, expounded 44
  significance of name 51
  structure of 35, 58
  supreme teaching 48
  title 32, 33
  and *trikāya* doctrine 60–1
  translation of 36, 591n
  two distinctive teachings of 62
  twofold message of 58
  worship of 58–9
White Tāra 121–2

Whitman, Walt 8
will to enlightenment, *see bodhicitta*
Wilhelm, Meister 86
wisdom 11, 261, 576; *see also pāramitās*, *prajñā*
  Bodhisattva of, *see* Mañjuśri
  faith equivalent to 49
  path of 59
  three levels of 11, 186, 585n, 603n, 607n
wisdoms, five, *see* five *jñānas*
women 47, 169
  capable of Enlightenment 46–7, 334–5
  disadvantages for 335
Wordsworth, William 375, 387
work, *see* livelihood
world 359; *see also saṃsāra*
  systems 39, 48, 198–9, 460
worldlings 193
worship; *see also puja*
  of the Buddha 569
  of the Dharma 571ff
  of relics 154
  of stupa 154
wrathful deities 71

Xuanzang 444

yab-yum forms 376
yak's tail 87
yakṣas 245, 344, 346, 348–50, 379
yānas
  as levels 62
  distinction between 77
  in parable of burning house 78
  three 40–41, 51, 61, 74, 489, 591
Yaśodharā 47, 65, 471
Yeats, W. B. 266, 611n
yidam 111
yin and yang 129, 148–52, 163, 175
yoga 231
Yogācāra 20, 61, 542, 544, 581, 631n

Zen 11, 37, 76–7, 92–3, 184–5, 218, 252, 255–7, 326–7, 608n
  art of statesmanship 477
  applied 475–6
  Christian 575
Zen-like approach 326–7
Zeus 191, 385
Zhiyi 84

A GUIDE TO THE COMPLETE WORKS OF SANGHARAKSHITA

Gathered together in these twenty-seven volumes are talks and stories, commentaries on the Buddhist scriptures, poems, memoirs, reviews, and other writings. The genres are many, and the subject matter covered is wide, but it all has – its whole purpose is to convey – that taste of freedom which the Buddha declared to be the hallmark of his Dharma. Another traditional description of the Buddha's Dharma is that it is *ehipassiko*, 'come and see'. Sangharakshita calls to us, his readers, to come and see how the Dharma can fundamentally change the way we see things, change the way we live for the better, and change the society we belong to, wherever in the world we live.

Sangharakshita's very first published piece, *The Unity of Buddhism* (found in volume 7 of this collection), appeared in 1944 when he was eighteen years old, and it introduced themes that continued to resound throughout his work: the basis of Buddhist ethics, the compassion of the bodhisattva, and the transcendental unity of Buddhism. Over the course of the following seven decades not only did numerous other works flow from his pen; he gave hundreds of talks (some now lost). In gathering all we could find of this vast output, we have sought to arrange it in a way that brings a sense of coherence, communicating something essential about Sangharakshita, his life and teaching. Recalling the three 'baskets' among which an early tradition divided the Buddha's teachings, we have divided Sangharakshita's creative output into six 'baskets' or groups: foundation texts; works originating in India; teachings originally given in the West; commentaries on the Buddhist scriptures; personal writings; and poetry, aphorisms, and works on the arts. The 27th volume, a concordance, brings together all the terms and themes of the whole collection. If you want to find a particular story or teaching, look at a traditional term from different points of view or in different contexts, or track down one of the thousands of canonical references to be found in these volumes, the concordance will be your guide.

1. FOUNDATION

What is the foundation of a Buddhist life? How do we understand and then follow the Buddha's path of Ethics, Meditation, and Wisdom? What is really meant by 'Going for Refuge to the Three Jewels', described by Sangharakshita as the essential act of a Buddhist life? And what is the Bodhisattva ideal, which he has called 'one of the sublimest ideals mankind has ever seen'? In the 'Foundation' group you will find teachings on all these themes. It includes the author's *magnum opus, A Survey of Buddhism*, a collection of teachings on *The Purpose and Practice of Buddhist Meditation*, and the anthology, *The Essential Sangharakshita*, an eminently helpful distillation of the entire corpus.

2. INDIA

From 1950 to 1964 Sangharakshita, based in Kalimpong in the eastern Himalayas, poured his energy into trying to revive Buddhism in the land of its birth and to revitalize and bring reform to the existing Asian Buddhist world. The articles and book reviews from this period are gathered in volumes 7 and 8, as well as his biographical sketch of the great Sinhalese Dharmaduta, Anagarika Dharmapala. In 1954 Sangharakshita took on the editing of the *Maha Bodhi*, a journal for which he wrote a monthly editorial, and which, under his editorship, published the work of many of the leading Buddhist writers of the time. It was also during these years in India that a vital connection was forged with Dr B. R. Ambedkar, renowned Indian statesman and leader of the Buddhist mass conversion of 1956. Sangharakshita became closely involved with the new Buddhists and, after Dr Ambedkar's untimely death, visited them regularly on extensive teaching tours.

From 1979, when an Indian wing of the Triratna Buddhist Community was founded (then known as TBMSG), Sangharakshita returned several times to undertake further teaching tours. The talks from these tours are collected in volumes 9 and 10 along with a unique work on Ambedkar and his life which draws out the significance of his conversion to Buddhism.

3. THE WEST

Sangharakshita founded the Triratna Buddhist Community (then called the Friends of the Western Buddhist Order) on 6 April 1967. On 7 April the following year he performed the first ordinations of men and women within the Triratna Buddhist Order (then the Western Buddhist Order). At that time Buddhism was not widely known in the West and for the following two decades or so he taught intensively, finding new ways to communicate the ancient truths of Buddhism, drawing on the whole Buddhist tradition to do so, as well as making connections with what was best in existing Western culture. Sometimes his sword flashed as he critiqued ideas and views inimical to the Dharma. It is these teachings and writings that are gathered together in this third group.

4. COMMENTARY

Throughout Sangharakshita's works are threaded references to the Buddhist canon of literature – Pāli, Mahāyāna, and Vajrayāna – from which he drew his inspiration. In the early days of the new movement he often taught by means of seminars in which, prompted by the questions of his students, he sought to pass on the inspiration and wisdom of the Buddhist tradition. Each seminar was based around a different text, the seminars were recorded and transcribed, and in due course many of the transcriptions were edited and turned into books, all carefully checked by Sangharakshita. The commentaries compiled in this way constitute the fourth group. In some ways this is the heart of the collection. Sangharakshita often told the story of how it was that, reading two *sūtras* at the age of sixteen, he realized that he was a Buddhist, and he has never tired of showing others how they too could see and realize the value of the '*sūtra*-treasure'.

5. MEMOIRS

Who is Sangharakshita? What sort of life did he live? Whom did he meet? What did he feel? Why did he found a new Buddhist movement? In these volumes of memoirs and letters Sangharakshita shares with his readers much about himself and his life as he himself has experienced it, giving us a sense of its breadth and depth, humour and pathos.

6. POETRY, APHORISMS, AND THE ARTS

Sangharakshita describes reading *Paradise Lost* at the age of twelve as one of the greatest poetic experiences of his life. His realization of the value of the higher arts to spiritual development is one of his distinctive contributions to our understanding of what Buddhist life is, and he has expressed it in a number of essays and articles. Throughout his life he has written poetry which he says can be regarded as a kind of spiritual autobiography. It is here, perhaps, that we come closest to the heart of Sangharakshita. He has also written a few short stories and composed some startling aphorisms. Through book reviews he has engaged with the experiences, ideas, and opinions of modern writers. All these are collected in this sixth group.

In the preface to *A Survey of Buddhism* (volume 1 in this collection), Sangharakshita wrote of his approach to the Buddha's teachings:

> Why did the Buddha (or Nāgārjuna, or Buddhaghosa) teach this particular doctrine? What bearing does it have on the spiritual life? How does it help the individual Buddhist actually to follow the spiritual path?… I found myself asking such questions again and again, for only in this way, I found, could I make sense – spiritual sense – of Buddhism.

Although this collection contains so many words, they are all intent, directly or indirectly, on these same questions. And all these words are not in the end about their writer, but about his great subject, the Buddha and his teaching, and about you, the reader, for whose benefit they are solely intended. These pages are full of the reverence that Sangharakshita has always felt, which is expressed in an early poem, 'Taking Refuge in the Buddha', whose refrain is 'My place is at thy feet'. He has devoted his life to communicating the Buddha's Dharma in its depth and in its breadth, to men and women from all backgrounds and walks of life, from all countries, of all races, of all ages. These collected works are the fruit of that devotion.

We are very pleased to be able to include some previously unpublished work in this collection, but most of what appears in these volumes has been published before. We have made very few changes, though we have added extra notes where we thought they would be useful. We have had the pleasure of researching the notes in the Sangharakshita Library at 'Adhisthana', Triratna's centre in Herefordshire, UK, which houses his own collection of books. It has been of great value to be able to search among the very copies of the *suttas*, *sūtras* and commentaries that have provided the basis of his teachings over the last seventy years.

The publication of these volumes owes much to the work of transcribers, editors, indexers, designers, and publishers over many years – those who brought out the original editions of many of the works included here, and those who have contributed in all sorts of ways to this *Complete Works* project, including all those who contributed to funds given in celebration of Sangharakshita's ninetieth birthday in August 2015. Many thanks to everyone who has helped; may the merit gained in our acting thus go to the alleviation of the suffering of all beings.

Vidyadevi and Kalyanaprabha
Editors

THE COMPLETE WORKS OF SANGHARAKSHITA

I FOUNDATION

VOLUME 1 A SURVEY OF BUDDHISM / THE BUDDHA'S NOBLE EIGHTFOLD PATH
A Survey of Buddhism
The Buddha's Noble Eightfold Path

2 THE THREE JEWELS I
The Three Jewels
Going for Refuge
The Ten Pillars of Buddhism
The History of My Going for Refuge
Was the Buddha a Bhikkhu?
Forty-Three Years Ago
My Relation to the Order
Extending the Hand of Fellowship
The Meaning of Conversion in Buddhism

3 THE THREE JEWELS II
Who is the Buddha?
What is the Dharma?
What is the Sangha?

4 THE BODHISATTVA IDEAL
The Bodhisattva Ideal
The Bodhisattva Principle
The Endlessly Fascinating Cry

5 THE PURPOSE AND PRACTICE OF BUDDHIST MEDITATION
The Purpose and Practice of Buddhist Meditation

6 THE ESSENTIAL SANGHARAKSHITA
The Essential Sangharakshita

VOLUME 12 A NEW BUDDHIST MOVEMENT II

Previously Unpublished Talks

13 EASTERN AND WESTERN TRADITIONS

Buddhism and the West
The FWBO and 'Protestant Buddhism'
Buddhism, World Peace, and Nuclear War
From Genesis to the Diamond Sūtra
Dialogue between Buddhism and Christianity
Aspects of Buddhist Morality
Buddhism and Blasphemy
Buddhism and the Bishop of Woolwich
Buddhism and the New Reformation
Alternative Traditions
Creative Symbols of Tantric Buddhism
Tibetan Buddhism
The Essence of Zen

IV COMMENTARY

14 THE ETERNAL LEGACY / WISDOM BEYOND WORDS

The Eternal Legacy
The Glory of the Literary World
Wisdom Beyond Words

15 PĀLI CANON TEACHINGS AND TRANSLATIONS

Dhammapada (translation)
Karaniya Mettā Sutta (translation)
Living with Kindness
Living with Awareness
Mangala Sutta (translation)
Auspicious Signs (seminar)
Tiratana Vandanā (translation)
Salutation to the Three Jewels (seminar)
The Threefold Refuge (seminar)
Further Pāli Sutta Commentaries

WINDHORSE PUBLICATIONS

Windhorse Publications is a Buddhist charitable company based in the UK. We produce books of high quality that are accessible and relevant to all those interested in Buddhism, at whatever level of interest and commitment. We are the main publisher of Sangharakshita, the founder of the Triratna Buddhist Order and Community. Our books draw on the whole range of the Buddhist tradition, including translations of traditional texts, commentaries, books that make links with contemporary culture and ways of life, biographies of Buddhists, and works on meditation.

To subscribe to the *Complete Works of Sangharakshita*, please go to: windhorsepublications.com/sangharakshita-complete-works/

THE TRIRATNA BUDDHIST COMMUNITY

Windhorse Publications is a part of the Triratna Buddhist Community, an international movement with centres in Europe, India, North America and Australasia. At these centres, members of the Triratna Buddhist Order offer classes in meditation and Buddhism. Activities of the Triratna Community also include retreat centres, residential spiritual communities, ethical Right Livelihood businesses, and the Karuna Trust, a UK fundraising charity that supports social welfare projects in the slums and villages of India.

Through these and other activities, Triratna is developing a unique approach to Buddhism, not simply as a philosophy and a set of techniques, but as a creatively directed way of life for all people living in the conditions of the modern world.

For more information please visit thebuddhistcentre.com